"Joy of joys! It is such a selection that one can open to any page and be richly rewarded. Never meant for publication, and therefore unfettered, it is surely some of Gellhorn's finest writing. It is also a barometer of the times over more than six decades of the last century—and an astonishingly apt predictor of conditions in the world today." —*The Buffalo News*

"If Martha Gellhorn had not existed, George Cukor would have probably invented her. . . . Given Gellhorn's iconic status, perhaps the greatest virtue of Caroline Moorehead's dexterously edited selection of her letters is the way it depicts the irascibly human personality behind the legend. . . . [A] fine collection." —Stephen Amidon, Salon.com

"If reading *A Life* left one with a hunger for more of Gellhorn's own vivid turns of phrase, the letters amply satisfy it. . . . This is a book of historic import, for it must be one of the last contemporary records worth collating of a very old expression of human relations—the intensely personal mix of ordinariness and art, chatting and pondering, that goes into the production of a 'proper letter.'" —Lorna Scott Fox, *Columbia Journalism Review*

"Compelling." —Susan Comninos, *Times Union* (Albany)

"There is much to recommend about this bountiful collection." —Scott Eyman, *Palm Beach Post*

"Compelling, enjoyable assemblage of letters. Gellhorn is at her most outspoken, fluent, hilarious, charming, and insightful in her energetic correspondence. . . . Gellhorn's peripatetic life was unusual and dramatic, and her dispatches are vital and exciting, empathic and gutsy, and brimming with choice metaphors, molten social commentary, and sharp analysis." —Donna Seaman, *Booklist*

Selected Letters of
Martha Gellhorn

Selected Letters of

MARTHA GELLHORN

EDITED BY

Caroline Moorehead

AN OWL BOOK

HENRY HOLT AND COMPANY · NEW YORK

Owl Books
Henry Holt and Company, LLC
Publishers since 1866
175 Fifth Avenue
New York, New York 10010
www.henryholt.com

An Owl Book® and ® are registered trademarks
of Henry Holt and Company, LLC.

Library of Congress Cataloging-in-Publication Data
Gellhorn, Martha, 1908–
    Selected letters of Martha Gellhorn / edited by Caroline Moorehead.—1st ed.
        p. cm.
    Includes index.
    ISBN-13: 978-0-8050-8322-4
    ISBN-10: 0-8050-8322-7
        1. Gellhorn, Martha, 1908—Correspondence. 2. Authors, American—
20th century—Correspondence. 3. Journalists—United States—
Correspondence. I. Moorehead, Caroline. II. Title.
    PS3513.E46Z48 2006
    070.4'333092—dc22   2006041168

Originally published in hardcover in 2006 by Henry Holt and Company

First Owl Books Edition 2007

Printed in the United States of America

10 9 8 7 6 5 4 3 2 1

Contents

Chronology

1966   August: goes to Vietnam for the *Guardian*
1966–1967   Writing *The Lowest Trees Have Tops*
1968   Builds house near Lake Naivasha
1970   Buys 72 Cadogan Square, London
1970   September 24: death of Edna
1976–1978   Writing *The Weather in Africa* and *Travels with Myself and Another*
1982   Buys cottage in Wales
1998   February 16: dies in London

Selected Letters of
Martha Gellhorn

Preface

Martha Gellhorn belonged to the age – perhaps the last age – when writing letters was a natural part of life. As a reporter and a novelist, with a precise eye for detail, she was also herself a natural letter writer, and all her life she used letters as a prism through which to filter what she saw and heard, and as a way of keeping close to her friends. She wrote more or less as she spoke, with humor and self-deprecation, full of fury about corrupt and evil governments. She wanted to make her friends laugh and she also wanted to talk to them, for conversation was what she really enjoyed. Letters were talk. "I felt like talking today," she wrote to Victoria Glendinning toward the end of her life, explaining the reason for her particularly long letter, "and felt like talking about books."

Because there was seldom a significant stretch of time when Martha was not moving around, letters were what held her life together. She started traveling at the age of twenty and never stopped. "I have only to go to a different country, sky, language, scenery to feel it is worth living," she told a friend when she was in her late seventies. Martha wrote letters every day, often describing the same particularly significant episodes to several people. When troubling things happened, she wrote them out, in long, anguished passages, as if only by writing could she lessen her own sense of grief. Then, often, she would write the whole thing again later, as a short story or novella or a scene in a novel. "The only way I can make it seem real to me is to write," she told Bernard Berenson.

In an afterword to the 1986 Virago edition of *A Stricken Field*, a novel about Czechoslovakia in 1939 and written at the time, Martha lamented the fact that she had never kept a "writer's compost heap" of diaries, journals, notes, or photographs. The archive of her past was "a poor thing, limited and fragmentary"; furthermore, her memory was terrible and she forgot everything. What she did not take into account then were her letters. And even if she did not keep them, others did. Read together, with her erratic spelling and her particular use of words, they provide an immediate and intimate portrait of a remarkable life.

Martha's letters are very seldom about social life, though she could be sharp and witty when in large gatherings. She loathed parties, formal dinners, and public life and was easily bored. She really did not mind what people thought about her and was not interested in trying to please. What she liked was friendship and love, in all their guises. To friends and lovers, to her mother, brother, adopted son and stepson, she wrote affectionately and often, though when angry, she could be harsh. She saw things in words, and liked to describe what she saw, heard and thought. Her letters are about the inner life, the excitements of youth and work and love affairs, the toughness of trying to write, the despair and loneliness of old age. Politics fascinated her: gossip did not. Malice, she would say, was not acceptable; hatred was. There are many references to American foreign policy, about which she was both highly critical and very apprehensive, long before the U.S.A. inspired alarm in others. It was soon after the war in Vietnam that Martha began warning about the rise of the Christian right and the dangers of American intervention in other parts of the world. A passionate liberal all her life and fired, from a very young age, by a strong sense of the injustice in the world, Martha could be impatient and intemperate over the question of Israel and the Palestinians; going into Dachau with the American army at the end of the Second World War had closed her mind forever against anything but the sanctity of an Israeli state, and many of her friends, both on paper and in conversation, preferred to avoid the subject. Apart from this, there were no taboos.

There are many letters about books and writers, those she admired – Joseph Heller, Peter Matthiesen, Henry James, Trollope – and those who she could never come to grips with, like Proust. But above all, Martha's letters are about survival, about the struggles of life, how to keep going, how to do no harm to others and attain some degree of happiness oneself. "From the onset of observation until death," she told her stepson Sandy, "life is a problem for one who lives it." George Kennan once said to her that her letters were her "real genre, and it is where you yourself come through most genuinely and convincingly."

The letters collected in this volume are a fraction of the number she wrote in her lifetime, many of them now held with her papers at the Howard Gotlieb Archival Center at Boston University. In order to include as many as possible, and to avoid repetition, I have cut, sometimes heavily, within the letters themselves. Major cuts are marked by dots; minor ones are not. One of her letters to David Gurewitsch, written over several days, runs to forty-seven typed pages; another, to Sandy Gellhorn, written over a month as a diary from Africa, to over thirty. In each case, I have selected just a few pages. Because Martha, particularly at the beginning of a friendship, often wrote letter after letter, day after day – exploring the limits of that friendship in a way more usual in a conversation than in a letter – I have included several examples, to illustrate how easy and pleasurable she found intimacy. Her letters to William Walton – briefly a lover but for many years a friend – in the 1940s and 1950s, and those to Betsy Drake in the 1970s and 1980s, belong to this category. Again, what appears here is only a fraction of what she wrote to them.

Martha had an enormous number of friends. Though she told Rosamond Lehmann that her five closest friends had all been men, and that the world she loved was one of "men, and not the world of men and women," she became increasingly close to women as the years passed, and it was to them that many of her most revealing and intimate letters were written. Though she repeatedly professed contempt for self-analysis, and at times displayed a remarkable lack of self-awareness, few people have written so perceptively and with such candor about themselves.

Martha's principal correspondents were: her mother Edna, to whom she wrote almost every day for forty years; Ernest Hemingway, with whom she lived on and off for eight years, though they were married for just four of them; Sandy Gellhorn, her adopted son, and Sandy Matthews, her stepson by her second husband, Tom Matthews; Hortense Flexner, who taught her at Bryn Mawr; Eleanor Roosevelt, who befriended her in 1936; Sybille Bedford, Betsy Drake, Lucy Moorehead, Diana Cooper, Robert Presnell, Leonard Bernstein, William Walton, George Paloczi-Horvath, and Moishe Pearlman; and, toward the end of her life, Victoria Glendinning, James Fox, Nicholas Shakespeare, and John Hatt. Many of them were given nicknames – Walton was Trolleycar, Hunk of Despair, Pieface; Hemingway, Bug, Pup-Pup, and even Mucklebugetski – though with her younger friends toward the end of her life she used terms of endearment. James Fox was "My favourite James in all the world." Affectionate and attentive with those she was fond of, Martha could also be unsentimental when they died. She dealt with partings and deaths with clarity, resignation, and a kind of brutality. When things ended – affairs, marriages, friendships – she packed, left, cut herself off, moved on. There was little looking back, few regrets. The only exceptions were her mother, whose death she mourned for the rest of her life, and her adopted son Sandy, about whom she worried constantly.

When she sold her cottage in Wales, a few years before her death, Martha made a bonfire of some of her more personal letters. In those flames went virtually her entire correspondence with her mother, and her letters to Tom Matthews, James Gavin, and Laurence Rockefeller. I have been unable to trace her letters to Nadezhda Mandelstam, George Kennan, and John Pilger, all important correspondents.

But most of the rest of her life – the wars, the books, the friends, the love affairs – is here, from the day when, at the age of twenty-two, she first arrived with her typewriter in Paris, excited, expectant, hungry for everything.

Setting Forth, 1908–1936

Martha Gellhorn was born on November 8, 1908, in St. Louis, Missouri. Her father, Dr. George Gellhorn, the son of a merchant from Breslau in Germany, was a distinguished gynecologist and obstetrician, an expert on cancer and syphilis, who had trained in hospitals in Berlin and Vienna before emigrating to America at the turn of the century. Her mother, Edna Fischel, was a feminist, a campaigner for women's suffrage, and a greatly loved figure in St. Louis, where she was born. Both her parents were half Jewish. Martha had two older brothers: George, born in 1902, and Walter, born in 1904. A third son, Alfred, followed in 1913. The family was close, prosperous, happy – and happy children, Martha would say, like happy families, have no history.

When Martha was twelve, the Gellhorns helped found a progressive co-educational day school, called John Burroughs after the naturalist, in order to provide their two younger children with a more enlightened and interesting education than anything offered by St. Louis's more conventional schools. By the time Martha moved on to Bryn Mawr, she was writing poetry and stories for the school magazine, and had been both Speaker of the school assembly and president of its Dramatic Association, two positions she would say later that had given her a taste for being leader. Although Martha was close to her father, whom she admired but with whom she quarreled, her real love was for her mother, who remained her "true north," her one point of certainty and unconditional love, until Edna's death at the age of ninety-one in 1970. The first letter in Martha's archive is to her mother, written when she was six. "Dear Mother. You are so pretty. Mother I love you. I think you are lovely to me." Their devotion was mutual. When Martha left home for Bryn Mawr, Alfred wrote to her: "She loves you so thoroughly it makes me ache."

Bryn Mawr and college life never suited Martha, and she did little to adapt herself to it. She failed one set of exams through carelessness, and, though she passed the next with ease, she had grown bored and left without completing her degree. However, it was at Bryn Mawr that she discovered the excitement of hard work, and the refuge it could provide, and she pinned up over her desk Mauriac's maxim: "Travail: opium unique." All her life she would repeat these words, to herself and to friends. Work was Martha's bolt-hole, as well as her duty, the place to which she escaped at times of trouble. And Bryn Mawr provided her with a lasting friend, and a second model – her parents being the first – of a happy marriage. Hortense Flexner, a poet little read today but much admired in the 1930s, was married to a small genial cartoonist called Wyncie King; she taught Martha English. They began to exchange letters, and went on writing to each other until Hortense's death some forty years later. Martha wrote to her as "Teecher" and signed herself "Gellhorn." She said that Teecher was for her the perfect example of "endurance, courage and gayety," all things she believed in strongly.

Dr. Gellhorn had taken his children to visit his native Germany when Martha was seventeen, and this visit, and others the family paid to Europe, had made her long to return. On leaving Bryn Mawr, she found a job as a cub reporter on the Albany Times Union, to cover women's clubs and the police beat, and when that came to an end after six months she knew that the moment had come to leave America. She was twenty-one, restless, impatient, and full of curiosity. No one was surprised to see her go.

Not long after Christmas 1929, Edna gave Martha the money for a ticket to New York, and from there she boarded a ship of the German Lloyd line, paying her passage with an article about their service to Europe. "I knew," she wrote later, "that now I was free. This was my show, my show." Dr. Gellhorn's parting words were affectionate. "I love you – not because you are my child but because of your essential honesty and sincerity and fearlessness and cleanliness."

When Martha reached Paris, with a typewriter, two suitcases, and $75, France was the leading economic power of the day. The city was elegant, exciting, full of possibilities. Cinemas were showing the films of Buñuel, Cocteau, and Man Ray; Josephine Baker, in a single pink flamingo feather, was the queen of the many musical reviews, more lavish and more spectacular than any seen before. The city was everything that Martha had longed for. She took a series of brief jobs – as a junior assistant in a beauty shop, as a copywriter for an advertising agency, as an occasional contributor to a news service. She had very little money but she was, if not beautiful, extremely attractive. She had also started to write a novel, later published as What Mad Pursuit, and which she rapidly dismissed as embarrassing juvenilia and suppressed. To write it, she went to the Riviera and found a cheap pension, paying her way by making up fashion articles and sending them off to magazines in America. A young lawyer friend from St. Louis, G. Campbell Beckett, took her to Morocco on holiday. Campbell Beckett, who would handle all Martha's affairs, fell in love with her. Many years later, she wrote about him: "I was the spoilt friend, the taker . . . He looked after people."

In the summer of 1930, back in Paris, Martha was introduced to Bertrand de Jouvenel, a left-wing political journalist who had not long before published his first book, L'Économie Dirigée. Bertrand was the son of Henri de Jouvenel, a newspaper editor and politician, and his mother had a salon in the Boulevard St. Germain. He was married to Marcelle, twelve years his senior, and was widely known in France as the boy seduced, at the age of sixteen, by Colette, his father's second wife, who, even as they were having an affair, was writing Chéri, the story of an exquisitely beautiful boy being seduced by an older woman. Bertrand was now twenty-six, a thin, good-looking man with high cheekbones and eyes that in some *lights looked green. He was also charming, perceptive, and intelligent. He fell in love with Martha. She fled to the lake of Annecy, near Geneva; he pursued her there.*

Their affair was, from the first, troubled. Martha's parents, and particularly her father, vehemently opposed the idea of her living with a married man, even though Bertrand kept promising, and trying, to get a divorce. In Paris, Martha and Bertrand lived together, but both were often away – Martha writing her novel in Bertrand's house at La Favière, Bertrand acting as his father's secretary on his official travels – and when apart they wrote to each other every day, sometimes more. In the summer of 1931, having broken with Bertrand, she persuaded the St. Louis Post Dispatch to take a series of articles about America, and she traveled through Texas, Nevada, New Mexico, and California, recording her journey in a series of letters to Stanley Pennell, later author of The History of Rose Hanks, *who had taught her English at John Burroughs school. Like Campbell Bennett, Pennell was clearly in love with her.*

From this early period, hundreds of letters from Bertrand to Martha survive, but very few of hers to him. Bertrand was, for almost all the four years they were together, the more in love.

To: Bertrand de Jouvenel

[?] 1930
Villa Noria
La Favière

Dear love:
There is four inches of snow. Joke. I've re-written the first chapter with what pain and I'll never be content with that chapter (the most re-done of the lot.) It moves slowly, setting no key-note and I just can't make it jell. I'll have the second re-done before I go to bed. I see the book pretty clearly up until the end and then I don't know what to do. Of course it's all going to be much more banal when I'm done with it; lots of the fire has flickered out.

I walked five miles in the wind today and my head hurt from the cold. I'm losing my appetite which is a good thing; why didn't you tell me I was plain fat these days. I shall come back to you as usual thinner and with gobs of discipline which I'll lose the instant I lay hands on you (I meant lay eyes on you but there you are – the subconscious coming out.) . . .

I listen for the telephone hoping it will be you and then I'm glad it's not because if you phoned I'd be tempted to come home at once and I must stay until I finish this damn thing. I love you passionately as you no doubt know by now.

I'm reading *Tragic America* and I love that old goofer Dreiser* for all his

---

*Theodore Dreiser (1871–1945), American novelist, whose harshly lit depictions of real life brought him up against censorship and popular taste.

cheap journalese style: he's angry and alive and that's pretty rare these days. On the other hand I think Hemingway is pretty bum from what he did in *In Our Times*: the story about skiing is written about an ex-beau of mine who used to ski with him. Hemingway makes him inarticulate simply because Hemingway doesn't know how to talk, and as a matter of fact that guy can talk in 9 syllable words all night long. So I'm not impressed. Anyway Hemingway has affected my style which is really too bad; but there you are.

Dearest you'll be very cool and stern with Marcelle won't you? I want so terribly to go to St Louis with you. Oh God if only that female will crash through with a divorce; she's hideously hopeful, isn't she?

Sixty seven kisses and a friendly greeting to the dog.

Marty

To: Stanley Pennell★

April [?] 1931
The Sunshine Special

Dear Stan,

I think life's damn funny. And almost fun. One ought to travel more – farther –. It makes one come alive. I got on the train in a brand new outfit – more chick than I've been for years – pretty dazzling – and there was no one to see me off. Such waste. I felt sad and alone till I began reading Evelyn Waugh's *Decline and Fall* which is magnificent not only in architecture but in his lovely distorted truthful diagnosis of (and non-conclusion about) this footling planet of ours. I wish I knew that man but would doubtless be disappointed. I see how he feels better than I can understand Huxley. It's all swill for Evelyn but laughing swill; and really people are only laughing swill and if one forgets to laugh swill becomes noxious unendurable, whereas it really isn't important enough to be that.

Dear, I think I am probably sexually repressed and all queer because I have scrambled sex and aesthetics and morals and fear into a fine stinking mess and I'm suffocation somewhere at the center. I tried, God knows why, to explain to Mother that exercising, sleeping properly, keeping one's bowels open etc. was scarcely enough if one's chief function was going to be deformed, shut off. But Mother even (and she's much smarter than anyone I know) can't rid herself (or ourselves) of little phrases such as 'how like the animals'. It's all getting me down. I think it's horrible to scare people about life merely because they are female and have the

---

★Stanley Pennell would later say that she had inspired him to write the best sonnets that he would ever write.

emotional make-up – in certain respects – of males, or what males supposedly have.

Am I making any sense?

A man with a horrid, jerky, apologetic, perpetual cough has been sitting next to me. And a man across the aisle with narrow, concentrated eyes whose mouth sags and would like to touch me or the girl next to me who sits with her fannie curved against the chair-back, and her legs folded off the floor – whichever one of us is easiest to touch.

I am drinking an orangeade and then I shall take a new dope Dad has given me which produced sleep and if one takes more than three a day one will sleep for five days quite unconscious and I may experiment with that too.

Darling everything a bit scummy. Apparently – unconsciously because I am not a sadist – I did to you exactly what a guy did to me (equally unconsciously). I hope to God that I don't stick in your guts the way he sticks in mine. I hope to God I don't turn out to be as much a blight for you as he has been for me. I hope you are shorter of memory. Because if you aren't – though you may hate me (as I am beginning to hate him) – nothing else will do very well.

Christ what a quaint situation.

I kiss you because that is pleasant.

M

To: Campbell Beckett

[?] May 1931
4366 McPherson Avenue
St Louis

Dear;

I am home. The word as you know has always had merely dictionary meaning for me. This is no longer true. I am home. It is like saying, rest, peace, honorable things. I love my family; their love for me is an unaccountable blessing. I feel protected from unnecessary ugliness and I feel that there is after all some meaning to my brief transit of this globe.

My fingernails are as beautiful as my toenails, and I have bought an outfit of that new dead-white jewelry which deludes me into believing myself sunburned. There are cornflowers in my study and when I return from an insignificant but pooping shopping tour, I find orangeade coolly on my desk. None of this implies vast histories to you. I have travelled so much, lived so thoroughly alone, that these piffling details of comfort and thoughtfulness come as a sweeping surprise.

I would rather not go to Mexico but shall go – in two days time.

Naturally. One doesn't die on jobs; and besides I shall doubtless be glad of it, as memory, if nothing else.

A letter from Audrey★ delights my risible muscles; the girl belongs in Henry James novels, and in music by Couperin. Two letters from Bertrand are almost more than I can stand. I have been unable to cope with my own optimism; though I wrote him that we might as well abandon each other because of his wife, I hoped – yes, hoped terribly . . . And now without meaning to he has so surely finished that hope, and his own blindness, his child-like refusal and inability to see what is what and what can be anything, merely adds to the piteousness and futility of it all. I have talked to Mother about this, and we have arrived at the conclusion – she wisely, I bitterly – that only work heals those stranger wounds, those sick deep wants that clamor in one's memory. I am not sure I shall do anything more about Russia next year; but probably try to get a job on a local paper; work, work, and home at night quietly. Some sort of anodyne; I have been counting my losses honestly and know that if I am to live with any joy or usefulness, without hideous waste of days and enthusiasm, I must forget all that B. means. Because he has meant too much. And I have spoiled months of my life already groping backwards, praying, weeping and wondering why I was doomed to this ignominious frustration. Enough about all this too. I am saying several 'goodbyes to all that' in this letter.

Dearest thank you 1000 times for your sweetness in N.Y. And for giving Kitten a good time, and for being alive, and wise. As for you – well, my old playmate, you will have to guess.

Write me here.

Yours, for probably always,
M

To: Stanley Pennell

May 8 or 9
Saint Luke's Hospital
St Louis

Stan – dear Stan:
I'm in the hospital. My right foot slowly ripens into red beef under a battery of lights. I bruised the bone it would seem – I remember – three o'clock one morning, hurtling down the mountain side above Ponte Tresa to Lugano . . . walking has always been a slightly dubious pleasure since.

I want to write – feeling uneasily that there is much to say: explanations; knowing also that you don't want words, that words are no good anyhow,

---

★Audrey, who had been at Bryn Mawr with Martha, went bicycling with her in the Loire.

all one can ever do is stroke someone's cheek helplessly, wondering why it is all such an inchoate thing, loving.

I want to say all sorts of things. And you will turn and say, 'Martha, you are a child aren't you'. I like your mouth, when it is almost surprised, and your voice, and I think you have eyes belonging to the truest fauns. But this is not to make you think anything at all – anything which has to do with you and me.

I didn't mean to say I loved you a little. You cheated – looking hurt and silent and rather obstinate. It isn't fair. It's like the children in the Luxembourg – I have no weapons for that.

Meantime, I take my code out of Hemingway. Unbelievable, isn't it? Do you remember *A Farewell to Arms*. The hero talks to the woman; she is worried about something; and he says: 'You're brave. Nothing ever happens to the brave'. Which is somehow enough – a whole philosophy – a banner – a song – and a love. And something to fill up time – busily, passionately.

Why do you care whether I go or stay? Can't you see with your eyes? you confuse stupid hair with inner loveliness or believe the former is productive of the latter. You are all lost – Wolfe's★ cry in the darkness – lost, lost, and so you build idols out of shaving cream and sawdust and worship looking inward.

A strange world, don't you think. I am in need of the far lands.

Martha

To: Stanley Pennell

May 19 1931
Bryn Mawr

Stan my dear;
Here I sit, alongside a lovely rock-gardeny tennis court, the country estate of vested wealth. They are playing tennis, but I have no social graces or I am waiting for you to teach me. A visitor; I feel now – as always – that I am like one of those Harlem nigs who look so like Spaniards that they are accepted into white society: 'going over' it is called. Parties on a yacht; maids busily unpacking my measly wardrobe, country houses, town dinners, and over all the cherry trees of Bryn Mawr, the gracious snobbery of undergraduate wit, my passion for trees growing. Why am I here. What is it that makes me one of these lovely useless people, who eat the world's fruits with never that indigestion-producing question 'Who am I to deserve

★Thomas Wolfe's autobiographical novel, *Look Homeward Angel*, had been published in 1929.

this?' Alone and happy, always – even on the bus, with another race, living
in a submarine gloom of not having enough and trying pitifully to bring
comfort out of want – alone. Does one ever find a class, a niche. Or is one
destined to be many things for many reasons, to be always somehow
dubious of what surrounds one. This thing called 'breeding' fascinates me.
I have no breeding. I am just plainly a freak of environment, and an ability
to giggle. But the 'bred' take me in as do the 'unbred.' And I feel always
like a spy, because I am watching them, thinking about them, never
accepting them, and someday I shall have things to say about them,
criticisms and laughter. But they have all been kind to me. Too kind, and
I am rotten with kindness. Yours as much as anyone's.

Thank you for your letter. I am glad you have a job, and for what cause
I do not care. If being brown-eyed and quiet can get you jobs, take them.
We must have weapons; we have no weapons of ambition, and rancour and
insensibility. Wherefore let us be brown-eyed and quiet – or blonde. And
let us take with both hands, since someday we may be giving all this lushly
back in words (between cardboard covers) and they shall see what we have
seen, and know wherein the joke lies . . .

My dear, I shall need you always, and give you nothing in return. This
seems to me sad; I have been in your place and know that you alone are
real, have heart to make the days bright. But I am no use. There is too much
space in the world. I am bewildered by it, and mad with it. And this urge
to run away from what I love is a sort of sadism I no longer pretend to
understand. And wherever I go there are people, do you see. For a while
these people blot out memory, and are a world and a life. And then I go
somewhere else, to make a new set of memories. So that Paris gave way to
St. Louis, and now St.L. is my memory and the East is my everyday; there
are girls here whose voices are more consoling than highballs and we have
the same jokes; and men who appear marked by Yale and Princeton, they
fill the evenings and are forgotten by the next noon. I shall be in New York
in two days where some extraordinary young *hommes du monde* are
digressing from Paris, there will be dinner parties and theatres and later this
will be brief memory. Nothing has a feel of reality; 'nothing endures', and
there are many countries I have never seen. Wherefore I am of no use.
Unless it be that you write sonnets to me, and it is good to write sonnets.

I am happy today and at nights I read *The Enormous Room*★ and lose my
own sense of loss and futility in thinking that some writers have brought
such gifts as would shame Prometheus. I am a nothing and know it; you are
somebody and should not waste your time on me and my earthly
irrelevance.

★By e. e. cummings, a fictional account of his four-month detention in a French prison
camp during WWI.

This typewriter has gone to my head, there are too many words here. Read what you like only.

A letter to be burned with the garbage. Forgive.

But a letter.

Yours, somewhat and sometime

Marty

To: Stanley Pennell

May 29 1931
The Barclay
111 East 48th Street
New York

Dear:

Not fine, not at all. Really you are wrong. And so bewildered; I had always thought life was an ecstatic business of drawing breath and beating the system. Now I am appalled, don't know what happens next, feeling empty. And worried about you, for fear – selfishly – I may reach out octopus arms and engulf you, to fill emptiness.

There are things one cannot say vis-a-vis. Listen: I have loved a man for almost a year. He didn't mean to, but he took me so completely that he left nothing of my own use. I have been colorless and undecided ever since. This is rather ghastly. I have marked time and wanted him and filled my suddenly purposeless days with activity. I love him terribly. But he is never to be attained. And doesn't realize that, loving as I love, with the peculiar intensity of those who have too much nervous energy, he is – in effect, the Angel of Destruction.

That's me – why I am, and what I am about. Take it or leave it.

yours

Martha

How you can even spit on me when I write letters like this is beyond me

Bertrand missed Martha. In September 1931 he turned up in New York on the Ile de France and they drove to California in search of work. Bertrand was looking for material for a book about the American economy. For a while they found parts as extras in Hollywood costume dramas, but Martha soon left and went to look for somewhere on her own to write her novel. After six months, promising Martha that he would make greater efforts to get Marcelle to agree to a divorce, Bertrand returned to Paris. Marcelle, again, refused and Bertrand sent Martha a telegram begging her to join him. "I want you," he wrote, "find out for yourself if you want me." *Despite the continuing opposition of Dr. Gellhorn, she soon followed him. "Every day I miss you more cruelly," Bertrand wrote before she joined him. "And I know more clearly that you are the very basis of my life." In the four years that they were together, on and off, Martha had two abortions. A letter from Edna showed the depths of her anxiety and disapproval. "'Rugged individualism,'" she wrote, "is for me as much to be feared in the social code of living together in an organised society as in the economic code . . . What more can I do for you? You speak of the possibility of coming to America together — I do not advise it."*

In France, Martha was now doing what she would do for the rest of her life: taking notes on everything she saw and heard, jotting them down in small, hardbacked lesson books, and later using them as the basis for articles and short stories. Already, it was the detail that caught her eye. At Argelès Plage near Marseilles one day, she noted that she ate "salmon trout with a little lake of butter, pale yellow-green asparagus, mutton chop and lettuce, Rocquefort & Gruyère, strawberries and white wine . . . In France, people sit down to this sort of lunch regularly; it is no wonder they prefer peace." In London to write about the opening of the World Economic Conference, she observed that the King had a "mild stammery voice and a true British schoolboy accent . . . exactly like a gentle and rather flustered lawyer reading the last will and testament of Papa to his respectful but secretly sceptical heirs." Most of all, she was enjoying herself. "I like working. In the end it is the only thing which does not bore or dismay me, or fill me with doubt. It is the only thing I know absolutely and irrevocably to be good in itself, no matter what the result."

To: Bertrand de Jouvenel

[late 1931/early 1932?]
Santa Maria
California

Dear:
I loved it so, all day. Beautiful, beautiful – shabbily I have tried to tell you how smooth and warm and alive and many these hills are.

Then Lady Jane★, fat red matron and slow on the towns, screamed like a beast in pain and broke – at 6 pm or so, 13 miles outside the town. I coaxed her here, with prayer and promises. She's broken 2 connecting rods – a hell of an expense – and here I'll be until noon tomorrow. I'll go very slowly, as the road winds trickily; but possibly I shall be at Carmel tomorrow night.

You'd be irritated by my inconsistency if you knew how much I'd

---

★A platinum-colored vintage Dodge Martha and Bertrand had bought for $25 and driven across America.

thought of you all day – and how much I hoped you weren't thinking of me. Mainly shame: you've given me everything and I've given you in exchange faint grudging thanks, so little warmth. My dear, forgive me. I wasn't meant for every day consumption: no one's ever been able to stand that great a dose of me – not even mother. I'm a holiday diet; I'm only bearable to myself – in solitude – as ordinary rations. You'll have to think of me as oysters – you wouldn't want oysters everyday for breakfast?

You have been more than gallant. My dear, only a nag – and a dyspeptic one at that – would criticize your manners or question your charm. *Sois rassuré* – I know they don't grow your equal at every corner of Sunset Boulevard.

Somehow – you will think me mad and unkind – I wish you'd have an affair, with someone beautiful, sophisticated, and attentive. I mean that. It would make me realize what I've made you forget – too many things.

I've repaid ardor with impatience and sponged your assurance with icy water. Please be a conqueror for a bit; forget me – I'm a shit face; and make yourself realize again what you knew before I came.

I'll write from Carmel. My dear, my dear – why do you have to be so good and I so mean?

love

m

To: Edna Gellhorn

[late 1931]
[Paris]

Matie* dearest;

Thank you for your letter. It's too bad you did that with the Stixes:† because of course I shall just go on being Mrs. and being accepted as such. Presently a diplomatic passport will cinch the matter once and for all. I daresay the news will be in papers sooner or later and why shouldn't it be. It's going to be awkward all round; though the only practical result probably will be that I can't come back to St. Louis. I do wish to God you and Dad wouldn't hang on so bitterly to woe and lack of confidence. It does seem to me that the years and my satisfaction with them ought to prove to you that this thing works and is what I want and need. Let people infer that you disapprove the match – it wouldn't astonish anybody and is doubtless correct anyhow. We've found the only way out – after some time – of the material awkwardness of unmarriage. Because we really are

---

*One of her nicknames for her mother, along with Fotsie and Omi.
†Parents of Johnny Stix, one of Martha's closest childhood friends.

married, the legal fact of marriage is here accepted without question. The friends in the U.S. who've heard the news also accept it. I don't ask you to lie but merely to keep silent, though probably now it's too late as you can't very well go back on that first statement. I'm sorry to be so peevish about this; but it's no joke having my careful building up just easily torn down that way, especially as all our plans for America hang on the veracity of that building up. Added to which it just all goes to prove that you no more understand or believe in us than you did three years ago and that makes me pretty hopeless. It's obviously no use trying either to explain or convince, and you won't let the facts influence you either. I regard B. as my husband and always have; my friends are willing to accept him as such – with or without legal confirmation. If you wish to go on thinking my life is ruined and that I'm a martyr to B's brutal selfishness that's your prerogative – but I have no sympathy with such an attitude. It's false and troublesome, as insulting to me as to B. If I were actually legally married to B. you wouldn't adopt such an attitude even if you felt it. I consider myself married, and resent your point of view towards my husband. I shan't discuss myself and B. anymore with you; it's no use. Also we won't worry you by coming to St. Louis; you apparently aren't willing to accept B. as a permanent factor in my life, and I have no desire to come alone and re-open stupidly a question which I feel to be finally and satisfactorily settled. We've evidently both got our prejudices and we can just go on having them. It's wasteful and painful; but it so happens that I love B. and intend to go on making my life with him; and no one but B. could ever change my purpose and it's doubtful if he ever will. And finally about the 'gossip' which you say will be inevitable in St. Louis; I don't give a damn about it. There's no gossip here; we have lived in such a way that people respect us and don't feel it suitable to whisper and criticise. Every time I came to St. Louis, I felt dirty and afraid: I've never felt that way anywhere else and the result has been that my life is easy and proud elsewhere. I'll never come back to that untrue and unwholesome atmosphere of terror and lying; of course people will make up foul stories if they feel one is cringing and apologetic. You and Dad have always felt that I committed mortal sin; the reward for such an attitude is all the gossip one can stomach and then some. I'm sorry for you; it doesn't touch me. Ever since I realized clearly that it was denial and falsehood and fear and creeping around and being anxious about Mrs. Jones's opinion, which was destroying me, and realizing that, stopped feeling or caring about those things, I have been secure and happy. Like the old families of the South, St. Louis can go on fighting my civil war long after it's finished and forgotten.

I'm sorry to write this letter; probably silence would have been kinder. But I want you to know how I feel, to know also why in future I shan't attempt to make you understand my life. Please show this letter to Dad, it's for both of you. And it's probably the last letter of its kind you'll ever have to read.

Love.

Martha

To: Bertrand de Jouvenel

[late Spring] 1932
[4366 McPherson Avenue
St Louis]

Sunday morning; it is raining. Cam [Beckett] reads my novel. Last night, after the Kings went home, I talked to him for hours. Talked? Well, I'm ashamed to say, I sobbed . . .

Bertrand: even with you, who love me – and whom I love, I have never had such a feeling of complete understanding. Finally, after three hours, I felt cleansed and quieted. And last night I slept.

I began talking about the Russian divorce. I told him he must help me to persuade the family so that they would give their consent gladly; so that they would realize that you were my salvation not my destruction. I told him I could never be happy if I were torn between my love for you and for them: that I needed happiness – or rather peace – because the mind and the body cannot go on forever, in doubt and struggle and uncertainty.

. . . I explained what it had meant to be a mistress; how you despised me for cowardice and conventionality; how it was – for me – like a Roman Catholic turning atheist. It was in my blood, my upbringing. I explained how I had fought my father's coldness and seen him sag and grow old before me. How I had been bitterly lonely with you – when, the mail arriving, the letters from Marcelle claimed you and unconsciously you turned away from me, giving your sympathy to her, regretting your desertion, and – again unconsciously – knowing that I was to blame. How I had failed you, being unable to give you complete joy in sexual love – because I was unable to attain that climax; and how I even faked it on occasions when you had tried and I felt your wretchedness at failure. And how I couldn't have pleasure: no mind so tortured by conflicting emotions – my feeling that you didn't really belong to me (there were Marcelle's letters) and that my family were agonizing – could be released and so release the body. And I told him how you had wept that night at Pascagoula, when I had let you swim alone – because I was no longer ME. And I said (listen now: here is the most important truth). 'If I am ever again the girl he knew at Annecy, at Sils, in Toulon, it will be after years of careful training. I have to be led back to my youth. I have to be melted – as if I were iron – because I have really grown hard and tired and old'. That is the thing beloved . . .

I'm no longer Marty who talked to you of Nietzsche at Sils Maria; and walked through life with hope, radiantly; I can't help it – I loved that girl, as you did – more than you did, because to me she was the flowering of old dreams. And she is dead. Do you understand. I shall tell you frankly that I am shop-worn goods now, I'm neither beautiful nor admirable. I'm tired and I'm bruised. Bertrand, I feel sick – spiritually sick. I feel old and bitter, faithless. My feeling for you is deeper than love. You are my only hope in life of being beautiful again; of living beautifully. Will you help me? Will you be patient and loyal and forgiving? It may take years: now, I feel that I am asking you to assume a titanic burden – I am asking you to marry a spiritual invalid.

Marcelle was your destroyer of peace. These last hellish months have been valuable in this respect: you have laid a ghost. Beloved, you wouldn't lie to me to please me – would you? You are too fine for that. You really mean that you are free of Marcelle, can now go with me, hand in hand, alone – as if she'd never been, as if you were born anew. You won't torture yourself and me with regret and doubt?

And my destroyer of peace was my family. Dearest, you will be free of Marcelle – and I, of my family. We will take each other's hands and make over life. We will learn again that there is joy, and hope, and – peace.

Beloved, do you agree?

Oh, say you understand! Say you love me, forever! Say 'Yes'.

Marty

To: Bertrand de Jouvenel

June [?] 1932
4366 McPherson Avenue
St Louis

Oh my beloved, my beloved: I've booked my passage today. I'm coming. It's going to be all right. Let's spend next winter in the Bavarian Alps – just we two, writing and getting husky . . . I have over $1000 – we needn't worry for a year or so. My love, be at Hamburg on July 1 for the President Roosevelt. I'll get off in my walking trip clothes and we'll start. Sweetheart, I've missed you so. I'm going to see a doctor about my lack of sexual reaction tomorrow and maybe I'll be just like a Frenchwoman when you meet me. Dearest, I must stop – I'm doing an article to make more money for us. I shall be keeping you! Three cheers.

Cam is going out to St Louis this weekend (the angel) to convince them that a Russian divorce will quiet their fears. Of course it's illegal in France and America but if they're happy, who cares? Oh my darling, I'm coming; I'm coming; I'm coming.

Do you love me? I'm almost happy for a change – if only these next three weeks don't drag so slowly.

Dearest Smuf

To: Bertrand de Jouvenel

February 27 1933
St Maxime

Dear love;

It's almost like talking – those very long talks we sometimes have (more rarely now and that's our loss) – to get a letter from you and then sit down at once to answer. This morning on the faded looking letter-head of the Rond Point came a letter which says many vital things and which I want to answer at once and in detail.

You had been reading your *Journal Intime* – and then '*nous nous sommes amusés à dire, au cours de ces derniers mois, que tu étais paresseuse, gourmande, nonchalante. Il n'est pas bon de perpetuer pareille plaisanterie.*' That's more than true; my beloved . . . '*il n'est pas bon*'. I really believe we are pretty much what we want to be and what we <u>tell</u> ourselves we want to be. This self-hypnotism or suggestion or whatever you want to call it is so continuous and almost sub-conscious as to be of lasting effect on our personalities and modes of life. (Forgive the horrible pedantic sound of this sentence but you know whenever I start thinking it gets solemn and deutsch.) For instance, when I met you, you told me I was a superman (I'm no more of a superman than I am a fat little girl with no greater passion in life than marshmallow sundaes but that is beside the point.) Telling me I was a superman, insisting on it, expecting it of me, I very naturally began to feel that I had an unshakeable obligation to myself not to be less than you thought I could be. Had I gone back to America – at the time of the *Journal Intime* – thinking myself a puffy, useless reader of thrillers, I should have behaved very differently in moments of strain; cracked under it; gained nothing from the most useful experience any human being can have: that human being's own immediate intense, personal (and because personal, mammoth) sufferings. Now, indulgence instead of expectation has become the tenor of our relationship. The instant effect of that is visible. I am not sufficiently strong to resist constant suggestion from someone I love and respect: I have one of the greatest inferiority complexes a person can well have, and a feeling of boredom and disgust with myself. I have grown to accept, with what diminution of vitality in living, with what lessening of a sense of triumph, this vision of myself as a cheerful bed-warmer. And, what is worse, I have been nothing more than a bed-warmer – the best I could do was to play my role well. You cannot be blamed for this: one thing is sure in life – we are responsible for our own existences; for their failures or success. Certainly you merely abetted a decay which I allowed to set in and continue. But decay it surely has been. I do not believe that happiness is a gooey emotion, nor a state of irresponsibility. I think of happiness (when thinking of it) in concrete terms: to me happiness is of the order of our first walking trip – I remember the bus ride up the Petit Saint Bernard, our 'drowning' (I couldn't swim like that now), hot afternoons on the road in Italy. I don't know whether you've ever noticed but the smile of joy is something bright and eager and sharply alive; the smile of contentment is merely sleepy . . . Mea culpa, dearest, I have been feeling for months that I was betraying my youth, my love and my dreams of life: looking back on the last ten months I almost find those dog-days in Saint Louis when I worked like mad and fought against despair and felt that I was fighting everything there was to fight to the limit of my endurance more desirable than the slow motion and gutlessness of myself in Paris.

Some people are goaded by what the world thinks of them; some people, by what they think of themselves. I do not believe that I have much need of the back-patting of the world. Pierre's* flattery is on the whole embarrassing. In my lifetime, I have wanted the good opinion of three people; my mother, you and myself. Of the three I need most the confidence of myself. Surely I am no superman; but I have to believe that my living is in some way fine and important, otherwise I am lost. I'm working on the chapter now where Charis says, 'One has got to feel important or go nuts.' A crude, inarticulate way of saying what I'm now trying to explain. There is surely no absolute vision of the universe outside science (and even there one can argue and new facts can change a recent picture.) There is certainly no absolute vision of our own place in the tiny corner of the universe which we fill. We make our own vision; it is either accepted by others, altered or discounted. What others do to our vision of ourselves is only important economically speaking. (Thus whether I think I can write books or not, my publisher's opinion thereon is what buys shoes.) But my vision of myself will control my actions in my lifetime, in the small part of the world which is my garden. And it is essential to me that I say, You have gifts which it is your duty to use; you have an imagination which is your own and through it you must find new ways to live and you must be courageous enough to live these ways. If on the other hand, I say, You are comfortable with Bertrand and you can go on living easily – accepting the warm pleasures of every day, making no effort towards something harder and more distant than these daily delights, then I shall have to face myself in ten years with the same horror I have been feeling in lucid moments recently: this soft and useless person who has abandoned all the old banners is really ME.

---

*Pierre de Lanux, the French journalist in whose office Martha had met Bertrand.

I am working now without joy but with just the steady will of a person who has a job to do and means to do it. I can't deceive or gladden myself with any dreams of talent; this is no picture of the struggles of genius. But I am grateful to the grey air, the cold, the loneliness of the days, because they are something to bite my teeth into; something to be ignored and overcome. These chapters are long and bad; I find my hands trembling with nervous rage at the slowness and dullness of my mind. And I shall stay here and sit through these interminable hours and get this book done. In the doing possibly I can leave behind this mask of self-indulgence which has hidden me from myself for so many months.

For three long pages I've written of myself as if I were something totally apart from you; a false and impossible assumption. But you must understand all these things I have been feeling. There is a funny little line in a poem called 'To Lucasta on Going to the Wars' by a Cavalier poet who had a light touch even when describing a very stern emotion. He wrote to his lady, 'I could not love you, dear, so much – loved I not honor more.' You see, sweetheart, I thought of you as making me live the hardest and finest and bravest way; I thought of our joy as being intense as suffering; I stuck to you always finding you stronger than myself. In softening myself, I've softened you. You realize this as well as I do. Possibly these months of easy content were a necessary rest after much strain; I am inclined to think that. But we are rested now. We must go back to what we were and go forward to being something more. We must find a way to be happy and to love each other, without weakening ourselves. I have been too happy in the security of your love, too happy loving you, to want to give that up for any reason. But what I do want is to combine love and the struggle for perfection. One can probably make perfection in whatever one is doing; I do not see perfection as a systematic denial of joy and gayety, a fanatic desire for tests-by-fire. I see perfection as a complete aliveness; being alert and eager, wanting all things to mean growth and intensity. Doing whatever one does with ardor – whether it's swimming or writing books or earning one's living. I want to keep my body and my mind muscular; surely one can do both at the same time? I want to love you actively not passively; enjoying you tremendously as a partner in triumph; not holding on to you fearfully as a protection against loneliness and boredom. We are still young: I see youth as the chance to cut the big, rough outlines of a statue in granite: when one is older one will perfect the details, having more technique but less strength . . .

My dear love, do whatever your job is in Germany with enthusiasm and do it splendidly. We shall meet again in a few weeks and go on with the determination this parting has given, and with the joy of being in love. For I love you very much – you must know that.

I think, for always,

Marty

To: Bertrand de Jouvenel

March 30 1933
Paris

These scratchy, useless days – darling darling – it makes me want to scream when I see time wasted. Money is nothing compared to time; there's always more money and even if by some economic miscarriage one is *sans sous*, what does it matter. But time; God how valuable it is, and how crazily one lavishes it on the dingy, squirrel-in-a-cage details of life.

Me, I'm feeling like a shoe-string that carries electric current (impossible image.) I've lost 2 kilos in four days – which is fine for my figure and grim for my nerves. I'm pooped and jumpy, wasting my substance as usual. A job will come as a boon; you needn't worry about my efficiency at Vogue. I regard my future career as *femme de ménage littéraire* with positive gratitude.

Saw the great Colette yesterday and found her lovable, really so. She is sweet to me, tender I think; she cherishes a strange *rancune* against your father – I should never have thought him worth while as a subject for endless bitterness. We talked of this and that; what impressed me was to come in and find her writing on a book, with such steady, bored persistence – so little flame and fireworks – but just the determined weariness of one adding up accounts . . . What wouldn't I give for that will and discipline. She asked me to come back; I hope she meant it because I should like to go. And she said, after I'd talked a little with her about my book, '*Je crains que vous êtes trop intélligente.*' I was properly astounded and slightly *méfiante*. Then she explained, '*Vous jugez ce que vous faîtes quand vous êtes en train de le faire; c'est fatale. On droit croire dans son travail; vous pouvez le critiquer quand c'est finit.*' At the moment, I can't do anything – my brain like my tummy feels desperately unsettled.

Sweetheart, your funny little dusty letters from Rome;[*] bored they are – bored and at a loose end. You are so accustomed to having your own life; to doing your work or playing as and when you like in your own way. Obviously, being courtier – which really only means waiting in ante-rooms and smiling like a well-bred statue and echoing the last three words of what anyone says to you – is no *métier*. I am sorry about those letters because I know that in your heart you looked forward to Rome, you wove brocaded dreams around it – the Palais Farnese and Diplomacy like something elegant and suave out of a book. You went wanting something and you are finding that the entourage of your father is as dreary in Rome as it is in Paris, as no doubt it would be in Eden or Paradise . . . One of the great sillinesses of life is that people like your father always live in places like the Palais Farnese

---

[*]Bertrand had accompanied his father, Henri de Jouvenel, politician and editor of *Le Matin*, to Rome on a diplomatic mission. The Palazzo Farnese was the French Embassy.

(they might as well live in a metro for all the imagination they bring to life) and that people who would revel in that gilt luxe, and manage to act up to it – being a cross between Cecil de Mille, Eric Stroheim, Oppenheim, and Hans Andersen – always live in small, neat houses in the *banlieu*. However, as I'm not there I can't know how dun-coloured it is, or the extent of your disappointment. And besides I don't long for rococo furniture and footmen in livery; I want flowers and sun and grass to roll in and air to breathe and sun and long, intensely empty days.

My darling my darling. Come back when you can. I shall be so absurdly happy to see you, for I take very little pleasure in life unless I have either you or country; and if I have both I am probably too happy to be decent.

I love you, Smuffy. I almost wish I didn't love you so much but on the other hand what a richness . . .

Kisses, as many as you want.
Marty

To: Campbell Beckett

April 29 1934
Villa Noria
La Favière

G. Campbell, dearie:

I write you today just because (do you mind being used?) I must somehow lead my mind back to the typewritten word, after four days of barren paralysis, with nary a key clicking on the whole peninsula. You see, I have started my second book; and therefore whether I write or not makes a hideous difference; and now I am going to be saddled with this wearying, half-finished, unquiet ache until the damn thing is done – a few years hence no doubt, what with publisher's rewritings and all the misery of transporting goods from manufacturer to consumer.

I'm writing about France, my son. France and the French and myself questing, dismayed and finally cynical amongst them. Or rather I'm writing about the Jouvenels; because I'm far too wise to write about the French. A very hard book to write, since I am trying to do it in the first person singular (a test in technique) and that is no cinch at all. You wouldn't believe how the world narrows in when you have to say <u>I</u> instead of <u>She</u>. But I must do it; because writing is more than just putting words down on paper to fill the time, hoping for money to come and a dash of fame: more than a job to ease one's conscience with against the empty passing of time. For me, it's my mind's and spirit's purge: there are things to be eternally rid of. There comes a time when one can no longer carry in one's brain, heavily, certain memories, certain aspects of the present. I did that once before: I wrote out of myself a lot of destruction. My father once said: blondes only work under compulsion. It must be true. I know what hell it is to write. I know how everything goes to pieces under the strain of it, the fear of not finishing or finishing badly. It never stops and there is never a moment – until the thing is out of one's hands into alien hands – that is really rest. Damocles sword – the unfinished chapter . . . I'm sure I'd only do this when I can do nothing else. That moment has come again. Because I am really sated with France; I have had all I want or can bear. And possibly I have had enough of the Jouvenels, the entire clan, for this life.

I don't know what to do about B. because I have turned coward. Not coward about him; I writhed too much over his pity ever to want to go in for pity myself. I'm sure on that point; pity is the one great crime because it destroys two people sloppily. Besides, his world stands firm around him; he fits in so tightly into his own pattern that nothing I could do would really run him off the rails. And then he's French (and here is where I draw conclusions) and the French are realists as neither you nor I nor members of our feeble Nordic lineage can be. We are people who go mad, or drift into gutters or suicide, from broken hearts. The French, at best, go back to their work, their life, their picture frame of place, position and reality. At worst, they turn hard and scheming and vindictive. But even so, they go on; with an eye to opportunity . . .

I should hurt him somewhere deeply; but that hurt is part of life and not to be feared. (If one has been hurt oneself and weathered the 'buffeting', one knows how time soothes all things, and how good an investment pain can be.) But in the end, what – he has a son, and a name which must go on; a place in his world which demands him, a role to play. And even if he doesn't love anyone again quite as he loves me, he may be happier with a smaller love; he will ask little because he has sources of riches elsewhere.

The cowardice concerns myself. I chalk up the accounts very coldly. I know it all, because I stopped lying or exaggerating to myself a long time ago; and have gotten a certain amount of steady joy out of knowing myself and where I stand. I am 25 which is not old if one has done something but is not the beginning if one's hands are empty. I have at this moment no name: I am called one thing and recognized unwillingly as such: but my passport says something else. And this is a handicap as only I can know. I have no world to go back into, or to go forward into. Because these years have cut me away from many things – from everything: not only materially, but also mentally, spiritually.

I have no money and therefore no freedom. One must not lie about these things: money is the only guarantee of privacy, the only way to operate one's fate. I should have to work – at some job which had nothing to do with me and used up more of this valuable vanishing time. I should be underpaid and harnessed. IF I could get work. It is laughable but true; I could probably only get work in Paris being a mannequin. They would all love having me: I am considered to be rather beautiful, with a good body – and enough of a lady to give that highly desirable amateur touch which all great dressmakers (the real professionals) so snobbishly seek. And how should I bear Paris, caught in it, seeing just the people who would be kindest, most inquisitive and pitying – in that role. What else is there. The ideal is a country where I am not known, where I could stay a few years until my life grew dusty in people's eyes, with the passing of time – and vague in my own mind too. But how? And what else: going home, my mouth buttered with humility and failure, to leach on their generosity? You see, I have chalked it up too well, and see where and how I am caught – and how tightly. Through ignorance, carelessness, pride and generosity: and the passionate desire to burn all boats, to prove that I had no intention of retreating. I pay for my own acts: mainly for my own pride. Because my own pride has been at the bottom of all this; possibly more than anything. Since I would not admit that I was licked by events or circumstances or people, and so – with my head down – I charged through. I shall pay for that, for a long time. Now, in a very numb and colourless despair – closely allied to indifference – I can only hope that I shan't have to pay all my life. If I did, it would not surprise me . . .

The root of the trouble is the body. I take it for granted that you would rather be drawn and quartered than share this letter with anyone. You know how I count on you; on your wisdom and loyalty. I am writing you because I want to see for myself; I am writing to myself through you.

It is a mammoth irony; I sailed against the wind, with incredible determination, and brought the whole house of cards down on my head: to sleep with a man – forbidden territory – a married man, and all of this most scandalously, bravely and openly – out of wedlock. So that it must be thought, she is a woman of great passion – with the needs of the body clamoring – and their life together must be a constant feast in honour of Venus. It has never been; that was the great error. The error of my pride – since I chose to give (out of pride – not wanting to save my hide or be afraid, and tenderness for his needs) I would go on giving. But one mustn't make love like that. It's terribly wrong: I – who have such a quiet cool body – know all that. I have a deep respect for what blood calls for, for passion, and satisfaction. Not that these things are mine; but that is my tragedy and my own fault. (And the fault of a loathsome education which did not teach me humbly to reverence what is the beginning and basis of all life, but only taught me to pass over lightly, or dispense with generosity, something which cannot be ignored and should never never never be a gift.) Bertrand has always, and still most terribly and completely, desired me. I am amazed at myself – amazed at the years that have gone by. Because I have no corresponding desire and have never had. But the years added on other things; he has always touched me more than anyone, I have always found such gayety and nourishment in his mind, and then there is tenderness – gratitude – and a kind of love that wavers between friendship and maternity. It is strong (foolish to deny that) and coupled with physical passion would make such a love as is rarely seen, and exists in old books and legends. Because I have suffered for him, and he for me; and very much alone we have gone together through endless rough country.

It isn't restlessness (the psychologists call this sort of thing repression but I find them wrong) which makes this all so clear. I am not turning from Bertrand, looking dimly or pointedly elsewhere. I have no desire for affairs. My body very curiously has no need of that food – not at least now. If anything, I turn away; into greater and greater detachment. I am happy with myself you see; that's an arm – shield and lance. I am very happy with myself, with land and trees and the smell of things on the wind; and with my typewriter. I have enough in me to fill my life. But all my life boils and simmers, stews and burns, because something is asked which I cannot truthfully give. And though I would – have and do – give it, when I remember; it is contrary to nature to remember with one's mind what ought to be a joyful instinct. And so, I forget – or don't notice – and then there is storm, rage, misery and a kind of maimed despair. And I can do nothing; because I <u>know</u> that it would be useless even to try to fake an instinct. And possibly – oh let me be very honest – there is selfishness deep in this too; the desire to save myself, the order and rhythm of my life, not to harness and throw out of key something which runs so smoothly – alone . . .

It can't go on; what is there to go on to? He can take mistresses; and now – provided he was graceful enough not to place them before my eyes – I shouldn't mind. How could I? He has a right to these things which I do not – and cannot give him. But what answer is that – more complication, more confusion, more people hurt in the mess, the growing mess. And all the time, he wouldn't really be happy, because in the end it is me that he wants. And we would be acting a life, and because we acted we would only be half-alive. Whereas we have that great talent: we can live – we were made to live. And I, at any rate – for myself, want to and must live; I feel that I have been a little hungry (not very, not badly or achingly so) for a long time; and I feel too that my lungs are not full – Great God! what an eagerness and energy I have to live; how much living I can stand and must have . . .

I am not lonely, living this way, because I have given up expecting that loneliness can be blotted out by anyone else; my loneliness is my own cherished possession and probably my only one. I feel, after the waste and nervousness of too many months, a kind of order coming back into my spirit. And I know I shall write – and maybe even write better than before.

The land is a gladness to my eyes; I feel positively dizzy with happiness sinking my feet into dirt, grass, sand; the pine forests smell like themselves and somedays the sun is hot and close, over this small corner of the world. Somehow inside me (and this is all I have gotten out of four years; but it is enough – the best) I have protection against passing events, people and circumstance. Somewhere within me, I know what climate I need for my own *vie intérieure* and have found it now (as I should always find it, with time, in the country). And so I live, profoundly glad of each day.

If only one needn't think: next month, next year . . . Because I don't know, and stumble in ignorance. What can happen next? I don't see any way out. So I shall just go on, with my own small garden. There is a book to write. And I shall write it. At the beginning of this letter, I told you how I used writing to purge me of memories; and I also use it as a wall between me and the present and the unpredictable future, and people, and fear . . .

Have you ever had such a letter?

Love,
Marty

To: Campbell Beckett

August 29 1934
Goodrich-on-the-Wye
Gloucestershire

G. Campbell dearie;

Have I written you lately – a thick letter full of this and that. Or haven't I? At any rate sometime (who knows when; time baffles me) I got a long, pretty glum letter from you. There is absolutely no answer to make. For a good many reasons; dreary, truthful reasons. To wit: we are both really very piggy people who are used to living alone and pleasing ourselves. We both expect too much. We are both fool romantics. What else. You know it all anyhow. You didn't expect me to say anything. I won't.

As for myself; I have fallen in love with England and a little with an Earl. I don't know if it can be the Earl (I only saw him for three days) or if it's his way of life, and his land. I'd marry him tomorrow if he asked me. Yes, you guessed it; I would like comfort, security, ease, unanxiety and a good digestion. The Earl has this great distinction; he is the only man I have ever met in my life who had any of this world's goods who didn't revolt me after five minutes. From which you may gather that he is intelligent and charming. Added to which he doesn't know I'm alive and I have no more prospects of marrying him than of espousing the Maharajah of Indore. But, I love England anyhow.

We have been having a grand time; weekending in great luxury in beautiful 'stately homes' (see Baedeker). Wandering around amongst factories and
fauna the rest of the time. We shall be off to London tomorrow. A week
there, being at once bright and busy and then back to Paris.

I am coming over alone around the 10th of October. I am quite blanched
with fear over the whole business. The Unknown and etc. But it must be
done. I think (if I have the guts) that it will be a definite break with France
and B. Nothing more can come of this union; it is getting to be destructive
in a bad, chipping-off way. Which doesn't mean I'm not fond of B. or that
I don't often amuse myself splendidly with him. It only means that the
whole biz is sterile. There is no place to go now. No future, as the girl sez.
And no future means something horrible to me; standing still and growing
old and hideously dissatisfied, with lines bitterly from the nose to the
mouth. I can't have that. I've cared too much about living in my day to give
up. So I shall come back. Tell lots of lies and fairy stories – or none at all,
and just refuse politely to answer questions – and start over again. It's a bit
frightening and a bit hard. But it must be done. I hate death in any of its
forms; even relatively pleasant forms.

Of course I want money more than anything else extant. I would do
deeds fair or foul to get same. I know about money; what it means not to
have it. And I'm finished with dependence. Forever. If I ever marry again,
I'll have a contract before I start – salary to be paid, and regular hours. As a
matter of fact, I doubt whether I'll be troubled with offers; I also doubt
whether my writing will ever go over; I also doubt whether I'll find a job
(unless it's being a mannequin.) The outlook is not brilliant. I have little
hope and less confidence.

What a droll life one has. One minute I'm being a kind of figurine out
of the Society column; supposedly rich as Croesus and only interested in
my clothes and the polite twitter of other Croesi. Then I'm supposed to
be a brilliant and hard working journalist; who has abandoned femininity
for brains. And then a devoted wife, given to yes-sing. And then a Noble
Savage, who prefers solitude, the simple life, and sunburn. And with each
personage, finances change. It is getting me down. I'd like to be the same
woman for at least three months in a row; maybe even a year. And I'd
love to have a home, some place to keep my winter coat and my books
and to read in bed in. Christ how I'd love that. My own home; quite
quite alone; with no one else in it. Well, sweetie, you can see: I have lots
to work for.

Love, and until soon
Marty

In the autumn of 1934, realizing that her long affair with him was over, Martha finally left Bertrand and Europe and returned to America, where Franklin Roosevelt had been in the White House for eighteen months. She had finished her novel – about a 19-year-old girl reporter doing much what Martha herself had been doing, having affairs, growing disenchanted – and, after rejections from four publishers, it was accepted by Frederick A. Stokes. By the end of October, she had been taken on by Harold Hopkins, a senior figure in Roosevelt's New Deal, to join a team of young researchers reporting from different parts of the country on what effect the Depression was having on individual people. He asked them for impressions, not statistics.

At twenty-five, Martha was one of the youngest reporters. She was paid $35 a week and sent off to the textile areas of the Carolinas and New England, from where over the next six months she sent back long, passionate, angry letters. It was in the mill towns that she found the writing voice she had been looking for: spare, clean, simple, a careful selection of scenes and people, set down plainly and without hyperbole, the tone one of barely contained fury at the injustice done to the poor and the dispossessed by the rich and the powerful.

Sacked by Hopkins after she suggested to a group of laborers that they break some windows to draw attention to the terrible conditions under which they lived, Martha was introduced to Eleanor Roosevelt, a college friend of her mother's. Mrs. Roosevelt was then fifty, a tall, ungainly woman with no chin, protruding teeth, and wispy hair, but with startling reserves of energy and determination. Hearing that Martha was planning to write a book about the Depression, she invited her to stay at the White House. The two became friends and lifelong correspondents. More than a hundred long letters from Martha to Mrs. Roosevelt survive; the replies, though often short, were affectionate, robust, and solicitous. Later, Martha would write that Mrs. Roosevelt had an "extraordinary presence: inborn dignity softened by gentleness . . . she gave off light: I cannot explain it better."

It was in the White House that Martha met H. G. Wells, there on one of his periodic visits to America. Wells was sixty-nine, a short, round man with a squeaky voice, famous both for his novels and for his books that translated the scientific discoveries of the age into language people could understand. Wells helped Martha find a publisher for The Trouble I've Seen, *her collection of four semi-fictional stories about the Depression. There are dozens of Wells's letters to Martha in existence; only a handful from Martha to him. The tone used by Wells – amorous and suggestive – has led biographers to claim that they had an affair. "A sunny beach," Wells wrote to her soon after their first meeting, "Stooge getting sunburnt, me getting sunburnt, Stooge very much in love with me and me all in love with Stooge, nothing particular ahead except a far off dinner, some moonlight & bed – Stooge's bed." Stooge was Wells's nickname for her – as in someone to fetch and carry. All her life, Martha emphatically denied that she had ever slept with Wells; it was just a case, as she told his son Gip, of "a young woman being charming to an elderly important gent."*

To: Bertrand de Jouvenel

December 2 1934
Providence
Rhode Island

Smuf darling;

Today is low ebb. The kind of dark day one passes, lying fully clothed on a bed, numb and doubting. Today I am hopeless about this country and other countries; about myself and find no suitable reason for going on, only an unlovely instinct called self-preservation, which has always seemed to be a footling reason for life.

I'm pretty dismayed about America. Just suffering, just misery wouldn't shock me. I've seen it before; it seems an integral part of our worlds of plenty; our luxurious frigidaire-radio-automobiles-for-the-masses civilization. To see people living sub-marginally is no new horror. Hunger isn't new: I remember years ago seeing the freight cars lying on their sides with vegetables and fruit pouring into the sewer water of the Mississippi; and knew then that forty miles away people were eaten and destroyed by pellagra (which comes because vegetables curiously enough are not obtainable, costing too much money.) But what is new is the clear realisation of this human material: and it's bad – it's underequipped and what will change that. Why should our serf class be a shining wonder when our ruling class is so vulgar, so unfit; so slow and so narrow and so piggish. Darling, the homes of the mill owners are only bigger and cleaner; but no lovelier, no richer, no quieter or more gracious, than the homes of the people who starve working for them . . . I mustn't let this despair cloud over other pictures, the memory of other unprivileged people. Oh yes, I suppose it's the same everywhere; horrible and hopeless. But what is the end, what is the answer. What world can be built on such foundations. You couldn't trust these people; they haven't intelligence and finally they haven't loyalty to each other or to leaders. I am constantly shocked at their unkindness to their own people; their suspicion of each other; their treachery. I am shocked at their leaders who betray them and whom they despise. But what can you do with them; half of the people I see accept this relief querulously; their only complaint is that a neighbor is getting more. What neighbor I ask; where; how many in his family; have you ever stopped to think that he may have a larger family, sickness; have been out of work longer; have less resources. No, and what do they care: he's getting more – that's all that counts. And I want it too; gimme; gimme because it's my right; I deserve to be supported (you deserve a job but this world should not be built on charity; should not be built on a few who pay for many.) And, my dear, often relief is better business than working; wages being what they are; hours; speed-up all the rest of it. The men I pity are not the unemployed;

I feel for those who work for $3 and $4 a week; in shoe factories and mills; and proudly avoid relief; would rather die than take it.

I'm all mixed up. And beginning to wonder this: is our disordered and hopeless world the final battle for the survival of the fittest? These people I am seeing – the unemployed – are (at least 50% of them) below normal intelligence; sick; unfit. We are keeping them; and they are reproducing. Their families mount more in these empty days than ever before; what is there for them to do. But they are the cancer now; I know this system is lousy; profits are a criminal menace to society and we are so geared that all our national life is one long yearning towards profit. But still, how about those unfit; how about the large percentage of the unemployed who would never be useful or competent human beings?

I needn't worry; we'll have a war (how horrible and terrifying the papers are; what are these criminals who rule the world up to). And this war will leave behind only the incompetents; and civilization will be keyed to them. I thank God I have no children and I want none. This mess is unworthy of new life.

As for me: I am ill – principally from nerves, and because my brain is rushing in unhealthy circles. And very sick at heart; and very alone. Another myth: America is beautiful. Oh Christ what a thought. It's ugly, horribly ugly; raw and unkempt; nasty, littered, awkward. The trees don't grow tall enough and the land is torn and dishevelled. It moves endlessly ahead, without shape or grace; and over it are spread the haphazard homes of a shifting, unrooted, grey people. I loathe the looks of it; every town and city I see is a fresh shock to accept. People are ugly too; ugly and vulgar; and poor, Smuffy. Poor the way I mean it; there are too few faces with warmth and intelligence, some harmony between experience and spirit.

It has meant more than I would have believed, to realise that my book* is a failure. Why should this matter; the reviews I have read have been immature and unreasonable. I have no admiration for the type of mind which conceived them. But it remains a failure; it has appeared; and disappeared. There is something quick-sand-ish about the whole performance; and when I think of what went into making the book, and see how little it counts, I am dismayed before the future. Moreover it is terribly hard now to write; this day has been wasted which could so easily have been recorded on paper. I do my reports; I write letters; I read all the papers; and so time goes . . . Not enough. I want so much more out of life. I want to give and take more.

Cam presents a very interesting problem; he has abandoned me. It is very

---

What Mad Pursuit had appeared, to mixed reviews, in the autumn. The *Buffalo Evening News* called her heroine "hectic," but the *New York Times* found "something fresh and appealing" in the book.

strange; no doubt his wife doesn't like me (I'm sure she isn't jealous.) But I think she 'disapproves.' And it's very curious how Cam's withdrawal has startled me; how it's made me feel that this world is not mine; that I will find nothing here. At best one finds merry folk with whom to drink and dance; at worst one finds pompous ignorant bores. But how about friends, and lovers; how about all the ritual and tradition of living. What do these folk use for blood; how do the years go by. Gawd, you can see I'm low; I warned you at the start. But if I write and send this, I shall be purged a bit. And I don't know anyone to whom I could send such a letter. I have no one here to talk to – think of it – 120,000,000 people; and the rabbit hasn't found a pal. Well, well, no doubt there's something wrong with the rabbit.

Marty

To: Hortense Flexner

April 10 1935
4366 McPherson Avenue
St Louis

Teecher dearest;
It is very late and I am very tired: the house is empty with Mother and Alfred visiting in your Louisville over the weekend. I have been sitting on my bed reading a great batch of letters which I wrote Mother during college. My darling, *où sont les neiges d'antan* . . . I must have a heavy dosage of semitic blood, and I do not doubt that somewhere an illegal ancestress was a sloe-eyed Russian. Melancholy comes to me more naturally than any other emotion.

Those amazing letters: in a handwriting that screams adolescence; using the English language thickly, as if it were marshmallow sauce. And such a capacity for absorption: everything I read, heard, saw, smelled, got its little note. And I think maybe one is not foolish to regret youth, which was evidently a painful and harrowed period. Because the mind, little pal, sleeps so quietly from twenty on . . .

I read the letter about my first solemn love affair (age 18 or 17, not sure.) It is such a documented screed and fills me with terror. The seeds (coming from which direction, on what wind) were already sown: and ripened into Bertrand and an attitude of mind which is going to land me in some pub, some day, being generous and tearful over a stevedore. What makes people? I spent most of this afternoon discussing with a doctor what made hair, but when you consider it who gives a damn. Whereas people, now . . .

Teecher lamb, how are you? Being a good little hero I know, and lighting up the world around you better than any Mazda lamp. But your former pupil and permanent adorer is noddinks. Scared cutie, believe it or not. Terrified of this slime I use for brain: of the jobless future; of the fact that I am twenty seven and have produced two stinking books only. And that the shining adventure which was <u>Life</u> at twenty is now an endurance contest. There aren't even sentences. I have written nothing for months. A few days ago, in fury, I began taking my days apart and writing brittle little pieces called 'Dirges', summarizing every hour, in as acrid prose as I could muster. But goddam it I want to write great heavy swooping things, to throw terror and glory into the mind.

Have you read Rebecca West's last. Such piffle: and so unreal. But it must be fun to handle words that surely, even if the very assurance and taste make the words die, like wired flowers.

Too weary. I love you. I wanted you to know at once . . . Today, for the first time, I went to a good Friday service in the Cathedral. The Bishop (who's a young man and a socialist and a pal) said these words, during one of the prayers: 'Oh Lord, deliver us from a cheap melancholy.' I find that a lovely combination: and it means something. But between the cup and the lip as they do say, there is only air.

Bless you and your man,
Gellhorn

To: Harold Hopkins

April 25 1935
Camden
New Jersey

My dear Mr. Hopkins:

I have spent a week in Camden. It surprises me to find how radically attitudes can change within four or five months. When last I was in the field, the general attitude of the unemployed was one of hope. Times were of course lousy, but you had faith in the President and the New Deal and things would surely pick up. This, as I wrote you then, hung on an almost mystic belief in Mr. Roosevelt, a combination of wishful thinking and great personal loyalty.

In this town, and I believe it is a typical eastern industrial city, the unemployed are as despairing a crew as I have ever seen. Young men say, 'We'll never find work.' Men over forty say, 'Even if there was any work we wouldn't get it; we're too old.' They have been on relief too long; this is like the third year of the war when everything peters out into gray resignation. Moreover, they are no longer sustained by confidence in the President. The suggested $50 monthly security wage seems to have done the trick. They are all convinced that $50 will be the coming flat wage for the unemployed, regardless of size of family. They say to you, quietly, like people who have been betrayed but are too tired to be angry, 'How does he expect us to live on that; does he know what food costs, what rents are; how can we keep clothes on the children . . .'

The leaders of the unemployed speak admiringly of you. They read about you in the papers (and one of the phenomena of this depression is the degree to which it has made this unread public avid for information: they follow every detail which deals with government or relief, and can give some of us pointers on what is going on in every branch of the government, as reported by the press.) They see headlines which indicate to them that you are telling people where to get off; and they feel that you still are fighting their battle. Formerly everyone used to ask me about the President, used to speak admiringly of him. He is rarely mentioned now, only in answer to questions. Local labor organizers and local unemployed council leaders say that if he were up for election tomorrow he would lose. They explain this by saying that labor feels the NRA [National Recovery Administration] has let them down and the relief clients feel there is no hope for them; industry will not take them back and relief is going on, as a mere sop to starvation.

I bring this up not because I think the politics of it will interest you (if in fact it has political significance). But because it is important in understanding the unemployed now. They used to be sustained by their personal faith: this belief made a good many things easier to bear and I think appreciably contributed to keeping them sane. Having lost that, their despair is a danger to themselves if to no one else. This is a hurried unjust country, and the people expect to be led into the promised land over the weekend. I am reporting what I see and hear . . .

Generalizing (probably accurately) the unskilled, uneducated laborer is probably getting used to relief. The middle-class white collar worker is taking it in the neck, horribly.

Housing is unspeakable. No doubt the housing was never a thing of beauty and general admiration around here; but claptrap houses which have gone without repairs for upwards of five years are shameful places. There is marked overcrowding. I have seen houses where the plaster has fallen through to the lathe, and the basement floated in water. One entire block of houses I visited is so infested with bedbugs that the only way to keep whole is to burn out the beds twice a week and paint the wood work with carbolic acid, and even so you can just sit around and watch the little creatures crawling all over and dropping from the ceiling . . .

Household equipment nil. Apparently what goes last is the unused overstuffed furniture in the front room. Clothes nil. Really a terrible problem here; not only of protection against the elements (a lot of pneumonia among children: undernourishment plus exposure) but also the fact that having no clothes, these people are cut out of any social life. They don't dare go out, for shame. The men feel it in applying for jobs: their very shabbiness acts against them. I am now talking primarily about the white collar class . . .

T.B. is increasing; the hospitals for mental diseases (State and county) have over 1000 more patients than in 1932, epileptics and feeble-minded are increasing. Malnutrition seems prevalent among children but not among adults; and venereal disease is more or less static though an entirely different class is beginning to come to the free clinics.

It appears that the depression is resulting in a lot of amateur prostitution. This is commented upon by the people who have to deal with the courts and care for delinquent children. The age limit is going down and unmarried mothers are very young. I was talking to a girl about this: she said, 'Well, the girls go out with anybody, you might say, just to have something to do and to forget this mess.' (She herself was on relief, getting something like $2.00 a week to live on.) I remarked that it was understandable, considering that at least they got a good square meal. And she said, very calmly, 'Meal? No, almost never. Sometimes they get a glass of beer.' It seems to me that this makes a picture: complete in itself. I've seen the girls. Obviously, they want clothes, and a little fun. It's grim to think what they're getting for their trouble.

The young are as disheartening as any group, more so, really. They are apathetic, sinking into a resigned bitterness. No good, most of them. Their schooling, such as it is, is a joke; and they have never had the opportunity to learn a trade. They have no resources within or without; and they are waiting for nothing. They don't believe in man or God, let alone private industry; the only thing that keeps them from suicide is this amazing loss of vitality; they exist. 'I generally go to bed around seven at night, because that way you get the day over with quicker.'

Yours sincerely,
Martha Gellhorn.

To: Hortense Flexner

[January 29] 1936
4366 McPherson Avenue
St Louis

Teecher dear;
Thank you for your note. This is something I haven't yet found the words for. And as for feeling it is like being stunned and knowing you're hurt, but neither where nor how. Death I suppose is the last thing one learns about.*
Even now, after four days which have refused to end, lingered through many winters and been slower than prison, it still seems unreal. I find myself talking of Dad as if he had only gone on a journey and I could write him a letter any time and tell him about all five of us, here missing him and wanting him to come back because it isn't good enough without him.

Mother is braver and finer than anyone has a right to be; always thinking of someone else, doing the superb and courageous thing without even having to make a choice. But she said to me, 'I don't know how to be now, I keep wondering what there is to be.' I never imagined anything about this. You see he had an emergency operation and miraculously got well. I went to NY on Tuesday, sure that he was all right and so everyone else thought and all their plans were made to go to Florida and get sunburned and have fun, every kind of plan, even long plans, for books to write . . . And Saturday I took the plane back because he'd died in his sleep, with his hand on an open book. His heart just stopped. It can't have hurt him, we all keep saying that to ourselves. And he must have known, during those three weeks after his operation, how much we loved him and how much all the other people cared and how glad they were for his being alive. Teecher, there aren't any more terrible words than 'too late.' I am beginning to be afraid of them.

I haven't any plans. My book is done and with the publishers. I don't know what they'll decide. I haven't a job. I'm staying on to see what Mother wants though she simply refuses to want anything lest I feel she's a duty. There is very little money and so of course I'll go right on as I have, being a wage earner (it's the only way I want to be, ever.) And I'll have to come east to be that; but not yet. It's very hard to think normally of tomorrow and tomorrow and Mother's face is enough to make me crazy with misery. They loved each other so entirely and so well, and for so long.

Always,
Gellhorn

---

*Dr. Gellhorn had died unexpectedly on December 25, 1935, after an operation. He had been very critical of *What Mad Pursuit*, but, to Martha's great relief, had read and admired the manuscript of *The Trouble I've Seen*, her title taken from the Negro spiritual.

To: Dr. Schumann*

May 3 1936
725 Park Avenue
New York

Dear Dr. Schumann;
This letter is late and it isn't going to be any better for having been brooded over. I want to thank you for having come to Saint Louis, and for the way you spoke of Dad. You were wonderfully generous of time and effort, and it was good to feel how well and understandingly you loved him. I can't write properly about this but I did want you to know that we were moved by your coming and that we all appreciated it deeply.

And since that time I have been job-hunting which is an experience everyone should have, because it makes you tender towards all humanity (except employers.) But it's an experience I have had enough of before and I loathe it. I feel constantly like a gold-fish who has been bought on approval; quizzical men behind desks saying doubtfully, 'what can you do,' are my idea of nothing at all. I got a job after about four days, doing a trial story for *Time*. Said job ran an average of thirteen hours a day and left me panting with weariness and feeling my years. I am to hear next week whether I am a permanent addition to their staff or not. If I do get it, I expect to retire to an old ladies' home after a year, with palsy. Meantime an American publisher has taken my book, having first made me an hour's speech about of course I couldn't expect anyone to read it etc., and only love of art spurred him on, and that left me full of cynicism about publishers (who are too transparently commercial for even the child-mind) but glad to have the wretched book berthed in this country. The life of the working girl is never dull, but I think I would rather be a farmer around now.

Gratefully,
Marty Gellhorn

Time *did not offer Martha the job, and the* New Yorker *turned down an idea for an article about Europe. But in September 1936* The Trouble I've Seen *was published to respectful and admiring reviews. In her syndicated column, "My Day," Eleanor Roosevelt wrote: "I cannot tell you how Martha Gellhorn, young, pretty, college graduate, good home, more or less Junior League background, with a touch of exquisite Paris clothes and 'esprit' thrown in, can write as she does. She has an understanding of many people, and many situations, and she can make them live for us. Let us be thankful she can."*

---

*A family friend.

Martha returned to Paris in the summer of 1936, thinking of writing a book about peace. In France, which had been hit by the Depression later than elsewhere, unemployment was now climbing above two million. There were strikes and hunger marches. Six governments formed and fell within two years. Martha had begun an affair with Allen Grover, a business journalist with Time *magazine, an energetic, gregarious man whose family lived in St. Louis. Grover was married and somewhat less in love, and when the affair ended they remained friends. Later, Martha would say that she never competed, never set out to get a man, never looked at a man and said: "that's for me." And, she added, she never knew the wives of the men she slept with and never slept with a friend's husband. She liked men, she said, because she was interested in what they did; the lives of most women she met were simply "not my bag."*

To: Allen Grover

August 6 1936
Banque Canadienne
37 rue Caumartin
Paris

My little plum pudding;
I wrote you a *crotte* of a letter yesterday, in a sudden dislike of you, thinking what a grand hit and run driver that boy has turned out to be. You see, I never got any letter from you that I know of. You will admit it comes as rather a shock to be rewarded so largely with silence, considering the circumstances. Today there is a volume on orange toilet paper and here you are again, infuriatingly seductive, always the guy who makes me laugh; and I could go out and beat my head on the accursed cobblestones of this vile picture postcard town, for not being there to laugh with you.

Lamb: I haven't done any very concise thinking about you and I don't believe I will. If I do not mistake me, we have done a certain amount of talking and decided you and I were what is known as a vicious circle or something. There are no ideas to have about you, and no decisions to make. I am much freer of you than I was last summer in Idaho. I think I can definitely consider you as the cream in my coffee, but not my breakfast. And I am damn glad I didn't spend the summer, slowly blistering with you: because I'd be a very caught unhappy girl by now, and you wouldn't like me worth a dime. The only terms on which to take you are the installment plan ones: or in other equally financial language, it is necessary that we both have bank accounts. At the moment your bank account is appalling and mine as usual consists in half a deficit and half a fortune in dubious investments. Christ the imagery. Isn't it awful. I simply won't get tied up with you: of that I'm sure.

I got my mail for the first time in two weeks today. There were two letters from Mother which break my heart. Now, unless she will join me here, I am going back to her fairly soon. My own life is not so important right now: I can write this book at home (with an effort) and I cannot bear to fail her the only time she needs me. Besides, this European jaunt has already done me a lot of good: given me a chance to take a deep breath, relax, and start all over. It's been good for my vanity which needs some encouragement from time to time, (I just swarmed with gents in London and got fine indecent propositions in Paris from what is known as the leading writers: all hunchbacks according to me.) I've seen some things and met some funny people and rushed about and re-learned French.

If my English lad★ can get a divorce I shall marry him. I think you'd hate him, but he's a kind of swell person and I am not bored with him. (Funny that in the end – I ought to know better after B. who wasn't boring but was everything else – I still want to be amused.) I doubt very much that he'll get a divorce. He is a Gentleman (vile thing to be) which means that unless his wife agrees he won't do anything. All this is about as secret as it comes. I should hate you if any word ever got out. I have a lot of funny standards about people I've discovered. For instance: I won't encourage that boy by promising to marry him. He's got to get himself free because he wants to finish one way of life; not because he wants merely to change women. I think that my reasoning is that I want to see what kind of guts and independence he has. (HATE people unless they are free of me. I want nothing to do with anyone except my superiors. I have a real physical loathing of people who are morally weak. A man is no use to me, unless he can live without me. Odd, isn't it. Once I'm sure he can live without me, I'm perfectly willing to deliver myself tied hand and foot. But Bertrand was enough for life of the little boy, who needs his nurse, to tidy up his soul and put his mind to bed.) Anyhow, there we are. It isn't very imposing because even if he can get a divorce (and God how I doubt it, I'm a jinx on divorces), it wouldn't be for another year. But anyhow I'm pleased to note that I've gotten around to the point where I consider marriage with anyone as desirable and not a new form of water-torture. I'm writing this very toughly (vulgarly?), and I don't feel it that way. I'm protecting myself as usual from a let-down which is inevitable and from the very obvious future which is going to be a future quite alone, with a monkey and a Dachshund for company. That's all. And you're the only person who knows any of this and I trust you to forget it.

Please write again my darling. I make myself a feast of your letters. I will never change at all in the way I feel for you. I still get quite crumbly with

---

★Not known who this is.

excitement thinking I shall see you sometime, before we are both too old
or dead.

Your little pal,
Marty

To: Allen Grover

October 4 1936
Hotel Lincoln
Paris

Darling
    . . . This afternoon I am going to the riots. What I love about France is
their sense of order inside a framework of anarchy. The Communists plan
a manifestation at the Parc des Princes, the Fascists automatically arrange a
counter-manifestation. All Paris knows (they just avoid advertising it under
'theatres.') One puts on one's Sunday black and takes the kiddies along. It
is sweet. They do not shoot, which makes it all gay but not nasty. At heart,
they are not so serious – having marvelous good-sense and real humor –
that they are prepared to die for anything. Except *la belle France*, in case
strangers start walking over it.

    I love this people: but Paris is rapidly getting as seedy and sad as Vienna.
It does not pay to win wars. England fatigues me very much, in principle.
I don't like the irrepressible commercial success, or the dignified balderdash
of her Eton-bred statesmen. The accounts of the Conservative party
congress make me rage. Casual, superior assumption that all is well. Band
of stinking ostriches. Everything is very damn bad. Everywhere. And
Gellhorn personally envies the ostriches, and longs for a dash of blindness.
I am, as usual, asking questions and reading. Tomorrow I see Delaisi* (who
is a partial French Keynes) who has asked me to come and talk about the
world. Wait till he sees me. Right now he thinks I am a *cher collègue*, 50 years
old, and spectacled. In fact I have reverted to Paris, with very long hair, vast
very painted eyes, smart unbecoming clothes and fingernails like a
mandarin. Just the old split personality –.

    We are in strikes again: the restaurants having closed because the waiters
are sick of it all. In fact, one enters by the back doors, eats behind closed
shutters, fast, pushed; badly cooked and over-charged food. Poor waiters.
Society gathers together, like a coiled snake, when anything <u>interrupts</u>. I
lunched yesterday, very hurriedly, with Bronwyn Clair, Névés' wife
Natalie Paley and some of the other gals.† And thought: my God, we are

---

*Francis Delaisi (1837–1947), journalist and economist, who started as a Communist but
later was regarded as a German collaborator.
†A group of women living in Paris, several of them American, whom Martha met through
Bertrand.

all ready to be massacred. Such a wonderful group of handsome, ornate amusing women – discussing communism and Agg's new mascara with equal fervor; so lovely. So senseless, so clever, so damned unreal. Then I went, with a famous actress and a girl who runs the cinema, to a slum to visit a fortune teller. We got fleas but slight prophesy. Last night I dined with Drieu la Rochelle,* who used to be a fine writer and is now in love with war (it ennobles man) and sexy as a satyr. And we visited the Louvre (it is open at night, beautifully lighted) and the Tabarin, and discussed women's breasts. The result of all this is that I feel increasingly fey, fake and oppressed. I don't belong in an air so strange, so languid and so intense. What did I do here, for five years? What incredible obstinacy or endurance held me amongst strangers for most of my adult life? – They are now decided that I am a lesbian because no men mar the scenery, because I deny the gloating satisfaction in physical love whereof they all brag, and because I have explained icily that in an unhappy life we can at least be calm – alone. (Love and politics, and literary intrigue, and the latest electric face-treatment: Christ, they do run around.)

I shall be ready for the long smoky, unexciting winter. And Europe is finished for me. A lot of things are finished. Which simply means growing-up, growing old, growing soggy and discouraged.

Angel –
Marty

To: Eleanor Roosevelt

November 11 1936
4366 McPherson Avenue
St Louis

Dear Mrs. Roosevelt;
Has Hick† told you my latest bit of muddle-headedness. It's very funny; and I was going to appeal to you to extricate me, but that seems too much of a good thing and I am going to be a big brave girl and tidy it all up by myself. It concerns that lynching article‡ which you said you liked (your last letter,

---

*Drieu la Rochelle, journalist and novelist, ended up among the Fascists and killed himself at the end of the war.
†Lorena Hickok, a newspaper reporter who smoked a pipe, played poker, and weighed almost two hundred pounds, had been appointed by Harry Hopkins as his chief investigator. She was a very close friend, possibly lover, of Mrs. Roosevelt.
‡The original article, written while staying with H. G. Wells in London in June 1936, had been sent by him to *The Spectator*, who published it. It would cause her problems all her life and provide ammunition for critics who said that she lied; but in fact it says more about the way that Martha, all her life, blended fact with fiction.

and thank you for it.) The *Living Age* pirated that – simply annexed it without so much as a by-your-leave; and then sold it to Walter White who sent it to you and presumably a lot of other people. He likewise wrote me a long letter and asked me to appear before a Senate Committee on the anti-lynching bill, as a witness. Well. The point is, that article was a story. I am getting a little mixed-up around now and apparently I am a very realistic writer (or liar), because everyone assumed I'd been an eye-witness to a lynching whereas I just made it up. I sent that story to my agent in London who sent it to Wilson Harris of the *Spectator* who published it. At which point Gellhorn, with $50 reward, ceased to remember the tale and went on to the next thing. It then appeared in Germany; was stolen by a thing called the *Magazine Digest* and published – very much shortened and confused – somewhere in the U.S.; and likewise was swiped and reprinted by the *Living Age*. Around now, I feel that I have attended twenty lynchings and I wish I'd never seen fit to while away a morning doing a piece of accurate guessing. The nearest I ever came to a lynching was being picked up late at night, somewhere in North Carolina, by a drunk truck driver, on his way home from a 'necktie-party.' He made me pretty sick and later I met a negro whose son had been lynched and I got a little sicker. Out of that, years later, appeared this piece. I have a feeling that I am on something of a spot but I can't see why exactly. Anyhow I shall write Walter White and tell him I'm only a hack writer, but not a suitable witness. Though God save and protect his cause, on account of it's a good one.

How was the lecture trip and how are you? Are you rested a little? I don't see how you could be, but you must have magnificent powers of recuperation as well as endurance.

I got a little off my chest about democracy, at the Book Fair. Together with every other writer in the Greater New York area, I spoke at that shebang. I was scared and it was a funny night; jammed, with a thousand folk waiting, a bad room, a curious eager audience, and a pulpit affair that wobbled under one's hands . . . Margaret Ayer Barnes★ made me mad by being complacent: sloppy babble about asking her husband what a bank failure was like so she could write one . . . awful, when women go feminine publicly, especially about a good trade like writing, a trade that's as sound and practical as plumbing. A wench named Sophie Kerr† got to her feet and read authentic letters from her readers; read them as jokes. Each one made me feel more miserable. They were the naive embarrassing letters of very little people, who want something far out of reach. It wasn't funny at all, I felt. A young actor mumbled about blank verse. And I sat and trembled all

---

★Margaret Ayer Barnes (1880–1966), playwright, novelist, and Pulitzer Prize winner, known for her aphorisms – i.e., "Character comes before scholarship."
†Sophie Kerr (1880–1965), U.S. writer of plays and romantic novels.

over with fear and nerves and wishing I were somewhere else. But the chance was seized to talk about dictatorships and democracies; and how we were responsible for democracy, if we wanted it we had to keep making it, and in this job writers had a part and readers an even bigger part, as they are the mass and therefore they are action . . . It seemed to make some sense to some people (though it certainly didn't to me at the time; I only heard my voice from a distance above the chattering of my teeth.) And you do know, don't you, that though I'm more grateful than I can ever tell you for all you've done on my book, that doesn't really count. What counts is that you're the kind of person you are, and that I love you for it. Now and always.

Marty

Hemingway and the Spanish Civil War,
1936–1942

In December 1936, Martha joined her mother and her brother Alfred for their first Christmas without Dr. Gellhorn. They went to Key West. One evening they stopped for a drink at a bar called Sloppy Joe's. Sitting at one end was Ernest Hemingway, "a large, dirty man in untidy somewhat soiled white shorts and shirt."

Hemingway was thirty-seven, large, with hard muscles and a weathered look. Already widely regarded as the finest writer of his generation, he was married to his second wife, Pauline Pfeiffer, a journalist who had written for Vogue *and* Vanity Fair *and for whom he had left his first wife, Hadley. Hemingway had one son by Hadley – John, known as Bumby – and two sons by Pauline – Patrick, nicknamed Mexican Mouse, and Gregory or Gigi. Bumby would say later that Martha was the first lady he ever heard "use the 'f' word." Hemingway was planning to go to Spain to write about the civil war for NANA, the North American Newspaper Alliance.*

To: Eleanor Roosevelt

January 8 1937
Key West
Florida

Dear Mrs. Roosevelt

I'm in Key West: to date it's the best thing I've found in America. It's hot and falling to pieces and people seem happy. Nothing much goes on, languidly a sponge or a turtle gets fished, people live on relief cosily, steal coconuts off the municipal streets, amble out and catch a foul local fish called the grunt, gossip, maunder, sunburn and wait for the lazy easy years to pass. Me, I think all that is very fine indeed and if all the world were sunny I daresay there'd be much less trouble as well as much less of that deplorable thing called officially progress.

I came down with Mother and Alfred to escape a Saint Louis Xmas and they went back and I stayed on, praying to my own Gods (they both look like typewriters) for some wisdom. I have thrown everything I've written out again. It is getting me blue as daisies but there seems nothing else to do. Either this book must be just right and as alive as five minutes ago, or it won't be a book and I'll sit and nurse a lost year as best I can. Anyhow, a week of steady mulling has produced a new and pretty good detailed plan for the book. The story itself is lovely and terrible and I know it's right: but I lack the technical ability to make it come right. So I just fiddle along, writing and hoping and tearing things up and making myself a nuisance to my peers and betters. Life will be a fine thing when all this is finished.

I see Hemingway, who knows more about writing dialogue (I think) than anyone writing in English at this time. He's an odd bird, very lovable and full of fire and a marvelous story teller. (In a writer this is imagination, in anyone else it's lying. That's where genius comes in.) So I sit about and have just read the mss of his new book and been very smart about it; it's easy to know about other books but such misery to know about one's own. So Hemingway tells me fine stories about Cuba and the hurricane and then I come home and sombrely drearily try to make a solid plan for a book which seems to be a think-book in which everyone sits down all the time and talks and broods and nothing happens. It is enough to drive the strongest one quite bats.

Going home at the end of the week, prepared to sit there and first freeze and then broil until this thing gets done.

If the madman Hitler really sends two divisions to Spain my bet is that the war is nearer than even the pessimists thought. It is horrible to think of Germany just this side of food riots and that maniac — no longer apparently even caring about history or facts, stopped by nothing, and protected by terror — being able to lead a perfectly good nation into something which will finish them up nicely. If there is a war, then all the things most of us do won't matter any more. I have a feeling that one has to work all day and all night and live too, and swim and get the sun in one's hair and laugh and love as many people as one can find around and do all this terribly fast, because the time is getting shorter and shorter every day.

I love you very much indeed, and I am always glad to know you're alive.

Yours,

Marty

To: Eleanor Roosevelt

January 13 1937
4366 McPherson Avenue
St Louis

Dear Mrs. Roosevelt;

. . . I've had a wonderful time with Hemingway at Key West. He does know the craft beautifully and has a swell feeling for words and is very very careful about them, working slowly and never using anything he doesn't think is accurate. He tells me what is wrong with me now is that I've worried too much and gotten the whole thing dark in my mind, and says the thing to do is simply write it and be brave enough to cancel it out if it's no good. We agreed that anyone writing ought to have time to fail and waste effort and not howl about it; but we also agreed that as the European war came nearer and nearer there seemed terribly little time to do anything. I maunder on terribly don't I. It seems silly to be so frantic over one little idea, one little book, one little life, when things are blowing up so badly everywhere. As a matter of fact, 1 suffer horribly from living here out of everything. I want to be in Spain desperately, because that's the Balkans of 1912. And if you're part of a big thing you feel safe; it's only waiting and looking on from the outside that makes one nervous and lost. For the first time in a long while I hate the way I live. But one has to stick by things until the end.

Love,
Marty

To: Pauline Hemingway

January 14 1937
4366 McPherson Avenue
St Louis

Pauline cutie;

Being here is worse than I had remembered possible. It rains and freezes on its way down. You cut your way through the smoke with an acetylene torch. Everyone has flu and you wait your turn patiently. It is like living at the bottom of a particularly noisome well. I am not content. But it is going to be brief. My new system of the daily dozen (pages, by God), is going to finish this book in no time. Then I shall flush it down the churlit and be a free woman. I am going places. I find myself boring and all the usual life about me sinister. Perhaps I shall take a cutter (now would it be a cutter) and sail about the Horn. Or maybe the Himalayas are the place for an ambitious girl. Or something, anyhow.

Look. Here are two photographs of Bertrand, so you'd know. Aren't they fine. They were taken by me with my little Brownie three years ago, I think, at Arcachon. Arcachon was funny; as we waded in off a boat we had rented, Marcelle (B's wife) and her lover Byron, seeing us, waded out at a point farther down and quickly took a boat away. Like a bad farce on the Boulevards. It was sunny and as the naked eye can see Bertrand was brown and well. Now he looks shrunken and tired and pale green, but once he was a pleasure to see. Send them back; that is also an excuse to make you write me a letter. But really. I have no others.

I had a very fine time with Ernestino eating the most superb steak somewhere and then quietly and sleepily digesting and admiring the vast head of Mr. Heeney.★ That man – Ernestino not Heeney – is a lovely guy as you have no doubt guessed yourself, long before this. I have also been reading his collected works but I am afraid to, because the style is very taking and I do not want to take his style, no matter how fine it may be and superior to all the styles I have been trying on lately. A lousy thing, but my own is my literary motto. In passing perhaps it would be as well to tell you that his collected works are pretty hot stuff not to say tops.

I loved seeing you, I loved Key West because of you and him and the sun and we will not omit Masters Patrick and Gregory who are seductive. All my thwarted mother love received a rude jolt because I went up in the car of Mr. Van Hining to Miami and his eldest daughter Jean was along, a girl who brings out the paranoia (spelling) in anyone. I said to myself, hell no, I won't risk it. My brats would surely be like this and not little gentlemen like the Hemingway young. And I'd be the kind of mother who went in for drownings, too.

What I am trying to tell you in my halting way is that you are a fine girl and it was good of you not to mind my becoming a fixture, like a kudu head, in your home. It made me very happy and if I kept a diary it would be full of fine words about you. I'll just remember it instead.

Please give my respects to the lads, and to you chère Madame, my affectionate souvenirs.

Devotedly,
Marty

★Tom Heeney (1898–1984), champion heavyweight boxer from New Zealand.

To: Mrs. Betty Barnes★

January 30 1937
4366 McPherson Avenue
St Louis

Dear Mrs. Barnes;
You may as well begin all over and write another letter quickly. What do you mean? Why are you going to Russia? For how long? Are you taking plenty of Laxatives. For me, Travel and Laxatives are one and the same. How are your Berlitz lessons going. What route are you taking. Would you like to have me visit and will you have a bathtub?

. . . Me, I am going to Spain with the boys. I don't know who the boys are, but I am going with them. I feel out of everything and I would like to organize a column, called the Martha Ellis† column. Perhaps a column of nautch girls is what they need in Spain, they have about everything else. I daresay one can't walk in Madrid for tripping over Great Writers, also debris.

I have no money so I am going to take a long trip, I also want to see Turkey suddenly and Iran (or maybe that is Turkey) and Persia and I want to make the same trip Peter Fleming‡ made because the mountains are so pretty in the photographs and I must get to Russia. Those trials worry me. I think I ought to understand them.

Here everything is simply wonderful. We take our acetylene torches and pickaxes, to cut our way through the coal smoke. The local gentry is as charming and wide awake as ever. I have renounced the society of my peers and live on the third floor like a Yogi. I work like hell, but it doesn't seem to jell. The book is half done and will be finished in a month. Which is to say that it will be written, but it will not be a book. Then I am going to Paris and begin all over, boring myself into a cocked hat and getting all the facts tidy once more. Then I am going to rewrite it. Then I am going to have an auto da fé, and begin to live again, free of this obsession, but having no book to show for it.

Mother is wonderful, so much better than anyone else that it is remarkable. She is in fine shape, gay and brave and busy. Alfred is superb, his blood pressure must be normal, he is so sane and collected. He knows a lot about medicine and will be a fine doctor.

. . . Mr Hemingway telephoned me from New York at intervals of five

---

★The wife of the author and journalist, Joseph Barnes, foreign correspondent and later editor of the *New York Herald Tribune*.

†Martha's maternal grandmother, a formidable and progressive woman from whom she inherited, she would later say, her feeling that it was a duty in life to pay back privileges and good luck.

‡*News from Tartary*, an account of a journey from Peking to Kashmir, had been published in 1936.

minutes because he was a little lonely and very excited about ambulances for Spain. He said Mr. Barnes was wonderful, about the best new young man he met in New York.

My love to both of you little ducklets. I am thrilled about Moscow, but you ought to explain it to me. Here I sit in the wilderness and no one tells me anything. I hope to be in New York about March first, sailing at once, if possible. As I say I have no money, in the end that sort of thing may hamper me, but I doubt it.

Love and blessings,
Marty

After Allen Grover, to whom she had sent a draft of her peace novel, told her that it read more like a political tract than fiction, she abandoned it and went off to meet Hemingway in New York, having decided to travel to Spain with him. Collier's magazine agreed to give her a letter identifying her as a special correspondent. The Spanish Civil War was now in its sixth month and Madrid, on a high plateau surrounded by the Guadarrama mountains, was besieged and bombarded by the nationalists, now fighting their way across republican Spain. Some 40,000 men, and a few women, from fifty nationalities, had come to fight in the International Brigades on the republican side.

Over the next two years, increasingly involved with Hemingway, Martha would return to Spain four times. In Madrid, they stayed in the Hotel Florida, the gathering place for visiting foreigners, where Hemingway kept two rooms. Other frequent visitors were Herbert Matthews of the New York Times, *one of the most admired reporters of the Spanish civil war, and Sefton Delmer of the* Daily Express, *a big man with a florid complexion. Martha also met Virginia Cowles, another young American woman ˙journalist, known for an interview for the Hearst newspapers with Marshal Balbo, the new Italian governor of Libya. They ate in the Gran Via restaurant, the only one open and run by the government, and on quiet days Hemingway, a familiar figure in filthy brown trousers and torn blue shirt, went out to the surrounding countryside to shoot rabbits.*

Martha wrote extremely few letters from Spain, but she did keep a long unpublished diary, recording her daily life in Madrid and her already difficult relationship with Hemingway. "Stupid day," she recorded, "grey, cold, nothing. Stupid day, stupid woman. I am wasting everything & now I am 29." She had not planned to send back stories on the war, fearing that she knew too little about warfare, but Hemingway pressed her to write about the things she cared about, the effect of the fighting on the civilians. Her first story, "Only the Shells Whine," was immediately published by Collier's, *a highly successful magazine which paid well and had a large circulation, and it launched her as a war correspondent. "I was always afraid," she wrote later, "that I would forget the exact sound, smell, words, gestures which were special to this moment and this place."*

*For all of them, Spain was the war they would remember. "I know, as surely as
I know anything in the world," wrote Herbert Matthews many years later, in* The
Education of a Correspondent, *"that nothing so wonderful will ever happen to
me again as those two and a half years I spent in Spain . . . it gave meaning to life;
it gave courage and faith in humanity. There one learned that nothing counted,
nothing was worth fighting for but the ideal of liberty."*

To: John Gunther★

February [?] 1937
[New York]

Herr Geheimrat
Right now I am supposed to be doing a fine article on the Beauty Problems
of the Middle-Aged Woman. That pays my passage to Spain. I would also
do a fan dance in Times Square for $300, or sing Aida in Madison Square
Gardens for $350. I am pretty goddam tired and it occurs to me that the
trouble with life is that it is long.

I had a good time with you and cannot remember much about the vino
or the exageration so you must have thought it up since. Everything seemed
on the up and up to me. I hope that if they don't give me typhoid (more
likely than neat romantic bullet holes) I shall be back as fast as the winking
of an eye. I do not even want to go. I want to go to Connecticut and sleep
for a long time, and wake up to find that my new book is in the hands of
the right publisher and my two pairs of stockings are darned and that God
is in his heaven. Anyhow, when I come back maybe you will amble in again
and we can go to a movie this time, they are easier to leave. And of course,
take skotch through a tube.

I sail Friday but have as yet neither ticket nor money. Someday I shall be
a great writer and stick to misery which is my province and limit my
reforming to the spirit and the hell with the flesh.
                              Blessings,
                              Marty

To: Allen Grover

March [?] 1937
[Crossing to France on the way to Spain]

Sir;
    . . . You ought to see me and how I go up in the world like a sky rocket.

★John Gunther, 1901–1970, American journalist and writer, who covered Europe for the
Chicago Daily News between 1924 and 1936, when he wrote *Inside Europe*, the first of an
extremely successful series of *Inside* books.

I have a first class cabin (the steward says the class here is 'mixte'.) It is enormous and cosy and hideous as is everything on every boat but notably on the French boats. There is a bath and a radiator which exploded once and was called for grumpily by two gents with cigarettes over their ears. There is a telephone which works on occasion and a bell which never works at all. The elevators are in a state of *arrêt momentané*, which means they won't work this crossing and probably not the next one either. It is unbelievably French and when the head waiter called Guy 'Mon Colonel' (thus politely advancing his title from Lieutenant le Comte), and said with tears in his eyes that he was desolated there were no more *crêpes suzettes*, would Monsieur find it in his heart to forgive him, then I felt quite bright inside as I had again come home, to one of my many homes. I never get over the French, they're the nastiest people on earth and probably the best. They carry their pride around with them and no one ever treads on it really, and they're sly and greedy and prudent and scheming, and with something so wonderful, a warm tangible set of values which makes *crêpes suzettes* far more vital than the immortal soul, in the end. (Sir, you cannot eat immortal souls, not this year.)

I am eating partly in bed, since I sleep until two or three, and partly in first where the food is better. I am amused by the engraved invitations to cocktails and dinner (boats are getting sillier every season) and by two thugs in first and a theatrical troupe of three blank faced lovely tough kids in Tourist. Nobody else. Mainly I am amused by sleeping which is a treat let me tell you, and by languid reading, and by not having anything to do.

This trip ought to go all right; I am in no mood to get involved emotionally with strangers and haven't really any desire to play around Europe since the fun is so high at home. I shall be rested when I arrive which is a guarantee of making some sense, shall leave if possible that same night for Marseilles and the border. Only Spain worries me; I am nervous of not understanding anything, getting side-tracked somewhere and confused in my thinking. That would be pretty grim. No use worrying about it in advance.

. . . Anyhow lamb I still think you're more fun than all the other members of your deplorable sex, lined up one by one and stretching from here twice to Tokyo. I also think you're a relief to look at and you have a good mind which goes places easily and a helluva lot of other things, but I renounce you again as I renounce you every time I go or come, and every time I see you, and at Easter also and also at Michaelmas.

Love,
Marty

To: Eleanor Roosevelt

June [?] 1937
726 Park Avenue
New York

Dearest Mrs. Roosevelt;
I'd have answered your fine letter sooner but we've been waiting to see
how the film★ shapes up. I am so excited about that picture. Two nights
ago we worked with three sound engineers in the lab at the Columbia
Broadcasting, and we made the sound of incoming shells with a football
bladder and an air hose and fingernails snapping against a screen, all
tremendously magnified and it sounds so like a shell that we were scared out
of our wits. That was lovely too, working there most of the night on
sounds, with these men, everybody doing it for nothing, only because they
love the work and care about the film and what it says, and everybody tired
but not minding. This goes on every day and people spring from the
ground who are eager to give their time and their talent to a good cause. It
makes me so proud of people that I now feel I am somehow the mother of
a million, and all of them doing well.

Meanwhile, I am a little dead with exhaustion because of the Bilbao
refugees. Do you know about this? It seems that 500 kids (those tragic little
dark ones I know so well) are waiting in Saint Jean de Luz to come to
America. There is passage money for 100 of them, and countless offers of
adoption. As you know, they are welcomed to England and France, the
governments there actually do the reception work. Here, it appears, the
Labor Department has decreed a $500 bond per child before they can get
in, and also demanded the approval of the Catholic Charities. I find it
incomprehensible, a Catholic lobby no doubt, but incomprehensible
anyhow. Those children are all Catholics, Basque children, but it is
embarrassing to find that they were made homeless and orphaned by the
people who wish to destroy the Godless Reds. That must be the root of it
somewhere, but it is pretty terrible. I happen to know (so it hurts more and
makes me guiltier) what those children come from, and it seems to me
amazing that only America should offer no sanctuary for them. I have been
at this since dawn, trying to think of ways to make this clear to the Labor
Department. It seems to me that it is two things, an injustice and a sort of
backing down on what America likes to think it stands for: kindness to the
weak. What do you think about it?

★*The Spanish Earth*, a documentary on the Spanish Civil War, filmed by Joris Ivens, with a
commentary by Hemingway.

I saw Anna Louise Strong★ at the Writers' Congress[†] (which was a wonderful show, Carnegie hall jammed − 3500 and more turned away at the door − only to hear writers. Ernest was astoundingly good and so simple and honest, and Joris' slices from the film had a great effect, and Browder[‡] was absolutely awful; and Muriel Draper[§] was dramatic and we felt (silently) kind of silly, but it was a great meeting anyhow.) Anna Louise wandered up and we met later; she's a great admirer of yours so I forgive her for being the messiest white woman alive and so overworked that she doesn't make any sense after four o'clock in the afternoon. It seems I gave you an erroneous impression: she challenged me on my facts. Apparently you thought I said there were 12–14,000 RUSSIAN troops in Spain, but I said there were 12–14,000 International troops in all. There are no Russian troops that any of us − the journalists − ever saw or heard about. I doubt if there are 500 Russians in Spain, not as many Russians as Americans. The Russians, like the Americans come on private initiative as volunteers, and it's a hard journey. The ones whom I saw (I saw ten in all) are all technicians, engineers and aviators and munitions experts and writers. I didn't want you to think I had been giving you wrong dope, I talked so much that I probably didn't make myself come out straight. But that is the figure, and has been checked by the English Commission from the House of Commons, and by the London Times and New York Times men, and by Brailsford and others, and there is no reason to believe it inexact.

I'm going away in about ten days to Connecticut to write. Here they are eating me alive. I suppose it is very flattering and all the rest but it is killing me and I do not know how to work diffusely, I get addlebrained and upset and I want to do one thing until it gets finished and then another thing, and I hate to speak at meetings more than I can say. If I don't have to work here, could I come with Hemingway and Ivens on July sixth, if that's a good date: I'd love to have another visit and I'd love to see the first finished showing of the film.

. . . How I ramble on. I'm so glad I live in this day and age, aren't you, even if it gets you in the end, there is never a dull moment. Will you let me know if July sixth is okay. And please know how very much and how very admiringly I love you.

Marty

★Anna Louise Strong (1885–1970), best known for books and articles sympathetic to Communism in China and Russia.

[†]The Second Congress of American writers, at which Archibald MacLeish called for help for those fighting in Spain. The next day, the Hearst newspapers called the Congress a Moscow plot.

[‡]Earl Russell Browder (1891–1973), leader of the U.S. Communist Party before WWII, who tried to run for president.

[§]Muriel Draper (1886–1952), enthusiastic writer and speaker for the Spanish Republicans.

To: Eleanor Roosevelt

July 3–4 1937
726 Park Avenue
New York

Dearest Mrs. Roosevelt
   . . . I accept your comment on being emotional, and your explanation of
the Bilbao children* business holds. I still think it is not unsound to take
children, briefly, as far away from the source of terror as possible: and from
the beginning it was planned that five Catholic Basque priests were to travel
with the children, so that religious objection would not be valid. But
getting money to them is perhaps the most effective thing to do. It is a little
harder to collect money than to obtain hospitality, however obviously it
can and should be done. The next time I get sore about something I'll wait
a week and see if I'm still sore. Emotional women are bad news. Reform
will now set in. And thank you for taking the time to tell me the other side.
It is hard nowadays not to get emotionally terribly involved in this whole
business. The attack on Bilbao is one of the nastiest things I can remember
having known about. And a great friend of mine was killed two days ago,
a lovely humorous man, and a writer whom I admire is dying of a shell
wound, and when I think of those people in Bilbao strafed by low-flying
aeroplanes with machine guns, and think of thirty shells a minute landing
in the streets of Madrid, it makes me sick with anger. Anger against two
men whom I firmly believe to be dangerous criminals, Hitler and
Mussolini, and against the international diplomacy which humbly begs for
the continued 'co-operation' of the Fascists, who at once destroy Spain and
are appointed to keep that destruction from spreading. This is emotional,
probably. But I don't know how else one can feel. You will agree with me
that the role of the Fascists in Spain is something one cannot contemplate
very calmly.
   It is grand that Allen Wardwell† is going to take on the co-ordination job
which is so badly needed and I am especially glad that a man of that sort will
be doing it. I can't bear having the Spanish war turned into a Left and Right
argument, because it is so much more than that, and increasingly it seems
to me the future of Europe is bound up in the outcome of that war. It also
seems to me that the future of Europe is our future, no matter how much
we want to be apart, man is one animal and our civilization is not divisable
into water-tight compartments.
   Right now, I feel personally terribly helpless about everything. I do not

---

*Mrs. Roosevelt opposed the idea of taking children away from Spain to escape the
bombing.
†Allen Wardwell (1873–1953), banker and politician.

really know how one can serve. I know what I believe, and I would do anything for a certain number of ideals and hopes about the world, and how man can live in it, but I feel very useless and unable in any way to be of help to the people I know need help. I talked on Thursday night to the convention of private librarians, people who run law libraries and libraries for corporations and foundations and such. And all the time (hating public speaking and being frightened) I kept wondering what use it was at all, I don't think one really touches people, they have to feel it themselves before they can understand. In the same way, you begin to doubt whether books or articles, or anything one does in any way explains and by explaining changes the way people look at facts. And if it is useless to work so hard at the different things which trouble me, then it is a poorish life. Because there isn't much time left for fun, for friends, for leisure, for enjoying what is lovely and can't be deformed. I've gone through this set of ideas until they sicken me, and come back to the conclusion that there is no choice; it is silly to talk of free will. We are what we are, by heredity and upbringing and because of the way life has hit us, and I suppose I will go on doing humbly and rather badly the kind of thing I do, whether it is purposeful or not, because I don't know what else to do, and because I can never forget about the other people, the people in Madrid or the unemployed or the seven dead strikers in Chicago or the woman who sells pencils in the subway. I wish I could forget, but I don't know the technique for that.

Always
Marty

To: Eleanor Roosevelt

July 8 1937
726 Park Avenue
New York

Dearest Mrs. Roosevelt

You did really like the film didn't you? Joris and Ernest were very happy about it. They were also impressed that you and Mr. Roosevelt said to make it stronger — that's what it amounted to — by underlining the causes of the conflict. I think Mr. Hopkins was very moved by it. You were heavenly to us and I hope you like my two trench buddies, both of whom I adore. And I am so glad you let us come because I did want you to see that film. I can't look at it calmly, it makes it hard for me to breathe afterwards. Those shelling scenes in Madrid get me and the women choking and wiping their eyes and with that dreadful look of helplessness, in the bombing of the village of Morata, and the grave waiting faces of the men walking slowly into the attack at Jarama: it's all very close. I think Joris did a magnificent job and it is a record of personal bravery that you'd get decorated for in any war but this one, which is a good one where they do not give decorations, and men do whatever they do for nothing. And I hope you liked the prose, the comment, despite that awful voice which mangles it. It is very beautiful: a good deal of it reads like poetry. Ernest has borrowed some money (he is now quite broke with paying for film and buying ambulances) and is going to pay to have that voice part done over, with someone who knows how to talk and has enough imagination to feel.★ I think the film will gain enormously. They are out in Hollywood with it now and I am hoping it works well there.

I am the scribe for that group and so am delighted also to thank you for them, warmly. They were glad to be there, and both so happy to know you and Mr. Roosevelt, and we have seen so many people who had neither understanding nor sympathy for Spain that it made them happy to see you. If I hadn't felt so like a mother with her two infant prodigies and been so nervous lest anything go wrong with the film, I'd have felt brighter. I was very nervous though, because I so wanted it to be good for you and so wanted you to like it.

Now it is just awful hot and kind of confusing here and I suddenly realise that I am not going to finish my book, that I can't even do it properly because it is really too close to me and I feel it all too hard and can't get away from it and look at it clearly. I think that I must wait which distresses me and I have really wasted my two months since I left Spain. But I can't seem to get quiet enough to work properly, so I am just going to enjoy Mother when she comes east, and try very hard to get myself a radio job in Madrid, working for one of the big companies here, and I am going to rework on the novel I did last winter. But the Spain book will have to wait. I couldn't have written about the unemployed in a month, after I'd only seen them for six weeks, so I comfort myself saying that later I'll do the book and not be too ashamed of it. Perhaps this is just rationalization.

What a poor letter. It's awful hard to thank you adequately for all the good things you do, only you know how grateful I am don't you. And how much I love seeing you, and the President. I hope you're cool in Hyde Park and getting a rest and I hope I can see you again before I sail. Thank you again, endlessly.

                                    Love,

                                         Marty

★The commentary was originally spoken by Orson Welles, but judged too theatrical and too polished. Hemingway himself recorded the final version.

To: Eleanor Roosevelt

February 1 1938
4366 McPherson Avenue
St Louis

Dearest Mrs. R.

I don't know what is happening. (Thank you for your wire, you're a darling.) It is like this. I have made some 22 lectures in less than a month, on Spain. I am not a lecturer and don't know how to do it, reasonably, saving myself and not getting excited. I see these rows on rows of faces, often women and sometimes men, and think: I have one hour to tell them everything I have painfully learned and to shout at them that if they go on sleeping they are lost. I have lost 14 pounds in three weeks and am shaking with exhaustion and perfectly ready to depart for a better and more restful world. (Cannot tell you how I loathe lecturing, the listening faces – I want people to talk back – the awful 'celebrity' angle which I have never met before and makes me sick – the flattery 'Miss Gellhorn you are an inspiration', Good God, I have been a not always admirable character but nothing to justify being called an inspiration – and the horror of those frightened, lost, uninformed, grateful, faintly slobbering people.)

So now my doctor says either stop it or you will crack up. So my agent says he will sue for damages. Blast him. I am really more busted than I've ever been. I've been tired before, but I was never a celebrity and celebrity I cannot and will not take. So now I am home, and out of bed long enough to write you. Mother is horrified by the turn of events. We do not break contracts in our family but we are also not celebrities. She understands that and then I look so awful, so she thinks I must not go on. (I wanted the money for Spain, but oh what a mistake.)

. . . I want very much to see you, you know that, I always do. It's just complicated. I am not much these days. Thin and exhausted and worried for that people I seem to have adopted. Also for my own people. If one is a writer, one should be a writer, and not a lecturer. That's about all I do know now.

My respects to your husband. And to you my love and gratitude for your telegram.

Always
Marty G.

To: Eleanor Roosevelt

March [?] 1938
RMS *Queen Mary*

Dearest Mrs R –
I wanted to see you, and hoped all the time you'd be in Washington and
that I'd get there. Then you were out west, and anyhow I decided on
Sunday night in St Louis to sail, & sailed Wednesday morning and there was
no time for anything.

The news from Spain has been terrible, too terrible, and I felt I had to
get back. It is all going to hell . . . I want to be there, somehow sticking
with the people who fight against Fascism. If there are survivors, we can
then all go to Czechoslovakia. A fine life. It makes me helpless and crazy
with anger to watch the next Great War hurtling towards us, and I think
the 3 democracies (ours too, as guilty as the others) have since 1918
consistently muffled their role in history. Lately the behaviour of the
English govt surpasses anything one could imagine for criminal, hypo-
critical incompetence, but am not dazzled either by us or France. It will
work out the same way: the young men will die, the best ones will die first,
and the old powerful men will survive to mishandle the peace. Everything
in life I care about is nonsense in case of war. And all the people I love will
finish up dead, before they can have done their work. I believe the people
– in their ignorance, fear, supineness – are also responsible: but the original
fault is not theirs. They control nothing: they react badly to misinformation
& misdirection & later they can wipe out their mistake with their lives.

. . . I don't believe that anything any of us does now is useful. We just
have to do it. Articles & speeches hoping someone will hear & understand.
And if they do, then what. The whole world is accepting destruction from
the author of 'Mein Kampf', a man who cannot think straight for half a
page.

I wish I could see you. But you wouldn't like me much. I have gone
angry to the bone, and hating what I see, and knowing how it is in Spain,
I can see it so clearly everywhere else. I think now maybe the only place at
all is in the front lines, where you don't have to think, and can simply (and
uselessly) put your body up against what you hate. Not that this does any
good either. . . . The war in Spain was one kind of war, the next world war
will be the stupidest, lyingest, cruellest sell-out in our time. Forgive this
letter: I can't write any other kind,

love
Marty

To: Eleanor Roosevelt

April 24 or 25 1938
Barcelona

Dearest Mrs. Roosevelt:
Your letter made me very happy. It was a kind of *de coeur avec vous* and what you say about the Neutrality Act★ is what, for a year seeing it work one-sidedly in Spain, we have all thought here. Right now, the Neutrality Act is of the greatest importance. Because the fight is far from lost here, but material is sadly needed. The much bragged of Italian advance to the sea was done with planes and artillery, against brave men who were inadequately armed. Whole divisions (amongst them the American Brigade) were surrounded and cut off, and fought their way through the Fascists back to Government territory, reformed their lines and fought again, again to be surrounded, again to fight their way through and reform. The military history of the period of the war since Gandessa, on April 2, is a story of men overwhelmed by planes and guns, who never saw enemy infantry, but who have somehow managed now (April 24) to reform and reorganize their lines and calmly, serenely and determinedly carry on. There has been neither panic nor disorder, neither in the rear – Barcelona – nor at the front. A retreat before impossibly heavy armaments was carried out with order, and the line now holds. Even the refugees – and they leave home often with a small bundle wrapped in a handkerchief, abandoning everything to get out – are quiet and patient on the roads, neither hysterical nor dramatic, but only determined not to live where the Fascists rule.

Just before the Fascists reached the sea, I was out on the road and watched for fifty minutes twelve black German planes, flying in a perfect circle, not varying their position, flying and bombing and diving to machine gun: and they were working on one company of Government soldiers, who had no planes or anti-aircraft to protect them but who were standing there, holding up the advance so as to permit an orderly retreat. That same day we watched thirty three silver Italian bombers fly in wedges over the mountains across the hot clear sky to bomb Tortosa: and anywhere and everywhere is proof of the huge amount of new material sent in for this drive, and everywhere is proof of the unbending resistance of Loyalist Spain.

And it goes on. It goes on in a way to make you very proud of the human animal. Franco will have to do away with about twenty million Spaniards before he could ever rule this country.

★The four Neutrality Acts of the 1930s represented the efforts made to keep the U.S. out of foreign wars. Since neutrality legislation applied only to wars between nations, Congress passed a special bill for the Spanish Civil War in January 1937, forbidding the supply of arms to either side.

Now, for instance, new plans are afoot for children's homes and hospitals, and no one thinks in terms of time, of war operations, but in terms of the future of Spain.

. . . This morning at five there was another siren rising and falling and wailing over the city, and then against the night sky the searchlights climbing up and bending back against the clouds, and the tracer bullets from the anti-aircraft slowly going up like hot red bars. And the searchlights crawled against the clouds and the anti-aircraft pounded over the city and when it was all over, I heard a man walking down the street, singing to himself, and the city was as quiet as a village before dawn.

I am writing this by the light of two candles, uncertainly, after a day out at a quiet part of the front. It has been one of the things to do lately, to go about and find one's old friends. To find them so sure, so unchanging, so excellent and humorous and simple and brave, is a good thing to have known in one's life. I find myself foolishly patriotic about the Americans – about half of the Lincoln-Washington Brigade is lost since this last push – I find that I love them immeasurably, am immeasurably proud of them, individually and collectively, and proud of their record and proud of the reasons that brought them here and keep them here. I never saw better men in my life in any country, and what they are willing to die for if need be is what you – in your way and place – are willing to live for.

You must read a book by a man named [George] Steer: it is called *The Tree of Gernika*. It is about the fight of the Basques – he's the London Times man – and no better book has come out of the war and he says well all the things I have tried to say to you the times I saw you, after Spain. It is beautifully written and true, and few books are like that, and fewer still that deal with war. Please get it.

My plans are uncertain. I am staying to see what happens next. Things look fine now, the Fascists are directing their attack on the other half of Spain so it is very quiet here, for the moment. I have a huge job to do in Czechoslovakia, England and France for *Collier's,* and my daily bread may drive me out for a while but then I'll come back. What goes on here seems to me very much the affair of all of us, who do not want a world whose bible is *Mein Kampf.* I believe now as much as ever that Spain is fighting our battle, and will not forget that night when we brought the film to the White House and the President said: Spain is a vicarious sacrifice for all of us . . . But I think Spain is maybe not a sacrifice, but a champion: and hope to God that America at least will not go on letting this country down.

And you know something else, this country is far too beautiful for the Fascists to have it. They have already made Germany and Italy and Austria so loathsome that even the scenery is inadequate, and every time I drive on the roads here and see the rock mountains and the tough terraced fields, and the umbrella pines above the beaches, and the dust colored villages and the gravel river beds and the peasant's faces, I think: Save Spain for decent people, it's too beautiful to waste . . .

This is very hard work, writing in this light, and I've written enough. But words are going to do nothing: Fascism has the best technique of words, the daring sustained lie, and it works . . . Around now, the people of Spain need airplanes. What a world we live in after all: it seems such a ghastly mess that one cannot begin to place blame. It is as horrible and senseless as earthquake and flood, and the faces of the people caught in the disaster – the old women walking on the roads, with heavy bundles, walking away from their homes, and stretching out their opened hands, wearily and desperately, to all cars, wanting only a ride to go some place else, away, though they do not know where and they do not care – well, one won't forget these faces, ever.

Don't know when I'll be back in America, have three months work over here at the minimum, and always wanting to see how things go, and why. There's a curious similarity between the endurance I saw in the unemployed – a kind of heroism in peacetime disaster – and this: and I want to write it.

Always,
Marty

To: Campbell Beckett

[Spring 1938]
c/o New York Times
37 Rue Caumartin
Paris

Dearest red lawyer,
I hope you'll finish by thinking all my causes are right . . . All I know is this: (and I believe it's somewhere in the Bible in different words), many scarcely live by bread at all. All the bread finally isn't worth a hoot in hell. What you live by is what you believe and what you are willing to sacrifice for, what you admire and love. And all money can buy is time. There is no security anywhere; only fools believe that God and man can be controlled into safety. But you can make a rich life out of trying, and that's what I mean to do. And you can learn, slowly and fairly miserably, to have respect for history and for your place in the making of it – I know what I'm doing. I waste time and energy, and lavish my heartaches all over the place: but I still know what I am doing. I believe in man. I want to be with those who work to give man a chance.

. . . And take care of yourself, and be happy, but don't forget how big the world is.

love

Marty

To: Edna Gellhorn

May 26 1938

[Paris]

Dearest;

. . . Ernest sailed yesterday and I am not exactly happy but am being what the French call 'reasonable.' There isn't anything left to be, I have tried everything else. I believe he loves me, and he believes he loves me, but I do not believe much in the way one's personal destiny works out, and I do not believe I can do anything about this. So I am hurrying, at last, on my *Collier's* job, and by tomorrow night will have finished collecting the material. I am allowing myself four days to write the piece. And then, by next Wednesday or Thursday, June 1 or 2, I hope to leave for London. With luck and concentration, I can get the London job done in two weeks. I shall not take the car to Cheko-S., but shall fly to Prague and try to clean that all up in two weeks too. My only desire now is to get this job honorably and competently done, and then work on my own mind, which is in a sorry state of ignorance and disorganization. I want to read and write and be very quiet. Shall not come back to America this summer, it is somehow easier to be really far from all personal problems, than to be within telephoning distance of something you can't telephone to. Maybe, I say this very tentatively, you would come over here. I have entered into negotiations for a house near Lavandou and maybe I'll get one. I would be happy to go back there with you.

Have to dress. Am, for my article, lunching with the Aga Khan who is eating a great deal these days because he is about to return to India where he gets his weight in gold from his poor misguided subjects who think he is a god. Then to the races, for the bright or social end of this article. Then a cocktail party, and then as reward for a long bad day, dinner with Herbert★ and two soldiers who are friends of mine, one of them Freddy Keller† – you remember his family – who is alive and out of Spain and only has two bullets in his leg to show for it. Tomorrow I lunch with Doriot,

---

★Herbert Matthews, correspondent for the *New York Times*. Hemingway later dedicated *For Whom the Bell Tolls* to Martha and to Matthews.

†Volunteer with the International Brigade, who rescued eighteen of his men by twice swimming across the Elbo under fire.

the Fascist leader and in the afternoon see Thorez, the Communist chief. That just about tidies up my work. I have quite a lot of stuff, if only my head will work well enough to allow me to put it into exciting shape. Dunno. Hope so.

My book* will be out in French in two weeks and finally, with much effort, I succeeded in getting the translation done well, worked over every line of it with the translator and scotched the cheap and sickening publicity they were going to do. So that seems fairly tidy.

I love you
Marty

To: Denver Lindley†

June 1 1938
18 Square du Bois de Boulogne
Paris

Lindley comrade;

I am just about gaga. Before I started to write this article, I threw out at least half my notes. Then I wrote it and cut it three times. Then I couldn't read it anymore and had it copied. Then I cut it again, as you will see. And it is still too long and I can't make sense about it anymore, having worked on it too long. Me, I am dead. I drove the length and breadth of France and can now give Baedeker pointers. I haven't started to say anything I want still to say, and see how fat this all is. Please. You manage it.

As for the pictures: I think the way to use them is BEFORE and AFTER. You know, the bad Spain pictures, with everything torn up, alongside a sweet Marseille picture. Then the cemeteries, and certainly the picture of the quiet and comfortingly high Pyrenees frontier. I do think it's well to show a brand new war, contrasted with peace pictures. Too tired to be sure of anything. But that was my idea.

Please CABLE me both comments and money. Gave my money away to soldiers like a goop, their need being at the time greater than mine, and now my need is fairly great. Let me know what you think of this article and what ideas you have for the others, if you have any. I am going to work faster now, seeing that this careful stuff only gets me in trouble and lands me with the Five Foot Shelf on my hands, instead of a *Collier's* article. I shall get the Cheko article off by June 18 and the English article off by July 10 at latest. Promise. You can count on that. I have learned my lesson. Very

---

The Trouble I've Seen, published as *La Détresse Americaine* and hailed as "one of the great books of the day."
†Editor at *Collier's* magazine.

damn sorry about being so slow and so solemn and etc. I got pretty well stuck in Spain, which I really needed as information, and this time I was horror struck and now I am a pacifist. But there's going to be a war all right, it's just a question of when the Germans get too cocky, go too far, and get slapped. They could do it next week in Prague or not for months. The real thing about it is that France's air force is absolutely nil: I have it on the best authority that only about 100 planes are worth a damn. They have been badly constructed and many are outworn and nothing they have is as fast as the Deutsch. And they are more scared of aviation than anything. The English it seems are coming on nicely, but the French are in a mess from the war material point of view.

I'm going to Prague now rather than later because of the elections next week, local color etc., and also because if it does blow up in Czechoslovakia later in the summer, I don't want to be there. I don't mind war but damned if I'm going to do it in any old country, and to be cut off there in those mountains with people who speak a preposterous language is more than I'll risk, even for my old school *Collier's*. You will be stiff with fury over the length, but you can decide better yourself what sections to cut out. It is written in sections and you can lift them out without having any rewrite jobs. Only I can't decide anymore. It is now four a.m. and I am very weary and this must go off on the Champlain tomorrow.

Greetings,
Marty

To H. G. Wells

June 13 1938
Hotel Ambassador
Prague

Wells darling

Am coming to London next Sunday to sweat out my life's blood on behalf of *Collier's* for one week. I do not invite myself to stay with you, because I do not think you like me anymore, but perhaps I could come to lunch in all cases, and see what we agree & disagree on. Shall call you up – hope you're in town.

This country is very interesting. If Hitler had stayed a housepainter, I think it might have become a model democracy. Anyhow they seem to have put the war off for a time & one must be grateful. Why don't you shoot Chamberlain, like a good citizen? What a man. With a face like a nut-cracker and a soul like a weasel. How long are the English going to put up with these bastards who run the country?

I am <u>very</u> tired, and have a bad liver from too much war, and wish everything would become reasonable for once so that honest folk could get a sunburn and cultivate their gardens.

Love, as always

Stooge

To: Eleanor Roosevelt

June 17 1938
18 Square du Bois de Boulogne
Paris

Dear Mrs. Roosevelt;
I got your lovely letter, and meant to answer it at once, but between now and then I have flown in and out of Czechoslovakia and had an exhausting if very interesting time. I wanted to write you, straight off, about that France-is-helping-the-Loyalists story. It goes on here, in France, very violently. Doriot, the not very promising Fascist leader, told me most seriously that there were 35,000 French troops, army equipped and officered, fighting with the Spanish government. I told him somewhat sourly that if that were true, the government would have won in Spain long ago. It makes me particularly angry in view of what is going on now: a massacre. I believe that some airplanes must have got in but obviously not too many, or else this heavy and general bombing by Franco would be stopped. I know the frontier well, having wasted two weeks of my time hanging about there at the end of the month of May, and having watched it, and asked questions along it at every entry and exit into Spain. And I've asked journalists stationed in Perpignan and all along, and asked homing soldiers, and everyone I can find, as well as authorities here: France is certainly not being the support it is supposed to be, and what does manage to get in is on largely private initiative. I only wish the stories were true, and would be the first to be noisily delighted. But there it is. Anyhow, they are now seriously considering sealing the frontier to what slight traffic crosses it, and in due time a blockade can win any war.
Czecho was amazing. The country is a fortress, and the atmosphere is of someone waiting in an operating room for the surgeon, who will come to work with a blunt knife and no anesthetic. I do not see how this armed peace can continue. Partly because of the disastrous economic burden and partly because of the wearing and abnormal psychological strain. And yet the Czechs seemed to have called Hitler's bluff with as pretty a mobilization as was ever staged, and quiet now reigns. It's David and Goliath all over again and the Czechs are dancing with pleasure about it. However it gives you a turn to see peasants working in the fields alongside black steel reinforced concrete pillboxes, to pass a Slovak peasant girl with red skirt and

high black boots, peddling along on her bicycle, with a gasmask slung over her shoulder, to see every road barricaded, guarded, and to know that all railway bridges are mined, and all the rest of it. People do not yet realise (because the mind isn't built that way) what war can be. They fear it but surely they fear it the way children fear nightmares, dimly, without definite images in their heads of how it will all work out. Me, it makes me sick, the whole business. By now, Europe knows that the former housepainter holds the lightning in his hands and it is ghastly to think that this one mad man can plunge us all into it again. Yet, Marx is still the sound one, tracing it all right back where it belongs: you can measure the rise of Nazism in Czechoslovakia exactly by the fall in export figures. And I am pretty sure those German minorities, who were 80% Social Democrat before 1935, would still be hardworking quiet reasonable people, if it were not for unemployment and hunger and the craziness that comes with a dole.

Ah well, I think the summer's safe anyhow. Have to go to England next week and ask a lot of questions. I am so depressed and disgusted with English foreign policy that I am beginning (stupidly) to feel the whole nation is a mass of cotton wool. This business of being a hack is fine for finances and revolting from the point of view of serious accomplishment. I am beginning to think in paragraphs and pretty soon it will be headlines, and when the day comes I shall hire out as a scrubwoman, which will be more suitable and honorable.

My love to you always, and please give my respects to the President.

> Devotedly,
> Marty

To: H. G. Wells

> July 7 1938
> 18 Square du Bois de Boulogne
> Paris

Wells darling;
I didn't call you Friday because I was sure you would be quite as hectic as I was: and no good comes of bursting in and out, with one's breath gone, and one's eyes wild. I'll hope to see you calmly someplace, but not in England. Gellhorn is renouncing England. It isn't enough to be beau-d about by bright but not imposing young men, it isn't enough to feel like the Queen of the May. I detest your ruling class, really thoroughly and seriously. I despise them as mercenary and without any desires except those concerned with holding on to what they've got. I find them horrifyingly shrewd and horrifyingly empty: and the worst of it is that the People put up with them, tip their hats, grin all over their faces, and are delighted to be

ruled, gypped, snubbed and lied to providing the gent who does it is a gentleman. Well, Christ. I prefer a lot of other countries: Spain is a paradise of reason and generosity and the finer things of the spirit compared to that green isle . . .

And as for a free press, mother of God. You don't need Goebbels.

Anyhow, I'm sick of the country and never want to see it again. I also loathe its comfortableness and its sloth: and reaffirm my dislike of islands and their effect on people's minds. So.

In all cases, I left England Saturday as one escapes from jail and have been just breathing in Paris which is quiet and a little shabby, except for all the horror that has been put up to spoil it in honor of the King. I've written my article on England (just whacking it out, and in such a hurry to be free) and shall soon be going somewhere to swim and sunburn and try to write a book. I won't move or earn money for at least six months, anyhow I hope so.

It was damned disappointing not to see more of you, but maybe you'll be coming in my direction sometime and maybe there'll be more leisure. I love you very much and find you always an enchanting guy. And am your humble servant as you know.

> Devotedly,
> Stooge

To: Charles Colebaugh*

> October 22 1938
> c/o Guaranty Trust Co
> 4 Place de la Concorde
> Paris

Dear Mr. Colebaugh;

About Beneš.† I got in touch with Jan Masaryk‡ as soon as you cabled me; we talked a long time from here to London. Masaryk said he did not think I ought even try to get at him; he said Beneš had not seen anyone, even intimate friends, since his resignation. For political reasons, he could not talk or write. The political reasons are that Czecho is now a Nazi vassal state and they dare not in any way offend Hitler. Beneš, aside from being unable to speak about the really shocking diplomatic methods that led up to the capitulation (an embargo which applies to all official Czechs), also enjoys the personal hatred of Hitler. Therefore, he fears to compromise the

---

*Editor of *Collier's,* a short and stocky Scot who set great store by good writing.
†Eduard Beneš, president of Czechoslovakia since 1935, had resigned after the Munich Agreement.
‡Jan Masaryk, ambassador to London between 1925 and 1938.

new dismembered Czechoslovakia by pleading its cause. Jan Masaryk also said: 'The important thing now is whether he will get out of there alive.'

So the minute I got to Prague I began on it. I saw Beneš' secretary, his chef de protocol Mr. Smutny at the Palace, two great friends of his in the Foreign Office, General Faucher and various others. The story is (it cannot be proved because by now everybody in Czecho is afraid to talk about anything) that Beneš remains a kind of prisoner at Cesimova Usti, because Hitler and Mussolini have made it clear that they do not wish him to go about the world spreading 'democratic intrigues.' That is probably in part true: another reason that he is in Czecho is that he doesn't want to give the impression of running away. No member of the Press had seen him since his resignation, no one could get near him, you couldn't even find out who – if anyone – did see him. I got a formal promise from Smutny to communicate your offer, explaining it to Smutny as Beneš' chance to win the public opinion of America etc. I did a very long and careful sales talk, but I am sure it did not come off. I would have heard from Smutny by now.

Then I hired a car and drove to his country house. The first thing that happened was the descent of the plain clothes police on me. I was well stopped at the gate of Beneš' house. I made a long sometimes indignant sometimes tearful speech, (not wanting to get arrested for any of the odd things you can get arrested for, in a troubled and distraught land) and at last they allowed me to send in my card. I made also speeches to the gate keeper and wrote on the card and waited. And waited.

I am not writing these things in my article. Perhaps I am wrong, but I have always tried to be as non-political and pictorial as possible for you, believing that was the way you wanted things done. The story of Czechoslovakia is, really and finally, the story of the dishonesty of the Chamberlain government and the cowardice of Daladier: but I am writing you a picture of a destroyed state, practically calling the lost sugar beet fields and coal mines and railroads by name, practically naming the refugees who are homeless and in desperate danger. It is the grimmest and most complicated story I ever saw: and worst of all, the war is now certain, and when it comes it will be a far worse war. And worse than that, Mussolini was at the end of his rope, and Hitler would have been finished after a few months of war, had it even come to that: but Chamberlain has given Europe to the dictators, and there seems very little hope that democracy will survive on the continent.

I am wiring you that I shall mail the story on the _Paris_ instead of on the _Bremen_. I have been waiting to try to find out what Hungary was going to seize; in order to get the picture complete. Now I don't think that will be settled for sometime. Probably another Four Power Conference to divide up the southern part of the country. Hitler doesn't want Hungary to have a common frontier with Poland but it is difficult for him to say so, and so the negotiations drag and that part won't be possible to write now.

But already the Left and Liberal parties have been outlawed in Czecho, and one 'National' Party established. Nazism. They will be saying Heil Hitler in the streets of Prague sooner or later; and they will be saying it grimly.

I am calling my article 'Mr. Chamberlain's Peace'. That seems to me a perfect description. But if you don't like that, I suggest as an alternative, 'Obituary of a Democracy.' Both are accurate.

At last a very nice little secretary-housekeeper kind of person appeared and told me in bad French that the President was desolated but he absolutely could not see anyone on any matter whatsoever. I had written on the card that I would not attempt to ask him any controversial political questions, but even that didn't help. The President (she said) knew I would understand that he was not seeing anyone at all; it had to be a blanket rule. I tried arguing but the police very politely and firmly saw me to my car and away.

I went back to Prague and tried it all over again and realized that I was up against something nobody could crack at this time . . . as long as he is in the country, he must keep quiet: both for the sake of Czechoslovakia and for his own safety. In this connection, it is interesting to note that most of the men I knew there – Beneš' men – in the Foreign office, press etc. – are leaving the country as fast as they can. They know that concentration camps are the next step.

So. I know the story of those days diplomatically; I got them from the documents of the state department, translated from Czech for me by an official who cleared out almost at once afterwards. It is a story like a third rate police court grilling; nothing so shocking that I know about in history. But someone official would have to write it, to have it believed. I wonder if the British Government could sue for libel (of course it is all true, exactly what the British did) but I shouldn't think Chamberlain would care to have it known. Amongst other things, practically every note was presented either very late at night, having given the responsible Czech ministers just enough time to get home, go to bed, and go to sleep for about an hour – notes were held so that this could be done – or presented early in the morning from 6:50 to 7:30, after all-night cabinet meetings. It was a sort of third degree of fatigue and beats everything. Likewise it is clearly seen in this documentary evidence of the events, that England planned to sell out Czecho all along, and that the mobilization of France, the mobilization of the English fleet, the mobilization of the Czech army (which was ordered by England) were all part of a vast comedy to terrify the peoples of the world and make the Munich Pact seem a last minute rescue of peace, whereas it was a long planned betrayal.

I am going to Morocco as soon as I get this story off. I want to see what is happening down there. It all sounds very curious and ominous. Maurice Hindus,★ whom I saw in Prague, announced one evening, 'I am going back to America as soon as I can; believe me, in Europe even the roses stink.' A very accurate statement, seems to me.

So you'll have the story on November 2. I trust you will like it. Czecho was much worse than war really, and the story is as moving as anything I ever saw. Evidently the four great 'artisans of the peace' never met any little people in their lives: but I still have the nightmares over the old Czech of sixty one who showed up at a frontier town with his front teeth knocked out and his ribs all but sticking through with the beating he got, and his hands black and swollen; and he was mussed up that way because he was a Czech and believed in having a president. He was only one of thousands on the march. It's some story.

This is a very long letter. There was quite a lot to say.

Sincerely,
Martha Gellhorn

To: Charles Colebaugh

December 6 1938
Paris

Dear Mr. Colebaugh;

. . . I am returning on the *Champlain* providing it runs, arriving December 20. I'll telephone you at once.

Meantime, the story that interested me in Barcelona is the one which will I believe ultimately decide the war: to wit, food. The army is okay and they are manufacturing munitions and light arms and the army seems astoundingly to get on somehow with a steady inferiority of heavy armaments and planes. The morale is fine and they have learned to dig: going along as is, without at least a German army corps and a few hundred more planes and countless extra artillery, it would take Franco forever to win the war and it is more than likely that he couldn't do it. This is politically tremendously important: being the first thing that has held up Fascism in Europe, since Fascism started. But the rub is food and the civil population. So I spent two very grim weeks going into vast detail on the life of the little man and his family and how they are facing the third cold hungry winter. It is a very moving story and of course, it is the real story about war. I took one typical Barcelona family (in general outline, the same things hold true of a Madrid family, or the average family in any

---

★Born in Byelorussia and emigrated to the United States, Maurice Hindus was a journalist and correspondent writing mainly about the Soviet bloc.

Republican city) and followed it through all the ramifications of a wartime daily life. So the story goes like a novel from a children's hospital where the seven months old kids have t.b. from undernourishment, to the front where the division commander is a fine 26 year old boy who was an electrician three years ago. I'm going to write it and will mail it, with luck, on the same boat as this letter, or if I can't manage that, I shall bring it along with me.

I got all the checks and thank you very much. I do think the Beneš thing will work in due time, and it will be very interesting to know (in case he knows himself or will say it) why he refused the offer of Russian aid and refused to fight. Even if he believed that Hitler really would make war – which very few informed official people believed at the time, it now appears (band of liars they are, anyhow, what with this and that) – he still has never explained why he didn't chance it. He's the only one who will be able to tell and I hope he does.

If you are in town before Xmas, I shall look forward to seeing you, and if not, I'll come around right after Xmas. I plan to go to the country and work on a book, at the beginning of the New Year.

Yours,
Martha Gellhorn

Convinced that there would be war before too long, and wanting no part in it, Martha returned to America in January 1939. She had been in Europe for almost ten years, writing, with no qualifications, as she put it, "except eyes and ears." She had decided to leave, she said, because she was sure "that the countries I cared about were lost."

Hemingway, still married uneasily to Pauline, asked Martha to join him in Havana, where he was working on a collection of short stories. Martha reached Cuba on February 18, 1939, and began to look for somewhere for them to live. In the local paper she saw an advertisement for a fifteen-acre property called La Finca Vigia – the Watch Tower – from where, at night, you could see the lights of Havana. It was now clear that Hemingway's marriage was over, and they spent the spring and summer together in Cuba, then went to Sun Valley in central Idaho, where the diplomat and banker Averell Harriman had created a resort with the hope of making Americans ski-conscious.

Hemingway was now working on For Whom the Bell Tolls, *his novel about the Spanish civil war; Martha was writing about a young American reporter witnessing the fall of Czechoslovakia.* A Stricken Field, *published the following year, started as a short story set in Prague and was Martha's way of writing out, as she put it, "the accumulated rage and grief" she felt by focusing on just one "small aspect of the ignoble history of our time." To a friend, she said: "I think that right now there is nothing to do about it except write about it . . . as an act of faith, believing still in telling the truth . . . and also write to save one's sanity."*

In October, Collier's *asked her to write a series of articles on Scandinavia.*

Stopping in Finland on her way, she reached Helsinki on the night of November 29 and next morning, at 9 a.m., the Russo-Finnish war began. Hemingway had stayed behind. They wrote to each other nearly every day and her nicknames had never been more fanciful: Rabby, Bongie, the Pig, Scrooby, Bug. She returned to Cuba after six weeks, to find him completing chapter 23 of his book — out of forty-six — and very reproachful about her long absence. She undertook not to leave him again.

To: Eleanor Roosevelt

February 5 1939
Naples
Florida

Dearest Mrs. Roosevelt;
I see by this morning's paper (The Tampa Morning Tribune, a strange sheet mostly full of local gossip about oranges and grapefruits and their prices) that the Nazi press is calling the President, 'Anti-Fascist Number One.' As I can think of no greater term of honor, I am hurrying to write and congratulate him via you. I am also thrilled to see that the Italians are in a fury. In these days, unless the Berlin and Rome press are insulting, you cannot be sure where you stand.
. . . The thing about Barcelona* is like having a death in the family, only worse. We have all been writing to each other, telephoning, thinking, and trying to understand it. I think the hunger had a lot to do with it; I know the inadequate munitions had too much to do with it: but I also think part of it was just the Catalans. The Catalans, to my mind, bear the relation to other Spaniards that a voodoo doctor does to a great scientist: they are sort of fake Spaniards. I hear now that the fine men, Lister, Paco Galan, Modesto and other divisional commanders, held where they had to, and the Catalans ran away on either side. When I first learned about cowards being shot at the front I was very, how shall I say, distressed maybe. Now I think that is okay. The cowards risk or sacrifice the lives of the brave ones. This time they seem to have lost everything. And I find myself thinking about Negrin all the time. I suppose he will fly to Madrid when it is ended in Catalonia and carry on there. Negrin is a really great man, I believe (and he can't stop being now), and it's so strange and moving to think of that man who surely never wanted to be prime minister of anything being pushed by events and history into a position which he has heroically filled, doing better all the time, all the time being finer against greater odds. He used to

---

*Barcelona had fallen to Franco's army on January 26, after which Republican soldiers made their way over the high passes to France. Juan Negrin (1892–1956), prime minister during the civil war, fled with them.

be a brilliant gay lazy man with strong beliefs and perhaps too much sense of humor. He was it seems never afraid and loved his friends and his ideas about Spain and drinking and eating and just being alive. Now he has grown all the time until you get an impression he's made of some special indestructible kind of stone: he has a twenty hour working day and in Spain you get the idea that he manages alone, that with his two hands every morning he puts every single thing in its place and brings order. Of course, he cannot hold a front. I hope he gets to Madrid. If they are going to be defeated, I still hope they don't surrender.

There's one thing in your letter I don't agree with, and you don't practise it yourself. You say: 'Stop thinking for a little while.' You don't stop thinking. I'm no use of course, don't accomplish anything, but if I ran away from it, tried not to know or understand, stopped caring (or being hurt or angry at how the world goes), then I'd be guilty not only of ineffectuality but also of cowardice. I <u>hate</u> what happens in these times, but ignoring it won't change it. And someday if I go on trying to know and understand, I may at last get it all in some sort of shape or order, be able really to see how it all works together and why, and then maybe I could write something that would make just a few other people think too. If democracy is good, it must depend on the constant concern of the citizens. God knows I don't recommend concern as it would surely be more comfortable to be a cabbage and the weather is always something to take pleasure in, and scenery remains pretty well unspoiled and there are fine books and sun and music and a lot of things (oh a lifetime full of things) always there to give pleasure. I don't ignore those things or deny them or minimise them. Myself, alone, I have a wonderful and privileged life and am deeply aware every minute of my benefits and good luck. But the only way I can pay back for what fate and society have handed me is to try, in minor totally useless ways, to make an angry sound against injustice, and to see what goes on around me that isn't as good as what happens to me myself. This is a very longwinded and confused statement of faith.

Love,
Marty

To: Eleanor Roosevelt

March 18 1939
San Francisco de Paula
Cuba

Dearest Mrs. Roosevelt

. . . Everything that has happened these last six weeks has been so heartbreaking that I cannot endure to think about it. Perhaps because I try to be a writer, perhaps because I am a woman, I cannot avoid seeing history always in terms of people. And I see this disaster in terms of the plain soldiers I knew, and the others who once were painters, musicians, dock workers or miners and became commanding officers, in terms of Negrin and the young man, a brilliant research scientist, who was his secretary. I keep thinking of Pasionaria*, and the peasant women and the little old servant who took care of me in Madrid and walked to work through bombardments, sighing to herself 'for the poor people and the dead.' And seeing it this way, it is intolerable. . . . In Spain itself, as the final disaster has neared and overtaken them, the fools, hysterics, cowards and liars have gotten the upper hand. I suppose it is inevitable. It begins to seem to me that the rewards of the good and the brave must be in heaven, since they are surely not on this earth.

. . . I have taken possession of my finca. I had a moment of acute depression bordering on despair yesterday, which was produced by protracted housecleaning and shopping at the ten cent store for kitchen ware. I'm not much of a house woman (*femme d'intérieure*, as the French so sweetly say) and the week's work of getting a place habitable seems to me far more trying than a week at the front line, or a week working myself to the bone getting an article in shape. I got very gloomy, thinking now I am caught, now at last I have possessions (and I have feared and fled them all my life), and what in God's name shall I do with this palace now that I have it. So I felt that the world was at an end, I had a house and would never write again but would spend the remainder of my life telling the servants to scrub the bathroom floors and buy fresh paper for the shelves. So I slept on it, and woke to look out my window at a saba tree, so beautiful that you can't believe it, and hear the palms rattling in the morning wind, and the sun streaking over the tiled floors, and the house itself, wide and bare and clean and empty, lying quiet all around me. And I am delighted, and feel almost ashamed to have all these wonders, and feel myself at last very serene and safe and I think maybe I'll get down to work at last and turn out the book that has been haunting me, but has never gotten written. It seems, somehow, shameful to be so well off in such a tragic world, but I console myself by saying that my money will run out in due course and I'll be back working hard for it, and paying again for this brief breathing spell.

When I was living in a $4 a week room in Albany, just after I left Bryn Mawr, working as a cub reporter on the *Times Union*, I never dreamed I would write myself into a grove of palms and bamboos and flamboyante trees, nor a terrace covered with bougainvillea, nor a swimming pool: and

---

*Dolores Ibarruri (1895–1989), key figure for the Republicans in the Spanish Civil War, whose words "The fascists shall not pass! *No pasaran*" became their rallying cry.

I can't believe it yet. I have a feeling I ought to put up a plaque to *Collier's* magazine.

Love,

Marty

To: Allen Grover

November 19 1939

SS *Westenland*

Darling;

We are anchored in the Channel as it is too dangerous to cross the minefields at night (I imagine them as something strange, like a spiky wilderness, or rather black mounds bobbing on the surface of a troubled sea, but it appears things are not as simple as that.) Up to now this trip has taken the cake for longevity. I would be able to tell you how long ten days at sea on a small, bored, waiting and uncertain boat can be. Sleep is a figment of the imagination, as that berth you sat on is made for pigmies and the mattress is full of nails. I am a little ill with loss of sleep, loathsome food and no exercise; and personally I think boredom can only be compared to malaria, as an evil.

Needless to say I know everyone on the boat and am the local toots. The people are quite funny, if you see things as a writer (I am very busy seeing things as a writer. As a woman, I would have stayed at home.) Now the situation is tense again. Simply we are at last approaching danger, that dull and violent and repulsive danger of accident and error, the mine that was not intended for you, the bumbling into something that might just as well float harmlessly for years until it was washed up on the shore of Holland and used by the thrifty Dutch as a flower pot. The radio announced early in the a.m. that a Dutch boat, one day ahead of us, bound for the West Indies and carrying 600 passengers, hit three mines in the channel and blew up with a loss of 150 lives. (You of course know more about it than I do.) Now the crew, stewards and passengers *chez nous* have sunk into a marked but inarticulate unease. I am so stupefied with boredom and liver and insomnia that I feel nothing except a vague resentment against the idiocy of fate and all wars. Still, we have to go through that mess these next days and you can feel the change in the people. As a writer (note) I am interested. I am getting a story out of this trip. I think it's a fair sample of a war of nerves, and I know what the phrase means. It means that you go stark dingo with *ennui* and any little noise at all would be welcome.

I still think I will be home early in January. We will become like neolithic man again. We will seek our caves and our own fires and our women (or our men). We will listen to nothing and we will not care. I am feeling, in myself, the beginning of one of those chins that Wells uses to illustrate pictures of his prehistoric men. I feel a very great indifference seeping over me. It is impossible to believe in anything much any longer. Did you know that a torpedo could weigh 1500 kilos and travel five or six miles. Men are too clever. It has really gone too far.

How are your teeth? Did they come out all right, that afternoon, ten days ago or however long, how bloody stinking and forever long ago? I dote on you. You are certainly a comfort in what is constantly referred to as a changing world.

Goodnight sweetie. We'll have a wonderful drunk celebration when I get back. But let's be gentlemen farmers or publishers or something. Let's get off by ourselves and be kind to everyone we see. But let's not worry too much about those large issues which apparently are the meat of the supermen who rule us, those shitlike creatures who can talk faster than we can.

I am your devoted colleague,
Marty

To: Ernest Hemingway

November 30 1939
Helsinki

Rabby;
I love you. That's the main thing. That's what I want you to know.

I arrived yesterday afternoon on what turned out to be the last plane. Everything looked normal. Diplomatic relations had been broken off with Russia but you know, one doesn't take these things too seriously. It was cold as hell and rainy and like Gary Indiana. I was very tired after another insomniac night and shivering with chills and depressed beyond belief. I went to bed at four and slept until eight and had some dinner in my room and slept again. Slept well for the first time since I left New York. At 9:15 I was dressed and ready to go downstairs to breakfast and I heard the siren and I thought, simply, well, I'm damned. Nothing more. I went downstairs and there was nothing to see. The people were behaving wonderfully in the streets, getting into airraid shelters but not panicky and it was a beautiful morning, and I stood in the street and watched. Then I saw a huge silver trimotor bomber go over at about 500 metres. Low and slow, just wandering around. It had dropped propaganda leaflets, it appeared later, which said (if you can believe it, it's too funny) 'You know we have bread, why do you starve?' Honest to God. They bombed the airport this morning. Lots of things happened as I learned at the foreign office but you will know all that from the papers.

The clouds settled down by midday, Helsinki weather is an almost permanent natural fog like London. Everybody felt very cheerful saying: now they can't come over. I didn't feel cheerful at all, as – flying in – I had decided that curtain of fog was God's gift to the Russians. They could stay above it and either bomb on instruments or dive suddenly: you would never see them. They have an airbase at Talinn which is 15 flying minutes away. At three o'clock, getting a belated lunch, they did just that; came in unseen, dived to 200 metres (imagine) and dumped the stuff. From the sound and the results they must have been 500 kilo bombs and they dumped thermite as well. I never felt such explosions; the whole damn place rocked. Must have been like March in Barcelona. I went out and there was a huge curtain of smoke rolling down the street and people were saying: Gas – gas . . . That was pretty awful I may tell you. I left my mask in NY and it would have been unmanageable anyhow and I really thought: okay we are lost. Then as nobody seemed to be choking, I went out with two Italian Fascist journalists (to whom I said frequently and bitterly, 'Now you see what it is like to be on the losing side, don't you gentlemen?') and we followed the smoke. There were three colossal fires, four big apartment houses – just plain people's homes – burning like tissue paper. Glass was shattered for six and seven blocks around these places. One house, by a gas station, had a vast hole blown in its side, a burning bus lying beside it, and a man shapeless and headless and dead the way our little man was on the corner of the Florida that morning. The raid took less than a minute; the siren began blowing as it was over, the planes were seen at 200 metres actually diving, and not before. Eleven bombers in formation of three with one ahead and one behind. It was just one of those terror jobs we know so well about; how well the Russkis have learned from their new friends. And anybody who tries to tell me the Soviet is the friend of the working man will have a hard time. Those were workers quarters, destroyed, and the man dead in the street was a perfect duplicate of our little guy with his roped soled shoes . . . So.

It is going to be very terrible Rabby. They are about as well off as Spain from the point of view of material. Nothing is to prevent the Russkis doing this three and four times a day. The people are marvelous, with a kind of pale frozen fortitude. They do not cry and they do not run; they watch with loathing but without fear this nasty sudden business which they did nothing to bring on themselves. I have seen too much in my life now: I promise you that I have never yet seen the innocent and unarmed other than hunted and destroyed. It is a very disheartening sight. If it's the unemployed or the Czechs or the Spanish or the Finns or the poor bastardly sailors on neutral ships; it seems to me they get it.

I have your little passport picture in my purse and I hope it will protect me. I am very alone here. None of the press is our people or extremely *sympathique.* I have bought books and hope to be able to weather this very calmly but it is bad. I know how bad now because I have standards of comparison. Apparently there are no more planes out and the Russian fleet has moved from Kronstadt so that I suppose the sea will become unsafe. I don't know either when or how I can leave. I cannot wire you because there is no cable communication. I am trying to get through to our old pal Peters who is now in Copenhagen and asking him to wire for me. Oh Rabby what a stinking mess. We should never have left Cuba.

Marty

To: Ernest Hemingway

December 4 1939
Hotel Kaalp
Helsinki

Beloved,
I got your lovely two cables today (December four) and am so happy you are proud of me – though what for? I'm just surviving – and you are my own and beloved and I knew you'd want to come but don't. The book is what we have to base our lives on, the book is what lasts after us and makes all this war intelligible. Without the book our work is wasted altogether. And as I love you I love your work and as you are me your work is mine. I could not have you maul that about and mess it up. We will come back later maybe, but now you must go on and finish this.

Besides that, if *Collier's* is willing (and perhaps if they are not) I am leaving next week. I have wonderful material, the best war stuff of this year – and no competitors in the field by Golly – and tomorrow at six in the night that never seems to end (six in the morning and six in the night are indistinguishable but this time the morning and Christ have I been getting up early and boy do I hate it) I am leaving for the front. No other journalist has this privilege but due to R's [Roosevelt] letter I am on my way. I think it will be quite something. War in the arctic is a very remarkable business. The climate is the best protection as are the forests and it is curious the way in the end the only way to fight man's inventions is with these uncontrollables. It snows and we are not bombed. The Finnish mist sets in and we are safe. The night begins at four in the afternoon and ends at eight in the morning, so we take to the woods at eight. It is pretty amazing and as you can guess pretty wearing. I find the cold absolute torture and love the snow because it is warmer then as well as safer. Anyhow, I shall have been here a week tomorrow and plan to be here a week more or almost that long and I will have – from Helsinki, environs, front, enough for three bangup articles if they want that many and will have stuff no one else has. Then one week each in Norway and Sweden and home, probably from Bergen but if possible by clipper. So you see, it is not even worthwhile joining me. You open our home in Cuba, as a Xmas present for me, and I shall return and wallow in sun and quiet and above all my Schatzy I shall be glad to be home with you where I belong.

. . . I think it can be a very long war and I think it is possible that – unless Russia sends an army of four million against these people – that the Finns will win. They have been steadily successful to date and their pilots are wonderful. And they can't be starved like our beloved Spaniards; they already produce 90% of their own food. Petrol is going to be the problem, and planes and munitions. But – though it seems fantastic – I'll put my money on 3 million Finns against 180 million Russkis. After all, they are fighting for their lives and their homes and God alone knows why the Russians are fighting. They don't even need the two possible strategic positions they can get out of this war.

So. Now I must go to bed. I have had a hard day. It has been quite alarming to see the panic amongst the diplomatic corps and the journalists notably American and English. Last night a real panic set in started by the English who began to evacuate their nationals (they have done it twice already) at 2 a.m. saying that gas would be used this morning. Geoffrey Cox* waked me and told me to beat it and I told him what the hell and went back to sleep. I had arranged with an Italian journalist (it is too funny being such pals with them, a story in itself) to go in his Legation's car out to the country at seven thirty in order to escape the probably eight thirty bombing which the Russkis must do one of these days in revenge for having had 16 planes shot down. I overslept which is really fantastic, and got up somewhat panicked at eight fifteen and went downstairs to find that I was alone in this hotel with the concierge. I called the Italians and they came around (I was supposed to telephone and wake them) and we beat it out to the country sometime after the raid should have started. It then snowed and I seized the occasion to have a lovely day walking through the snow, and came back in the early afternoon. I have the curse and am somewhat wore out but I got in my exercise and I needed air and a change of scene and talk. I have been sleeping in town every night, while the English speaking contingent pulls out and am feeling very snotty and superior. But Rabby, my God, if they begin being scared pissless of probable dangers now, what are they going to be later when it really breaks loose on them. I am scared when it is three minutes off and am scared blind three minutes after, but would be sick by now if I thought about it all the safe time. Besides that, the Finns give a very good example of taking it and

*Sir Geoffrey Cox, foreign correspondent for British newspapers in the 1930s, and later pioneer of television journalism and first news editor of ITN (Independent Television News).

keeping the trap shut and I learned from you not to have the vanity to think the planes were looking for me and all bullets had my name on them.

I am tired Bongie and wish I were with you. When I get back I shall go to Washington briefly to talk to R [Roosevelt] about this and then hurry to you. That will delay me one day; it is my sort of repayment to these people for their goodness to me and their elegance and courage in undertaking this war rather than be kicked around. We have seen an awful lot of kicking around and I like those who deny it and fight. The little nations are rather more first class than the big ones I think, these days. But peace will be lovely. I have a steady pain in my head from thinking about the folly of mankind. I love you so much that it is almost hurting to think about it and I try to behave as you would want me to, and hope I am not mean to anybody though you know people sometimes think you are being snotty when you are only in a hurry, but I try to be good and I try to be very serene and I do my work hard and as well as I can and hope I am a credit to you and a sound workman. And soon I will be with you and where I want to be, and Bongie let's never never leave each other again. Or rather, I'll never leave you and you can go anywhere you want and do anything you like, only please, I'll come too.

Goodnight my dearest love. Sleep well. And take care of Mother for me. I cannot write and wire to you both so hand on everything in the way of news to her and keep in touch with her and keep her unworried and all right. This is the biggest thing to do for me. Because she is ours too, like the book, something we have to take care of together.

I love you.

Bongie

To: Whom it may concern

January 19 1940

San Francisco de Paulo

[Cuba]

GUARANTY

To whom it may concern (I guess it concerns Mr. Warp Dimpy Gellhorn Bongie Hemmy)

I, the undersigned, Mrs. Martha Warp Fathouse Pig D. Bongie Hemingstein, hereby guaranty and promise never to brutalize my present and future husband in any way whatsoever, neither with weapons nor pointed instruments, nor words, nor uncalculated sudden phrases nor looks. I guarantee (providing my future and present husband does not wake me from a sound slumber when I am not in control of all or even half my faculties) always to express the appreciation I truly feel for everything he does for me, gives to me and means to me. I promise equally to cherish him so that he knows I am cherishing him, and not only to cherish him so that I know it. I also state for witnesses that far from putting him out of business, he and his business are what matter to me in this life, and that also I recognize that a very fine and sensitive writer cannot be left alone for two months and sixteen days, during which time many trying and unlikely things are put upon him, voluntarily and involuntarily, and that said fine and very fine and very beloved writer should immediately be in a state of perfect calm and confidence and that, in so much as I, involuntarily, was a great cause for his uneasiness of mind during this long period of solitude, I am deeply sorry therefore and shall attempt (with a few relapses due to general stupidity and personal lack of intelligence) to make up to him for the wretchedness he has gone through, and shall also attempt to protect him against same wretchedness in future. This statement is given of my own free will and in my rightest mind and with love.

Signed:
Martha Gellhorn Hemingway

SECOND GUARANTY

I the undersigned guaranty also that after marriage I will not leave my present and future husband not for nothing no matter what or anything.

Love,
Martha Gellhorn Hemingway

THIRD GUARANTY

I, the undersigned, further guaranty not to divorce my husband (previously named, see other page) not for nobody, only he has to be a good boy too and not love nobody but me. But he will not love nobody but me. This is an unnecessary guaranty.

Love,
Martha Gellhorn Hemingway

To: Charles Colebaugh

January 21 1940
San Francisco de Paula
Cuba

Dear Charles;

Let us talk money first (alack aday.) You will find herein enclosed, neat as a pin, an expense account. I kept it good in New York but after that I had very little time as you can imagine. I got a note from my bank saying that $6000 had been deposited from Collier's. That would be for the first four articles, would it not? There is still another to come.

When I got back here it was very fine and all the pelota players were down at the dock and I had a good fast argument with four stewards on the boat from Miami to Havana about the Spanish war, which made me feel at home, and everybody said to me warmly, happily, and affectionately, 'Marta,' they said, 'How fat you have become, how big, healthy and fat.' This is usually a very flattering thing to say in Cuba but I can do without it. Then out here at my house the boy from the farm next door who manages my swimming pool pump, came over to tell me (as always, nothing changes) that the pump was broke. Then he said, also with delight, 'But you are wondrously fat, it is a magnificence.' I said, sadly, that war did this to me. Oh, he said, war? Yes, I said, I have just come from Finland. He took that silently and then said, with interest but some doubt, 'They have war in Finland, is it not true?' Yes, I said, in fact they have war in Finland. Well, he said, in Cuba all is tranquil. (You can see what a hell of a fine country it is.)

We are being slightly troubled by some climatic disturbances: I understand there is a blizzard or whatnot all over America and people are freezing to death. Here they go about looking pinched and alarmed and tell each other in admiring tones that it is the coldest day in all the history of Cuba. The coldest was 68. I can stand it okay.

It is perhaps wrong to be so happy in this present world, but My God how I love this place and how happy I am. There are eight huge mauve orchids, blooming right out of the trunk of the ceiba tree that grows on my front steps. Some country. I cannot recommend it highly enough.

Will you please tell Mr. Chenery★ all the things I would have told him, what a wonderful trip it was and how I enjoyed making it. I see even the Danes are getting uppish and preparing to fight. By now any little country feels pretty sure it can lick anybody else, I guess. The war I will really love covering (hope I am not old and gouty) is the second Spanish war. This Finnish business gives me great hope. Maybe all the little guys will get their own back.

Have a lovely time in Florida.

Yours,

Martha (Gellhorn)

To: Hortense (Flexner) and Wyncie King

March 29 1940
[Cuba]

Dearest Weakies;
If you go to Taos, we will stop in and see you on the way west, next

---

★Bill Chenery, a distinguished Scot and editor-in-chief of *Collier's*.

September. The Pig and I read a book about vice in tourist camps. It was called something really original like 'The Scarlet Trail.' It sounded far too good to be true. So this time, going to Sun Valley, we are going to allow three weeks and drive and stay in all the Tourist camps and make an authoritative study of the question. There is almost no place you can go to, where you could escape us. We are ever present. Go to Alaska, for instance, and presently you will see us, because I have just learned to my horror that there is terrific shooting in those permanently frozen wastes. Try China; try Pitcairn; try anything. We will follow you. Taos sounds good though. Are you really going. Avoid Mabel Dodge Luhan;* a bigger phoney and larger stink I almost never met. Her Indian husband is nice though (he smells rather strong the way Indians do.) He just grunts and leaves the room, when bored.

I would like to see you two guys wrapped in blankets, loping on piebald ponies across the moonlit desert.

I love you very much and I can easily see that my last letter was very bullying, by the humble tone of Teecher's reply. When I bully, the thing to do is send me a telegram, of one four letter word, or one four letter word, with 'you' added on to it. Then I will know I have been a bully and will be more respectful next time. I have the soul of a Hun and need to be stepped on.

(If the Pig knew I was writing a letter this morning he would come in and hit me with a shoe. I am supposed to be writing. People are disgusted with me because I lack discipline, am wasteful, lazy and complaining. I have started to write again. Am doing five finger exercises. That is what we call them and they are very good. If you see something, you write it, to give the exact emotion to someone who did not see it. You can concentrate on your failings: with me for instance, I cannot write dialogue, nor can I write anything funny, nor can I write about sex. So now for two weeks I write these things, practicing dialogue, sex or humor as the case may be. They do not have to be stories (no plot), just a complete picture of something. At present I am happily working on a wonderful drunk I went on with the pelota players last week, that ended at five thirty in the morning – I was still drunk the next day, Easter – in which we sang our way happily through Havana and quite miraculously attached to ourselves a man from Miami and a French whore he had picked up somewhere. It was a great evening. If I get it right, I will send it to you.)

I am now suddenly a mother of three and I must say I love it. It is certainly a lot more fun to be a mother of three (without ever having to lose

*Mabel Dodge Luhan (1879–1962) was a rich heiress from Buffalo who married a Taos Pueblo Indian and held a salon for left-wing intellectuals and pacifists. After WWI she set up an artists' colony in New Mexico and wrote several volumes of autobiography.

your shape) than being a mother of one, your own, and not knowing how the brat will turn out. E's three sons have turned out very very good. They are all just as funny as their papa, which is saying something. The littlest one is eight, and dark and with a wonderful smile and bright black eyes, and you ought to see him shoot craps. He is called Giggy, but known as the Jew due to his great respect for money (the whole family is just waiting for him to grow up and support them; he has such an acute sense of silver. His brother Patrick, aged eleven, says, with admiration, 'I never saw a man more careful of his pennies.') Giggy knows all the dice language, never bets more than a nickel, consistently wins, refuses to play when he doesn't feel 'hot,' and addresses the dice with friendship, saying, 'snake eyes,' 'little fever,' 'Richard,' according to the points, and also sits there mumbling to himself, 'Seven, Seven, treat me good, dice and I'll do the same by you.' He is very funny. He is also fine to watch when shooting. He shoots his brother's gun, and has to sit down and balance the barrel against his leg to get his aim, and then the recoil knocks him over backwards, but they are all children without signs of fear. He just sits and takes his time and he is death on pigeons. He told me that Patrick read aloud to him, but it bored Patrick because he could go faster reading to himself. He said, 'Mousie (that's Patrick) is about the biggest reader anywhere. He can read a book as fat as the *Green Hills of Africa* in one morning.' The way you describe all books is whether they are fatter or skinnier than the *Green Hills*. Patrick read aloud, with emotion, (we overheard this) parts of E's new book to Giggy, and they told Ernest they thought it was 'terrific' and very interesting and would sell a lot.

Patrick is the jewel of them, a beautiful little boy, with such a good swift mind and such delicacy and so funny as I almost never saw. He is a great gambler too, and a fine shot, and we have all taken up tennis together, which is almost too exciting to bear. And the oldest, Bumby, who is sixteen and taller than Ernest and has a body like something the Greeks wished for, and to make you cry it is so lovely, is a boy who concentrates on one thing at a time, and just quietly thinks it through, and never has any problems because he never thinks about himself, but only about trout fishing, tennis, fencing, and sometimes he thinks about the one act play he is going to be in at school. So that, riding in the rumble of the car, you will hear the Bumby reciting, in different voices and with feeling, all the parts in his play. We are very good friends and have long interesting talks on a variety of subjects, but mainly I take such pleasure in looking at him that it is enough for me. They all think I am a sort of colossal joke and one of the boys; and refer to me as 'The Marty', and I think it all goes very fine. Anyhow I am nuts for them, which is a grand thing, and they are no strain, each one having a very full and busy life of his own; and they love the house and the life here, and I am hoping they will be around a good part of the time.

As for Frost,* Teecher, he is a relic, and I would certainly not worry about an elderly relic who was satisfied with New England all his life. You are a damn fine poet, as far as that goes, and you have the great thing of the professional which is discipline and persistence and passion. You have another thing which you probably don't give a damn about, but in that entire ivy covered ruin of a college, you are about the only one who can make the youthful mind come alive. I regard that as a great talent, not as a teacher, but a talent as a human being.

Now I have to do some work myself, to justify my existence. Such as it is. Tell King I challenge him to write me a letter. I do not believe he can write. I know he can read because I have seen him reading the papers, but I am not at all sure he can write. I bet he has to print. I will give him a quarter if he writes me. You two beloved darlings. I love you very much indeed, always. I love you for having all the guts and all the laughter.

> Your devoted dopey old pal,
> Gellhorn

To: Hortense (Flexner) and Wyncie King

> [Spring] 1940
> [Cuba]

Darlings;

This is only to explain my wire. It seems to me that what you need is a spring vacation. The climate here is something you would hardly believe. And this palace, clean and orderly at last, turns out to be a pearl among houses. It is lovely. Do come and join me.

And Teecher, I will tell you someday about how real writers are, as I have just been seeing it at work. Himself is in a *belle époque*, as he says, and doing a fine story. It is exactly as if he were dead or visiting on the moon. He writes and when he is through he goes into a silence. He protects himself from anything and everything, takes no part in this world, cares about nothing except what he is writing. He handles himself like a man who is about to do the world's championship boxing match. He has been I may say about as much use as a stuffed squirrel, but he is turning out a beautiful story. And nothing on earth besides matters to him. You see, that's the way to be. That way you get writing done. He likewise believes in himself and his writing as if it were the tablets of stone or the true God, and that's another essential. I learn a lot as I go along.

If King can go to New York and get drunk with the girls, he can come

---

*After his return from England to the U.S. in 1915, Robert Frost wrote narrative and lyrical poetry, drawing its imagery and characters largely from New England.

here and get drunk with me. What rot to talk about my work and fame and allied nonsense. In five months, little woman, I have written two Collier's articles and nothing more and one wasn't published. In five months, do you hear me. If I'm a writer, my colored cook is Gauguin. As for fame, ho ho. I am almost the only person I know who never knows a soul, never meets anybody, never goes out, and lives the perfect life of the Benedictine coupled with elected-most-likely-to-fail-class-of-1930. If I could organize, the retired life I lead would produce work. As it is, it usually produces gloom and acute attacks of loneliness. But things are looking up. This house pleases me. Of course, I shall never pack up this furniture or these odds and ends. When I leave, they can be seized by the first comer. I am happy to live comfortably but am not going to have possessions, no matter what.

Please come if you can. I would so love it. Kisses to you both. It's very hot, all you'd want is white clothes and one thing a little heavier. There's no reason ever to dress either. I wear around Havana cotton dresses no stockings or hat and a pair of underpants when I remember. Of course, they treat me like the unemployed but who cares. Love again.

Gellhorn

To: Allen Grover

[Cuba]
March [?] 1940

Dear Allen;

As a suite and finale to our telephone conversation:

There were two things in that incredible page★ about me which were damaging: the first was the opening sentence (*Time*'s new trademark: I should think it would make you very unhappy to see your magazine slyly, with its own little phrases, entering it, the field of, competing and defeating the Hearstlike press with its brand of phrases). The second was the statement: MG returned to SF de Paula where EH is wintering. That is of course a libelous statement, and I would like to know who dared risk it, and with what knowledge. It <u>cannot</u> have come from the Havana AP. So where did it come from?

I will not insist on the damage, it is plenty, and you know that. I will not even insist, full of outrage and contempt, on the shamefulness of having a Book Review department which has so little understanding or respect for books that they can handle books by making a *succès de scandale* of the author. (This, in fact, is what really revolts me the most: not only because I am the

---

★In the form of a book review, *Time* had published a gossipy piece about Martha and Hemingway together in Cuba.

writer in question. I love books and I have a passionate respect for writing, and I think it is absolutely horrible that cheap, small people, who could never work through the hardship of writing, can destroy the goodness and the effort of writing, by reporting the personal problems of the author. I do not know anything about the personal lives of those who discovered ether, the circulation of the blood, the spirochetes: the work of a writer is a thing as apart from himself as the work of a man in science: I think it is barbarous, and the mark of microscopic minds, to confuse the man and his work: as long as the man, in his own life, is not the enemy of the commonwealth (but only a man, with a man's troubles and failings), and his work is definitely done for the common good, the common knowledge, the common progress.

The damage is all done and I will get through it all right because there is no damage anyone can do to me which will be permanent. I have lived my life exactly as I thought best and it is a perfectly good life and I don't give a goddam what anyone, who could be influenced by *Time*, thinks about it. But, because I have work to do, I would like if possible to have as little interruption, as little useless messiness as possible.

. . . So what I ask is this: that you issue a blanket order that when I am to be mentioned in *Time*, the copy be submitted to you first. I do not wish to jeopardize your job, or ask you to do things which are impossible for you. But I wish to be warned in advance, so that I can take my dispositions, before the next little vile story appears.

I do not like to write you about E. because for E's sake I would like to keep him well separated from that horrible whorish photograph of me and that horrible whorish write-up. E. is in Camaguey, where I hope he is peaceful and undisturbed to do his writing. (Allen, it is absolutely horrible that that man, who is one of the best writers in the world, and writes as he does because he has a very delicate instrument for a brain, should have been so hounded – because everything comes back, you know, with interest, on the personal angle: use your imagination – that his writing, the writing of the finest and most large and rich book of his career, should be jeopardized: especially as he is ending the book, was writing smoothly, with ease and magic and like an angel. I <u>love</u> writing. I think to do that to someone like E. is a stinking crime. E., you know, can take anything that comes his way, quite as easily as I can: and laugh at it and laugh at the tadpoles who do the damage. But at the end of a book, after a year and three weeks of unremitting work, he is open to all comers. You can lose a book, if people make you enough trouble. He will not lose that book, but the times are being made as tough as possible.)

Well, it is the first lousy luck I have had for some time: that Tom Matthews* was away and you did not see the copy.

---

*Senior figure at *Time* magazine.

The thing is all over now and we don't have to write about it or talk about it again. I don't believe in dwelling tightly with the disasters that can come. But I would like, if possible, to be a little less startled the next time.

Best to you and good luck

Marty

P.S. I think my writing will go on a long time, and stand up okay, and I can live down any rotten lousy confusion. Only it's hard to have nine months of stiff work, and what you most believe in, made so cheap: when it isn't cheap.

M.

To: Charles Colebaugh

April 3 1940
[Cuba]

Dear Charles;

I have been thinking a lot about the next job, and what would be good for the magazine, and I want to talk this over with you when I come up.

As a writer, I am pretty much getting branded as a disaster-girl. This has certainly not been my fault, because nobody lurking around Europe these last years could have arrived at any very happy conclusions, and one would have to be blind not to see the sorrow and despair and cruelty which I have seen. I do not know of any place that would have given me a chance to write happily about happy people, because though in Spain (and only in Spain) people were often wonderfully gay and loved life while they had it, the first fact was that life was more than hard and life was ominously brief. In articles, it is not possible to delve into every variation of feeling and one must honestly record whatever is the predominant atmosphere.

. . . But if you see only disaster, and write only disaster, there is the danger of being regarded as one who is blind to everything else, or even an inventor of catastrophe (in order to suit one's special talents) and finally people will say: she always says things are terrible, they can't be as terrible as she says, it's just her racket – or her style of writing – or her own psychological approach. Then the force of the facts is weakened by the personal brand one has as a writer.

This is very damn bad. I can't change Europe, and I can never write with hearty optimism about events which I find blacker than night: but I can look at some things which are fine, entertaining, good and pleasing. As I myself always have a fine time.

So I would like to do some writing about America, because I have a lot of confidence in America and enjoy the country and the life very much indeed. America is far from being entirely bad, and is not without hope, and a lot of the people are pretty happy a good deal of the time: and I would like to write about success, for a change, rather than about failure and defeat.

Also, I think such articles would make good, lively, entertaining reading. For instance; I want to drive west this summer, taking a lot of time, and stopping in tourist camps and small towns. It is not at all hard, in any place, to pick up pals and see what goes on, to see how people amuse themselves, what the country is like, to join the local rabbit hunts and swimming parties and Lodge dances.

Anyhow, you see what I mean. I see about three bang-up American articles, which are cheerful because the subject matter is cheerful, and full of odd enlivening information, and written gaily and happily.

I think it would be good stuff to have in the magazine; and I think it would be very good for me to balance my other work, to give more importance to my future European articles, and to give me a more sure and just literary rating.

There are two kinds of articles about America, both valid. One is to show what is wrong, in warning, because we cannot afford to have things wrong, as we are the last large so-called civilized country on earth with a lot to save and a lot to lose. And there is the other kind of article, which shows how America is good, and what there is to love and be happy about, and what is worth all the effort of keeping.

I'd like to do the latter.

Will you think about this? How's everything up there? Here it is getting lovely and hot, and I am writing short stories with great pleasure, and playing bum tennis, and going to the pelota games on Saturday night and being indecently happy.

Yours,

Marty

To: Hortense (Flexner) and Wyncie King

May 17 1940
San Francisco de Paula
Cuba

Darlings:

. . . E bought a very costly radio a few days ago so that we could get our disaster shrieked at us, fresh and on the minute, whereas previously we got it four days late on the mail boats. Still, I am very calm, brooding over maps and watching this disaster with a feeling that I have met it all before. To me, truly, the battle was lost in Spain and in Czecho. I do not think any nation can countenance the steady betrayal of all others, and remain unbetrayed. In the end, England is weakened with the treachery of its leaders, accepted by all Englishmen. It had to be something like this.

I suppose we will get in the war because we are fools like everybody else and man seems to carry the seeds of his own undoing in his pockets, generation after generation. Yes, I daresay we will be in the war and the movie house will ring with the loud courageous voices of the three minute speakers and women will walk the streets selling Liberty Bonds instead of useful services and all will be simply ideal and Barbara Hutton will knit like a madwoman in Palm Beach, rough little mufflers for doughboys. But I am not going to fool with any war from that angle, neither now nor ever, and if I cannot believe in a thing I am at least not going to spend my days gagging with disgust at the dishonesty and bad taste of all concerned. As soon as we get in the war I am lighting out for France, where I shall get myself (God willing, though it is going to be a serious drawback to be a woman, it always has been but probably worse now than ever) attached in a journalistic capacity to the armies of the Third Republic. I do not mind the French, in action, because they are sane tough people who do not sing hymns and every *poilu* is given two or three litres of red wine a day as his human due. I would enjoy very much being a journalist as near the armies as they will let me go, when said armies are marching into either Italy or Spain. The country is beautiful in either case and I would take an unholy pleasure in doing great damage to Franco's Falange and as for Italy, with Ernest, I believe that on the whole one has less chance of being killed when around Italians. But I am going to avoid both my country and countrymen because I can still remember as a small child how awful it all sounded and even now, ahead of time, I feel a definite nausea at the sound of all the words. Patriotism is surely the most revolting emotion people go in for, and as a nation we can do it as well as the English when we get started.

I read the last parts of E's book last night. He is like an animal with his writing; he keeps it all in one drawer, close to him, and hides it under other papers, and never willingly shows it and cannot bear to talk about it. It is of course an absolute marvel, far and away the finest thing he has done and probably one of the great war books of always. It is so exact that it becomes truer than life, and yet it is all invented. And in places it is so funny that you scream with laughter and E screams with laughter and embroiders from the book, telling you all the other things they said that he didn't write, and it is as if they had said them and were real people. Also it is very beautiful and breathlessly exciting. I think he may have it finished in a few weeks, though we have been living with it so long that I consider it as the basis of our life and I do not really believe it can be finished any more than one believes breathing can be finished.

Crandall* delights me. I never knew the old crow was a Catholic but in fact that explains many things about her. So women shouldn't go to a war because they get in the way and *Wind Sand and Stars*† is the nuts. She should have seen us taking care of the author of W.S. and S in Madrid, where he spent one day and night and then beat it. He is, so some French aviators I know tell me, a very swell guy, but he is not used to ground artillery and when the hotel was shelled at six one morning, as on many other mornings and was hit five times, he stood in his doorway, an inner room (I lived across the hall and patio facing the street and did not know how dangerous my room was until it got blown up one time when I was away from Madrid) and handed out grapefruit, in a state of intense nervousness. He had a lot of grapefruit and he evidently thought it was the end so he was sharing his wealth. She also should have seen me cooking for the menfolks and taking care of a typhoid patient, when of course I do not know how to read a thermometer but someone had to take care of him. You might tell her that under menace of death, chivalry is a very outdated idea, and though men put themselves out for the woman they love (which is normal in peace or war) no strangers spend their time throwing their cloaks over the mud. The only place a woman is not welcome for reasons of her sex is in the lines immediately before a morning attack is going to begin, because the men are going to the bathroom (in agony of spirit) in all the trenches and up and down the countryside and supposedly this would embarrass the woman. I can't say it does. It is a damn sight more trying to have a company of infantry come on you, in a similar position.

I have two stories I am mad to do if I can ever finish this bloody one. I want to do a story about Finland, about an aviator I met there and a woman who should be somewhat modelled on Clare Boothe Luce† whom I have never met. I want it to be a story of pure sex (because I am so bad at handling that), with the man full of a bitter and hurried contempt, and the woman trying to understand life by handling the body of a man who deals exclusively with death. I write it horribly now but it is some story as I see it. The aviator was a wonder. It gave me cold shivers to look at him. I suppose he is dead now. And then I want to do one about the first day of the war in Finland when I ran through the burning streets with an Italian who had bombed the niggers in Ethiopia and flown in Spain, but never seen what a bombing was like on the ground. That is quite a story too, and

---

*Regina Crandall, Bryn Mawr administrator who started their writing program.
†English translation of *Terre des Hommes* (1939). Antoine de Saint-Exupéry, magnificently turned out in a vibrant blue satin dressing gown, had been at the Florida Hotel in 1936.
‡Clare Booth Luce (1903–1987), married to Henry Luce, publisher and founder of *Time, Fortune,* and *Life.* During a successful and frenetic life, she was by turn editor, playwright, politician, journalist, and diplomat. She won a seat in the House of Representatives as an ultraconservative isolationist.

I liked that man better than anyone in Finland which goes to show that we never know what we are talking about.

Oh hell. I wish I were at the war this minute and didn't have to write and work and learn to think and learn to read and discipline myself and lead a decent life. I wish E and I were roistering and running about with all the other overexcited loonies who live in the moment. But maybe there are no more wars like the ones I have attended. Maybe they talk at these wars now, and there is nothing to do at them except die.

Give my love to King. Tell him to cheer up. There is <u>much</u> worse to come. Tell him to drink more. No one can even guess what a difference scotch can make to the world situation.

I love you <u>very</u> much

Gellhorn

To: Hortense (Flexner) and Wyncie King

June 8 1940
San Francisco de Paula
Cuba

Sweeties;

Have just finished my day's work, five typed pages, about 1250 words, and am both exhausted and in a state of deep doubt and soul searchings. Soul searchings are not indicated for the novelist at work; what you need is a blind and bubbly confidence. So. I have been thinking about writing until I am dizzy and a little ill. And have decided that what I have is patience, care, honor, detail, endurance, and subject matter. And what I do not have is majic. But majic is all that counts. Or do you spell it magic. I am a little mixed up, due to Czech street names. And so I am feeling fairly gloomy. Because, with magic, I have here a little tale to break the heart. And without magic I have here a set of facts, damning and terrible facts, but without magic who will weep and who will protest? Oh hell.

Tomorrow we lay off and go on a boating peekneek. It is with the pelota players, eleven Basques and us. They bring the food: Ernest and I are being invited. We go on Ernest's boat to a cove and drop them and they make a fire under the trees and cook a chicken-with-rice which is made in a dish two feet across and has everything in the world in it, as well as chicken and rice, and we wash this down with wine from gallon straw-covered jugs and later we all get blotto drunk and they sing Basque songs, which are like hymns, except gay and fighting.

Then someday, when I am surer of myself (because either I am going to learn to write or by God I am not going to write at all), I shall try to put down on paper what it means to have lost the war in Spain. Not being a

Spaniard nor a lover of war and hating Fascism only very specifically for what it does to human life, I find it rare★ that I should every day of my life, in my heart and mind, hurt because that war is gone. Nothing in my life has so affected my thinking as the losing of that war. It is, very banally, like the death of all loved things and it is as if a country that you had worshipped was suddenly blackened with fire and later swallowed in earthquake. I think this feeling must be carried by all of them, somewhere, in their minds, or wherever feeling rests: and I know it because I have it every day. Czecho made me fighting mad and sick with rage: but Spain has really broken my heart. I haven't the faith of a flea left and am acquiring that detachment which Wordsworth, the old bastard, preached: due to the indifference resulting from having lost what I cared about. Also, I wonder if this can be true, can you love land that is not your own, more than any other land. Spain of course looks like the west, only eaten with history and used with all the life and blood and cruelty and gentleness and hope of a complicated, childlike people. But there come days when it seems to be utterly unbearable to have lost that land, those bald, always moving, forever hills, the claw sharp mountains, the green plains that go down to Aranjeuz where they grow strawberries and asparagus. I don't know. Maybe that is not a book but a poem. A lament.

I am reading with interest about the Napoleonic wars. And living here, like the gent who loved Thais, stuck up on a pillar in the desert. And writing. And torn with doubt about the writing and wanting so fiercely to have it right. But where is the magic? You can't breed it into people and you can't learn it. Ernest has it. He doesn't know how it comes or how to make it, but when I read his book I see it, clear as water and carrying like the music of a flute and it is not separate from what he writes, but running all through it. I fear I am German. Well. Goddam.

Kisses to you both. I have been reading about the Writers' Congress,† and suffering that such worthy ideas and such hardworking people should appear such poops, in print. For folk with dirty minds (like me) there was plenty to laugh at in the reported speech of President Donald Ogden Stewart who is not so much a comic as an ass.

I dote on you,

Gellhorn

★A word often used by Hemingway in *For Whom the Bell Tolls*.
†The 1939 Writers Congress in New York had ended with accusations that it was dominated by communists. Donald Ogden Stewart (1894–1980) had edited a book about the Congress, *Fighting Words*, which was seized by the FBI. In 1950 he was blacklisted.

To: Charles Scribner★

July 7 1940
[San Francisco de Paula
Cuba]

Charlie my dear (that's how you start letters):
Your letter had our household in what is called gales of laughter. You are very cute and far too jolly to be an English country gent. This is not a letter as I have nothing to say. Only that I am not coming to New York, so you won't need to build up health for future destruction. E is coming alone as soon as the book is done, sometime between the 15th and 30th of July, and going to do his business quickly and return. You and Max† however take good care of him and see that he doesn't get in the papers. The bridge is blown, or did I tell you, and is _very_ exciting and worth waiting for.

I have been writing about the local Nazis and now that is finished and I am not pleased with the article but relieved not to have to go to town every day and return with my clothes sticking to me and the general feeling of having crossed the Sahara on foot. We had a good hot time at the pelota the last night of the season due to one of the big Nazis getting above himself, with their defeat of France, and talking too much and too loud. But he wouldn't fight. He sounded awfully big until E called him and then he evaporated, but it was good while it lasted. I think a war against those guys will be a necessity someday and something of a pleasure, but I do not think we ought to bother with having France and England for allies: we stand a better chance to win doing it on our own, and on our own territory. I must say, though, that Nazis individually or en masse call out to be shot at. It is curious that people can be as unattractive as their philosophy.

You will be impressed to hear that our mango and alligator pear crop are record breaking, that arsenic judiciously sprayed has liquidated the cater-pillars that were eating the bougainvillea, and that the pigeons are doing very well except there are too few females and so life in the coo factory is kind of like a dance at Yale, with far too much courting and rushing around. We are going to buy some new ladies and put an end to the belle-system: those lady coos have to settle down, marry and reproduce, like in the novels you appreciate. I like life on the farm. It is the only life I ever saw that didn't get to be troublesome and every day nature offers up a diversion. I would keep permanently busy just tidying up after the daily acts of God.

Don't know when I will see you but sometime. Perhaps we will come to NY in the fall. I don't imagine we will meet you riding over a mountain in Idaho?

Always,

Marty

★Charles Scribner was Hemingway's publisher in New York.
†Max Perkins (1884–1947), the legendary editor.

To: Eleanor Roosevelt

July 20 1940
[San Francisco de Paula
Cuba]

Dearest Mrs. Roosevelt;
I hope the next four years will not be the hardest ones yet,* and I suppose
one ought to pray for miracles for the sake of the country, and all of us, and
especially for you and the President who will have the toughest job of all.
When will either of you get a real rest, or even a good breathing spell? It
doesn't look as if you would at all, but I hope you do.

   Mother is here now and has been telling me of seeing you. She is another
of your great admirers (our family is full of same.) We are trying to give her
a good rest, which she needs. We have been out fishing in the Gulf and
yesterday had a terrific day, seeing a whale shark – which is very rare – that
swam right by the boat. It was as big as the boat, and you can't even believe
anything so big is true, it is as if something from the Smithsonian woke up
and began plodding around the ocean. Said monster has a mouth twelve
feet wide and all it likes to eat is sardines. We also saw a pair of marlin
playing in the water, playing as fast as pursuit planes, and diving and racing
after the light blue flying fish. We clambered up and down the side of the
boat and swam miles in the clear green water near shore, and Mother has
already turned a nice salmon color from the sun, and looks very cute and
fresh and gay. She's a wonderful woman, wonderful company always, and
loves to laugh, and right now I am glad of the unreal calm and the great
beauty of this place, because she can't think much about the war here. In a
way I think this time of history is worse for people who remember the last
war clearly: she of course remembers it all. I think you can feel as protective
about your parents as they felt about you, when you were a child. The only
thing is that you can't really take care of anyone, though I wish I could sort
of develop great solid wide wings, and keep them around Mother.

   . . . Yesterday we ran into one of the local Gestapo in a bar which we
frequent. We've known this man for a long time: he is a German and a Nazi
and a pretty good sample of what they are like. He doesn't surprise either
E or me, who know the type, but Mother curiously enough has never met
a real Nazi. She has only seen the people who were victims of the Nazis. It
was very strange and interesting, because the Nazi gave Mother the horrors.
I've never seen her so uncomfortable with anyone: it was the same sort of
reaction people have to seeing repellent sights, buzzards eating, or mashed
bodies. It proved to me again the difference between seeing with your own
eyes, and reading: and it occurs to me that the mentality of the English, up

---

*Roosevelt had just secured a third term.

to the war, may also be explained by the fact that they were stay-at-homes by and large, and reading about the Nazis is not the same thing as seeing them.

This Fifth Column stuff is a red herring. When you look at France, Norway, Spain, you can see that the real destroyers of a country are natives of that country. I only hope Americans will realize this in time, and recognize their enemies. No redheaded hairdresser on the Bremen ruins any country: it takes Quislings, Lavals, Juan Marches and people like that to do the trick. The established and respected traitors, who belong to the best clubs, are the ones to fear.

Greetings to Tommy, and Hick if she is still there. If Hitler would only die from being hit by a thunderbolt, the next four years would be easier, wouldn't they?

Love,
Marty

To: Charles Scribner

August 23 1940
San Francisco de Paula
Cuba

Charlie darling,
I am not near married at all, and even if I were that is scarcely a reason to become formal with me. I find the prospect of matrimony frightening enough without your doing that.

We have been working very hard here. Duran's★ corrections of Spanish came yesterday and so everything will be perfectly tidied up and ready for you on the date you named.

Now about your suggestion. E had talked to me about it, and I thought it was a very sweet picture, the two of you sitting there making up plans for Marty, and thinking of good things for me. I do appreciate it, darling, very much indeed. I don't see how I could do it though. Perhaps I can explain and perhaps not. You see, I write with a great deal of difficulty, partly because I am lazy and partly because it is hard to write. The only way I write well at all is to be very excited about what I am writing. The Collier's articles are always easy because I go to a brand new country which is usually in the midst of some stupendous trouble and I am excited by everything, from the food to the disaster. I go around for two or three weeks all day and

---

★Gustavo Duran, composer and friend to Capa, Ernest Hemingway, and John Dos Pasos, became a lieutenant colonel in the Republican Army and later escaped with the help of the British. He never returned to Spain.

most of the night, collecting every known kind of information and putting it in notebooks. Then I sit for two days and try to bring order out of the notebooks, and then for two or three days more I write. By that time, the excitement is pretty well gone, but the article is done, and it is only hard work, but always it is sustained by the pressure of the newness and if there is any danger then I am really lucky because I function well under such conditions and feel lively in the head.

I have published three books and written four (one huge one still in my drawer, not good enough: it took one year of study and one year to write and I nearly died over it, but I lost the excitement almost before I began and just plodded on and it was a poop.) I have never been not writing, since I can remember, something or other, but there is very little to show for it because most of it is not good enough. I could not do a book (a book, Charlie, think of the high pile of bare white paper that you have in front of you before there is even the beginning of a book), unless I believed awfully hard in it. Unless I wanted to do it so much that I could sweat through the dissatisfaction and weariness and failure and all the rest you have to sweat through. I really and truly could not write a book to order. And also, I really don't want to.

You see, if I had to for money, I would do anything from scrub floors to write corset advertising and I would never think that was hard or remarkable or anything: only doing whatever anybody has to do to eat and have a roof. I used to do that when I had to, I wrote fashion articles and I wrote about face-lifting and I wrote about the festivals for Jeanne d'Arc in France and about the Dolly sisters and anything else you can name. I wrote nothing but corset advertising really, because I had to. It was okay and I did not mind. Only now I am older and I have worked through that. It took me almost ten years. I was lucky to get it done that fast. I don't need to do for money anything except articles for *Collier's,* or for somebody else, but that same kind of article, what is called foreign correspondence, and if lucky war correspondence. I like that work very much, and am of course delighted that I can earn my living doing a sort of hack writing that interests me.

The books I do are what I earn my living for. Very odd sentence. I mean it would depress me a great deal to earn my living just to eat: I earn it very well and as fast as possible so as to have time to do the kind of writing I want to do. This writing so far does not pay too much ($1500 advance on the last novel: that is what I get for one *Collier's* article). But it is what I want to do, and all the time I try to learn so I can do it better, whether it pays or not. I simply could not write a book for any motive more serious than that I wanted terribly to write the book. I am a writer of very serious books, because it is so hard for me to write at all that I can't waste my juice on anything that isn't very very important to me. Do you see?

This is not to say that I do not appreciate very much what you suggest.

It might be that one day E and I made some kind of odd and rare travelling and then I would want to write about it. But Cuba is not odd and rare to me, it is lovely and interesting and where I live: and I could not set out cold to work up a book from it. (That is to say, within the limits of the gravity, that of course I could and would if I had to. But I don't. And *Collier's* being after me all the time to set out for the wars again, I don't imagine I will have to.)

We were talking the other day about you and publishing, and me and my next book. Now you have up and offered yourself as my publisher. Do you remember the things you said against publishing two people in the same family? Another thing makes me feel shy about talking publishing with you. It is that we are pals, and I would not want to be published because you liked me. I think Charles Duell very probably hates my guts, but he thinks I am a good writer. (I do not think he necessarily knows, but that is his impression.) So it is just professional and non-feminine. I am somewhat the enemy of the feminine, you know, except in a strictly limited field of personal relations. Oh well, this has been a very long letter indeed and it begins to meander and go nowhere.

. . . We have been very gay here, with that letter. Duran said (to compress it), that the book was a Spanish book, and he Duran recognised the place and the people, the voices of all the men and their way of thinking (the obscure manner of thinking of my people, he said) and the road to the attack and the place where Robert Jordan★ was wounded, and the look of the early morning coming through the pines in the Sierra, and said Duran, I felt as if Robert Jordan were me, and Maria is a girl I only had once in my life and long ago. He said 'the situation is authentic and the scene exact.' Oh he said a lot, and all good. You see Duran commanded that attack (which E did not see) and being himself a Lieutenant General of the Republic and a Spaniard, what he says is the real and important thing to have said. If to him everyone is real, everyone is someone he has known, the war part is so true it is as if he had lived it, then there is nothing more to say about it. You will be glad to know this. I myself never doubted it for a minute and did not need Duran nor anybody else to affirm it.

It is really a whiz of a book.

The third of September will be the beginning of vacation. I think it is needed.

E is working beautifully and easily.

Always
Marty

★American hero of *For Whom the Bell Tolls.*

To: Hortense (Flexner) and Wyncie King

August 25 [1940]
[San Francisco de Paula
Cuba]

Teecher sweetelpipes;
Are you interested in dreams? Normally I am not so crazy about dreams myself but we have been having a lot of spirited dreams around this house, whose symbolical meaning is indeed dark and various. I had a very trying dream, from which I woke, twisting and straining and muttering with rage. I don't know where it happened exactly and I was quite alone. But what had happened was that I was wedged tight, up to my neck, in a huge tub of lard, which was studded on the outside with precious jewels. Now, Teecher, what do you think?

Right now it is pouring rain, and the sky is winter grey and there is a wind beating the leaves off the trees and a steady stage-rumble of thunder. It is winter already and I feel it coming and I hope the fall is lovely enough, out west, to make up for the always yearly despair of having the summer end. I wait every year for summer, and it is usually good, but it is never as good as that summer I am always waiting for.

Mother was here for five weeks which was the longest vacation she has taken since she left college. She got younger right in front of us, and a lovely browny-pink color and the lines went from her face, and she slept well and long and was jolly and contented and relaxed.

So that way, it has been a good summer. I love her very much, and I feel older than she, and tougher. I know I am not, not in any real way, the way of enduring and believing and patience and wiseness. But I am certainly less startled by evil than she is, and not being a very good person myself I can take a lot of non-good. I always want to protect her, which goes to show that life is surely some kind of goofy circle: and in one way or another, we have all the emotions before we are through.

Meantime Scrooby's book is nearly finished: that is to say really finished, as Scribner's set it up in type the minute they got their hands on it. We have been reading and correcting galleys and as it is about 200,000 words long that is no joke for anyone.

But it is very very fine indeed, oh my what a book. It is all alive, all exciting, all true, and with many discoveries about life and living and death and dying: which in the end is all there is to write about. I am proud of it and so is Scrooby and maybe we can rest easy for a bit.

We are going west now. (I know just how that lard-tub idea started: I feel almost unbelievably safe and I am not a one who is nuts for this safety racket. We will have to get into some sort of serious trouble next winter or I will curl up and melt. I like my catastrophes; I like to feel myself a small blown and harried part of a great havoc. The times being havoc, I have no desire to live in a sort of superb cotton wool, all the year round. At least four months of something tough, says I, so that I don't choke on the ice cream.)

We'll be in Sun Valley as of September 8 or so, and through to the end of October. Address simply: Sun Valley, Idaho. There is also much divorce talk going on, and probably it will actually materialise in due course and I will be made an honest woman. Gellhorn, the first of her class to sin, the last to legalise. They ought to put it in the year book. I am engaged right this minute which I enjoy like mad; being married for three years it is very nice to be engaged simultaneously. It gives you an impression of permanent youth. I have a ring that is all bright with dimons and sapphires and snappy as hell and the only problem is not to wash my hands with it on and get it all mushed up with soap, but unaccustomed as I am to jewels I can scarcely even remember and my day is partly given over to picking at my bauble with a safety pin to get the Lux off it.

Have you noticed the way our friend Archie MacFlees★ is going in for vulgarising patriotism. Get a can of MacFlees patriotism, good for everything that ails you, only fifteen cents at the nearest *Time* vendors. Myself, I can not bear patriotism and feel certain that if we are going in for that (and evidently we are) I am going someplace else. War is not the worst thing that can happen; but by God war on the home front is worse than whatever could happen anywhere.

Oh hell. If there is a war anywhere I want to be at it. But I do not want to hear too much about it.

Since my book came out, I have been asked by two Councils of Jewish Women to make speeches. I am flattered and tell them I would rather be shot at five paces than make any more speeches. But that is what I got from my book. I better do another. The *Trouble* netted me invitations from Social Workers. Maybe on the third book I will get invited by the League to Protect our Feathered Friends.

I hope everything is dandy in your woods.

Love

Gellhorn

★Their name for Archibald MacLeish, who had been appointed Librarian of Congress, and was exhorting writers not to present a critical or disillusioning view of war.

To: Allen Grover

September 6 1940
4366 McPherson Avenue
St Louis

Allen darling

I have been missing you now for quite a long time, in a ruminative way, like a cow, chewing on the missing of you and thinking maybe that is how things are or get to be, but I do not like it. I do not think we had better lose each other, no matter what, because there is always so little time and nobody ever comes along who is the same thing, and then it is very lonely to have once been really at home with someone, and then not have them anymore.

I think for instance that never in my life was anything better than how we sent each other off to Finland: and I can remember one summer night sitting not quite listening to the radio in your partially dismantled apartment, and all the other times, and then I get so lonely for you I feel sick. I love you very much, I really do: even if suddenly things get said, sort of oddly, as if dictated from outside like the voices of Jeanne d'Arc, and whatever kind of people we two may be, we have always been satisfactory people to each other. We have, haven't we? I was bad in NY because somehow distraught inside myself, and so out of the world and so hating not to be part of history (I don't want to be elected to anything or mentioned in the papers, I just always want to be where history is happening, to see it, to know about it for myself, to do whatever small goofy usually futile thing I can do in order to make some minor events easier for unknown people). So I felt nasty and was nasty: and that never matters to me, except it does matter with you. I need you: you mustn't ever think I am nasty permanently.

It is a little complicated even to write these things. I would not want to seem a critical and disloyal bitch. You can tear letters up, can't you, quickly, and not remember anything except what they told you? E wants me for himself, altogether. He has me too, and need not worry. But you know, you do know, how people get hurt when you don't mean to hurt them, and think things are rivalry, when in fact it is two different and uncompetitive kettles of fish. You do know. I don't have very much privacy. I don't really have any right now. It isn't worth while to write me a very good letter, because you can sort of figure that it will be shared. (Do you suppose I would be that way, if E had a woman who was Allen to him).

. . . I'm leaving by plane tomorrow for Sun Valley. I had planned to stay here longer and wanted to. I am very tired. E's book has been an agony, like having children without interruption for months and months. I am tired in my head with it. I don't think anyone can be a great writer and do great books without pulling down the pillars of the temple all over the place. But I have to hurry out, because he is lonely, he feels abandoned (I have not seen him for a week), and besides I evidently have to read the proofs again. In principle we are marrying this summer. In principle. I have a quiet horror of marriage. I have seen the women getting their divorces and if that business is linked to marriage, boy I can do very well without marriage. I would rather sin respectably, any day of the week. E thinks of course that marriage saves you a lot of trouble and he is all for it, and practically he is right. But Allen, it is awful isn't it, the way you can make someone pay you in stocks and bonds and furniture and Christ knows what all, for not loving you. I thought if people stopped loving you, you went into a corner like a sick animal and held yourself very tight, so as not to break. But on the contrary, it seems you get the best possible advice and see how you can ruin the son of a bitch who no longer feels the sun shining inside him, when you enter the room. This is all deadly private and to be torn up. I count on you. I do not and cannot speak of it with anyone. Myself, whatever grand things I have gotten from men, I did not consider that you could deposit any of it in a bank: equally with the bad things you can get from men, but since when can pain be paid for in dollars? Or then, what class of pain is it that can be bought off? Anyhow, I like it better clean: I think sin is very clean. There are no strings attached to it. There is all the deadly intense obligation of one human being to another, but there is no insurance. You are probably less free, socially, but anyhow you feel awful simple and straight in your heart.

The book* will be out in November and then, having done what I could to be helpful during all these months I want to get back into the life I care about, seeing how the world works, and how the people in it behave with their disasters. I am really more interested in seeing France than anything else. The cradle of civilization, as I recall. Well, I believe in the French, and I want to see whether that is true or a mistake, and whether a people can remain, despite their government, and their defeat. I want to see whether all the minds stay good, no matter how they issue official proclamations of idiocy from Vichy. For the sake of history, it is more important to know whether the Nazis can conquer the minds of the French, than to know whether they can take any amount of ground, or any set of fortifications. I am crazy to go: all this time I have been wanting to, but we have our small personal jobs and must stick with them. Mine will be done when that book comes out. I wish I felt in myself a more valuable and necessary person: then I would be able to think that I had a duty to society, and that I was anointed of God to keep the record straight, to the best of my ability.

The west is very lovely, do you know it. The land goes on so long and

---

*For Whom the Bell Tolls.

looks so brand new, and untouched, that you have a feeling perhaps man is not as powerful as he seems, and in these days that is a happy thought. Also I like the people. I like them very much because they are proud without being insolent, and individuals without being Dali. They are good, being still so close to the time when every man had to help every other man, or they would all be wiped out. So I like that and feel okay there, but it would be even better to be working, doing my own work again. However, in November: and that is not too far away.

What are you doing? Are you very thin and brown and are you interested and happy: and what do you think we should be doing about this war and what do you think about that strange Mr. Willkie★ with his honest homespun hair and that complicated cruel mouth, and those odd flowing utterances, as if he did not know himself, when he said something fine and when he said something that made him sound like the Burns Detective Agency, strikebreakers on the side . . .

I love you. I love you a great deal and always. And I have to know you are there and sticking with me, and that we have each other in our good way, our being at home over lunch in the Gotham way.
Take care of yourself.

Marty

To: Hortense Flexner

October 30 1940
[Sun Valley]

Hello Teechie darling;
I have just been out riding, for the first time since the flu started almost two weeks ago. I feel pink and shaken up and fine. The high hills are covered with a grey frozen snow, very thin and cold looking and the sky is made permanently of asbestos roofing. That is what Sun Valley is like this year, But I didn't mind today, being so glad to feel alive and to breathe some alternative to steam heat. I rode with a fine girl named Tillie† who, with her husband, is the Camera Shop. She comes from Nebraska and is I think an unafraid woman, and she is good and tough and speaks a colorful English untroubled by grammar, and we galloped along shouting to each other about what sons of bitches, dungs and bastards various people whom we know are.

★Wendell Willkie, nominated for president on the Republican ticket in 1940 and defeated by Roosevelt in the election. Roosevelt later sent Willkie as a special envoy to Britain and Russia.
†Tillie was the wife of Lloyd Arnold, Sun Valley's chief photographer. Hemingway regarded her as the best cook of game birds he had ever met.

Then I came home and found your letter and I love your letters Teechie and maybe you don't know what you and Wyncie are to me. I could tell you all right but I am always a little scared of telling. You're <u>my</u> friends. It is very lovely to have had you all my life for myself, for no reason I could ever see and not because I deserved it you were my friends, just like that, for me. It has always been good and happy and safe for me, and as I have been and often am and probably always will be quite lonely a great deal of the time, the knowledge of having you, and getting the letters, is something I very much count on. That's the selfish part. The other part is that I admire both of you, what you are, what you stand for and the way you never give up goodness for any cheap rewards. I admire also what you have made together, the thing that is the two of you (that's the loveliest finest and last thing people can be and few can ever get there, but you have. My mother and father too. It takes great class and very clean hearts to do something like that.) I hope I never lose you.

I haven't much to write about. I go on working, drearily, without much confidence and with no ease. The Finnish story goes on and on, I know about war and about Finland but it is doubtful whether I really know about the people I am writing about. Technically it is quite a good story and it has some handsome writing in it, but I am not sure I believe it. It is the last story in the book. I wanted to speak to you about it, but I wanted to be sure it would be done first. I <u>think</u> it will be done now, God knows it is awful far along, so maybe it is all right. I am going to break with Dull, Slum and Pus (Ernest's name for Duell Sloan and Pearce), because they depress me and I am tired of putting my books in a vault instead of putting them on sale. I believe Charlie Scribner will publish me, anyhow he has said so often enough, so I think I can guarantee that the book will appear. Those two ifs being settled I would like to dedicate it to you and Wyncie, if okay with you.

The little girls on the campus who think it is wonderful to have a fine book dedicated to you (and it is wonderful) should however realize that like everything else in life you do not get it for nothing, and tell them to try sticking around with a very fine writer during the two years he is doing a difficult book and then after that they can decide how often they want books dedicated to them. I myself will settle for once, in that I am still a little shattered from the books and there are moments when I find Bug just as goofy now, when it is all over, as he more than frequently was during the writing of it. In any case, it is not an exact bed of thornless roses either to write or to watch writing, and I am always amused at folks's idea that whatever good happens to you in this life is just that much gravy. I never saw anything that came as a gift, except trouble, which one rarely has to work for. Bug is perfectly unaware that he is probably the talk of the town; he is deeply engrossed with duck shooting. We never heard anything about Dotty* writing the movie and she will not do so, or anyhow over Bug's dead body, as he has less feeling for her writing than you have. [Ingrid] Bergman is taller than I am, I crossed on a boat with her. In all cases the movie won't be made until next spring or fall and I hope to Christ that I for one have nothing to do with it. It was mad-making enough just to listen to the deal being settled and gave me nervous indigestion for days. If Greta [Garbo] were a braver actress I think she might do Pilar, without eyelashes, but with all the strength there is in her, unused and never to be used. Averell Harriman who owns this five million dollar dump is asking for a job as assistant cameraman and if we are all going to get sucked into the making of this movie, maybe they will let me take care of the horses.

The Burma Road is out, *Collier's* has sent someone else, some other girl, one who is free I suppose. It nearly broke my heart, as nothing has for quite a long time, and I wanted that job as one would want Xmas or a hope of heaven. None of the rest matters to me much. All the sudden money is just figures on paper, I want nothing really and Bug wants such funny small things, like a rifle and a pair of binoculars and a new sleeping bag, and thinking very hard I have decided I would like an ice box for the Cuba house, but beyond that we don't want anything really. It will be nice to give hunks of it away and Bug does that better than anyone I know. But all I wanted was the Burma Road and my own work and getting back to a life I really do understand. So I guess it will be Bucharest or some filthy hole, but anywhere that's hard and the work is hard and I can just live and look and get my work done will be okay. Quentin Reynolds of *Collier's* has changed his first war assignment (England) into the most extraordinary exhibitionism I have ever seen and from letters and reported New York talk, you would think it was not London being bombed, but just that hero, Quent. It sickens me and I must learn to keep my trap shut. I do not want any of that, I want to be very far away from where that sort of cheapness and wrongness is going on, and I look back with love to Spain, where all men were equal and all were serving and none were getting photographed or writing heroic letters home which are then retyped and sent to every gossip column and magazine editor in town. Teechie we live in cheap times, that is the worst of them: the dignity of man is getting smeared out. I want to be back with the plain people, who never heard of publicity and are not so busy buttering their bread that they have no time to believe in anything.

Now I have to write to three papers to send subscriptions to a guy I never saw who is in a Canadian concentration camp and also send him some

---

*Dorothy Parker. The film was eventually made by Paramount, starring Gary Cooper and Ingrid Bergman. It was nominated for an Oscar in almost every category.

dough, and then a few more letters of that general nature and then it will be time to bathe and drink whiskey.

I love you both dearly.

Gellhorn

To: Averell Harriman

November 8 1940
Sun Valley Lodge
Idaho

Dear Averell

E is out shooting pheasants (naturally). I feel today a little uncertain due to a birthday party for me which we had last night at Trail Creek and we all became definitely hilarious and I drank only limited quantities and feel worse than anyone today (except maybe Tillie). Our old pal [Robert] Capa of *Life* has come today to make a picture biography of Ernest for that magazine; I wish you and Cathleen were here and then we could do group pictures. Otherwise the only news is that there has been snow all over the place and everyone skis and it is very cold. If you have any errands you want done, Boss, just let us old timers know and we will do them. We are divorced now, did you know?, and E is a bachelor for the first time since he was 20, and I think it is a very good change for him. We are going to get married as soon as we find out what state it is okay in, because as E says there is no use getting legally divorced and then get married in some state which is not in agreement with you, and just get in trouble.

E says he is going to write you a letter. I think the letter will be written in pheasants' blood.

See you soon.

Marty

Martha and Hemingway were married on November 21, 1940, in the dining room of the Union Pacific Railway at Cheyenne in Wyoming, after which they ate roast moose for dinner. Martha was thirty-two, Hemingway forty. One reporter called it a "pairing of flint and steel." Hemingway wrote to Edna Gellhorn: "Everytime I see Marty, or hear her voice, or hear her thunder feet approaching I am so truly happy and I know how lucky we are to be happy that way, and never to be bored alone together." The first printing of 75,000 of For Whom the Bell Tolls *sold out within a couple of days of publication, and the* New York Times *called it the "best, deepest and truest book" that Hemingway had written.*

Soon afterward, Collier's *asked Martha after all to go to the Far East to report* on the *"Chinese army in action."* She was to start her journey on the Burma Road, the 715-mile track along which traveled the only supplies into China. Hemingway agreed to go with her, and to wait for her in Hong Kong before visiting China together, where he was to write some articles for PM magazine. Jokingly, he referred to their trip as their *"honeymoon."* Many years later, Martha would describe the journey, with humor and affection, as one of the horror journeys of her life. Martha herself, obsessed by the news of the war in Europe, was desperate to get back to active reporting, and deeply ambivalent about what she witnessed in China.

To: Eleanor Roosevelt

[December/January] 1940/41
The White House
Washington

Dearest Mrs R –

The changes in the enclosed letter are the name (add Hemingway) and the places to which I am going. My passport is validated for Japan, China, Hong Kong, Netherlands East Indies, French Indo-China, Thailand, Burma, Australia, New Zealand, Straits Settlements, British Malaya and New Guinea.

Perhaps easier for the President just to put 'Far East' which is good for all.

I love you. Will write later. The French are against us (can you believe it) because E is supposed to have signed a manifesto against Vichy. Oh boy. It all amuses me.

I love you again
Marty

To: Charles Colebaugh

March 1 1941
Hong Kong

Dear Charles;

Hongkong is the busiest place I have ever been in. So now I will write you very quickly in order to get this off on the Mar 2 Clipper, and tell you all about my works and acts.

1) I returned yesterday from Lashio. Lashio is at the Burma end of the

Burma Road. It takes about seven days in a passenger car if all goes well to drive from Kunming to Lashio, and the plane trip is three hours. I got in to Hongkong on Saturday Feb 22 on the Clipper and got out on Monday night (Tuesday a.m. really) at 4 a.m. to fly the round trip Hongkong-Lashio, as I cabled you. That is the principal run of the China National Aviation Corporation, a company partly Chinese (55%) and American (45%), with five American pilots to fly it; and it is the third lifeline of China, and the connection for Chinese brains and Chinese money with the outside world. It is the outfit that flies Madame C [Chiang Kai-shek] and all the big shots to and fro, over the Jap lines, to Chungking: it carries an average of 12 million Chinese dollars a day into China: and etc etc. It is the damndest thing you ever saw, being as no plane takes off except in weather which grounds all other planes in any sensible country, and you fly at 10,000 feet in an ice and hail storm over mountains at night (to say nothing of over the Japanese but that is very minor) to get to China's capital. We waited on the field at Lashio for the Japs to finish bombing Kunming with 27 bombers, three hours air distance away. We came into Kunming as soon as possible after the Japs left and the town was burning and we flew over it and saw the smash-up which was some smash-up. Our pilot, an ex Indiana boy, was the personal pilot of the Generalissimo and Madame and flew them out of Sian when the Generalissimo was kidnapped. He is a very nice boy who makes puns all the time; he is the damndest aviator I ever saw. Point is: I am doing a story on this line, how it works, who flies it, what it means and it is such color as I have not seen for sometime. I think you will like this story very much. I am getting pictures. There is a famous citizen named Newsreel Wong and I have bought three pictures from him, and I got permission to have Norman Soong go to the local airfield and take pictures of takeoff, plane, passengers etc. Have not seen them. Am trying to get them off on this Clipper but cannot guarantee.

2) Remember Press Wireless, which I used from Amsterdam? They function out of Manila and their rates are 4 and ½ cents a word which is nice. When I wire stories, will try to use them, but you remember you have to keep in touch with them in New York because they have a tendency to hold copy in NY and not let you know at once.

3) We have been keeping very close tabs on the Singapore end. You have probably read about the Jap officer shot down outside Kunming who had plans on him showing the Jap projects for an April push. Very likely the Japs know his plans are public now, so that doesn't hold much anymore. But the local authorities, both US and GB feel nothing is apt to happen for four to six weeks. They think the Japs will want to wait until they see how things go with the Germans. The GB ambassador is going to Singapore at the end of March, not before. On the other hand, everyone agrees that the Japs are not reasonable therefore not predictable.

4) There is a very good story right here. It is Hongkong. I don't know quite how to describe it to you, though you will see when it is an article. The city is jammed, half a million extra Chinese refugees. It is rich, and rare and startling and complicated. It is vastly important and it is surrounded on three sides by the Japs. It is color in huge bright letters and it has its own significance.

5) With our military attaché, E and I are arranging to get front passes to the Chinese war, the front near Ichang. As far as I know, the press does not get to the front, only Edgar Snow★ who has been with the Communists. This is a non-Communist front. It will be very remarkable to get there and some trip I fancy, from the slight bit of travelling I have done (which was luxury, all things considered). The Japs very evidently hoped that there would be a civil war in these parts, between Chiang and the Communists, but the civil war did not come off. The Japs were taking it easy for a time but have now started up again. I am sure the American public would be interested in an accurate first hand account of Japanese methods in the field, for future reference. So there you are, that's two more articles.

So, if nothing blows up sooner to the south, we will be here for 2–3 weeks, then the front in China for 2 weeks if passes come through as planned, then we will head out in the direction of Indo China and Singapore. Chungking, which I visited en route to Lashio, is no story for *Collier's* now. There have been no bombings for some time and the situation is static. I think we will try to come out from Kunming over the Burma Road by car.

Hope all of this letter meets with your approval. Have never been happier in my life (aside from the fact that I picked up some kind of a throat and can't swallow but what the hell).

Hope all is well with you. Love and kisses,

Martha

★Edgar Snow (1905–1972), writer and journalist from Missouri and one of the only Americans allowed to roam freely in China during the era of Mao Tse-tung. Snow was the first Western journalist to interview Mao after the epic long march and his *Red Star over China* became a classic of modern reporting.

To: Alexander Woollcott★

March 8 1941
[Hong Kong]

Mr. Woollcott darling

I would do almost anything to oblige you, but please do not make me return at once from China. The only thing that baffles me is why I did not come here sooner, as it is evidently heaven on earth, and aside from that, I wonder why you are not here. I thought you were going to pop up from behind a malarial bush on the Burma Road? And where are you? Rotting in America when you could be out here, racketting about like a loony.

I have been to the Burma border and back by air (which is twice the distance of Chicago-San Francisco), just as soon as I staggered off the Clipper. The purpose was to write a piece about that airline, which flies at night over the Japanese lines and the most beautiful and godawful mountains, only in bad weather, usually at night, and just ducking in and out of airfields between Jap raids. It was a very jolly trip and I have written seven thousand of the soundest words about it (probably too sound, I am in revolt from the Haliburton cum Hearst school of war correspondents), and am pooped. Life is awful jolly and I have never been happier, only a little weary. Ernest goes about really learning something about the country, and I go about dazed and open-mouthed, just seeing things and not having an idea what anything means or might prove. He has a good friend named General Cohen, who used to be Mr Sun Yat Sen's bodyguard and who looks like a gentle retired thug. He was born on the wrong side of the tracks in London, and addresses me as Moddom and I love him. Ernest also drank snake wine (with the snake right there in the bottom of the jug) while out on the town with a policeman. I have done nothing so drastic. I am just trying to keep some pieces of my liver, for future use. Whiskey is so cheap here that we do not see how they can afford to sell it, they ought to give it away.

I wish you were here. You would like it very much indeed. Nothing is at all like anything else. Everything smells terrific. Someone once described the citizens of this country (in a moment of genius) as China's teeming millions. My theory is that they have children every six months, being smarter than other people, and liking to keep up the population. I have not yet seen anything at all like any of the books I ever read. Miss Smedley,† a

---

★Critic and founding member of the Algonquin Round Table, a group of writers who met regularly at the hotel, which was across the street from the *New Yorker* offices in New York. In 1939 George Kaufman and Moss Hart used Woollcott as their hero in *The Man Who Came to Dinner*. Martha had met him at the White House.
†Agnes Smedley (1892–1950) was a journalist, feminist, and political activist who wrote about China in the 1930s.

well known and distinguished writer, is here. You would love her. She is like a sociological Edna Ferber.★ Same trouble that I think you once attributed to Miss F. There are others. There is certainly never a restful moment. Among the other dire results of crisis (quote and unquote), the women have been shipped out. Of course that leaves about seven hundred thousand lovely Chinese females in town, but strictly speaking there isn't a woman in the place. When I am old and entirely on the skids, I am going to look for a colony that has shipped the women out. The few remaining ones have Zuleika Dobson lashed to the mast (if that is the expression I mean.)

I miss you anyhow. Take care of yourself. Are you back in residence at the White House. They will have to put up another plaque in the Proclamation of Emancipation room, saying: Alexander Woollcott gives breakfast parties here, when in residence. What do you want me to bring you back from here. Just name it.

Much love from your old White House classmate,

Gellhorn.

P.S. I love you dearly. If you ever feel like writing to me do so to U.S. Consulate, Hongkong. They will forward.

To: Allen Grover

[July] 1941
Finca Vigia
San Francisco de Paula
Cuba

Allen darling;

I dictated a letter to you when I was in New York, at the beginning of June. I was there for two days, submerged by suitcases and conversations of a business nature with *Collier's*. I did not even try to call you because there was no time, and besides I was too gloomy to be any gift. Am still gloomy.

So. And how are you? China was awful in case you want to know. So was the whole Orient. I do not feel cosy in places where the poor literally never straighten their backs, and seem to be born, live and die in mud. The wage scales sadden me, and being a pukka sahib is my idea of an absolutely stinking time. Then too I don't like the English. If you are not nuts for the

---

★Edna Ferber (1885–1968), novelist, short-story writer, and playwright, winner of a Pulitzer Prize, whose book *Giant* became James Dean's last movie.

English in England, you are close to vomiting over the English in the Orient. Also there is so much shit written in our business that finally you feel very ashamed: you cannot write the straight truth because people resent it, and are conditioned (by the shit) not to believe it. So, finally, you write a certain amount of evasion yourself, carefully skirting the definitely dung features of journalism. But it isn't very satisfactory. You know how it goes. Madame Chiang* that great woman and savior of China. Well, balls. Madame Chiang is the Clare Boothe of Cathay, different coloring, different set of circumstances. Perhaps more health and energy. But far far far from Joan of Arc.

Anyhow, I find I tire more easily every year of the nonsense. You have to be very young, very cynical and very ignorant to enjoy writing journalism these days.

I cannot write you about the war. Maybe you know what you think. I certainly don't. But it is far worse not to know what to believe. If you can just tell me what stands firm and is absolutely decent and good, so that I can trust in it, and believe that the future will not be as filthy as the past and the present, I will be very grateful. It only seems to me that this war to save democracy (this second war) is going to finish democracy for good and all, win lose or draw. I can only see that as usual the innocent and ignorant get it in the neck. I definitely do <u>not</u> believe that England is the perfect standard bearer, any more than I believe that the Nazis are human beings and capable of living in a world of men. So there we are. Full of fun and games and a soul serene and at peace. You might tell me what you are tying on to, in these so-called troubled times, so as not to have such a disgust in your heart that you can scarcely bear to think or read.

And isn't Mr. Ickes† a pain in the ass, to get down to facts.

Do write me.

Love,

To: Charles Colebaugh

July 17 [1941]
Finca Vigia
San Francisco de Paula
Cuba

Dear Charles;
You don't seem completely consistent. You ordered this Nazi piece in

---

*Later, Martha would say that she had not been altogether honest about Madame Chiang Kai-Shek in her article for *Collier's*, because as a guest it would have been bad manners.
†Harold Ickes (1874–1952). Governor of New York and strong supporter of civil rights, Ickes had been appointed Secretary of the Interior by Roosevelt in 1933.

New York:* you thought (and said) it would be amusing to have an article showing up the Nazis as hard working little fellows who were not getting anywhere. There was no talk between us about 'important revelations' of Nazi activity: that was not the assignment. I then write the story and you say it is light and you don't want it.

It would have been easy to write a sensational Hearst-type article with the material I had here. There are 770 Germans here (how many in Mexico) and 30,000 Spaniards who are organized into the Spanish Fascist secret society, the Falange. I could have played these facts up (and you would have had an article called Swastika over Cuba). Instead I explained the facts: explaining the system of the Fifth Column, how work begins in a country, and the utility of this work as part of a larger scheme.

If I tell you that the American Ambassador is constantly and intensely concerned with local Nazi activities, and that the English minister is equally so (my facts were all checked with their people and I talked with them at length), you can see that there is another angle. They feel that while Nazi activities here are small, they are a perfect sample of how it begins and they think it significant that Cuba, itself useless, should attract Nazis and they are following all their work, and the Falange, very closely. I still do not believe that one should cry Wolf, Wolf: and I think that such a treatment of the subject is going to do great harm.

. . . Aside from the money question, there is also a professional question. I naturally do not like having enlisted the services of practically every important person on the island (all of them being perfectly serious about this question), and then having the work discarded. A good deal of work.

You say, 'Don't feel badly about this.' I was acting on instructions as regards the tone, and I was giving you accurate facts and a sound approach to a question which has been generally handled by people without previous experience of Fifth Column activities and how they grew. You may remember the young thugs who drove around Madrid in taxis taking pot shots at almost anyone, until the government supposedly 'could not maintain order'. How do you think the Sudeten Henleinists looked one year before they got the go-ahead order. They ran around wearing white stockings and behaving like Peck's Bad Boys.

Yours,

Marty

---

*Many of the large Spanish colonies in Havana were openly anti-American and pro-Axis, and Hemingway had persuaded the American ambassador, Spruille Braden, and the local FBI agent, Robert Leddy, to contribute $500 a month toward equipping the *Pilar* to hunt Nazi submarines. *Collier's* had said they would be interested in an article. The tone of Martha's letter indicates the new, firmer, and more confident stance she was now beginning to take with editors and publishers.

P.S. This all, the foregoing, has sounded pretty upset, Charles, and fairly cross.

. . . I think great service was done the Nazis by those people who have been saying their 'war of horror' would be the worst thing mankind has ever seen, and that no man born of woman could survive against them. I think it would have been perhaps luckier for the French if some writers had pointed out that they used Stuka bombers in Spain, and people survived. In the same way, I think it serves the Nazis to give the Fifth Column credit for being a full blown deadly international organization: that we are already rotted from underneath, from inside. I think it is more useful to a nation to explain always <u>exactly</u> what is bad and exactly what they must face, and never to give the enemy the unpaid aid of making him out more fearsome, appalling and above all successful than he is.

I have a letter today from John Gunther which interests me. He is talking of Ed Taylor's new book, *The Strategy of Terror*, and he says: 'It's a very acute analysis of the sources of defeatism and how they may be stirred and fed. Things seem very wrong with our democracy just now. There is a lack of stamina and fibre.'

I think that one of the ways to produce defeatism is to tell people that the enemy is superpowerful, in every way, and that we are not ready: and then make it clear how fast the enemy works, whereas we democracies move like snails, I think that if you say there is a lack of stamina and fibre, presently there is a lack. And I think knowledge is wonderful, but fear is a disease: and one way to make fear is to blacken the facts until a storm looks like an inescapable devastating hurricane. . . . None of this has anything to do with me. It's just a general line of reasoning: borne out by having seen Fifth Columns at work in Czecho, Spain, France and Sweden, and knowing who ran them, how they started, and were developed, and what they could do.

I'm not cross anymore. I'm just doing sound thinking.

Your old pal,
Gellhorn

To: Hortense Flexner

September 22 1941
Finca Vigia
San Francisco de Paula
Cuba

Teechie dearest
I forgot to write or wire the President about his mother's death and I will have to do something now, too late, and it is very grim and I cannot yet

face it. As I have a honey of a HANGover, one of the real ones, with burning stomach, the shakes and all (y la gloria), I think maybe wait a bit before writing to the President expressing sympathy over the death of that old lady who he must have loved since she was his mother, but surely there was not a goddam thing about her that any outsider would work himself up into a frenzy about.

I am living here in bachelor splendor and though it sounds very disloyal, I was a bachelor for a hell of a long time and it is a thing I understand and no one on earth appreciates it more fully, as I have actually about as much reserve, sense of convention or understanding of public opinion as an ink-fish, and when I am a bachelor, all unrestrained, my Christ how I enjoy myself. So lately I have been out on the town with the boys, drunk as a goat I may say in passing, and dancing until six in the morning. When you are married you do not do such things because you never can stay awake and maybe you don't both like to dance or something and if you were dancing very happy and drunk with some exceptionally handsome young man who seemed very fond of you, there would be trouble and serious scenes. Whereas, the idea is not to have any trouble and nothing serious. I go out only with the Basque pelotaris, who combine – to me – those beauties of the body which the Greeks (I understand) wrote about, with a simple direct and comic mentality that keeps me absolutely shaken with mirth. They have no shame, which is the first sign of honest people, and their language is at once so clear and so brutal that anything you say in it gives you an electric shock.

We went from one dive to another but the first dive was the best. Always the writer (like hell) I observed with fascination the effects on my old friend Pachi of a whore who looked like a sharecropper's wife, with pellagra and no teeth and Sears Roebucks's cheapest sleeziest silk dress, not troubling to dance, or follow him, but simply rubbing herself all over him with an energy which would also reasonably churn butter. There were wonderful obscene jokes in Spanish, they have words for everything, and Pachi delighted with the jokes and not giving a damn and the whore roaring with that strange high hurt insane laughter. It went on fine, fat negresses doing a conga such as they do not do anywhere that people pay to see it, and all doped to the eyes and happy as grigs, because too stupid to be anything but happy.

I saw it all, drunk and sober and all the rest, and saw the 45 year old American who had strayed where he did not belong, solemnly taking flashlight pictures of simple orgiastic nig dances, while his wife and daughter, ugly, pale, silent and hating, handed him new bulbs and did not speak or look at the dancers. There were fights in the lady's rooms, and a wonderful air of not caring about anything nor even remembering who you were, and I kept thinking: heigh-ho for the life of sin and lechery. I know what I want: I want a life with people that is almost explosive in its excitement, fierce and hard and laughing and loud and gay as all hell let loose, and the rest of the time, I want them bloody damn well not to get any place near me, I want to be alone and do my work and my thinking by myself and let them kindly not come to call.

It is, Teecher, a grave but not important error that I happen to be a woman. I do not think that history will, shall we say, suffer: that mass destinies will be altered and blackened because of this. But on the other hand, what a waste. I would really have been a very something man, and as a woman I am truly only a nuisance, only a problem, only something that most definitely does not belong anywhere and will never be really satisfied or really used up.

So, to my permanent disgust, I am not a man, and if I am a woman I am going to make the most of it and not let this biological accident hamper me any more than is necessary. I can resign myself to anything on earth except dullness, and I do not want to be good. Good is my idea of what very measly people are, since they cannot be anything better. I wish to be hell on wheels, or dead. And the only serious complaint I have about matrimony is that it brings out the faint goodness in me, and has a tendency to soften and quiet the hell on wheels aspect, and finally I become bored with myself. Only a fool would prefer to be actively achingly dangerously unhappy, rather than bored: and I am that class of fool.

This (all, by the way, more secret than the tomb from which no traveller returns, or whatever, and you be careful, see) is ever more odd because my man is another hell on wheels character, and what is so christed odd is that two people cannot live together, with any order or health, if they are both hell on wheels, so for the mutual good, and the sake of the party, they must both calm themselves. And that is a loss, but I have not yet found out what to do about it. Ernest and I, really are afraid of each other, each one knowing that the other is the most violent person either one knows, and knowing something about violence we are always mutually alarmed at the potentialities of the other. So, (I think, but I do not do much of this sort of thinking) when we are together we take it fairly easy, so as not to see the other burst into loud furious flame.

The other night, before I started on this wonderful epoch of drunkenness, laughter and dancing, I was home here being decent and elegant and all the rest. (The rain was what bitched me; it has rained for five days and finally I was driven into town to escape the dampness and the awful slow sound of it, and now I wonder if I will be sober again before I leave. It would be funny to be drunk, wildly happy and careless in Saint Louis, where I am going next. There is no one in Saint Louis good enough to be drunk with, there is no one with enough blood to merit that lavish outlay of energy and jokes.) So that night, the quiet night, impressed by Brahms which was playing on the Capehart, I started to write memoirs, addressing them to you, since I can always talk to you. But the memoirs cooled off, because I knew what I was doing; and if there are any rests left, on paper, of my life, they will have to be like this, disjointed and uncertain, done for no reason, and put in an envelope to mail. I cannot do the other. When I start to think, I freeze. And when I freeze I write like a lady who came from a clean, honorable, intelligent and quiet home. And what sort of writing is that?

E is at Sun Valley and I will leave here October 2 and spend about 10 days in St Louis seeing Mother and doing dentistry and then I will go there too. I hate it like holy hell. It is the west in an ornamental sanitary package. But maybe by that time I will need sanitation and anyhow I am going, because that is my job. I am an old woman now (33 in November) and unregenerate and in my heart still as curious and generally angry and anxious for trouble as when I was young. But I will have to get over that. There is no sense in allowing one's own arrested adolescence to become a problem for the general public.

I love you. Have a hell of a good time. I don't really know what else is worth having.

> Always,
> Gellhorn

To: Max Perkins★

> October 17 1941
> Sun Valley Lodge
> Idaho

Dear Max;

I think the book is <u>beautiful</u>.[†] I never saw one that looked so fine, and we are all enchanted with it, and I treat it as if it were some marvelous piece of decoration, a thing to stand on a table and look at. The cover is far better than any of the books I have seen recently and the book itself, the cloth cover and the print, is a joy. Ernest thinks so too and so does everyone who has seen it.

Now maybe some critics will like it and maybe they won't. . . . I always envied Ernest when a book came in, because it made him so happy, and when mine came in I just generally felt sick, and always disappointed and sort of scared inside and usually regretting the whole thing. But this one,

---

★Maxwell Perkins had now taken on Martha as one of his authors.
[†]*The Heart of Another*, Martha's first collection of short stories. Critics suggested that they seemed to have been greatly influenced by Hemingway.

no. I know it is more grown-up than anything I have done before, and am very surprised to do anything grown up, and therefore full of hope. The weak story is 'Slow Train to Garmisch', which brings back that old familiar sick feeling. But I can read the others and could never before read anything of mine in print, could only sort of look at it, and then tell myself I would do better next time. Still, don't get the idea I am just wallowing in smuggery and thinking all is for the best. There is still everything to learn, and everything to do sharper and tighter.

It is very handsome out here with the mountains like lion skin and a marvelous cool blonde light over them. We went on a disastrous duck hunt yesterday and sat and watched thousands of ducks, as high as bombers, flying somewhere else. Only Giggy shot really well, but today the two children and E have gone out again and will go to a good place. Bumby is a fisherman as if the whole fate of mankind depended on it, which is probably the way to do anything. He occasionally relaxes from his high destiny and plays tennis with me, or with better people, and he is very lovely to look at and a very gentle and very young and very good boy. I think Mousie is the most interesting character of them all, but they are none of them slouches and it is very impressive to see that rare and inexplicable Ernest bringing up his children as he writes, with genius and not obeying any of the rules and doing exactly what he intends to do, and bringing it off better than anyone.

I would rather be a writer than anything else on earth, including a shot or a tennis player, but I am lazy and there are communal demands on time, and then besides, I feel very troubled in the head and heart. It is as if all the time one was boiling inside with some kind of helpless indignation, enraged to see such a good-looking and possibly decent world always going to hell, and going to hell with such cruelty and waste. If you liked horses (which I do not) it would be as if you had to watch people beating and abusing them, every day, everywhere. And could not even scream out, or throw a bottle. But I must say I was very disgusted to see that Dos [Passos], at the P.E.N. congress in London, said that writers should not write now. If a writer has any guts he should write all the time, and the lousier the world the harder a writer should work. For if he can do nothing positive, to make the world more livable or less cruel or stupid, he can at least record truly, and that is something no one else will do, and it is a job that must be done. It is the only revenge that all the bastardized people will ever get: that someone writes down clearly what happened to them.

Have you read [Elizabeth] Bowen's book called *Look At All Those Roses*? I am not sure what I think about it. It seems so shiny and impressive, technically, and so empty and yet not empty. It is as if she almost told you something very surprising and new and then did not tell it, because she did not see it. It is as if she made a big mystery out of something, so it would look important: and all the words are wonderful but when you study it closely it is false, and none of the people are alive and none of it happened or matters. It is kind of like Kay Boyle★ and Katherine Anne Porter† who have that great talent too, making you so excited and eager and alert, and watching all the time, and finally there is nothing to see, and what the bloody hell was it all about. But it is a talent: it is like a blind story teller, somehow, crossed with a conspirator.

That *Oxford Companion to American Literature* is a bunch of dung, frankly. Have you seen it? I think it is the Oxford Companion to American Literature for Rotary Clubs who want to know about books without reading. I think it is a shame. There is a whole thing about Ernest in it which is as silly as anything I ever saw, and looks as if it were taken from the blurbs of books or cheap book reviews. And the way he retells the *Bells* in one half paragraph is a marvel of bad writing and taste. This awful condensed culture is one of the horrors of our time, surely. Do you think people have to be cultured, if they aren't really and don't feel like it? I don't think they even have to be educated. Like Mr James M. Cain, and the book we call Mildred Pus.‡ It seems to me fine that Mr Cain is nothing at all, except what he appears to be, and if he could think better or feel better and avoid those godawful endings he always had, he probably wouldn't even write the first halves of his books and that would be a loss. Look how easy you can learn about the restaurant business, just reading a bad novel.

I must stop maundering on.

Thank you very very much for all the trouble you have taken with my book. Please tell Charlie how happy I am about its looks.

Always,

Martha

★Kay Boyle (1902–1992), novelist and European correspondent for the *New Yorker* in the late 1940s, and active in progressive movements in the U.S.
†Katherine Anne Porter (1890–1941), Texas-born novelist and short-story writer, best known for *Ship of Fools* (1961).
‡James M. Cain (1892–1977), American journalist, scriptwriter, and crime fiction writer, whose novels *The Postman Always Rings Twice* and *Mildred Pierce* were made into classics of the American cinema.

To: Eleanor Roosevelt

October 17 1941
[Sun Valley Lodge]
Idaho

Dearest Mrs. R;
I am sending you today the first copy I have of my new book. Will you like
the book, I wonder? It is the first time I am happy about one of my own
books, and that makes me nervous because perhaps if I am happy about it,
it is punk. But I never could read what I had written and this time I can,
without that awful sick gloom of someone knowing they did not carry it
off as intended. I think there are grown-up things in this book, and so I am
happy. I think it is getting more like an iceberg (which is the aim of all good
writing): one ninth of it shows, but there truly is eight ninths submerged
and you can feel it there.

And, you know, it is just a book. It is a book of stories about people. It
is for no purpose. And for the first time I feel I did say what I meant, just
writing about people, without any special point of view, only wanting to
understand them and tell about them as truly as I saw them. So finally, it
occurs to me that the human heart is what lasts and what always did and
always will last; and maybe the human heart is the proper field of study and
the only undeniable concern of writers. It's all there, after all: it isn't because
a thing happened in 1841 or 1941 or any of that: it's because people are how
they are. Now, with this war, we must all be expedient, as the thing to do
is to win. But the war will not matter in the end any more than all the other
wars (and there have been too many), but what happens to human beings,
before during and afterwards, is all that matters. And it is by God not a
question of democracy, nor of nations, nor of any of those abstract words:
it is a question of human lives, and they have names and places where they
were born, and jokes and sicknesses and despair and jobs and children and
taxes and hopes, and they die: and they are all that matters. Life must be for
them and about them. I think our time is so unspeakably lousy because
human beings seem so completely forgotten, and the rules do not consider
them, nor the rulers, and the human race seems to be living on sufferance,
whereas it should live in full possession of the earth.

That's my politics. I wish I knew who my co-religionaries were, and I
wish we could organize. I wish people could stick up for themselves, for the
absolutely real and concrete dignity of human life, and nothing else. I am
sick to the nausea point of all the idiot things men have been shouting about
in their ignorance, one way or the other. The British Empire seems to me
as foolish as Nazism is horrible: and when people say we must do this that
and the other about America what the hell are they talking about. What
America: a geographical expanse, a section of society which is their own?

Or what? A country is only good, where life is a dignity, where each man has his dignity and need not scratch or kick people around, to live. The only real reason for this war is to remove, if possible, terribly and finally, a system which makes life as bad as life can possibly be. But that does not mean anything positive; it does not mean life has been made good. It is like cutting out a cancer and leaving a tuberculosis, which need not be fatal and is surely not painful. Still the tuberculosis is there. There will have to be a great deal of work after the war. I am afraid all the good people will be either dead or tired, the way they were after the last war.

Well, here is a very long letter and you cannot have time for very long letters. I love you dearly as always. I wish I could hug you and tell you so.

Always,

Marty

To: Alexander Woollcott

January 22 1942
San Francisco de Paula
Cuba

Dearest Woolkie;
Having a bad pain this morning I think I will write you for a little while. Is it true you have been ill? I do hope not.

I am not very well myself but that is due to the fact that I got all mixed up and hurried yesterday and forgot to eat after breakfast but on the other hand went to a cocktail party (a feast here that begins at 6:30 p.m. and ends at 4 a.m.) and drank a certain amount. This is my second big party here in five years, and perhaps the fifth party in all. I think I would like to be a philosopher, being as I think such deep thoughts after parties and in fact any time my stomach is distressed.

However, as a philosopher (this morning) I think parties are really the last refuge of the empty and shrivelled brain, and are more destructive to the body than cocaine and more destructive to the spirit than jail. I have such a good time during them for a while, going about showing off in the cheapest and most repugnant manner, shocking citizens whose emotions (whether of shock or otherwise) surely should not concern me, and making a kind of belligerent tough-joking conversation which is found amusing only by me the maker. I had a fairly pleasant interlude last night with a little man named Igor Cassini* who earns his living writing poisonous and

---

*Igor Cassini (1916–2002), journalist and gossip columnist, who wrote for the Hearst newspaper chain under the name of Cholly Knickerbocker. In the late 1950s Cassini claimed a readership of almost 20 million.

painful things about fashionable or famous people in some second rate Washington paper. He is a little man with a mouth which I like to think looks like a hog's ass in fly-time though I never saw that phenomenon but only imagined it. He has a great deal of matted waving hair and a little short doughy body and perfectly flat black little eyes, calculating and about as warm as ball-bearings. He has also a wife who looks like a Russian mannequin formerly employed by Patou until she opens her mouth and then I do not know exactly where she comes from as I do not get around much but she asked me if I was American and was terribly surprised to find I was. I went to this party with Bumbi, Ernest's oldest boy who is four days this side of the army. Bumbi is blonde and very good to look at and 18 and sweet and six feet and one inch tall. (Ernest, canny to the last, put himself to bed before the party with a sore throat; he seems fine today.) So I told Igor Cassini that Bumbi was my son and that I had had him when I was twelve, an act which had startled the medical world internationally and been very painful but rewarding for me. I also said that of course the boy had not been legal at the time but we had since given him a name. Igor was horrified to hear anyone breezing skeletons around like that (he evidently thought I was Bohemian and knew no better) and the little ball bearing eyes gleamed with pleasure at this item. So I was happy for a bit.

But now I feel hungover and sick in my soul: think of the wasted time of these parties, think of the wasted money; think of people meeting each other day after day, drowned in flowers and martinis, with nothing to say to each other but all talking like parrot cages. I shall not go again anywhere for a year and the horrid effects will wear off.

. . . I am still writing my story and still happy with it; but this hangover is no condition in which to produce that pure and gemlike literature we like to see. Why don't you ever write to me? You are a sloth not to. Or don't you love me any more? Have you taken up with a new bride? Please answer.

Ernest sends you regards. I guess you got his story all right for your toilet paper anthology. I wish I saw you sometime. Give Mrs R my best love when you see her again.

Always,

Gellhorn

An Honorable Profession, 1942-1945

After the Japanese bombing of Pearl Harbor on December 7, 1941, and the United States' entry into the war, Collier's *contacted Martha to ask whether she would do some more reporting for them. The American military, however, remained totally opposed to women war correspondents on the front line, and it was not until the summer of 1942 that she thought of a "sideshow" where they were unlikely to notice her presence. In July, she set off to roam the Caribbean and report on submarine warfare.*

To: Charles Colebaugh

February 3 1942
San Francisco de Paula
Cuba

Dear Charles;

As you say, it is really too late to do anything about my sex. That is a handicap I have been struggling under since I was five years old, and I shall just forge ahead, bravely, despite the army. Probably, when anything happens, and we want very very badly (both of us) for me to get there, maybe I can arrange it. No sense fretting in advance though. I do not observe any note of frenzied haste in your letter: and do not feel any special violent urge to move right now myself. That South American story will only grow riper and better with time, don't you think? And I'd really like something a little more active, when the time comes. I mean, more like the good old days, like Spain or Finland. This is going to be a nice long war, and sooner or later they are going to want to make it popular, and then folks like us can work.

Meanwhile I do my homework, like a little boy getting ready to take West Point entrance exams. (A little bigger boy than that, really.) It is very instructive. I split the rest of my time between trying to write (which is the soundest occupation I know) and trying to shoot 20 out of 20 live pigeons, flying like hell bats with a big norther driving them. We have a measly little international championship on live pigeons, down here in a few days, and

I am going to enter, mainly because I am the *fille du régiment* of the shooters, being the only female on the island who hangs around the club, shooting as solemnly as the oldest shoot-fools in the place. They all make loud sad sounds when I miss and rush out and shake my hands and say that I made a shot of surpassing beauty when I bring down the birds. It is very jolly, and there is a kind of formal Spanish joking that goes on all the time, with people addressing each other as 'Caballero' and 'Senor', and bowing, and making huge fun of each other.

I shall be right here and you can reach me any time you want me.

Your devoted servant,

Martha Gellhorn

To: Bill and Annie Davis★

April 17 1942
San Francisco de Paula
Cuba

Dear Man and Wife

. . . Things are about the same here. We went goggle fishing only there was such a hell of a storm with rain and what not that we could not go down into the reef. I was sick mostly and have renounced the sea. E got a huge white marlin, about two hundred pounds, up to the boat three times and the boatman muffed the gaffing and finally broke the line. This was a moment of great drama, as we had had our brains beat out for three days and the marlin was to be the reward. However.

E is working. I am being made very jittery and wretched by the horrors of the servant problem, which leads me to decide, as always, that possessions are the undoing of man. If we had no possessions we would not need anyone to keep them clean and then I would not have to make myself into a fury trying to find and instruct domestics. On the other hand, E says I am a fool and people have to have a house to write in, and taking care of the house is just what you have to do, in payment. So. But what a bore it is. Of course, people would not be servants if they had more brains, but really the lack of brains can disrupt life badly.

I have to go to lunch. E is writing and happy. His pigeons are doing very well.

Love

Marty

★Old friends of Hemingway's with a house near Malaga in Spain.

To: Bill and Annie Davis

[June] 1942
San Francisco de Paula
Cuba

Dear Guys,

Ernest is asleep and I want to talk. It would be even better if one could write; make something with a shape to it in words. But the writing seems all dried up and gone and only letters remain . . .

Have just finished reading Richard Hillary's* *Falling Through Space*. Now it settles down on top of all the other books: the books eaten every day, a new one every day as if you were afraid to stop reading for fear you would starve. I never lived through books before, but now they seem to be the only nourishing substantial part of life. And at last, very slowly all kinds of books mixed together in an unbalanced diet, I am beginning to get something from them.

I think (though perhaps wrong) that am beginning to understand how to take this war. We were the wrong age, absolutely; we are neither young enough for this to be the first time, nor old enough to have the relief of feeling it to be the last time, at least a last time personally . . . I think we, of course, were and cannot help but be specially deformed because of Spain. Spain was where our adult hope was (the sum total of the remaining hope of youth, with a reasoning and logical hope of adults) . . . Spain was a place where you could hope, and Spain was also like a vaccination which could save the rest of mankind from the same fearful suffering. But no one important cared. So the hope was killed, and mankind was left to suffer it all, and the suffering of Spain was as lost as the hope. That is exactly what I mean. Because we saw that, we were specially deformed. I think if Ernest had been older the last war would have done the same thing to him; he was too young to harm . . . But after Spain, I at least felt such bitterness at how the world was run that I wanted no part of it in any way; and I felt such a despair for the human race that I thought they were forever bitched, in any language and any country· we were all victims, the evil ones and the fools would always triumph. The last active thing I had the energy to do was a protest, in the form of a novel about Czecho which was already lost . . .

. . . But if you have no part in the world, no matter how diseased the world is, you are dead. It is not enough to earn your living, do no actual harm to anyone, tell no lies (so as not to be responsible ever for any treachery however small), help a few people with money or kindness when the occasion presents – and without too great hardship to oneself. It is not enough. It is okay. It is not dirty. But it is dead.

---

*Richard Hillary, a British Spitfire fighter pilot who had been badly burned when his plane was shot down. He wrote about his experiences before returning to active duty. He was killed soon afterward, at the age of twenty-four.

Then this war, the worst bitterness of all, because if Spain had not been sold out, truly this long and hideous killing could have been avoided. It was clearly the visual daily payment for the evil and foolishness of the past . . . I have been shut up and cut off and violently refusing and unable to see or think; the rage over the past making it impossible to function in the present. It would be better to have an attack of amnesia and forget. Because there is only now; and no matter how this war came about, no matter how it is run, it belongs to us. 'Because I am involved in mankind'. And one must remain involved in all mankind, even uselessly, and even if one is intellectually conditioned to doubt and despair. Otherwise one might as well be dead.

I am trying to work out a modus vivendi somehow; and it is a curious process which would be easy if one were at the front, any front, because there you do not have to think. It is very hard to shape your mind at a distance, in peace and great ease, relying only on the mind and not on the heart, and learning not directly but through books. It is like being blind and having to see through the perceptions in your finger tips. But I have a feeling that the mind must be whole and unshaken; must be wiser; must seek out a pattern that is acceptable and believable. It does no good to save one's body or one's comforts and I never gave a damn for the soul . . . The mistakes also concern us all; we are in no position to regard them with rage or contempt; that is too aloof, too apart. We must either understand exactly how they are made and try, however ineffectually and humbly, to stop them; or we must somehow take them with the others who suffer them; we must not get off free.

It remains to be seen how. I have no ideas and no plans. At present I am going off this summer to the Caribbean which will be pleasant and pointless, to work for *Collier's*. I will enjoy it very much but it answers nothing, except the need to work. But that is work as opium, nothing else; though of course agreeable and always brings in money. The dreadful thing is that I only know how to write (if that) and I do not believe writing is of much use. I mean, as a thing in itself. This boy Hillary (who started it all) has written a wonderful book because it is like a pair of glasses if you are getting nearsighted. But he did not set out to write a book; he did not burn to a crisp to get material. The book as product is useful (see *For Whom the Bell Tolls*.) It is inadmissible as an end in itself. And of course I do not believe in journalism; I think it changes nothing. Though perhaps if enough journalists wrote the same way about the same thing they might affect 'public opinion' (quote and unquote, a nebulous factor it seems to me). But with censorship and what all, even that is doubtful. So my trade seems to me a non-entry into the business of sharing. I do not want to tout war and do not believe it can be properly reported. I want to be part of what happens to everyone.

Ah well, maybe after squirming around like a stuck fly, I shall know how to think and then finally how to act. But all I am sure of now is that there is no escape; what is now is what we have; and we belong in it. Not in the red tape and the uniforms at the Stork Club, not in the garbage of war, which one must ignore since one cannot correct it. But from where I sit, all I see is that garbage and I know that is wrong. The garbage makers, collectors, eaters, will remain so for themselves, always, at any time of history: and they will not be troubled, being used to the smell and taste of the product. They need not really concern us. And it isn't even a question of winning or losing the war, though it must be won; because what little we do or do not do is not going to affect that. It is really that 'any man's death diminishes me because I am involved in mankind.'

Well, so long. Hope you are keeping well. I probably need a bottle of tequila. No, probably not. Love,

Marty

To: H. G. Wells

June 14 1942
Finca Vigia
San Francisco de Paula
Cuba

Darling I always feel like writing but you know how it is: I must have got some sort of quirk through living in Europe which makes me rather rat-eyed and glum when I think the people at the next table are listening, and I do not like to have letters read (even the most innocent, honorable: anything that does not begin Dear Sir is private) and besides I know so little. My world is really small: part of the time it is an island thirty by eighteen miles, which I invented (thus horning in on God), and the rest of the time it is ten or eight acres, I forget which, of this finca. I concern myself in the way the bougainvillea is cut and look with dismay at the rain washing the new whitewash like milk from the house; I discipline the cook who slips past economy most graciously, with obeisant senoras and absolute agreement, and no economy; I hound the butler, a dark man who should have played poker for a living, since he has that face, and had he been white would have driven Humphrey Bogart from the screen, and hound him and he nods (usually with a toothpick in his mouth) but cleans no silver, brass or windows. Things like that. And dentists for the children and equipping and packing them to join Ernest on a fishing trip. And answering all our business mail and lately I have had Paramount with me, via the cable and the long distance, since they are such people, Paramount with organ voices intoning the splendors of the unseen film FWBT (censor: *For Whom the Bell Tolls.*) They want us to come to NY all at their expense, to be present at what is called the woild preemeer, on Basteele Day (no less), but of course we cannot and really we would not if we could.

The writers I now admire are Koestler,[*] Nelson Algren,[†] Nicolas Aldanov and Ira Wolfert[‡]: I think they are full of juice, with good sharp new eyes, and not enough comfort in their bellies to make their minds boring. I recognize them too: they are part of a lovely lost life, when everything was at once harder and easier. The kind of life is the one that drove you to suggest I get a new dress, that dead old black wool was so worn and shabby and almost smelly (or perhaps entirely smelly?) That's the life I mean. Maybe it is only one's youth one is talking about, and of course the poor and the struggling stay young longer.

One thing time has not removed from me, the last toughness of my youth, and that is to live alone. I am glad of that; I would be scared to death if I found I was really needing people, needing the comfort and reassurance, since one's own society though varied is not exactly soothing. But that is left, may God be thanked, though my God I am getting soft otherwise. And I read so badly. Do you read well? It was a talent I always coveted and thought I could acquire but apparently not. I wish my memory were better and my brains less languid; I would like to read fiercely and learn from it and remember. There's so much to know. But it leaks away, or else the cutting edges of my brain are blotting paper.

Perhaps we'll be in England together now that spring is passed. That would be very rare. I have a feeling that it is years late to go, though the heroic days may be coming again: but that not having seen the beginning one will never entirely understand the end. However, even a grain of understanding is better than a blankness.

Goodnight,

Marty

To: Nelson Algren

June 24 1942
Finca Vigia
San Francisco de Paula
Cuba

Dear Mr. Algren;

I just want to tell you how terrific your book is, and it ought to be the best of the best sellers if books sold on a basis of their goodness and you ought

---

[*]Arthur Koestler (1905–1983), author with a wide range of political, scientific, and literary interests, was imprisoned as a Communist by Franco during the Spanish Civil War.

[†]Nelson Algren (1909–1981) had just written *Never Come Morning*, a novel about poverty and crime, which had been banned by the Chicago Public Library. Algren won the first National Book Award for fiction in 1950 with *The Man with the Golden Arm* and had a seventeen-year affair with Simone de Beauvoir.

[‡]Ira Wolfert (1908–1997), war correspondent, screenwriter, and Pulitzer Prize–winning novelist.

to get one of the big prizes again if they gave them rightly; and if you get none of these things it will be because people are dopes, which is just possible. It is very hard to talk to writers about their books; it always is embarrassing to listen to other people doing it. So please forgive anything which sounds strained or shy. I think if a book shows you a whole world, that you never knew of, and makes it so real that this new world sticks with you, in your mind, as if you had been there, then the book must be the real thing and the only thing that is worth writing. Yours certainly does all that. It terrified me to read, naturally, and just as naturally made me furiously angry, knowing it was all true and knowing that none of it need be true if we weren't really such slobs and fools and such careless little-minded people. But aside from that, and as writing, the way it was written was as exciting as new country; wonderful new sounds you've got hold of, and wonderful quick and sort of desperate ways of saying things. I can't tell you about it properly, except to say that it can't be forgotten and that I hope nothing in the way it is received will depress you for a minute and please know also that you have here a permanent reader, waiting eagerly to see what you do next, and remembering with the greatest admiration what you have done. If I were you, I'd be so swollen with pride I would be unable to walk. How did you feel when it was done? You must have felt very very good indeed.

Ernest has been spreading your book around Cuba, and you have many devoted readers here. They think Chicago is certainly some place. I think it is too, and it sounds a good deal more terrifying than the jungle.

Yours respectfully,
Martha Gellhorn Hemingway

To: Ernest Hemingway

June 29 1942
Bacons on the Sea
Fort Walton
Florida

My beloved Binglie,

. . . Yesterday we drove over to a town called Crestview in the afternoon. There's a field and you pick up soldiers and give them lifts. On the way home we picked up two boys from Brooklyn New York who asked us if we had ever been to NY. I said out of curiosity, that a lot of Brooklyn boys had been in Spain. Yes said one, that was that Jewish outfit, the Lincoln Battalion. They must just have been soldiers of fortune, said the other, you don't see any of them in this war. They weren't fighting for a cause or anything just Communism versus Fascism. I asked him if they talked much about the war in their mess, what it was about and so on and he said you never heard anyone mention it, they just all hoped it would be over as soon as possible. I thought it was gruesome and very interesting. I am very sad most of the time.

. . . We saw Garbo's latest, *Two-Faced Woman*.* It was tragic; I hope she never makes another. Or at least that they don't have her doing comedy any more. She looks as if she were in terrible pain when she smiles; her laugh sounds like a sob. She is old now and the beauty is all gone; the beautiful mouth is ruined, everything is bad, lined and terrible. And they spoiled her hair with a huge permanent and curly bangs, and her bosoms are long and flat and her *derrière* wobbles. It is enough to break your heart. The most beautiful woman of our time just hideous and ruined; with nothing left. She is about ripe to play Queen Victoria or Eliz. of England now; those seem to be the two roles which remain. The camera is a cruel thing.

The week ahead seems to me the longest unit of time yet invented. What are you doing? Oh please write me? I need a big hugalug,

Always your mopey wife
Marty

To: Nelson Algren

July 11 1942
San Francisco de Paula
Cuba

Dear Mr A;
. . . The more I think about the book the more terrific I think it is. That you should have had no luck out of doing such a fine job is just the way things work. Ernest is a sort of optimist, about writing anyhow, and is convinced that in the end with good writing you conquer the earth, at least as much of the earth as you could care about. I think he is probably right in the long run. There are very good precedents anyhow. I know you're a good writer; all you have to do is survive.

. . . I hope you will not think that I am one of those elderly women with grey marcelled hair and sweet determined smiles who set out to mother young artists etc. And I am afraid I may sound very bumptious and butting in and bossy and god knows what all. It is probably a terrible weakness to care so much about writing and be so goofy with pleasure when I find anything first rate. The only way I know to judge a book is whether I wish I could have written it myself. (Bad sentence.) And I wish I could have written yours.

---

*In 1941, Greta Garbo was 36. After scathing reviews for *Two-Faced Woman*, she retired from films, remaining a recluse until her death in 1990.

The joke in all this is that none of my books sell at all. I must have the smallest and most rare reading public on record. I do not find this odd at all; the books are extremely gloomy reading. But it makes me sore as hell that you do not sell one hundred thousand. It is not only for your sake, but because I think it would be good in a general way if one hundred thousand people saw what you have seen.

I am off to the Caribbean in a few days on a two months assignment for *Collier's* (that's how I earn my living; the books are what I do when I have made money. No, that's a lie. The books are what I do when I have something in my head, instead of the usual disorder, laziness, confusion, rage and poopiness. If you have something you intend to write, you write it somehow or other. I wrote a lot more, though it was worse writing, when I was earning $12 a week in Paris.) So I shall be contentedly percolating through the hurricane zones for the remainder of this summer.

Good luck to you. Though you've already had an enormous amount of it, with that book to your credit.

> Yours,
> Martha Gellhorn Hemingway

To: Charles Colebaugh

> July 16 1942
> San Francisco de Paula
> Cuba

Dear Charles;
The letter of credentials and the radio card have come. Thank you. I am now all set. I am just holding my breath until the Saturday plane and the joy of working again. The radio card is made out to Martha Hemingway. That is okay. But don't get mixed up; my articles are always to be signed Martha Gellhorn, always. That is what I always was, and am and will be: you can't grow a name on to yourself,
I'll make it as fine a trip as I can Charles, as you know.

> Always,
> Marty Gellhorn

To: Ernest Hemingway

> July 23 1942
> Port au Prince
> Haiti

Bug dearest;
It is now four o'clock and the mountains and the sea and the sky are all grey, but the sea shines, and there is no air. This is the bad part of the day, waiting

for rain. . . . Since lunch I have slept. Now, if I can move my limp string muscles, I shall go up the road a ways and then climb into the hills for a bit to see a small village which they tell me is lovely and truly country. After that I will go to the Chargé d'Affaires' house (he was in Prague when I was) and have cocktails with some people who run mosquitoe boats . . .

The mountains are real mountains, four thousand and upwards. I talked with an American who has business here, he is also agent for shells, and he tells me the duck hunting is unbelievable, teal, pin-tail and mallard, more than you ever saw. I saw some pictures a man had, which he said were poor and modest, of a flight at the edge of a lake; it was very imposing. They have also here blue pigeon (I do not know what that is) and guinea. The American says they are great fun to shoot, he says you can drive the guinea and make them fly like pheasants. He also says there is fine tarpon fishing and sailfish.

Meantime I have got together the things that interest me and it is more or less like stringing beads, no single place will be enough by itself. It is interesting to think of the beautiful now deadly sea (deadlier than one knows) bordering so many lovely and peaceful lands. The land is calm and rich in the heat, and the water is like the jungle or else the water is the modern world.

Meantime, the Dominican republic has not given me a visa and if they don't give me one tomorrow I shall just go on without stopping there. They are very fussy and silly; they make a sort of performance of keeping one waiting, without a purpose. I only want to go anyhow in order to see what a modern city is like without any gasoline; but it will not break my heart if I cannot go and I am certainly not going to sit about waiting. I would like to move about from there in some sort of small inter-island sail boat but nothing seems to move specially; it is too spooky apparently and everyone advises most strongly against anything of any size. But you can see that it is hard to give an itinerary.

. . . I really have loved this place; there hasn't been a dull or useless moment and at any hour, even now, stifling in the grey heat, it is beautiful. If this job keeps up so well I will be a very lucky journalist. The war is really like a great pebble or a depth charge, thrown into the world at one spot and widening out from there. If I could be as detached as God, it would be a most amazing spectacle . . . At the same time there are Germans here who have not been back to Germany since the last war. They sit in an internment camp and worship the Führer and believe every one of his lousy and repulsive theories, which they have studied by correspondence course, or learned through pamphlets and they are as ardent as if they were party officials in Germany. These Germans have all been well treated and happy and successful here for years, but they are not content; they want to be the master race. It was amazing to see them, and I also get the feeling they are insane, in a most dangerous way, because you cannot put a whole nation in the loony bin. There are Italians too and I find them harder to understand; perhaps it is just that they are a little weakminded. They do not seem to have the fierceness and meanness of the Germans. They seem foolish rather than dangerous.

There are some wonderful little birds, which I think are swallows, though of course I don't know, playing in the sky like seals or pursuit planes, outside my window. But oh my, how I love the South Seas, how I love to travel light and with no plans and have every day come as a surprise. It does not make for depth or wisdom probably but it keeps the mind light and limber and full of jokes. And I think I would rather feel young than be Jane Austen.

love
Mrs Bug

To: Charles Colebaugh

October 4 1942
San Francisco de Paula
Cuba

Charles dearie

I think this piece★ runs about 3000 words but if it is longer you cut it darling, or get your hatchet men to. I can no more. I have enough stuff for three articles. I could write one about the escaped French convicts, their stories, how they came to join de Gaulle but the planter Chandon had already left with 140 men and there were no more boats, how they came across the Marowyne river, hanging on to bits of wood, swimming along between Tommy gun bullets, what it is truly like to live in that place, what the prison community is like. I could write one about the bushniggers, who pan gold and cut down vast trees (the U.S. Engineers use them, asking for the wood and leaving them alone, since they don't take bossing) and fear spirits and eat their own fleas and the Moravian Brothers, the missionaries, and the old white Deaconess with her four adopted bushnig kids and their savage odd little thoughts about war and peace. I could write about the Dutch and Paramaribo and what it is like to live in such a place and how it can be done and all the weird and rare and sometimes wonderful people. Without even mentioning life at a gold mine in a jungle, where you dress for dinner, and take your bath in a tin wash tub and have to put on boots and change to evening shoes when you get to the main house, from the guest house (and both houses are sewers) and how strange it is. (And how

---

★"A Little Worse than Peace" appeared in *Collier's* on November 14, 1942.

the gold doesn't come in as it used to – but why?) Without even mentioning the gold train and the Dutch sergeant with his native girl and curious cargo; and without mentioning travel by native canoe on the rivers. So much, so much. But there's no time: it won't change the course of the war: and there is not enough paper. Only I wanted you to know, because I've tried so hard to hold down.

I am enclosing also expense account; the first part of it was sent you before. Where are we depositing dough now; New York or Cuba? Could you let me know so I can keep my accounts straight and not overdraw more wildly than usual.

E has convinced me that I deserve a trip to New York and Washington, and though I probably should not do so, I am so anxious to find out what America is like (or rather what New York and Washington are like) that I am coming.

I hope you're pleased with this last trip Charles. It was quieter territory than I am used to, but it was wonderful too. I hope some of that got across in the articles. It seems almost sacrilegious to say so, but life itself (apart from war, oh remote from war) turns out to be rare and exciting to watch. Only I don't suppose people are interested in just people and living right now.

Anyhow, we'll have lunch won't we?

Always,

Martha Gellhorn

To: Allen Grover

October [?] 1942
The White House
Washington

Dearie dearie

The reason I was so non-committal over the phone is that I do not imagine the phones are entirely un-monitored. I know that some kind of mysterious folk sit on the 3rd floor doing something electrical. See?

I told you I had Lincoln's room and how I felt ashamed to be in his bed, so I also told Woollcott who's up the hall in my former room (mine and Churchill's) and Woollcott said the bed had already been desecrated by Edna Ferber so what the hell.

I am sick in bed again and thoroughly fed up with myself and life and I think this cold is incurable like cancer. Living here is also like convent life; just Wollcott and me here alone and both ill and maybe the Lunts* to tea

---

*Alfred Lunt and Lynn Fontanne were the best known and admired stage couple in the U.S., never appearing on stage separately.

(if we can get them through the guarded gates) and nothing to do but cough and write notes on this costly paper. I feel particularly bitter about Tuesday evening: I wanted to be sleek and shining and just make eyes at you like an eye-making machine and dance and be as gay as all get-out. Also I have not seen the autumn at all – just some golden leaves outside my window now. And not really seen you. What a trip. What <u>did</u> I do? I haven't even got a new dress. And meantime Allen, <u>how Rome burns</u>.

My love
Marty

To: Ernest Hemingway

October 23 1942
The White House
Washington

Dearest,
I'm sick abed again. What a life. I don't feel too awful but just sort of depressed & hopeless as if I had an incurable cold.

. . . Last night the light over Washington was that lovely deep purple blue it used to be, November afternoons, over Paris. It was so soft & gentle it made me want to cry. Then driving in over the bridge to the Lincoln Memorial & then the beautiful Cleopatra's needle & the pools in front. It was at 7 o'clock & still and with that lovely light & it made me think of the Seine & the Bois (where I always specially noticed the light) and I was all sad & homesick but happy to be seeing again. I have grown as blind as a business-man, or else I am like a paid psychiatrist, listening and figuring. And really I would like to be like a poet and have fresh eyes & be in no hurry . . .

love
Marty

To: Charles Scribner

February 26 1943
San Francisco de Paula
Cuba

Dear old Crowned-Head;
You ought to stop all that money-making nonsense and being bank presidents and such rot and dedicate yourself to Art. What can you do that is more important to the world than concentrate on getting good books to the vast public and getting a little money for your stable of writers (none of

whom have bank presidencies etc on the side to keep them rich, you loathsome capitalist.) (Or directorships of companies or whatever the hell.) You write a good letter, son; full of news.

We are raising cats but it is not much of a war effort and no matter how bad things get, we do not intend to eat them. We now have nine. They all eat ground up filet mignon every day in a most startling manner and none of them is ever going to do a day's work in exchange. Ernest bought some mice for them, as a big treat and hard to get they were too, thinking the catsies could have a sort of hunting party: but they all blanched with fear and fled under beds and the mice stumbled around, stunned and uncomfortable with no one to chase them, and finally we let them loose. I hope they are making out well somewhere around the property.

My book is not the one we talked of; perhaps I will do that too someday. This started out to be a short story and is becoming a novel and you will like it, it is full of love and sex. I won't write to you about it because that is bad luck and besides I have struck several snags and am not as full of conceit and that feeling that pooh, I can do this with my hands tied, as once I was. But it goes along and sometimes it is vast fun and sometimes it is the grimiest sort of work; and I do not think the course of the world is going to be changed but it looks like a fine story.

Bug got an offer to write one chapter in a symposium published by some nameless robbers-of-writers called 'The Ten Commandments and a man named Hitler'. What a dung-making title anyhow. Bug was to write 15,000 words of a chapter entitled 'Thou Shalt Not Kill', for $500. Wonderful text for Bug also. They enclosed a six page contract. Bug wrote them saying: 'As far as I am concerned you can take your symposium and your contract and make a package of them and stick them you know where.'

No news from here. All goes along fine. Very quiet peaceful household. I wish I were in North Africa but cannot be a wife and a writer there and so will stay here, anyhow until book is finished. Do not know whether they permit correspondents of my sex to get around any more anyhow. A few tedious bitches in my trade have caused so much trouble where they went that they might easily clamp down on all females which would be a foul injustice.

It will be a fine thing if paper rationing makes books smaller; they were getting to be as bad as illuminated manuscripts and you practically couldn't travel on planes with them. I don't know why books aren't gotten out paper-backed like the French ones anyhow and sold for 75 cents so that everyone could read. The volume of sale would compensate surely for the smaller revenue; why don't you start that as a patriotic suggestion?

Please write again; tell me more of your life and works. I am very fond of you. I still feel badly about having died like a poisoned frog on you that evening when we ought to have been jolly as grigs and instead I was a mass of suppressed influenza. But perhaps we can try again and actually stay to hear Maxime.

Always
Martha

To: H. G. Wells

[Spring] 1943
San Francisco de Paula
Cuba

Wells darling;

How are you getting on? Has [Somerset] Maugham sent you any more food packages?

I have just finished three books by Henry James. Never read him before because the type is always terrible. They are *The American, Portrait of a Lady*, and *The Europeans*. I find them fascinating: James seems to me a classical Michael Arlen. Classical not because his people are any realler or his situations more moving or true, but only because he writes with such unique care. I think the style is often ridiculous, don't you: and there is an old-lady quality to it that amazes me. Old lady, not fairy. I read *The Europeans* as if it were a thriller, so anxious to see what became of the people. Nothing becomes of them: you never know them, or else there is nothing to know. The Baroness (what a damned funny idea, James's 'morganatic marriage' or were there different arrangements in those days and not Magda Lupescu and Carol?*) is rather less interesting than the Vicomtesse de Noailles† (the young or youngish one, not the dead big-eyed countess). James was enchanted with her and I kept trying to see why, and what there was about her. Like all his characters, she emerges from nothing and to nothing she returns. James reminds me very much of a philosophical discussion Ernest once had with Scott Fitzgerald. Did you ever read Scott? He wrote one fine book called *The Great Gatsby*. At least it was fine when I read it. Scott lived a great deal in Cannes and Antibes and was very much impressed by whatever he considered Society. He once said to Ernest, in an admiring wistful way, 'The rich are not like us, Ernest.' And Ernest said, 'No, they have more money.' So that is the way James makes me feel too. The man was in love with aristocracy (his word, and his meaning); but I can never see how the aristocrats are so astounding, except that they talk very

---

*Magda Lupescu (1896–1977), mistress and later wife of Caroll II of Romania, and accused of exerting a corrupting influence on Romanian politics.
†Marie Laure de Noailles (1902–1970), patroness of the arts who financed films by Buñuel, Cocteau, and Man Ray.

fancy and spend more money. Am I all wrong? Anyhow, James makes delightful war reading.

I am writing a book that is nothing but a story. This is a new idea for me. I have gotten humble, or at any rate I have come to the wise conclusion that I do not know what I think, and that perhaps I never thought very well. I know exactly what I feel; but that is something else again. So this is a story about people, and a love story which is slowly working its way to a sort of frittering off ending. Not one of the love stories where everyone falls on a sword and dies. That's the great kind of which you see very few examples around you, during the daily marketing etc. I like it and on the whole, except for bad stuck exhausted doubting periods, I have had fun with it. I would like, from now on, to write better if not bigger. It is quite an occupation and I am as absorbed as if I lived in the bottom of a beautiful well with no company except a typewriter.

This summer, maybe, providing *Collier's* and everyone else official agrees, I am coming to England. In August if I can arrange it. I want to write some things. Not that it appears there is much relation between what people write and what gets done. That curious hiatus between the written word and the urged deed must depress you sometimes, doesn't it? Depresses the pants off me. I miss you very much and send you a big juicy kiss.

Love,

Stooge

In the winter of 1942, Martha had started work on a novel about a beautiful mulatto girl living on a French Caribbean island. Hemingway was often away, cruising in Pilar off the shores of Cuba, hunting for German submarines. His letters to Martha, and her replies, were loving, but his were also apologetic, for on his rare visits back to the Finca Hemingway would drink heavily and become quarrelsome. "Rilke wrote: 'Love consists in this, that two solitudes protect and touch and greet each other,'" he wrote to her one day. "I haven't protected you good, and touched you little and have been greeting you scoffingly. But truly I respect and admire you very much and on this date and hour have stopped scoffing; which is the worst of all."

Martha was not unhappy on her own. She loved the garden, exotic but tamed, and their cat population was growing rapidly, with nicknames as fanciful – Furhouse, Friendless's Brother – as those she gave to Hemingway. There were also several dogs, three tree ducks, forty-two pigeons, and six love birds. "I do not like dogs," Martha wrote later, "but am addicted to the grace, speed and general uppityness of cats."

To: Nelson Algren

[Spring] 1943
San Francisco de Paula
Cuba

Dear Nelson A;
    . . . My book goes very slowly now; though sometimes still with much pleasure. And even when there is no pleasure and my mind is full of flypaper I always feel good when I have worked and bad when I have not, so it proves to me that writing is a fine thing. I wonder if you will like the book; perhaps so and perhaps not. I wonder, in the long run, how healthy it is for a writer to live all over the world but never at home: and if one is not going to be in one's own country, should one then establish a substitute country and take root. I have never wanted to take root anywhere and have loved the places I lived (with the sole exception of Spain) for the <u>looks</u> of the place and not for the life in it. I mean, I love it here because I love the land and the weather; and I loved France for the same reasons and also for the looks of the cities which used to excite me so (Paris notably) that I felt as if I were seeing visions, on the good days when I was able really to see. And I never loved England because it is a kind of land that does not hold me; it is too used and lived over; and London's looks depressed me. But it is so extraneous to build one's devotion on appearances. Aside from that, the best I seem to get out of places is a curiosity and amusement about the people which is like attending a play: one sits and watches, but does not really share and certainly one does not belong. Only in Spain it was different: and as it seems to me I was happiest there, I suppose that really one needs the feeling of belonging and living entirely with the country and being of it. Still this is not a thing you make to order, since it is a feeling. It is amazing what a substitute weather and scenery can be for people. Anyhow, the life I have led and am leading is perfect training for being shipwrecked alone on a desert isle, so if ever I get shipwrecked I will be okay,
    You are quite right that I cannot think (you put it better but that is what you meant) and probably you can't either. E has always cheered me on that score saying that no novelist can, or ever has, and as I think about it I believe it to be true. It is not their racket; their racket is to understand which is quite different. There is order and judgement implied in thinking. When you read Tolstoi's thoughts (not his novels) he sounds like a street oaf, a wordy dope. I am trying to decide whether Stendhal could think or not, and I decide not. Mark Twain certainly couldn't. He <u>felt</u> wonderfully; and rightly; but his judgement must have been a joke or he wouldn't always have been in such a terrible personal financial soup. And his political opinions are fine because they are so angry (which is always a tenable position about politics) but they are not thinking. I suppose that the best

writers have some magic kind of understanding which is then wisdom, and good eyes, and honest ears, and very lively hearts. Painters are even more untroubled by brain. I know nothing about musicians. Henry James, as a writer example, could not think for dirt but he wrote very amazingly and he had a great eye for what interested him. I think most of his people are vast jokes, and I wonder if any of them ever lived at any time, but he can get an atmosphere — a sort of stew of color and feeling and appearance — describing a party, which is unique. I have never been able to read Proust, but intend to before I die; what I have read leads me to believe that he is no thinker either.

Do you read a lot? I did not formerly but the taste is growing on me like a disease, so that now I have a hunger for it that never gets satisfied; but I am still too lazy to read well and my memory needs training before I read really usefully. However, now, I get all my excitement that way. It does seem odd and it makes me feel very old. It is the accident of being here, instead of someplace else, in this present time that makes reading so complete an ersatz for life.

This letter is too long. I wish you would read a book I wrote called *The Trouble I've Seen*. It may be very bad. They said it was good at the time, but reviews are balls if you ask me and never to be trusted. I'd like you to read it because it is the only one I ever did about America. I'd like to see whether you think there is anything sound and durable about it. The other novel about Czecho, probably would not interest you. It has good flashes in it; but I do not care for it. I know so well what is wrong with it that it embarrasses me. What is basically wrong with *The Trouble I've Seen* is that everyone in it is good. I have always found it almost impossible to write about people I did not like; or else I grow to like them while writing and then feel so kindly towards them that I pass over their faults. That story 'Portrait of a Lady' was an exercise for myself; trying to write about a creature I despised. It is stupid and lop-sided to be so generous towards one's people: I hope to outgrow this excessive charity. It's easier now; when I was younger I had such firm principles that I knew right from wrong whereas now (except for Fascists), I simply think people are people and have no ideas about how they ought to behave.

Give my love to Mrs A. I hope you are no longer snowbound. But how would you know it was spring up there; do snowdrops push up from the paving of the Triangle?

Always,

Martha

I saw Savold fight Billy Conn (unless I've got names mixed) in Madison Square Garden. At the end he looked like raw meat. It was very ugly. Billy Conn fights as pretty as a statue whereas Savold was of the ape school.

To: Hortense (Flexner) and Wyncie King

May 20 1943
San Francisco de Paula
Cuba

Darlings;
The hell with the dogwood but oh my, how I would like to be someplace where someone else had to run the home. I am apt to develop into the permanent guest, any day now; my housey has me on the run. Here, we have no dogwood, but all the trees (named flamboyante) are now scarlet, with great waving hunk-like flowers. A purple lily, about two feet across, grows somewhere on the property, and another lily that is shell pink and a cluster of flowers about a foot wide grows from some dopey looking leaves behind the pump. On the whole, I think I would take dogwood. What I would really take is some competent servants, or a nice hotel room. You know how it is. After a while it seems too goddam silly to eat, if you have to think it all out.

The social life here is limited but odd. The only people I have met of consequence are the pelota players. Pelota is the best ball game I ever saw and the pelota players are all Loyalists and mostly Basques, a fine folk anyhow. So about two nights ago I found myself with five of them, and Scrooby, sitting in a cafe after the game, talking with the one who had played that evening, fast as wind, and by the time he reached us, sheet-pale and caved in. He was a lovely boy with such a mouth as you never saw, who had fought for a year in the north, in the San Andres Battalion, on that mountain which the German aviation set alight with thermite bombs, after they had practised at Guernica. He retreated with his battalion back to Bilbao, and thence to Santander; and afterwards there was nothing to retreat into except the sea. 'I then retreated to Brussels,' he said. He spoke of the other men, the Basque soldiers in his battalion. '*Muy valiente,*' he said, 'When they heard the guns they stuck out their chins and rushed forward; the aviation turned them into heroes, any little noise would start them fighting. Wonderful men,' he said, 'very brave, unlike me. Me,' he said, 'I sweat very much when I play pelota, but man, it is nothing to how I can sweat when there are machine guns.' I liked that citizen.

I get on with my book; it is more than half done. Scroob says it is good. I hope he knows. He has often told me stuff stinks, so I do not believe he is just being a pal. I am worried all the time and will get drunk for a week when it is finished. What one needs is confidence: I can never be sure, for five minutes, that I have said what I wanted to say and as I desired. My own writing always seems to me peculiarly flat compared to anyone else's and my vocabulary bores me stiff. What keeps me going is the story (which I do not believe I will do justice to), and the background, which is the terrible and usual thing of a people on the march, the awful, now common, but unbearable and unbelievable flight of the refugees across Europe. Also what keeps me going is dog determination and pride. But by the end of every week, I feel light in the head and churning in the stomach, and the empty pages ahead frighten me as much as the typed pages behind.

Have you read Comrade Steinbeck's latest?★ I think it is very good. (It is not nearly as good as they say, but now the fashion is superlatives and no harm done.) Whenever Mr. S. confuses himself with God and writes like Tom Wolfe and the Saint James Version, seeing all, with a heart as big as a lake, it is pretty dead. But fortunately he has a story and comes back to it and tells it and his people are alive. At the end of course he goes off his rocker in a way that first takes your breath away and then makes you roll on the floor with laughter. (The critics all, to a man, got dewy-eyed over this. The critics are a bunch of you know what.) Still, I keep wanting to write him to ask him how in hell he happened to do anything so lamentable and odd. He goes along fine, close to a truth, sticking very tight to his material and his people, remembering all the details which prove it and make it moving: and then he has to end up in a rain soaked barn, with a girl who has just produced a dead baby, feeding a starving stranger from her bosom. Oh boy. I guess you have to live in California to fly so high and so haywire. Keep out of California, I sez to myself, avoid all the big German heritage, read a little French now and again to tone yourself down, remember that in the end people are only people, and can be killed by one falling brick or by slipping in a bath-tub.

I love you desperately. I don't know [W. H.] Auden, I know [Stephen] Spender. We saw him in Spain. He was always very upset about the dead and blood and what-not. Most people try not to think about these things, because there they are, and what can you do about it. But he thought and thought and wrote poetry. We heard him read it one night in Paris; we thought it was bad poetry but especially we thought he was being awfully gloomy about that war. I criticized him, and Ernest said, 'Well, he's a poet isn't he. Can't be too tough on him. I guess poets gotta be sensitive fellows.' That of course looks like nothing now on paper, but it was satisfactory at the time.

Love to you pearls. This is a godawful letter. I have a headache and it is hot as stink and now I have to write out the week's menus.

Blessings,
Gellhorn

★John Steinbeck had recently published *The Moon Is Down* and *Bombs Away*.

To: H. G. Wells

June 9 1943
San Francisco de Paula
Cuba

Dearest Wells;

Your letter came today. It came (since these are the times we live in) as a parachuted package of food into the jungle, as a nice passing empty rubber boat to what they call 'survivors.' I deciphered the letter, having almost lost that art, and added on to it and continued in my mind whatever it began. I am so dying for talk. There is a big hollow longing for talk in me: you would find me a far better listener and learner and giver than I was that winter when you were like a snowed-in teddy bear with me in Connecticut.

. . . I am reading Stefan Zweig's *Autobiography*, with such a passion of understanding and pity that I almost can't read it. It seems to me unbearable in every line, knowing that the man killed himself for no personal failure or despair, for no lonely human reason, but simply that without his arranging it, the world exhausted him and that he was actually driven too far. I do not know exactly why it seems so tragic that a Viennese Jew should kill himself in Brazil but it does: that is too far from home. And finally homelessness is unendurable for others, since that is what torments them. I see it all the time, and keep thinking: my God, it is a small thing, to want only to live on some particular piece of ground. They do not even ask or expect to live well; they do not imagine they can cheat disease, be free of money, look beautiful, work superbly: they only want to suffer and struggle in whatever way they must, on a recognizable soil. It is very little for people to ask: a bare minimum.

My own book ought to be finished in a month. I don't know about it. Maybe it's all right. I must have a wide cowardice in me somewhere because I find confidence very hard to come by. It is difficult always to write with a doubt inside you: and the conviction that no matter what you do, you meant to do something much more. As for the love part, I do not believe these people are in love: my people that is. Or rather they love other things, but finally not each other. They ought to have two words for love instead of one, and then everyone could think straight. There's friendship and passion: if you mix them in proper quantities you get a very strong brew which is apt to be satisfying for some time. But love? Anyhow, as my people mooched around and grew, it became clear that they could not be friends because they were not equals: and I have a horrid hooting inability to believe (perhaps because of the times we live in) in the enduring force of passion alone. I think people simply get interested in something else. This is all wrong obviously: we have been raised to believe that people roll on swords and etc for passion alone, but I think this must be before they have slept together for any length of time, not afterwards. Oh hell, what do I know? I guess, that's all. But the man is something like me, and I know damn well his job would come before his life (if you can call passion a life): so I think I guessed right in this case. I am very sorry for the girl in the book, but on the whole I am sorry for women. They are not free: there is no way they can make themselves free. Glands no doubt, and whenever I have time I will have to study biology and find out, if I can. Anyhow, if the book seems any good I will send it to you.

Wells, save me time will you? Time to talk until all the saliva dries up, as well as the ideas. I also knew (or learned later) the meaning of the word Stooge. The meaning is wrong but the sound is different from the meaning, and a funny amiable pleasant sound. If you prefer darling, I will however remain your adoring,

Martha

To: Eddie Marsh★

[Summer 1943]
San Francisco de Paula
Cuba

Dear Eddie;

I was reading around our shelves today and I found an anthology of poetry gotten out by Ezra [Pound] in Paris in about 1930. It contained a poem Ernest had originally published in a magazine called *Exile* in 1922. This is the poem.

> Neothomist Poem
> The Lord is my shepherd.
>   I shall not want
>   Him for long.

I think it is very wonderful and it has made me laugh all day. And all evening I have been reading Mark Twain and laughing. I am alone here for the moment but I am doing all right. I have a very good life; it does not prove anything but there is no shit in it.

Have a good time in the army darling. And my God after it is all over there may be no beautiful cities left and nothing very fine or healthy, but my God let us somehow all get together and make the best of it.

Always,
Marty

★Sir Edward Marsh (1872–1953), civil servant, scholar, and patron of the arts.

To: Ernest Hemingway

June 26 1943
[Cuba]

Dearest Bug;

I have been writing every day fiercely all day, never wrote so long or so hard, and I believe it is good. It makes me feel good anyhow, both during and after, and for the moment that is the only standard I have. It feels inside of me like juice coming up in big fountains; and in four days the book will be done. It seems good now; these last chapters seem very good.

. . . I saw a showing of Noel Coward's *In Which We Serve*, the only bad thing was Noel Coward who has found a way to act in which you do not have to move a single muscle of the face nor vary the tone of your voice. It is really ludicrous, Noel's idea of how a gent and sea-captain behaves. Though as I remember that was always his style. His part is so unsympathetic that you have to steel yourself not to dislike the whole film; but the little people are not only marvelously photographed but marvelously written and it adds up to something solid and moving. Of course the shit about the ship was so overdone it gave you real shivers; and by God, according to themselves, the English not only never say a mumbling word they scarcely say a word. I don't know, you'd have to see it. It's got everything that is right and wrong in it; but as a race they suffer from constipated minds, neither ideas nor words will pass without a grinding effort.

Will you be able to come back and celebrate with me? You must be nearly nuts now, in your floating sardine box, with all those souls and all those bodies so close to you,* I admire your patience more than I can ever say. You are a disciplined man.

I love you Picklepot. Are the childies having fun?

Marty

To: Ernest Hemingway

June 28 1943
[Cuba]

Bug my dearest;

How I long for you now. My cats are very good to me but fortunately or unfortunately they can neither read nor speak. I say to them: is it a good book; and they chase-chase over the table and roll with the electric wire and Friendless, with her dynamo purr, sits briefly on my lap.

---

*Hemingway was away, German submarine hunting on the *Pilar*.

I am enjoying Alicia who does the typing. She is surely the most unicellular female I ever had dealings with. Today she said, 'Martha I <u>hate</u> men.' I believe it too: the way labor hates capital. She finds my books 'absorbing'; she loves Marc's 'reactions.' How odd it all is; how odd is life. Who ever would have thought that I, who started out with the dream of writing (and that dream at least never changed) and lived in a *maison de passe* alongside the Madeleine and romantically, self-consciously, bought a bunch of violets to wear, instead of buying breakfast, when I went looking for jobs (I was twenty), would end up here in this perfect safe beauty, finishing my fifth book. Alas. I do not want to grow old; not even if I write so much better, know more, and have an enviable instead of a rather shoddy uncertain life that only my posturing could dignify. I do not want to grow old at all. I want it so little that I would trade that wretched first book, right now, for this perhaps excellent fifth one: to have, included in the exchange, the fear and the surprise and the hope of twenty.

There are no real rewards for time passing. And I was not beautiful when I was young and no one said so and I never found myself so; and God knows it was a mean row to hoe. I have so much now that it startles me: blessings overflowing, and I had nothing then. But I don't really like what I know; I don't really care for wisdom and experience. I would rather believe, and beat out my brains, and believe some more. I do not like this safe well-armed woman I have become. The loud bleating disheveled starry reckless failed girl was a better person.

I wish we could stop it all now, the prestige, the possessions, the position, the knowledge, the victory: and that we could by a miracle return together under the arch at Milan, with you so brash in your motor cycle sidecar and I, badly dressed, fierce, loving, standing in the street waiting for your picture to be taken. My God, how I wish it. I would give every single thing there now is to be young and poor with you, as poor as there was to be, and the days hard but always with that shine on them that came of not being sure, of hoping, of believing in fact in just the things we now so richly have. Well, shit. I am a fool.

Where was I? I've had dinner now. I write the best letters and the worst books at night. Or maybe you don't think so? Perhaps, and very naturally, you would prefer the morning letters, the cheerful known thing. I am not cheerful and I never was, I have none of that truly inside me. But much practise and much fear have taught me how to hide, so I seem just about as comfortably unconscious as the next one. Only it's not true and I despise unconsciousness: I want life intense whether it's good or bad, but I never want it other than intense. I want to know it's happening, every minute of it.

Marriage is a rare thing, since it happens everywhere in nature and always has, since it is more an instinct than otherwise, it must be good. But it is a brutalization too. You've been married so much and so long that I do not really believe it can touch you where you live. That's your strength. It would be terrible if it did, since what you are is very much more important than the women you happen to be married to, and certainly more important than this institutionalized instinct. But it is an odd performance. One is safe: two people live together and know they will find each other at certain hours within some kind of walls. And slowly, for each other, they become the common denominator: they agree without words to lay off the fantasy and passion, the difficult personal private stuff: they find some common ground, which is green and smooth, and there they stay. And they may be quite odd and burning sort of people: like all the fancy ones of legend; Icarus and Prometheus and Leda and who else: but they are two people who have agreed to polish all the edges and keep their voices low and live. At what moment, together, can they be as wild and as free as they really are; as they are inside themselves where they never heard of an organized society and the serene considerate practical institution of marriage.

I would like to be young and poor in Milan, and with you and not married to you. I think maybe I have always wanted to feel some way like a woman, and if I ever did it was the first winter in Madrid. There is a sort of blindness and fervor and recklessness about that sort of feeling, which one must always want. I hate being so wise and so careful, so reliable, so denatured, so able to get on. Possibly why I have always been happiest at wars (and also because I have never been hit) is that war is the greatest folly of all and it permits the participants to throw away all the working paraphernalia of life, and be fools too. If that is being fools? Depends on the values I guess.

I will almost bet twenty dollars that this letter makes you angry, my Bug. Doesn't it? What does she mean, you will say, complaining and crying for some other time, and place, and life? What the hell is the matter with that bitch: haven't I enough problems without her? But I am no problem, Bug, never think that. I am no problem. I have a brain locked inside the skull bones, as have all, and this is my affair. I only write to you as I now tonight feel or think because why not: we cannot be so married that we cannot speak.

Marty

To: Ernest Hemingway

July 9 1943
San Francisco de Paula
Cuba

My dearest beloved Bug;

. . . I am in such a state I can hardly write you. This afternoon Mother comes. If one leaf falls the absolute concert pitch perfection of the place will be marred; I have never seen it so dazzlingly beautiful. I would be very happy if I could be as sure of words as I am of things: I mean sure of handling them so they produce the exact desired effect. It is terribly conceited to speak this way, but perhaps it does not matter because I do not find it anything very valuable and am not proud of it: it is just a fact. The house is a lovely pink; it never was prettier; around the pool looks like I don't know what, something so light and fresh and sweet. And Mother's room is really a dream. It is all shone up and faultless, nothing can last this way, but it is good to have all the effort coming to a point (like finishing a book) and have it so really exciting to look at.

And I not only finished the book but also corrected the two carbon copies (a dreary three day job), and all of that is as done as I can do it until you return.

Oh my I love you and oh my I am homesick for you. I want to fix up your beard in beautiful braids and you like my Assyrian.

. . . It is going to rain and make a mess out of all this perfection. I think I better try to rest a little. I could not sleep for excitement last night and have absolute shakes of same now. Have not seen Mother for six months; and have a big huge stock of loneliness anyhow, waiting to expend; or a hollow place waiting to be filled. Do not believe much in loneliness (same way you do not believe in suffering), never thought it was a thing to pay any mind to and certainly not a thing to get fussy about, and really believe it is man's fate, in whatever doses it comes. But simply note now that it will be very fine to have her there to look at, and talk to; and know there's a body moving around seeing all this finery. And it will be shall we say fine (what word is there?) to have you here my honey bear. Oh how I love you. Will spoily you like a goat. Also spoily childies. Will be very good and unjumpy by the time you get home. Live alone makes jumpy; live on tiny boat with eight guys probably makes jumpy-ier; we will unjumpy ourselves junto in the six foot bed and all the long hours talking by the pool. I give you a big damp kiss, like when practising how to make kisses. My bug.

Bongie

At the end of the summer, her novel, Liana, *was finished and with the publishers, soon to make the bestseller list. Martha agreed with* Collier's *that she would return to Europe to report on the war. She pressed Hemingway to go with her, but he told her that he preferred to stay in Cuba, German submarine hunting. By September 1943 she was in New York, waiting for a passage. The moment she reached London, she started looking for the kind of subject she most liked: small, individual stories about people, through which she could write about the larger picture.*

To: Ernest Hemingway

September 16 1943
Hotel Berkshire
New York

Dearest; my typewriter is broken so I am in Max's office while he is in Baltimore and am writing you my dearest love. There is so much to write that I am afraid I will forget everything so I will put the little things first so as to get them in.

. . . Now here is what I most want to write about: the movie.* Bug, the reviewers are crazy. It is a fine picture; as a picture it is perhaps one of the best, the most adult I ever saw. You cannot think of the book; it is another medium. I will never be able to understand any kind of reviewers; God knows what motivates them.

First, politically, it is not the mess they said. Three times the Nationalists are mentioned; not using the word Fascist. But throughout the band speaks of the Republic and Pilar's love for it is completely clear. You do know where the picture takes place and what the two sides are. Physically, most of the Fascists depicted are definitely unattractive. When Ingrid [Bergman] tells of how her mother and father were killed (in your words) it is the most heart-breaking moving thing you could ever see; the most winning of sympathy. After that, the flailing scene makes curiously little effect, and the faces of the people flailed are all bad (morally bad), and it is clear that the flailers acted in passion and regretted it. I would say that, for Hollywood, the politics were clear and anyhow they are good. The only bad place a speech of three lines which Gary [Cooper] makes, in answer to the question of Fernando, why did you come to Spain. This speech is a little jumble of specific words, which explains nothing. They could have put in a speech, much less clear (he names Italy and Germany on one side, Russia on one side, Spain in the middle etc.) which would have given the essential lacking emotional motivation to Jordan's character. That is my only criticism of the politics. And you know me and how I criticize.

Then, Gary is wonderful. I feel sick for him to have had such unfair and

---

*The film of *For Whom the Bell Tolls* had just opened.

lousy reviews. He plays it all down; he does look tired and not a kid; but he must play it down, for contrast, to balance the others, and because really he alone knew the complete gravity of the whole situation. His love scenes with Ingrid are more beautifully done than anything he has ever done before; his hand on her hair is enough to make you cry. And my Christ her hair is a moving thing, so lovely so lovely. He did with his eyes, his smile, his hands, as beautiful and restrained a piece of acting as I have ever seen. It is a tender love story, not the grab-all passionate fake of Hollywood, and I could not have believed he would be capable of such quietness and gentleness. For the rest, his voice has little range but I did not find that bad. I found it restful (in that welter of accents) and good. I again don't understand the criticism of him.

The man who plays Pablo is colossal too Bug; amazingly good; uglier than I had imagined, or dirtier, but so good. And Pilar, though a little stagey at moments, is fine and her voice and diction are terrific. All the characters except the gypsy were really fine. The gypsy is played for comic relief; I said he was like a Jewish comic and Jane said no, he was like the Italian barber in European farces. He was simply awful; and the audience adored him, laughing like goats at his every remark.

It is long; but I did not find it so and the audience was spellbound and silent. You can't smoke; I think that is what strains people; almost three hours without a cigarette. If you could smoke I am sure no one would remark the length. This audience, which is of people who do not read reviews, is really with it every minute; and of course the film is a huge financial success not that we give a hoot. They give no passes, because all seats are sold.

The dialogue is lovely, most of it is you. It sounds too beautiful and accurate, never stagey, never difficult. Ingrid, when she says, 'I always wondered where the noses would go,' when they kiss, is something honestly Bug that you almost can't bear, it's so lovely. She is anyhow, in this (and only in this) one of the really rare beauties of the world; she got thinner, and her body looks so long, so fine, so strong, and the child's mouth, almost no make-up and the smoothness and goodness. You'd be really *exalté* to see her.

I think the plot builds up very good, and rich and in a straight line; and the interval where Augustin (is it?) tries to get the message through is terrific. With Marty really murderous and insane and finely done; and the character of Kharkov, coming in for a second, a thing to give you shivers of delight at one of the finest performances I ever saw. Gary always seems tired; but he <u>would</u> be tired, as Jordan, and as Jordan why would he be given to giggles and gayety. But never let them say that Jordan did not love Maria; for he did.

Now: the color is terrible. You know it is a thing not yet perfected. And it is horribly picture postcard, to me it was never good, always too blatant, and because of it, when they did have to use manufactured sets, these showed up as papier mache. In grey and black, they would have looked fine. But the color brings out the fake, and also in make-up. So that both Pilar and Pablo look made-up; their dirt is stage dirt. None of that would have happened in grey and black and it is a huge pity. But the audience adores it and the color, for Ingrid, is perfect; the blue of her eyes the tawny hair the brownish glowing skin are all perfect. However, it is nothing to be ashamed of; it does no dishonor to the book; and for me it was a wonder and I was crazy about it. And I went prepared to be disgusted and furious.

. . . I so love you and so miss you and so admire you and am so proud of you. I am so glad you are not here in a specially made suit being noble in bars. I am so glad you are the kind of man you are and do your life as you do.

Last night I went to see the musical Fats [Waller] wrote and the music is divine. More tomorrow. Yours really always and forever,

Mooky

To: Ernest Hemingway

September 30 1943
114 East 52
New York

Dearest Pup-pup;

Your wisdom is more apparent to me every day. Not for nothing did the cooniest men always refuse to have anything to do with theatre or movie people. Yesterday I went to see Miss Helburn* at her Guild offices. I sent you her letter to me; meantime she read my book and made the appointment. First she kept me waiting (which is okay) and then rushed out several times and six secretaries rushed in, signed checks, answered phones, dictated, and put on such a huge act of business executive that she began to seem far busier than the President. I was smugger than God. Was so nice to me, so lordly-nice. I always wanted to meet you Miss Gellhorn (it makes me mad now when people call me Miss Gellhorn though it used to make me mad when they called me Mrs H.) I knew someday you would write something talented for the theatre (implication being: not yet written.) What other work have you done, haven't you published some short stories in magazines? What year at Bryn Mawr? Did you know Kate [Hepburn]? On and on, it went. The alleged piercing eye, which sees all and evaluates character between winks, meantime fixed upon me, studying.

---

*Administrative director of The Theatre Guild which had been founded after WWI to bring on new actors and playwrights.

The book had such lovely color, was such a lovely romantic story. Of course, however, it is a book about miscegenation. (Imagine. What crumb would write a book about miscegenation.) I said, you know I always thought it was a love story myself. To the brutal reader, she said, it is a story of miscegenation . . . She put me in the position of explaining and defending my work; of being a supplicant pleading for Guild attention. I became helpless and speechless and lost with anger. Miss Helburn truly thinks she runs and owns the world. I will not see them again at all; if they want to buy the book they can but I am not going to talk to them or anyone else about it. It's done; I'm not going around saying whiningly that it is not really a book about miscegenation (hateful word), while they say, but after all the heroine is colored. My lovely Liana: a miscegenation queen.

. . . Today I went to George's who gave me hell about my week's absence and found me again stiff and awkward. He says my body is dreadful and my thighs grim.

. . . Buggy the letter where you say that these are the worst two weeks of your life and that you feel you are going to die of sadness is too awful. If you like I will give up the English thing and come back to you. You matter more than anything in the world to me, I can't have you dying of sadness. I just can't be party to that. If you see that you truly cannot bear it, I think we better just call everything off with *Collier's,* and I'll come home. I may say that I do not find myself roaring around either; there's a hole of loneliness too, and no amount of people are any use. And I'm getting my belly-full of the mechanics of life; the business of living in the world and having a place in it. I don't want anything except you and to write well. Oh Bug I love you. You tell me what you want me to do and I will do it.

Your wife,
Mook

To Ernest Hemingway

October 21 1943
New York

Beloved Bug,

. . . It has happend like a whirlwind; I heard I had a place for Saturday morning at ten; and simultaneously I heard that *Collier's* had gotten none of my visas; but none; and that without the Portuguese one, which they cable back to Lisbon for, you can't go. Honestly, it is the most godawful sloppy shop, but I have $2000 expense money in my purse and a fine open field ahead and I will have a very interesting and instructive time . . .

. . . My dearest Bug, I just make talk to amuse us if we can. Just a little bit of gossip from the Rialto. What I want to say is goodbye for a while,

Bug. Take care of yourself for me. Take good care. And have the great good luck that you have earned. And maybe come to me if that happens and if not I will come back to you. Please know how much I love you, how well, how admiringly. You are a much better man than me but I hope I am not too bad a wife, even if I have gone away when I thought you would be away too . . . And you are so good and generous and always want me to be happy and I feel ashamed of being happy unless you are. And tonight, just going, just feeling ahead already the strange places, I am happy like firehorse. Awful to be happy like firehorse but I am. But like woman, and your woman, am sad: only there isn't anything final is there, this is just a short trip and we are both coming back from our short trips to our lovely home and our loving catsies. And then we'll write books and see autumns together and walk around the corn fields waiting for pheasants and we will go to all the palaces and be very cosy in them, and we have everything both now and to come. I don't mean to write you any kind of sad or dramatic letter or anything my Bug but I just want you to know how I love you.

Goodnight
Marty

To: Ernest Hemingway

October 29 1943
Estoril Palacio Hotel
Lisbon
Portugal

Beloved: We have been here 2 days – maybe we will leave today or tomorrow or who knows when. The Estoril is a beautiful place, more like San Raphael than Cannes, and it is a little colder than one likes . . .

. . . I have danced 2 nights. I love that & find I am good at it again. I go about with a cuadrilla consisting of the Clipper captain, the co-pilot, a tall acne-masked gloomy young radio engineer, & a very sharp young man from Montana who heads our scientific research bureau in London (better ways to exterminate). Of these the Captain (who has a hideously scarred & deformed forehead – with a piece of that frontal bone evidently gone) is the only adult. But they are solid & cheerful drinkers, good dancers & very attentive to your wife, and I have a fine brainless time.

Last night we went to a Russian place and the vodka was really beautiful. I never had better. There was a fine accordion man who went from table to table playing what you asked for. We were surrounded by Hennies.* They look awful, Bug, with weary sated cruel faces. Really bad – not my

*Germans.

imagination; but wicked bad. They asked for crying sentimental music of course. One of them was fat, blond & very dandy in a pin-striped grey suit. When the accordion came to our table I said play *The Last Time I saw Paris*. The accordion man played the music (flicking his eyes over to the Hennies who were very silent). . . It lilted out like a really marvellous insult to the heavy, weary, dead-faced men, and here it was, back again, defiant & wonderful in a marvellous song. Half the room applauded like nothing before; & they were silent. I almost wept with pleasure. You could see them memorising all our faces. And of course, just seeing them, makes one feel absolutely murderous. They cry out to be abolished. There's no one in the world quite like them.

. . . I love you my Bug. I'm really very happy. I guess one's tastes change very little. I adore moving – am a very superficial girl. The only real roots I've got, or want, are growing in you & mother. But do not think I do not love our home . . . It's just that it's such fun to see the world, at 250 miles per hour.

A big loving Portuguese kiss,
Bongie

To: Ernest Hemingway

November 10 1943
American Airforce
Royal Air Command
Woodhall Spa
Lincolnshire

Dearest Love,

Now I am sitting. Like war, where you sit a great deal. This is very weird here. I came last night to see how they work but the weather was bad, so we sat – five of us – in an ugly room in a very large country house & drank & drank & I made them laugh. (I have that value). The great neglected gardens stretch out in front; all the proper furniture has been removed & there remains the ugly makeshift furniture of officialdom & war; the food is regular at the most; and we laughed & talked & were great friends. Today they are getting ready again. It's a fantastic atmosphere, like a convent & a hospital: so quiet, so determined, non-committal & lost. I am stunned by the atmosphere; one wants to lower one's voice & walk on tiptoe. They are sitting in their sort of reading room, like good quiet children, reading and waiting. Some sleep. The air is full of the roar of planes. A little earlier, pale tan & close to the sun, a squadron of planes from somewhere else flew across the sky. We watched them from the rose garden.

I'll be spending the night up so now I am going to sleep. The sun is warm even in this dismal cold room. It is very hard to understand – one cannot truly, not having been there, know what goes on in the heart of another.

. . . Thus far am very popular; no cobra blood has appeared . . . Everyone asks after you; everyone speaks with passion of *The Bell*; everyone admires you. You are a big hero in England & I only profiteer on the glory & power of your name. I am very proud of it too. But I really think people like me because you chose me, & thus put on me the mark of a superior approval. I don't think they'd notice me otherwise.

I love you Bug. Kiss all catsies. Take care of yourself for me.

Mook

To: Ernest Hemingway

December 1 1943
[London]

Dearest Love;

. . . Ginny* is a boon to me. I see her every day and most evenings, when I get back very weary, and she is helpful and loyal and jolly and I am devoted to her. I don't know what I'd do without her. One does need a good close pal to count on, and tell all one's stories to, and she's it.

. . . I had dinner with [Arthur] Koestler a few evenings ago and I cannot stand him. I almost never took a quicker and firmer dislike to anyone. He has all that ghastly Regler-ish abstraction talk but without Regler's† sweetness, and he evidently thinks that he alone has a corner on the Light and the Way. I absolutely loathed him and made it clear, and it was mutual. Cyril Connolly‡ was there too; he's the ugliest man I ever saw, practically, very involved, very somehow not all wool, very attentive but basically doesn't like one (you know what I mean), and not my dish of tea. They both claim to admire you extravagantly and maybe they do. I had no confidence in them as people. Now I am finished with writers, having met [Evelyn] Waugh and Koestler: it's too disappointing. In future I will just read what they write.

. . . I'm reading Vansittart's§ book; everyone criticises him like mad, saying he's a brutal extremist but I do not find this so, and have not found anything yet that seemed to me inaccurate and much that is about as sound as one can

---

*Virginia Cowles, with whom Martha had been in Spain.
†Gustav Regler, German novelist who had been in Moscow during the first purge trials and became a political commissar with the International Brigades in Spain.
‡In 1939, together with Stephen Spender, Cyril Connolly had founded *Horizon*. His best-known book, *Enemies of Promise*, had been published that same year.
§Robert Vansittart, English diplomat, had become an uncompromising opponent of Nazi Germany after meeting Hitler in 1938 and was an outspoken critic of appeasement.

hope to see, and all he proposes is the occupation and supervised re-education of Germany, based on the assumption that the Germans will never voluntarily reform themselves. It seems the absolute minimum to me, and I do not understand the hostility against Vansittart. It is curious and odd. I want to see him and maybe write about him. He's got a lot of stuff that is new and interesting and the importance he places on Laval* is something I hadn't realised before. The book is called *Lessons of my Life*, it is written with an irritating facetiousness but is still worth reading if you can get it.

Now I have to go back to bed. I feel too awful. You are always quite right in your judgements (unlike me) and what you say about staying where you are as you stayed in Spain when Joris went to China, is probably right. But if there were any reason to change that idea, you would come wouldn't you? It is also good to see this; you would see better than I do and understand better, as you always do. But there is a vast amount I want to see; it would break my heart to miss the final stages, and I would like to be the first one drinking Tavel on the rue Royale. I think it is all going to go quicker suddenly, just a feeling as like everyone else I know nothing at all. But the bomber boys are certainly giving it to them and so are the Russkis, and they cannot take it forever.

Please excuse awful dull long stoopie letter. Attribute to aches and pains. I send you a big kiss, carefully kissing you someplace where you won't catch flu, and a big hugalug and solidarity and wish you much luck and good fishing and a fine weather and everything you need.

Your loving wife,

Bongie

To: Ernest Hemingway

December 9 1943
Dorchester Hotel
London

Dearest Love; your second letter came today. I love you and I miss you and I wish you was here where you would be the darling of all, and as you are so much smarter than me I would not have to work so hard because you could do my thinking for me. I so wish you would come. I think it's so vital for you to see everything; it's as if it wouldn't be entirely seen if you didn't. I restrain myself from sending you cables saying my dearest Bug please come over at once, for fear you'd think I was sick or something and that would be a dirty trick on you. But that is what I would like to do.

---

*Pierre Laval (1883–1945), twice prime minister of France and later head of the Vichy government. Laval was executed after the war.

I hope to be able to do seven articles in all, which will be pretty damn terrific, considering how painful and slow I get my material. I think they are all well chosen and are a good range of subjects, and if I can manage it – without dying of exhaustion – Collier's ought to be pleased and it will make a nice little family nest egg too.

I'm a little fed up in London and I am definitely weary of important people with big intellects. The hell of not being at a front is that you never really see anyone continuously or long enough or well enough to know much about them; even if you do run into fine guys at air stations it's just like being one of those reporters who stop people in the street and ask them what they think about communication with the spirit world, or something of the sort. I like to have lots of time, and to live with the same bunch until I feel that I belong and understand them, and then write. But those are ideal conditions, and there isn't time, and besides as journalists do not function that way usually, but function on a basis of the most speed and the least comprehension, it is not too easy to arrange. And of course the only thing around here that fulfills the conditions of a front is an air station, which I have already written about anyhow. So what the hell.

. . . Yesterday at Ginny's I met Duff Cooper and wife and I like them.* She is over fifty and so beautiful you wouldn't believe; looks perhaps forty but ageless with huge blue eyes and lovely profile and then the fine thing about her is that she is really funny and amusing and adores him. He's a little guy in an absurd high collar with a fine honest head and with the physical courage behind him, in the last war, and the moral courage strongly with him in this war. They are off to Algiers and thence when the time comes to *la Belle France* as ambassadors and I think he will be a good one. Ginny is really wonderful. They dropped in and she usually has little or nothing to offer in the way of drinks, which is usual around here anyhow; but at the time she had taken off all make-up, had cold cream on her face and her hair in curlers. Nothing upsets her complete calm and I must say I almost never saw a girl who proceeded more entirely on her own, in her own way. She's not at all interested in guys now, and treats them all fairly badly, but still has dozens of beaux if she wants them. The brother of that awful man, next door to us in the Palace is still her main interest, but all her friends agree that he could scarcely be a worse shit and is abominable. But she's got him like a disease. I think if you get sick, and ill and grey and exhausted due to the life a guy makes you lead, the guy is wrong for you. That seems a very simple yardstick but I believe in it. Look at me; the only time practically that I am healthy is when I'm with you. I realise that, left to myself, if I

---

*A celebrated beauty, Diana Cooper, née Manners, would become one of Martha's closest lifelong friends. Duff Cooper had resigned from the office of the First Lord of the Admiralty in protest against Chamberlain's Munich agreement.

hadn't had you all these years, I'd probably be dead of ulcers or something by now but I am more stupid in managing myself than Ginny anyhow. I don't think her problem is like mine, which is that I simply cannot seem to manage any other paces than sleeping and running away, as you once said.

Well now I have to work my beloved Buggly. I can't bear to think of this article, about all the poor burned guys, and it has no shape in my head and I'm worried about it, and have those panics of thinking I'll never write another line. I wish you were here with my whole heart. Is there any tiny possibility?

Goodnight dearest.

Mooky

To: Ernest Hemingway

December 13 1943
Dorchester Hotel
London

Dearest Mucklebugletski; Today I got four letters from you so it is a national holiday.

. . . I'd like to explain to you about journalism but don't know whether I can and am maybe too sleepy. I see perfectly that it is bad for you; as it is not really a good enough trade for you and it has also a faintly or permanently non-grown-up thing about it. But it is good for me. It gives me many things for my eyes and mind to feed on, and they need to feed on actual sights rather than reading, simply because they are not first-rate; but that is their best food. It gives me a chance to meet people I would never otherwise meet, and I want to know them. It has been wonderful knowing the bomber boys, the plastic surgeon and those men out there, the slum kids of London. Really wonderful. I would not miss it; I like them and I am fascinated by them. Besides, deviously, everything I have ever written has come through journalism first, every book I mean; since I am not Jane Austen nor the Bronte sisters and I have to see before I can imagine, and this is the only way I have of seeing.

Then there are two other things, less personal and perhaps not tenable, and I am not always sure I believe them. One is that if there is anything to public opinion, there is surely a place for this sort of writing. I do not mean that anything I write produces direct action, or action of any kind; but I like to think that it makes a sort of climate, that it makes a little more receptivity in people who read it. The other is negative; if such as me did not write, far worse people would do so. I can only guarantee the truth of what I write, not ever saying that I write the whole truth, because I never know the whole truth and if I did no one would publish it. But I know I am conscientious and serious, and fake nothing, and I think really that I do a sort of negatively useful thing, in employing the space and paper that would otherwise go to someone far worse.

I know it does not harm me to do this work. On the contrary. It tires me physically but as I do not take myself solemnly I have no chance of believing myself to be a prophet or a power. I feel and act like a hardworking stenographer and I feel kind of happy about it in a grubby hardworking way. I do not think you need ever worry about me turning into a walking dead: on occasion, when with shits, I try very hard to throw weight around since that is all they are impressed by, but am never very successful at it. And I'm not a walking dead because it is a great big world and I love to walk about it and look at it; and if you consider it, dearest Bug, I am very lucky as a woman to be able to do this because most women can walk nowhere and see nothing, and they become mittens characters and their husbands get bored and then where are they.

I do not suggest this is either good or necessary or desirable for you. But I do think you would wish very much to have seen, the other afternoon, the tiny little silver balloons like elephants floating against a pink red sky, over the city that is now so shabby and still quite lovely. I think you would have liked the black Lancs going off into the black night. I think you would like the cold long train rides, listening to the people talk. I think it is not disgusting to look at the world and at the war; because someone must see, and after all we have trained ourselves to see. It is an honorable profession. You are a very great writer and what you see gets pressed down and compact and one day it becomes a book. I am not a very great writer and function more like colonic irrigation, with things coming in and out at top speed. But I am on occasion very mildly pleased with my articles and even when not pleased with what I write, I am immensely pleased with what I have understood. My mind feels good now, lively and digesting with ease.

. . . I love you dearly. I won't urge you any more to come, though I do think you will regret it and I think it will be a great general loss for future time, for all people who need and love to read. But I will not speak of it again and I perfectly understand how you feel now, and I know it is hell for you there alone but I have to ask you to be patient. You have a life there because you have a useful work; it is what you believe in and feel right about doing. But I believe in what I am doing too and regret fiercely having missed seeing and understanding so much of it in these years and I would be no use to you in the end if I came back before I was through. I would give anything on earth to be part of the invasion and see Paris right at the beginning and watch the peace and see what they are going to do to Germany; but I know all that is out of the question. Only I have to live my way as well as yours, or there wouldn't be any me to love you with. You wouldn't really want me if I built a fine big stone wall around the finca and sat inside it. I'm the same person who wrote articles for a steamship line trade paper to buy a third class passage to France in 1929. I'll never see enough as long as I live. And though my vision of the world is a Cook's tour vision, and yours is *en profoundeur*, you are fair enough to concede mine as I respect yours.

Goodnight My Bug. God I'm sleepy. The day isn't long enough nor is the night. I'm a lovely shape anyhow now, fine and thin and with huge hollies in my cheeks. And very jolly when not exhausted.

I love you,

Mook

In Cuba, Hemingway was getting increasingly impatient with Martha's long absence. His letters to her, which in the early autumn had been affectionate, were now angry and reproachful. "Maybe will see you soon, maybe not," he wrote on January 31, 1944. Martha decided to go home, pausing on the way in Algiers, where Duff Cooper had been appointed British representative to the French Committee of Liberation, with the prospect of going on as ambassador to Paris after the war. Martha stayed with them and Diana Cooper noted in her diary: "A packet of fun, yellow hair en brosse, *cool slim lines and the most amusing patter imaginable." Between 1938 and the early spring of 1944,* Collier's *had published twenty-six of her articles, in which a new voice, clear and more authorative than in the past, had emerged.*

She reached Cuba to find that Hemingway had grown a bushy pepper and salt beard, that the Finca was a mess and full of his hard-drinking cronies and that he was in a sour, quarrelsome mood. What was more, he had changed his mind and now proposed to go to the war in Europe after all, having secured a deal with Collier's *that effectively demoted her. They fought. It was Hemingway who now got a priority flight on a seaplane, while Martha, terrified of missing D-Day, eventually and with the help of Allen Grover, found a berth on a Norwegian freighter, carrying amphibious personnel carriers and dynamite.*

To: Eleanor Roosevelt

April 28 1944
Gladstone
New York

Dearest Mrs. R;

Thank you very much for letting me come down. The White House is certainly a fine rest cure place, and I slept more than I have for weeks so returned here freshened up. Am now right back in the frantic stage, of endless errands and what-not. Actually I am getting almost sick with fear: the way it looks I am going to lose out on the thing I most care about seeing and writing of in the world, and maybe in my whole life. I was a fool to come back from

Europe and I knew it and was miserable about it; but it seemed necessary vis-a-vis Ernest. (It is quite a job being a woman isn't it; you cannot do your work and simply get on with it because that is selfish, you have to be two things at once.) Anyhow, due to Roald Dahl* – who has been angelically helpful – Ernest will get off to England at the end of next week. But I have been shoved back and back, on the American Export plane passenger list, and we do not know whether the RAF will consent to fly me over (it's different for Ernest) and there I am. In a real despair and a real fear. It's so terribly ironical too, because I had it all worked out, just how to cover the Invasion, and during all the winter I was learning and learning so that when the great time came I would be better able to understand it and now God knows what happens. It will take an awful lot more humility and good sense than I now have at my command to make such a great disappointment bearable, in case it all works out for the worst. However. Anyhow Ernest will get there and he can always tell me about it, as if that did any good. Enough of this. You can see that I am not in a jolly state of mind.

Thank you again darling for letting me come down. I'm always happy just to think of you, and what a person you are, and the good it does simply to have you alive and going about being yourself.

Devotedly,

Marty

To: Allen Grover

May 7 1944
[at sea]

Darling, when I said I knew all about loneliness and it was just a thing people had and shouldn't make a fuss of, and that I expected nothing anymore and could get along fine, and all that other big talk, it was not so much whistling in the dark as it was positively screaming in the dark. It is all rot as you no doubt knew at once. And what I am, as all the other times, starting on all the other trips, is sad and by myself and frightened. It seems very awful, if not unendurable, that you will not be there to make the going not so hard, to make it gay, to make it part of all the goings when you were there and I knew I would come back and you would be there too. I could never tell you what you mean to me. I don't even know exactly because it is such a big thing and has gone on so long. But I love you and that will always be true.

Marty

---

*Roald Dahl (1916–1990), specialist in macabre ghost stories for adults, and bestselling children's author.

To: Hortense Flexner

May 17 probably [1944]
[at sea]
c/o American Embassy
London

Teechie dearie;

God what a fine time I am having. I have just written seven pages of a short story that is going to be good; very good I think. Oh heaven help us, I hope it is going to be good. I am all sweaty and weary and feeling fine, the fine flying feeling, or as if one could walk on water. I hope it will be good. I hope I am not slick; I hope I do not make it work too easily. I hope this ease is the final result of having worked a long time, and being professional and knowing how to handle the tools; I hope it's not slickness.

. . . Meantime here we are. It is one day over the time the Lord took to make the universe. I feel quite sure time did not move any slower even in His day. I have slept so much that days do not exist any more, there are just periods when I happen to be awake but it can be night or day. Yesterday it was clear (all the rest of the time fog) and suddenly there were three icebergs. So yesterday is the Iceberg Day. The other days have no names. I had never seen an iceberg and they are more beautiful than you can believe and very wild. They fit into the ocean, they are wild and strange like something of another age before things got organized and spoiled. One of them, through the binoculars, looked like the wings of a white pigeon which had fallen head downwards to die, the wings peaked up and flaring. One looked like an enormous monumental Aladdin's lamp, with great high architectural sides, smooth and high and hard, made of granite if granite were diamonds. One was a great peak, a conventional iceberg, with a high fang of ice cutting up into the sky.

The convoy is cute and odd. It gets all mixed up, like musical chairs, when there is fog and when the fog lifts all the ships scurry about like children in grey school uniforms, trying to get on the chairs again. Sometimes, when it is in order, it looks like a toy from Mr Schwarz's toy store; an enormous number of unlike little grey skips sewed to a big flat piece of cardboard; and later someone will take them up and play a Navy game with them on the floor. It so happens that this miniature tub on which I am the only passenger is carrying a great deal of stuff which would go BOOM if the very slightest thing happened. One cannot even smoke on deck. I think that is damn funny; one cannot smoke on deck and meantime we wallow around in this fog, blowing our whistle waspishly at everyone (the whistle says, for Christ's sake don't run into me, you baboon, I'll explode.) It is the first place I have found for a rest cure in years. There never was so much sleep, so much time to read, dream, write, and just sit.

The captain, who is the only person who talks to me, is a homespun Norwegian, a really kind and considerate man, though his conversation is of a type that practically maddens me. But he is such a good man that one must overlook that and as he loves to talk and loves company I drive myself up to his sitting room for a while every day. But the rest of the time is mine and very wonderful it is too.

I've read a fine book called *The History of Rose Hanks*.* I don't know when it will come out but get it and tell Geismar to get it. The boy who wrote it is an old friend of mine; from the book I gather he was a great deal more. Charlie and Max made him cut the book in half (Scribner's published) and take out the entire story about me, because they thought Ernest would kill them. I think on the whole they did well, though I disapprove that attitude, because the wonder of the book is the way that boy writes about the Civil War as if he had fought in it. I don't think Crane† is as good. I have also read first version of *Lady Chatterley's Lover*, with a foreword by Freida Lawrence. If you want to be made good and sick, read that foreword. Women are really too bloody awful. It is one of the most godawful tasteless mindless things I ever read. The book is quite interesting, though for my money Lawrence cannot write at all. He is a dreadful writer. Dreadful and undisciplined. But I found the book this time a real book, quite a good psychological novel, a study in boredom and marital distaste. I wonder why he went on writing it until he got that highflown pornography at the end version.

I am terribly happy you loved Ernest, as he deserves it. He is everything you said about him and he is more. He is a rare and wonderful type; he is a mysterious type too and a wise one and all sorts of things. He is a good man, which is vitally important. He is however bad for me, sadly enough, or maybe wrong for me is the word; and I am wrong for him. I don't know how it happened or why, as one does not know these things, they are some curious chemistry like the oddities that go on in one's blood cells. You must of course never speak of this. As far as I am concerned it is all over, it will never work between us again. There may be miracles but I doubt it, I have never believed in them. I am wondering now if it ever really worked; I am wondering what all these seven years were about exactly. I feel terribly strange, like a shadow, and full of dread. I dread the time ahead, the amputating time, I do not see how to manage it. I do not want the world to go dark and narrow and mean for either of us, and the world has been very unlovely in my eyes, and I very unlovely in it, ever since I got home from Italy. I wish there would be a beautiful mistake in compasses and this

---

*By Stanley Pennell, Martha's teacher and friend from St. Louis.
†Stephen Crane (1871–1900), best known for *The Red Badge of Courage*, which depicted the American Civil War from the viewpoint of an ordinary soldier.

ship would deposit me in Italy instead of in England, so I would not have
to go through anymore of the hardness and hurtingness. It is, note, my fault:
I am the one who has changed. Or maybe I was changing all along, so
slowly that it was like getting a callous; but now the callous is there where
there ought to be softness and trust and love. And I am ashamed and guilty
too, because I am breaking his heart. It is as if, quite unknowingly, he
sharpened a sword and then it up and stabbed him. We quarreled too much,
I suppose. He does not understand about that; he pays no attention to
quarrels or to any words said in anger. He expects each day to be new and
the mind new with it. Unluckily mine is an old mind, which keeps all
things about as they were; and the angry words have been ugly wicked little
seeds which have taken root I guess and there is a fine harvest of mistrust to
be reaped. It is all sickening and I am sad to death, and afraid, and as I said
guilty and ashamed. But I cannot help it. I only want to be alone. I want to
be myself and alone and free to breathe, live, look upon the world and find
it however it is: I want to escape from him and myself and from this
personal life which feels like a strait jacket.

Well enough and enough for always. I want my own name back, most
violently, as if getting it back would give me some of myself. Please use it
always from now on, writing to me. And do not worry and do not feel
badly. We are, basically, two tough people and we were born to survive.

Have a fine time, you two. You really do not know how lucky you are:
having had the world's bad luck piled on you with a shovel, having been
hurt by crooks and with God sending germs from time to time in order to
make all easier: but you have the heart's good luck. It is the rarest kind
surely, and without it I am not sure there is much value. There is a great
deal of interest, fun, excitement, pride, triumph, I suppose; but there is a
hollow as big as a house. There are no hollows in you two; you are all alive,
there are no dead cold places. If there are any people to envy, then you are
those people. Only not envy, Teechie dearest; you are two people to love
and to thank God that they exist and that, in a way, because they have such
a home I have a home too.

> Love,
>
> Gellhorn

To: Allen Grover

> May 27 1944
> [at sea]

Darling, we've been out just a little longer than Columbus. So we wallow
through the interminable sea, mostly in fog, and are just a ducky little bunch
of firecrackers.

The convoy however is rather impressive. I feel myself that man is mad and the phrase quo vadis is engraved upon my mind in neon lights, and very little makes any sense to me anymore: but nevertheless the convoy is impressive. It is enormous and slower than erosion, and to look out and see it all, every day, grey, shabby, humble, manned by soiled weary bored determined or simply resigned men, is quite a something. It is more like a work of nature, it has the same inevitable feeling. We will in due course get where we are going and before us, hundreds of others, thousands, have done the same; and there will be thousands after us. I wish man were less mad. I wish this vast slow will were always used and used for happiness, not for death. I wish peace would be at least as purposeful and moving as war.

I cannot thank you enough for this ride. It is what I needed. I have slept as if I needed (as indeed I did) to wash out something. I have been very alone, also healthful. I am happy because when I write I am happy and in an odd way, I am very happy simply because I am alone and there is nothing I can do and even worrying or dreading is pointless. Please never abandon me. Just be as you always have been, if you don't mind, a distant warmth but always a warmth. It is a very odd feeling, at 35, to be beginning your life all over, sort of naked only rather tireder. On the other hand, whatever happens is what happens and God knows one will manage it.

There is nothing to tell you. The days get mixed up, due to sleeping in such a jumbled way, into the days and into the nights. Nothing goes on. Every once in a while there is a sudden thing about the wind that makes one feel alive and strong enough to fly. The food is dreary; I see no one except the captain, a very ownerly man. I do not see him much. The time passes. And in some more time there will be England and all the mess and doubts and hurts and difficulties to be gotten through, before one can simply lose oneself in work and in hurry. What an opiate hurry is. I have been taking it as dope my whole life.

I would be very happy if now and again you could write to me; just to say hello perhaps, just to say anything. I love you very much but it needn't worry you. The only way one person can worry another is through wanting to make a place, wanting to tie on, make roots, nests, whatever. But that I have given up; I am never going to try that again. So I can love you okay, without being any sort of problem, as plants live on air if you get me. Goodnight darling. I want to go back up and see what is happening in our curious oceanic life.

                                                                Marty

Because of the rules of the U.S. army, which permitted only one correspondent from a paper or magazine to report in combat zones, and in any case did not allow women reporters at the front, Martha was effectively barred from the war again. Threatened with deportation back to the U.S. if she disobeyed orders, she went AWOL from D-Day until the war ended. Having smuggled herself onto a hospital ship and taken part in the Normandy landings, and written an excellent piece – more evocative and less self-indulgent than the article by Hemingway which appeared in the same edition of Collier's *– she kept moving.*

In Nijmegen in September, a military policeman of the 82nd Airborne division stopped her and, finding she had no papers, suspected her of being a spy and took her to his commanding general. This was James Gavin, the youngest divisional commander in the U.S. army, a good-humored and boyish-looking man, at over six feet in height, tall for a parachutist. Gavin laughed when he heard her story, and told her that if she was foolish enough to be there he would pretend that he had never seen her.

Over the next few months, Gavin tried to find her again, and finally caught up with her in Paris. They started an affair. Over the next two years, both of them constantly on the move, they exchanged dozens of letters. All but one of Martha's to Gavin are missing, but his to her, either typewritten or in a large curving hand, survive. He wrote to her about the fall of Berlin, about his regiment, about the intricacies and politics of the army, and about Berlin itself, where he had been sent to command the American forces. "I have always thought that love like this was something that imaginative people wrote about in books," he told her, "but something that never really happened."

To: Colonel Lawrence

> June 24 1944
> Dorchester Hotel
> London

My Dear Colonel Lawrence:
I want you to know that I sincerely appreciate the understanding assistance of yourself and your staff, and that I am writing this letter not in criticism of persons but in criticism of a policy. As you know, General Eisenhower stated that men and women correspondents would be treated alike, and would be afforded equal opportunities to fulfill their assignments. This was later qualified to mean that, when American women, military personnel (in this case Army nurses) went to France, women correspondents would also be allowed to cross. As far as I know, nurses were working in France towards the end of the first week of the Invasion, but though eighteen days have now elapsed since the landing, women correspondents are still unable to cover the war.

There are nineteen women correspondents accredited to SHAEF; of these I know that at least six have had active war reporting experience, and at least two (of whom I happen to be one) have been war correspondents for seven years. It is to be assumed that SHAEF accreditation would be given to no one who was not recognized as capable, and with only nineteen cases to consider it would seem fairly easy for each individual case to be studied, if there were any doubt as to the fitness or previous experience of the individual concerned.

The women correspondents have not appointed me their spokesman and I do not wish to imply that I am writing this letter on behalf of anyone except myself. I simply call attention to the general problem, because there is an injustice here which affects nineteen people.

Speaking for myself, I have tried to be allowed to do the work I was sent to England to do and I have been unable to do it. I have reported war in Spain, Finland, China and Italy, and now I find myself plainly unable to continue my work in this theatre, for no reason that I can discover than that I am a woman. Being a professional journalist, I do not find this an adequate reason for being barred. The position in which I now am is that I cannot provide my magazine, and three million American readers, with the sort of information and explanation which I was sent here to obtain.

. . . I have, too frequently, received the impression that women war correspondents were an irritating nuisance who, very tiresomely, kept asking to be allowed to do their job. I wish to point out that none of us would have our jobs unless we knew how to do them, and this curious condescending treatment is as ridiculous as it is undignified.

. . . Finally, returning to my own case, I cannot continue to fail in my mission, through no fault of my own. It is necessary that I report on this war; the people at home need the most constant and extensive information, and my share of that work – humble as it may seem – is my obligation as a citizen. Since I am helpless to fulfill my obligations here I wish to return to Italy where I always found the greatest cooperation for the Press. Though Italy is now a secondary phase of the war, it is better to be allowed to work anywhere than to be refused permission to work at all. I do not feel that there is any need to beg, as a favor, for the right to serve as eyes for millions of people in America who are desperately in need of seeing, but cannot see for themselves.

Yours sincerely,
Martha Gellhorn Hemingway

To: Hortense Flexner

August 4 1944
[London]

Teechie dearest; I saw it all right. The takeoff as you say. What happened with me was that an airforce type popped into my bedroom at six a.m. or something and said it's happened and I said don't be silly, waking up good Christians like this, and he said no really. Then later I went languidly to the greatest press room of the world, where I was summoned (and they practically searched us) and we were locked in there while all the serious types pounded out a thousand words a minute saying nothing. Suddenly the doors were unlocked and we were allowed to pour out into the world like the germs from Pandora's box. I went out to my taxi and told the driver; he was the only person I could find quickly to impress. He said, it's not true they wouldn't have started it without telling me, why I'm on 24 hour duty. I never found out what duty. I then went around London looking for reactions. There were some American colored troops sightseeing in Westminster Abbey; they'd heard it and it was all one to them. There was a very old woman freezing outside the Abbey selling red cross pins, because it was the day of the Drive and she said she didn't think anything about it because it was very wrong to think anything about rumors. I got discouraged and went home to sleep.

Then the next day I went down to one of the embarkation ports and that was wondrous exciting. I saw the first prisoners to arrive on the shores of England, and wrote about it. They were a damn sorry master race. Everything was very lickety split and cheerful and you could get a ride to France easier than you could get a taxi. I went over myself the night of the second day on a hospital ship, and worked so hard I almost forgot to come up on deck and inspect the world. The wounded were very wonderful and I loved working, not writing or looking, just working. I went ashore looking for wounded too and it was all sort of mad and ominous and dangerous and, in a way I can never explain to anyone, funny the way war always is funny. I really knew a lot about it, at the start. Then there was all the excitement in bars and low dives; it was a sort of cummuters war and very nice and human the first week. People rushed over and back and someone brought a bottle of French sand to the jolly hideous French girls who run a basement bar where all us folks hang out, and they tied red white and blue ribbon around its neck and wept and everyone was drunk as skunks.

After that red tape set in and I lost track. I got awfully cross because it appeared there were rules about women correspondents going to France. I had not heard of them and kept very silent. But it was all a bloody bore; too many journalists and far too many officers detailed to help and actually hindering; and a headquarters staff about the size of Cincinnati.

I was bored and grumpy and couldn't find out what was happening and life was a dark thing until the pilotless plane which momentarily sped everyone's blood around and was quite exciting. Oddly enough it did not frighten me, it seemed so much less than any secret weapon I expected. I slept without a quiver in my eighth or top floor room and sometimes when the noise was really too bad to sleep went up and watched them from the roof. Sometimes during the daytime they made you a little cold in the stomach. You couldn't hear them if you were in a cab and it was a shock almost to drive into one.

Then I left for Italy which I had loved before and how right I was. This is the ideal theatre, it is successful and beautiful and the weather is good. Rome is very heaven; I cannot think why I did not know this before. I've never been more bewitched of beauty than these days. Have been working very hard and having a marvelous time. Just returned, complete with ptomaine poisoning from ten heavenly days roaring around the Adriatic front with the Poles. The Carpathian Lancers are my newest loves and what a lovely desperate bunch they are.

I'm now off on another fine exciting assignment, one I gambled on and which I look forward to with absolute joy. The only sorrow is that there is only one month of summer left and it has gone too quickly; I am hungry for it still and feeling cheated. There never was enough time and there never was enough summer. But the spring and early summer this year were a time of such small grey eating sorrow that I can find nothing really very happy in them to remember. Now in July life has resumed its fine old pace, like a run away train, like a comet, and it is funny and careless and all alive and I am happy again. I think I'll stay in this part of the world until the end of the war, but I think the end of this war is not far off. No later than November I should think and maybe sooner. And afterwards there is that wonderful thing I had forgotten and which Rome has reminded me of, Europe in peace. I had forgotten how beautiful and free it is, and how simply to enjoy oneself is a fulltime occupation. I want to see so many countries still and so many people. And I love this rare racketing job, which makes every day into a grab bag.

The only danger is that of seeing too much and finally feeling too little, but we can avoid that. Yesterday I saw the worst thing I have ever seen in my life; it was so horrible that it passed the point where the mind or spirit can comprehend it. They are digging out of the catacombs the bodies of 320 hostages the Germans shot in reprisal for a bomb once thrown in Rome which killed 32 Germans. The smell was something utterly unimaginable and that garbage of human bodies, with nothing of human dignity left was the most ghastly sight I have ever seen. A great pit full of decomposing bodies which had melted into each other, and shrunken, and outside the people of Rome had made a sort of shrine and there were pictures pinned up, of real true people, imagined to be somewhere in that pit where nothing was real and nothing was people.

The Germans it seems are always very correct, only they shoot hostages everywhere they go and Ginny – who is with me – tells me that in all the villages she has been going through in the north there are piles of hastily murdered unburied dead.

What a race are these Germans: considering that we have tried to exterminate the anopheles mosquito I think we could most easily devote time to exterminating the German who brings surer and nastier death.

The war must also stop soon before all the lovely small old humble villages of Europe are smashed into grey rubble. But how can the Germans ever pay back for all this? How? I think there is no answer. And I think maybe the reason one is so very gay in a war is that the mind, convulsed with horror, simply shuts out the war and is fiercely concentrated on every good thing left in the world. A doorway, a flower stall, the sun, someone to laugh with, and the wonderful fact of being alive.

I love you both immeasurably. Take care of yourselves. We will all eat ourselves sick in Paris one day before we die.

Always,

Gellhorn

To: Allen Grover

October 30 1944
London

ON BRIEF REST FOUND YOUR CABLE STOP WHY NOT BRING YOUR BODY OVER AND WILL THERE ATTEND TO LOW MIND STOP FEELING PRETTY POOPED MYSELF ONLY SOLUTION IS CALL FOR LOUDER MUSIC STRONGER WINE STOP WRITE ME CARE APO 887 PLEASE DARLING AND DO COME OVER LOVE

MARTHA GELLHORN.

To: Allen Grover

November 2 1944
[London]

Darling, it is 8 o'clock and I have dined alone and am about to go to bed. This is revolutionary; in a year nothing like this has happened and God knows I have dined with fools. But I always had enough hope to go on dining. I feel myself very forlorn, since now returning to London after four months absence, I am so without hope that I will take no chances and will dine alone. It is like Dotty Parker, who sits and Suffers and never picks up the telephone.

Please come here and soon and even at once. I need you. Is that enough (I would not think so.) Who shall I talk to and who will tell me why I am doing what I am doing. Darling, it seems to me I had better get divorced. There is no one to marry, and if God has any benevolence for me he will spare me further horrid errors of the heart, when one tries to make permanence. I wish only to be unmarried; it seems neater. I am so free that the atom cannot be freer, I am free like nothing quite bearable, like sound waves and light. But I think it disorderly to be so free and officially, legally, attached. There is a kind of theatre about this deal which is displeasing. I resent being asked after my husband and pleasantly lying: he is well, with the First Army . . . when I have no husband and it is all fake, and I want no husband, and why ask me.

On the other hand I want a child. I will carry it on my back in a sealskin papoose and feed it chocolate milk shakes and tell it fine jokes and work for it and in the end give it a hunk of money, like a bouquet of autumn leaves, and set it free. I have to have something, being still (I presume) human. But how does one work that out? My God who made it so hard to live, or does one weave this out for oneself every morning like a spiderweb (useless spiderweb catching no flies.)

Darling are you tired? My Christ I am tired. It's got me at last, I cannot bear anyone else dying. Though no doubt it is worse if legs and private parts get blown off by mine, and still one lives. Certainly worse. I can bear none of it. Nor the very pale big-eyed faces of children too small to talk, wounded in hospitals (in the cellars where they keep them since the town is still shelled.) Nor none of it none of it.

I also do not believe in what I do, realising too well the fine protective layer of the human mind and heart, a thing made of ferro concrete and built to resist knowledge. I write like someone screaming, my articles are horrible, and unread and inefficient. I do not even know what I scream against, except the barbarousness of the human animal. I scream for kindness. Let there be kindness. There is bloody little and never at a high enough level.

What shall I do with myself? It is not enough to suffer for everyone, to have everyone's story like one's own personal guilt, to wake in the night sick for the people you know and do not know but can well imagine. (The ones I know are all dying; it is not worth while making dates.) One cannot stop anything or help anything and only finds oneself a little mad – with always the fine shrewd disgusting self protection that halts madness before it becomes heroic – and lonely and afraid not of the usual things, but of the unseen things, the dark series of days, the long days and the long years and all the time ahead which will be no better than this time.

I think anyhow get divorced and at least go down alone, at least have the consolation of pride, which is to say that one will sink or swim without benefit of clergy, a borrowed name, and nothing and nothing besides.

Or else be able to write but I am too tired to write, too driven, too screaming inside. I feel too fiercely to write, even to talk. It is no good to be alone either; though one makes no noise the screaming is all there.

And what happened to the fine gilded hopes when one expected to be like other people, with a place to come back to, someone to trust, someone to whom one could say anything without shame: what happened to the desired never existing always comforting loving trusting arms that were to be guarantee forever against nightmares. What a shitty business: who invented marriage since it fails. Better never to have thought of it and then one would never feel so cheated.

I am in good health, you will be interested to hear. I am a witty dashing woman who can vamp any young man (specially if he is at the front and there are no women for miles around and no tidy small mouthed boring decent little girl who is exactly his cup of tea but now, due to high explosive, lacking from the scene). Oh Allen come and hold my hand and I will hold yours. Life is as long as war.

I do love you and always did.

Marty

To: Edna Gellhorn

November 14 1944
[London]

Matie dearest; it's been weeks since I wrote you. This will be such a bad letter now that I wonder whether it is right to bother.

If only my own life was a mess and a sort of boring dismal failure, that would be bad enough; but I cannot separate anything and my horror about the war has gotten beyond the place where I can control it. There is no use going into that: writing of it only makes it worse and there is no sense in dumping it onto you. But every dead seems to me to be part of me, and I have a feeling of such absolute and unutterable despair that I can scarcely handle it. The Catholics brand despair as a mortal sin, and they are right. For them, it is to despair of the Lord, to be without faith: but my kind of despair is a loss of faith in life and it is surely as bad.

I do not want to stay here and I do not know where to go. I would like to go home and there is no home. Home is something you made yourself and I have not made one. I feel so rootless now that it is fantastic; one cannot be as free and live. You are my only link I think with life, because I believe in you and you go on; but since no one can help me, except myself, I must find my way out of this alone. Perhaps writing is the answer; I shall try. If only I can find a place to live where the mechanics of life are endurable (one is too cold all the time).

There is something you must not repeat to anyone at all: Bum* has been wounded and captured. It is pretty awful isn't it. I think E must be at wits end and hearts end. He has a girl, not a good one unfortunately, but she will seem so and he will try to make a life with her. I wish him such luck. I have grown so queer that I really wish to see no one and I do not know how to make time pass. And how I love you every minute of every day.

Marty

To: James Gavin

[?1945]

Dearest Love, dearest Jimmy and darling; I have thought of nothing but you all these days and everyone and everything seems very flat in comparison. I think of you any number of ways: and I mistrust myself and I fear all this deeply. Because you see, you will fall more in love with me as I am more and more in love with you; I know this is so and unavoidable. And I will make a wonderful story about you in my mind, making you into many people you are not (as well as the person you are), and I will live with that story and count on it. Meantime, you, being more intelligent, will simply count on me. On what you know or understand of me, or on what you hope of me. I suppose love is like this: done with the most beautiful mirrors in the world. But when I can make any sense, which is not often nowadays, I recognize this all for folly and very dangerous. Because it could go on, through separation and time, and suddenly we would find ourselves striving towards each other and towards permanence: we are both strivers. And we'd get it, if that is what we set out for: and it would not work . . .

I simply could not be a good army wife. I'd be dreadfully bad at it, I know: it is sickening to realise that two people alone are not a world nor even a life; we live in a fixed specific world (I, on the other hand, am only happy if living in every available world and obeying the rules of none), and we live with countless people. I am too definite and too old and too spoiled and too intolerant to be a good wife when good wife principally means good mixer: and though I could take you anywhere with me – for all my worlds would be enchanted by you – you really would find me burdensome in the end. If not a good deal sooner. I'd be bad for you, and I'd be bad because I'd get bored and impatient; I'd only like the wives I liked and see no reason, finally, to act otherwise. I could not do a wholetime job of the army.

This is an effort to be honest for us both, and as a warning. I write it when I love you so much that these days are rather fuzzy dreams and I am

---

*Hemingway's oldest son, John, known as Bumby.

living suspended in time, waiting for you to come. All my desire is to follow you, so I can be where you are, where your voice is and your funny face is, and all the things that delight and surprise me about you. But really, I ought to let you go entirely. I cannot see, now, where I belong; I think possibly I am doomed to live alone because there is no place where I can imagine living. But I am already depressed by this life I see ahead of me; the best that can be said for it is that it will not irritate me: it may easily freeze me to death. My feet are cold every night, without you, and presently I suppose I will be cold throughout.

I am trying to say that nothing short of perfection is good enough for either of us now; I would have to believe I could guarantee it, and I fear that I cannot. We don't really need to make a Big Plan: the Big Plan is already made, we have made it with the years of our lives. We may always be in love, some way; but we won't be able to make a partnership that will last day after day and day after day.

And I love you and kiss you.

Martha

Washington, Cuernavaca, and Sandy,
1945-1954

On April 15, 1945, the Allies entered the concentration camp of Bergen-Belsen, where a typhus epidemic had left thousands of skeletal bodies rotting in the open. Martha had been hearing about the camps for months, and wanted to see for herself the legacy and victims of Nazi rule. Early in May, a few days behind the liberating American troops, she went into Dachau. She wrote very few letters about what she saw, beyond telling Hortense Flexner that she would never lose a sense of guilt about the fact that "I did not know, realise, find out, care, understand what was happening." But, she would say later and repeat many times, "a darkness" entered her spirit. The article she wrote for Collier's was despairing.

Soon afterward, Martha returned to the U.S. But not for long. She was thinking of buying a house in London, for though James Gavin was pressing her to marry him, she did not believe that she could cope with army life. To Diana Cooper, she wrote: "I am more dependent on laughter, or even giggles, certainly giggles, than anything else: and somehow J. and I don't seem to make them happen." She went to Nuremberg and wrote an article for Collier's about the men in the dock, and early in the New Year of 1946 she set off for the Far East. She returned to London to write a play with Virginia Cowles, Love Goes to Press, about women war correspondents in Italy, then settled down to write a novel about the concentration camps. She called it "willed forgetting."

She wanted, as she put it, to be "relieved" of the memory of Dachau, counting on her terrible memory and her habit of losing information the moment she had no need of it. If she wrote out Dachau, she reasoned, she would forget it. She finished the novel, about Jacob Levy, a young soldier in Germany during the liberation of the camps, in a motel room in Florida. She had wanted to call her book Point of No Return, after the technical phrase used by pilots to mean the moment a plane must head back or run out of fuel. Max Perkins, her editor at Scribner's, said the title was too bleak and she accepted, reluctantly, The Wine of Astonishment, having leafed through a Gideon Bible in her motel room and come across the words: "Thou hast shewed thy people hard things; thou hast made us drink the wine of astonishment." In later editions, she reverted to the title she liked.

Jacob Levy did not relieve Martha of Dachau. She remained haunted by what she had seen all her life. It changed, she wrote "how I looked at the human condition, the world we live in." Dachau was her own point of no return.

Like many others, Martha found the end of the war hard. She felt aimless and alone. "War was always a solution to life," she wrote to Diana Cooper, "because one's own life became such a pleasant casual joke and one was always absorbed in what Americans call the big picture." London did not work out and she returned to live in Washington, where she started an affair with William Walton, who had parachuted into Holland with the 82nd Airborne, covering the war for Time *magazine, but she was soon driven away by McCarthyism and the witch hunts against the left. The first of seven visits to Israel followed before she settled – for a while – in Mexico.*

A bitter, furious letter from Hemingway closed all doors between them. It was, he wrote "something to see how your ambitions had shaped and how you had played them; for what dough and for what ends . . . Good night Marty. Sleep well my beloved phony and pretentious bitch." While Hemingway frequently spoke ill of Martha to others, Martha herself remained silent, apart from a rare and for the most part humorous aside. Talking, years later, about Mary Welsh, whom Hemingway married as soon as the divorce went through, she said that Mary was "Countess Tolstoy and the Count should not have had me along the way."

To: Charles Scribner

July 29 1945
4366 McPherson Avenue
St Louis

Dear Charlie; you are not – repeat <u>not</u> – to put this letter in the files, nor are you to tell Max [Perkins]. Do you promise? Very vital. It's a gossip letter between us, concerning Mrs. Pennell. Charlie, she's too grisly. It's not to be believed and I am so sorry for Pennell, who is bound to realise the soul shaking gaffe he has made, if he doesn't know it now. She's hideous to start with, but really hideous: harlequin glasses and dreary hair done in sort of curly bangs and common clothes and a large hefty kind of body. Then she's a sort of rummy (I must say they both drink like nothing on earth and considering he's had a hell of an operation, I should say she was either a fool or a pig to carry on that way.) Then she's one of those bores who will <u>not</u> shut up: the bore who insists upon telling her life story, which though in outline is fine, when told is just a nightmare of tedium and somehow embarrassment. You know that awful feeling when you're sweating shame for someone else. She has a huge sense of grievance about her years as a WAC; was not properly used and so on. No humor about it or herself: oh God, what a dreary girl.

She has taken the one of two possible attitudes towards me: it would have to be love or hate so she's taken love. She's not a mean woman at all; probably has a heart the size of a house and solid gold (which is not enough in this life, a little charm helps.) I don't know what Pennell is nowadays: the interference is too great to find out. He still has the fine taste about books, and the fine interest. He looks absolutely terrible, sort of gray green and rather bowed over (results of operation, which he is curing by straight bourbon.) He seems sort of mannered and uncertain and with too many hates. What in hell is the matter with writers? Why do they have to be so goddamn <u>touchy</u>: I remember all E's touchiness and phobias and enemies and what-not. It seems such a furious waste of time. I find myself being a kind of Pollyanna and telling them to leave things alone and forget it, one hasn't time in this life to be so full of resentments and angers. Or rather, one shouldn't have them personally: one should use up that set of emotions on causes, and try to be a jolly person in normal life. Anyhow, I was rather bored and definitely a stranger: and I felt badly for Stan, who has such a fine eye. This lady has been married twice before, I reckon her to be early forties; and how she got two other men beats me. Maybe she's something colossal in bed but one would have to be blind. (How wicked.)

Now, tear this up immediately like a nice man. It's a shocking letter; no doubt the local rocking chair atmosphere has already corrupted me. I'm fine myself, if weary from the social round and chores. But I love my mamma so am happy to be with her.

And I am your always devoted caviar companion.

Marty

To: H. G. Wells

August 25 1945
4366 McPherson Avenue
St Louis

Wells darling,

You are the greatest man in the world. There was probably no reason to doubt this and you will not be surprised by this statement, but the atom bomb has convinced me once and for all. As you are right in everything, I am now looking forward gloomily to living underground in an air-conditioned artificially-lighted tunnel and eating vari-colored pills (instead of spam and brussel sprouts as it used to be in the fine old days).

I have a house in South Eaton Place and am returning to it on the Clipper on September 21st. If London after the war is as wonderful as it was during the war it seems to me a place where a permanently rootless one might take roots, for a while at least.

Did you know that E and I were getting divorced? Change and decay in all around I see, in case that is the accurate quotation. How are you darling? I wish you could foresee something agreeable for the world, as you seem to have influence with history.

Love,

Stooge

To: Robert Sherrod★

February 14 1946
[Singapore]

Dear Brother and Robert;
The weather here is delicious and exciting. There is a wind from the sea and many ships in harbor. If there are ships one need not go anywhere; it is like not worrying when you have money in the bank. The streets are clean and the trees have personality and the land is not flat. Also the night is a beautiful color.

I have the bridal suite at Raffles a cosy room like a skating rink with stained tobacco colored curtains and it is both cool and quiet. Tomorrow I leave for Penang; I am now considered a VIP which means special rooms and very easy plane space. Since you pay for everything in this life you pay for VIP-dom with civility. Unlike Jap guilders this is a currency of which I have none. I grew bored at dinner last night (ladies bore me quite a lot) and talked too much and afterwards reproached myself and worried and suddenly thought: what possible difference does it make and why should I ever reproach myself again. I suffer from talk as poor Don Birnham† suffered from drink; it is a European failing but I have complicated it with American enthusiasm. All right; I refuse to see bats and mice anymore, I abandon myself to the failing.

I have found a phrase: the pale empty color of the future. Good phrase?

Also have bought khaki and having clothes made; you will be dazzled. Also had a hairwash with authentic hot water and look as bad and bushy as before. Am now going swimming. Will inform you of conditions in Penang. But I must be alone a bit; I am all shredded inside.

How are you brother? Take care of yourself.

Your ancient comrade,

Martha [Gellhorn]

★*Time* and *Life* correspondent, who had helped Martha with introductions for the Far East.
†The hero of Billy Wilder's *The Lost Weekend* (1945), a struggling alcoholic writer, played by Ray Milland.

To: Robert Sherrod

February 21 1946
Penang

Dear Brother;

. . . Like Manchuria and Abyssinia, the pre-patterns of war, that stinkhole of Indonesia is probably the pre-pattern of after war. Its niggardliness is what now strikes me most, the absolute lack of grandeur. Everyone is too tired, of course; there is meanness left, enough energy for meanness, but not enough for splendor. I guess it's why I haven't any sympathy for our little brown brothers; they truly lack stature. (You should have seen my beautiful Spaniards fighting for *Libertad*.)

I've done my *New Yorker* piece, working over every word like carving cherry stone. This does not mean the words are any better; it only means I have the proud sensation of being respectable.

I loved your letter but I am appalled by Clare [Booth Luce] being converted; she will not give up politics, she will simply be urged by the Mother Church to continue in the Right Path, and from being just a minor upset she will become part of a dangerous machine. I oppose it all. If on the other hand she has — at her age — embraced that consolation, that shutting of the eyes and cowardice of the mind, and means really to renounce all else, then I am terribly sorry for her. Life must have been too much; each time you were given a huge red apple, having worked so hard and singlemindedly to be given the apple, you found it tasted sour and had a worm . . . But sad, that is. If one is ambitious enough, and intelligent enough, in the end one must despair.

I am loving this cure of silence, but must leave here Sunday or Monday because really it is a damned imposition on the poor Colonel whose house this is. I guess I'll toddle back to you and those glum Indonesians. Maybe after this I'll go to Italy; I love Italy and perhaps someone would pay me to write a fine piece about the Polish army, whom I love too. There is no sense hanging around the Orient. I never want to write another line about it. It is hopeless and shitty; give the country back to the ants, I say.

I think what I really want is a little white home with a picket fence around it and some toddlers. If so, I should really have thought of it sooner. No pickets and no toddlers, it looks like to me: only Residencies and Palaces and the society of the semi-important middle-aged.

I miss you too brother. There's no one between here and Paris besides you that I want to talk to. However let us not grow to depend upon each other's society, for we are the hardboiled ones who love vacuums.

Always,
Your brother [Martha]

To: Robert Sherrod

March 22 1946
21 South Eaton Place
London SW1

Dear Brother; I've been too paralyzed to write. The trip back was something: travel steerage by air. The poor little children vomited and wept and laughed and ran up and down and sang and talked to themselves and never never stopped. It was really terrifying, though I loved Cairo and got ten cartons of cigarettes at Karachi. Then, returning, I found that my house was not ready (we knew that) and that I employ more people than Henry Ford, to less effect clearly, and that it was all in such a huge muddle that one wanted to sit on the nearest packing case and blow out one's brains. It is Friday now and I got in Monday night and since Tuesday a.m. have done bugger all except householdery. I shall I think be living in it within two weeks which is not bad (it has only taken ten months to achieve this state.) What surprises me is that the little sewer is quite lovely; not the outside, which looks like a camera study of blasted Europe, but the inside which is so elegant and white and so old and so entrancingly shaped. I am going to make a lovely place of it, but this is my last effort; it is my eleventh domicile – eleven times before I have started from nowhere and fought my way towards that shining and always diminishing goal: roots, a place of your own, peace. This time I may have found it, because I really do love London. By some alchemy, I am unhurried and at peace in this shabby rain sodden burg. I find it so restful not to have to be anyone or get anywhere, to telephone your friends when you feel like it, to know a few people who are always the same, to live in the curious atmosphere of London – somehow they all seem to feel that just living here is achievement enough for anyone. And I know I can write here and I am not lonely, though I am much alone. So – because also the winter has passed (I shall never be able to endure their winters) – the outlook is a lot less horrible than it was. Financially, it is a shocker, but you can't have everything. And there are women here I like, and you can't really live without women. This is almost the only place I like women (I like three in Paris), and I must say it is pleasant to find the girls again, all so worldly and so funny, disabused, unexcited, uncomplaining and a pleasure to look at.

Today Ginny and I were commanded to the presence of Mrs. Carol Brandt of New York and Brandt and Brandt. Mrs B buys books, or plays, or the people who write them, for Metro. Mrs B had on a star ruby the size of a tumor and a diamond and gold bracelet like something to handcuff a galley slave to a galley, and a chic and pressed dress, and neat hair, and the endless energy, charm, assurance, hurry, and smell of cash, which to me marks New York. Ginny and I, suddenly looking very small, absolutely quiet, unutterably well-born, shabby, sat on a rich couch in a Claridge suite and did not know what to do with our hands, let alone say with our tongues. Patently Mrs B was disappointed with us, so she became even more gracious. We left, having accomplished nothing (we did not know why we were summoned nor what we were meant to accomplish) and sailed off down the hall – rain spotted stockings and uncombed hair, – and crouched on the bench by the elevator and shook with laughter. And we agreed, driving off in Ginny's tiny tinny car, that we were happy to be who we were and where we were, we liked this easy-going rundown island; we were unsuited for American life, because we simply never would get ahead, being unable to see where the getting got you . . . We have absolutely lost out on this play; the producer has been a swindling shit but I suppose that happens to all beginners. We are going to write another, as soon as I get in my house, about the House of Commons, and this time we ought to make some dough. We both need it, but another great feature of London is how little one worries.

. . . I got fine funny letters from Bill Walton, mainly about the 82nd Parade. Capa and Collingwood★ are wowing Hollywood. But another pal of mine, such a beauty, who is also wowing Hollywood writes that, if you look and even if you do not look, there is no paucity of shits in this cardboard village. So I am still pleased about not being there, in the old country I mean.

Write to me darling, and come home via this place. And we will drink in nice pubs and go walking in the Green Park or by the Serpentine. Nothing is solved, and I feel happy. Maybe it will suddenly work for you that way too. By the way, Ernest and Mary [Welsh] married last week, read it in the papers. And I am getting my passport changed to Gellhorn and I feel not resentful about anything, but only spared and free.

Love. Your Jogjacarta playmate,
Marty

To: Robert Sherrod

May 4 1946
21 South Eaton Place
[London] SW1

Dear Beautiful Robert;

. . . Last night I was trapped into the 50th anniversary dinner of the Daily Mail. Representing the US were Mr. Luce and Miss Gellhorn. None others. I saw him from a distance, looking old and with skin like blotting

---

★Charles Collingwood, of CBS, whom Martha had also met in London.

paper and was full of pity mixed with contempt. Everyone was rich and famous and there was not one good warm generous mouth in the gathering, plus a very strong odor of decay. Everytime a speaker said 'Free Enterprise', 500 fat throats said, 'Hear Hear.' I had a great personal success (though I was so busy saying SHIT that I scarcely had time for it) due to wearing a 12 year old backless Paris evening dress; from the speaker's table talked about by Mr. Churchill (who said, 'Ah so it's Farewell to *his* Arms,') and today Lord Beaverbrook★ telephoned to invite me to that dreadful palace of his next weekend. If my bosom had been bare too, I have no doubt I'd have been made a Peeress.

Next week however I am going to America. Isn't it silly? I want to see Mother and Jimmy Gavin (because I must straighten that up; I can't go on being romantic and wasting his time) and also get some clothes and furnitures. Also a favored nation treaty with Collier's – 4 stories a year, my own time, place, subject matter – because I have to have papers to live here, they are getting tough on unexplainable foreigners, who eat three tiny loaves of bread per week. Rightly. The trip is free and I shall be gone 3 to 4 weeks and then return for the opening night of our play which comes on on June 18 at the local version of the beginnings of the Theatre Guild. A nice outfit, with no fairies in it, which is a rest in London. After that, by Christ, I am going to write, as I have been a nonsense for long enough and it is giving me sort of ulcers (soul as well as stomach).

But the happiness that had to come, has come. With the spring, and with this house, and with a sort of feeling that the past – good, bad, and only mediocre – is past, and I am fit to live and not really frightened about anything. I hope this lasts, as it is heaven itself.

The news is not to be pursued for a while; one's body and heart and spirit need some kind of strengthening. I would wish for you exactly what I have; a bit of dough in the bank and an inexpensive life (I live well for less than $80 a week) (maid and char and part time secretary included), and books and victrola records and long hours of the day and the night. And in one's mind a good warm feeling towards everybody but no desperations.

Brother, be calm. Your spring is bound to come too. I send you an avuncular kiss.

Martha

★Max Beaverbrook (1879–1964), proprietor of *The Daily Express* and once described by Iris Tree as "this most attractive gnome with an odour of genius about him."

To: Eleanor Roosevelt

[May?] 1946
South Carolina

Dearest Mrs. R;

Mother and I are off on a grand wild outing. We have her car which is seven years old, a small Plymouth. We both love it because it is like a steady old horse, and neither of us has any idea what goes on inside a car, what its hopes and fears might be. In this charming antique, we are driving to Mexico. Every once in a while we look at the Atlas and add up the mileage and having now discovered that it is farther than crossing the Atlantic we are very impressed. At the same time, we are not especially go-getting about driving, and have a tendency to settle down as soon as we see a nice place. This is apt to happen every three days, for after three days at the wheel (and it's an enormous day if we do 300 miles) we feel we have already crossed the country in a covered wagon.

At present, we are taking up the squatters life at Myrtle Beach, South Carolina, and adoring it. There's a huge white sand beach, and a huge grey-to-blue sea and we found a hotel which seems to us divine, being clean comfortable quiet and cheap. So here we camp: I have been writing an article, Mother has been reading, in between times we walk along the beach collecting shells for grandchildren, attend the local movies, and gossip together. We have a portable travelling cocktail shaker, and every night sit cheerfully on Mother's bed and have our evening drinks, and launch forth to dinner giggling like a pair of Peter Arno charladies. It is a very good life and I will be astounded if we get to Mexico before June.

. . . In a moment of madness, I seem to have bitten off the most godawful assignment for next winter and I am already dreading it. I told Collier's I wanted to go from Finland to Greece – Poland, Czecho, Jugoslavia, as way stations – and report on how people really live behind what the press is pleased to call 'the fringes of the iron curtain.' As I am thoroughly and heartily sick of the idea that people necessarily eat babies just because they don't operate on a basis of free enterprise. Maybe they do eat babies, but I want to see it for myself before I'll believe it. And it occurred to me that all we ever hear is the solemn badinage of statesmen and I want to know what ordinary humans are saying and feeling, shop clerks and college professors and plumbers and truck drivers and farmers. Not that I believe such as they, the majority of the earth, control the policies that make war and peace. But for my own hope and sanity, I prefer to keep in touch with them, for on the whole I have found them good. It always beats me that there is such a difference between life and politics, and between people and those who represent them. On the other hand, the thought of plowing through snow up to my neck, all winter long, gives me the horrors: and also, unluckily, I never really believe that my reporting does the slightest good or informs or educates anyone. So in a way, I am not sure why I do this: there are easier ways to make the necessary money. However, there it is, and that's the next plan.

And I've got a novel, written once but badly, which has to be done over and finished this summer. This is the only work I really care about, so I'm delighted. I've been panic-stricken about it several times, and decided to abandon it, because whereas men apparently have no nerves in writing about women (from Madame Bovary to Kitty Foyle),* the reverse is rare, and I found myself launched on writing about men as if I were one. Suddenly I said to myself, come, come, you might as well admit you aren't; and then the panics set in. But Max Perkins, of Scribner's, who seems to have a sort of literary divining rod, tells me I better do it, that it's okay, and as the highest compliment 'I wouldn't have thought a woman had written it.' Now why that should please a female writer, I don't know: in a way, it shocks me that I am pleased, for it's so unrealistic. Perhaps it's because I've never lived in a proper woman's world, nor had a proper woman's life, and so – feeling myself personally to be floating uncertainly somewhere between the sexes – I opt for what seems to me the more interesting of the two. Or is that right? Women are just as interesting as men, often more so: but their lives seem to me either too hard, with an unendurable daily exhausting drab hardness, or too soft and whipped cream. The home, in short, does not look as jolly as the great wide world. Anyhow, I am going to try to get the novel right, and if I don't there are always matches available wherever one is, and a manuscript burns very nicely.

I was astounded by New Jersey, Pennsylvania, and Maryland, as we drove through them, with everything bursting into flower and the little towns so clean and sound and gentle; and I thought, if this is what they mean by the American Way of Life, they have something to talk about. (Then of course we hit the coastal part of the Carolinas, a garbage country if there ever was one, and doubt set in.) I love you enormously as you know, and think you are an absolute blooming wonder, as you also know.

Always,

Marty

To: Campbell Beckett

September 12 1946
21 South Eaton Place
London SW1

Darling; Thank you for your long letter. Life is a package of trouble isn't it?

---

*Heroine in a movie about a poor woman struggling to succeed in a white-collar world.

I am off to Nuremberg and Paris in two days, for two weeks, hoping to make some money (knowing it: $3000 and expenses). I am really broke and realise to my horror that since March I have spent $10,500 and all on this house, for myself I am just about walking around barefoot. . . . It's been a funny year and four months, since the war ended in Europe; not really happy though parts of it have been very fine. But such a desperate scrabbling for roots, trying to buy myself into a state of mind. The greatest possible folly. And all that happens is that now I have a town house and a cottage in the country, a car and a miniature Pekinese, three servants scattered around and a secretary and a cable address and no money and a feeling of light-hearted madness, wondering how I got into all this and how will I ever get out.

. . . The novel has been abandoned for this year; I was not up to it. I am doing instead a book of short stories, to get some confidence back, and some feeling for real writing: and then of course I shall have to put in another three months later on, making money for *Collier's*. The play was a financial failure; it is apparently going on in NY where it probably won't make money either.

But I work for myself all the time, and that is both wrong and unsatisfying. I keep the wolf from no door but my own, and slave for no cause except the cause of my own prose style. That is not a good way to be or live, and I do not care for it. And beyond that, there is this dismal question of being in love, a phrase I handle with extreme caution as if handling six snakes and a live wire. For in the end, how do I know what love is, and where sex starts and ends, and love (for me always an operation done with the biggest fanciest mirrors in the world) comes true and is not my own invention, invention of need and loneliness and the terrible boredom of looking after oneself. James is coming to me next month; and I am hoping that something will be clearer; but I doubt myself terribly, and in a way I doubt life. I have E to thank a bit, for there was such an investment of illusion and it paid off so shabbily, that I am frightened and doubtful, and everyone who touches me must suffer. With luck, these matters will become solved and with luck they will do so painlessly. I should dislike, more than anything, hurting James, who in no way deserves it. You should have married me off when I was young, Campbell, and kept me from getting so many confused and difficult ideas.

Much love, always

Martha

To: Hortense (Flexner) and Wyncie King

> June 22 1948
> Cuernavaca
> Mexico

My dearly beloved Weakies;
Teechie's letter arrived and would have been answered in the minute, were it not for that fact that I am no longer captain of my soul nor master of my fate. I am fixing a house again (the equivalent for normal women is the torment and delight of romantic love) and I am obsessed. It's going to be quite a charming house, costing of course double what I intended, and will remain (with the help of the Almighty) in my possession, at least as winter quarters. I have got to stop finding and fixing houses; it eats huge hunks from my life and equally huge from my bank account.

Destiny has only smiled on me in one way. I've never had a really happy love affair. But boy, the luck I have with servants. And, on my more icy-minded days, I feel a good maid replaces a man or does better. No man ever looked after me the way these maids do; nor was so sympathetic to my caterwauling about the horrors of life. I've got another dream, called Maria, and you better come down and visit me. I also have a jeep.

Did I tell you that, one day, I said to myself: what is honor. I thought about that for a few minutes, and decided honor was a luxury I could no longer afford. So I wrote a pure bilge story, with such ease as shamed me (and enjoyed every minute of it) and bunged it off to my agent who sold it immediately to the Satevepost for $1500. Have I told you? So I bought a jeep. Then I thought: here is my future income, I have a naturally bilge mind, and only the greatest control has made me into an honorable and gloomy writer. So I wrote another, in six hours, laughing like a goat; (though the story is awfully solemn and cosy at once) and bunged it off. The agent reports it is a sure sale to Goodhousekeeping. You see? I'm fixed. Live in Mexico and write *ordures*, there's my life span. Started high and settled down into crap and comfort.

And Mexico might actually prove a haven because, after more than 2 months, I like it better every day. That's unusual. On the human side, it's a bit thin; the quality is fine but scarce. I have two beaus now, one is 27 and one is 32, so I feel like a kindergarten teacher. To my delight one left for Central America and the other lives two hours away over the mountains and is too poor to travel. Otherwise I see rarely a collection of people, the best being a marvelous painter called Siqueros, who is a living volcano and vast fun. But mainly I live alone, like any other nice old maid, and the mountains and the weather keep one company.

And you meantime have been plunged in other people's tragedies. You know, I don't believe that one about it being better to have loved and lost.

Damn sight easier just to scrabble along, without the pain of memory, without memories at all. It's what I am doing; and for three weeks or more I have not read a newspaper.

About Camus, I've read the *Plague* and found it superb (he's much better than Sartre and so are his plays) but I don't know *L'Etranger*. Will get it, in due course. Otherwise what should I recommend; Woolf's new essays *The Moment*, Geoffrey Gorer's *The American People*, wonderful, nothing else. I read very little and mainly war books (to see what the competitors are up to; and am happy to report, not much). I'm a failure right now on literature; simply haven't time to read. I run about all day doing house errands and by night collapse with a detective story.

I'm going to be here all summer. You better come down for Christmas. I'll write another bilge story and we'll buy a plane.

Your ever loving slob-friend,
Gellhorn

To: Lew★

July 6 1948
Avenida del Parque 14
Cuernavaca

Darling, my darling, very darling: I cannot write to you or telephone you or see you, and you are gone. You must be gone and stay gone, because I do not know how to share and I also would not know how to make you matter so little that it wouldn't even be sharing. What kind of luck is it that makes you suddenly, unreasonably, love a man, and that man not free, not returning the love (and why should he?) and that man locked in his own torments and doubts and perhaps happinesses, asking no help and wanting none. But what am I to do? Knit and think. Think: maybe the telephone will ring, and if it does, what differences does it make. Maybe suddenly the cowbell at the gate will start tinkling in its incompetent way; and it will be Lew. Lew is no use as a name, I do not think of you with a name. I think of you as what I want, and mine. And know that is untrue.

I dug this grave with my teeth; made my bed full of nails and must lie in it. I should have stopped before there was any starting, instead of which I have now the hunger and the wanting and the pain. And no future at all. It is much harder to be lonely, when you have for a while (three nights and two days) stopped being lonely. I was used to having only myself, cold and

★Lew was an American film producer, passing through Cuernavaca. He was married, and nothing came of their affair, but Martha's note of need and attraction was new in her letters.

hard as that is; I could live with it. And now I wait, for a voice, a face, a body, that is not going to be here, is not mine, does not in any case wait as I do, nor share this homesickness.

You didn't understand about bed; and it has broken my heart. I think, surely, you have had so much better. And how could I explain all that it is and means to me, for the many years that happened before you. How could I explain that I taught myself to be tough and indifferent, because it mattered too much and learned not even to weep in my mind not to notice. And then, because of the piled up loneliness and the failure, I learned to think I didn't matter; all I had to do was see that the act of love was pleasant to another body . . . And finally, that I cannot give my body as entirely or easily as I gave my heart, and yet my heart is the more valuable of the two because I haven't taught it any tricks.

Come back come back come back. Come back because I need you so. And you do not need me and why should you come back your life is good and full and why should you come back. Only because I want you and need you; and if you come back it will only be worse. It is bad enough to love once but unendurable to lose twice, to lose with every departure, to have every leave-taking be an end.

I was so sure I could be as cloud-like as you; that I could seize my joy and forget it; or I wasn't sure and I hoped and gambled. And I can't. I am wretched. It is better to have nothing, which is normal, than to have this wanting, and the telephone silent and the gate bell silent and no letters in the mail and no day, fixed, when you will walk towards me.

July 6; bad bad day.

To: Lew [?]

October 9 1948
Avenida del Parque 14
Cuernavaca

My darling;
You cannot help yourself; you are forced to break my heart without meaning to. A broken heart is such a shabby thing, like poverty and failure and the incurable diseases which are also deforming. I've lived with it for what now seems to me like years, though it is only a fourth of a year or less; and I hate it and am ashamed of it; and I must somehow repair this heart and put it back into its normal condition, as a tough somewhat scarred but operating organ.

You cannot feel what you do not feel; you cannot be blamed for that lack. But, to me, there is something so chilling, so really kiss-of-death in our relation that I've got to stop it altogether. We spend the night together and I go away. And afterwards there is not one telephone call, not ten minutes in a busy day when you are impelled, you must, you need to talk to me. Or even, not as much as that: ten minutes when you think it would be pleasant to chat to someone who loves you . . . It's too lopsided and I am afraid I cannot bear it. Since there is no way to cure myself by seeing you, as you suggested, I think the only way is not to see you, not at all, to decide in my mind that you are gone for good, and slowly to decide that you were never here. (And indeed, were you?)

I wish you everything you want, the old dream come true, the great excitement of making films, making the life you want. I know you will and that you cannot fail. I wish you every happiness for yourself too, long or short, deep or shallow, however you want it and find it.

I have a strange feeling of saying goodbye to a turned back, but I say it nevertheless, with love,

Martha

To: William Walton

December 25 1948
Avenida del Parque 14
Cuernavaca

Darling; Christmas got itself over in record time this year. I imagine (it is six p.m. of Dec 25) that you are now surrounded with your young, making that train run. And snow, by God. Whereas I spent the morning, after feeding my three animals and doing the housework (I sent Maria to Jojutla, firmly, for the holiday season), sitting naked in the sun, wearing a large sunhat and reading a very frivolous novel.

Luckily, on Thursday, Maria told me that Xmas Eve was the next day or I wouldn't have known it. And yesterday, Xmas eve, I had an amazing experience. I could scarcely believe it. As I had forgotten what it means: to be moved to tears . . .

I went to a tiny church near the market, called the Church of the Mats, the smallest I've ever seen, all white and red and gold and pink and lovely dressy saints and a modern square grandfather clock (you know with different colored woods). Outside there was a throng of little boys; at the front there was a handmade rickety litter, carrying the figures of Mary on a *burro* and Joseph dressed up like a Spanish grandee. Both of them wearing tiny little straw hats such as you buy here in the market, above their satins. Two little boys, in red dresses and white surplices, with candles bigger than themselves, stood at the front; and right by the church door there were about ten little boys, clustering around a dirty printed paper, on which words were written and they were singing. Wonderful voices, and wonderful music, tremendously gay and easy to sing and yet with that great thing songs sometimes have, the thing of being like water flowing. They sang, on behalf of Mary and Joseph, and suitably enough Joseph did all the talking as a man should. The boys' voices rose, singing the simple wonderful words: 'My wife is feeling very poorly, please let us come in.' From inside the church other boys' voices rose in answer, so that the church and the courtyard were light with sound: 'We are very poor and we have no room, we cannot.' Finally, outside, the boys' voices, climbing up the night, said the great words: 'But my wife is the Queen of Heaven.' And then the doors opened and the children burst into the church, everywhere, all over, singing and singing, while the Holy Family was carried to the altar by two little creatures looking like Mexican Huckelberry Finns. And I stood in the back of the church, weeping. I who have never found anything in a church except architecture, and sometimes (Midnight Mass at St. Etienne du Mont in Paris) the great beauty of the music, the organ. But I never really felt that anyone loved God and Mary and the Infant Jesus and even poor old Joseph; and suddenly here they were, being loved like members of the family.

. . . Yes, I find our gin rummy game very odd. Or rather, I find us quite wonderful people, you and me together; because I don't quite see how we could have done that, what we felt like, what was suitable, and carried it off without any anguish or embarrassment or anger between us. Men and women aren't generally so sound with each other (and that may be why you and I will certainly love each other until we die, faithfully, through every- thing: which is something different from the pain and folly and fireworks and also joy of being in love, a thing which − for me − can never be maintained, as it burns too hard and bright). We know this now: what we have we will always have, we will have no more and we shouldn't have any less. It's a very good quality. I am richer because of it. But you need, and will have, the Mesdames Churchill, Tree, Pitcairn, because the sexes were also put on the earth, with their different construction, for the purpose of providing each other with excitement.

And I will always be there, year after year, certainly the best giny- rummy-partner-in-bed that a man can find, don't you think?

I'm writing again, and think I'll have a book of short stories ready for next fall, though I don't care if I do or don't. I want to do a very long story, and am brooding about it ineffectually, on Ernest and the cats. I've got a wonderful picture growing in my head, a composite man, which would delight me to get down; but I haven't seen the woman yet. I'll write that just as long as I want it, letting it find its own size as it goes. And try not to sell it anywhere, only for book use.

. . . Goodnight darling. I hope you have the happiest New Year imaginable and that everything you want, happens.

love always

M

Martha was happy in Cuernavaca. She liked her house, with its stone floors, large windows, and the views over the mountains, and she loved the clear blue days when she would sit in the garden under the bougainvillea naked or in a bathing suit, writing what she referred to as "little, little stories, like a small wind blowing." To make money she began what she called "literary whoring," finding in herself an unexpected talent for stories composed of "fudge, high life, virtue and women wearing carefully described clothes."

Cuernavaca also provided her with two new friends, with whom she would correspond for the next thirty years. One of these was the scriptwriter and director Robert Presnell, son of the famous Hollywood producer and married to the actress Marsha Hunt, a man of great charm and a passionate liberal. The other was Leonard Bernstein, already well known for his work as a conductor and composer, who rented a house not far from hers. Bernstein talked of their friendship as "our own peculiar sexless love affair which can never be erased from the books." Martha was now forty-two; Presnell and Bernstein several years younger. They played tennis together and one night experimented with marijuana. When Bernstein married, his wife Felicia became an equally good friend.

Martha had always envied those of her women friends who had children. "It's what one needs," she wrote to Diana Cooper. "Someone, or several, who can take all the love one is able to give, as a natural and untroublesome gift . . . As for men, they seem to me on the whole confused and feckless creatures, who are necessary, for a variety of reasons, but who are certainly not reliable." Encouraged by Edna, she went off to Italy, with the idea of adopting one of the many thousands of war orphans.

To: Eleanor Roosevelt

June 22 1949
c/o American Express
Rome

Dearest, dearest Mrs R.

I talk of you so often, think of you so much, love you so greatly, and I never see you or hear from you. It makes me sad. I wish you weren't always so far away and that I never knew anymore what you're thinking and feeling. Where are you this very minute, I wonder; half past twelve on a hot summer's day, June 22, when I am in Rome, thinking how dreadful it is the way one loses the people one loves.

Have been in Italy for two months, working most of that time on one article about Italian children, the ones who paid, are paying, will always pay for the last grown-ups' war. It was heartbreaking work and I don't know what good it is; the readers of the Saturday Evening Post may feel slightly heartsick on the subway – but what else, what more? Now I have one more to do, an easy silly one, and then I don't know. Look at the world, I think, with special attention to the incredible beauty thereof. And in the fall I go home, to Cuernavaca, and the sun and the silence. It's a very privileged life, really, and I am almost too lucky.

All I want really is children of my own; about six of them, I think. I don't feel I have to bear them, just have them around, and worry about their eating and sleeping and having shoes. It is such a fierce bore to worry about oneself, only.

Please please write. It is more than a year, I think, since I've heard from you.

Love,

Martha

To: William Walton

July 16 1949
Rome

Beloved, distant Pronto;

You take your time all right about communicating with the outside world but when you do, no one can kick. I had just about decided to send you a 300 word cable collect, to teach you not to plunge into silence. And then your wonderful letter came, which I have memorized, and I do not feel that you have been gone for ten years (previous feeling) and that no less than eight oceans separate us.

I hardly know what to tell you about here so will begin with the joyous news that my Capri article which was a solid mass of shit was described as excellent by the Satevepost and bought. Thus I am solvent. I wrote you about Capri and perhaps about Edda Ciano?* I left her to the last day and have regretted it ever since. Terrible woman, naturally, but nothing dull, nothing weak. From her, one does get some idea of how they must all have been. I wish I could see her again. Then I must have written you that I went to Pescara with a gentleman and behaved much better than Saint Catherine

---

*Edda Ciano (1910–1995), daughter of Benito Mussolini, whose husband, Galleazzo Ciano, became Foreign Minister and was executed on her father's orders.

of Alexandria, if she is the one who got so disgusting about Christ and always wanted to exchange rings. I didn't exchange anything and came to Monte Circeo, quite a lovely joint by the Pontine Marshes, and wrote the Capri piece for the third and final time. Was robbed by the hotel and it was there that I started getting bored. I know now how this works. At some point I stop seeing or hearing people (really) and of course a huge boredom sets in. I also stop everything else and go about in a slightly soured daze. Now I am deep in that and Rome is so hot (yes) that it makes me both sick and angry.

But the real thing is the adoption business and I am keeping a detailed record of it and someday I am going to write a honey of an essay. The Eyeties act as if I wanted to eat the baby not adopt it. This is due to being a non-Catholic foreigner, both states being regarded as willful criminality. Today, when I was nearly in despair I discovered the Italian Protestants and all may be well. If you can believe it, these lambs have been lurking around in the Piedmonte mountains for about six centuries, being absolutely completely and determinedly Protestant. I am of course drawn to them like anything, with my usual tenderness for minorities. They think it is lovely for me to adopt a child if only they have one I like. So that is the next step. Off to the mountains with the waldensians. The law has now been pretty well doped out and can be handled. I am going to try to be named guardian of the child – quicker process and more chance of winning. Later, any number of years, it will also be easier to adopt; a sort of fait accompli angle. But I am tired and bored and it is drab work.

Meantime I at last seem to know buckets of Italians. It stems from Mary Roberti and they are all the ancient nobility who, I may say, have remarkable powers of survival everywhere. They think they are poor and are still richer than everyone else; have the same beautiful houses and lands; and the same absolutely idiot lives. They are very pleasant and infinitely affable. No men. I don't know what's happened to men; they seem to be a disappearing sex. They imagine they are men but cannot fool me. Last night I had dinner with Uggucione di Sorbello and went afterwards to his flat on the Via Due Macelli (the rent is 1000 lire or $3.50 a month for 4 rooms; frozen rents.) It looks like a stage set for a really gloomy Chekov play; incredibly Russian and dirty. He is quite sweet and mad and full of aches. Sybille [Bedford] left yesterday for Ischia with her beloved. Her beloved is six feet two, wall-eyed and talks like an early American primer. Sybille cannot bear her any longer. There is nothing I do not know about Lesbians except how they make love; I couldn't bear to ask that for fear of hearing. I do not see any of the others. It is too hot and I did not come this distance to consort with sad fools. Also today I moved from the Inghilterra out of sheer loathing, into the Anglo Americano. The difference is that whereas my walls at the Ing were like dried blood here they are like dried mustard. It is a tiny bit quieter and no cooler but the view is better. I am also pleased to see a different lobby.

I am going to Florence to see the Mooreheads★ and Protestant orphans in four days; thence up to Piedmonte; thence to Venice to a palazzo; thence back here for more wrangling. I do not know how long I can stand it and am longing to get to England, sell everything, see everyone, and return to my delectable white house in the mountains. Am homesick. People are fine but not as exciting as when I was younger. I hope I will wake up again and be able to look at the world around me. I have done no sightseeing here, and am a lump. But this adoption thing obsesses me.

Am also fat as a pig; and my clothes are on the whole an outrage to God and man. The only good thing is my car which I better go and garage before it is pinched. I do love it and it makes a great difference. Not trapped anymore. But it does not replace you; what I want is you and the car. I also resent the idea that you find me comfortable, but am delighted with your other remarks. Do you really miss me? Do you really prefer me (at least spiritually) to all those girls with huge breasts? (Anyhow if I gain another ten pounds, I'll be bosom to bosom with the best.) I feel sure you will marry some chit of a girl (such a hideous expression) and forget me and our *amour d'automne* will go up the creek. But you know I love you; you last.

M

P.S. What do you think Ernest has done now? He told the Mooreheads he paid me $500 alimony a month, which explained why I travelled and had such a fine life. You know, he may also be quite quite crazy.

To: William Walton

[Summer 1949]
[Rome]

Dearest Vietato Fumare;
I realise that, since you are gone, I have <u>looked</u> at nothing. How lucky that you were here at all; otherwise I should finally leave Italy (a fairly welcome day, whenever it comes) without having seen any more than if I had spent four or five months in Oshkosh, Wis. It is terrible and criminal and I feel at once ashamed of myself, bewildered and helpless. I drive blindly through the country; I struggle in this heat (how fragrant and cool my tropics are,

---

★Alan Moorehead, the war correspondent and writer, and his wife, Lucy, who had a house in Fiesole.

by contrast) and am a monomaniac with no room for the things of the spirit or spert, as we say in the American Express.

But, out of this, something has come; I've found my child. At last. I calculate I have seen about 52 orphanages and institutions for children. In Pistoia, which is a small boiling town 25 miles from Florence, there is a shabby Foundling Home and therein dwells my heart's desire. His name is Allessandro. You must immediately think what his name should be: Christopher, Timothy, Thomas, Robert, John. His age is either 14 or 17 months; the birth certificate will have to be verified. He is as fat as two sausages, blonde like Botticelli folks (gilt shining blonde) with grey eyes, a snub nose, a delicious mouth, and bow-legs. He is covered with prickly heat and normally dressed in an old UNRRA flour sack. He walks, waving his arms and grunting with pleasure, like an old gent who has palsy. His smile is not to be believed; it looks as if he had invented the whole idea of smiling. He waddles forward and clutches my knees. The other day I was passing a happy morning with him on the floor; we were playing a distinguished game of tossing his rubber teething ring back and forth. All of a sudden, he found this so absolutely perfect and satisfying that he sighed with delight, a huge fat sigh, clapped his hands, and lay down to laugh better. I cannot tell you how I dote on him; it makes me come over weak to consider the fat character. I do not even ask for a medical exam or an intelligence test and do not give a hoot about his parentage; I just want him. He may grow up to be very short and stout and of a moderate brightness; but I think he is always going to be happy, and sow happiness around him. He's a complete optimist. And in this tragic jungle of warped children, with sad pinched little faces, who either scream all the time or compete like fierce animals for love and attention, he alone is serene and generous and taking it easy.

Legal complications have set in. I felt my mind going; it's been so long and so depressing and so exhausting a search. So I have fled for a few days to the home of the Gherardesca family, and you would adore it. I miss you doubly because it would be such a pleasure to giggle with you. They live in a renovated antique, which has housed their line for 1100 years. It burned down in the 19th century and like fools they put it right up again. It is so dark at all times that you feel your way along the corridors. There are almost no windows. There are 4 inner staircases so your chances of finding your room again, once you leave it, are nil. The furniture is a vast mish-mash of ancient horror and the old Count has, for 40 years, been collecting the most hideous and extravagant majolica that the world produced; antique hideousities in the form of plates and jugs. The house literally sags under them. The house by the way looks like a smaller watertight version of Uggucione's castle.

Herein dwell the old Count, aged 75, who is I suppose the final example of the feudal lord. (By the way, they own something the size of a county hereabouts. A double row of cypresses, five kilometres long, leads to the house; the land is too incredibly beautiful, including mountains, and a wild empty strip of beach several miles long.) The countess must be Baron Wrangel's sister, a Russian; and her sister, Princess Kuraki who has been living here since 1917 when booted out of Russia. They speak French together, still, in the ancient way, and still make mistakes in same. The old Princess is painted like the Madwoman of Chaillot, with those huge black lines under the eyes and the rouged cheeks, and in her late sixties, rides daily, sidesaddle naturally, with her long pearl earrings afloat. Then there is a Greek princess called Semira, who is about 60 and looks like someone's governess, and another antique Marquesa, about 70, who looks like someone's cook, and a strange elongated gent called Monsieur Felici, who speaks five languages and is silent in all of them, who is here for bridge. That is the older generation.

Italy is a huge sweat box, with a wind like hair driers, and the land bakes brown and mosquitoes the size of ponies. Not a leaf stirs. And at night, what air there is cannot enter the endless 14th century windows. I hate these houses; I have never been more uncomfortable than at the Villa Diana (where I stayed a week with the Mooreheads who are plainly angelic and whom I dote on) and here and the glamorous country houses in England. I am so homesick for the comfort of Cuernavaca that I could weep. But the plan is just to hang on and hang on until I get that child, and make plans from there. Anyhow someday I am going to get him, and put him under my arm, and jump into a plane, and settle down in my walled garden. It's all I want. I think I may have to come via New York and maybe should stay over and take the baby to a first rate doctor to be sure he is okay. If so, will you come to NY to see him. Such a dreamboat. I love you. I miss you.

M

In the autumn of 1949, Martha collected Alessandro from a lawyer's office in Florence. He was nineteen months old and ill with measles, but Martha was overwhelmed with pleasure. "I know I can make him strong and well," she wrote, "and I think happiness is built into him." When he had recovered, they embarked on a 28-hour journey to America "something Dante would have loved to describe." Sandy, as she called him, was teething and Martha had never before changed a nappy. "I longed for wars, any wars, those dear past comfortable wars," she told Mrs. Roosevelt, who had provided her with the references she needed for the adoption and who later helped to get Sandy American citizenship.

Not long after returning to Cuernavaca, Martha was introduced to David and Nemone Gurewitsch. David was a doctor, and a close friend of Eleanor Roosevelt, whose private doctor he later became. By the time he left Mexico, a week later, Martha was in love, and desperate. Between April 4 and April 11, 1950, she wrote him six immensely long letters, streams of consciousness about her life, her past, and her feelings for him, adding to them at different times of the day and night, with a sense of need and urgency she had never experienced before. The first ran to forty-seven typed pages.

To: Diana Cooper

October 26 1949
[Rome]

Darling, I went through Paris with the speed of light, lingering only long enough to get my hair cut (practically shaved off, too dreadful), catch a cold, and talk to a very old girl friend who seems pretty low in her mind. Then, feeling cheated but breathlessly excited, I jumped into the plane to come and call for Alessandro. Upon arriving in Rome (feeling like drowned Gorgonzola) the lawyer informed me casually that there had been a legal delay and I would not get Allessandro until November first or maybe November eighth, not sure yet. Whereupon I had a good bawl, something that has not happened since V-E night in Paris when I bawled for all the world instead of for the horrors of adopting a child; and have now retired to the country to sleep. It is all a shame and a scandal; I could have stayed in Paris and come to see you at Chantilly and as it is I will not see you again for a year which is a long piece of time. I am sad about it. Maybe next year at Garda?

Italy may or may not be lovely. I wouldn't know. I have been given two bibs and bought one, which is all A's trousseau to date. I cannot see him until he is given to me legally which drives me nuts. I lie awake worrying about rickets and how to change diapers. If adopting a child is such a torment I wonder what having one can be; a four star hell, I should think This will all be fine when once I get the small fatty safely back to Cuernavaca and we can both settle down to a life of sloth. However, seven months to adopt is already two months better than making, and I should not kick.

M

To: William Walton

December 7 1949
Avenida del Parque 14
Cuernavaca

Darling, darling; do you remember those lovely cosy wars? When one didn't have a thing to do except scrounge for one's comforts and write a bit of shit now and then. When one owned one musette bag and lived like the religious bums of Burma with their begging bowls. When each day was complete because one was not silly enough to look ahead. Ah me. And obviously there will always be wars because enough people, everywhere, can think of nothing finer than getting away from home.

I tell you, I hadn't a clue about motherhood, neither its pleasures nor despairs. Both astound me. Pleasures first, because otherwise it would seem so ungrateful. Pleasures come under the heading of love (Love); the little chap has acquired a greater passion for me than anyone ever had, except of course Mother who has been proving hers (and continues to do so, every minute) for forty one years. I find myself absolutely starry-eyed and absurd just because he rushes whenever he hears my voice and of all conditions prefers to sit on my lap, sing and hug me. Pleasures also consist in the fact that he makes me laugh, which is a miracle as I am generally in such a tempest of unquiet and nerves that laughter could hardly pierce that wall. . . . And I never pick him up (except when in a rage because he is crying for the sheer fun of it) without feeling rather stunned that this fat little body is in my care from now on. And I love his looks, and am proud as a fool about his cleverness. All that is pleasure. But there is a lot more and it hounds me.

For a beginning, his nurse is *a lata* (Spanish word meaning literally tin can, and used to refer to disasters.) She is too stupid and tactless and mindless and due to her washing his hair at night, a cold night, she has had hell's own cold for a week. I have no ease or confidence with her and that means we are nannies too; obsessive work. Second there is this damn cold which won't go. Third there is a miserable diaper rash (and I spend my reading hours with the baby book, not getting around to more refreshing fare.) Fourth there is the fact that he hates to sleep, or rather to be left alone in a closed room. I cannot think; I cannot separate myself for an hour from the gnawing problems of how to manage him.

. . . Also, my staff has swollen immeasurably. Last year Maria and I lived here. Now Maria and the gardener have felt Love's Burning Breath and both live here; there is Maria de la Luz, the nurse, and Sandy and Mother and me, and the laundress who luckily does not sleep in. I can tell you that Mr. Ford, surveying River Rouge (if that's its name) never felt he had a bigger plant to run. As for the cost, we will pass it over in discreet silence and prayer. A child is clearly twice as expensive as a yacht and a built-in mistress.

I think of your visit constantly and have a studio for you, which was a problem because you could hardly move inside this crowded sardine box.

. . . By January it will be nice and hot. The land has already been burned, more than I remembered, at this time of year, and is lion coloured except for the mountains of pine, and something else which stays green. The gardens are of course beautiful and lush because watered. I find it too chilly to swim but not too chilly to sit naked in the sun if ever I had time. You must come; it really is, to me, the most beautiful land in the world; beautiful wild, not beautiful civilized. And I think the Indians the most attractive people to look at, and everything they do is enchanting to watch. I wouldn't swop it for Italy, nor even for England which remains the place where the heart is warmest to match the anguished chill of the body, no doubt. And we eat and drink fine.

I'm weary. You write me now. Quick. Love,

M

To: William Walton

[? December] 1949
Avenida del Parque 14
Cuernavaca

Darling, darling;

The trip was terrific, marred of course by work, which I have grown away from. I cannot stand going about asking strangers questions; it seems such an intrusion. And of course I know the absolute folly of journalism which at best reflects the vision of one person, and pretends to give an 'over-all picture.' And I hate to write it; and only want to do short stories. So in England it was rather rough as I had to work very hard, and was not interested in any of the subjects; and alienated my friends by never having time to see them, which seemed to them all (rightly) too vulgar Big Business. But Israel was bliss. Sun, to begin with, and without which I find no life valuable. And there was Capa, standing at the bar of the hotel when I arrived. It reminded me of Spain, of all my youth; one worked so hard, leaving every day at dawn, returning every night late, exhausted, but still ready to go out and look, listen, drink, laugh. It's a hard uncomfortable country, with one million individuals in it; you'd never have known how many different kinds of Jew there are, until finally there is no such thing as a Jew. But their stories, ah William, this affects me as the sight of Italy affected you; a gold mine of stories, the equal of which I've never before seen. And then they're brave, or they wouldn't be there and alive, and because they're brave they are gay (I am now certain that gloominess and cowardice go together) and face the more than uncertain future with a steadiness which delights and dazzles me. They are proud, which also is earned, and some of them are beautiful; notably an oriental tribe, called the Rabanim, Jews from the southernmost part of Arabia; men with long thick curly tresses and eagle noses, women walking like gypsies in colored silks, their eyes darkened with kohl, tied round with silver ornaments and their straight hair braided into hundreds of long tiny braids, like glossy snakes. . . . I laughed more than I have in years and my mind reeled, between the glories of Crusader ruins (history, there, is so tangible that you feel yourself really moving, not dislocated, but small and inevitable, in a procession of centuries) and the corrugated tin huts springing up on Mount Carmel. I want to go back. If I could, sometime, when Sandy's older, I'd like to live there a year and collect those stories; although now is the time to go. Because the stories will become legend, not immediate fact, and be dimmed or lost; they will become a race of farmers, as they must to survive, pioneer farmers, fighting sand as the Dutch have fought water. But what a place. If I had to move from here, I'd only want to go there; I like drama or sleep, and nothing much in between.

I fell in love with no one, anywhere, which saddens me – surely part of a journey, of tourism, ought to be falling in love. But I can't any more. I was also appallingly homesick, sorrowing because I missed the sudden change-over from babyhood to boyhood, in Sandy. And thrilled to be home, here, where I still love life best, in this green flowering place, living quite separately among all the small quiet lives. The child is a grandeur, always more beautiful, more exciting, more charming. He cannot keep it up; it doesn't seem possible. But he goes from strength to strength and it is not only my blind mother love speaking. And he's happy, always, so that it is like having the sun built in to one's private world.

I love you and wish you a _very_ happy New Year,

Martha

To: William Walton

January 30 1950
Avenida del Parque 14
Cuernavaca

William Walton; Do you know what I have done since January 8. I am going to tell you for I feel sure that in all your acquaintance there is no one so prolific as me except Edgar Rice Burroughs. I have written two 6000 word articles, revised another article, gone over with a fine tooth comb, changed and cut that Polish story you read so long ago (the Atlantic bought it, paid for it, set it up in galleys but the ending has been worrying me for six months so I just started all over again) and written a book review. How about it? Isn't it soul-shaking. Now I am going to devote myself to the care of the body which has been neglected for as long as I can remember; and lose ten pounds and play tennis and get so I can actually bend my back bone which is presently made of old arrow-heads from Aztec tombs. And once that is accomplished I have two enormous short stories in mind; one about Israel and one about Dotty★ in Mexico, and I can hardly wait. If I could bring myself to use a short story based on Flavia's† family-in-law and their castle, a monumental job of work, I'd have a book of short stories. But I think I better wait until the old people die, as they might just see it, and it would hurt their feelings; and they did take Sandy in to recover from the measles, and although writers are by definition shits, there is a limit. Isn't this all stupendous. I haven't got anemia any more clearly but this energy scares me.

On top of this I am at last legalizing our position in Mexico and buying, for a mild $7000, proper papers as '*rentista*' for Sandy and me, so we can not be thrown out of the country. I am also seriously looking for a house with enough land, to buy, and if you look hard enough in this country you find; so I think I shall be a land-owner in six months or less.

Honey, isn't it wonderful to be interested in one's work. It's happening to me again for the first time in three years and by golly it's like a love affair only much more solid. I am almost nervous about it; it seems too good to be true or to last. I've got a room, far from this mad little nest, which I go to every day for four hours or more; and maybe the fact that it is hard to get time is what makes the work time so exciting.

What did you think of [Irwin] Shaw's‡ collected stories. He gave me a copy too, with a dedication: 'To Martha, who is welcome anywhere we are, on any continent, anytime' and that gave me a turn, just the way your dedication did; it made me realise I had been appearing and hanging about quite a lot. About the stories: I read them all, one right after the other, which is the way to see what they are like. He is technically hot stuff; he writes a fine smooth readable prose; he has moments of goodness. But you know, Hollywood or something, has muddled him on endings; they are

---

★When Dorothy Parker visited Martha in Cuernavaca, Martha grumbled about having to look after such a "dreary creature, not given to the ways and means of life."

†Flavia della Gherardesca, whose family estate near Livorno, Bulgheri, Martha had stayed in.

†Irwin Shaw (1913–1984), scriptwriter for popular radio programs in the 1930s who went on to write novels and short stories. *The Young Lions* (1948) brought him money and fame. Martha had met him at the end of the war.

too slick, you can see them in close-up. I agree with him that a short story should have a plot; but I do not believe the ending should be engineered, so as to close the plot up neatly. And he is very sentimental and he has a sort of cast of characters; their names don't matter too much for they keep re-appearing. (Just like my woman, generally dark-haired, who is always travelling and has slept with everybody.) Now sentimentality is something I do not quite understand; I do not know what makes it. I am sentimental about Israel, from excess of admiration. And myself, I find it hard to write about bad people, evil people; in life I dislike almost everyone and can hardly bear to waste my time with the human race, but when I write I always see what is okay about them or how they got to be un-okay, and that makes my writing too kindly towards the human race. Maybe that is sentimental too. His sentimentality is different; I cannot put my finger on it. The best simple example is the way the hero of *Young Lions* fell dead, by a werewolf's shot, in a field of pink flowers. Know what I mean?

As people I agree with you, those Shaws are like coming home. I really love them and feel good and lively with them, despite my deep psychopathic hatred of New York, which makes me miserable with almost everyone there. And you know about Allen [Grover] and me, he has renounced me; he did not call me in New York, nor send one of his $20 Xmas cards as usual. This is because of politics, I reckon, if politics is the right word. I informed his little woman over the telephone that I sure hoped Time, Life Inc would not sweep the country, as a new party, and get us all into the most hopeless of wars. I restrained myself from saying that it was curious how none, not one, of the senior people in that outfit, including of course Luce, had ever heard a shot fired in anger, nor closely inspected any battle field; their boyish enthusiasm for war may stem from their protected lives. And I really think that gang has become hateful and dangerous. Since Allen is completely sold to them, one would naturally have little in common any longer. It takes a long time for history to interfere with friendship, but eventually history always gets around to doing its job.

Have you heard the repeated new gossip about the dashing Hemingways. It appears there is truly (kiss truly, belch truly etc) a nineteen year old girl in his life, and a menace to Mary's chances of the inheritance which is her only hope. Lenny Bernstein, whom I met in Tel Aviv, said he had met a sad-eyed glamorous dark 19 year old beauty in Venice, called Baronne Francetti (very poor family, Flavia says, bought Papal title) who goes into a meaningful silence when Ernest's name is mentioned; Venice reports they are 'linked.' And poor Mary; there she's been over a hot stove all these years, and what would she get. Mr. Bernstein by the way is a something. He is reported to like men (also women and goats), and is actually beautiful, which is an odd thing for a man to be, and about as natural as a 20 minute permanent wave; and full of talent and neuroses, ai, such neuroses. Of course he liked me; you know my unfailing appeal to men of talent and low character; or just of low character. I saw myself suddenly, through his eyes, as a beautiful placid middle-aged woman, a farm mother, honest as trees, capable of making butter and patching pants and giving out homely wisdom like Carl Sandburg.* Very funny. He threatened to come to Cuernavaca, but I doubt it. This is a place people only threaten to come to.

In a way, you and I are the two most eccentric people we know; we regard money as a commodity, not as a sign of prowess, and we live outside the moving staircase or rat race of competition, and do what we want to. I daresay we will somehow get bitched for this; since it is almost too sane and pleasant to be allowed, forever. You say nothing about your social life, those bright evenings of waltz clubs and what all; please tell. For unlike me, I am sure you are no Carmelite. I have finally discovered what keeps me chaste: nothing but boredom. I cannot bear the endless repetition of it, repetition without illusion; and the language depresses me, it has grown so jibbering, since it is without any possible trace of sincerity. Capa, giving me one of his better lectures on the subject in Tel Aviv, said he thought of course it was terribly embarrassing, all these goings-on with strangers, but that it was necessary to embarrass yourself in life; anyhow the alternative was worse; one really got <u>very</u> queer from chastity. I don't know. I think one can get very queer from anything, and surely it cannot be advisable to take sex as a pure purgative, with a bad after-taste?

I've read nothing I like very much but have been too busy to read well. Have you any suggestions? I shall get the new Greens and Faulkner's *Collected Stories* but I wish there were anyone as good as the early Waugh or Orwell, writing now.

I love you, William.

Martha

---

*Carl Sandburg (1878–1967), socialist poet and writer who won two Pulitzer prizes and in later years kept a herd of prize-winning goats.

To: William Walton

February 3 1950
Avenida del Parque 14
Cuernavaca

Darling; I have your letter and I will answer it, sentence by sentence tomorrow and I kiss you. But just now I have to write you about Ernest's new book;* have you bought your February copy of *Cosmopolitan*. If not, do so now.

I have just read this first installment, with a whiskey to help me, and curiosity to spur me on. I know I am biased and unjust; but I find it revolting. I also realise he will never have to write his autobiography because he has been doing it, from the first novel, chapter by chapter, each book keeping pace with his calendar years, building up this dream vision of himself. Now he is a fifty year old Colonel of Infantry with high blood pressure, a great education, and a passion for duck shooting. The women get younger and younger; so that now the woman is an olive haired Italian (perhaps Princess, by the next installment) of nineteen. And I feel quite sick, I cannot describe this to you. Shivering sick. I watch him adoring his image, with such care and such tolerance and such accuracy in detail, 'He walked with the exaggerated confidence', and such abject bottom-licking narcissism. And I feel sick, and you know what else: I weep for the eight years I spent, almost eight (light dawned a little earlier) worshipping his image with him, and I weep for whatever else I was cheated of due to that time-serving; and I weep for all that is permanently lost because I shall never, <u>really</u>, trust a man again.

You must read it and tell me if, anyone not me, not knowing who sits for the portrait, (with an expression of reverent self-love on his face) will accept this and find it fine. Perhaps it is. To me, it has a loud sound of madness and a terrible smell as of decay.

. . . As for my American acquaintances, they are bleeding fools. Do you suppose they think one can only love (and stick by) what springs from one's own loins, thus linking love to narcissism. Whereas, my son is what I would have made, in case the womb took specific orders. But it doesn't; and he has everything a child of mine wouldn't have, including the sanguine nature and the irresistible laughter and the passion for everything and everyone about him. He's an education to me and I've grown quite cheerful to keep him company. And I love him, oddly enough, much more than I ever loved anyone except Edna. I reckon it will stick. I only hope he loves me, when he gets old enough to know his mind. He may think me a blight. Just now he thinks I am divine, which is very satisfactory.

---

*Across the River and Into the Trees.

. . . Do write more. Go on being happy; do not marry any dark woman without my permission. I kiss you and miss you much more than you seem to know.

Martha

To: William Walton

February 15 1950
Avenida del Parque 14
Cuernavaca

Darling; I have been wondering: is Marx as funny as Freud? I find Freud perfectly killing and suddenly thought: maybe I've missed Marx; endless worlds of unexplored merriment. Tell me.

I was just telephoned from Mexico by a man (unknown) called George Bluementhal. His history is: tax evader, hotelier, and the repulsive man about town who squires the visiting starlets. He informs me that Clare Booth Luce and Margaret Case* intend to lunch here Friday. This is perfectly extraordinary since I know neither of them and have not invited them. It is like Henry the Eighth, commandeering lodgings as he progressed through his kingdom. It is more like the Regent. Anyhow on Friday there will be here a nice middle-aged (plus) doctor and wife from St. Louis, whose claim to my attention is that they loved my father. I think that will be excellent company for Mrs. Luce.

Oh Lord I am bored. I was happy as a mudlark a week ago; but suddenly and for the first time, there have been people all this week. I cannot stand it. People are for four reasons: 1) to make one laugh and to laugh at one's jokes (you note I put this first); 2) to give a jet propulsion to the mind because their minds are richer, faster, stranger, deeper; 3) love; which means that one is happy simply to sit in the same room (and applies to almost no one); 4) to go to bed with. Aside from that, I know no purpose to human huddling together.

I wish they would all fuck off to the US and leave me in peace.

Why don't you write, you cow?

Love,

M

---

*Editor of *Vogue* and voted International Best Dressed Woman of 1964.

To: David Gurewitsch

April 5 1950
[Mexico]

David, David: you couldn't have been named anything else, could you? It is so lovely and so right. I am in my workroom, but there is no question of work. I can only think of you. And I do not know what to think or how to think; there is only this longing for you which is uncontrollable, frightening and quite useless. Now I have decided that I cannot burden you with daily letters, my love must not be heavy on you; so I shall write for myself and keep the letters here in a drawer. Perhaps talking to you this way will make the days easier.

There was no word from you this morning; Tuesday and Wednesday have passed too, and you must be drowned in work, all the telephone calls, the people asking questions, the unread mail, the patients. You are too busy to think, I imagine. I see you, so thin and so calm, going through that driven routine, never appearing to be in a hurry or cross or worried. Driving your body by will and nerve, the lovely delicate body; and giving everyone what they need. I imagine you putting off thought and remembrance; but it is possible that, as you said, you found yourself there again and that is the real world and you remembered the sky here and the bougainvillea creeping up the walls and cascading from the trees, and you remembered us, and it seems to you now a dream, improbable, impossible, not to be renewed and lived, any more than dreams are. If this is so, my beloved, I can understand it, I promise you. Only tell me; only tell me. Hope is so new to me and so rare, please do not let me live in hope mistakenly. If now we seem a dream, then my dearest please only write me to say goodbye. For I could not bear to go on, letting the hope grow until it fills my life, and then have it wither. I always must know what is truth; it is the only way I can live. And I would understand: it happened very suddenly and quickly; behind you, you have a settled, sound pattern of life. I would understand that you could find no room for me; but I must know so that I can arrange myself to live, without waiting in such passion for the future. Then I would have to change how I was and felt; and take my nourishment from those fifty hours past. And I know I would be grateful, David; and manage somehow. It is really better to have known what there was to know, once, however briefly, than never to have known. Not right away; right away it would be almost too hard. But I know now that I won't die, mystified, thinking there was a secret I never learned, thinking there was something very strange and ugly about me because I, alone, could never find what I was looking for. I have found it; it is not in my power to do more than recognize this. I cannot make anything happen. I can only live and wait, if you want me; or live and not wait, but cherish and remember, if you do not want me.

I have thought of you so much that my mind is tired and blurred; but there was not a look, a word, a gesture that was wrong in that time; I had to make no explanations to myself, no excuses to account for even a momentary failure; I was not lonely. What else is there to know? I am very ignorant about love, very new to it; I do not even know what one must know, I have no way of comparing; I have no one to ask.

I have gone over all my past very carefully, to try to trick myself. I do not want to lie to you or me, and I have gone over it, as best I can, trying to see whether possibly I ever felt this way before and have forgotten. I am going to write it all down, more for myself than you, because perhaps there will only be one letter from you, the one which wakes from a dream and says goodbye, and then I would never send this.

You see, David, I never made up my mind; it was made up for me. So of course, I could never have been sure; only I did not know enough (until you came) to know this was wrong, this was the germ of wrongness in everything. I am sure of this because I am such a writer, and have been writing all my life, notes to myself, diaries, letters unmailed; I have been talking to myself on paper since I was a child. And there are records; there are notes of all the beginnings.

. . . [After Bertrand] I was alone then for almost two years; first working for Harry Hopkins, then writing that book, a part of which Mrs. Roosevelt showed you, then back in Europe, working and studying in the Weltkriegsbibliotek in Stuttgart. I moved steadily; I was everywhere in America, and then roaming about Europe. There were men. I think I must have been pretty or had something men wanted, because I never did learn how to be a flirt (early training being against); I never knew how to 'get men', and after the six years in Paris I had a sort of revulsion against appearances so I was very careless of clothes. I thought, with horror, that I must give off a smell of a fallen woman, or something of the sort, or why would men, so many men, reach out for me when I did not reach out for them. No one reached out for me, really, not for what I was or wanted to become; but grabbed for my body, or that was how I saw it. I cannot quite explain this time. I was lonely, that of course. I also loved gayety (everyone in France was always old, no one laughed, no one danced, no one moved on whim as I did; and in America the men were my own age, and strong and gay too, and drank too much perhaps, but anyhow liked suddenly to drive all night to Atlantic City and swim forever in the dark and laugh and eat hamburgers and drive back to an office.) So some men gave me that, company, laughter, movement, the sense that life was an open road and you could run very fast on it; and then they wanted me. And then, I think, I paid my debts. I returned quid pro quo; I had had my pleasure, now they had a right to theirs. It was also never any good. The only part I ever liked was arms around me and an illusion of tenderness. But I could not make much illusions, and arms didn't last; and the rest happened to someone else (it always was painful).

. . . I think Ernest was something I deserved; because I made no judgement of him in relation to me but only in relation to the world. In Spain, the judgement was high and admiring, and with reason. After that, I could never escape; I was in too deep; and perhaps a little like you and N. – because his wife then started, with her friends, a campaign of fearfulness against me, horrid lies, beastly insinuations, and that made me very angry. But also perhaps there was always a bad weak point in everything: I did tend to collect kings. Bertrand was a king of his time and place and kind (although I only knew this later, slowly, I had not known anything about him or how one could be a king, when that started. I did not know enough about snobbery when I was 20 to know the value of a name; but France taught me that, fast.) Ernest had always been a king in my mind, for his writing; and surely was – as anyone could see – in other people's eyes. I grew to hate that part of his life, with a really sick hatred, and I would never take it for myself.

. . . Mother said to me once, 'When you were very young, what interested you was France, and you found or were found by the most complete Frenchman available. Then you were interested in writing, so you found or were found by what you thought the finest writer. In the war, finally, you were interested in bravery and you found or were found by who was considered perhaps the bravest of all. But someday you will find a man, and not someone who represents something.' More or less accurately remembered and reported; and it was a kind way of putting it.

This is terribly long, even for me, even for me to think, write and read. But it is doing something very good and clarifying for me. I cannot see that ever (and to tell you the shocking and unpalatable truth, David, I do not even know how many men there have been in my life) I myself <u>knew</u>, I never decided, things happened, I drifted, I got in deeper and deeper, and something like love, some odd angle of love, came along spasmodically, to make a relationship bearable or to keep it going. I loved <u>something</u> about them, sometimes; and that apparently was all I imagined one could get. And I was always lonely, always. I can remember sobbing that out, to both Bertrand and Ernest, before we were finished, in helpless final despair; I think both of them were repelled or irritated.

This account sickens me, so I must go on with it. It sickens me because it is such a pure record of waste. What was I doing with my life? Why didn't I have it all more in hand? I think of course I must have been living <u>outside</u> myself; the whole world was my garden, what happened to others, masses of others, strangers, was what moved me. I worked a lot, six books and hundreds of articles, trunks of stories, notes, poems; I moved so far and so fast that perhaps just the moving took up most of my energy. But still, that does not quite explain why my own life was so disordered and futile and casual. It never seemed to affect me much; because it never changed me (until Ernest; and the changes he made are evidently not final, because there is you and I can feel honorably and entirely for a man). It should have showed on my face, or in my manner, or somewhere; but presumably it didn't. I suppose I did not even pay enough attention to it, to be marked. It is incomprehensible.

. . . There is very little more to this document and there is never time. I feel I have lived, in the last few weeks, a whole exhausting life, and am washed up on the shore, panting like a fish. The weather can be blamed somewhat; you will see; it is airless; one feels sucked dry. And more than that, really my body is in poor shape; too many cigarettes, not enough sleep; so that sometimes I have to move and speak very carefully or I will start shouting at people, at the foolish hurried days. I am in terror lest you will find me as I now feel (what I hope is that, seeing you, I will not feel this way and it will fall from me): ugly, driven, tired, and somehow uncollected. I could not go on being so desperate about you; so I had to put you farther away in my mind, as if you had happened long ago and would happen again sometime far hence. I had to make a wall of time around you, or wear myself out with emotion which had no place to go. We must learn to live with love as a joy, which we have both said, and not as if we were being driven mad and starving to death. We have both got to learn how to live in love.

And now I will finish this long story: because that is a habit, one finishes writing what one has started . . .

In three years I have been away from here 11 months; but in all that time, here and in Europe, I have actually conceded to the nervous needs of the body, or the depression of the mind (it was either or both) exactly nine times. I tallied it up, so I could tell you. Out of 1124 nights, it is a pretty good record; I wish it were perfect. I wish I had been stronger still, but that was as much as I could manage. And I hated myself and did not enjoy anything but it was somehow like taking a big dose of sleeping pills after you have battled insomnia for some time. It was almost medical.

So for three years, you see, I had given up one sort of hope: I did not think there was a man for me, or perhaps that I was not meant for any man, and I had decided that was the way it was going to be, and since life is not perfect, one must be grateful for all the good things one has and not weep if something profound is lacking. I worked it out, and generally I managed; I functioned anyhow, and I do not think I was a weight on anyone. And if I got too sad or too lonely, then I read some more or walked farther and went to sleep, knowing that I would wake up and start my life over again and do it as well as I could.

. . . Then you came; and this, this mountain of experience which has not been experience, and failure and finally the rejection of failure, is what you found: looking quite normal and respectable in a cotton dress . . . I cannot see how it will end. I know nothing. I think it depends more on you than on me. I do not think I have it in me anymore to struggle and fight and suffer; I want to be quiet and happy.

. . . Like you, looking at pretty girls, I have always looked at men. Not undressing them in my mind like the New Yorker cartoons, nor wanting to go to bed with them; but wanting them to be there, walking around the world, wishing that there should be real men alive in it, straight, tall men, with good faces who looked as if they knew where they were going and were glad on the way, not the bowed, the harried, the prideless, the mean. I always loved London because the men were handsomer there and seemed delighted with themselves, with the act of being men. But now, I am only looking for you.

I did not tell you this last book of Ernest's was good prose; it is appalling. I hate to be in that book specially because it is so disgustingly written. I think it is filth, all of it; and the picture of a maniac. But he had grown more and more a maniac; I left him absolutely when I saw that, and knew he wished it so. I do not even think *For Whom The Bell Tolls*, dedicated to me, written on top of my slavery, is good. But the stories and the early novels are a discovery in the use of words. I hated his toughness, because I know it for what it is; the brave do not have to be cruel, the brave can be gentle. The toughness is a pose to get away with being nasty, and ungenerous (it allows you to mock everyone and everything). In Spain, he was not tough; he was kind. He was never kind to me, even there, because I was the woman he wanted which meant the woman he intended absolutely to own, crush, eat alive. But he was good to soldiers, to poor people. For a very short time, he tried to live up to the image I had made of him; the image I have to have, since I cannot love without admiring. Then that tired him, and it all fell apart. I would not have left him, because I believed those words one says, if I had only been unhappy. I left him because he became contemptible, apart from me; and I could not stop him nor protect anyone and I despised him. I beg you to understand this. Ernest had a theory that brutality was all women understood; if they seemed recalcitrant (like me) they only needed to be beaten more. You must never never do this; all my terror is centered in just that. I have been, myself, really neurotic about it so that I could hardly stand to be close to anyone for fear of the slightest <u>intentional</u> hurt. It was, until you came, like a shellshock of the soul and I thought I would never get over it. I was afraid to try to get over it, lest something happen and I start really to bleed again. I had honestly thought that Ernest would drive me mad with cruelty; and since he didn't, I thought first that I had become inhuman because I had to be inhuman to survive, and afterwards I knew I had become a coward, I could never again take a chance. David, I beg you to remember this always. If you are angry with me or disappointed or I do things wrong, you can tell me (Mother does); if I hurt you, you must know it is by mistake, through lack of sensitivity, or ignorance, but I will never hurt you on purpose, and you must tell me, cry out, warn me. I have been ridden with a harder bit than anyone can stand; and now, if the reins are pulled, I go crazy and bolt. I know this is so because it has happened; it happens even in casual relationships; suddenly I am no longer there for I feel, like sickness, a beginning, an intention of cruelty. It is asking a great deal of you because I do not know myself and I do not know what I do, nor how I am cruel; but if you tell me, then I will know, and change.

You said E. was a king in something; and you are a king in nothing. Darling, listen. You and I, we are the same kind of people. I reject the notion of my being a queen. I know, I think I have always known, that I was one of a kind; in a profound sense, and always with pride, I have been and am a displaced person. There were any number of worlds, ready and waiting; I had only to go in and sit down. And I never could. The English are my easiest friends because they have all life taped; they take you as you are and find a name for you; they consider me, in their own words, a 'gay eccentric.' They left me alone and welcomed me; but I have never belonged except with individuals, at given moments, in certain places, for certain states of emotion and mind. I feel you are the same. I do not expect to belong and I had given up expecting to belong with one, which was the most I ever hoped for. I expect to move wherever I like, easily, watching, laughing, loving, raging; but I always came home to loneliness and accepted it. Now I do not accept it for you are there. And I am sure this is the same for you. I know this absolutely. I was born with perfectly good roots, and I have none; it is not an accident that you have none either. We can, either of us, live anywhere and (this is shameful pride but there is no use faking modesty) more people have loved us than we have been able to love. I have been able to live alone because it is only making literally true what is really true. When I left London this time, Ann Rothermere*, in whose house I was living, gave a farewell dinner party and invited my fourteen closest friends. I felt so lonely I thought I would scream; I behaved so badly that I am still ashamed and embarrassed, I had a real fierce *crise de nerfs*, there on the spot. I was out of my wits because here they were reunited because they had me in common, all acting as if my going away was like dying, all giving me advice, all begging me not to be a fool and hide myself in Mexico when I belonged there with them, all offering me love, shelter, homes, anything.

---

*Ann Rothermere, wife of Lord Rothermere, proprietor of the *Daily Mail*, later married to Ian Fleming. She was a renowned hostess.

And I felt so apart and so far away from them that I was in terror; because if they were not my home, my world, then what was?

. . . No, I did not know you were a Jew and I dismiss it in this sense: to me, that term is only valid as the term Catholic, Mohammedan, is valid. It is a religion; if one believes it and practices it, one has the right to take its name. Racially, as blood, I have always thought it the most miserable nonsense. I do not believe in categories: people are always foolishly talking about 'the French', 'the English', as if all of them were a unit, feeling and behaving alike. This is clearly the sloppiest thinking; people are if nothing else unlike, each one a secret. External conditions evidently form people; if one is born in an English country house and goes smoothly to Eton, one will react differently to life than if one was born in the Warsaw Ghetto and escaped to the forest, via the sewers. But that has nothing to do with the internal core of the individual; this is what life does to the individual.

. . . My hair is curious. If it were not on me, I think I would be quite pretty. But it has very little to do with me. I will try to get a snapshot but maybe will not have the courage to send it. It would be too awful if you hated me with short hair, as there is also that other part, that very vital part about you feeling randy. (I must look up the word.) And I think I am very randy, David. You don't know what a surprise it is to me. You must explain it all to me; you must explain everything. I lie in bed at night and think about you and think about how you were there two nights and I cannot sleep at all and get a sort of pain or ache inside, in my privates. What is it? I hope it is not queer. I know nothing, David, nothing; I feel a fool to know so little because there have been many men. Eduardo, who is a strange lecherous old man, has been brooding about me for three years. About two weeks ago, he finally discovered what he was looking for and he said to me: the secret about you is that you are a virgin. I roared with laughter, and pointed out to him that this was hardly possible. And he was very impatient and said, 'They mean nothing. No man has ever had you; you have never had a man. Everything that is wrong and strange about you is from being a virgin.' (It was his intention to correct this sorry state of affairs.) I thought about it, later, and decided he was right and I felt terribly about it; I would never have admitted it to anyone. But I don't think I am a virgin any more. Only of course one can't go from 22 years of virginity into being an accomplished lover, just like that, all of a sudden. I am so afraid I won't be exciting enough for you, or knowledgeable. Maybe there is something I could read? I have no idea how to give you pleasure, but only to receive it. And from all the talk I have heard from the boys I know very well that some women are considered 'wonderful in bed.' It is their great charm or strength. I want to be, for you, but how do I go about it? All I ever did, really, was sit about and men made decisions about me; it is not a good training. I want to be everything; I want you to love me so much that there will just be us, as man and woman, in the whole world.

. . . David, have I neglected to say that I love you or have you seen it in every word, every comma? And David, if it is not bad for you in any way, please come back to me as soon as you can. And if it's a weekend, we will treat it as if it were a year and live in every moment of it, not looking ahead or back.

Entirely yours
Martha

To: William Walton

April 5 1950
[Cuernavaca]

Darling; This letter is secret, equals U.S. Topsecret. Really. I count on you. Something unbelievable has happened. I have fallen in love. I know so little about all this, due to my failed and sheltered life, that I am bewildered, rather frightened, very wobbly. He says he loves me; I do not see how he possibly can in the same proportions. Maybe he will change or forget. It all happened so fast, on sight really; suddenly he arrived with a wife and two days later we were alone. We had fifty hours. Now four days later I am able to eat again, and sleep via Secconal, but am somewhat blemished by a fever blister and the interior sense of being at once elated and in despair. He is not here; lives in N.Y., where he works, hard. He is a Russian. I had not, until this minute, realised how funny and suitable that is. A pre-1914 non-political Russian, but Russian anyhow. It is different from everything else because, instantly, I trusted him and could say anything and know he knew what I meant; and whatever he said I understood as if I had always known him. I did not have to make any excuses to myself for anything; with Jimmy, I was always explaining things away, and telling myself the fine and good things to make up for the loneliness and the starvation of where the minds would never meet. I would marry this man tomorrow if he could, or wanted to. And in a general way, as you know, I am irrevocably opposed to marrying anyone. I do not see how he could possibly feel all this as I do, and I may be arranging for myself an intolerable degree of heartbreak but there is nothing I can do about it, except live it all through, waiting and hoping . . . I do not know if you would like him, I do not know if anyone I love would. I know nothing about him except his name, which I remember how to spell after some thought, and whatever it is that counts between people, but none of the things one usually knows.

I cannot get over my amazement and joy. I thought I would never feel this way in my life; I thought I had wasted or missed all my chances and

that, besides, I would never really get over the nightmare of E., and the fear
and mistrust it left.

Love always

M

To: David Gurewitsch

April 28 1950

Avenida del Parque 14

Cuernavaca

Beloved; I love you so much, so much, that I can hardly stand it. I am NOT
frantic or doubting or hysterical or anything that I was before, in the awful
first separation; but just wanting you, just missing you every minute. What
worries me: Can it be possible to go on feeling anything this strong; would
it fritter away and become routine in ordinary life; would it become no
more than a pleasant habit? I don't know; I cannot tell; I know nothing;
you know much more about living together than I do. And then: if one
does feel so strongly, how CAN one do ordinary life? I am like tight strung
wires all the time; concentrated only on you, unable to concentrate on
anything else; almost unable to take rest, which is not concentration, but
just spreading, loosening, drifting. . . . And then what? Wouldn't one
explode? I simply don't see how one handles an emotion like this. I am very
afraid of it, while at the same time I clutch it to me and need it desperately
and only want it. Do you find this is neurotic?

It is absurd to turn into a clinging little woman at my advanced age, and
with my kind of past: but there it is. Do you hate it? Do you feel already
that you have a sort of huge human barnacle growing on you? Oh tell me,
tell me.

Now there has been a lapse of two hours while Robert Rossen who
makes films and is now hounded and ruined by the Un-American
Committee and Lenny [Bernstein], came for drinks. I have had three
highballs and am a little drunk which means that everything is heightened,
not deformed . . . Dearest, my David: I realise I am a very special kind of
snob. No external badges work with me; I am really not impressed by what
people wear as their identification. The Duchess of Kent strikes me as
grotesque and tedious: Gary Cooper is my idea of a fairly good hearted
boob and a man to avoid with care: I thought the President (how one says
that, as if FDR were the only one) a genius in his field, and I was never
taken in. But I am a snob anyhow. Only my standards are my own: and they
are based on some curious instinctive requirement of aristocracy, nothing
to do with labels. I am not sure if I could define what my aristocracy is but
it would certainly have something to do with the body. Then it would

encompass a <u>shape</u> of mind, a way the mind worked. Then it would move on and make demands and judgements about the soul. You will see that this is the most arrant conceit: who am I to set such standards; and who am I to feel that these standards must be met, and that I belong within them. But there it is: and I always feel lonely, although others do not feel lonely with me, except when I am with what I consider my own kind. . . . And also, after talking too much, too well, too honestly, with those who are actually strangers to me, I feel ashamed: and they feel delighted and falsely (because I have been false) believe they belong. This is a bad décalage in the personality: and I have never written this down, because I am actually appalled by my own arrogance. Lenny, being intuitive and clever, knows it: he says that he identifies himself with people and needs to please them. But I, says Lenny, do not identify myself and have some mysterious inner scale of élite, and do not give a damn whether I please or not because mostly, I do not care about the people, and do not feel the same, not identified at all, but apart and gladly apart. . . . How vague and diffuse this is; how boastful; perhaps what a sign of uncertainty. I don't know. I never want to lie but I have never really examined my bases of life enough to know what they mean: they are there, I operate on them. They take funny external forms: I cannot curtsey, for instance (this is a ten cent store drama which used to take place often in Europe when there were de-throned kings and queens all over the lot) – I cannot, physically, curtsey: yet I could curtsey very easily to Einstein, if that were the form, and with joy to many of the dead, it would give me enormous pleasure to curtsey to Tolstoi, to Flaubert, but something inside me refuses absolutely the notion that anyone is superior, without having proved it, by virtue only of a label. . . . How I ramble on: it is scotch whiskey no doubt. But it is to say, basically, that a great involved complicated snob, like me, is entirely satisfied, in every aspect of her snobbery, by you: nothing you do displeases all those delicate antennae of perception and judgement. And I have suffered in my unanalyzed snobbery, terribly, before: I used to sweat with shame for actions, words, attitudes, of Ernest. I used to wish, in a passion of disloyalty, that I could shout: I am not like this, I do not agree, I am not responsible for this. It was a very great effort to be loyal, against those internal clamorings. And now there is no problem. I am always delighted.

Dearest dearest dearest, do you feel too that although we have all the time in the world we can hardly afford 13 days apart?

I love you,

M

To: David Gurewitsch

April 29 1950
Avenida del Parque 14
Cuernavaca

My beloved; I have been lying in the dark for an hour and cannot sleep. I lie and say to myself, David, David, David.

. . . David, if I do not love you as I think I do, it will break my heart. But you know that, don't you? It will be the failure of me; it will prove to me that there is no one on earth for me and that I am not good enough to be a pair, to belong to a man. I think I love you terribly, I believe it; but way behind somewhere is a suspicion of myself: am I capable of love, am I capable of permanence; is there something unruly and solitary and perhaps even deadly in me, which does not fit with happiness and steadiness and joy? Is there some inborn panic which would make me run away even from what I want? I am not trying to worry or frighten you; I am as usual saying whatever comes into my mind. I have been alone so long, in fact always, that I can hardly credit this sense of not being alone: I adore it, I romp in it; I bathe in it and bless it; I would rather say 'I love you' than anything else I could say, and I mean it, and I dream of you and I miss you so much that it is not even sane or normal (you behave much better than I do). And a devil inside of me says, 'I do not trust you, Martha Gellhorn; what do you know about love; what do you know of its meaning and cost; what makes you think you are able to undertake anything so tremendous?' I wish I could trust myself as I trust you; I wish I could count on myself as I count on you. Will you not let me waver, or doubt, or stop; will you just tell me to shut up and come back to your arms where I belong and was always meant to be?

It is extraordinary to talk like this; and a proof of love, because I could so easily terrify you or turn you away from me. What man wants a woman who is unsure of herself? But I love you, you see that, and I must tell you everything so you will be warned against me; I want to protect you; and all the time all I want, really, with my body and my heart, is to have you there, like a beautiful rock against the tides of one's own mind. How abominably I write; I would kick myself if I ever produced such prose for public view. It is very hard to write what you call 'accomplished language' when everything inside you is in a state of joy, and fear and bewilderment.

And how does one sleep, when so desperately in need of sleep, and how does one stop thinking and say: I know. I have always known about Mother; I know about Sandy; but knowing about you baffles me because I feel so selfish – I want you for myself. I want them for nothing, I want them just to be alive and happy and let me look at them and hear them and know they live. But I am greedy about you; I am full of greeds. I want to touch you, I want to be reassured, I want to find peace in you, and excitement; I make demands on you all the time and I do not make demands on them. And love, I imagine, must be selfless; but I am not selfless. I can never see what I give to you, but only what I take from you.

You said you wanted me to tell you what you meant in my life. How can I? You are probably the first occasion I have ever had to feel like a woman. I have felt everything good as a daughter and a mother; but as a woman I have just started. You are probably giving me what a human being must have, as a human being (not necessarily as an artist, or even as a functioning member of society – more or less functioning): a center of gravity. I have not even thought of myself as a woman much before. Other people did that, but not me. I have never wanted to depend; I have never wanted to plan life with anyone; I have done nothing but fail, as a woman, because I never felt like one really. I know about vanity – the pleasure of attracting men and being admired, but that is quite different. I have consciously used what I suppose must be sex appeal (but what a cheap thing it is: all women have it) for vanity, from loneliness, from doubt, or simply to exert power. But this is the first time I can begin to imagine what women feel. I always thought, or felt, vaguely, that it didn't matter too much about men since there were always more men. They were expendable and easily replaced; and one did not need them, nor need any special one. I could always get on, by myself. I could live. Now I am beginning to understand what it is when that is not true: there is one man, the man for you, the only one, and it is impossible to imagine getting on alone any more. But I am scared of that feeling, scared that some ancient brute will rise up in me and say: Nonsense, you don't need anyone, you were born alone and will die alone, and there is no path you cannot walk without leaning on a man . . . Oh do you see? Oh how badly I explain.

. . . But David, my darling, my darling, can you just hold me and teach me and keep me faithful to love?

Goodnight, I must sleep; and please you sleep and sleep, I am already sickened by the thought that between May 15, night, and June first, we will not be together.

M

To: Bernard Berenson*

May 31 1950
Avenida del Parque 14
Cuernavaca

Dear Mr B;

What can you see from the Prince de Galles, except across the street? Or do you get a high-up room and look over the city. I cannot remember. When I was a girl, in World War Two, both those hotels (the Georges V too) were the hang-out of the biggest set of punks and grafters possible, all very braided, non-fighting generals; usually in super echelons of quartermastery. I remember going to a few fiestas there, where it was hard to retain one's sense of self interest (needed a new tire or cigarettes or a piece of signed paper), and not make furious speeches about vulgarity and boredom. My dream has always been to be very rich, for perhaps two weeks, and get one of the huge front rooms at the Crillon where one could watch the Place de la Concorde. But then I love the Concorde as if I'd built it, due to rioting there in 1934, leaping in and out of dry fountains with the Garde Republicaine on horseback and scared into nastiness, and everyone shouting *à bas* something, and I very unclear as to who Monsieur Stavisky† might be. Oh dear, I did have a lovely youth; all riots and strikes and wars, and a wonderful lightness owing to not expecting to last and having no one to support and being very vague about supporting myself, since croissants and café crème were so filling.

If I trusted you which I don't (and what claim would I have on your trustworthiness) it would be pleasant to write you enormous self-revealing documents; on the other hand, I know that self-revealing trick and see it for what it is, the most appalling lying flirtatious salesmanship. So I've kind of given it up, and besides it is doubly bad because one lies to oneself in the process. As for you, I have a big curiosity about you but know I will never learn anything. You are too *fabriqué*, too perfectly hand-tooled, and unlike most, you must be a man who knows his own secrets and therefore will certainly not tell them. So I guess that's how we'll stay; with the curiosities hanging.

But I feel surprised that you should decide, from one letter – written in temper, boredom, despair – that this is the wrong place for me, that I am

---

*Martha had met Bernard Berenson (1865–1959), the art historian and critic, while she was looking for a child to adopt in Italy. Berenson, known as B.B. to many of his friends, had settled at I Tatti in Settignano, outside Florence in 1911.

†Serge Alexandre Stavisky was a swindler associated with the municipal pawnshop of Bayonne which, in 1934, sold a huge quantity of worthless bonds, leading to riots and the fall of the Daladier government. Stavisky was found dead, in mysterious circumstances, in Chamonix.

an 'American uptodater' (hideous invention, that word), and that I should pull for the shore. What shore do you suggest? What shores are there? The one country I can find no *querencia* in is my own; there is no American way of life that I ever saw which I wish to share and no place where I feel so ungainly, as if I were eight feet tall and always walked backwards. I don't like it, in short. And Europe isn't right just now; I can't make much out of the present and am bewildered or blinded by too many memories, so I feel there like a ghost who died young, but a ghost anyhow. This is all right for me; no place is perfect obviously. On a low incompetent level, I am in search of my education like Henry Adams. Only I think it useless to pursue same from Chartres to the Rocky Mountains, from London to the South Seas; I've already been there and if I learned anything I never took time to find out. It seems to me best to sit very still and wait and pray.

Do you really know, even you, who your own kind are; and what is your clime?

Have a lovely time in Paris; hateful city to live in and the best to look at, I think.

Always

Martha

To: David Gurewitsch

June 24 1950
[Avenida del Parque 14
Cuernavaca]

Darling

... I am reading Peter Moen's Diary, the diary of a 42 year old Norwegian Insurance salesman, caught by the Gestapo, beaten, put in solitary, and picking out his words with a pin on toilet paper, from the need to communicate with someone, himself in this case, or leave a record which is always man's need. It is very ordinary, ordinarily written I mean, and terribly moving. The human heart never fails to astonish me, it is only a bore when it's all hidden or gives its answers like a gramophone or a parrot. And by accident I find myself reading books, at once, about Shaw and Wells; very large luminous often loud personalities, but neither of them of the first order, I think, as people or writers. The two don't often go together; and a writer's first job is to be a writer. Of the two, I think Wells the more important. What interests me most in these books is the quality of hero-worship in the biographers; it is quite different from love, admiration, tenderness, it is a childish quality, with judgement suspended – except for superficial, show-off, snappish little judgements which only makes the writers seem like ants writing about what they can see of men's feet.

Do you think I will ever write again? I think I will manage, until I die, always to have a previous engagement. I seem vowed to a struggle to fill my time so that I cannot do the only thing I want to do or was meant to do.

Sandy fell down some steps yesterday on to his face; I was terrified and behaved very calmly (such good training in fear and how to behave with it) and actually he only cut his lip inside and out, nothing. I must get used to all this too; much harder to be a mother, so easy to be careless of oneself.

Darling, a tentative kiss

M

To: David Gurewitsch

June 24 midnight 1950
Avenida del Parque 14
Cuernavaca

Do you remember when we first met that I told you you were stronger than I, and I was glad of this. You said you felt it too, felt it with me; with Nemone you felt crushed. (This puzzled me at the time and puzzles me now; I wonder if you know what you mean by it?) I think I have always been looking for a man 'stronger' than I; a psychiatrist would at once trace this to my father, I am in search of my father who shall not only sustain me but approve of me. It is so damned easy, this kind of analyzing stuff, and once it is done, where are you? The fact remains, I have looked for that man . . . And I know this search comes from my own weakness, but I am not ashamed of it; I have been made to be, first by myself, then by circumstances created by myself, stronger than I want to be, stronger than I feel I actually am; and I long to rely, to rest, to renounce some of my power to someone else. Then I gave up that search which had gone on for some time, gave it up as hopeless. For, in my intolerant way, my ignorant way, the man had to be stronger than I in my own fields, stronger than my kind of strength: there are as many strengths as weaknesses, but he could not excel in his own, he had to top mine so that I should feel safe. I began to understand this too, because I was able to recognize the different superiorities that many men have had to me, but at some crisis I felt myself not only abandoned, (exactly as if someone turned and ran from danger) but sustaining us both.

. . . In the two weeks, what appalled me most was the feeling that I had destroyed your strength, for the moment only I hope, and that this strength was exactly what I needed and turned to, so that it was like loving a beautiful face and throwing vitriol on it. And I had not only destroyed it, but done so at the very time when I needed it most. I felt then that somehow, although my own supply was gone, I had to lead us both (lead us where and to what, I don't know); that I had to be strong for two. And I know, of course, that I can't, not ever; I need what I have, like water in a desert; and can exchange it, but if I give it away, without return, then finally both perish, because there isn't enough to last. The images are terrible but you will see what I am saying. This also happened to me before, too often, I do not know why, unless I am a destructive human being; and I know or recognize my own emotions, which are first of all fatigue and then bitter resentment. I find myself alone, thinking: no one can help me or carry me; luckily I can walk by myself; but this is a very long journey and uphill, and the best I can do, since I am not really strong, is to give a helping hand from time to time, to someone I pass on the road – but the long walk has to be done by myself.

Think about this, David, for me.

I know that I have actually hated cowards, in war, with a real hatred; but if I had been easily and completely brave, I would have been able to feel sorry for them – instead I hated them because I feared them; cowardice is infectious, they could have contaminated me, they could have destroyed my willed, not natural courage. I have despised weakness in ordinary life, when I should have felt compassion and understanding; despised it because I have to fight against it and if I, weak, can fight against it why can't others, instead of crying and crawling for help? These are all absolute signs of cowardice and weakness and I know it; and I know that the determination and the effort to make oneself strong, or to live as if one were strong, can never be stopped. If I stopped, I would melt, and I do not know who I would be.

. . . I use the word strong as a symbol; it means so many things to me, almost more than I can list or describe but sometime I will have to try. But briefly, it probably means to me: walking one's own path, on one's own feet, using one's own eyes and mind and heart, despite one's own fear, to find one's own goal.

I am reading Spender's* Autobiography now, very well written, full of little discoveries, but he is nobody really, or rather an immensely talented nobody; he is scared, I think, to the marrow of his bones and always has been, and he is trying to cover his fear with handsome words.

Goodnight, darling, sleep well,

M

---

*Stephen Spender's autobiography, *World Within World*. Spender had been in Spain during the Civil War, and had been told by Harry Pollitt of the Communist Party to "get killed; we need a Byron in the movement."

To: David Gurewitsch

[?1950]

[Cuernavaca]

. . . Is anything happening in the world? I never see a paper – lucky you didn't mention my story to Pacciardi.★ It embarrasses him. He behaved much worse, much randier, than I wrote. And he was a handsome man then & great fun. And determined Italians are something serious to beat off, in no-man's land at night. He took me back to Madrid in his car – in the back seat – he kept trying to get me to put my hand on his privates which filled me with terror and horror. And he laughed merrily at me & all my scruples. So brave about rifle & machine gun fire, so frightened of sex! Very odd story. And then the one time I loved Ernest, really loved him, was because of Pacciardi. We met him in Valencia, in civilian clothes. The government had disbanded the International Brigades (to please that cheating non-intervention Committee) & cashiered them – carelessly, without thanks, or money, or papers or any future. And Pacciardi was going back to France – stateless & penniless; and his eyes were tragic; he was heartbroken, but he never said a word, not a complaint, not one objection. Ernest & I were going upstairs to the desk afterwards (as an air raid was on) to our room, & all of a sudden I heard Ernest, leaning against the wall, on the steps, and crying. I never saw him cry before or since. He was crying for Pacciardi, whom he'd hated as a rival, saying, 'They can't do it! They can't treat a brave man that way!' I really did love E. then & it had a long influence on me – it took him seven years to ruin finally that impression of instinctive generosity & compassion. So you see, Randolfo Pacciardi has lots of funny corners in my life – I saw him often in Rome, but a War Minister has to be discreet about blondes! I like his wife immensely. Il *la trompe à faire claquer les vitrines*. But she loves him.

And I love you. Oh God God when will you ever get back here I wonder? Maybe this next week (by a miracle) something final will be settled.

Goodnight my only one

M

★Randolfo Pacciardi (1899–1991), cofounder of Italia Libera, the movement of antifascist excombatants in Italy in the 1920s. Pacciardi became commander of the Garibaldi Brigade in the Spanish Civil War and Minister for War in Rome after WWII. Martha used him as a character in *The Heart of Another*.

To: David Gurewitsch

August 8 1950
[Cuernavaca]

Darling;

. . . Yes, we must be happy. It is ridiculous not to be, in whatever time remains for the world, and blessed as we are, so richly blessed. I must point out to you, my beloved clot, that I was really very happy until I met you, having solved my problems to date. My heart was fed by my child; my mind was fed by the beauty around me and by books; I had discovered a painless way to earn my living; I was not troubled that I did not really work. I was floating on quite a smooth sunlit sea, a bit sex-starved no doubt, but able to cope. I think the condition of happiness is to be <u>entire</u>, to be at home in one's skin, whatever one's skin is. I think, for me, the condition of happiness is to have life simple and very concentrated. Life is still simple but less concentrated, because part of me stays with you – therefore no place, in the sky, dispersed; I cannot imagine, now, any greater horror than having the man you love away at war, where you cannot follow, not even in thought; and living only in a state of <u>waiting</u>. In a much milder degree, I too wait. And I know it won't do in the long run; one cannot wait, one must live as one goes, however that living is. Luckily (from my point of view) no shape is fixed in life; the pattern can change without notice. But there is a present pattern, always, however impermanent, and one has to live that entirely. Not a piece of oneself here and a piece there.

. . . Sandy is thirty nine inches tall and weighs over 40 pounds, which is very good, isn't it for a chap who is three years and three months old? I hope he's going to be a very tall man, that being the kind I prefer. You didn't send me the promised picture of Grania. And of course you miss her; you must miss her terribly. There isn't anything so rooted in one's heart as a child, with imperishable roots. I think it would be extraordinary to have a daughter, I can't imagine it. My imagination doesn't go beyond three year old boys, thus far.

. . . I love you, David, as far as I know. It still isn't <u>comfortable</u> for me to love you. I guess I can't accept it, or agree to it entirely; I have been alone really most of my life, and I suppose I cling to that because it is so much easier. But whether I want to or not, I imagine I love you. Anyhow you are always in my mind.

A kiss or many,

M

To: David Gurewitsch

December 25 1950
Avenida del Parque 14
Cuernavaca

Dearest: It is Xmas Eve or rather Xmas morning – perhaps 1 a.m. We have had a perfect evening. We dined, Flavia, Mother and I, at the Lennys, and everyone looked very handsome and the turkey was delectable and Lenny was in top form and made us laugh until we cried (mascara all over the napkin) and then we sang Xmas carols and then we went off to Yiutepec, the little village where you and I have so often walked, on the road to Tepoztlan and there saw perhaps the loveliest ceremony I've seen in Mexico, or ever in a church. A procession formed in the churchyard, children dressed up, as angels, as virgins, as Wise Men, and there were men in the rare masks that village uses, and moved slowly through the night – such a night, with the stars close together and close over us and brilliant – singing, lighted by candles. Beautiful, beautiful; and everyone so happy and so happy with the night, the air, the smell of jasmine, the happiness of the Indians and the gay and loving way they celebrate this night.

Only me, only Miss Gellhorn, not so happy, I think . . . My dear David, I think you are going through, now, what I went through in June: a state of panic and horror. I understand it; I understand you better than I understood myself. I want so much to reassure you; you <u>must</u> not be afraid, there is nothing to fear. You do not have to worry about being in your house and not telling Grania; you need never tell Grania. You need never do anything, anything in this life, that you do not feel is right. You must not accept pressure from anyone ever, David; if only I could persuade you of that. No one can make a life, like a sandwich, the life being a thin strip crushed between conflicting pressures.

And about New York, David, truly I have come to the conclusion that it would be a fatal mistake for you to leave. It was a dream we had, for you had it too long ago; and a lovely reckless fine dream; but it won't work. It is not a thing you can ask of yourself; I do not ask it of you. There is also nothing good in sacrifices, nothing good at all. Except for saints, perhaps; but we are not saints; and sacrifice is surely not the way to earthly happiness.

You must stay there and work as you've always wanted to; you must take on the Blythedale Hospital in my opinion; you should work to the hilt and have all the joy of that and all the reward and all the certainty. And with my blessing and my complete understanding, too.

It seems to me we have given each other a great deal, something very rare that we never had before; we can still give each other much, but probably not all. We have our lives; they are formed; we are formed. It is a pity, but we are not twenty. We can be lovers as long as you like, as often as you like; and that can and should be a source of joy. (You remember: I believe in joy.) Love is based on fact, isn't it; we must recognize the facts which are that our lives are two and can run like parallel lines which meet in infinity, but they cannot be joined.

I am grateful to you for everything you have given me and I am immensely sad. But darling, I would rather be sad without you than sad with you, and I am afraid those are the only choices.

Please do nothing foolish and think nothing foolish, but go calmly and well about your life, managing it in your own way, guided by your own feelings and certainties. You are a free man, Davilita, and I take back my freedom. I hate to lose the dream of us, it was a wonderful dream; but it is somehow lost. We have not enough faith, either of us, to make it come true. So we must not muddle our way into disaster, but recognize our limitations and accept them – perhaps these limitations are strength in other ways – and love each other in peace, without trouble, or anguish, without plans, within the limits of time and space.

I love you David and you love me and I don't want that to wear out with misuse. It is our dreadful bad luck that we didn't meet fifteen years ago.
Goodnight darling,
                                                  Tinky

To: Eleanor Roosevelt

June 28 1951
c/o American Express
Rome

Dearest Mrs R.

I think everything seems harder than it really is, just now, because of being tired and harassed which is a silly way to feel. One of the things I find hardest to do is talk about David, basically because of a terror of bursting into tears. I do not feel that I am the size or shape of a woman who should burst into tears about anything ever. But I'm not bitter; I'm also too old for that and if that were my habit I'd have been bitter as vinegar long ago. I'm appallingly sad, in a way I have never been, which frightens me because it feels like a sickness. And I am running from that sadness as hard as I can, hoping a new place and a new life will cure it. I find no easy way into or out of emotions; I wish to God I had no emotions, being unequipped to handle them with detachment. I feel myself constantly and with real conviction that David and I would have been fatal to each other; we would have made impossible demands (or I certainly would have) because neither of us had inside the really satisfying food for the other. But this does not make the failure of hope any easier to bear. And it does not give me much courage and gayety for the future. Time heals all things, it is always said; I am an idiotically slow healer.

That's all. I'll never speak of this again. But I felt the silence between us and it saddened me even more.

. . . Thank you as always for everything, and for being you.

Love

Marty

Once it became clear that neither of them would or could take the steps that needed taking Martha and Gurewitsch parted. Many years later, Martha would say that she had at last understood why the "single greatest sex frenzy of my life turned into black ice: lack of tenderness." "I do not comfort you because I cannot," Martha wrote to him sadly. "I have nothing to give, just now, to anyone." Having decided it was over, she was impatient to move on; and with the end of the affair came an end to Mexico.

Sandy was now five. She thought briefly about moving to London, and contemplated France. Then she settled on Rome. She had several good friends in Italy from the months she had spent searching for Sandy: Sybille Bedford, now working on her first book, A Visit to Don Ottavio, *with whom she talked about writing as she never had with anyone before; Flavia Gherardesca, with the house at Bulgari; and the "middle-aged madcap set" of expatriates, presided over by Princess Margaret's friend, Judy Montagu, and Jenny Crosse, Robert Graves's journalist daughter, "both driven and aimless, introspective, somehow insatiable" as Martha noted critically. Through Flavia, she rented a corner of a house at La Storta on the outskirts of Rome. A collection of her short stories,* The Honeyed Peace, *had appeared and she was trying to get down to a new novel, while churning out "bilgers" for the* Saturday Evening Post *to keep herself and Sandy financially afloat.*

To: John Gunther

December 27 1951

Avenida del Parque 14

Cuernavaca

Dear John;

I have been meaning to write you for months, to thank you for your semi-annual letter; and now I want to thank you for your handsome Xmas card.

Also I want to ask you for the name of an agent who places articles, in advance; gets an assignment in short. I mean to go to the Middle East about the middle of February and to my horror Marty Sommers of the Satevepost (my last journalistic connection) tells me they are all full up on the Middle East. This scares me considerably as I depend basically on my annual journalistic jaunts and besides I need them for myself; have to see the world briefly but intensely once a year – and am then always delighted to return to this garden. I had in mind to do two pieces: one on how the rich live in those parts – Egypt or Syria; and one on how the poor Arab lives. I am interested because I have no idea how either live; all I ever see is weird political stuff, which is all situated in the clouds because of not knowing what the people look like, say, eat, where they live, what they earn etc. I want to go from Egypt to Turkey, maybe dashing in to Iran and Iraq too. Have you any idea whether there is such a thing as an agent to get assignments? I never had call to need one before, but surely do now. It is clear that if you stay out of New York (my only wish) you get very lost in the shuffle. But then we must eat so I can't afford being lost. Dearie, if you do know a name, please tell it to me.

What are your New Year's wishes? I've got only one. Peace on earth; a year at a time suits me, six months at a time is gratefully received. I cannot believe there will be a war because I can't believe in suicide, but I avoid reading the papers so as to hang on to my illusions.

Love,

Martha

To: The Van Mooks*

March 18 1952
Sint Maarten
Curacao

Darling Family Van Mook;
I am again on Dutch soil, the islands of Sint Maarten which I bet you didn't know you owned. Above my mosquito net hangs a photograph of the old Queen when she was a Victorian lass, very touching with her short frizzed hair and corsetted waist.

I found this island ten years ago while snooping about in a sail boat looking for submarines on behalf of *Collier's;* and always wanted to come back so here I am. Am resting my soul (rather battered) in this complete solitude and trying to write. I do write, hours every day, and I loathe increasingly each sentence as I make it, which is bad luck. I wish I were an easy, happy writer; but there it is. On the other hand, I only write half the day and the rest of the day I walk to deserted beaches and loll naked on the beach or in this clear lovely water. When I say deserted, I mean they ought to be; but two days ago, a huge yellow crab who conceitedly imagined I was making the mating call with my hand in the sand, jumped on me and

---

*Lieutenant Governor-General of the Dutch East Indies, whom she had met on her travels in the Far East in 1946.

nearly frightened me silly; and today a semi-colored gentleman emerged from a rock, as far as I could make out, while I was lying bare as a stone watching the sky, and I snatched my skimpy towel around me and he bowed and I bowed; but if this sort of thing continues I may have to dress.

The local Dutch are good as gold and heavy as lead; I cannot take them. Nor, I would imagine, can they take me. They treat me with great courtesy and hustle away, as if I had the evil eye. The ladies no doubt find my solitude and sleeveless clothes shocking; and perhaps the gents feel that only whores wear mascara and lipstick; or perhaps it is my alarming conversation.

Have you read *Julius Caesar* lately? I always think I cannot stand Shakespeare so every time I am going off the map, I haul him along to try over again; and this time I am bowled over by J.C. Think of that man having understood the whole danger, the whole feeling, of the dictator, when he did, such ages in time ago. I think it the most wonderful writing, so mysterious, so full of unresolved questions: for who, in the end, is right: Brutus or Antony or neither. Oh me, it has given me vast excitement for these last two days. That's another beauty of remote places; one has time for discoveries.

I am also greatly exercised about the problem of the soul, speaking as a complete non-religionist, that is to say one who cannot believe in the supernatural. But the soul concerns me; and I am beginning to wonder whether it is wise or useful to spend so much time searching for one's own. Who is profited by that tiring journey; and wouldn't it be better to be an optimistic boob, like most of mankind.

Well darlings, goodnight. I think of you often and I love you well,

Martha

To: Hortense Flexner

May 18 1952
Avenida del Parque 14
Cuernavaca

Teechie dearest; This is not the real dark night of the soul; I've had that one for 1952 and am through with it; this is only the winter of our discontent.

. . . Last night I was so broken down that I got enough nerve or resignation to re-read for the first time the sixty odd pages of my novel, written on the island . . . I was afraid to, and I am just as afraid now. I think I see what is wrong with it; I think I know how it should be made right; I am not sure however whether, making it right, it would be right anyhow. Do you understand?

. . . What worries me is: am I off on to something I can't do – on to something perhaps not worth doing? I think (note the permanent uncertainty) that my idea was to give a sort of mental picture of a woman – these words are terrible – to show the form and habits of a woman's mind, sketchily, as it developed over a period of say 30 years. The only reason for this prelude was to situate the later action, which is to be detailed and specific, against this woman's mind. The action itself, a love story, only has significance (I thought) if one knows for how long a time that mind was getting ready for it . . . Basically this story is all about the failure of communication between people; I am not talking of loneliness (a sporadic disease) or of aloneness (a permanent incurable condition) but simply of the fact that people – in this instance a man and woman – are impenetrable to each other, and very likely impenetrable to themselves, no matter how much they desire to communicate, no matter how articulate, honest, etc. they may be: there is a mysterious and final block, a secret, as if the mind itself worked involuntarily to close itself upon too close approach of an other mind. Again these words are appalling.

What I am trying to say is that my most repeated and certain observation about people is that they do not and cannot know one another; finally I believe it impossible to know oneself; the only one who can ever know is that false God, the novelist (let us say) and the more he is sure of knowing, the falser he is . . . I believe this impenetrability to be the real tragedy of life, the universal tragedy, and also the secret inside the secret; and that all personal human effort is expended trying for the impossible – to join, to be one, to know.

Anyhow, save this letter for me, will you? I can never write notes for myself but this is as close as I've been able to come to what I think I am about. And God knows how I am to do it. Between the dream and the performance stand those pedestrian sentences, and the terrible feeling of cliché and déja-vu, and a feeling of impotence.

Love always and until soon

Gellhorn

To: Sybille Bedford

August 19 1952

L'Olgiata

La Storta

Sybille dear creature;

. . . Today Sandy went into Sheila's* room and did his best to strangle her canary. We do not need Freud to explain that one. I tell you, the child psyche is a lot rarer than the adult one, being so close to simple passions like

---

*The nanny.

murder. He thought it was a goner, I imagine, and announced gleefully to Sheila, 'Your canary's dead.' Even Sheila caught it and came to me presently in tears, the poor wretched creature. I feel like beating Sandy's brains out as I am tired of a baby Hamlet around the home. Sheila is going to stick until Sept 15, at which time 'we will see.' But he has now decided he doesn't like anyone at all, including our friendly peaceful help. He also kicked the cook and maid today. As a result, I am going to Elba on Saturday for five days and expect to return to charred and smoking ruins.

No work. I feel very tired. I am interested in house beautifying which is an unconquerable itch with me. You'd think I'd have learned better, on my 12th permanent residence. I cannot resist it; and so now I mooch around buying odds and ends and re-arranging. It is going to be very pretty. But not very pleasant in case Sandy has some profound subconscious loathing of Italy – the memories of the womb – which will keep him in a state of boiling hatred from now on.

Don't answer this. I use the typewriter instead of visits or telephoning, neither of which are now feasible, but it is just running off at the mouth, do not notice it. Get on with your work which is what counts.

> Blessings,
> Martha

To: William Walton

> September 11 1952
> L'Olgiata
> La Storta

Darling Napoleon Slice; My telephone was at last installed today, one month in the country without same teaches a body to admire modern inventions. Anyhow it rang, for the first time, and it was Shim,★ Capa's partner, and he had Miss [Ingrid] Bergman in tow and they are coming here any minute to drink (my one bottle of scotch) and I know what will happen: tomorrow, after seeing Miss B. again, I will start on a much needed diet.

. . . Well, here there has been a long pause. They came and wanted eggs and cheese which of course we do not have, in the country one has (as in Mexico) the eggs of the day, nothing extra; besides it is the cook's first day and I did not want to frighten her; so I gave them whiskey and at ten, now, they have gone to eat elsewhere. I am not necessarily going to diet being

---

★Shim, or Chim, was the nickname given to David Seymour, the photographer who together with Capa and Cartier-Bresson founded Magnum, the photographic agency, in 1947.

not one whit bigger than Miss B; who is also taller than I am, would you believe it. She was very nice; easy and laughing; I have never found her glamorous, not being male; and surely not witty; but very nice and Shim is a darling, everyone's uncle. So I have had a pleasant dull evening and I am better than I used to be at this sort of thing; I do not try to force life where none is, nor bring light where all is cosy twilight.

The house would enchant you, I think; consider it as Italian George-town. It is tiny and roomy; all rooms very small, some panelled in wood, some with fireplaces; wood floors. The windows are large and look on to landscape; simple landscape, trees, a gravelled road, a curving yellow hill. Around us there is ever more and more land, farmed, squatted on by huge oyster white cattle with vast ornamental horns; and race horses. I am busying myself (exhausting myself) to bring into the house that odd something, which comes from a flower vase, a curtain, a print, a book, an ashtray, the set of a chair – charm, livability. I do not know why I care so much except that I am an egotist and a perfectionist. There will be even fewer people here than in Cuernavaca; I shall enjoy this alone. For myself, I live where I now am, in a wee cell with fireplace, bookcases, a day bed covered in cretonne, a solid oak table, a handsome small chest of drawers and another smaller one beside the day bed: my work room. Two doors shut me from the house, I have a bathroom next door. It is on the second floor, a dead end, there is nothing here but me and the attic. From my window I can see the children (shabby Renoir children) swinging on the swing I had put up, riding their small bikes over the green sward, and to the left a tiny domed honey colored church, where every Sunday the farm folk come, for their weekly and easy-going ritual. There is a kindergarten, ochre colored with clematis over it, and a bell; in due course the bell will toll and the farm children will plod up the hill (and Sandy will ride on his bike) and they will sit all morning in that cosy place, heated by a stove, and do God knows what. It is very good.

My love, William. Certainly no one makes me laugh as you do; in the end, that's my vice. I want to laugh more than anything.

Martha

To: William Walton

November 17 1952
L'Olgiata
La Storta

Dearest Brother in Eggheadery;

   . . . I have done two new short stories since being here, both huge, but the one finished yesterday is a novella, as long as for instance *The Old Man and the Sea.* That story, mine not his, was done in a total of ten days; I cannot believe it. All I did was race my fingers over the page, trying to keep up with it. I think it is completely successful which dazes me. The heroine is a middle upper class English lady called Moira; her lover is an Italian lawyer named Enrico Chiaretti, the key figure is a Hungarian pederast astrologer called Signor Kollonic; need I say more. It is a horror story and at points makes me laugh out loud, which is a novelty in my writing you will agree. I am <u>very</u> pleased. The book is a collection of short stories, eleven or thirteen of them, depending on whether I keep in or throw out two of which I am not entirely sure. It is called *The Honeyed Peace* for obvious reasons; just look around you. That is also the title of the first story which I love, an old one printed in 1948. I think it is a very good book; very alive. And now, as soon as I get it mailed off and do my Xmas shopping, I am going to start on a novel. As you can see, life in Italy is a veritable dynamo.

I see more of Mr. Berenson than seems to me reasonable; he claims that I treat him like a pickpocket (sic) and I have an awful feeling that I am storing him up for future use, in a story, though I do not yet see how or when. It can only be that. For others, I see few; do you remember Sybille Bedford. She has become my bosom companion (not literally of course); she is the best person to talk writing with that I have ever found; she loves going over, by the hour, words, effects, motives; she is such a help it isn't even true; has a fine literary education so one can listen to her; and I like her own work. She has written a travel book about Mexico which is as funny and as perceptive as anything I have ever seen.[*] It is that lovely English trick of being so cultivated – all their jokes come off on a vast underground structure of culture which I adore.

I miss you. Who are you in love with these days? Up to no good, I am sure. Whereas I am as chaste as Mother Hallahan.[†]

Love always,
M

To: Hortense Flexner

December [?] 1952
L'Olgiata
La Storta

. . . Life, I suppose, goes on in these parts but not in any way I find inspiring. Times are dark grey bordering on lousy. I think I will go to bed and thus terminate another uneventful day.

---

[*]*A Visit to Don Ottavio.*
[†]Margaret Hallahan (1803–1868), founder of the Dominican Congregation of St. Catherine of Sienna.

Oh Berenson. I don't like him, you see. I think he is an inexcusable sort of failure. He has a learned mind but it does not seem a mind to me; I never heard him on painting and he may be extraordinary but you know I doubt it. I doubt if one can be really profoundly extraordinary about art, unless one has a certain fire and richness inside. He hasn't; he is a little Tanagra man, spoiled all his life by smart second-rate people. He's not interesting nor inspiring; I always felt <u>less</u> of a human being after seeing him. Did I tell you that he said to me that no one had so attacked him in his life, except Gertrude Stein. I found that funny; this came after I had carefully explained to him that I didn't trust him and he wasn't my cup of tea. You can always bet on Miss Gellhorn; she was born to make friends and influence people. I think he ended by not liking me though God knows he tried hard enough to be bosom pals. Anyhow now he's gone and forgotten and I do not plan to see him again. In my life, there has been an amazingly quick turnover of folks and on the whole I only regret the ones who died young, without meaning to.

Yes, I must fall in love; I need this most of all; and your picture of the right man is no doubt the suitable picture. But none of it will happen. I grow stranger and more remote all the time; fixed in habits which I don't even like but which have the power of law. I am superior to a degree you cannot imagine, it is like some sort of horrid test and if people quail before my awfulness I let them go; they have to dig through layers of pomposity, impatience and dogma, the work is up to them. None of this corresponds to any feelings of mine, but is an accident, only that is how it is. And I seem to meet such unlikely men anyhow and to be through with them before they have stated their name, age and occupation. But my life is odd and queer and not right; it is unheard of to sit in a tower in the country, alone with a perfect child, writing, not really reading, not studying, not learning, not seeing anything, and numb with joylessness. It is sick and luckily I have neither money nor time to consult a psychiatrist (besides they don't have them here, just priests).

Love to you always

Gellhorn

To: Sybille Bedford

December 31 1952
[L'Olgiata
La Storta]

Sybille dear; I got your note this morning and it adds to the strength you have already given. And I am grateful.

It occurs to me that in my youth, grown-ups were always saying the most unseemly things to me to explain the nature of gratitude: that one could never return what one had been given; that one received and gave away, but the operation was never neat, tidy or mutual; and in a way, I suppose, (in my German moral way) I thought that was a sound reason for taking as little as possible, since one could not give back. I now find myself in that position with you, to a degree I do not remember; I take everything, I take greedily, with both hands, without consideration, sparing you nothing; I feed upon your help, your concern and understanding. In fact, I feed upon exactly nothing else. And I am unable to do anything for you; and it alarms me. I am afraid of draining you, of distracting you from your own work, of intruding in your life and swallowing hunks of it; I am afraid of being a vampire on your mind. You must not allow this; you must issue warnings and ultimatums. Because, you see, there is absolutely no sense in my being in Italy except this astounding, unexpected sense of having you to do my work with.

Today, the last day of the year when I solemnly make my annual moral and financial accounts (it is almost impossible to be as neat as I am), I want you to know what you mean to me, and also to know that I do not wish to be a heavy, leeching burden. If one cannot return to those for whom one feels gratitude, one can at least avoid killing them.

I have swum along, full of doubt and grinding out words, these last two days; I do not like what I am writing nor how I am writing it, but, driving home Monday night I saw, as if interior headlights were at work, the line and direction of the story for some four or five chapters ahead. I may lose that vision, probably will, but it was very exciting to have it. And now I am working on happiness; and it is damned hard to do; but I am helped because I remember Cuernavaca as my old German* remembered Tubingen, a small silent town dreaming in the sun, in another life. I find also, (and hope to God this keeps up) that I am going to be able to write about this love story; I have gotten out of it enough to be able to remember and to re-feel, and Sarah Kent† is in love, I think, really in love. If I can do only that, if only I can do that, I will feel that anguished year and that unhealing disappointment were worth living through. There are still days when I would blame God if I believed in Him, asking why people are taught only to lose, only to know what they have missed and bitterly lack.

Martha

---

*A German maid who worked for the Gellhorns while Martha was growing up.
†Heroine of Martha's novel *The Tallest Trees Have Tops*.

To: William Walton

March 28 1953
L'Olgiata
La Storta

Darling; I have just, as usual, renounced my morning's work in confusion of spirit. I spend hours and hours and hours, staring at one sentence; I lie awake at nights brooding on order. I am nigh nutty, truth to tell. Therefore I am going to Ravello tomorrow to join Capa for a few days while he snaps lovely pictures of a movie band – Miss Jones, Mr. Lorre, Mr Bogart et al – who are making a film which that daft little gnome Mr. Capote is writing.* This will hardly solve my insoluble literary difficulties but may stave off madness.

Yesterday, Sandy and I went to the Zoo. The Roman spring is going to everyone's head (as well it might after the hideous arctic winter) and it has sure done things to the animals. I watched two brown bears making love, and it gave me a turn; the male, with bored rather glazed eyes, mounted the female who snarled, roared and did her best to bite his head off. The bear's penis, in case you did not know, is tiny; the giraffe's which was also on exhibit, is absolutely terrifying. I have never, off hand, seen so many private parts displayed at once; it leads one to wonder what the Romans themselves are up to, in this aphrodisiac air.

Now the sky is clouding over; probably there will be snow in Ravello when I get there. God how I hate cold. I am a fool to live anywhere but in the pouring sun, since weather does matter to me more than anything else in life. Would you, when America becomes intolerable, like to join me in the Maldive Islands and be the modern Gauguin?

It does not really matter whether the General [Eisenhower] appoints Mrs. Harrison Williams† to Paris, or whether he sends the entire staff of Vogue to represent us at the Coronation. In these matters we only look ridiculous which is an old American prerogative. But you cannot kid me into thinking only stupidity is the matter with the U.S. You cannot calm me at all. I follow with horror the organized and growing and successful attack on the mind; the new American meaning for the adjective 'controversial' is enough to scare the hell out of anyone who remembers any recent history.

Mother arrives on April 9 which will be too lovely. I plan to take Ma on splendid jaunts around the countryside and also to find a summer house on Lake Garda. We then move, like the 19th century rich, with cook, nurse,

---

Beat the Devil, odd, quirky, cult film directed by John Huston and starring Humphrey Bogart, Gina Lollobrigida, and Peter Lorre. Truman Capote wrote a draft of the script.
†Famous American socialite and fashion icon of the 1940s.

playmate for Sandy, and no doubt icebox. One's life changes so much that one can hardly get used to it. But I think mine has taken its final shape and will never be much different. I shall live in varying states of isolation, writing and writing; I shall be an expatriate forever; I shall be an old maid; I shall always be running houses; I shall always be trying to get good weather and be complaining; I shall always have just not enough money to do what I want but exactly enough to live. I see it like that; scarcely exciting. If I were a first rate writer, I wouldn't mind a bit. What does depress me is this: it is so desperately hard and so obsessive and so lonely to write that, in return for all this work, one would like a little self satisfaction. And that is never going to come, for the simple reason that I do not deserve it. I cannot be a good enough writer. You see? I call it grim. But the future looks awfully clear to me.

As for a war, here we only hope the Americans will not start one; that the lunatic fringe will not win out. No one believes much that the Russians will; they have more sensible methods, more effective ones. Civil war, at most; but even that seems unnecessary. In Italy I am steadily surprised there are not more, rather than less, Communists: it does not matter in the least that Communism does not work, nor bring economic justice and happiness; hope in the unknown is always powerful if the known is dreadful. Were I a rich Italian, I would be worried to death; no amount of crash-helmeted police in jeeps would reassure me. The inequalities are too evident, too unfair, and too cruel. Even the stupidest Italians can see this is not the case in America; but stupidity (not the right word: greed, maybe) is great here too, if entirely different. Only the English are smart enough to know you have to give up something, to retain something. I have a feeling England is the stronghold of civilization. What do you think?

Myself, I wish I could write this novel. I have become the greatest ostrich alive. I am sick of this silly world. I don't want to know about suffering which I cannot change and I don't want to think of the willed evil which I despise. I just want to do my work, for no reason whatsoever except the doing of it, and have as much fun as I can, and look at all the lovely things (done by man) which are still standing . . . Yes, the Maldive Islands; you be Gauguin and I'll be a tropical Flaubert.

I love you. Write to me more. Tell me all. Do you think age has anything to do with one's fussiness? I keep thinking men have changed but doubtless it is me; and how do you find women? I know: they still have bodies and why ask too much?

A big big kiss,

M

To Sybille Bedford

[Spring] 1953
L'Olgiata
La Storta

Sybille dear

How are you? I am in bed allegedly with flu but really with Humour, Spleen, Melancholie; however since I have not got the Seven Year Itch and Dropsy, I mustn't complain, must I? The thing is I must have a change and go away, there is nothing like travel to resign me to the home.

. . . I am always making homes but I was never made for homelife. The certainty of the shape of the days drives me mad. I am reading Mme Bovary* & his description of her life in Tostes is almost more than I can bear to read, I feel each day in my nerves. But you know I don't think his writing as such is remarkable except for clarity, accuracy & economy. But why did he spend his time scanning and intoning and chanting his sentences since there is no music in them anywhere. Hard and clear, and the glory of it is his eye for detail (the Bovary's wedding being a Breughel miracle).

. . . I wish I were a young man, setting off for London with my clothes in a bandana tied to a stick, and my cat at my heels.

Life is not long at all, never long enough, but the days are very long indeed.

love
M

To: Adlai Stevenson†

[Spring 1953]
Via Pinciana 37
Roma

Dear Governor Stevenson;

I am going to write bits of conversations, as I remember them, facts, stories, repeated rumors and gossip: all the floating words that make an intellectual and emotional climate. You will be able to sort it out and of course you will be able to check my report against what people say in France, Germany and England. I am not dispassionate. Having spent my

---

Madame Bovary, Gustave Flaubert's best-known novel, provoked something of a scandal on its publication in 1857.
†Adlai Stevenson (1900–1965), governor of Illinois and close friend to Mrs. Roosevelt, had been Democratic candidate for president in 1952. He was defeated by Eisenhower and would be defeated again by him in 1956.

youth reporting on Fascism in Europe, I have a haunted sense of déjà vu, as I watch the ugly, pointless, witless process beginning at home and spreading back to Europe.

I think the effect of McCarthyism★ on anti-totalitarian Americans abroad is as important as the effect on Europeans; but this is arguable. The effect on Americans is classical. We saw these changes in personality and behavior overtaking European liberals in the early days of Fascism. Americans now practise caution and reserve when talking with other Americans whom they do not know; they feel extreme anxiety about future developments in America, coupled with a feeling of personal insecurity (having to do with one's papers and one's job.) And, as a new experience, they realise what it is to suffer from moral shame for one's country. There is adequate reason for all these unattractive emotions.

You know that there are already American refugees: these are people chiefly from the cinema and radio world, who have of course never been tried and convicted of anything; they have generally been named by someone as being Communist and cannot therefore get work in America. The number grows and Paris is their center, but sometimes they show up here. They stick very much together, are hostile and touchy with other Americans, evidently feeling that they are being martyrized early for all of us. This is exactly like the first German intellectual refugees, some Jews, some not, who appeared in France from Germany around 1933–35. The fact that such a being as an American refugee exists, alarms other Americans seriously.

. . . The main effect of this specially American exile – the flight from unemployment towards the hope of a job – is fear: there, but for the grace of my own obscurity, go I. For no one any longer imagines McCarthyism to be other than a general attack on the free mind. We remember so much, you see; and we remember that the European 'eggheads' had to be squashed, one way or another, first. Meantime it is considered very courageous to befriend the refugees, to take them into one's house or be seen . . . there is the praise for anyone who speaks up.

There are also the transients, passing Americans, who divide into three groups. The first group approves of McCarthy, the second group denies the importance of McCarthyism and says the whole subject is exaggerated in the press, the third group shows signs of shell-shock. The third group is apt

---

★In February 1950, the Junior Republican senator from Wisconsin, Joseph McCarthy (1909–57) alleged that he had the names of fifty-seven "card carrying" Communists in the State Department. McCarthyism, the practice of accusing individuals of belonging to communist organizations with little evidence created a sense of "red menace" and helped win the 1952 election for the Republicans. Stevenson had asked Martha to report on its repercussions in Italy.

to be the most alert and informed and includes people who have had previous experience with European or Oriental Fascism. We, the residents, see these travellers and they all leave their mark differently. Everyone coming from America now seems a stranger coming from a very strange land.

. . . Heaven forbid that I should lecture you, but I want to resume my impressions of what McCarthyism is doing to Americans abroad. They are learning suspicion of each other which is a hideous novelty in American relations; they are afraid of this unseen thing, denunciation; and because of their fear and disgust they are turning into different people. They grow to resemble those European liberals who were waiting for doom in the nineteen thirties. They know this themselves, they feel it with horror; and Europeans know it too.

. . . And now to the effect of McCarthyism on Europeans. Mrs. Roosevelt was speaking mildly in Athens when she said that she felt 'senator McCarthy has done great damage to my country.' Morally, our stock goes down every day; it is really to the credit of Europeans that they regard our toleration of McCarthyism with such contempt.

. . . Writing this to you, I have a feeling of hallucination. I remember the enormous moral credit we had in the world at the end of the war, and I think that capital has been recklessly thrown away. It seems to me that no amount of gift money is going to buy it back, and no amount of gift tanks; but that we will only regain and retain admiration (and with admiration, co-operation, one supposes) if we stop being so horribly frightened and rub out the signs of that fear from American life.

I know that intellectuals are a tiny minority all over the world, but I also know, with passion, that when that tiny minority ceases to be free to think, talk, work, move, believe, argue, disagree, protest, then all is lost. For it would seem that this minority, if it remains operative, is the guaranty against tyranny. Intellectuals are the first who must be silenced; they were silenced for a time all over Europe.

. . . Since there is no God who saves Americans especially from human folly, I don't believe that McCarthyism which is a power movement will stop unless it is fought. Then the point remains (and this is the one that baffles me): do the majority of Americans want to fight it? For intellectuals, who can gauge the danger, are never a unified fighting group: it is a tall order to ask them to protect themselves and the freedoms which all Americans must keep. I doubt if they can do it. Then who will?

. . . I was honored and flattered that you asked me to make these notes and I hope they will be of some use to you. But I think that Orwell and Kafka, in collaboration, are the only writers who could have done justice to this miserable story.

I was happy to see you and hear you. If ever there is any way I can be of service to you, I would be grateful if you would tell me.

Sincerely,

Martha Gellhorn

To: Bernard Berenson

July 27 1953
Hotel Excelsior
Dubrovnik
Jugoslavia

Dear B.B.

Everything looks too beautiful for me; I never saw such a place anywhere and I have not been so happy for years. Joy, which I thought was gone for good, has returned in flood tide; and accomplishes its own miracles. One feels so wonderfully well, one feels also *en beauté* which is almost as good as really being *en beauté*, one is given to courtesy and friendliness as a general rule, and this easily, not as an act of will (the way I grit my teeth in Rome and force myself not to blow up with irritation). I love these people; I imagine they are the same people you knew and Rebecca West knew and everyone has known; they have had too many regimes for the regimes to do anything much to their own quality. Beautiful, beautiful; the sea and the sun and this blessed pouring heat which I adore, and the long warm nights with the moon. I love the town so much that I would really like to spend all my time, when not in the sea, mooching around it; it will be very hard to work. I don't give a damn about work any more. Only about being happy.

Night before last I went, by full moon, on the ship to Kotor. You know it? Think of coming in, on an absolutely flat still sea, through those mountains, all silver in the moonlight, to the little city. I have new friends – the ship's officers (two young men, very good looking, very funny, and with what seems to be a native quality of absolute self reliance and pride and dignity), a taxi driver who was a marquis, and is a wonder without a word of self pity, and very good at his new metier; some women who are uncomplaining new poor, but they used to be the equivalent of the Volpi★ girls and one can hardly imagine the Volpi girls behaving with this good humor and compassion. I know one Communist, and like him too; he became a Communist when the Austrians put his father in jail, when he was

★The daughters of Count Giuseppe di Misurata (1877–1947), governor of Tripolitania and Mussolini's Minister of Finance.

a child; if all Communists were like him I cannot see what anyone would be excited about; he is, to my mind, exactly like my British Labor friends except he is really mainly interested in art and his children. And I am fascinated by them all; they tell me new things about the past and the present. I have recovered the power of seeing and hearing, which I thought were gone for good, worn away by boredom and the kitchen of life and a kind of contempt for most of what I heard and saw. This is all such happiness to me that I can hardly believe it; and my only anxiety is the thought of returning. I would love to do a book on this country but would need six months to travel and six months to read and think and where am I going to get the time?

. . . I probably will do no work, except to write a bilger for money as I want money now, so as to spend it, quick, on travelling. Travelling is the final joy of living, I think; the delight of surprise, the delight of glimpses into lives, the lightness and freedom, – I see no reason why, since the world is so large and one can never run out of it nor learn enough – why one can't travel almost steadily. But no, it would be wretched for Sandy and I must control myself.

When I was in Bled I heard that Mrs. Roosevelt was at Brioni so I wired her and she asked me to meet her at Lublijiana. With Mrs. Roosevelt, to my complete and shaken surprise, was an old friend of hers who had come to join her in Greece; he is the one man I was ever really in love with.* (Private and confidential, not to say top secret between us.) I have not seen him for a year and seven months, when I broke off what was planned to be marriage; and I could not marry him (nor anyone probably), but I never got over the feeling of loss. Not the loss of marrying, but the loss of a way of feeling; and it had ended sadly, bitterly, and that was terrible to bear. So we met and it was as if we had been separated for a few hours; it was pure joy and magic; and I fled, knowing I could not again start a life of loving someone at a distance and knowing I could never share his New York existence, that ugly slave life they all lead there. But it was an unexpected gift and some weight has left me; I did not imagine I would have this also, to be able to love someone, and go on loving, and not have him and be finally at peace with him and with the fact of separateness. It is going to be much easier to live. The sorrow of my life was the way Ernest shut all the doors on the past, made it hateful to me, would leave me no chance to keep the good memories; and I was afraid it was a sort of doom I carried round – a sort of forced emotional amnesia. But now the past can go on, as part of my living, and this man who probably will always have a magic no one else can have remains part of my mind and feelings. I write this very badly and perhaps you will not know what I am talking about. I feel as if I had

---

*David Gurewitsch.

been given time back, given back two years of my life which were rubbed out in misunderstandings. And given something to keep me company, a memory: things need not work (practically into the future), they must only go on living beautifully in the mind.

Always,

Martha

To: Bernard Berenson

August 9 1953
Dubrovnik

Dear B.B.

I am touched by your letters and by the appreciation you shower on me, but really I do not deserve it. I think my letters are very human stuff.

Evening melancholy. Do you suffer from it? It is of course only the product of fatigue, but there is no use being reasonable about it. I have spent three hours working on a bilger and feel morally exhausted. Three hours' work on good serious stuff leave one exhausted but elated; three hours on this *merde* leave one exhausted but sick. However, I should not complain, and if I do, I merit to be smitten down by God's angry hand. For surely it is the easiest way to earn a living that can be imagined; and if it ruins my good name, I cannot help it; and if it ruins my ear and my eye and my vocabulary, that will be my own fault.

I am sure you are right and I ought to give Rome *la ville* another try and perhaps I will. But from a sense of duty not a sense of joy. The fact is that one lives by the curious whims of the heart, which sometimes work and often change. And one of those whims, a powerful one, is the sense of instant sympathy with strangers. I feel it for these Slavs; I felt it for the Mexican Indians. I certainly do not feel it for Romans, and on the whole not for Italians. Which is sad and my loss; but there it is. I feel the violent reverse of it for Germans, and I feel it intensely for the English. These are either genuine irrational emotions, or prejudices; I wouldn't know which. But they guide and color life. So I return to Italy glumly; and will leave here with real regret.

Once you asked me why I left Mexico and I blubbered a bit. I invented a lot of good tangible reasons, all of them true and all of them invalid. In fact, I left because of that ruined and ruinaceous love affair; because my house had become a sort of mausoleum to me and the whole countryside was unbreathable for memories. For no other reason. I probably made a mistake; it was a moment for discipline and not for flighty despair. Yet I did no work there, during five years, except the essential drivel-writing to keep us eating. I was too well, too benign in the sun, too lazily contented, and

the days flowed like water and one could not hold on to any hour long
enough to turn it into work. Then the great problem arises: what should
one do with one's life, live it or work it. I don't know. I really only want
to live; and I think I am a writer because I have never never been able to
get enough living. And then of course, as I am inclined to forget, I always
did pay my way; and writing did it.

And why are there no men, B.B.? Can you tell me that? Why in heaven's
name can't they make them alive enough and brave enough and funny
enough and good enough to use up a woman's life? But there aren't. They
don't exist. And they seem paler to me every year, until I could weep with
despair, thinking how ghastly women will become in this world of
inadequate men. So, enough melancholy for one evening.

Always

Martha

To: Bernard Berenson

September 17 1953
[Rome]

Dearest B.B. I got a good letter forwarded from Dubrovnik and this
morning your letter in which you speak of my book. How does one get
confidence, B.B.? I am grateful for your letter and for your reassurance, and
I need it. But all these years I have been writing against myself, as it were,
and envying the writers who could give themselves importance and believe
in the value and necessity of their work. I only write because I have to, and
I don't have to steadily, but life frays and falls apart and the only way I can
make it seem real to me is to write. Then I do so. But I never have any time
of certainty, of self-belief, of feeling that it matters whether I write or polish
shoes. And of course I have very little success; it might be that outside
success would bolster up the feeble confidence inside me. Once I did have
a lot of success, when I was about 26, but I failed to notice it (so stupid) so
it didn't do me much good. Maybe if I'd kept my eyes open then and
noticed it and eaten it I would have formed the habit of self importance and
self confidence and then the whole business of work would be easier. You
see, it does take so long and it is so alone; and then finally it is finished and
published; and then what? Now, in my advanced years, I read reviews (I
have seen three) of this book,[*] where unknown people are in the delightful
position of snubbing one with sentences which really do not make much
sense. They, on the other hand, seem very sure and successful to me. So
someone says, 'All Miss Gellhorn's stories start with a climax and work very

---

[*] *The Honeyed Peace*, her collection of short stories.

seriously towards an anticlimax.' I don't know what it means, but it is certainly snubbing, isn't it? And then they always inform me that I am a good journalist, so finally I begin to believe these unknowns and wonder whether I am a teller of stories at all and whether I had better not change and start writing something else – but what, how, how? It is terrible to float like this, in one's work; terrible. And of course, I have never myself been satisfied at all; and it is not true that good writers are not satisfied. They are satisfied like billy-goats. I know, I've seen them. And being satisfied is what gives them courage and strength to go on. They <u>love</u> what they do; they really think it is better than what others do. I wish I could ever feel that, even only for a week. It might make me into a hardworking, undoubting writer.

Well, now I am doing nothing but run about like a headless chickie. Sandy cut his eye on Sunday; today is Thursday. He was perfect, as he always is, absolutely unexcited, uncomplaining, untheatrical; in fact he did not speak of it and I only realised what had happened on Monday morning when I saw his eye swimming with blood. The doctor, following the new fashionable system for brutality in medical men, said: *molti bambini perdono gli occhi cosi.** You can imagine, can't you, what Monday and Tuesday were like. Or you can't imagine because I could not have imagined; I never felt such fear before, I didn't know anything about fear until Monday and Tuesday. Now the doctor swears all is well and the eye will be healed by Saturday.

By the way, B.B. I wrote 'Venus Ascendant' last October, when I thought I loved Rome; it's a prophetic story isn't it? And you know, Italian men have a horrible way of being mass products, at least as I see them. But I do not think my men are ever much good. I wrote a war novel, only men really; and as if I were a man, being a man all the time in my mind. I have never known how that turned out. I do not like it, but that is not a judgement on whether the men are real or not. I think I know absolutely nothing about men, having spent my whole life with them, living their lives, doing their kind of work. I know something about women, although God knows how, because lately it seems to me I never <u>see</u> anything. It must be by osmosis. I never know how to get round men (which is what women do know and jolly well should know) and I never know what they are thinking except in relation to themselves: I mean I only understand a man when he has become an impersonal human being, trying to look at himself with the stern eyes of God, to see where and why he has behaved shabbily. But, qua men, I think I am doltish. If I like them, I magnify them until they are splendid giants (very uncomfortable for them); if I don't like them, I ignore them. But understand, study, observe, realise – never. So it follows that men in my books must be rather ghastly.

---

*Many children lose their eyes this way.

You know, it occurs to me that the answer to all this is that I am not only a Biedermeier Boche Romantic, born 150 years too late, but also that I am astride the sexes, having the mind (and tastes and instincts) of neither a man nor a woman, but a scrambled mixture of both; well, under those circumstances, it isn't odd, is it, that I find it rather difficult ever to get settled in life?

I will be sorry to go so far away from seeing you, and who knows what London will be like. Perhaps just another city.

Love,

Martha

In September 1953, Martha decided that she could not face another solitary winter at La Storta. She had finished a collection of stories, writing "at white heat" for eight hours a day, telling friends: "I am not living much; I am working. It turns out I cannot do both at once, and right now I must work." Just the same, in the evenings, she hurried into Rome in search of English companions, saying that she found no race more "dotty, hierarchical, demarcated and unabashed," while Italian women were too ladylike and Italian men "too old and brittle." It was to England that she now turned for their next home. Leaving Sandy with a nanny, she set off for London to see what it might offer. She returned to Rome only to pack up and collect Sandy. The Italian chapter of her life ended.

To Sybille Bedford

September 23 1953
20 Albert Hall Mansions,
London SW7

Dearest S.

It is <u>too</u> wonderful. I cannot think why. And I don't care not yet anyhow. Just love it, the friends, love the voices, love the hideous grimy city, love eating a huge lunch and <u>immediately</u> afterwards, a huge tea. Everyone makes me laugh. Also marvellous work ideas – immediately. You know I want a job now – not being alone. So a series (*Sunday Times*? *Observer*?) on juvenile crime; like Ruby.★ You see, back to my favourite kind of reporting. Virginia wants to write another comedy – maybe – but the feeling of bustling and belonging, at once . . . Everyone so nice. Can't tell you. One doesn't ever count the change. Taxis very ruinous but my only expense. And too excited to sleep. Being in the middle again. I love it. I imagine I'd got (after so many years) scarred and saddened by remoteness.

Only thing is: I do worry about Sandy. Please make the telephone calls,

---

★Character from *The Trouble I've Seen*.

with <u>detailed</u> questions about his eye. Also if he has sore throat or cold. If <u>anything</u>, make her go to doctor at once, please Sybille.

Blessings to all

love – M

To: Evelyn Gendal★

October [?] 1953

L'Olgiata

La Storta

Evelyn dear;

This is a little secret final letter between you and me which must absolutely be kept from that angel, that adorable sweet watch-baking angel, Sybille. I do not want to leave unless I am sure that you two would have no immediate financial disasters. I count on you naturally to let me know whether anything grave happened when I am not around, but meantime there could be anything, a brief sickness, a need to get to Paris, the necessity for more Queen Bee Juice, how can I foresee; and since Sybille is in the hands of monstrous crooks, as publishers, and since they manage to get her as little money as possible and always as late as possible, I am worried about the chance of a gap between money coming in (it will ALWAYS come in) and money going out. Just that: a gap. And she must not be anxious and harassed for tiny sums, while doing her work; it is vital that she finish her book as calmly and happily as possible. So I am sending you this little check which is only insurance against gaps, and you use it if and when you need it, and do not tell her please because she makes such a ghastly thing about money. When she gets an honorable publisher, when the recipes start being printed, there will be no gaps; but there just might be and I wouldn't be near at hand and no one would tell me about anything small. But the small things can ruin one's nerves and concentration, as I know with my whole heart.

I cannot ever thank you enough for your great generosity, which is that of the heart; for your sweetness and patience and kindness. And I wish I were Carnegie so I could endow Sybille with a chair (a big cosy chair requiring no work at all but allowing her a beautiful room with a view and all the time in the world.) She is a real writer, and there are few. And besides that, she is the most lovable human being imaginable. Take care of yourselves. And always keep me posted please; reports from the tiny room.

Blessings,

Martha

★The separated wife of the American writer and artist, Milton Gendal, who was now living with Sybille Bedford.

To: Bernard Berenson

October 26 1953
L'Olgiata
La Storta

Dearest B.B.

. . . My astrologer (cf. *Venus Ascendant* for life size portrait) told me that Saturn had been flopped over me like some sort of cosmic fried egg (or so I understand it) for months and months, thus 'blocking' me in every way, but Saturn rolled or dripped off, says he, on October 22. This is glorious news, so nice and comforting to know it was Saturn all the time and not me, and truth to tell I feel like a new woman without a lot of glum stars in the voisinage. I have come to the novel conclusion that people need a bit of success to buck them up, like sugar in the diet; and have therefore decided to get some. Also arrived at this age-old conclusion (a surprise to me) because of being rather annoyed by the American reviews of my book. Iris★ says she imagines they did not know what I was talking about, which is one way of looking at it. But I am bored by now with the condescension of my inferiors, those unknown word-haters who seem to write reviews, and have decided to do something about it. Be successful for instance. And am looking forward to England, where I mean to work, rush around, make a face like someone who believes all the claptrap everyone pretends to believe: you know, success, doing well, isn't everything grand, we are all here to stay, what we do matters, look look how important we are. I can play that one too, having decided to. I always thought it was a bad joke before, but have changed my mind. Or rather, it still is a bad joke but the only one to play. So as to keep one's inferiors in their place.

I would so like to know Rosamond Lehmann;† would you write her a note and tell her I am a nice affable harmless woman and her great admirer. Maybe she'd get in touch with me, or maybe I'd dare get in touch with her then; although I do not know where she is.

Sandy is perfect and beautiful; he has moments of such loveliness it can't be believed and I gloat and also mourn, knowing no one ever is as beautiful as now, with this shiningness of being so new to life. He is delicious company and always more so; I am very lucky indeed. But who knows what he will think of London. And really, one should force oneself to settle somewhere just because very young men are conservative and do not approve of changes.

★Iris Origo, novelist and historian, whose *War in Val D'Orcia* had appeared in 1947.
†Rosamond Lehmann's novels – *Dusty Answer, Invitation to the Waltz,* and *The Weather in the Streets* – had already been immensely popular. The author was only seven years older than Martha.

Dearest B.B., I am so really sorry not to be seeing you this time, but think how rich I will be, now that I've decided to be a success, so I will have plenty of money to take airplanes to Italy to visit you any old time. Greetings to Nicky.*

Love,

Martha

To: Diana Cooper

November 18 1953
215 Ashley Gardens
London SW1

Dearest Diana;
I cannot thank you enough for Mrs. Woolf's *Diary*.† It has made a huge effect on my life. Poor Mrs W. was no better off than any of the rest of us. It has cheered me up so much to realise that she didn't, by any means, always know what she was doing either. I am also astonished at her interest in, and care for, and score-keeping on, fame. Fame, mind you; that's the word she is constantly using. Well, you know, it has brightened me. I feel we are all minnows in life together; and one cannot ever feel comparative about work, because that's useless. She is also full of helpful little tips; oh a splendid book. But I would not have liked her. Did you know her?

As for all that cosmetic aid, I again cannot thank you enough. Cremene is no doubt the ideal food for Babies; your Lotion makes me look marbled and fine and takes off my skin, in gentle strips, but I go on using it anyhow out of love for you (emulation department) and the soap is a present joy. What I really need is a whole new face like criminals get, when fleeing from the cops (or so I have read in the more lurid newspapers.) A whole new face, a whole new body, inside and out, and Duffy's happy outlook on life. Or Sandy's.

It is really so nice here, smog and all. I am getting happier all the time. It's slow, which is what I like; all the advantages of living in the country with none of the drawbacks. My inspired cleaning woman has made this place bearable and now I have found a small soiled kindergarten for Sandy, so he is fixed. It's cosy and easy, being here: what is the secret of this place? I feel I never want to move. Nana says it is too wonderful, except for the sky. I am adjusted to the sky and never look at it. Eyes fixed on the

---

*Nicky Mariano, close friend, companion, and secretary to Berenson. She later edited Berenson's diaries and wrote *Forty Years with Berenson* (1966).
†*A Writer's Diary* by Virginia Woolf, edited by her husband, Leonard Woolf, and published by the Hogarth Press in 1953.

pavement, I go happily through my days. Sandy is in love with the Regina; saw a picture of her (for taking home) in the Army and Navy Stores and mooned in front of it, muttering to himself, 'Ah dat Regina is berry nice, how nice is dat Regina.' New angles on English life. I never thought about the Regina at all, before, and now she is steadily in the home.

Please come back. We will go and look at a crystal Aztec skull in the British Museum which I am reliably informed is the most beautiful object in the world. I miss you. I dote on you. Love to Duffy.

Always,

Martha

To: Edna Gellhorn

January 4 1954
[London]

Dearest Fotsie

. . . Then there's Tom.* Ah me. I think probably it is best to marry him. I'm not in love with him, but my being in love is always fatal, whereas my taste in friends is very good, and he is a friend. I think it might make life easier. Around now, that is what I want; things easier, just less damn trouble. And how funny and unexpected life is. Ten years ago, at this time, I was in England, at bomber stations, reporting on the men who nightly raided Berlin. That was my climate and how very well I functioned in that; I found it so easy to do my work that it cannot have counted as work, and I believe I did it – such as it was – very well. I was also very popular with the chaps; it was cold and uncomfortable and we were really semi-starved, on a diet mainly of bread and margarine (the diet is now bread and butter), but I suppose happy because one was doing one's job well. I guess this life is not my job and I do not do it well and as a result I am never really happy. Terrible thing to say. Probably I was no more meant to be a mother than Olga† was to be an international journalist; I have entered a too difficult profession, I am simply not up to it. Which does not mean that I shall abandon it, or do it any less well than my very best; but it does mean that I will always do it with something close to agony, never ease, and that I will never feel that I, as a person, am really functioning. This is appalling talk but alas, I am afraid it is true. Under these circs, I might as well get married. I am too old for the life I loved and knew how to handle; I might as well pool my few advantages and many failings with Tom; if one is caught by time and love in domesticity anyhow, it is surely less hellish to have someone to

---

*Tom Matthews, former editor-in-chief of *Time* magazine.
†Olga Gellhorn, married to Martha's younger brother, Alfred.

do it with. But hellish is what it is, basically; plain hellish; it is not the death of the heart but the absolute death of the mind, and the wearing-out of the spirit. Unless, perhaps, as a couple, and doing things on a rather lavish scale . . . maybe, that might be easier.

Goodnight my dearest Fotsie. It's no wonder you hardly know me any more, because who am I? And what have I become? But what would I have become anyhow, at forty five? Hard to know. I feel ten years older than God.

Love always,

M

Tom Matthews, 1954–1963

Tom Matthews was a widower, American, and a former editor-in-chief of Time magazine and Martha had met him briefly in New York in the 1930s. He was fifty-two, a keen tennis player, and he liked to give and go to parties. He wrote poetry and was slightly deaf. He also had four sons: Tommy, who was twenty-eight and an Oxford scholar like his father; Johnny, twenty-five, who worked for Radio Free Europe in Munich; Paul, twenty, who wanted to paint; and Sandy, eleven, then living with an uncle and aunt in America.

Martha and Tom were married on February 4, 1954. The witnesses were Sybille Bedford and Moura Budberg, H. G. Wells's long-term companion. Martha told Diana Cooper that she and Tom planned to take care of each other, and that since both could be "very merry on occasion" they would be like a pair of cheerful clowns, no bad thing as "you know what a soured human yoghurt I am." Sandy Gellhorn was delighted to acquire a father. For their honeymoon, and while they bought and did up a house in London, in Chester Square, they rented a cottage in Oxfordshire. For the first, and only, time in her life, Martha now embarked on an intensely social life, which she hated, both for itself and because it prevented her from writing, but the intimacy with Tom made her initially happy. "Knowing that writing is all I have to look forward to is not enough," she wrote in her diary. "Because I cannot take what I write with sufficient seriousness: it isn't important enough to be a life." However, she did not find family life easy, and the swings in her feelings toward Tom and his sons came out in long, impassioned letters to her mother and to Sybille Bedford.

Martha's closest woman friend at this time, apart from her mother, was Diana Cooper, with whom she exchanged hundreds of letters, often about appearance, health, and states of mind, topics that run like a humorous refrain across their forty-year friendship. They compared ailments, symptoms, remedies, and diets and swapped doctors and antidepressants. "Have all the pains and aches gone?" Martha asked one day. "Was it anything like the year you decided your heart was weak or the year you had cancer?" On another, she reported: "the wrinkled skin of my eyelids is steadily dropping over my eyes. In ten years the way I look will frighten even baboons." Martha called Diana "my essential girl friend, the only person in the world with whom to moan."

To: William Walton

[March 1954]
92 Albany
Piccadilly W1

Darling; I cannot tell you how relieved I was to get your crisp little letter this a.m. I feared your silence was intentional, or perhaps you had not understood my mysterious and somewhat military cable. I thought you had cast me out, without even a curse on my retreating back, and was very glum. Now all is well; you simply think, as I imagined, that I have taken leave of my senses, but you are used to that.

The main thing to keep firmly fixed in your mind is: Tom is NOT Ernest. Correspondence will reach the addressee, unopened. Lunch will never be *à trois*. Passes will be freely received in the spirit in which they are delivered. All is well. No purdah, no chains, no scenes, no one shooting out the living room windows. Times are different now. Times are, in fact, perfectly idyllic.

This all happened very fast and much to my astonishment. I was not feeling at all predisposed to marriage, which anyhow I never am; and when after some weeks of Tom nattering on in the same vein, I croaked out (being in bed with laryngitis at the time) that I would join up, it was decided to get through the ceremony in such secrecy that even I would not know when it was to happen. This is because I have a justified feeling that a little more Wolf, Wolf stuff on marriage, from me, would sicken my friends; and besides I have hitherto shown a certain tendency to bolt from nearing altars. Instead of which that miserable Evening Standard snoops around Caxton Hall (have you ever been to Caxton Hall, it is like a cut rate funeral parlor), and C. Hall posts civil banns which we did not know, so we were announced in the papers before we had told anyone and the further insult and complication was that I was quoted, as if I had a hand in that blabbing, and the result is that Lady Reading sprang to the telephone and told me I was a swine, and elsewhere a shirty silence reigned, so my pre and post marital condition is one of constant apologizing for not having confided in one and all, which is very silly, is it not?

We are honeymooning *en famille* in the Birkenheads' house in Oxfordshire, a dream rabbit warren, which we have until spring. Then they return (cutting their way through the ice?) and we are roofless again. It is awfully happy and easy, I never imagined marriage could be like this, it is a cosy, giggly improvement on being alone. I am of course unspoiled, considering my honeymoon in the Brown Palace Hotel in Denver, and greatly touched and grateful. You are not <u>obliged</u> to like him, but I think you will, if ever you take time off to see him.

He has a flat in Albany on Piccadilly, do you know that long cloistered bachelor's dump, wherein Byron, Macaulay and others hung out (throwing champagne bottles across the inner courtyard.) Women have been allowed in (wives only) for about thirty years, I believe, but still no children or dogs. Sandy cannot breathe London air anyhow, so we always have to have two dwellings which I think a dandy idea. In July we return, the three of us, to spend the summer with Tom's youngest son, aged 11, and also called Sandy (isn't that remarkable) and Paul his 20 year old and Mother. At Newport, where Tom has a house. You will be able to come over and see us on the wrong side of what I imagine to be diamond studded tracks. In the fall, we return, because Europe, with England as base, is where we are going to live luckily. The two Sandys will live with us, the other three Matthews sons are of an age to be on their own, but I know two of them and find them very okay, so that's all right.

I envy you being able to work, as I have not set pen to paper except for two bilgers done in Dubrovnik, since last April. But when we return to London, in about two weeks, I am going to start a new life on Clapham Common which I take to be a sort of Brooklyn of London. A most amazing murder was committed there some months ago, by a gang of very young boys who called themselves the Edwardians; the murder had to do with a lady's honor, as one of the gang felt his girl to be insulted at a London County Council dance. I have been obsessed with these youths for months, and arranged with [Stephen] Spender to do a detailed study of their lives and times for Encounter (do you ever see it; it isn't really first rate because of the American influence which will only give them dough if they have a certain amount of anti-communism, thus articles by Koestler, lamentable). However, it gives one space, up to 10,000 words, to roam around in and one can write as literately as one knows how. So I hope to wend my weary way back to the desk and discipline, via Clap Com. Life is simply an hysterical mess, without work; maybe funny, maybe diverting, but basically all wrong, like chewing of marshmallows or ashes, or both mixed together, but nothing really nourishing. I long to write; and think marriage may easily be a great help, not hindrance.

Oh, you did ask what family and friends thought about this. Sandy and Mother are beside themselves with joy; even my granite Englewood brothers approve, as they met Tom when he had to fly back, about two weeks ago, for his father's funeral. All my friends hereabouts (London, Paris, Rome) are almost insultingly delighted; it makes me think I must have lost my looks completely without knowing it, and have given the impression of a witch on a stick. They seem unanimous in feeling I have done something admirable and clever, like pulling off a great bank robbery. Flavia and Diana Cooper especially. We are in fact surrounded by surprise but approval; not so much, I gather, from Tom's American connections who evidently feel he is marrying the Whore of Babylon, or some such provincial nonsense. Can you believe it, they are upset because I have been divorced; whereas getting married and divorced is the one respectable legal action I ever took. But of course I exaggerate so do not report to the Jet Set that I will be stoned by angry friends of Tom's upon returning to the U.S. Darling, write, write, write; also paint.

I love you

M

To: Sybille Bedford

March 4 1954

[London]

Darling S;

The touch system? How brave, how incredible. Surely in a way like learning ballet dancing late in life? It must give you the shakes. How is it coming? And where, I do wonder, are you?

Please do not be in a despair about a) your quality b) your writing. I will stand absolute guarantee (and I have the objective eye, therefore far more reliable than yours) for both; also at the Bar of Heaven, if it's there. Although I think those fierce black soul searchings are as much part of writing a novel as, simply, typing and retyping. Unavoidable, and the biggest price one pays.

I've been to Clap[ham] Common yesterday and as soon as I pull myself together am going back today. Too odd. Did you know (of course not) that it is covered with sea gulls? That is already one of the biggest surprises I ever had, clouds and drifts of wheeling settling sea gulls. Then strange seas of mud, and left over houses from the war, with now chiffon ruffled curtains. There is a bandstand (where the trouble started) and a wide cement circle around it where the London County Council dances took place, and a refreshment house, rustic; in the morning it is in a traffic jam of prams, with all the mothers having a good hot cup and the babies cooing and slobbering. The Victorian drinking fountain, where the stabbing began, is a huge bronze group, a gracious veiled daughter ministering to her Victorian Daddy wearing a rug, as far as I can make out; the ideal of young Victorian womanhood? Maybe it's allegorical, I would not know. One side of the common has the most beautiful Georgian houses, like the very grandest houses in Georgetown in Washington, then it drifts off into Victorianism and modern blocks of flats. The commercial part is strangely American, small middle western town, shabby, garish, but homey. Today I must pull up my wits and courage and start ringing doorbells. Yesterday I picked up the chief reporter of the Clapham Observer, a tall charming tolerant young man, who believes this all came about because of the clothes which the youths affected; a dandified English version of the zoot suit; 20 pounds per suit. Mad, isn't it? And you know, its Dostoyevsky; they did not know the boy they killed. He apparently spoke ill of Ronald Coleman's suit. 'Flash bugger,' he said, or some such; and died for it. This is where boredom leads, you see, and boredom is the modern world's real sickness; it has led everywhere, thus far. The young bored are the armies of destruction; it is proved; they will be again. I wonder if people are bored in Russia? Or is it Slav despair which must be so much more interesting.

But I do not see any form for this, nor any end in sight; I only know that I need this, as if my lungs were slightly collapsed for want of air; I do this entirely for myself. It is at once easier and stranger. I realise also how immensely lucky I was never to have any money; I thank God for that; I always imagined it was a good thing but did not know it was bedrock vital. It turns out that money you earn belongs to you, and is a kind of passport, and free money is a sedative. I intend to make nothing at all of this, so don't worry about it; I am not going to get queer and have to start proving stuff all over again. But it is a fact; I am not so much easy, as slowed-up. It is no doubt jolly good for me to be slowed up, and I am still not slowed up enough. I'd like to be what they call relaxed, but (money or no) I churn, I always churn.

. . . Well, those are the problems. Otherwise none. It is Lent (a fact you would know at once but a novelty to me) and Tom is off the booze, as always each year, and I am off to keep him company and to save my stomach.

. . . Also I love him more every day, so that it scares me, because you know there are the two things about love, (I feel this always with Sandy), the kind of revelation and the sky opening, and below that or around it a steady terror, lest ill befall the loved one, lest anything harm them. I finally understand Diana Coop[er] who began crying on her wedding journey for fear Duffy would die sometime, thirty or forty years later. I begin to know what she meant. And beside loving him, which is a climate I believe, and a feeling of almost choking tenderness all the time, I am fascinated by him; he knows me far more than I know him, I have to dig and dig and pry and guess, for perhaps he does not even know himself. It is all a miracle; I am sure I am very changed although I cannot see it myself. But values perhaps? I don't want to see anyone, just him; I resent the need for giving and receiving dinners, and every telephone call is a blight, and I lie and squirm to keep us alone. Unsuccessfully; as everyone takes him all too fast and well (I wondered about that, you remember.) His friends seem perfectly deadly to me; that hasn't changed; and the sister-in-law who wrote the snotty letter is really inimical and I await a lot of dreariness in America. But he and I, together, seem to me incredible; I never never dreamed one could live with anyone like this, feel this way, not want any day to end and yet also very eager to wake up so one can start the next day. I am all too careless about how I look (too much to do), but I take infinite pleasure simply in looking at him. Now how did I have the sense to do this?

I love you and admire you, as you know,

M

To: Edna Gellhorn

February 18 1956
Hotel Bon Sol
Palma de Mallorca

Fotsie dear; No word from you, probably my letters have bored you so much you couldn't answer them. Here all goes from strength to strength, though the weather remains cold, dismal, and unlikely. But we are happy, both of us. Sandy is settled into this new life and finding it good. He has four American chums, who live practically in our laps; and Juan Graves,★ in Palma, whom he dotes on – he is there now, spending Saturday and going to a Spanish movie. Sandy does not want to go back to London until the end of his spring vacation, though a week ago he was wishing to return at once. He works by himself in the morning and I think does more than he does at school and as I am a hard task master he does it quite well. He looks really fine, and has stopped that neurotic gorging which I so hated and so feared; he eats like a normal child now, not like a boa constrictor.

. . . And as for me, I am happy. Really and for no reason, there it is, like a tea kettle singing away inside me. I had thought that was gone forever; and now I think I was actually sick. Sick with that house, and sick with Tom's children, and sick with our life. Whereas now, here, in a small bare hotel room that reminds me of Mexico, as everything on this lovely island does, with my small petroleum stove to assist the weak hotel radiator and my work table and the light bulb I bought for over my bed, I have all I need or want, and am happy. The walking is wonderful, the air is lovely, everything of the land is beautiful to behold, as is the water: and Palma, which I have scarcely glimpsed, is a joy. When the weather softens, and Tom comes, I have many bus and toy train trips that I want to make, looking at the island. Meantime, here I stay, full of joy, doing nothing except walk, read, dream, write letters (too many, mostly to Tom) and occasionally work. But I wake happy, and all day I feel happy, and I go happy to bed: and that's like being re-born, Lazarus raised.

And Tom is fine too. The best of all is that this separation has not made

---

★Having spent WWII in England, the poet Robert Graves returned to Majorca in 1946 with his second wife, Beryl Hodge, and settled there permanently. Juan was his son.

him grumpy, gloomy or bitter; he loves me, he says, and he is having a fine time. He is, for one thing, seeing people which we never do together and which he needs and likes and should do. Seeing lots of people.

My main occupation is losing weight, which I am doing without pain and well. I haven't had a drink since leaving London, I eat no dinner, a very light lunch, and a careful breakfast. I do indoor exercises and plod over the hills. I mean to lose 12 pounds in all; the 12 pounds I have gained in these last two years. Those pounds are a symbol, and I am getting rid of them. Fat and trapped; thin and free. That's how it looks in my mind.

. . . I love Tom really, but the lead he gives in life is a disaster. He wrote me in a letter that came today something he has often said: 'everything in me says "die" and then the little something left says "live".' If anyone else said that, you'd think it was bad theatre; but with Tom, it is the exact truth. He told me that the first evening he took me out in November of 1953 (in different, even stronger words) and I was speechless with anger, and made a note in my diary that he was the finest and nicest man possible, but dangerous and to be avoided because he depressed, he darkened life. I think it is his disease, inherited, or infected into him when he was tiny and helpless; but I do think it is a disease. And since he is stronger than I am, his deathliness prevailed over my desire to love life and laugh. I am not strong enough to cure him or to fight off a sort of miasma that comes from that secret hidden sickness. Then I must flee; there is nothing else. Because I don't want to die, except one day without any fuss: I want to live every day I am alive and every day unlived is a misery and a crime.

So I flee in little bits and all the happiness comes back, and if I can keep him away from his appalling tendency to spoil fun and life by doing unnecessary duties, and worrying, and expecting nothing good, then that's fine. And when living with him has (from nothing cruel or wrong that he does, but from what he fails to do, a basic lack of vitality and hope) again saddened and depressed me so that I no longer care about living, I will flee again, and get my happiness back. And so on, da capo, if that is what I mean.

. . . I have put Sandy to bed, and on the strength of his having lied to the Graves – saying he had had his birthday on Feb 12 and what lovely presents he got – I made him a long speech, trying to explain the difference between telling funny stories (after which one says: 'I was fooling') and telling lies. And it seemed also the occasion to speak to him as earnestly and terrifyingly as I could about stealing. He stole 1 pound 4 shillings from Mrs. Roxburgh, our secretary, which I naturally and quickly repaid, and never spoke to him, as I was worried about him then, I thought he was going round some bad bend. But now I know he's all right (but oh Fotsie, it's going to be hell's own job to drill the most simple sense of morals into that one) so I brought it all out. Let us hope. Anyhow, the next time he steals anything, if he does,

I will punish him terribly severely, because the matter has been stated clearly. (It has been before, but I assume he was too young to get it.) And the next time he lies, I will treat him with contempt. And let us hope that he will neither steal nor lie; but he listens to me very little if what I have to say is disagreeable. I can't remember that I stole or lied – did I? – so it's harder for me to understand what to do.

Goodnight dearest. Write some time, I love you,

M

To: Diana Cooper

March 17 1956
Hotel Bon Sol
Palma de Mallorca

Darling Beauty;

I am a convert to Mallorca; I love everything about it (will spare you nature descriptions but my goodness they are something) and above all I love living in a hotel. What a wise, benign and God-given thing is a hotel no matter how badly it runs.

. . . Tom and I planned to go to the Feria in Seville until last night, when we dined with the Graves's and one of their cuadrillas of young skunks, and the young gents began that bullfight talk which I can hardly bear (it is even worse than balletomanes) and I said to Tom: do you think we could endure this, all the streets of Seville full of such jerks showing off their quarter knowledge and talking about bravery? And he said well no. So instead we are going over to the mainland on April 6 and work counterclockwise as it were, starting from Madrid to Granada and timing it to get to Seville after the feria and the fiends are gone. Meantime here we have a motorized pram called a biscuter and pronounced beescootair, which has one spark plug and wheels from a kiddy car, and looks like those things at Fun Fairs which run into each other, and in it we sputter about the island at 40 km. per hour, mad with delight, and causing children to hold their sides all over the landscape.

. . . You will (I trust) be dazzled to hear that I have lost twelve pounds and am down to my fighting or pre-marital weight and my goal is one stone off. I feel wonderful and can wear pants again without shame. Also, owing to sun and a dash of daring peroxide in the soap, I again have yellow hair instead of mud or seaweed and all these things combine to make me feel that life is full of hope. It was very odd the last year because my only concern was in growing old well (like brandy in a cask, perhaps) and how to die triumphantly. It now occurs to me that I really hoped I would grow old quick and die soon, as I was so fat and bored, and so sick of my bloody house; and all that has gone, evaporated with the lost pounds, and melted in the sunlight. It is also, I am ashamed to say, absolute heaven to have no sons present on this island except little Sandy, who is a comic character and a wiseman and by nature a realist and realistically dishonest, and never a bore. Sons are arriving, in April, but I think I am recovered enough to take it. And Tom is fine, very beautiful, very cheerful, pleasure-bent. . . . You haven't heard such sounds from me for years, have you?

But somehow – where? when? – I must see you. You know my astrologer in Rome. He told me in 1954 that I might as well go to bed for two years, since nothing valuable was going to take place and everything I turned my hand to would immediately dissolve into ground glass. But as of 1956, he said, Saturn was moving off. That star, which is apparently the total son of a bitch amongst stars, has indeed moved off. I feel everything will be fun from now on. Would you like to do a tandem bicycle trip somewhere?

Always, with mountains of love, as you surely know,

Martha

To: Diana Cooper

[? 1956]
20 Chester Square
London SW1

Dearest D;.

Iris Tree★ was brought here a few nights ago by Raimund and Liz[†] and it would have been fine, I think, just the five of us, but alas almost at once Ivan[‡] arrived with his new future bride (the fourth?) (such a quick worker.) The future bride is really hell; Tom and I instantly took against her so much we could not even look at her. I think Iris (I call her this improperly) is too kind, too loving, too detached and also busy with her own business, to notice much; but if she were a noticer or thought sons' wives were here to stay, I bet she would think that girl pretty rough stuff. It is a new kind of horror girl, which they have here in London: the intellectual arrogant type, but no intellect really. I also think Ivan pretty much of a poop. When he is funny, he is fine value, but basically he is a poop you know; spaghetti in place of bone. Raimund, our hero, seemed tired and dim; Liz I am

---

★Iris Tree (1897–1968), poet, actress, and painter and the daughter of Sir Beerbohm Tree. A close childhood friend of Diana Cooper, her unconventional and exuberant family caused a departing governess to say: "*Quelle famille de serpents!*"

†Liz and Raimund von Hofmannsthal: she was Lady-in-Waiting to Queen Mary and very beautiful; he was the son of Strauss's librettist. They lived in great style in London.

‡Ivan Moffat was Iris Tree's son by her second marriage to an American photographer, Curtis Moffat. A successful screenwriter, he was responsible that year for *Giant*.

beginning to think is a disinterested Machiavelli, if you get my idea; she waits to see who is going to win. I would really have loved to have talked with Iris as I admired her. Her eyes are fine, aren't they, and I like the childish gum-showing smile (like Jenny [Crosse]), and the laugh. I think, a guess only, that she was self conscious about that grisly oncoming daughter-in-law. And there was also a curious awkward thing in that they wanted, or thought they wanted, to talk about Jim Agee, a young man recently dead, and a man Tom really knew (a man apparently almost impossible to know) and really loved. And Tom felt about that (Ivan saying, 'Didn't you adore him?) the way I always and furiously feel when people who don't know and didn't really feel it, speak about my sacred deads. I freeze and I hate the speakers and I always want to say, 'Never heard of the fella' in order to shut them up for good . . . But my real conclusion, after our champagne evening for the Thurbers★ and other piddling events is that I do not care a bit, not one rap, or worse I loathe, social life. I only love friends and very few of them, and on the whole I would rather see them alone. I can't bear that quark-quark kind of nattering which goes on, in company. Anecdotes are bliss; any old rug seller from the bazaars who will sit down and tell me a story about anything or anyone is what I love. And I love also the sort of talk where people say trustingly what they are thinking and feeling. But I despise social talk, and can no longer waste my time and energy on it.

News note: Jenny discovered a drug called drynamyl, small blue heart shaped pills. I got some. They may kill us all but they are wonderful. You take one in the morning, and a kind of insane spastic energy attacks you and furthermore you lose your appetite. If I take one early enough, I can get going by ten o'clock in the morning, which is dawn patrol by my standards. Also by lunch time, instead of feeling faint and like a tiger in a dry plain, I feel a pronounced distaste for the coarseness of eating. Soon, I shall jump out of my skin, with this selfsame drug, but meantime, I have lost three pounds, only cutting out bread. So. I'll send you some in an envelope if you want.

But darling please appear sometime, if only for a noggin of vodka, between the 15th and the 20th. My mama is nice, you know; and then here we are, a housefull of your adorers, and besides I hope we might run into each other in the summer, if we had a hollow tree somewhere to leave messages in.

Love always

Martha

★James Thurber, the *New Yorker* writer and illustrator, whose *The Secret Life of Walter Mitty* had been published in 1932.

To: William Walton

May 26 [1956]
20 Chester Square
London SW1

Darling;

I miss you. There is really nothing to say beyond that, as far as I am concerned. I do, I will. Oh come. I could not possibly find you a studio, who could? But I can feed you, which is a novelty in this house.

I cannot imagine what has happened to your brains unless they are undergoing that sea change which evidently transpires constantly in the U.S. to the mystification of the entire outside world. Harriman instead of Stevenson? Surely, no matter what Adlai may not have or have lost, he still has more than Ave? However. I think this is all academic. We will have that rubber dolly Father Figure, whom the Americans love, until such time as constant rest and fearsome care succeed no longer, and then we will have Dirty Dick.* Meantime, here, we will no doubt have that lady the Italians called Clare Boothey Luchay. So all is well with the world.

I am not really interested in anything except Israel and Nasser. I dislike dime store Hitlers as much as the $1.98 variety, and Nasser is a plain pustullant sore. And of course the life and death of Israel is like the life and death of the Spanish Republic, and is one of those simple issues: justice versus injustice. I dread having to attend another war, but if that one starts I shall have to comb my grey hair and go. Meantime I am going in September as it is just a step from Greece. You will not be surprised to hear that it terrifies me to think of being any place within sound of small arms fire; perhaps another reason to go?

I have solved the servant problem (marriage remains, as usual, insoluble, a sort of Rosetta stone in human affairs) by searching out and importing two glorious Spanish women, whose mother I have become. They are the nicest people I've known since my beloved Maria and Bartolo in Mexico, and from the way we all feel, they are for life. Meanwhile they do not speak one word of English and since I am the only bi-lingual around the joint, you can imagine what my life has become. I work far harder than before, at housewifery, but the work shows some results; so I feel less awful. And I actually have an assignment to do a piece on the Old Bailey for the Satevepost (my first assignment in about 5 years) so, though I have no time free from domestic translating, I look forward with joy to one day getting out on the streets with my pad and pencil. My book of course stopped long ago. Oh shit. It was easier to live when I had to write in order to live.

---

*Averell Harriman was now governor of New York. In the 1956 elections Adlai Stevenson lost to General Eisenhower, as Martha feared. Richard Nixon did not win the presidential election until 1968.

Mother is here, very good, sweet, and tired. Tom and Sandy bloom, owing to having a feminine and kindly woman on the premises for a change, instead of a tiger. (But what a sleek tiger, I hope to retain this shape until the autumn of 1957. I've lost 15 pounds and now weigh in at 126. Also my hair, due to exhaustion, lies flat and shiny on my empty skull. I even have good clothes. Unrecognizable. And nasty.) Tom is fine, I think. Sandy is fine, I know.

I see no one. Where are they? Who are they?

Enough or more than enough. You will find me on a rock-bound Greek island, panting for water, from end of July until approx middle of September, then panting around the Negev. Back here for the happy school days. I would give a great deal for days of you; but perhaps you would not like me any more. I can hardly stand my own presence.

Love always,

Martha

To: Edna Gellhorn

October 24 [1956]
20 Chester Square
London SW1

Fotsie dear;

I had, before I got your letter, consulted a child psychiatrist; I wanted advice about the tutor, and ended arranging for Sandy to go twice a week for 'play therapy'. The woman is a nice woman, German Jew, mother of two, lives in a small modest house, and seems to me solid.*

She believes (first ideas, may change) that his trouble comes from the earliest times, from an insecurity based on having been abandoned – there is a raging 'why?' she believes, at the bottom of it all. She does not think he is afraid or feels unloved; but underneath all there is this nagging doubt. And she attributes his need to have a superiority complex (that is his sulking when he fails) and his temper, to this: the doubt and the pain of his beginnings. I understand none of this, and I am not sure I would believe in it all (it has a certain magic, white or black, quality) were I not seeing, before my eyes, the amazing effect of <u>freeing</u> which such therapy is having on Tom. I really cannot get over it, with Tom. And, in a funny way, Tom had a lot of Sandy's problems, including sulks.

. . . I think you have gotten one point wrong: you seem to think I don't love Sandy now, find him a burden and am turning my affection away. Well, that is not true. I am attached to him in a way I cannot even analyse

---

*Sandy kept putting on weight, and Martha and he now fought constantly about food.

or describe myself. Perhaps if I said, we sink or swim together, that is the nearest I can come to it. Sometimes he drives me mad with anger and fury (when he behaves in a way that I regard as mean in spirit, or bullying), often he charms me in a way nobody else can, and always, always, he is the deepest concern I have. I cannot be at peace, I cannot draw a free breath ever, unless I am sure it is well with him. He might even be better off at a boarding school simply because he would be released from the appalling pressure of my attention. But if that attention does not spring from love, I don't know what it springs from. And then there is the other thing: in a funny way, I admire him as much as anybody I know. This is an odd way to talk of a child, but I recognize as a fixed point in my nature that I do not love without admiration.

. . . Our life is much changed, this last week, owing to endless social goings-on. Two lunches and four dinners, all invited out. All my friends. Tom behaving perfectly; gone the panic, the stoniness, the source of quarrels. In the end, we may even become quite an easy social unit. We lunched at Ann Fleming's yesterday. I was alarmed, at the beginning, to find us with two Cabinet ministers and an old friend of mine, a dotty Lord, alarmed for Tom who used to panic shockingly as soon as he was with what he thought of as 'celebrities.' Nothing of the kind happened; lunch very quick and funny. Tom enjoying every second. I work with him constantly on his book.★ He said, 'I don't know where I'd be without you' and frankly, neither do I. Which I do not say. But heavens, how I do work, advise, soothe, suggest; I think after this book is finally done and published, he will be on his own but just now he needs my strong motherly hand. I am very very pleased about him; I think that, somehow, I am doing a good job there.

For myself, I feel as I always do in London, like a piece of cheese. Too many cigarettes, too much drink, too little exercise, too little sleep and too many daily concerns. Never mind. I thought all was a failure. I have done two thirds of my job: Tom and the house. Now I have to see Sandy somehow better settled, and then I will lean back, take a deep breath, and go to sleep for a month. Or read thrillers.

Tonight we are dining with the Crawleys,† because Bertrand and Hélène‡ are staying there overnight – B. is speaking on BBC. I have been going all through old papers and filing them, and for days have been reading B's letters. My own past seems to me more incredible, foreign and distant than the history of the ancient Hittites. This is very odd. I do not feel, now,

---

★His autobiography, published as *Name and Address*.
†Martha's journalist friend from Spain, Virginia Cowles, was now married to the writer, broadcaster, and member of Parliament, Aidan Crawley.
‡Bertrand de Jouvenel and his second wife.

being who I am and doing what I do, that I have any relation to that fierce strange girl of long ago. I guess I am really old.

Darling darling, well, this is quite a letter. As usual, you are the one to talk to.

Love always,

M

To: Hortense Flexner

November 26 1956
20 Chester Square
London SW1

Teechie dearest;

I return to this saga. And now, in this holocaust, in this deep November of the soul, I might as well go on with the poodle. The poodle returned. The Poodle's name is Soot of Aldebourne, called Sooty. After two or three weeks at his country mental home, he seemed physically well and as the vet said, 'His mind's all right.' He immediately deepened his mother fixation on the cook, whom he will not leave for one single minute; he accepts Sandy as another poodle, he is too frightened of Tom to bark and only slinks away, and barks his head off whenever he sees me. This hurts Tom's feelings, God knows why. So we have been living like that, the poodle keeping himself to himself on the basement floor and hurrying up to bed, ignoring us; and we polite in the upper quarters. Today arrived Miss Green, a young woman who goes about clipping and shampooing poodles. On the house intercom I explained that he was to be clipped the same all over. Presently Rosario,* the cook, telephoned from the kitchen to say that Sooty was very ugly and it was a disaster. I asked for the dog who arrived, with a shaved face, except for beard and pompadour, shaved feet, huge fur trousers, and a body like a black sausage; completed by a grayish tonsure just over his tail. I rose in my fury and went to Miss Green, who had come accompanied by her own poodle, another neurotic who cannot be left alone. We then worked over this ghastly coiffure for an hour, trying to repair the worst horrors. Cook restraining tears, me promising that nature and time would repair the disaster. This poodle is going to complete the state of paralysed aching wild wretched insanity I am getting into, owing to Suez, Hungary, America, and the way Eden hasn't got the guts to do a proper smash and grab. I do not at all mind the smash and grab, but I am

---

*After a succession of disasters with an ever-changing cast of servants, Martha had been to Pamplona in Spain and brought back Rosario the cook and Lola the housemaid. She called them the Pamps.

sick at heart about the smash and the failure to grab. In its way, Suez — stopped both too late and too early — is a folly like Gallipoli.

I won't write you politics; we live them here all day long every day. The horrible sense of being helpless is what I mind most. I have gained 4½ pounds in a week, not from eating but from misery, and broken out in bumps, and taken to insomnia. If only I could rush to the fires; it is always all right at the front.

Kisses to King. Love always
Gellhorn.

To: Leonard Bernstein

November 30 1956
20 Chester Square
London SW1

Dearest Lenny-pot; Too long a silence. What are you thinking? Some world, isn't it?

. . . I think of Chim★ all the time. He was meant to live; he loved living; and he had a private system that would have made him grow old really well (which none of us may achieve.) I keep going over that imbecility, the jeep driven fast down the road by a reckless young Frenchman, the last English lines <u>not</u> marked (muddle again), the paratroopers calling out, neither Chim nor the Frenchman understanding what they said, passing the Egyptian outpost, where of course the Wog was lying low, taking no chances, even against two unarmed men in a jeep, and then the rattle of machine guns against the windscreen. I above all hope Chim was killed then and there and didn't in fact drown, wounded but conscious, in the canal . . . Useless to think. I tell you, given half a chance, one could spend one's time mourning for the whole race of men, living and dead.

It looks very bad to me; I think it's about 1936 now. And Hungary is a new style Spain, and like Spain, it will die. No one ever helps in time. But there is a sort of hopelessness, or madness, or something loose on earth; no one is in control, no one at all, anywhere.

Love to you and Feli. Write to a sad old friend.
Martha

★Chim, David Seymour, had been killed by Egyptian gunfire near the Suez Canal.

To: Iris Origo

October 13 [1957]
20 Chester Square
London SW1

Dearest Iris; Bain is a better bookseller than ours (who <u>still</u> hasn't got your book;* we must switch) and I thank you very much for sending it. I have read it all except Allegra, which I have read before; and congratulate you as always on the quality of your prose. To me the best parts of it are: in the Mazzini piece, the feeling for Carlyle and Mazzini, the understanding of their contrasted and related qualities, the sense (comes through to me, there) that they are both alive, and you have seen them, really did get into the air between them. And then the beginning of the Marie Leneru piece, the part about her ghastly illness; again I feel <u>inside</u> those emotions, and you have a paragraph of what I think the great luck in writing (not luck, but you know what I mean) where you put your finger on a truth – that all of us, unbearably, have flashes of foresight and hindsight about ourselves, see suddenly and with horror that there is no accident, this is how we are, this is where we are going. That is a sickening set of emotions, and true, and as you point out, happens seldom because we could not bear it. But you have that down, and made powerful by the horror of that girl, <u>knowing</u>. After, after her 'recovery' (how complete?) she dims to me; but the early Leneru I think has the quality of a fine novel, when you are really feeling inside the character. Those are my favorite parts.

Now, about the Carlyle play. Where IS a play? For 14 years, they all <u>waffled</u>. I am bound to say that I find all three of them repulsive characters (I might vary my feelings about Carlyle if I knew his writing; I shall now read some; never have.) Carlyle seems to me of a disgusting weakness; absolutely unable to take any clear line; unable to dominate Jane, unable to shake himself and her emotionally free if that is what he wanted; unable to know what he wants from Lady Harriet. Lady Harriet is a glorified Victorian version of Kay Halle (whom you don't know) a bright-saying Washington *salonnière*, who needs a court, astounds only those capable of being astounded, idle, surely vain, less stupid than most people who spend their time getting people together in drawing rooms. The generosity is very *de haut en bas*; I dislike the Carlyle's sycophancy; but you are right about that, it is in the air, blood and bone of this country, the way malignant malaria is endemic on the Burma Road, nothing to do. Jane, I find pure hell. Waspish and conceited, or if not conceited not <u>anything</u> enough to be

---

*A Measure of Love, Iris Origo's collection of biographical essays, including one on Byron's daughter, another on the Italian patriot Mazzini, and another on the Carlyles. Origo greatly admired Carlyle's attention to truth.

it, only with an idea of herself which makes her snarl Me Too (by what right?). I have no sympathy for long suffering; I do not share what I think to be your feeling – if marriage is an endurance contest, there is final virtue in simply enduring. (I feel, by now, that the form of marriage should be maintained, if there are children, <u>for</u> the children.) (Children are an obligation; they did not start things themselves.)

But aside from the fact that I really do not like any of these people (although I like Carlyle best of the three), what I cannot see is: where is the peak, the intensity, the concentration that you have to have for a play. I see a play as this shape.

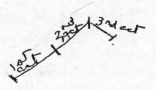

No doubt wrongly. However, I see the Carlyles' life as a long series of wavy bumps; and the basic cause for all the bumps seems to me lack of honesty, decision, and guts.

Now tell me where I am wrong; or tell me where you see a play. Mazzini, by the way, is not a minor character (I wonder why you did not write those two pieces as one?) since Jane, so maddeningly offended and sorry for herself, did have a playmate. Also, why can anyone think her an intelligent woman? Can you imagine sitting down for 14 years under a nagging jealousy and not finding a way to fix everyone? What is the intelligence for, if not to survive with?

Do write. (I beg you to do so on a typewriter.)* I shall read C's essay on heroes and maybe a life of C. But unless you have much more dope than there is in the piece, some central event to change people's shapes and way, or to crystallize them, I don't see a play. A play is an artificial thing which has to move on action, of some clear sharp kind, be it in head, heart, or body. How could one ever get drama out of 14 years of hanging about? I am ready to be convinced; but you see what my doubts are. Big ones.

Maybe you've got the wrong couple? I do think a play on marriage is a good idea; not, as I insist, that I can write a play.

I am deep in painting. I go to the Chelsea Polytechnic to a beginner's drawing class. I am also writing a story, with difficulty. It started on a wonderful and quite funny burst, and has now bogged down into heavy narrative. It has all one color, about now, and it strikes me as about to become an irretrievable bore. But I cannot deny that fiddling with words is the real thing; the thing that drives one bats and at which one cannot

---

*Iris Origo's appalling handwriting was legendary.

succeed; but there it is, the <u>itch</u> is there. Yet I have damned little to say about anything and wonder why I sweat.

How are you all? How is lovely Rome? When are you coming here? I await word.

Love,

Martha

To Rosamond Lehmann

[?] 1958

68 bis rue Charles Laffitte

Neuilly-sur-Seine

Dearest Rosamond:

. . . What you say about my stories fills me with happiness. The story* you like best, this year won the O.Henry Prize in the US – supposedly best short story published in the year – a joke of course although considered great honour, and first time in my life I ever won any prize, including in school.

Bara is, in personality, in everything as much as I could do, Capa, the war photographer, killed in Indo-China in 1954. The story is all mine, an invention, based on a long surmise – to his friends it seems so true, and at last so explains Capa, that they believe I knew it, he told me, and are disappointed to learn this was not the case. I suffer (and am also thrilled) by this constant accusation that I am reporting what I have seen & been told. Of these stories Robert Graves wrote that of course I had changed people's names but the absolute truth of the stories made me realise they were beautifully done case histories – true life, in short. And every one is made up from start to finish. I want, of course, to be patted on the back for my intuition, and instead am praised for being such a good journalist. Embittering.

I loved Capa with my whole heart – but not the way you mean. I met him in Spain in 1937 and he was my brother, my real brother. (I was his brother too); there was never, not for one minute ever, the slightest sexual attraction between us. We counted on each other. He needed me less (yet I was the only woman he ever had as a friend and perhaps the only friend he had who knew him); I needed to know he was alive in the world. We never wrote, nor made plans to meet; we always found each other – all over the world – by a kind of miracle accident when we were really in need. I took his advice, and only his, as if I knew it to be absolute truth – a mystery. And we laughed – oh God, how we ambled about, very poor when young, and then both incompetent & bothered by increasing material possessions

---

*"Till Death Do Us Part."

and cares, and we saw everything. I miss him every day I live. It only grows.

I had, all my life, and in different degrees (Capa was the best, the nearest in every way) five friends – men – I don't know if you have friends with men, when it is as if you were nearly the same (I think I am, very, largely, a man anyhow) and perhaps because of them I always had a feeling of being at home in the world; they were there; I could always find them and they me – although I didn't find them much, I only *knew*, and when actually needed, one had only to stretch out the hand. But they were alive in the world. They are all dead, violently; only one died of a peacetime accident having survived near death from wounds in the war. I often feel like a remnant, and always strangely old – as if I had outlived my time and place.

I still have a few friends, men, (not quite the same as the others, the first ones) and they and the dead have always mattered more to me than any lovers. Lovers somehow never seemed serious; there was something I couldn't quite believe – and even in the most anguishing intoxicating depths of a love affair, I would always rather be with my friends, who were my own people and where I belonged. I found this very queer (I bet you do too), very unwomanly & probably neuter of me. I only loved the world of men – not the world of men-and-women. I only loved the men as they were themselves, not as they became in relation to women. Perhaps I am simply a born visitor – meant to go, as a stranger, into someone else's territory, having none of my own.

Someday (I have never been able to) I will have to use myself in a story; and no one will believe that – and will, say, whatever next, what *nonsense*.

Too long a letter. It's because I can't do any real writing and (for the first time in very long) unlimited time and nothing I can do *except* write. Also an overpowering need to write, so it comes out in heavy letters such as this. Forgive and forget.

love
Martha

To: Leonard Bernstein

July 4 1958
Mexico

Lennypot my dearie one; I waited for the right time to write about West Side Story but probably the exact right time will never come, so now on a rainy (can you beat it?) Cuernavaca morning, I shall begin. But I know I am not going to do it well enough.

How can it be called a 'musical comedy'? It is a musical tragedy, and were it not for the most beautiful music, and the dancing which is like flying, people would not be able to bear to look and see and understand. Certainly they would not pile into that giant stadium, paying huge sums, in order to be wracked by fear and a pity which is useless because how can help be offered, how can a whole world be changed? Tom and I found it beautiful and terrifying. But he and Omi must speak for themselves. Omi had seen it before, found it more enthralling the second time. Enough about their feelings.

I was literally frozen with fear. Do you realise there is no laughter in it, no gayety that comes from delight, from joy, from being young? You do, of course, and all of you knew what you were writing about. The immensely funny song, 'Please Officer Krupke' (I will get these titles wrong, but near enough), is not laughter, but the most biting, ironic and contemptuous satire. And I felt it to be absolutely accurate – not the perfection of the wit, in music and words – but accurate as describing the state of mind of those young. Again, the Puerto Rican girls song, when one longs for the beauty of home and the other mocks, is not laughter; but the hardness of life, the rock of life, a dream of something softer (softer inside, where it counts) as against the icy material measuring rod of modern big city young. The love songs made me cry (they had before, when I heard the whole show twice in one day, listening to [Irwin] Shaw's record in Switzerland.) But this time, with the visual picture there, and the murderous city outside, and <u>in</u> America, where 'West Side Story' becomes a sociological document turned into art, they made me cry like a sieve, from heartbroken pity.

But what stays in my mind, as the very picture of terror, is the scene in the drug store, when the Jets sing a song called 'Keep Cool, Man.' I think I have never heard or seen anything more frightening. (It goes without saying that I think the music so brilliant I have no words to use for it.) I found that a sort of indicator of madness: the mad obsession with nothing, the nerves insanely and constantly stretched – with no way to rest, no place to go; the emptiness of the undirected minds, whose only occupation could be violence and a terrible macabre play-acting. If a man can be nothing, he can pretend to be a hoodlum and feel like somebody. I couldn't breathe, watching and hearing that; it looks to me like doom, as much as these repeated H-bomb tests, with the atmosphere of the world steadily more and more and irrevocably poisoned. I think that drug store and the H-Bomb tests are of the same family.

. . . It shames me to speak of music to anyone, owing to my hopeless ignorance and to the fact that I do not hear it, only feel it. I love your music – everything you write (much more than I like anything you conduct.) It may be part of my loving you, but it wouldn't work entirely. I love some people whose writing and painting I deplore. No, it isn't that personal at all. I think I love it because it seems to me <u>real</u>. You'll have to figure that out for yourself.

I think you must write music, more and more, and I think you will. Americans are fools to fear age. It is needed and proper; all one must certainly do is change with one's age, live one's own age, let one's shape (inside and out) alter as it should. I think that, being you, you had to have the great hectic period of doing everything, being everyone and going everywhere. I think that's raw material; and you had to swallow it all, for you will need it. But I also think you will chuck it, without effort or regret, in time; because that will be the time to work on the raw material yourself, draw your conclusions, make your own private gift out of all you saw, did, heard, felt. I think you will really write music, and be concentrated and used by that, in perhaps eight years from now.

When in N.Y., I seem to have gone mad. Within a week (thinking that I knew what I was doing) I arranged four book contracts, two for Tom, two for me, and five articles for me. People leapt to offer me these contracts, paying more money than I have ever before received. The reason for this is that I really do not want to do any of the work, and I certainly do not want a cent more money than I have. The result is that I have to finish my book of collected war reporting by September 1. Beginning in October, and going through until April, I have to do two articles on England, one each on Poland, Hungary and Czecho. My only hope is that I won't be able to get into the last two countries. I am surely mad. The only good I can see in it is that it forces me back to work habits, which I have lost, and will be a long dismal training for my muscles.

Love always

M

To: Hortense Flexner

February 4 1959
20 Chester Square
London SW1

Darling; It's my FIFTH Wedding anniversary and the sun is shining and my room looks as if I were Maria Callas (that hideous fraud), being awash with red roses, and I am hung over from having dined with Polish Communists last night; and your letter arrived. Great relief. I thought I might have enraged Wyncie, but as long as I didn't, then all is fine. I have an immense amount of my grandmother's blood, alas; and have a tendency to beat my cane on the floor and call everyone to order. The remaining blood in me is my father's and he was a man who used to inform people that their doorbells were broken, and run his finger thoughtfully if silently over dusty surfaces and also look at people with friendly interest, as though they were under microscopes, and tell them they looked as if they drank/ate, or whatever, too much. You see what I mean.

I agree with you about Mrs. Matthews – Tom loves her, and love blinds as we all know. But between us, I think her very guilty and probably guilty of that dread sin, stupidity; she should have protected her children better, from their father. It seems she did not even protect herself. I do not regard it as Christian, angelic and feminine to lie down under a steam-roller. I regard it as the act of a fool. But I keep my total lack of sympathy to myself.

My intervention has, I believe, largely denatured Tom's chapter on sex. I feel badly, as one would if one bound feet. But on the other hand, I think there is a point where one must restrict one's honesty for private consumption. Tom is so incredibly honest (and in a curious way which I cannot define, curious and specific, so naive) that he does not foresee what happens when you make honesty public. I may be all wrong on this, but I don't think so. Of course, enduring art has always been terrifyingly naked. But, perhaps, one ought to die first before publishing, in that case.

After abject misery and constipation of mind, I managed to get the 7 first pages of my book down (having chucked out already something like 60 pages of false start.) I think that's the right start. Nothing says I can go on. But I hope I have evolved the outlines of the character of the woman; the man is very clear to me, although I don't understand him.

Well, Teechie, here we are, slaves to our itch, which is to make something from nothing and bring order out of chaos. God's work, in principle, and we shouldn't kick if it causes us trouble and belly-aches.

Love to youse,
Gellhorn

To: Alvah Bessie*

January 22 1960
20 Chester Square
London SW1

Dear Alvah;

. . . I thank you for that long and very kind review.[†] It is impossible for me to explain to you the condition (borderline? hairsplitting?) between a sense of reality and despair. I think one lifts one's puny hands and feeble voice, as frequently as possible, against stupidity – which is the root of all

---

*Alvah Bessie (1904–1985), New York writer and novelist who served with the International Brigades in Spain. *Men in Battle* (1939) was based on his experiences there.
†Probably a review of *A Stricken Field* (1940), Martha's novel about the fall of Czechoslovakia.

evil – but I think one does not expect much result, one only expects to stand and be counted and so keep the record a little straighter. As for progress, I think that is an abominable joke; and anyone who reads history at all must agree: change, yes; and some like the present changes and some do not, it's a matter of taste; but progress my foot. I happen to like being alive and the daily spectacle of the streets of this city (it's a matter of taste) fascinate me, also sadden me, also make me laugh. But I'm damned if I think London 1960 is necessarily a happier, richer, gayer, warmer, more ennobling place than London 1690.

. . . Yes, Alvah, Spain will rise again but not for a very long time and perhaps neither in the way you expect nor for reasons you would accept. It will also fall. This happens, dammit. I am glad, and will be glad all my life, to have been young and there, at that time; I think we got something out of history that is more than anyone has a decent right to hope for. We got that fusion, so often attributed to the human body (but so rarely achieved except in literature) of body and soul; of living one's life and believing with one's whole heart in the life around one. Very special, I can tell you.

I will buy the new edition of *Men in Battle,* next month. Glad it's coming out. It's the main comfort for writers, to stay in print. Penguins bought one book of mine and won't buy any more, as they didn't do well enough. Occasionally I see it in railroad stations; I never see anything else anywhere and rarely have. Seeing it gives me an odd hallucinated feeling; I say to myself, maybe I really am a writer.

Xmas was its usual hellish self but thank God it's over. I have had flu ever since, what an annual waste of life. I feel ugly, stupid, heavy, boring and second rate. But spring will come. And I am your devoted admirer also,

Martha

To: Diana Cooper

> February 2 1960
> Hotel Krone
> Solothurn
> Switzerland

My darling and loved beauty;
How are you? Where are you?

Please speak; please give me your news. It is one of the many sorrows of my life that I never get an unsigned pencilled document from you any more.

As for me, all that anguish of the winter in London, and the miseries of the Xmas hols was not, as I thought, middle-aged neurotic frustration. When Tom and the boys went back to London, I crept here to Solothurn, where an old medical chum runs the hospital, and asked if I could put my neurosis to bed for a time, since I really could not bother to move about on my pins any more. He quickly diagnosed and then proved by x-ray that I have a good-sized active hernia of the diaphragm. Ever heard of it? I hadn't. The stomach has burst out, it seems, through the walls (or whatever) of the diaphragm and now floats in a small poisoned sack, with the oesophagus all out of place and everything a huge and <u>chronic</u> mess.

Oh Diana, Diana, these are real intimations of mortality and the ugliest sort. This is something I had never never thought of: ill-health. The shamefulness and the boredom of it, and the dreary limiting of life. I have always looked forward to my old age, being more and more convinced that it would be far funnier than this neither fish-nor-fowl period of middle age, which I am bound to admit bores me. I saw myself as a ghastly old woman, fat as a pig and not giving a damn, not doing anything which bored me even for a second, with a mean tongue and a lot of equally tough old chums, sitting about making derogatory comments on the human condition, with a whiskey bottle at my elbow. What I will have at my elbow is a bottle of milk, no doubt; and I will be too busy with my various pains even to think of snide remarks about the human race. I cannot bear it. I feel at the very bottom of a pit and trap of gloom.

. . . The only good thing about this is that at last, finally, at my age (can you beat it?) I have begun to understand something about what life really is. How it really works; and how it decays; and what people have to learn to put up with. I have decided the whole human race (except me) is heroic; how do they stand it? It may make me a wiser writer, if nothing more. On the other hand, I wonder if one does not go a bit gaga, having to look after oneself all the time, and then write like a loony?

Love always
Martha

To: Mr. Lemay*

April 4 [1960?]
20 Chester Square
London SW1

Dear Mr. Lemay; Thank you for sending me *The Disinherited*. I have been away and found your gift on my return; I'm sorry to be so slow in answering because I want to talk to you about it.

I greatly admired *Child of Our Time*; it was finely written, tight, built on rock, and <u>finished</u>. I think it an exceptional book, one of a kind. That

---

*An editor at Alfred A. Knopf who published *The Disinherited* that year.

strange short fantasy, *The Guitar* is also a remarkable book, and also finished. Two weeks ago, I read in French a novel of Castillo's;⋆ I cannot even remember the name. It was a sketchy and jaded triangle story. And now this book.

I do not think it is good enough; not good enough for Castillo, who is a real writer. In intention and feeling, it is first rate; the workmanship is bad and I attribute it to haste. There are great chunks of the book where the author is speaking directly, not having had time for the digestive processes of art. The people are not real; they are symbols; it is like the first draft of a talented, and wonderfully sensitive writer, but a writer who must make many drafts before the work is finished. I emphasize this word: finished.

A writer writes too much for two reasons, I think: inner compulsion and the need to eat. If he can eat enough, and that need is satisfied, he can discipline his inner compulsion; he can take the time necessary to wring out of himself the very best he has in him. That boy is full of the very best; but he is writing far too many books and obviously far too quickly. I believe that you, his publishers, have a serious moral obligation towards Michel del Castillo, both as a human being and as a writer. (You and Rupert Hart Davis together.) I think you should make him an allowance, in the form of advance royalties or any old way, which keeps him alive, warm, clothed; and which gives him the time to finish his work. You have a real writer on your hands and a real human being; he is not only worth cherishing and saving; I say, simply, you <u>must</u> do this. But then I am not your conscience nor yet your literary yardstick. You asked me what I thought and this is what I think.

I'd like to see that boy work very carefully and slowly, and get it all down (what is in him) in depth; I think he has the makings of a great writer, if he isn't shredded to death young.

Yours,

Martha Gellhorn

To: Hortense Flexner

May 14 1960
Marbella

<u>Teechie</u>, you admirable half pint, WHERE ARE YOU?

. . . Tom is in London, having the usual ghastly time of someone trying to get a book finally polished and off. He doubts himself, it and indeed the

---

⋆Michel del Castillo, Spanish-born novelist writing in French, became famous at the age of twenty-four for a short novel, *Tanguy*, which, though written as fiction, was based on the months that he had spent in Mauthausen concentration camp.

universe, as is normal. I meantime to my great surprise have suddenly rented myself a small house; Lord it is all so easy. I saw it yesterday afternoon, moved in this morning, and by early afternoon was all unpacked, with huge vases of flowers everywhere. This is a new part of Spain to me, the coast an hour and a half from Gibraltar. I am mad about it. There's something I can't place (some emotion, no doubt literary) which happens when you look to the left and see the great rock of Gibraltar rising from the sea, and across the way, the Atlas mountains of Africa. That's a thrill all right. And the sun.

Life is unspeakably cheap and one tries not to notice the poverty of the people. Sun is what keeps them alive, too. And probably olive oil. The beach is not much hereabouts, but the views in any direction – the satin blue sea, the curve of coastal mountains, the Rock and Africa, and inland a miracle – high stone mountains with the sharp edges of Mexico, led up to by tumbling interlocking green mountains, and an agriculture that makes my heart beat: orange and fig and olive, gold wheat and little fountains of vines. I adore it, and here I mean to buy land and probably build a house. I've done everything else except build from scratch; and there's a good way to stop writing for a long time . . .

Tom will kick. Jack Spratt Matthews likes and thrives on grey weather. Mrs. J. Sprat Matthews is made ill every year and iller and iller; I have wasted a minimum of four months a year in ill health or plain sickness, in each London winter. I'm not going to live long enough to afford that; hence the Malaga coast of Spain is the answer. But he is really allergic to mosquitoes; he does not itch, he develops boils: and flies make him hysterical; and he sweats like a poor horse; and too much sun makes him dizzy. Whereas I . . .

Anyhow I am here now, in a state of bliss; and soon I will have to write out of self defense. I know no one, have talked only to two house agents in two weeks, and after I've burned myself brown and rushed around gaping at the land and the little whitewashed villages, I'll have to work, having nothing else to do. And I saw a valley today which is so beautiful that one would not know which way to face one's house, since all views are a delight. (I have solved this in my mind – a shaded terrace running all round, and move one's chair.) There's a sort of bluff, with fig trees, up above a rocky river bed: across the river bed is more rising land and a bouquet of trees, edible in their loveliness. Down the river valley is the sea, like beautiful blue syrup. Inland, are the tumbling little mountains, and the great mountains behind. And all around the up and down hilly agriculture. The orange groves smell like all the weddings in the world.

Yes, yes; this is for me. Immediately, of course, I get involved in real life, despite my constant desire not to. I was staying at a glorious luxury hotel, the other side of this sweet little village, on the beach. I walked on the beach which luxury hotel people do not; they stay around the lavish giant swimming pool, in their golden ghetto. Instantly I had the company of about twelve children, thin, alive, funny, and naked under whatever dirty torn piece of clothing they owned and wore. Their fathers are fishermen, whose boats now make a necklace of light across the sea.

I have been regaining my figure, which was lost; eating like a bird, and nary a drop of booze. I reckon I have lost a lot (at least my tum) and can get into my last year's summer clothes. But I am lard, from waist to knees, without a muscle to hold the lard in place; and I have to work at this. Vanity does not rule me; I think it is some moral quirk. I feel that a sloppy body is hand in glove with a sloppy mind; I cannot bear it. On the other hand, my mind is grotesque.

Do read a book called *Spinster* by Sylvia Ashton Warner; a jewel. And a book (I don't know where you'd get it) called *One Man in His Time* by N.M. Borodin. Fantastic, shiver-making, can't be put down. And have you read Chekov's letters, as collected by that witch Miss [Lillian] Hellman? Wonderful.

Do write me.

And love always,

Gellhorn

To: Leonard Bernstein

September 5 1960
Villa Candida
Marbella

Lenny pot my dear one;

. . . What can we do about our world? Ah Lenny, if I knew. It may be that Gellhorn's See-Saw Law of Marriage works for everything; in times when life was close and small, public influence was possible. Perhaps that period ended forever with the last war. Now, owing to the horrors of modern communication, we know everything and can do nothing. Like those awful dreams, where one screams and is unheard . . . I am convinced that government (politics) has nothing whatever to do with real life and real people any more. Bears no relation to, and hardly serves: but is there, like cancer, infecting us all. One never thinks in terms of good, but only in terms of least bad: Kennedy preferable to Nixon, but imagine having such a miserable choice of manpower. I also think that our rulers, everyone's rulers, inhabit some dream cosmos of their own, isolated from daily reality and the majority human condition, and in a trance – themselves troubled by such failings as wickedness, greed, ambition, and stupidity (failings of everyone) – they decide events, which in any case do not obey them but turn out even more nastily than expected. It is out of control, Lenny, that's what it is. It looks to me like schizophrenia: on the public scale, it is chaos and dark night; on the private scale the peasants of the Levante, hereabouts, are gathering the grapes, which they enjoy doing, and setting out great trays to dry in the sun into raisins. We belong on the private side, which is still not only sane but little changed really, it has the comforting quality of being rooted in unchangeable human needs: the need for food and shelter, the care of children, the hope of love. I am so wearied or embittered or realistic, I don't know which, that I come to the conclusion one can only stay sane: it is a public duty, as well as a private necessity. Never to flop hysterically with any herd, never to shout slogans, never to call for blood. Cultivate one's garden: if it's only two inches big, at least that much is saved from the jungle. In fact, what can one do: cling to one's standards, and see oneself as a dodo, probably, but maybe a useful dodo, handing on a few dodo ideas to a few young dodos.

Comforting? The Dark Ages seem positively neon-lighted now. We continue, Lenny. That's all we can and must do. You make good music for people; no evil has ever come from listening to good music, and maybe some refinement of soul which is eventually translated into some refinement of action. I don't know. I care about sentences, partly from love, partly because I know that the human animal can only think in words: if he is to think at all clearly, ever, he must respect the order and meaning of words, his only tools. And I cultivate my tiny garden, as you do yours, and ward off cheapness and ugliness from it, and cruelty. And revere and adore the miracle which is nature.

Love

Marthy

To: Leonard Bernstein

September 7 1960

Marbella

Lenny pot my love;

. . . The summer is ending, how sad, how sad; and there are sofa cushions of weed in the troubled sea and medusas a foot and a half wide, and soon we all go back to city life and winter dark. The trick is to keep life from becoming real and earnest and I don't know how to do it. It needed universal cataclysms to keep me loosed from all the damned daily kitchen I so hate; I never really found my own private disorderly place in the world except in the general chaos of war. But now nothing will ever shake me free again. I'm so tied, so many people depend on me, and I suppose I would not really want again to be an untrammelled solitary. But I still dream of surprises and derringdo. I long to set off into Africa from Tangiers, alone in a jeep, and see that continent somehow, however it happens, disasters included. Tangiers by the way is the closest I've come to the Arabs for some time and they are not endearing and I cannot understand the English phobia for them. Depressing and idiot, is my feeling, and inimical as well. I see perfectly why they hate Israel; it's too clean, and it makes some sense out of real life. Whereas the Arabs are lost in a loony dream, mainly to do with heaven. Those miserable veiled women and those tedious gents in dressing gowns, who pray five times a day, yowling for heaven, and indifferent to behavior in the here and now. Not my cuppa. But I would love to see the desert and love to see the real Africa, and the strange negroes, and all the unknown mountains and rivers.

Instead, I am going to the US where I will see a lot of motels, high schools, country clubs. Heigh-ho.

I love you,
Marthy

To: Diana Cooper

November 1 [1960]
20 Chester Square
London SW1

Darling; I forgot to send the letter yesterday so open it to add, having finished your book* altogether. I don't think you know yourself any better than anyone else knows himself/herself. There must be some reason for this almost universal non recognition of self. You think you are a cowardly bunny; all three books have been full of your fears. Yet you always did the physical act which roused your fear, always; sweated, swigged, and did it; that's not cowardice you know; and as for the non-physical fears, you have always behaved in a way that looks like a model-to-the-young. I think you are quite amazingly brave, and I judge by results which is the only way to judge bravery.

Then I also think the melancholia so odd; do you realise the pattern. The first suggestion of change fills you with horror, whereupon in no time you adore the new place and life. Look at it: everything from Bognor, Dorch, to Singapore, Paris, you always loved it at the end. Chantilly too; think how you hated the place a few years ago and now really there are heart wrenches about it. To me, this is the happiest way to be, so much better to love at the end than hate at the end. Oh Diana, what if really you have a golden and blessed nature? And have been happy as a sandboy (what is that?)

---

*The third volume of Diana Cooper's autobiography, *Trumpets from the Steep*.

always; surely unless you are lying in your teeth, the sum total of your life is an add-up that gives 89.99% to life-loving and therefore happiness.

As for me I am covering the Lady Chatterley Trial★ so at once feel happier. The real thing is that what makes me happy is to watch events which do not concern me; I am a voyeur. This trial is the Monkey Trial (remember, anti-Darwin in the Deep South) in Oxford accents, very high tone. The Judge is 54 and looks 70, a dried withered man with a lipless mouth; he purely hates sex, you can see it has been his lifelong enemy and my theory is that it has been his lifelong stumbling block (insuperable.) The prosecuting counsel speaks; 'She was an over-sexed adulterous woman,' – talking with such hate of Connie Chatterley that he might have known her personally, and she cuckolded him. It is weird. I think that all people who hate and abuse Jews, negroes and sex have something very wrong with them, are psychopaths of a dark kind. Sex is surely here to stay and ends up by being a matter of private taste; but if you could hear the Judge asking questions, you would think that sex was a perverted disease, something like cholera only much muckier. Most interesting. Also it's like a veritable lit. whirl down there, everyone on hand as they say; saw Rupert[†] for a second in the hall, and all the names, some giving evidence, some sympathizing. My element; only lasts day and a half more. Tonight a din at the U.S. Embassy.

Darling, I thought: of course I must not come to Chantilly because you have no slaves and I do not want to push one extra house burden on you. We will meet in Paris only let me know your local voltage.

Love,

M

To: Leonard Bernstein

January 17 1961
20 Chester Square
London SW1

My darling landed gentry;
    . . . Being, myself, a fantastic financial and otherwise practical brain, I have managed to pour $18,000 of my hard earned savings, like rain on the

---

★*Lady Chatterley's Lover* had been banned in the U.K. In October 1960 Penguin decided to publish and challenged the government to prosecute under the new Obscene Publications Act. The trial, held at the Old Bailey, lasted six days and ended in a victory for Penguin which sold 200,000 copies on the first day of publication. Witnesses for the defense included bishops and leading literary figures. The judge was Mr. Justice Byrne and the case is remembered for the words of the prosecution counsel, Mervyn Griffith-Jones, who asked the jury: "Is it a book you would even wish your wife or your servants to read?" Later, Bernard Levin described the trial as a "collection of symbols for the decade that was beginning."
†Rupert Hart-Davis, the publisher.

desert, into Spain, where all is stopped and I have a badly constructed shell, roof and walls, to show for the agonizing effort and the cash. I put it out of my mind; it may stand there forever like Ozymandias, King of Kings. Instead I am installed in a divine squalid bed-sitter in Ebury Street, where I work. It is rented by the week (payable in advance, to a basement caretaker out of Hogarth); it heats – dimly – by an electric fire which eats up shillings slipped into a meter. I come in the morning, and when hungry I heat (generally boil over) a can of soup on a ratty electric hot-plate. Somehow this is the very air of home, the beautiful scenery of all work. I never liked London more. I never exercise and smoke 40 cigarettes a day, and it's dandy.

On the other hand, the work. This amazes and shames me, and I cannot explain it. I have evidently had a moral change of life; I am becoming a dime store Jane Austen, the poor man's Nancy Mitford (with vermiform conscience). My English publisher tells me that my tiny novel, called *His Own Man*,★ is 'a winner', by which he means it will sell. I cannot believe that but feel shaken anyhow. I write to amuse myself; and it's disgustingly easy, and I lollop along, not only on the surface of things but perhaps several feet above them, being entertained. Instead of caring, I mock; and I have taken up the most shocking faults – I invent people about whom I know nothing, and then sloppily browse through the Encyclopedia (picking out the jokes) to bolster up my backgrounds. Thus I learn about splendid events such as papataci or sand fly fever, which I am sure is no joke if you have it, but serves me well. Isn't it awful? I am going down the drain.

How can I write about the great problems of mankind when I have no part in them, when I sit on my ass like a Virginia Woolf lady most of the year, and have a horizon as wide as half a silver dollar? How can I take seriously the problems and difficulties of the sort of people I know and see: I never did take any problems seriously unless they were life and death, and done by cruelty to the innocent. The rest (including my own) are to me the self indulgent whining of the overprivileged. Just as the cure for a finicky appetite is hunger, so the cure for boredom and stylish neurosis is a season in real hell – Poland, say; or maybe a frontier kibbutz; or the refugee camps in the Congo where children starve by hundreds every day – hunger is a slow and painful death, it must be quite something to watch it happen to children. Being, as I am, furiously angry about the world I live in, I have two choices: either get out and in it and fighting; or accept my diamond-studded destiny, sit on my ass, be a reliable wife and mother, and write acid little tales. So.

★Based on the relationship between her old friend Judy Montagu and Milton Gendal, whose mistress, the wife of one of the Olivetti family, gave birth to twins. *His Own Man* was withdrawn in the U.K. after Montagu protested.

I'm not unhappy; but deep down I feel like a plant which is going to burst out, one day; maybe a dragon's tooth plant. Then again I may be wrong; my bursting days are over, I am bitched by chronology; no matter how I feel, a sober middle-aged lady can no longer get a job on the barricades, looks too silly and she wouldn't move quick enough.

Pazienca. (Spelling?)

At the end of April I go to Israel for the Eichmann Trial. No other plans.

Work hard, my darling one, write like an angel. I love you and miss you, but never lose you.

                                    Marthy

To: Paul Matthews*

                                 January 17 1961
                                      [London]

Darling old child; I have not written you since who knows when because I am so out-of-step with your times, so dissident, so far away; and besides nobody asked me to stick my oar in. Now I think I will; an unwanted oar can easily be shoved aside.

What I want to say is: I do not agree. I do not agree with this dangerous abominable party line: 'poor Paul is having a terribly rough road to hoe', 'poor Paul looks a little better but still very haggard,' and the resultant mental and physical activity which is to treat you as if you were stricken with a fatal disease and loony-bin material yourself. I do not agree. I think it is shit and will kill you. I think you won't amount to a damned thing as a person, if this keeps up, and also never paint your way out of a paper bag. And I also think (this will make you mad as hell, it is exactly what would and has made me mad as hell) you have a suicidal streak of self-pity in you anyhow, the unkempt, mute, helpless, appealing, far too young man, who rouses and enjoys the protective instincts of others. I wish to shriek a warning: look out before it is too late.

Nobody would deny that your marriage could hardly have been worse or ended more hideously. Okay. It's a fact and can be accepted as a fact. I should think you had sound emotional grounds for hating Bryarly; also for hating yourself, which makes the operation reasonable. But for God's sake don't forget some other facts: you and you alone insisted on this marriage in the manner best described by W.S. Maugham in *Of Human Bondage*. You wanted it and you got it; and now you are paying and that can and should and must be chalked up to experience. The harder you learn the more you learn. What are we put here for, except to learn? What are any artists about,

---

*Tom Matthews's third son, a painter, had recently broken up with his wife.

except learning? The price is stiff? You are goddamned right. Whoever said it was meant to be easy, or could be had at bargain rates?

. . . I wish to God you would stop lolloping about the countryside, seeing loving and sympathetic friends and family. I wish you would sit anywhere and wash yourself out, for the time being, and <u>work</u>. I wish you would get clear enough and tough enough to accept the minimum contact with Bryarly or her doctors: sadism and masochism rear their ugly heads in all this, and you aren't doing any good, anyhow. I wish you would not only bite on the nail but swallow it and digest it, and get on with your life, for Christ's sake. You are supposed to be a painter, not an unlucky, good, innocent, and (I insist) always too young man, whom life has hit on the head with a bottle. Use your eyes, hands, brain on your job; it's quite amazing about work, it cures everything, it's what counts. That is: if you love the work. And if you don't, then hurry up, hurry up and find the work you love. The ugliest fate is not to have your marriage, after who knows (except you) what shame and anguish, end in a mental institution: marriages are expendable. The ugliest fate is to go through life not knowing how to use yourself, and all of yourself, in the doing (in the service, I would say, this being my only religious area) of something that is bigger than you are.

I personally think you ought to get divorced as soon as the law allows; but in any case, I think you ought to get cracking and the sooner the safer. Otherwise you may get the habit of all this; and then you are buggered, my boy, and buggered for good.

This is enough, not only for now but for always, of the unwanted oar. I've said what has been on my mind for a long time, and though I doubt whether you will take it, it keeps me from feeling like a crook. It's very important, as I have been trying to say, how you feel about yourself. From my point of view it's better to be loathed than conniving. From your point of view it's better to accept whatever happens, and go on, and no cozening allowed.

I don't know how much I love you but I know that I sure as hell care about what becomes of you.

Always,

Martha

To: William Walton

February 8 [1961?]
20 Chester Square
London SW1

William dear; Thinking back over our life together, which began on a sled in Luxembourg, I find that it has never been dull. This may be due to my almost constant absence. (Stay away and keep your friends is the cry.) But confidentially (as the Senators never stop saying) from sled to White House in fifteen years is tasty, is it not? I loved our last visit, including your elephant yawns (so nice that you never change) and my Chas. Adams hair and looks and fatigue; and our din in the W.H. [White House] charms me every time I think of it.★ I tried to tell Tom why I was potty about this young Mr. Pres. and the nearest I could come to making it clear was to say that it was as enjoyable with him as in the Cellar in Krakow. This may not mean a lot to you but does to me, as the cellar is the coal hole of the former Potowski palace where a jolly group does such things as a strip tease of the statue of Stalin and the cops arrive; you do see the connection, don't you. It's deeper than meets the eye, really: I find the Mr. Pres. has the makings of my favorite qualities, which are to be brave and learn quick and laugh and also remember the human race. When people get high up (not that I know all that many of same) these qualities are apt to become dim; and then of course a tedious number of people never had any of them to start with.

Tom says the Limeys are all in love with Mr. Pres. and to such an extent that they are beginning to get tired of Mr. Mac.† They now wish he was younger and peppier, poor soul, and would stop saying all is well and start exciting changes. It is so pleasant to be back here in this marvelous climate. You know where you stand in London. The sky is always dove grey to slate grey and the temperature stays at 60. I had a brief impressive time in the Carnegie with Lenny; can never get over the extent to which Lenny is a pro, maybe the most pro I've ever known. Fantastic figures appeared on the stage, to sing and play, in auditions. Not one piece of music, not one note, was unknown to Lenny; from noon until five he listened, always kind and polite, making brief steely accurate notes on each performer (yellow block on knees). I love to watch him at work; hate to watch him conduct before audiences.

And I dined with my stepson Paul because I am a great duty woman; I cannot remember being 28 because probably I never was; or rather that's the year Hemingway the lover entered my life and I was writing a monumental novel and I thought constant trouble was the natural condition of man.

Darling, it was blissful fun.

Thank you for taking me along.

Love as always,

M

★William Walton had taken Martha to dinner with the Kennedys at the White House.
†Harold Macmillan had been prime minister since 1957, after Anthony Eden's resignation. His "wind of change" speech in Cape Town in 1960, acknowledged the inevitability of African independence.

To: Alvah Bessie

April 13 1961
37 Via Pinciana
Rome

Alvah dear boy;
. . . Spain. I am giving it up. We are foolish; we forget real life. 22 years of corruption do not improve people; it infects them. 22 years of enforced mindlessness do not make people bright either. Do you remember one of the most beautiful lines of someone or other: 'Hope deferred maketh the heart sick.' That's what's the matter, basically, in Spain. But the sort of people we loved – our first love, therefore strongest, longest, blindest – are not the same people. 22 bad years have passed.

I mean to go back within the next two months, board up my half built house and leave it; some day someone will buy it because the land is so lovely. But I am through.

What am I doing? Just now, nothing. Frivolity. I go to Elizabeth Arden and have beautiful elegant hair; I amuse myself by painting my eyes à la Picasso. I fritter. My child is here in the hospital getting thin; he suffers from the curable disease of obesity, forty pounds overweight. Tom thank God has gone to Jerusalem to the Eichmann Trial. I am counting on the Jews doing for him what nothing else has: opening his eyes to the great world which is bigger, fiercer and nobler than anything one has privately. I too am going: Jordan and Egypt to do a piece on those poor wretched refugees who are Egyptian cats' paws; and then the Trial. Myself, I only want to go up the White Nile to Victoria Nyanza, and thence by jeep to Dahomey. I want to make long slow rare voyages, look at new landscape, new people, think other thoughts. I am tired of virtue and nearly dead of over anxiety.

In short, what I want now is joy. The whole poor damned world is sickening for lack of it. One had better start getting it oneself. Joy may be infectious too.

By the way, I am mad about the new young Mr. Pres. Dined with him in Washington and thought him first class. Gives me much hope for the U.S. Brains are fashionable again, and so is laughter.

Bless you dear boy. Always,
Martha

During the first years of her second marriage, Martha wrote little: no novel, only a few articles and short stories. But she read a great deal, and she thought constantly about writing. "It's awful to be a writer," she told Leonard Bernstein. "You not only must know how to write, but you have to be privately, personally, sound at the core. Not sane; but sound. If not, it always shows. Slight smell of cheese in the air, and the work gets a limp, rotting, glazed look."

*She was, once again, restless. Both Sandy Matthews and Sandy Gellhorn –
with whom Martha was continuing to have fights over weight and food – were
away at boarding school, and she felt increasingly harassed and bored by the social
life that Tom enjoyed. From the beginning she had loathed – and said so, loudly –
running a large house; she described the "servant problem" as being like "having
one's fingernails torn out." "Two and a half years in the trenches," she wrote
gloomily to Diana Cooper, "24 servants mooching through the premises, all fools
or fiends."*

*During the Christmas holidays of 1961 both Martha and Tom caught colds and
a "general air of martyrdom" hung over Rosario and Lola. Martha had sold a story
unexpectedly to television for $3,000 and she decided to spend it on exploring Africa,
on her own, to "travel for pleasure, the most daring idea yet." She took with her a
hot water bottle, wool trousers, a large Spanish fisherman's hat, paints, cards for
playing solitaire, a portable typewriter, binoculars, a bag of detective stories, Jane
Austen, and a large selection of medicines. She expected to be away three months.
Africa, she was soon telling Tom, was perfect: "Like Livingstone, I don't mind
fighting for survival; I just hate arranging gracious living."*

To: Adlai Stevenson

January 4 1962
20 Chester Square
London SW1

Adlai dear;

I plan to set out for Africa on Jan 21, armed with a pair of binoculars and
every known microbe, which are raging in me now, having been put there
with a hypodermic needle. Never felt sicker; I hope it is as wonderful as I
imagine. The journey is unplanned but I mean to start at the eastern side,
and work across the Sudan to Tchad, Camerouns and Gabonn. Looking at
animals and going to see place names that charm me. Two lady anthropologist friends of mine said that everyone in Africa knew and loved you,
and it would not hurt to have a letter from you, in case of wishing to get in
or out of some country. Personal letter; private letter; this will introduce my
dear friend who is making a journey through Africa, to look at animals and
etc. Or what not. Could you bear to? I would only use it in case of need. I
do not want to see people; I am sick of them. I only want to get past their
complex and boring visa business and maybe if I seem not to be a dope
runner, spy, or white slaver, because of being so well connected (you) this
would help.

Would be very grateful if you could manage this.

All well here; the snow is melting and 1962 already seems far along. Tom
has resolved to work more and I have resolved to work less.

There are signs of a very respectable Fascist party starting here; called The National Fellowship. Ah well.

Love,

Martha

To: Hortense Flexner

January 25 1962
Hotel des Cocotiers
Douala
Cameroun

Teechie dear:

You will be happy to know that in the Hausa language 'Oho' means 'who cares?' . . . Thus far, I've not found Africa; but only something that looks and feels like the lesser Caribbean islands, or the Guianas. I must find Africa. Hard to do. The airplane has rendered land travel extinct.

Last night I finished *Out of Africa*.* Obviously, though incredibly, I was too young when I read it 20 years ago. It made no effect then. Of course, it is a great tragic story. Telling it with a reserve that amounts to secrecy, the woman is explaining that she had everything she wanted and loved in the world – a country, a home, a way of life, a lover – and lost them all irrevocably, nearly 40 years ago, I reckon. She has lived in Denmark, since, with no one ever replacing Denys Finch-Hatton, or Africa.

Her husband (whom I knew, a big, brutal man) gave her syphilis as a wedding present when she was 18. She has suffered torments from the undiagnosed disease; and bits of her spine have been removed over the years. She is smaller than you and weighs about 80 pounds.

Her attitude to and about God somewhat chills me. It is as if she felt that He and she were both well-born. But in the end, I decide she has earned such snobbish intimacy.

How shall I escape from this boring scrofulous layer of white civilization, and get the sense of the country? I'm off inland tomorrow, but without much hope. May have to abandon this country (though, somewhere, it still has real and varied native life) and head for Tchad. And it may be too late, Teechie. Mexico is almost totally corrupted now; not our country any

---

*By Karen Blixen (1885–1962), who, in 1914, married her cousin, Baron Bror Blixen-Finecke and moved to Kenya to start a coffee plantation. Denys Finch-Hatton, a white hunter with whom she fell in love, died in a plane crash. Karen Blixen (known also as Isak Dinesen) returned to Denmark and became a writer.

more. It may be too late everywhere. I haven't a kind thought for the 20th century.

love

Gellhorn

To: Hortense Flexner

May 17 1962
Yacht 'South Wind'
Bouncing over the Aegean, with Turkey to starboard.

Beloved Teechie; I've been a silent pen-pal for months. I think of you and long to tell you the story of my life. Nobody will listen anymore. They only listened briefly in the beginning, but now I have but to say 'Africa' and all eyes glaze, including Mother's. Still Africa was a high point and that rare thing – a dream come true, of course not at all as I had dreamed it. After the boredom of the West Coast, it got progressively more fascinating. The hardships are very special; unlike those of any other place, and of a category I enjoy. The streak of Tarzan in me was pleased. I found the Africans maddening and funny; they found me exactly the same. And I did a very remarkable journey too, in my ignorance, by myself, and at the end it was like being young again and climbing over the snow Pyrenees in a cotton dress without a guide or a clue. The best was East Africa which is even more beautiful than Mexico; I can't say more. It took about 7 hours of hell-driving to do 100 miles. I did 3000 miles in a beat-up landrover with a Presbyterian Kikuyu pansy, named Joshua. He was supposed to be the driver. As a driver, he was as useful as typhus, and I ended driving myself. I was frightened every day, all day, of being lost – no one passed, no one knew where I was, and Joshua could not tell his left hand from his right and became hysterical over insects. In Africa there are insects the way there is rain in England.

In two months, I had meals in company seven times; and the odd thing is that I adored this light-house keeper's existence. I'll go back next winter. It is a pity that I found Africa so late in my career, and in its. Those black people will make a sewer of Africa (from our point of view) in no time; they don't mind sewers. But though I think them largely half-witted, I'm on their side. The whites either have to become chummy with them, or get out; otherwise (as will happen in South Africa) they'll drown in blood. But no one learns from history; and common sense is the rare human attitude.

Then I came home for Sandy's spring hols. He is very charming, and lazy, and addicted to food which is the opium of kiddies. He is now completely square & weighs 25 pounds more than I do. If he has any problems, he is inarticulate about them, but he's 14 and adolescent. I explained to Tom that we had to treat him as if he were mentally ill until it passes . . . But he's got a happy nature, is successful at his country-club school, and will become a man of the world with a monocle aged about 16. You should have heard me discussing sex with him, no one ever treated me to such calm realistic chat; I wanted to spare him all the high-minded nonsense that I absorbed. Probably I did all wrong; he's a romantic. Anyhow I said sex was fine and normal and there were only 3 essential rules: neither give nor get venereal disease; do not make girls pregnant; and never lie about emotions and make false promises.

Then Mum came to London and on May 1 we flew to Athens and we set forth on our yacht, like millionaires. We laugh like goats over the hardships of the rich, are flung about like bean bags; have had to have a very sharp talk to the crew – getting sloppier and more unwilling to do anything we wanted by the day. Greece is not my favorite place by any means. The deserted coves, in the little islands, are lovely; two islands are very pretty and with charming white cube villages; Rhodes is a medieval dream (but the rich yachts are anchored side by side, like a caravan park; the golden rural slum.) I'm glad to have done this; I always imagined it was a heavenly way to live.

. . . In Rhodes, a huge steam yacht anchored next to us, and we were asked to drinks; a man I knew, a woman Tom knew. There were 8 people in the party – including Franny Hand and her husband. Haven't seen her since college; didn't recognize her. I've no idea how I look (pretty bad and pudgy) but I am sure my facial expression cannot have reached the stage of hard, haggard respectability that hers had. She was never a girl who saw a joke; but she's a matron (married for 29 years) who oozes correctitude. I attended this party in old shorts & shirt, while those grey-haired, well coiffed ladies had on summer evening dresses, pearls & diamonds. I got drunk so as not to notice the terrible dryness of their minds. Tom says these are the sort of people he's known all his life – 'friendly, ill-meaning people'. To me, it's a world more vulgar and depressing than any other.

. . . Ma and Tom sail for the US on July 5 – and I, God willing, go off somewhere alone & write. I want to write about Africa. And finish a book of short stories. Maybe I'm going to get a permanent work-room in London. If I had such a place, I'd like London better. There's a good line in Doris Lessing's new novel: 'I don't enjoy pleasure'. Personally I enjoy surprises, and work. But it's alarming, Teechie, to grow less and less gregarious. I can hardly bear social occasions; I feel as if I'd written the script long ago.

I love you very much
Gellhorn

To: Leonard and Felicia Bernstein

June 6 1962
Corfu

Darlings. I've had writer's cramp in the head for months; but silence does not mean forgetfulness . . .

Yesterday, in a three day old paper, I saw that the Israelis had done what I hoped they would – executed Eichmann quickly, without advance publicity, and scattered his ashes in the sea. Have no idea what repercussions there are to this in the world, but I am sure they did the right thing. People do not realize that this monster was a Joan of Arc to the Arabs and to all the remaining (plenty) Fascists everywhere. Dead, he can not be a rallying point – hardly even a memory. Alive he was a curse on the soil of Israel and a potential danger. I feel a curious sense of relief; obviously there was no punishment to fit his crime, but there is such a thing as cleansing the world of those who have lost all right to be members of the human race.

And I am against capital punishment, too. But this was a different (indeed unique) category; and I continue to brood on what is to me a new idea: a man can be perfectly sane, and perfectly inhuman (ie insane). I hope Israel will not release his memoirs – not now; but will preserve them, for students of human behaviour. It is just possible that somewhere inside that document a future genius – a Freud of sociologists – will discover the root germ of anti-Semitism.

I love you very much. I want to see you. But in view of my incurable allergy to New York, I never want to see you there, for I feel myself to be a bad-tempered, wretched mess – unable to give or get pleasure . . .

your loving
Martha

To: Adlai Stevenson

June 6 1962
Corfu

Adlai dear boy;

. . . I read your Lake Forest Speech word by word. Being an inverted snob, I never expect people in power to know beans (a polite way for say 'ass from elbow') about anything. On the contrary, you do. Obviously you walk, or float, on eggs; and speak carefully . . . Of course none of us will be around in fifty years to note how Africa is faring; but in case I'm seeing ectoplasm, I'll eat my ghastly hat if Africa is in any real order by then. (Two hundred years seems nearer the mark; and even so they'll be a lot faster than we were).

There are two points I don't think you considered.

To wit: what is so hot about white civilization that they should aim for it? They may prefer the muddle and mess, African style, to ours. From my travels, I think the least civilized (ie contaminated by whites) of the Africans are not only the happiest but the best adjusted to life on that beautiful murderous continent. They may, you know, work out something entirely their own. I bet it will be tough and bloody; but so is ours.

The other point is this: we always talk of 'helping' them. Psychologically, this is all wrong. Children don't grow up by taking their parent's advice; but by disobeying and learning the hard way through their own experience. I think the Africans will have to do that. Individual humans waste a lot of time that way; so do nations. And no other procedure works. Also I think we better sit tight on our bottoms and our money-bags, and wait until they ask for help; and then be very very accountancy-minded when we provide it. All people want something for nothing, if possible; all people have a huge supply of leech blood. Since Africans are, en masse, the most illogical lot you could find, these two tendencies are exaggerated in them . . . And their own powers of inventiveness, concentration, self-reliance (not top grade, you'll agree?) will wither even further away if a lot of spoon feeding is the order of the day.

The local medical wallah I saw told me that the whole black mass was half-alive – by our standards. What with syphilis, malaria, bilharzia, and any nutritional ailment you can name, they'd be dead if they were us. But they aren't dead; and they don't need psychiatrists.

. . . I think a great deal of waiting, and a minimum of enthusiastic action, would be our greatest kindness to Africa. But then, I never fear the Russians. I don't fear them because I think they are worse boobs than we are, and to know them seems – everywhere – to get a belly-full of them. Their goods are shoddy and their manners a scandal. And the Russians could never organize the Africans. I don't believe anyone can (not even the Africans). I'd think it funny to watch the Russians try.

But I'll go back to Africa in January; and go every year unless the local whites make such a balls-up of it that the blacks knife anyone with a fair skin on sight. It isn't that I'm mad about Africans; I'm not. They're far too different, as why shouldn't they be? But I am mad about their landscape, and the emptiness of it, and the animals, and the happy fact that they really haven't joined the 20th century. It doesn't seem to me to be the best century on record; we have to live in it but escapes are a joy.

. . . We were on a yacht for three weeks, did I tell you? A yacht is a millionaire mug's game. Only the rich could dream up such an expensive way to be bored and uncomfortable.

love
Martha

To: Leonard Bernstein

September 22 1962
Chateau d' Artigny
Montbazon
France

My dearest Lennypot: In the station at Tours, I saw *Newsweek* with your picture on it, so have read about you and the Lincoln Center.★ That's why you had to go home early and Feli needed Paris dresses. It sounds very big and exciting. I always love pictures of you, since I imagine I see many things in your face which are hidden to the multitude, and I am devoted to what I see.

. . . I am at present in a place such as you never say in all your puff. It is a palace, copied from Versailles, by M. Coty *le roi des parfums*. Not unnaturally, M. Coty got the horrors upon seeing his finished work, and sold the vast pile for a hotel. I came upon it yesterday, for I have been taking a long slow walk through France in our Mini-Minor, and am now established in a room the size of a house, decorated with marble lining the walls to a height of ten feet, and Empire furniture and scarlet and gold satin. It is blissfully funny. Whereas the whole Loire valley pullulates with the most beautiful and genuine chateaux, which poor mad M. Coty might have bought – I see him now as a *petit bourgeois* Oxymandias.

Except for two weeks when Sandy joined me at Duino, I've now been alone for just over two months. This last week, in the golden September weather, roaming without aim through parts of France I'd never seen before (but how had I missed them?) and which are miracles of God and man – land and villages – has been the best. The natural world is what I love, and have faith in; and the aimless life of a gypsy is all that now charms me. All the weeks of fasting, silence and prayer produced 200 typed pages not one of which is worth reading. I may have come to the end; can't yet take this in, but the thought sits in my mind – no longer as a screaming sound, but as a stone. It seems to me that art, great and small, is similar in one respect: it is an affirmation. It is a statement of hope. The finished work, I think (thinking hard) is the one tangible hope in the world – it is almost as if hope took form and could be touched. I find myself unable to affirm – anger itself is an affirmation, you know, an affirmation of disgust against what is stupid and corrupt and spoiling of life.

. . . It is strange not to know what next. A paralysis of the will feels like sleepiness and amnesia. Probably I will return to journalism, although shuddering, as I really do not want to see any more of humanity's folly. The

---

★The opening of Philharmonic Hall in Lincoln Center for the Performing Arts in New York on September 23, 1962.

newspapers – seldom read – look to me like the blatant record of a mass death-wish. I am out of sympathy; the great world rolls on insanely taking no account of what is real in life – the quiet back country everywhere, with slow people in the fields, slowly doing what they have always done, harvesting food for the continuation of life. To report the death wish. That's what journalism amounts to now.

I'd like to learn so much, but wonder if my memory is an adequate tool. I'd really like to learn botany and biology and Swahili; for no purpose except to see Africa better. But I cannot write about Africa – I tried and tried and it all came out like cement – and isn't all life exactly like the digestive process, so one must swallow for use, not simply swallow? I don't know. It may also be that one has to come to terms with disappointment. Or that despair is the beginning of wisdom.

Tom arrives this evening: I haven't seen him for two and a half months and am rather alarmed. It's become as natural and right to be alone and silent that I don't know how I can shift over to company. I was horrible to Sandy, for which I shall never forgive myself: he is fourteen but not nearly as odious as he has a right to be at that age, and I behaved with unjust harsh criticism, my nerves writhing like Medusa's hair, and was so ashamed of myself that I felt physically sick, and relieved like a fish thrown back into water when I was again alone. It bodes ill for being a member of the human race.

Did you write the Lament for the Dead? I hope so; and if you did, you are a wonder.

You won't have time to write to me, so do not worry. I wish you everything good. I see great sadness in your eyes (do I imagine it?) but that seems to me inevitable and probably right. Sadness but no hardness. You must have moments of joy, or you could not live and work as violently as you do. It's the one vitamin pill that no one has yet bottled, and which is essential: joy. I wish you that brief, rare, magical shining – you deserve it.

Give my real love to Feli; I think of her often.

Always, as you know,

Marty

To: Sandy Matthews★

> [October ? 1962]
> 20 Chester Square
> London SW1

Dear old boy; where to begin? I look with pleasure and astonishment at this pen-pallery springing up between two lost souls.

. . . About talking: I suppose it starts in the family – mine was a talking family. My father was a brilliant man and talker, and held that since communication between people was largely done by words, the words should be exact, interesting and lively. We were trained to think and to talk; we were forbidden to talk about money or gossip, two subjects my father found unfit for human exchange. But all else was wide open. I think we had a very odd upbringing, too noble (though there was no sanctity in it and God was never called on), too active in the head, and too peculiarly our own. We have none of us ever fitted into any set or society, as a result; my father simply mocked the conventional ways of feeling and thinking of average bourgeois society. I talked for fun when I was very young; then I talked from hope – a great, intoxicating hope. It was always like holding out one's hand to the possible friend, the possible love; it was always saying I'm here, where are you, tell me. That's worn off, or died, well and truly. I am, oddly, happiest when alone for weeks on end talking to no one there, talking in my mind to the imagined listener who perfectly hears, perfectly understands, and talks back with equal truthfulness. In daily life, since I cannot avoid it entirely (but I avoid it most of the time, hard on Tom who is uncritically gregarious) I talk out of despair. I find the talk people bat about so slow, so dull, so approximate that I cannot endure it; and I talk in the despairing effort to make it less intolerable to me. That does not, however, work; only leaves me feeling wearied and empty, or a clown, as the case may be. I learned about drink, in order to be able to listen a bit and talk a lot about nothing much to people who don't matter to me. What I like is to listen to people who talk better than I, and more truthfully; I have found only a few alas, and they are not readily at hand.

When you find the one you can trust with your heart, you will also be able to talk to her. If you can't talk to her, run away. And if she can't talk to you, be sure there is something deeply wrong. Not that most people either know this, or try for it, or find it; but most people are accepting with grace and sometimes with pleasure a compromise; or else they are frozen in their loneliness and without hope of escape.

★Sandy was Tom's youngest son. Initially neither Martha nor Sandy found their relationship easy, but this letter is one of the first that marked a new friendship between them, which would over the years become very affectionate and important to both of them. Martha wrote hundreds of letters to Sandy in the next thirty-five years.

I don't really think I am getting old, nor even that I am growing up, which would be desirable. But your pop does, as I constantly feel, so I take it he knows. And of course there are the facts, the chronological facts; and if I look closely in the mirror I can vaguely see myself, only vaguely – I never saw myself which is why I've always hated photographs. But for myself, for my own private self, I feel dismayed because there is so much to do and be, and clearly there is not unlimited time; but what is worse – the things I want to do and be are exactly the same as they were when I was 18, only clearer now, more urgent, and they are no doubt quite mad. So, to keep myself in line, I tell myself I am growing old. And to prove that's a lie, I still do things which I could have done at 21; and take the derring-do chances of the category I enjoy, and daydream and hunger, just about the way you do. It's hopeless, Sandy, take it from me: there's no way to win. You get what you ache and perish for, in tiny unexpected bursts when least looked for; and sometimes are so blinded with your hunger that you can't even feel them as they happen, but only know afterwards, in despair, what you lightly took. But sometimes you do know, for a minute or five, or three days or a week, and it only whets the insatiable appetite; but there is joy. I know that much. Not frequent or enduring, but there. The only reason I know to go on hoping.

. . . I am going through a patch of coal black darkness, almost paralyzed, as if trying to find one's way in the galleries of a mine without a lamp. I cannot write at all. I can hardly bear to see people, and talk (again) is an appalling effort. I am trying to find a work-room because it will help to be out of the house, which feels to me like a handsome tomb built over me; and I shall try to paint, my happy baby-work. Or maybe lie on the floor. Or maybe read. Though reading also has become hideously difficult; if one can't write, it is agony to see how beautifully others are managing. A bad time. You are not alone.

You may never become comfortable in your skin; but console yourself with thinking that you have a long time for the struggle. It is the only good news I can give you.

I took your last letter as one of the greatest compliments I have ever received; and thank you for it with my whole heart.

Love,
Stepmum

To: Adlai Stevenson

November 8 1962
20 Chester Square
London SW1

Dearest Adlai; This is a day when it would have mattered to be together.*
To weep. All the weeping for Mrs. R. should have been done years ago,
starting seventy years ago. Not for her, now; she'd never have been afraid
of dying and would have hated to live, ill and dependent. I always thought
she was the loneliest human being I ever knew in my life; and so used to
bad treatment, beginning with her mother (she spoke of her mother with
love; I hated her mother) and going right on that it did not occur to her to
ask for anything for herself. Not ever. I've wept for her often; and been
shaken with anger for her too; and I never liked the President, nor trusted
him as a man, because of how he treated her. And always knew she was
something so rare that there's no name for it, more than a saint, a saint who
took on all the experiences of everyday life, an absolutely unfrightened
selfless woman whose heart never went wrong. And her hunger to give
love – she who had never gotten it when she should, from those who
should have given – is hardly to be remembered; you will find it mad that
I felt she was younger than I, and I was twenty six when I first knew her
and felt it then.

Today we can weep for ourselves. I feel lonelier and more afraid;
someone gone from one's own world who was like the certainty of refuge;
and someone gone from the world who was like a certainty of honor.

Words are no use. Weeping's no use either. There it is. I know you feel
this too; I wish I could have spent some of this day, which happens to be
my birthday, with you.

Hands across the sea, dear boy; from one in need to another, helplessly.

Love,
Martha

---

*Eleanor Roosevelt died on November 7, 1962, at the age of seventy-eight. Martha heard
of her death on the 8th – her fifty-fourth birthday. She had met her first on her twenty-sixth
birthday, in 1934. Later, Martha wrote: "There has been no other woman of her stature in
public life and probably never will be again."

To: Adlai Stevenson

December 26 1962
20 Chester Square
London SW1

Adlai dear boy; Thank you for sending me those fine essays you spoke about Mrs. R. I can't write you more about her; I said it all that first morning when I so terribly wanted to talk to you. Life closes over the dead like quicksand; they sink into death and the surface is smooth above them. Everything goes on. We are, of course, all moving on that quicksand. There are moments when I think it may be restful beneath it. In any case we can do nothing about the dead; miss them, because one cannot help oneself, though missing, like regret, is an agonizing and futile emotion; and try to be a bit decenter in their name and memory.

I follow with indignation and disgust the latest of your trials and tribulations. How awful to have to be a grown-up which you are in a country of incurable adolescents. What is to be done? The people of the United States of America need suffering to learn dignity; but I hope to Christ they are spared it, simply because they would not suffer alone and the rest of the world has had enough. Everyone's politics stink, as a matter of fact; perhaps it is simply a revolting profession, essential like garbage collecting and sewer cleaning, but revolting. I do not know why this should be.

Spent three weeks in Germany and I shall never go again. They're incurable people, in my opinion. At present they are in the phase of being quiescent sheep and tigers; but only because they are overweight with butter and cream. Remove those and they will become insane blood-loving sheep and man-eating tigers. The young are sometimes pathetic; and the best Germans are alone, despairing, condemned to their country. We can count our blessings, few though they are. Anyhow, we're not Germans.

Am off to Africa on Jan 10. Golly, so much writing these days, but I look forward with a wildly joyful heart to sun and the beautiful animals.

Love,

Martha

To: Nikki Dobrski★

April 4 1963
20 Chester Square
London SW1

Dearest Nikki;

No word from you. You are using this house, aren't you? Please say yes.

I saw George Jellicoe† at a party the other night. Didn't recognize him but I never do, nor remember names either, and my mind is going. He looked bouncier smaller and uglier than I remembered. He had with him an older, better bred version of Patsy, called Princess Carraciola or some such. I loathed her but talked politely. Solid Fascist Eyetie, rich as cream the way they are, and unimproved by defeat. My God weren't we fortunate to win the war.

Love to both,
Martha

★A close woman friend who lived in Switzerland.
†The 2nd Earl Jellicoe (1918–), longest serving member of the House of Lords. In 1973 he resigned as leader when he admitted to casual affairs with prostitutes.

Africa and Vietnam, 1963-1974

Sometime in the early spring of 1963, Martha discovered that Tom had been having a long affair. Her reaction was one of outrage, as well as disbelief that she could feel so jealous. She decided, instantly, to leave. "I will never try it again," she told Diana Cooper. "We'll be single ladies (you with countless admirers) and I earnestly and fervently believe it will be gayer." She asked Tom for a divorce and took off for America to spend time with her mother, whose health worried her. Edna was now eighty-four. They drove for a holiday to Florida.

Whenever she could, whenever she was not with Sandy or visiting St. Louis, Martha now escaped to Africa, most often to the coast near Mombasa, where she could snorkel, swim, and lie in the sun.

To: Adlai Stevenson

May 22 1963
Destin
Florida

Adlai dear boy; This American Apartheid is a disgrace. What can be done? I don't honestly see how we can bellow about democracy, freedom and the American Way of Life while this beastliness goes on. Mum and I drove through Miss. and Ala. on our way here, with the motor literally burning itself up. (I mean to get a job in a Mombasa garage and learn about cars for myself; mechanics are worse than quack doctors.) You do not see negroes. Every so often there's a wretched shanty; there they live. But they vanish from streets and roads, like the Jews in Germany before 1938, hiding in their houses. There's something Freudian and ugly in it too; this haunted notion that the white men have about negro lust for white women. Certainly the white men must be lusting after negresses. I've had chats with negroes, revealing, strange, but they are cautious, and rightly frightened. How do white women usually treat negro men, I wonder. It must be abominable. Anyhow it all makes me ashamed, both to be white and to be American. And what the Africans must think. No amount of AID is going to counteract Bull Connor.★

I wish I hadn't wasted time with you talking about personal things and depressing you. The world is far more interesting. I'd have liked to indoctrinate you properly about Germany, for we are folly-bitten there too. Putting all our money on a profoundly unstable horse. And about Nasser and the Middle East. By now, one should give up caring or having ideas or being enraged by the US doctrine of expediency; as if expediency ever worked. But I cannot stop, though I know my fury is futile.

I wish you well, dear boy. And I am sorry to have saddened you; and selfishly sorrier still to have misused time with you.

Love

Martha

To: William Walton

May 24 1963

Destin

Florida

Dearest Pissoir Attendant;

I think of you with love. I also think a lot about what the quality is in a man which makes him entire. This is not idle rumination; as I wish to be damn sure to locate that quality in future; even the briefest walk-outs must not take place with cripples. Do you feel you know anything about women, after all these years of study and experimentation? I thought I knew quite a lot about men but see I was wrong; so now I am back at work, determined to learn. Having absolutely no one to talk to or observe, my learning is a matter of memory. I have to think about what I've known and try to sort out. I told you that you and Jimmy [Gavin] were the only two men I was sure were grown-ups, in quite different ways of course; it seems significant that you both remain friends, James slightly handicapped by having to treat me as if I was Agent X-77 of the Ogpu, but his heart is in the same solid place. And William, how wise you were not to marry. Of course you had the children, as your main concern; but how wise to know you couldn't combine things; how sensible to have seen the children through, and be available to them at need, but now free. Your gregariousness helped you, I suppose, and your endless ability to be amused by whatever comes. If you have ever been lonely, it has not showed. Then too, I imagine, life with your wife was a shocker, and dread remained. You could not be sure enough of never having to repeat a day of it. Yet you do not fear or dislike

---

★Bull Connor (1897–1973), an outspoken segregationist from Selma, Alabama, who turned the dogs on civil rights marchers.

women. It is a most interesting subject of thought for me.

The Gulf of Mexico is beautiful and so is the white sand, and that's the end of it. Americans are the greatest despoilers of scenery that the world has ever known; I cannot believe that any nation, at any time, had such a reckless lack of care for beauty and such solid bad taste.

I adore sunbathing with a book; and the water is bliss; there is nothing in it for Mum. She's been variously ill; even this tiny journey seems to me too much for her. Yesterday we went to a dentist in Fort Walton and she had two teeth pulled. It never ends; it fills me with fear of growing old; I will not have her uncomplaining elegance and resignation. I know what I'll do; I'll bump myself off. And all in all, this violently costly almost four months' exile in my native land has been futile: a loss of time like a loss of blood, and all the money I've earned this year (a good year) gone – not on pleasure, not on work, but just on living. My stay has not effected miracles; I haven't been able to make her well physically or lift the awful disappointment – that's what heartbreak may be – from her mind. My anger against Tom is enormous; he deceived her even more than me, and he pretends to love her totally. And I am the one who is left with the sorrow of it and the helplessness and hopelessness and self-destruction of trying to tide her over. This has been the lousiest phase of my career which no one would call a bowl of cherries, all in all; but nothing like this ever buggered up my life before.

. . . I'm trying to line up lucrative magazine assignments. If only I could get started on my new life, all would be well. What is killing me is this interminable wait. It is almost ten months now, since I began to live in definite limbo; it is three years that I've been living in semi-limbo and unable to understand what was wrong, because it never occurs to me that people lie.

Ah well.

If you have never read a glorious book called *Henderson the Rain King* by Saul Bellow, do so. I couldn't give you a better tip. Pure joy.

. . . I love you dearly, and look forward to seeing you again in three or four or five years time. And of course, I wish you wrote letters; but I see that American life precludes writing letters, so abandon hope.

Love always,

Martha

To: Diana Cooper

> June 15 1963
> 118 East Hamilton
> New Jersey

Dearest Diana; My mother is dying.* What else do you think matters to me? Day by day, unafraid, in despair because she can't finish it once and for all and not be a 'burden', never talking of herself, thinking only of others; and her eyes are something to break my heart all day long and all night long. I'm dying with her in small pieces, longing to keep her company, horrified by the loneliness and how love (real love, this) cannot reach.

As for Tom, you know nothing about him and me and our life alone. You know that wonderful party-line he's been selling all these years. And then he has such a talent for arousing pity; it's like a talent for growing roses. Remember B.B. [Bernard Berenson] and 'life enhancers'? Tom may enhance many lives; for me he has been slowly and then finally, definitively, a life-destroyer. I mean to live somehow, not die; so that's that.

I don't know when I will get home and home will be my 18 foot wide work flat on Caxton Street. If there is any hope of joy left in the world, let's have some of it together. I am spending the summer in England in a loaned house near Oxford with Sandy and his favorite American boy cousin. So shall see you sometime.

> Goodnight, darling
>
>   Martha

To: Sandy Matthews

> July 26 1963
> [?]

Darling; Just a quickie because I MUST get down to that damned German article. Your splendid letter arrived this a.m. I need time to read it again and think it over before making a proper reply.

But I am specially interested in you and God. You're not alone in your searching and feeling; you will find literature full of just your kind of want. I do not feel it; never have; we are probably entirely products of our environment and upbringing. My grandmother was one of the founders of the Ethical Society. Ethic, says my dictionary, 'Relating to morals, treating of moral questions, science of morals, moral principles, rules of conduct, whole field of moral science.' . . . Humanism, again says the dictionary, is 'Devotion to human interests, system concerned with human (not divine)

---

*Edna Gellhorn recovered.

interests, or with the human race (not the individual.) . . .' Well, I guess I am an Ethical Humanist, though all definitions seem to me limiting.

I would hate to believe in immortality; I would be afraid to die if I thought I would have to live forever. I would also hate to be afraid to die. I expect to die sometime (any time, no one knows) and return to dust, and some of me will live as long as anyone remembers me or is influenced by what I did and thought in my life. No more. I like that. It's a great comfort to me to know that nothingness and rest will follow the more and more complicated struggle to be and to become.

There is a mystery at the very beginning of life: why did the gases explode, why did the waters recede; why did man develop from the carnivorous weapon-making ape Australopithecine? I have no idea. I do not give the name God to that mystery. I just know there's a mystery.

God is too limited by man, for my taste; and besides, even if my nature allowed for considerations of a supernatural Being, I would be finally and absolutely put off by all organized religions. They seem to me largely based on fear (Save me Save Me, Me, Me) and on hypocrisy and cruelty too. Pretending to practise what one preaches (no one does) and bullying others to agree. I know what the sense of worship is, because I worship nature: one is flooded by gratitude and wishes to give praise.

The Ten Commandments, except for the one about God which I cannot understand or feel, strike me as perfect ethics. They are the best thing about Christianity; and though no Christians or anyone (I expect; no there must be exceptions) fully obeys them, they are a first class guide rule. I believe passionately that we are responsible, here and now, for ourselves and our acts; there is no escape from that; and punishment, I also think, is meted out here below, as are rewards. Not necessarily punishment on time, or even to fit the crime (that would be ideal justice) but in some fatal way it arrives; equally, the rewards, which are interior, also arrive. With this tiny set of thoughts, I stumble along my way; always remembering – sooner or later – how much I have been spared, and fearing (often) that I will be spared less and less. Because we are also here to learn (I can see no other reason.) What we learn, or a tiny fragment of it, flows into some general river of learning, and helps those who come after. The process is slow and wasteful; but exists. I also imagine that we learn best, being ornery animals, by having our brains beat out – I am not talking about war; therefore I suspect the soft and protected lives, I think those learn too little; they have somehow not paid their fare.

Make what you can of that.

Anyhow, if God created man, He can hardly object to someone taking man seriously; and caring deeply about human behavior.

It seems to me that the Jews invented God out of their loneliness, and that everyone's God basically is needed for this: we are alone, we do not know why we came here; we want to feel protected, that Someone is interested in us and cares and will keep a loving eye on us. I'd have thought God would be so busy keeping the planets and stars from crashing into each other, that that was enough. Besides, I think it is pure glorious luck if ever, if even only for a little while, one can escape the truth of loneliness. I don't like it, but accept it; and that gets easier as the years go on. Cheering note for you; though you may have the luck to become really, totally, two-in-one some day. It is what everyone seeks.

I love you, old boy; and will write more when I've got those Germans off my mind.

                                                                    Stepmum

To: Sandy Matthews

                                                      August 1 1963
                                                              [?]

Dearest old boy; I'll tell Sybille [Bedford] about your reaction to The Trial of Dr. Adams.★ She will be pleased. It's the only reward writers get; to feel that they did something exciting to another's mind. She's here for the Ward Trial;† staying at 20 Chester Sq. I called her this a.m. because so shocked by Ward's attempted suicide but she was running for a train and will call me back this evening. I've been following that trial (Sybille will write it up for Esquire so look out for that number in a month or so; she is <u>always</u> worth reading and specially on law.) It's been a horror; it seemed to me that every tart in London, if young enough to move and prejudice a jury, could walk in and say what she liked – applauded by the detectives, whom I deeply mistrust in almost every criminal case – and Ward was helpless. Clearly he's a fool of a man, a permanent adolescent; no matter what anyone says it is a sign of being arrested to whore around with teenage girls when you are middle-aged – but that doesn't make him a criminal. It casts doubt on his taste and intelligence; yet he was not married, was deceiving no one, and I have the impression he was quite nice to those beastly tarts. Young Miss Keeler strikes me as a dangerous liar, and with the soul of a cobra. Now the poor man has just about killed himself; and maybe he will not recover. Miss Keeler can congratulate herself on the destruction she has done at an early

---

★An account of the Old Bailey trial of John Bodkin Adams entitled *The Best We Can Do* (1958). Dr. Adams was a doctor from Eastbourne accused of murdering a patient.

†Dr. Stephen Ward, a fashionable osteopath, was charged with living off immoral earnings. Christine Keeler, a twenty-one-year-old call girl, had had relations with the Secretary of State for War, John Profumo, who resigned after it was revealed that she had also been sleeping with the Russian naval attaché. The Macmillan government almost fell. On the last day of the trial Ward took an overdose and died three days later.

age. I'd say all the men involved with her were fools. Sex is one of the most interesting subjects in the world: for a few instants of pleasure, people are willing to risk their whole lives, the whole structure of their lives. There's some link-up, which I do not decipher, between self confidence and sex.

Don't fear death, my Sandy; that's a sure way to cripple life. Don't fear anything if you can possibly help it; or anyhow think about your fear and get it into shape, where you can handle it. Fear is a hideous burden and useless. Fearing something does not stop it; it only makes the time of living ugly and menaced. I believe in working against rational fears (look at Ban the Bomb; goodness how happy those people must feel and rightly so), in trying to spare the world threats and suffering. (Which is why I keep on mumbling warnings against the Germans; no, that article is for the Atlantic if they finally dare take it.) But I think one has to fight fear in oneself _for_ oneself. Self fears are really diminishing, to one's dignity as a human being, to one's chances of living hard and fully.

I'm actually sweating; you wouldn't believe England. We've had 10 days of perfect sun. I never saw the like. Now I have to go off and interview a pub keeper for my East Hendred article ($1000 for Vogue.) I wish you were here.

Love always,

Stepmum

To: William Walton

November 23 1963
Mombasa
Kenya

Dearest William; I only heard this morning.* One feels the sun must stand still and the sky turn black. It is impossible to take it in; such shock, such horror stupefies the mind. I know it is true and he is murdered but cannot believe it yet; takes time to get used to anything so wicked and vile and wasteful. And so horribly dangerous to all the world.

. . . Cannot begin to think of the future; what will be undone that he did, what disorder and stupidity will pour in; oh it makes one too sick in mind and heart; too stunned. I feel also a loss; that intelligent altogether alive charming charming and decent human being gone, as if we could afford it for a minute, as if one's own life will not be poorer – together with everyone else's.

I wish I could be near you. I feel very frightened; man is his own enemy

---

*President Kennedy had been shot on November 22, in Dallas.

to the point of stark fatal madness; there is no other enemy. One is afraid to live among such a ravening species.

Will write to you again later. You know how I feel for you, for you as his friend; and how I feel for all of us everywhere. Amputation: that's what it is: the life of our times getting suddenly amputated.

Darling, a loving hand across several seas.

Martha

To: Jacqueline Kennedy

December 24 1963
Mombasa
Kenya

Dear Mrs. Kennedy;
You will have heard millions of words and read millions of words, many of them noble and all sincere, but it seems to me words are hopelessly futile. For a month and a day, I have been thinking of you and that uniquely fine man, your husband, and can find no words for a steady passion of grief. You are most beautifully worthy of him; I hope the country will become worthy of him. But we are all poorer, and always will be.

Martha Gellhorn

To: George Paloczi-Horvath★

February 5 1964
Mombasa
Kenya

George dear; You know what would be interesting to write about? The nature of happiness. You know about it without knowing, because you are yourself, a brave man, an extravert. (The brave have a better chance for happiness than anyone else which is the best recommendation for bravery. Otherwise bravery is a mug's game; you stick out your neck and the frightened chop it off. There are more frightened people so their ability to chop off is extreme.)

I know little about happiness and am suffused in it, just now, bathed, floating, almost alarmed by it. For no reason. That's why I think the subject

---

★George Paloczi-Horvath, a Hungarian writer who had been arrested in 1949, tortured, and imprisoned for five years by the Communist regime, and later wrote an account of his life, *The Undefeated*. He and his wife Agi Argent became close friends of Martha's. They had a son called Georgie. George was, Martha wrote, "a man who understood what I talked about, what haunted me." They were "world watchers" together.

interesting. The nearest I can come to a reason is that I've got a good borrowed portable gramophone and all of three LP records – Brahms, Beethoven and Chopin (our local music shop sells Pop and Hindu bleating love songs.) But surely, just because the silence has been filled with this glory, is not enough reason for me to rejoice, the way the saints are supposed to do, who praise Him. What else? The weather is like being kissed. There is a star, whose name I do not know, to the southeast, so glorious that it makes me feel faint. What else? My establishment is miraculously pretty, luxurious, comfortable (I have never been so comfortable in my life.) None of these are reasons. I've just returned from Uganda, where Buss★ proved to be a prime shit, a scientific fraud, a man lusting for publicity, mean, conceited and a bore who ought to be put down for that reason, like a mad dog. I spent my time in such physical discomfort as you can only find in war, and bored to the point of insanity. No reason to be happy: I have written the piece and doubt if it will pass and I damned well need the money. No reason to be happy. And yet I am.

Tell Georgie, who will then respect me, that I have been charged by a lion (owing to Buss's vanity.) And have slept in a mud hut on a canvas cot 12 inches from the ground with a kerosene lamp before my front door to keep off hippos and lions, and they made more near noise than London traffic. I am not impressed; I was only cross. No big murderous animals scare me beyond the actual moment when they could kill you; and that's brief and I have no pre-imagination and no memory. What gives me the shakes in Africa is the insects. I was eaten by safari ants and pepper ticks and driven insane by clouds of lake flies so thick they dimmed the stars. That's all that worries me. They can have their dime-store mutinies until the cows come home, and all the offended wild animals can, understandably, take against the smell of man. But the insects give me the horrors. I sat in a small plane to Kampala with my dress around my neck, picking off pepper ticks with an eyebrow tweezer and having the horrors.

What's the matter with Agi? I know she has nothing to do in her office except knit. So why doesn't she use her time to write to me? Tell her I feel abused.

I love you all

Martha

★An animal scientist Martha had gone to see – he was an expert on elephants.

To: Diana Cooper

February 25 1964
Mombasa
Kenya

My dearest and only Diana;

. . . Of course I have no feelings about your going to Tom's; every day if it amuses you. I'm just so very glad I am here, not there. As for Magouche,* I daresay she was his bedfellow at some time, I daresay any lady he took out a few times was, or he tried; he hasn't anything else to do except play tennis. (Didn't you think Pam† a joke? It is awful to have one's husband enamored of someone that neither oneself nor one's friends would care to have a hot meal with. So much nicer if you could be rather proud of the lady.) But one thing you can do, darling, and that is tell Magouche or anyone else that I <u>long</u> for and crave divorce.

. . . Tom's the only part of my life that I regret which is odd since my life is positively starred with mistakes. But they all had value one way or the other. The dread Ernest taught me things about the world I'd never have known, and living with him I wrote more than at any time before or since, which is reason enough not to regret him. The time with Tom was solid exhausting waste. I so wish I had it back; and so wish I'd come here instead of taking Sandy to Italy when he was four; I wanted to but lost my nerve due to him, his age. It would have been far better for him, every way, he'd be better off now; and I'd never have run into Tom again. Well, it occurs to me that there is always a penalty for cowardice, for any form of it and any degree of it. So that was the penalty: nine years wasted.

But it is a piece of luck anyhow to have gotten here, however late, and after what insane and pointless misery. (That also seems so strange; I cannot imagine why I agonized over Tom.) I'm not only really at home in my skin, at last, but the skin is spiffing. It's so wonderful to feel free — and this is freedom: I see absolutely no one and it's total liberty to find you can live day after day on your own resources and like it. And so wonderful, magical, to feel so well. I now weigh 123 which is 3 pounds more than my best so am getting back to that; and my main sport is browning all over, naked by the pool. Bottom and bosom are very hard to cook. It's the best 5 months I can remember, though the first ones, slaving on the house, were so awful I've forgotten them.

I'll have to tell you about Mombasa but I don't know what description will mean. I live outside the town, 5 miles, on the beach; and the scenery is South Seas. A lot of Vervet monkeys live on my place too and eat the

---

*Magouche Phillips, once married to the painter Arshile Gorky.
†The widow of General Vladimir Peniakoff "Popski" of Popski's Private Army in WWII.

fruit of the wild almond trees, perched on the garage; sometimes perched on my window sill watching me type. The sea is right there, two minutes away, blue like the Mediterranean with a line of surf over the reef like the South Seas. I can't see any other houses or hear any voices. It is hot, I live in a bikini, dressing in shorts for dinner. There was a young black mamba in the sitting room a few nights ago and when a bat starts creeping up my mosquito net, I hit it with a library book. There are insects of every possible variety; one fights them hopelessly. I only travel if on a job, expenses paid. Here I write, read, putter on the place (outdoor men's work), swim, sunburn, attend to my cottage industry, and sleep. It makes no picture does it? Now I am going swimming. And I love you and can't wait for our reunion.

Martha

To: Alvah Bessie

April 11 1964
Mombasa
Kenya

Dear Alvah; I'm not <u>only</u> a writer alas – I'm a mother, daughter and employer and worrying about my troops and trying to support them, and organize their lives, occupies a good deal more of my time than writing. And the writing has been largely hack, to make money; but around now I'm so glad to be able to write that I don't mind that. I only mind how hard it is (eating a ton of shit) to get the assignments and how desperately hard to please these editors. I'd gladly write beauty cures if that paid and I knew any. The difference now is that I'm a working writer instead of a bored and harassed wife and hostess. Never bored any more.

The book (the only pleasure) is just mailed off; guaranteed not to please. Three long stories entitled *Pretty Tales for Tired People*

. . . It's so odd, when at last you get straight in your mind about yourself, thus reaching an incredible unhoped for position of calm and serenity, you find that you have to worry about others. But again, that's preferable. No, I shall never again try to live with anyone, it's not my cuppa; I like living alone, I do not enjoy shared daily life, and think marriage the original anti-aphrodisiac. I like excitement from men, all the kinds there are; and you can't get that Sunday through next Monday. For daily life, I like it calm and uncomplicated; and with time in one's own hands. Ideally I'd spend 9 months a year alone on this sort of sunny desert island, writing, and three months gobbling excitement. Ideally. That never arrives.

Bette Davis is right: one is guilty of attracting the wrong people (wrong for oneself.) Guilty of weakness too; I think I've learned enough to waste no more vital time. . . . Does your wife hate her job? Otherwise, I'd say any woman is better off with a job; nothing more cage-like than the home and housework. So, signing off; I'll be back here in July (I said so?) and in the interval scurrying like a managerial rat in a trap. Blessings,

Martha

To: Nikki Dobrski

June 14 1964
London

Nikki dear, I'm here until June 26 when I get divorced (heaven be praised); then join Alexander [Sandy] and young cousin in Rome and take both to Africa for the summer. I'll stay on there anyhow until next May.

News of the Rialto. I saw George Kennan* twice, Annaliese once. He had jaundice all winter, now recovered, going to Japan to lecture, then to Norway where he has a sailing boat. He's adorable, so naive really, so gentle, so conscience eaten that he feels he ought to suffer every minute for the US but really wants to get off like me into outdoor wildernesses and enjoy life. Annaliese thrives, adores the US; not so George.

Alexander has lost 25 pounds, his own will and handiwork and grown. Also nearly totally emerged from that teen age tunnel where all is cotton wool. Become good, thinking, loving chap; a delight; I see I am going to have a friend. Best thing ever happened to both of us is Tom's finally getting pasha power drunk; otherwise I'd have stayed forever, never really happy nor really well and Sandy with taint of spoiled little rich boy. Altogether different now; we are very much in it together. He's been so good about new school which he loves; but that is a rooted New England world and he is an outsider and he suffered but I explained that all best people in world are always outsiders, too awful to be labeled, ticketed and safe and he could just join me in a gay life of being an oddball, so now he seems to think that is splendid. I am looking forward to the summer which is new as I really loathed that teenage biz of dealing with a demanding zombie, as I have no sacrificial blood.

My mum also glorious, just got an honorary doctor of laws degree at 85. Complains she tires easily but I have long since collapsed before her. We walked for four hours around World's Fair (marvelous) and I had to lean on her to get out.

I am as happy as a gaggle of larks though looking forward with dread to

---

*George Kennan (1904–2005), political analyst, adviser, and diplomat in charge of long-range planning in the State Department and architect of "containment" strategy. Martha met him in Prague in 1939.

sordid English divorce where you have to answer questions in court which you would not answer in the dark if put by your best friend. Tom insists: seems he feels he wouldn't be legal otherwise, maybe I'd rise up after his death and contest his will? I think maybe he is mad – so lucky to be out – as he has behaved with notable lack of human concern throughout but just wrote my mum that he would always love me. No relation between acts and words; is that not a sign of insanity?

London is really fun for the first time in 10 years, fun as it used to be. I adore my tiny flat and never adored the house. What I like is being free and healthy and lots of work behind and ahead and friendly beaux and can make any plan I want or make none and also own as little as possible. The Pamps (my Spanish maids) are in Africa waiting and terrorized by weather and insects, snakes, lizards, bats and what not. Will send them back to Spain for a sabbatical in the autumn if their fear persists.

Much much love to you and Bear.

Martha

Sometime early in 1964, Martha had been introduced to Laurence Rockefeller, brother of David who was chairman of Chase Manhattan Bank, and of Nelson, politician, governor of New York, and later vice president under Gerald Ford. The Rockefellers were enormously rich, philanthropic and had been influential in setting up such supranational bodies as the Trilateral Commission and the Bildberg Society. Laurence, whose interests ranged from financial institutions to wildlife parks, was two years younger than Martha and had been married for thirty years. He had four children. He also had a mistress of fifteen years' standing.

Martha, to her friends, called him "L." She loved his lack of pomposity, the way he laughed at himself, as well as his generosity and desire to do good. He once told her that he felt so privileged that he would be ashamed ever to be unhappy. Martha would say of their relationship, which lasted until her death, that it had such "lightness in weight that it would hardly burden an ant." He regarded her, she said, "as a great spiritual luxury, or like maintaining a rare game park." As ever, she was brisk and did not complain. "This is one area in which seek and ye shall not find," she wrote to Robert Presnell. "But people do not generally get what they want and there is no need to be tragic."

Though they met no more than a few times a year, they spoke at length on the phone. Years later Martha would say that Laurence had been the "best and longest" relationship in her life, "some sort of golden gift of good fortune" and that it was strange and wonderful that accident, "which has always ruled my life, brought me such unexpected joy when, nearly 60 years old, a woman could hardly expect that kind of blessing."

To Agi Paloczi-Horvath

June 27 1964
Hotel d'Inghilterra
Rome

Agi dear:

It's over. Decree nisi. Now, after October, I'll be totally divorced and get my own name back on my passport.

The time in court – on the witness stand – was more detached than a dream. It was so unreal that I could not believe it was me nor my life that was talked about. My eyes did not focus and I did not exactly see any of the many faces. I heard the questions from a great distance and have no idea what I answered. Like being in a play. Very weird. It is an ugly and indecent business but did not matter.

However, on the bus to the airport, suddenly I began to vomit – discreetly and steadily – into the *Daily Telegraph* which luckily I had with me (never a more useful newspaper). Vomiting the whole thing, I expect.

And now it's gone and over and done with. Never to be repeated. Never to be remembered. A wrong long piece of life which I have survived.

My darling telephoned me here today for half an hour. So heartwarming. It seems I'd signed a letter to him 'Always (I mean that)' and he said, 'I'm so glad you wrote that because it's how I feel.' Wouldn't it be funny Agi, if now, so late, I was having the totally impossible great love of my life?

Be happy in your splendid new home.

love always
Martha

To: Hortense Flexner

August 17 or sometime like that [1964]
Mombasa
Kenya

Teechie dearest;

. . . You're wrong about this election* being dull; it may be as vital as the German elections of 1933. On the one hand we have the usual, inadequate, but best we can do American style democracy; and on the other chocolate covered Fascism, which is of course how Fascism would have to

---

*Vice President Lyndon Johnson had been Kennedy's host in Dallas on the day of the assassination. Immediately sworn in as president, he later gained a record 61 percent of the popular votes in the 1964 election against Barry Goldwater.

be introduced to America. Unless there's a Johnson landslide, the country and world will know how many incipient and energetic home-grown Fascists we have. I never for a moment feared Communism in the US but have always feared Fascism; it's a real American trait. This is a vital election and be sure you vote. Every vote matters now.

What can I tell you? I've played more solitaire this summer than Napoleon ever did on Elba; like him, caged and beaten, I wait for time to pass. In future life when the interviewer asks me how I managed to maintain the fine balance of my mind, I'll say 'Solitaire.' Though hanging by a thread is a better phrase than fine balance.

Work? Don't be silly. I sit like a frozen mummy, sending out powerful waves of will, directed on Sandy. My mind is an absolute blank from nagging, cajoling, encouraging, bullying. He arrived a pimply obese little boy and leaves with clear tanned skin and having lost 22 pounds so he is normal and good looking for the first time since childhood. He will also have done his required reading, with Mum hovering daily, asking if he's worked and going over, inch by inch, his ghastly book reports. To do this job on Sandy has left me dry and drained; all joy gone; Africa just another place. I feel I was booted out of Paradise for doing my duty.

Thank God he goes in another three days; I might be netted otherwise and carted off to an African loony bin. Then I send the Pamps back to Europe on Sept 8, a year's paid hols. Then and only then I may be able to find again what I so loved and have lost: the great wide sky and land, the serenity, the sense of time to live, not live through.

We have had constant dramas and how they bore me; left to myself I can take drama in my stride, but not with the Pamps having hysterics of fear and Sandy a bit scared too. Sandy however is so self centered that he doesn't notice much.

Anyhow, more snakes; and I have at last invested $15 in a snake bite kit, having no confidence in it whatsoever. We have been robbed; the camera Laurence gave me and my radio gone. But worse, the thief was built in, a presence meandering around us in the night, night after night. I naturally sleep through everything; the Pamps are sleepless. So I've had 2 police ambushes which a child of two could have managed better and terribly costly night watchmen who are useless too. Then, the dog was savaged nearly to death – I still do not see how he lives and I have to take him to the vet every day – by some wild animal on the premises. From the Pamps description of the beast, seen at dusk, and from local gen, and the appalling extent of the damage, it is pretty clear it was a Servel cat, African wild cat. It's been with us too for several nights, but now seems to be doing its murderous business elsewhere. Well, I shall be here alone as of Sept 8 and screaming with joy; I really cannot undertake any more nanny-dom for others. I've put in for a firearms license, a 410 shot pistol – which would be good for snakes and marauders, and with that and my snake bite kit and an African houseboy whose emotions I will never know and therefore not have to consider, I hope to get my life back. Patience is something I haven't got; and I'm not sure I care for patience – it seems to me it may just be another name for inferior metabolism. But endurance is something I get more of every year.

If you have never read anything of William Styron (I hadn't) I wish you would get a paperback called *Set This House on Fire* and tell me what you think of it. I am dazzled by these young writers. Their world is entirely personal and introspective, violent, but they know more in their thirties than I shall ever know. They know about evil, a subject that has always baffled me. And they write like angels, it comes out like lava. I feel very young and inept and scared; how dare I undertake a novel when my youngers and betters produce these strange marvels. To me, everything I think, say, do, feel seems most pedestrian. Yet they have seemingly soft little lives – Styron went to Italy on a Guggenheim, I'd never have done such a thing in my life – and out of that cocoon, they bring forth tigers.

There's a real heartsickening tragedy going on in our family. You must not know about it or know I've told you; I tell you because Miss Edna may be pretty well out of touch for a time, or writing odd letters. Alfred's second to youngest daughter Maria – a doe-like creature with a talent for painting and a personality all her own, not Gellhorn brand certified – is aged 18 (I went to her 18th birthday party in London) and she is dying fast and in pain of incurable cancer. I've known this since May and it has haunted me every day and hour; my time in London was spent acting the buffoon for that tragic family, to give them all a change and breather – and I used to drink before, during and after each meeting. I can hardly bear this story but again it has taught me much: I think I got as close as possible – without being there – to feeling what gas chambers were and how the parents must have felt when they could not protect their children from a cruel death. But now I know much more. This waiting and watching is too terrible; Olga's eyes look as if she had been struck across them with an iron bar and Alfie has the tragic quiet face of a saint who will not complain of torture. And now the little girl, who does not know, is at last beginning to feel fear; and that must be unendurable. Just know this but never mention it.

. . . My loved one telephoned me (awful, circuits breaking in the middle) and though he cannot write a letter he writes delightful cables. But I imagine he will tire; how can one keep a love affair going at such a distance in time and space. He's the only amusing bright thing in my life, just now; the only thing that keeps me from feeling I really have lived too long and it's too damn dull and/or painful to go on with.

. . . There must have been worse summers than this but off hand I cannot recall them.

Bless you darling; let me know when you're going back to Louisville. I like to know where you are.

Gellhorn.

To: Hortense Flexner

August 31 1964
[Mombasa]
[?]

Teecher dearie one; I am half drunk on a judicious mixture of despair and two whiskies. Meanwhile a Mozart concerto is whisking out of the gramophone; in fact I cannot endure Mozart; it seems to me all brightness and no feeling, a permanent child prodigy, clever as hell, and never was there, not a clue to the human condition. It's like mathematics, the way that smart fellow writes music. I like my music written from the viscera.

Someday, and very soon I feel, instead of pursuing a lifelong folly, the passionate desire to find someone to communicate with, I shall simply write. I will at last admit to myself that it is a mug's game, there is no one to hear and no one to talk back, and the last and good resort is the white page and the faceless strangers who may or may not hear. I will talk to myself on paper; I have been talking to myself, in my brain, silently, all my life.

Love costs too much. That is to say, I have to pay so much for the odd and inadequate quality of love that I have ever received, and so much for the pleasure of loving, that I think I can hardly afford it any more. My son just now (hopefully, not forever) is a disaster; cold as ice tea, selfish beyond words, dull beyond imagining; so I have made a simple self protective resolve not to suffer any more. I cannot help my mother, whom I love with my whole heart, the only saint I ever had the good luck to meet; but then she has the awful hardship of being a saint. No one ever kept her company, the most was my father, but I know he also failed her (she would never think anyone failed her); I am there, for her, always, but what she's going through now will finish her and there is nothing I can do. My loving servants have eaten the marrow from my bones.

. . . Mr. R. [Rockefeller] does not need me as I need him, it stands to reason. He has an overabundance of demands, public and private, on his time and emotions; he has hardly time to live. And also he has that indoctrinated selflessness, not saintliness, more nearly a loss of identity, which royalty has. I think I must be by now just one thing more, for Mr. R. whose cup is running o'er. And no one but me would have imagined that a love affair could be kept going on a basis of absence, a year at a time. (But then I do not think love affairs can be kept going with presence either.)

Anyhow he was more generous and more disinterested than any man before him; and I am grateful; and though I think he has bid me farewell, I harbor only loving sentiments for him; and also know, inside me, that I will never find what I am seeking, so disappointment grows less with the years.

'Whether or not we get what we are seeking
Is idle, biologically speaking.'

So quoth the bard, Miss Edna St. Vincent Millay,* in my infancy; and the truth of her couplet rang in my child mind with all the force of the funeral bell. As did a phrase of Mauriac:† *Travail, opium unique*. And I was not deaf to my father who informed me, at the age of about eight, that all people are forever alone, separated by the bones of their skulls. I heard what I had to hear, very early on; though I have spent a lifetime trying to disprove what I know to be truth.

Ah well, I live a tiny silly life, placing goals for myself month by month; and fiercely determined to make the goals.

. . . Yet, Teecher, we are the privileged of the world; we are not hungry nor roofless, our passports are in order, we write in the language to which we were born. We are lucky, lucky, lucky, in a world which is like a steel trap and a jungle at night. I never thought the business of living was easy but what surprises me is that it gets harder, with every year; I imagined, foolishly, that it got simpler and saner.

Take care of yourself. Music and solitaire, I now think, are the opium of the people. Try them.

Love always,

Gellhorn

To: Hortense Flexner

October 14 1964
Mombasa
Kenya

Teechie dearest;

. . . Styron‡ is a jolly sun-touched Boy Scout compared to some of the others. I got a book by one William Burroughs, read about forty pages and thought I would be literally sick. What a scurvy thing. The printed and glorified (by critics) work of a dope addict; filled with ugliness and hate.

---

*Edna St. Vincent Millay (1892–1950), first woman to receive the Pulitzer Prize for poetry in 1923.
†François Mauriac (1885–1970) who won the Nobel Prize in 1952. Martha first quoted this phrase while at Bryn Mawr, and she continued to write it all her life to friends.
‡William Styron's novel, *Set This House on Fire*, about Americans in Europe after WWII, had been published in 1960.

There's another, much admired, called John Updike; I did plow through *Run Rabbit Run* and was again amazed at the total recall these chaps have – no detail too small to forget or note – but bored; and could not even dream of reading a book called 'Centaur.' Also, regretfully, I have put *Augie March* back on the shelves, though I loved Bellow's *Henderson the Rain King*. We're old hat, Teecher, we're squares. I like the murder stories better; beautifully written nowadays, and with an implied jollity – such fun to be alive and track down murderers. The good new writers would glorify the murderers as the only people who had the hang of it.

But they have got talent and superb working minds; and their memory is what really dazzles and daunts me. They remember everything, seen or heard or smelled. I remember nothing.

I've just read Hannah Arendt's *Eichmann in Jerusalem* and have the greatest respect for that ice-cold absolutely rational mind. And am about to read *Cooper's Creek* by [Alan] Moorehead, having read a thrilling and terrifying excerpt in the Atlantic.

But nowadays I am having an orgy of sloth and loving it, though worried. For four days I've done nothing but sunbathe, read thrillers, drink beer and watch the view, take repeated peeks at the night sky, and listen to music. I hope I don't turn into melted fat as a result. But what joy this is: to be alive, not to be hounded by anyone, to have time, to feel well.

Oh about Tom. Yes he's marrying his long-time lady friend. She is a large insignificant woman and she could not cause trouble on a desert island where there were only sex starved men. Tom caused the trouble; it is always that way. Never believe about the siren who lures the innocent husband. I've been around; husbands get lured (in fact they hurl themselves at the 'other woman') because that's what they want. You cannot lure a man who is pleased where he is. I do not object to adultery; I object to lying. Tom's one remaining crime (a big one in my eyes) is that he will not return my letters. I cannot get over the caddery. Write soon. Take care.

Love

M

To: Leonard Bernstein

November 9 1964
Mombasa
Kenya

Lennypot darling; I think you are on the great wicket, the only wicket or anyhow the greatest. I think music has got everything, but Brahms and Chopin stand up best to the African night. Are you surprised? Beethoven sounds too loud, too forceful, and the others, Rimsky Korsakov, Ravel,

Debussy, Schumann even Mozart sound slightly fishy. They are fine by daylight but cannot compete with the night. I have nineteen records and by the end (whenever the end is) I may recognize them, note by note, though without knowing what a note is.

I'm making such discoveries as daze me. The discovery is happiness. I have no idea why and am quite certain that the way I live would drive anyone sensible crazy. Now for conversation I have perhaps five Swahili sentences a day, if that, with Kimoyo and Kibia my Kamba servidumbre. (I wonder if all Kambas have names beginning with K. Charming if true.) I have an African dog and two African cats inherited from the Pamps, who drive me potty with their need for a love I do not feel, and the problems of their feeding. And I have 24 hours a day, the one inexpendable – time; and I revel in them and worship them and know them. This is so very queer that maybe I am slightly bonkers; but on the other hand, if the recipe for happiness, a private affair, independent of anything, is to be bonkers, then I am all for it.

The weather is like being stroked with feathers and hammocked in silk.

I wish you well with every breath I draw. And I do think you were blessed to spend your life with music. It is such a clear business. It is great or shenzi; and you are involved with the great. Love,

Marty

From the summer of 1961, American policy had sought to build up the South Vietnamese as a barrier against communism in Southeast Asia. Attacks by the Vietcong had led to heavy bombing of the north, and by the summer of 1965 the U.S. had 125,000 men on active duty in Vietnam. Martha opposed the war from the start, and it came to preoccupy her more and more as the casualties mounted among Vietnamese civilians. She spoke of the war to friends as a "stone on my heart."

To: Lucy Moorehead

May 16 1965
Hotel St Moritz
New York

Lucy darling; I am sinking into a cross between melancholia and frenzy. Melancholia on the personal side. I see my Mum 4 days out of 7 and I think amuse her and give her pleasure. Myself I shiver inside, seeing her so desperately frail and old; not her mind, always gay and always courageous and always interested in the whole world. But she really can't walk without

an arm to support her and she sways with dizzy attacks; and I make jokes
and <u>ache</u>. I take her off for weekends and then there are Wednesday
matinees. Sandy got into Columbia not Harvard; and I have to arrange his
summer job, summer living quarters, autumn dormitory. After that, by
God, he can stand on his own feet or live in a Bowery flop house. That lot
(teenagers) do nothing for themselves out of idleness; no kitchen of life for
them. And L.R. Just called this evening; our life is largely on the telephone.
Overworked, exhausted, it is frustrating and pointless, not joyful like last
spring. He deplores it too, but there's no life in this city really; only success,
duties, importance. So personally I am wretched; hate the place; bored,
weary, lonely, sad and bankrupt as well.

The frenzy comes from Vietnam and Santo Domingo.* I cannot endure
this hideous wicked stupidity; to be at once cruel and a failure is too much.
Our President is a disaster and will get worse; never trust a Texan farther
than can throw a rhino. There are protests everywhere; I give money to any
group that is protesting; not enough to do. I feel like a Good German,
saying how bad the rising Nazis are, and doing nothing. Been trying to get
myself sent to Vietnam, to write the story about how we are making this
people homeless and dead instead of free; but no takers. Sick with it; sick
with shame to be American. Santo Domingo is a dime store version of the
war in Spain; we are the latter day dime store Nazis, supporting the Fascists
and calling the others Rebels and Communist-inspired. I feel I've lived too
long; and God knows where this will end. Power ill becomes this country,
there's no wisdom to balance it; and the morals of our government are
revolting hypocrisy. We really are the backers of reaction everywhere. The
government is; and the government, supposedly, in a democracy is <u>us</u>. We
have as much influence as the citizens of a dictatorship as far as I can see;
Washington is astonished and irritated that the citizenry butts into policy
and soon will suggest more openly that all us dissenters are Communists if
not traitors; they've started that line.

I don't know when I'll get to London, but surely see you in September
in Italy, if not in London. I do know about your feeling displaced in
London; as I do here. Out of step. I don't want all this mindless haste.
Wherever I'm going will be reached if at all with patience and endurance;
and I do not give a damn for fashions and the latest thing, and most people
weary me and bore me. And here there's no laughter that I can find, or
maybe I quench it.

Sex. Well, love is not separate from sex, is it? I think men and women
are completely different in this matter anyhow, biologically and therefore
emotionally. Their sense of love follows sex or is dependent on it. No we

---

*Fear of a communist takeover in the Dominican Republic, as in neighboring Cuba, had
led the Americans to intervene in the civil war that flared up in April 1965.

can't compete with 20 year olds but no man I know wants 20 years olds. Not being half wits. But they do want (need) the reassurance and excitement of sex; and so do I. Quite impossible for me, without emotional connotations. (Love. But what is love?) Not impossible for them, or anyhow they build the word love after the fact of sex. That's all. I think it has something to do with a loneliness of the skin, a primitive sense of the terrible solitude of being a human; one needs the close physical contact, as one needs fire. Something like that. I wish I were a nymphomaniac, so much easier. Instead am fastidious and faithful. Awful.

Love
Martha

To: William Walton

May 19 1965
St Moritz-on-the-Park
New York

Lover-boy:
(But I hear Lady Bird is your lover, too! The company you keep!)

Have had a shivery sickening experience: Carlos Baker sent me 4 mss. chapters of E.H. official biography to vet for errors. My God. It made me suicidal just to remember E.H. – couldn't bear it. Have never read any of the E.H. bandwagon biographies & won't read Baker's. You ought to see how I come out – sort of Babe Paley* war correspondent; apparently attended the wars with wardrobe trunks & Eliz. Arden to fix my face. Golly. All I want is out. Mary [Hemingway] is more than welcome to him; she can have him from 1936 on, with my blessing.

I've finished a joke Mexican novel. Off to London on June 19.

love
Martha

---

*Babe Paley (1916–1978), famous American beauty and one of a group of four women referred to by Truman Capote as his "swans." Capote also said of her that she had "only one fault. She was perfect. Otherwise, she was perfect." She was married to the founder of CBS, William Paley, and is credited with the phrase: "You cannot be too thin or too rich."

To: Robert Presnell★

July 20 1965
39 Candos Court
Caxton Street
London SW1

Dearest P;
   . . . I could not dream of having such a far flung correspondence were it not for the airgram, and also it limits the time I can spend on letters. I have written enough letters to make as many volumes as Dickens, and am a fool.
   Ah yes, it is fine here and believe me I note every passing second and hope I can remember, when the inevitable dog days return, that for these dark grey summer weeks in London I was merrily at peace. All that is lacking, to make it heaven here and now, is a lover. The need for concentration – so sadly lacking in my work – applies to emotions: I need to be emotionally and physically fixed on one man at one time in one place. L.R. telephoned this a.m. – just when I had decided he had forgotten me, after 3 silent weeks, and that our love affair had now passed through its last rose of summer stage and entered the sere and yellow leaf bit. But I feel lonely about him: he is forever walled off, the limits are so set, the amount of capital – in time and feeling – he has to expend so rigidly rationed that I feel as if I were always pressing my nose against the bakery store window. And that's a chilling way to feel, in the long run. He matters more to me than I do to him: the only antidote is to find another lover. Easy to say, nigh impossible to do. One doesn't 'find': people happen. And obviously they happen less and less frequently. Men, I think, use the sense of power to substitute for love: power is surely a fine, nourishing illusion. They thus keep busier and busier, because if they stop they will have to think and judge and that would be terrifying. For romps in the hay (when they have a minute) they not unnaturally prefer beautiful girls who present no problems and ask no questions. Everyone, except you, strikes me as ready to play it safe now; everyone is tireder or more settled; this is the penalty (for such as us) of being chronologically older while remaining emotionally about as eager and experimental and hungry and interested as when 20. I see no answers. There aren't any. Only means, not ends; only ways, not goals. Since there is nothing I can do about anything, I do nothing.
   Yes, the Vietnam war would be better if those turds who govern us (all four of them) said simply: America Uber Alles, and were honest turds. I cannot endure the words spoken and it amazes me that everyone is not deafened by echoes – this is the very language of the Nazis, the Soviets, and

---

★Scriptwriter and playwright, married to the actress Marsha Hunt and living in California. Martha had met him in Cuernavaca with Leonard Bernstein.

squeakily from the East, the Chinks. It's sad that this British government has to bottom lick on behalf of the pound; sad and shaming. We used to live in a fearsome world, where the choices were absolutely clear; we now live in a smeared odious world and I can understand why the ostrich buries its head: the view is too sickening everywhere.

Dearest P, I do envy you <u>working</u> on Bolivar. I am not working at all. I think I am afraid to try.

Love always,

Martha

To: Alvah Bessie

October 17 1965
4961 Laclede Avenue
St Louis

Alvah dear

. . . I am fretted by Carlos Baker, the chap Mary Hemingway picked to write E's official biography. I have stayed well clear of all necrophilia about E., neither reading any of it nor contributing towards it, but foolishly agreed to see Baker some time ago, since he wanted to ask about E. in Spain and this was the official work. That was a pure maddening waste of time; Baker got everything wrong, starting with being unable to understand the feeling of Spain, and the emotions of everyone involved. And he took most of his information (all about me anyhow) from Sidney Franklin,★ a very cheap type of liar; and the whole Spain period in Baker's book is tinged with that cheapness and all of it that I saw, anyhow, is basically wrong, and hideously superficial. Now he's again written to me, asking permission to use a note – I said send me the Xerox copy of the original or I'll sue, because I didn't believe the note – and found out, from the Xerox, that he'd edited, and it cannot be innocence, to make the thing different from the original. Well, what the hell; I am doomed to go down to posterity as some sort of second rate witch in the Master's life, and the Master himself is probably getting what he deserved, for he did fake things – events, people, emotions – himself, so one can't be surprised if the survivors fake about him.

You live under the charming delusion that I have what they call 'outlets', that anyone wants to publish me, that a public waits breathlessly for my words. Honey, I am nearly as bad off as you, the only difference being that

---

★Sidney Franklin was a young American bullfighter who had become a protégé of Ernest Hemingway when he was in Spain before the Civil War writing *The Sun Also Rises*. During the siege of Madrid Franklin acted as his major-domo and secretary.

I don't write the stuff which doesn't get published. You're very brave to go on writing, and you're right to do so. I feel little urge and am never urged. For journalism, my last effort was the Six Day War, for the Manchester Guardian, a job which took me six weeks, and cost me around $1500 to do and for which I was paid $200 and the editor, being suddenly against Israel, edited my pieces so as to make them as unsuccessful as possible. I've written nothing since.

Now I have decided to live for pleasure, trying out the strange ancient saying that happiness is the absence of pain. I find I want an absence of pain badly, realising it was not feasible to live without joy or ease or pleasure – it's a mental attitude, you know, one has to discipline oneself, like choosing a camera angle, in how one looks at things. I now take the Pollyanna angle, for me personally; and for the world, I adopt the position that if I am not able to do something positive about an event, I will not torment myself endlessly, will try consciously to shut off thought. For instance, I literally dare not think of Vietnam, literally, for the sake of my own mental health. In entirely different ways, Spain and Vietnam are the same for me – it's as if my intestines were twined around those wars.

. . . Now I must pull myself together, with shivers, and write to that tricky Carlos Baker. Hopefully, for the last time; and you can read his book (not me, I won't) and report to me.

Love to you twain,

Martha

To: Leonard Bernstein

December 7 1965
Naivasha
Kenya

Lenny love; If you'RE STILL FEELING DEAD, JOIN ME?? I (oh really fuck this typewriter and indeed every machine and everything in my happy home) feel so dead that it is a wonder I am still breathing. I'll go anywhere (have Traveller's checks, will travel); what'S THE odds? Maybe Bombay. They say it is so awful that it might shock us alive. Maybe JAPAn, maybe Hongkong, dear old Hongkong, we could buy ourselves masses of handmade silk things like pyjamas, shirts, underpants. We could get drunk and stay drunk. I cannot stand much more of myself; or of my house which is like some demon's curse, tiny gremlins operate constantly, everything breaks or is broken, my Africans are more half witted than is possible; I want to scream, do murder, flee. I scarcely even smile at giraffes when I meet them on my road.

So. What next? I know that the only thing I want to do is go to Vietnam, with a photographer; and work 20 hours a day in all the places I know, to collect again all the ghastly facts of how we, the greatest self advertising and self loving democracy on earth, have mutilated, exterminated, destroyed a distant people, none of whom ever menaced us. It is the one ruling concern of my life and the only work I want to do. But nobody wants it; I am plainly too old; there are newer younger chaps and of course by right they must have the field. I would pay any magazine to publish what I wrote, with pictures: but that is not at all how it works. I am aware of not being necessary or even useful. And it is killing me. To say nothing of the fact that my own writing (this novel moving like a stream of cement) isn't good enough, isn't good enough.

Listen: if one cannot be effective in the only cause one cares about; cannot do one's own work in a way which gives one joy, amusement or pride; has neither sex nor love, I ask you what the hell is there? Travel. But no longer alone. I travelled everywhere alone for all my life, not realising that I expected to be, and was, picked up everywhere; I didn't even recognise, until now, that that was what was happening. I travelled alone but never stayed alone.

And now? Duff Cooper said so rightly, 'The older we get, the harder to please and the less pleasing.' And Lenny, there are hardly any jokes any more. Where shall we meet? Aden, Karachi, Bombay, Dar es Salaam? I've gotta move or fall on my sword.

                                          LOve,
                                          Marthy

To: Lucy Moorehead

                                          December 23 1965
                                                  [?]

Lucy darling; What about that book, *Talking to Women*.* You said these were not like you in your time. In what tone did you say that? I was filled with contempt for these young puddings, these non-creatures. First of all, can you accept that illiterate speech? It isn't funny (as for instance the speech of Wolfie in *At Play in the Fields of the Lord* a marvel novel by Peter Matthiessen.) It isn't the fast almost secret jargon – originally from Harlem – of the way-out young. It's just bloody illiterate; repetitious, unparsed, banal in language, studded with misused words. It enrages me. I wouldn't have talked to any of them for half an hour. When one girl does seem or

---

*Its author Nell Dunn, whose first novel, *Up the Junction*, had attracted considerable attention in 1963, had interviewed nine women about, as the jacket put it, "sex, babies, morals, men, abortion, eroticism, freedom."

try or hope to be daring and uses the word 'cunt', one is embarrassed: a poor little genteel girl trying to keep up with the smart boys. Ah pfui.

As for their minds: I wince. They're not young, they're young middle aged, crazy mixed-up old kids: and in fact they are suburban housewives, really glorying in pregnancy, babies, their cooking (OH THEIR COOKING), their houses and things; and with that, as if the Pankhursts had never lived, they'd still like a bit of a career if they don't have to 'lose' their men, or neglect their babies, or affront their world. Jesus. It's more alarming than juvenile delinquents because presumably this wizened little lot are the privileged. Except for the barmaid and I was thrilled to learn there were heaps of Lesbians in Battersea; I think that's really funny.

Is this book being taken in any way seriously in London? Of course London really is such a village that Nell Dunn's being Mary Campbell's daughter and old Dunn's no doubt is the cause of interest and chat. But does anyone who doesn't know the parents' world or the 'women's' world pay heed to this: the triumph of the tape recorder.

All the editors of women's magazines are right. Women aren't worth shooting, if this type of mind and emotion is the generality; and I jolly well bet it is.

They sure as hell aren't a bit like me, when young; and I hope and pray I won't suffer from their type of anemia as long as I continue to bother to draw breath.

What breaks my heart, on the other hand, is that all the good young writers are men, every damn one. As if women were wilting back or out; or maybe honestly women never had a chance, due to their inescapable biology. I would have died rather than admit this, twenty years ago; but I'm beginning to fear it. There can never be equality, and only the very rarest women, in a sui generis way, can ever match the vitality and courage and humor and inventiveness of the best men.

Lavender and dirty nappies, that's what this lot smell of to me. Whereas I still want both men and women to smell of fire and to laugh like demons and to take chances, all the chances.

I detest this country and I fear it, too. Not death; it.

. . . Having seen the newest smash hit of Broadway in NY last week, have decided I will write another play with Virginia; the smash hit would do well for the Birmingham Junior High Players; Virginia and I are Voltaire in contrast. And it will be nice anyhow to do something with someone, though we quarrel and I consider her tasteless, but she's good at plots, complications, and I love writing dotty dialogue. I must find a niche for myself in London; I mean a job – not a money job but a mind job. Maybe something to do with the Society for the Prevention of Cruelty to Children. The only thing I can finally believe in is that: the weakest minority should not be pushed around. If all life is a repeated scandal of cruelty and stupidity, then anyhow children ought to have a few fear-free years.

News notes on love life; poor L. was made so guilty by my daft uncontrollable fidelity that, to release him, I popped into bed with a handsome old lover who was de passage here. And told L – no details, only the fact; and it cheered him up intensely, increased his ardor, and interest and passion, and also made him feel bird free. So a very good thing. Meant nothing to me. I wish I had the nerve (or the certainty of my taste) to write truthfully about sex; and I must read Kinsey on women, not that I believe it can be solid but to see if any of my suspicions are confirmed in any way. . . . Though L. is still the favorite of all time, and we have agreed not to mention Vietnam lest I have a stroke. He makes me laugh, covers me with absurd gifts and thoughtfulness, is more generous really in spirit than any man I've ever dealt with. But it is a rigidly limited relationship; maybe that's for the best, maybe all should be. It can be nothing but fun; would stop at once if the fun stopped. I won't live in this country; he won't and can't change the shape of his life. We will always be brief visitors, like space capsules meeting, in a hotel room high above Central Park.

Ah Lucy, such a pleasure to chat to you; I trust I do not bore? Why not take February off and come away with me; it's a filthy month everywhere except Caribbean and East Africa.

Love always.
Martha

To: Lucy Moorehead

July 18 1966
London

Lucy darling: When B.B. was about 90, I said to him, 'What IS life about? You ought to know by now, if anybody does.' He said, 'Work and love.' Ed note: work came first. 'Work is the building and love is the windows.' I thought it too easy; I was looking for something more subtle, tricky, hard to figure out. Well, I suggest to you that what's basically wrong with you and me is that we're out of a job.

You have to see that, mainly, women's work is <u>people</u>, and notably then their own families – only area in which they can work steadily, with reason. They are the prop or stilts on which men build their careers, they make and rear children. Trouble is: the job runs out. Your life is not totally wasted, idiot. You did superbly a full-time job: the success of your job is not <u>your</u> life, but what you made for others. Alan is a monument to your work, so are the children; not only that but all of them still need you. It would be nicer, clearly, if they needed your spirit, soul, mind – or rather cherished same – instead of needing your service and attention. Where the grief comes in is this: men are extrovert – competitive outside, in an impersonal world, and doing an objective job; women, by nature, chemistry, biology, custom are vice versa. The woman's job is more quickly at an end: men die very soon after they've 'retired' from their work. I never understood why men worked themselves to death, if they didn't actually need to. I understand now. They fear the void. We know all about it.

My agent here is not keen on my book and dawdles about reading it; she would hardly do that with Saul Bellow, Alan [Moorehead], Irwin [Shaw], Len Deighton etc. Three NY publishers have said my Mexican novel is 'charming but not strong enough for today's market'. See? As old fashioned as pantaloons, I am. One can vanish before one dies; if one's work is not wanted, and one has no place to be, that does look like a tunnel without end.

Of course, this could happen to a man; and I threw away ten years of keeping my place in a relay race. I am, naturally, scared to death – you realise I talk to you as to no one else. Pride and a rudimentary sense of self preservation keep one from telling all; last week I wandered around whining, but this week I know that is absolutely fatal. Will howl inside, silently, alone.

But all we can say is that we <u>did</u> our jobs, the best way we knew how, as long as we had them; if they were a waste of time, so is every job a waste of time; all lives are wasted. Would one do any better? Is there any way to win?

I think (or suppose) that one must find palliatives. Nibbling at philosophy in the Encyclopedia (I can only understand it at all, if it is canned or simplified) I find that Spinoza held that <u>to be is to be doing</u>.

What terrifies me now is the sense that I increasingly am <u>not</u>; and the answer is that I am not doing. A job, almost any job: it is the only palliative I can think of. Oddly, pleasure and the pursuit of same is the dustiest answer of all; pleasure is a side effect not an occupation. I also discover that I am basically weak: I can hardly write if no one wants to read; it is like talking to oneself, and instils fear in the heart. A doubt of one's sanity, a real emotion of isolation, solitude, not chosen, but there and inescapable. Sometimes I think I'd do best really to become a hermit, externally and in fact and all the time; because I am so nearly a hermit anyhow, so cut off, so unanchored, so unable to join anyone or anywhere. But what must be done, to stay sane, is to find work that is in some way communal, joined to other workers.

I tried, with Amnesty. There is absolutely nothing for me to do. The office is run by kids, and is splendid, heroic, grave, brave, intelligent. I am not a kid. Alas. I am trying like mad to get to Vietnam. Thus far, no one wants me; polite sounds, polite rejections. My clientele of company is always smaller; I am not the most popular debutante of 1966. Not: I am too good for this world therefore unwanted, BUT: I am no good so naturally no one is interested, I am past my prime (like Miss Jean Brodie.)★ Well. There is nothing to pull oneself up with except one's own boot straps. Mine are short and frayed.

. . . As to Sandy, I'm now going to write my sister in law, with another idea of how to find him. My heart breaks for him – alone at 18, and for me – a failure in this vital relationship. It is awful, and successfully adds to the darkness in my mind. But there is nothing to do. Possibly the last and worst lesson is to learn resignation. I never had a drop of it.

Very long letter – yes, like the 18th century, to talk by mail. I've been doing it ever since I can remember. It is one of the sure signs of the solitary. And for a writer, it is madness: it should all be put into form, into real writing; and I don't.

Dearest Lucy, how wonderful if we could be like those gay old hags I remember from my early youth in London, old chars I expect, happily drunk together on gin in the pubs, loud and coarse and tight as ticks, living in the minute, enjoying the gin and the pub, having a small sure thing to look forward to at the end of every meaningless day.

I am devoted to you. But I think we will have to take steps, since to be is to be doing.

Love,

Martha

In the summer of 1966, Martha finally managed to persuade the Guardian *to take a series of articles on the war in Vietnam, providing she paid her own fare. Before leaving London, she wrote two letters, one to her mother and one to Sandy, to be opened in case she did not return. She reached Saigon on August 17, to find casualties rising and civilians burned by napalm. For most of the time, she kept away from the military and other journalists, preferring to wander on her own, writing not about military battles and tactics, but about hospitals, orphanages, and refugee camps.*

Six articles appeared in the Guardian *in September, and were then printed as a booklet. The carefully detailed picture of the wounds and the casualties, written with Martha's particular tone of cool precision and reined-in anger, caused a stir, for newspapers at the time were still not often so openly critical of the war. Martha used the press tour of eight British cities planned to launch a collection of her wartime pieces,* The Face of War, *to talk about the immorality of the American military that she felt so passionately about. Moving from station hotel to station hotel for the tour, she was always cold and used her mink coat as a bed jacket.*

Martha had come back from Vietnam saying that she would cover no more wars:

★*The Prime of Miss Jean Brodie* (1961) was the title of a novel by Muriel Spark about an Edinburgh schoolmistress and her group of favorite pupils, her "Crème de la crème."

she could no longer endure man's inhumanity to man and would in the future study wild animals, "dream predators" who did not torture but killed only for food. She was now in correspondence with other critics of the war. In July 1967, she received a letter from George Kennan: "We simply slither and stumble down the precipitate slope of events. Perhaps God will be good to us and we will survive. But it will have to be God, because we have lost control."

To: Edna Gellhorn

August 9 1966
London

My best beloved, my dearest little Fotsie, my one lifelong companion: I hope you will never get this letter and I do not think you will. But I am nearly thirty years older than when I went to Spain and far tidier: if by some accident I did not return from Vietnam I would hate to leave you without a word. Especially as I shall have been deceiving you, for the first time in my life and only for your own good and peace of mind, by <u>not</u> telling you that I am going to this evil, insane war. And I feel guilt about this, and guilt about going for your sake (though one can always drown in a bath-tub); but I believe you will understand why I must.

I cannot live with the sense that I have not done all I could (and small enough it will be) to protest against the war in Vietnam, protesting on behalf of Vietnamese, Americans and finally on behalf of the human race; since now folly and wickedness are more terrible than ever. It may be that the human race is on the way out, a failed species, and anything one tries to do is futile. But I think that even if I knew that was true, I would still believe that each individual is responsible for his conscience; and must live by his standards of right and wrong, as long as he breathes. All I know how to do is write: the only way I can write with any authority, in the hope of influencing even a very few people, is to write from first hand knowledge. You will understand this, and respect my motive; but that won't make it any easier for you. So I ask you to understand and forgive, should you ever get this letter; and know it is not any lack of love for you that allows me to take chances with my life. It's that I cannot live it, feeling, thinking and fearing for the future as I do, and <u>not</u> take the only action open to me.

I love you best of anybody; I always have. I'll love you as long as I live, and more grateful to you than I can ever say, because you are yourself.

Your

M

To: Hortense Flexner

April 1 1967
St Louis

Darling

. . . The English jaunt was incredible: 8 cities in 5 days: Birmingham, Manchester, Leeds, Newcastle, Glasgow, Edinburgh, Belfast, Dublin. 8 Press Conferences, 4 telly interviews, 2 radio interviews; I never saw anything more ghastly. I fooled everyone by never mentioning my book but talking only about/against the Vietnam war: a solitary Billy Graham. And learned a lot because now I know, as fact, what I've always surmised: our rulers travel like this on a grander scale, everything arranged, straight from train or plane into waiting car to waiting reception to press conference to talk with one or more of their own kind. You never see the people in the street, you never are in the street; one place is like another; there is absolutely no contact ever with daily reality, with the strains and stresses of real life as lived by real people, and you are always the star, always telling, never listening, never learning. No wonder they rule us as if we were punched cards for a computer and they the computers. They don't know anything else.

. . . Now I am about to add to three of my Guardian articles for a small national Catholic weekly; just because I'm glad to reach 50,000 young liberal Catholics; glad to reach, or try to reach anyone. The Ladies Home Journal thinks they might want another article on wounded Vietnamese children and I've proposed one to them, we'll see what they say.

Love
Martha

To: Meyer Levin*

November 13 [1967?]
4961 Laclede Avenue
St Louis

Meyer dear boy; I looked for you in Israel in August but you were gone and I've just been in NYC for three days but didn't know your address. So there we are.

---

*Meyer Levin (1905–1981), novelist, journalist, and playwright, best known for Compulsion, about the Leopold and Loeb case, had sent Martha a play he had written about Anne Frank. He had been refused rights to the story and though he eventually won a jury award against the producers of a rival play, the bitterness of the trial made him enemies in Jewish and literary circles. Meyer claimed that he had been discriminated against because his play was "too Jewish."

. . . I am returning by ordinary post your copy of the Anne Frank play. It grieves me to realise that old Oscar Wilde was only semi-right; it seems to me that each man doesn't so much kill the thing he loves as kill himself – but perhaps that amounts to the same thing. You'll never forgive me for telling you truthfully that you have wasted your nerves, gayety, energy, and surely your wife, on nonsense, it simply isn't a very good play, Meyer; not that the one shown on the stage was very good either, though they are astoundingly similar. That the author of *Compulsion* could have written this play is in itself odd: like two different people, and the author of *Compulsion* is a tremendous writer, whereas the author of *Anne Frank* is a good honest man, who has made a pedestrian play, and stuffed such boring speeches into the mouth of a 13 year old that one can't quite believe what one reads. I suppose we are all mad; you surely are.

. . . Irwin Shaw has a loony need to write plays, get them put on, and watch them fail with inevitable speed and thoroughness. He goes on doing that, and I take it to be like a tic or hobby; but fortunately he manages to grin, bear it, do some good work and then start again on this play bit. Henry James also was mad to write plays and equally incapable. You're a novelist, which to my mind is something far harder and rarer than being a playwright: and believe me, love, if all you'd ever written was the Anne Frank play, I doubt if you'd even be considered a writer.

So there we are and you will never forgive me. Probably the best character in the play is the ghastly Mrs. Van Daan; and I kept thinking of those early Jews at Masada, and how enviable their lives and deaths.

Two things are unendurable, both happened in our lifetime: the indescribable horror of the Nazis, and what we are doing to Vietnam, and have done. And the righteousness of both the Nazis and ourselves is beyond my powers to condemn, an abomination on the earth. Today I am going out to see a little Vietnamese girl, aged 8, size of one aged 4, but too weak to walk: she has half a face, one dead eye hanging out one side . . . the other half of her face is lovely: the Vietnamese are beautiful people, very rare in the Orient to my mind. She would be better off dead, as would literally hundreds of thousands of children in Vietnam; and it goes on, day by day, while the cheap non-men who rule us talk about that war as if talking of some abstract theory of geopolitics and the mass of America wants it over, I suppose (maybe they do and maybe they don't), but is not lying awake in anguish of soul, sick with guilt, with sorrow, with despair for the cruelty and the wrongness.

. . . No sense in reporting it; I think the world is so adjusted to horror that finally nothing, not even photographs, really impress. Once, the idea was that swift and total communication would make us empathetic brothers; but instead we are only glazed or hostile strangers largely. But then, we are a predator animal species and should not expect to be saints, heroes or even good men.

Love always

Martha

To: Raleigh Trevelyan★

December 26 1967

St Louis

Dear Raleigh; Thank you for your note, and for your kindly continuing efforts with Sphere. And for *Titania*.[†]

About a year before the lady[‡] died, we were in Denmark with letters to her from Diana Cooper; my husband wanted to meet her. I left him at the door of her house and drove off to wait in a nearby café, knowing – by instinct – that she'd far rather be alone with a tall good-looking man, and by golly I was right. Also right in not really wanting to meet her; I know about writers. The thing is to admire their work and avoid having a hot meal with them.

As a person, I find her odious throughout this admiring, girlish, superficial biography: a labor of love. Is it not typical that Tania Dinesen wanted a book written by just such a woman, literate and adoring, not a biography so much as a paean of praise – though very occasionally a hint of doubt crept into Miss Migel's mind.

It had always irritated me the way Isak Dinesen behaved as if she, God, and some royalty were all members of the Jockey Club – I had to love *Out of Africa* despite what I felt to be a certain parvenu quality in the author's mind. Now I wonder if God (her celestial chum) wasn't punishing her, though she never thought of that, for marrying a man she had no feeling for, wanting however very much to be called 'Baroness', by making that man the instrument of lifelong suffering – for we all knew that Blix gave her syphilis. As I read the book, I must say I found myself thinking she'd asked for it all – and as usual remembering that great talent (not even genius) has nothing to do with great humanity.

And how I understand those young men who fled from her, feeling her to be a cannibal. She sure was: the ego is the most insatiable tapeworm that exists.

I'd be interested in what reviewers see in this book when it appears; save me some reviews to read, please. I'll be back for a few days in February on

---

★Raleigh Trevelyan, publisher, writer, and historian.
[†]*Titania: The Biography of Isak Dinesen* by P. Migel.
[‡]Isak Dinesen (Karen Blixen).

my way back to Kenya. My hope is to build a very small house in the Rift Valley where I can spend about 7 months a year looking at a large empty world and circumambulating animals so as to recover from what I feel to be the unbearable disasters of the present.

Do you think it's at all sensible to wish anyone a Happy New Year? I think the best one can do nowadays is just to wish that we all survive, year by year; and the Vietnam war is like a darkness hovering over that wish.

Yours,

Martha

Martha now had a routine to her life. She spent a couple of months each year in St. Louis with her mother and split the rest of the time between London, traveling to new places, and Africa where, in the late 1960s, she decided to build a house. She chose a site on land belonging to friends in whose house she had previously stayed, on Mount Longonot, Naivasha, 7,200 feet above sea level and eight miles from the nearest road, in the "vast silence of Africa." It took her a year of infinite problems to build the house and the wind and the altitude oppressed her, but she loved the skies and the openness and the animals. "Normal people," she told a friend, "depend on other people . . . I roam in space."

Often, in these years, her letters were sad. Sybille Bedford sometimes hesitated before opening them, feeling overwhelmed by Martha's despair and her anger against governments and the war in Vietnam. "Dearest Girl," she wrote to Martha one day, "A cheerful letter from you reads like another's De Profundis." Faced by misery, Bedford herself went on, she retracted, while Martha lamented. From sixty to seventy was a terrible decade in a woman's life, Martha would say later, "a second adolescence when you are neither young nor old, not knowing how to behave, not knowing who you are."

To: Sandy Matthews

January 27 1968

[?]

Darling;

Listen to me: your elder, if not your better (though I begin to respect elders for a novel reason; they have survived <u>this</u> longer, and deserve respect for endurance.) I have decided the following, as a final conclusion: in every generation, and at every age during that generation, from the onset of observation until death, life is a problem for the one who lives it. Every person is trying to <u>become</u> and <u>be</u>. The form this effort takes is as various as thumbprints. It is clearly neither easy nor successful, for almost everybody, almost everywhere, almost all the time. But no one is better off, or has it made, at any age: we struggle like beached fish until we die.

I am incapable of being jealous of <u>your</u> youth. Often (now, it's a recent malady and will probably get worse) I long for my <u>own</u> youth, which was harder than my life now but also far funnier, more daring and exciting. Jealous isn't the right word, but if I am jealous – no, covetous – it is of Martha Gellhorn, who knew so little, did not value what she had, took for granted – and was splendid to look at, lively, involved, and totally unabashed: I covet <u>that</u> young woman – but would not willingly be young with you chaps. It's your kind of problem and time; what haunts you and how you live and struggle is understandable to me, from the outside. But I don't feel it. It's the <u>only</u> condition you know, therefore the best and worst (one is, most truly, only young once.) I think the thirties were a more tragic time in history and a more terrible, (also beautiful, fierce, committed) decade than now. I'm glad I had my youth then; I wish to God I could do it twice. But I wouldn't want to be twenty now; now, for purposes of ease (and because I detest my lined face) I'd like to be 45, say, just because it's prettier – not because it's grander. But I don't find this a grand moment in history, I find it, really, pathetic. The evil stems from stupidity rather than evil; only a loony would equate Hitler and Johnson, for instance.

But you're getting to be elderly yourself, aren't you? You'll have to decide in a few years whether you're going to be a crew cut kid (the way a woman has to decide when she will stop wearing girl's clothes) or accept the full biz, good and bad, of <u>seeming</u> to be adult. We adults largely <u>seem</u>. I've known so few genuine adults in my life that I could name them. All an adult does is renounce certain freedoms of youth, bites on the universal nail to a certain extent, agrees that time actually does pass. You'll come to that, or be Daddy to teen-age chums.

My range of company with the young grows, to my surprise, for I do not flatter, and definitely do not think that youth, by itself, is a positive good quality. It's a condition everyone passes through; some young are interesting and valuable, but not just because they're young. Some are sinister bores. I fear these young like me and seek me out because they think I'm an eccentric. I do not see myself that way, and don't wish to be charming as if I were an elephant who could dance the waltz.

. . . As to that Sandy: I am well aware that your generation neither plans nor writes letters. At your age, I also did not do many things my parents did. Nothing odd about this. Only I loved them, and as I loved them I stayed in touch – for their sake and for my sake. Sandy knows, because I have so gulpingly swallowed my pride that I've told him, that it breaks my heart never to hear from him; I feel unwanted, unneeded, despised – and also I feel desperately lonely; and on top of that, anxious. I <u>need</u> to know something about him; and months pass and he cannot even bother to pick up the telephone (surely no heroic effort?) and call me, collect. Nothing will explain this to me except the obvious explanation: he doesn't care how I feel. There is no rule which says he should or must care. I only say: he doesn't. Tough luck on me. No doubt I should have been a better mother; I couldn't have been a better mother than I am a person. Okay, I should be a better person. Not for want of trying, life-long, but we have our limitations. (I also wish to God I'd been as fine a writer as Stendhal and I'm not.)

Love always,

Martha

To: George Paloczi-Horvath

March 16 1968
Naivasha
Kenya

Dearest George; Oh yes, I know all about it. The depersonalized despair. Because one is actually too old to despair for oneself, it's too late to worry. One can fret, one can be itching with frustrations and a sense of time running out, like water in a sieve, and so little joy to pay for the time. But in the end, in the end, one has probably made a bargain with personal hope, asking less and being less disappointed. But the depersonalized despair can drive one mad. I meant it: mad. I thought I was getting there, no longer sure that I was a bit like other people who seemed to work, eat, play, gossip, sleep as if life was assured and the air wasn't polluted with murder. I myself felt as if I were living under a very low and totally black sky, could hardly breathe and could speak in no voice other than a scream . . . Waking up was the worst and all I liked was another day done, and I could sleep with Secconal. I kept thinking how essential it was not to go officially and certifiably insane; I reminded myself of people everywhere somehow living each day and able to live the next. I decided to keep my body in shape (dreary thrice weekly gym) because if one is going to die, it must be by decision and not by ugliness and neglect. But really I was frightened for my sanity, and remembered everything I had read about melancholia – a slow slipping into grey and shapeless dark.

So I fled. Is it true, do you think, that it is better to live and run away, and thus be able to fight another day. I'm not sure about fighting any more. I am filled with hate and anger, and also with weariness as if weariness was a defined disease like cancer. I pity the young beyond words and only reassure myself with this: they are young, which prevents them from knowing just how filthy this world is. Youth is an armor; I remember that much about being young. It is something like armor-plated invincibility.

One is not tired; one has not had time to despair. I despair for them. This is the Greater Dark Age, making the previously historically designated Dark Ages seem like a happy garden suburb.

And of course it is unnecessary. There is no need for all this evil stupidity. I think man must be descended from the lemmings, not the apes.

I have tolerance only for the young, the helpless, the victims; no tolerance for those who ought to know better. As for love, I think maybe with me its highest form is an anguish of pity. I wish for more joy, for myself, for everyone in the world, and I doubt the chances. But my eye rejoices here and that's a lot. Love always,

Martha

To: Dr. Raymond F. Dusmann★

[? 1968]

Dear Dr Dusmann;

To my surprise and sorrow I suffered the reverse of what happened to St. Paul on the road to Damascus: I lost my faith with a bang. As you know, I set out on my ecologists' hunt – who is doing what and where – full of faith plus hope and charity, eager to learn and ready to admire. Instead, within nine days my first unexpected doubt had turned into something far more grave. I have not compiled a directory, or even started to do so; I have piled up a series of questions, colored with indignation.

Not being a scientist, there is nothing useful I can do except hand on my questions to you and a few others, qualified to ask better questions and with the power to expect convincing answers. Not being a scientist, it is also possible to be a booby but I cling to the notion that anything rational can be explained in simple declarative sentences, and that even the lay mind ought to be able to understand what field ecology is about and why. I spent 17 days in the Serengeti, one of my favorite spots on earth and left with the status of Typhoid Mary. I do not expect my opposition to what is going on will move mountains; I only hope, like one hurling (not throwing) a pebble into a pond, to create some effective ripples. As far as I am concerned it's over to you chaps – if you see any worth in what I have to say.

There is a small number of purely behavioral ecologists, who patiently and skillfully (and also bravely) observe animals and do not kill them. I admire and respect the pure behaviorists because they do not harm (and this is a rare talent in itself). An example is Hans Kruuk, who has been in the

---

★Dr. Dusmann of the Conservation Foundation in Washington, a body funded by the Rockefeller Trust, had asked Martha to do a report on the ecologists and animal scientists working in East Africa.

Serengeti for five years, studying hyenas. The upshot of his work is that the hyena is okay in his environment, belongs there, and the relation of prey and predator is working as nature intended. This is good news for the hyena as it prevents one of the nice Park Wardens from shooting hyena on sight on the grounds that they are nasty and there are too many of them. And the behavioral ecologists, even if there is nothing more positive they can do for wildlife than prove scientifically that it ought to be let alone, acquire knowledge which is fascinating and useful to us – an extension of our insight into our own behaviour. (Hans Kruuk and I agreed that there was an awful lot of hyena in people.)

But the patient men are few, as I've said, while the killer ecologists increase and thrive. Nothing has convinced me that this killing for science is justifiable. I have no authority to say that most of the killer experiments seem to be nonsense as science, but they certainly seem like worse than nonsense from the point of view of the animals.

. . . Since I do not want to spend my African months haranguing the killers in vain, I am bowing out of this job. I have returned the Rockefeller grant in toto, with the enclosed report as explanation. Report is too fancy a word. At my age, learning more about human behavior does not leave one sadder and wiser. All that happens to me, when I stumble on another area in which mankind is behaving dubiously, is an increase in anger. However, all is not lost. I have acquired the latest thing in collapsible canvas safari bathtubs (suitable for bathing an infant) which leaks like a sieve.

. . . So here I am, shooting my bolt, hurtling my pebble, and it is all that I can do. I find that I am passionate about conserving the East African National Parks, for I believe they are the last such land on earth that can be saved. If we spoil them, through stupidity and arrogance now, our heirs and descendants will have the right to spit on our graves. If I am completely wrong, you have a handy wastebasket. If I am even partly right, you can do something about it.

Yours sincerely
Martha Gellhorn

To: Diana Cooper

March 28 1968
Private Bag
Naivasha
Kenya

My darling Diana and sweetie one;

My life story (I now think) is one ceaseless record of making homes (nests) and leaving them. By count, I am now engaged on doing simultaneously my 16th and 17th. New York City, Albany, N.Y., Paris, Washington (twice), Corsica, Cuba, London (three different ones), Portugal, Mexico, Italy, Mombasa, and now here in the Rift Valley. For a nomad, I evidently do not like tents. I've been loaned a house which is divinely set near the lake, with such a view; and the house suits me so perfectly that I am building a copy of it – one wing only – but the insides were something to make one cry.

(I do not count the half built house in Spain, four of life's worst months, nor the two summer houses I did over also in Spain. Dear God.)

At this moment, I am also engaged in such esoteric shopping as roof tiles, folding interior steel shutters (security), and wood flooring. My new house will, God willing, be done by July. No guest room; can't afford extra room and bath. Just veranda, sitting room, bedroom, bath, kitchen, store room, carport.

. . . But I adore my mountain top, 15 minutes drive from nearest house; and way up there I see all four horizons, clad in mountains, with the lake in the valley below: and not one sign of human habitation. Every time I go up I meet 4 ostriches, evidently a devoted set of couples, and a herd of Tommy gazelle, and when staking out the position of my house, a Steinbok, a tiny reddish antelope, leapt from under my feet. Giraffes frequent the area – just now, perhaps due to the rains, they seem to have wandered off – but it is their territory. African cattle, humpbacked and gently bellowing, roam the hills, and Masai herdsmen, camped farther up the side of the volcano, have complained that they cannot sleep at night for the roaring of lions.

The birds, down here in my present dwelling, are incredible. The starling, in Africa, like everything else, is special: orange-red breast with white collar, and royal blue wings. All starlings I knew previously were a sensible black. I've got tribes of baby parrots living in my fever trees, and crested hoopoes, and various others I can't identify. On the mountain side, I am assured that if I put out seed and water, I'll collect an aviary in due course.

When, if I ever get my house done, I may even become a writer again. For the moment the best I can do is paint; and I have at last discovered what my style is in painting: Eisenhower, crossed with Nigerian primitive.

. . . And I begin to have hopes that this filthy evil war will be brought to an end because I think the country is getting sick of LBJ, who is the worst President in US history, the most damaging. It is a terrible pity that Nelson Rockefeller decided not to run – obviously because those mad Republican party hacks prefer to lose with Nixon rather than nominate the one man who would surely have been elected. It also seems to me that [Harold] Wilson is a British version of LBJ, ghastly in his own English style. But one cannot work up enthusiasm for [Edward] Heath either; I met him in NY at

Lenny Bernstein's and we all thought he was either a pink-cheeked neuter or an ageing pink-cheeked pansy, and somehow he seemed silly in a complex way.

Sometime, whilst lying in bed, could you write me your news? I think of you with joy, rather like a Tibetan hermit reflecting on All-that-is-Good.

And love you constantly and look forward hopefully to summer movies with you.

Always,

Martha

P.S. Don't you think my address is stylish? It is, in fact, a huge canvas mail bag with a huge padlock.

To: George and Agi Paloczi-Horvath

April 22 1968
[Longonot
Naivasha
Kenya]

Darlings; Short of cancer, there can be no more hideous experience than building or rebuilding a house. If I had put as much time and effort into books as into housebuilding, I'd have written the same number as Simenon.

I have such hands and finger nails as you never saw and am too tired to read at night. I spend at least 10 hours a day on the fascinating and insane task of trying to make something grow on this windswept mountainside. Nothing likes wind; and the soil is volcanic ash, and the bore hole water (when it arrives) has very tough unfriendly chemicals in it. But I have been digging, (with 3 Africans), sifting soil, watering, raking, burning; learning. I haven't a gardener, only people with more muscle than I — but I get more muscle daily — and proceed partly from reading, partly from asking questions, partly from logic. If in the end anything blooms, I think I'll feel prouder than of any other act in life.

Before this, I was on safari for 3 weeks, finding out to my fury and horror that ecologists are not noble either. There are good ones — the behaviorists — who watch animals with patience, skill and often courage. But they are vanishing. A new lot arrives, young shits out for a Ph.D. or a fancy paper in a fancy scientific journal: and for no reason that will ever help the wild animals, they kill. (Like the experiments in Dachau and Auschwitz clinics.) So I set off, in my Toyota small truck, an entire safari in the rear and an African in front with me, and learned something else new — which is how to operate alone, in a tent, in the wilderness. I am very pleased with this knowledge, an extension of physical freedom. Meantime I learned as much as I could – a non-scientist – about these chaps, lazy (it takes time not to kill), ambitious, not giving a fart for the beauty and rarity of this last place where wild animals live. I then (with the worst sort of writer's aching duodenal) sat down and wrote and rewrote a report. But to my surprise the gesture has not been totally in vain; I have started trouble, questions, doubts. Maybe I'll save some wild animals. Maybe I'll at least for a minute slow the usual contemptible activity of man, which is to destroy.

Laurence once asked me what I'd do in Africa now my house was built. I am up and dressed by 7 a.m. and not sitting down until 7 p.m. Covered with dust and dirt, hardly ever out of gumboots; I think I have never worked harder. But it is a different work, and I am doing something very amusing – keeping one jump ahead of Africa.

I have to drive 32 miles to get my drinking water, for instance, which I get from the petrol station in Naivasha: the bore hole water up here is undrinkable and not even very good for cattle. I set out with plastic jerry cans of 4 gallons each, and stock up.

But the house is charming inside and slowly will become charming outside, that is if anything grows. And it is a triumph: no one can find it, the roads remain terrible; I do understand the Pharaohs, I have built myself a small pyramid.

I am waiting for Josphat, my Kikuyu man of all work (house) to produce an inedible dinner. Alas, how I wish I knew how to cook. I only know how food should taste but not how to make it. However, I do not starve; and have a madly misplanted vegetable garden (that gardener was sacked when I returned) which is full of huge old vegetables, enough tomatoes for Campbell's soup. Weird life, maybe the one I was looking for. Dear God, I have looked long and far and how I hope this one lasts.

Always
Martha

To: Hortense Flexner

April 26 1968
Naivasha
Kenya

Teecher dearest

I sorrow for you, and for my Mum and also for myself. This is the first day when I have felt that perhaps my veins were not crawling with hooked and slimy viruses, for I have <u>again</u> had malaria, the entire month of April. I've had a nasty 26 days.

. . . But never mind, as they say. What's the use of minding. We grow old, we grow old, we do not even wear the bottoms of our trousers rolled. Would it not be the greatest thing that ever happened for mankind if just one traveller could return from that bourne whence no traveller etc, to give us the straight and definitive gen. Either say: my friends, there are the eternal fires of hell, or say: my friends, there's nothing to it, or say: my friends you'll meet all your old chums like a regimental reunion. Just say something. Then there would be no doubt in anyone's mind and instead of sitting around while one's body falls apart, one would take off, as if on BOAC to London. But you know, the longer I live the worse I think absolutely everything is arranged and the more convinced I am that if God is not dead, he sure hates us.

Anyhow I am writing again; suddenly, although slightly shaky with the tail end of malaria I sat down and wrote for 12 hours and produced a short story which has something in it. I wouldn't like to say how much because I've no idea. And am well along in the second, with the third clamoring at the gates. The only snag is I am enjoying it too much so it cannot possibly be right. (Calvinism, deep in us all.)

. . . I lift my head from my thriller and behold a male monkey with black face and delicate black hands and pale blue balls, who is sitting on the low wall by the swimming pool and eating a papaya for lunch, hungrily. He eats away, then scampers up the papaya tree and picks off another ripe one; this time he heads for a bushy tree and settles out of sight in the shade, only his tail hanging down. And around here it looks like the south of France but one should never be fooled by the houses and people; when I drove on the near road, a long black mamba was crossing same. I respect this country; it really impresses me. Write sometime. Get well. You know I love you,

Gellhorn

To: Sandy Matthews

April 27 [1968]
[Naivasha
Kenya]

Sandy darling: No vitamins have arrived or I should have thanked you instantly. You are sweet to have thought and worried but you need not. I am in bursting health.

The secret of happiness, in private life, I have decided, is manual labor. I have become a gardener on this patch of volcanic soil where man has never before laid hand. In all time. It makes one think. Everything is against it: gale force wind at 7000 feet altitude, alkaline bore hole water (which is ruining my skin, thins the cattle and does not cheer plants); and then the soil itself.

I have suffered over every single page of *The First Circle*. And am sure it is a great book, judging by the pain it caused me. We are muddled by Russian names – very hard to keep the people straight when the names are so difficult for one's memory. That doesn't matter. I also think [Aleksandr] Solzhenitsyn is a hero. Really a hero. The bravest kind of man alive. To have lived all that and still be able to write: not scream: not go mad. And I have realized also that I was wrong to think Fascism and Communism different in that Fascism allowed the old rich to go on (as it does and did: all my ancient acquaintances in Italy and Spain). But of course I never realised that Russian Communism had created a new rich – silk underwear, and all. That rich is surely less secure than the Nobles' Trade Unions of Fascism; but is altogether similar in every moral sense.

The Lord God created the dinosaur too; and allowed it to perish by itself, by its own lack of brain. Why should we be other, the most recent experiment in a species? I think when the destructiveness of man outweighs the creative then we are done for.

I have also read with interest and disappointment the second volume of [Bertrand] Russell's *Memoirs*. In the terrible years – 1933–1939 – he mentioned Spain only once in a sentence in a letter. Nor does he speak of the rise of Hitler, the plight of all good men in Germany and the Jews. I know he was very old but he protests too much about staying out the war in the U.S. True his son was only five but so were millions of English children. Somehow he comes out as not quite good enough; one had imagined more. I think it splendid that, in a letter, he attributes his happiness in life to the fact that he defecates twice daily without fail.

And finally, dear boy, I think philosophy is a parlor game. I do not see how it relates to life at all; nor to the condition of man. It is a very high-toned entertainment between men of equal and detached intellect. And in a way, it repels me. I think more highly of Florence Nightingale who did something about human suffering in hospitals than about any philosopher. For where has philosophy saved; and where – when possible – has it not been used for evil ends. (Think of Hitler and Nietzsche.) I am an admirer of Galileo, who discovered a fact, and died saying: *E pure si muove*. But not philosophers. Finish your stint and leave it. Join the endless chain of people living here on the ground: we are lost, but the best we can do is, each one, be the boy with his finger in the dike. And somehow, I find the higher flights of the mind very cold. And if they hadn't flown so goddamned high we wouldn't have the H–bomb either.

You know the worst invention of all? The airplane. Though I think all the communication media a disaster. Nothing but spreading fury and untruths and envy and contempt among all peoples, via cheap transistors.

Also cheap music. I think I believe in Gutenberg; but not in linotype machines. Ah well.

Now, if you have not, then immediately read *The Last of the Just* by Schwarz Barth. Another unbearable and great book.

Love always,

Martha

To: Diana Cooper

May 20 [1968]
Naivasha
Kenya

Dearest beautiful Diana; You write the wonder letters and this one was so moving, all the right and rare adjectives to mourn Iris.★ Cancer is surely the worst way to die: like being in the death cell at Sing Sing, waiting for an appointed day. And the pain, and the ruin of the body. Science, which will take whatever loonies so desire to the barren moon should everywhere and with all money available be concentrated in finding a cure for that. And Iris' longing to live, and hope for miracles, is something my brother, the great cancer specialist, has often told me about, when I speak firmly about refusing to endure old age (like my lovely Mum). I think it is not fear of death, but horror at not being alive – curiosity must be like breath, to keep one always wanting to see what next. The only good way to die surely is suddenly and without warning. It is those months of knowing and waiting which break the heart. And then there is the loneliness for the survivors. My cancer brother doctor watched his 19 year old daughter die of cancer, slowly, for seven months. One can hardly bear to think of any of this.

My Mum fell in her apartment on April 30. She broke her hip, but what she did was manage to summon her maid, get up, get dressed, sit at her table dictating letters (among which one to me, in which she did not mention this fall) until finally she decided she really did hurt too much and telephoned a doctor. I cabled, asking if I should not now come back; and left the coast, where I'd spent a month being steadily ill; only to be hit by a second attack of malaria on the road. So had to pull into the nearest hostelry and flop into bed; this open (not masked) malaria hits one like a bullet but is preferable, I think; because I took huge doses of the antidote and was able to drive on the next day. Here, I found cables from Mother and Alfred (doctor brother) saying progress splendid don't come.

. . . Finally, there is my house. A disaster. Friends were supposed to supervise it. I came back here to find a bathroom in which perhaps a cat

★Iris Tree, Diana Cooper's lifelong friend, had just died at the age of seventy-one.

would comfortably have bathed, and in the whole house room for 7 feet of storage space; this to hold clothes, linens, luggage, and all the odds and ends. SO. I have ordered a bedroom wall torn down, a bathroom wall will have to be made of wood (ah, the sound) so as to get more room; the cement somehow has to be chipped off; and I have hired a Sikh for technical supervision but will have to buy all materials, arrange their transport and be on the site daily.

. . . My one desire for the summer is to go to Holland; I wish to see Amsterdam. I've got a sudden intense curiosity about it, and a vast presently suspended and dragging story needs some authentic Amsterdam stuff in it. How about that, a new country to me, and you'd love the pictures. We could take your car on the boat to the Hook of Holland and spend 10 days fooling about. Does that appeal? Sometime in August? Could Doggie go?

. . . On our favorite subject: all this combined illness has had an amazing effect: I have to <u>force</u> myself to eat. Never happened before. And yet I do not waste away, also a surprise, but stay around 123 pounds, dreading the thought of the next necessary intake of food. My face is tomato red, splotched with the brown spots of solar kerotosis and the lines on my forehead look either like scars or the lines resulting from steady torture. I cannot tell you how hideous I am. And I must say, it is lowering not to have a man waiting for one's scribbles, as you say: or scribbling himself. My loved one wrote me perhaps three letters in five years, an act of unheard-of devotion on his part since he cannot write. But he used to cable and telephone: this time, nothing. He is no doubt engrossed in the political career of his brother; he is also far less involved with me. I can't say I feel abandoned because I never felt the opposite; I simply feel time's winged chariot sitting on my neck. Whenever I go back to N.Y., he will have flowers in my hotel room, telephone perhaps every day, squeeze me into his overcrowded life by coming for lunch and the afternoon of love-making: delightful, like a Christmas present maybe. Not enough however to keep one's spirits up or make one feel of any special value.

. . . Now I must hasten into the village to buy 15 bags of cement and a barrel of creosote; then return and pick up my houseboy who is hard-working, slow-witted and speaks English. So it goes. I may lose my mind. However, this awful immediate kitchen of life keeps one from thinking too long and hard about the state of the world; and that does definitely drive me insane. Can you imagine a <u>friendly</u> country, using artillery, helicopter gatling guns, bombs, in the midst of a friend's crowded city, to root out a small number of enemy? The Germans didn't do better on London.

I love you. Please let us have some time together in the summer, for a good groan and a lot of movies.

Love love,

Martha

To: Edna Gellhorn

August 23 1968
[?]

My only beloved; I have been thinking of you and Dad all these last days and trying to gain some courage from your example. It's not much good; you're the brave one, you always were. You were four years younger than I am now, when he died, and I remember your saying to me, perhaps fifteen years later, that you'd give everything you had or were or ever had been or could be to talk with him for half an hour. I know you missed him every day, and it only made you even gentler with others; somehow, beautifully, you must have kept him with you always and not let the loneliness numb you. You always said your children kept you alive. My darling little Fotsie, you've kept <u>me</u> alive; you've been my country and my compass and the one true warmth for my heart.

You've often said to me that I made life harder for myself, as indeed Dad did. And now I have made it unbearably hard for I should have come to you at once, early in July, and stayed, quietly, not taking up any space or interfering with anyone, but just being there, day after day, to see you, to hold your hand and kiss you, since we've kept each other company all our lives and now it's your company, your presence, that I so hopelessly miss.

I feel we are both living in a dream. Your dream is far off and no one can accompany you, but I hope the dream is radiant and peaceful. I know no one on earth who had a life with nothing to regret: all of it lighted by love given and love received, and all the work in it good work, that stays and remains, that makes the world a less cruel and less ugly and less stupid place for those who come after. Your life is the only faith I have; it's a light that never failed and that has kept me warm. How can I thank you, Fotsie? You must know that I have been thanking you all my life.

My life now is a dream too, semi-detached, it seems to happen to somebody else. Perhaps it will make you smile to yourself to know that I have taken cooking lessons, and plod about in my nightgown today practicing and experimenting on what I learned. Such a sad joke; after all these years, your daughter has made a salmon mousse – who would really want to eat such a thing? And also learned to sandpaper and varnish furniture, another occupation of this day. This flat is the only place I've ever cared for; it comes next to the one perfect place, our little house in Cuernavaca. My beloved Fotsie, my only beloved, you will be with me every day I live, just as Dad has been with you. It's been hard for you, Fotsie, it's hard for me. I'll try to copy the perfect manners of your heart.

I love you now and always more than anyone, ever.

M

In April Sandy, Martha's adopted son, was about to be twenty-one. There had been
terrible battles between them, over his weight, his refusal to study, his failure to write
letters or stay in touch. Martha's feelings and behavior toward him were by turn angry
and affectionate, accusatory and guilty, rejecting and beseeching. This ambivalence
poured out in her letters to him, as he went through bad spells with drugs, as he
abandoned his studies and later walked out of the army. When he was in serious
trouble, she was anguished; but she could also be cold and censorious.

To: Sandy Gellhorn

September 6 1968
London

My dearest boy; I've had a glorious holiday, the best since my long lost
youth. I cannot remember (within living memory) when I felt so healthy
and carefree; it was as if the uptightery of the years fell away while I walked
around Switzerland. I went to the Jura, our country, the hill land beyond
those little lakes we visited. And must have been a strange sight, a very tall
elderly lady, clumping through the landscape with a knapsack. The first six
days were hell on my legs, and have convinced me that I shall do this blissful
cure of body and soul every year. I walked like a Chink lady with bound
feet, each step being wrenched from my knotted leg muscles. Then, when
I had almost lost hope, deciding my body was beyond salvation, my muscles
lengthened and I became a strider. I walked 170 miles in two weeks, and
loved it all.

The country is adorable, no other word. The forests are full of wildflowers, the high pasture land full of pale tan and white cows with blonde
eyelashes, wearing bells on necklaces; and sleek brown horses. There was
never anyone around but them and me, and when I got lost (often) I would
ask my way at a farm. I liked the people, and the superb cleanliness of
German Switzerland. I fetched up, exhausted, in any little village and found
a clean bed. Oh lovely, lovely: this is the first way I travelled in Europe and
it remains the best. And as I walked, I talked to myself. Talked a lot about
the novel I now know I will write – and it may be the last one, but I want
to write it finally, and I see its shape more clearly. And I praised the
Creation, the beautiful world, which the human species has not known
how to cherish, but which is the one consolation of the mind and spirit. I
realise how much I needed happiness and freedom, because both have so
changed me.

And I thought about you, and thought about you, and thought about
you . . .

There are things I must make clear to you. I want you to know that I
admire and trust what you have made of yourself. I think it a triumph that

you have so disciplined your body that it has become beautiful and strong and your servant: a real triumph. (And no one believes more in the body than I do. I <u>know</u> the body comes first. If the body is healthy and strong, the mind follows; the mind by God does not leap and sing in a damaged body.) I realise perfectly what an effort it was to lose all the sludge of the years, to exercise your will and strengthen your muscles; and I respect this deeply. And also I am glad for you, gladder than I can say.

Beyond this, I admire intensely what you have made of the army, how you have survived all the pressures and the boredom, and used this time to learn. It seems to me that you have taken what you could get – training in a very exact skill – marvelously; and for the rest, you have been teaching yourself. Teaching yourself interests and tastes, books and music; and developing your always great talent of understanding and appreciation of people.

You have grown yourself up, and I think you have done it beautifully. You have set your own compass straight on its own true north, so you will grow and survive, and that's what life is about – growing takes in all giving, as well as all getting; survival means surviving as someone real and complete and alive.

Your relations with me are something quite apart from what you are, have made yourself, and my rejoicing over that. I do not understand your relations with me. I wonder if you do? I feel that now you are too aware to punish me by casual neglect; I cannot help feeling that now you are punishing me by intention. Like a Kafka character, I feel that naturally I deserve punishment – we all have many sins, conscious and unconscious on our souls; but like a Kafka character, I do not know what exact crime I am being punished for nor do I know the term and extent of the sentence. Of course I am hurt, as much as I am baffled. And it seems to me a sorrowful waste, for if only you would talk, surely one could straighten out this emptiness. Straighten out is not the word; surely one could somehow fill this void. Unless you have decided that you do not want or need me as a mother. But if that is so, would it not be fair to tell me?

Unless I see you, in October before going to visit Omi in St. Louis, I would have no chance to see you again until next June. The thought that a whole year of silence would pass frightens me; out of self protection, I would have to train myself to grow away from you. Is that what you want? Alienation, rejection, all the new fancy words for lovelessness and loneliness?

There are material things to discuss too. I have had a brainwave which I think you will find good. It has to do with London and living conditions; I think for the first time I have come up with something very sound and satisfactory. Meanwhile I want you to know that, if you come here at Xmas, you can have this flat.

I brought a portable typewriter back from the U.S. for you; it's that good one L. gave me. It needs to be serviced, but you can take care of that when you want it. It is waiting for you here. And there's a gramophone for your sounds.

Oh Sandy, I do love you and cannot believe you really want to disown me, by silence.

Mum

To: Sandy Gellhorn

November 19 1968
St Louis

Honeychile, I do hope that this time you'll somehow get in touch and stay in touch because it would be so dreamlike to meet in London for Xmas.

Meantime, to make you howl with laughter, I take 'discotheque dancing' lessons, with Mary Hall, grey-haired Mum of Fred Tompkins,* from an 18 year old lassie named Pam. It is funnier than you would credit and I must say it has jogging beat, as exercise. You should see your old Mum solemnly learning steps entitled Funky Broadway, Tighten Up, Pearl, Boogaloo, Shingaling, Stomp. I specially admire that basic gesture, the heart of the matter, which most closely resembles a male dog in the act of procreation. Anything anything to make life here a little less dismal. Have finally decided what I think about St. Louis: I think it is castrated.

. . . And I think of you, my favorite cameraman in the whole world, a new creature, with a fascinating profession opening up.† I remember the beauty of *A Man and A Woman;*‡ but of course I see films differently from you now, not with the professional's eye. I remember the beauty of the woman's face and scenes by the sea; I remember being very weary of the auto racing, tired finally of those speeding, skidding cars – too much of a good thing. But there was an interesting and maybe profound and maybe unintentional piece of psychological observance in that film: both the man and the woman had loved their previous mates – I cannot remember if the man loved his first wife, who killed herself, as much as the woman i.e. you love and lose and the one love is the only and best. But I believe in fact it is true of humans: and the people who marry and marry and change and change actually never loved, never have learned, they are always looking for what they can't do. They have no model of feeling and behavior. I am sure, for instance, that this was true of me, until L. L. happened too late, in

---

*Family friends from Martha's childhood in St. Louis.
†The U.S. Army was training Sandy to be a cameraman.
‡The English version of *Un Homme et Une Femme* (1966) starring Jean-Louis Trintignant and Anouk Aimée.

practise, for my life: too late to make over the shape of my life, I guess I mean. But not too late to save me from dying in ignorance. I know now more than I ever did before: and it is very simple – an unquestioning and total delight from the sound of a voice, the look of a face, the peace of a body: and the longing to make the other happy. Who learns that young is lucky: I begin to feel that love, like art, is a talent which has to be trained – yet one cannot organize to train oneself.

A huge kiss,

Mum

To: George Feifer★

Rainy Easter [1969?]
[St Louis?]

Dear George;

Mao may well be barking mad; Stalin was; Hitler was. Personally, I feel LBJ is – paranoia. Surely absolute power (or as near as dammit) must make people insane; no one dares contradict them. Mao's wife also sounds pretty loopy to me. Chiang was not as crazy as Madame Chiang but neither of them thought of people as human beings: only as things. That's what madness really is, isn't it?

This country gets scarier by the minute. You of course remember nu-speak and double-think? Well, that is the way it operates now, entirely. I do not understand the press; where is the great enlightening role of journalism. There's only Walter Lippmann to be counted on every time; and a few other columnists occasionally; and two newspapers editorially. Otherwise, blind or compliant, the press plays the game. This is a country almost as isolated as behind any iron curtain but self-isolated by a combination of conceit and fear. Very strange; also awful.

Do you know, I think what we do and care about and feel is hopeless; the barbarians are sweeping the world, from one direction or another. A man named, I think Pierre d'Harcourt,† wrote a book about being in a concentration camp; maybe Belsen. He said the only thing that mattered finally was a man's hanging on to his own standards, his own integrity; it was the only thing to save or worth living for. (I got this from reviews.) I think that's right and cannot imagine any other reason for going on. In fact, one goes on because one cannot stop, for by stopping, one has agreed with the enemy; one is *not* silenced simply as an act of presence, a gesture.

★Writer and journalist in the U.S., author of books about Okinawa, Lenin, and Solzhenitsyn.
†Pierre d'Harcourt, member of the French resistance in WWII and author of *The Real Enemy*, an account of his four years' imprisonment in German reprisal and death camps.

I am altogether too low in my mind and need the natural world to re-establish some joy in living. Hence Costa Rica which I hope will have empty beaches and a warm blue sea.

Love to you three,

Martha

To: Sandy Gellhorn

September 5 [1969]
London

Poor Sandy: one day we will all die, or perhaps just move away and you won't know, you'll be out of touch, no one will have your address so no one can notify you; and at last you will be totally alone and entirely free, as you've been trying to be for so many years . . . You know, old boy, parents turn like worms. I have turned. Good and hard. Signing your second letter, 'I love you totally' annoys me as much as one day your words, not your acts, will infuriate a woman who expects you to be real, not a pile of soft verbal stuff.

I am also tired to death of your behavior towards life. You are always bored, idle, impotent, no matter where you are. The one true phrase is 'No motivation.' You were trying, a bit, not much, to write or practise with film, but gave it up – no motivation. You bet. Motivation comes from <u>within</u>; the world was not invented to amuse and satisfy you; or make your way a bed of roses. Motivation comes from guts, imagination and will, <u>within</u>. You have none. You are a poor and stupid little fellow in my eyes. I'd be so damned ashamed to be you, I'd want to jump off a cliff. For God's sake when are you going to start <u>to be</u>, instead of waiting for something, someone, <u>outside</u> to arrange all to your taste and to your order?

I have no respect for you, and at present little affection. You pay no debts, none, of any sort or kind (and there are many kinds of debts; and honor always demands the repayment of debts.) You have absolutely no style, your mind is as interesting as blotting paper, you *do* nothing, you are unable to make anything of the days, the life, the places. You are a perfectly average nonentity. Perhaps Vietnam would have been fine for you: motivation in plenty, simply to save your skin.

. . . If you're interested in me, you'll have to earn your way back. Become interesting. Do something with your time; <u>learn</u> something. You have just about everything to learn since you know damn all. Stop protesting love, at your convenience, and prove it by concern for others. I am tired of you, Sandy, deeply tired. You have ceaselessly shown you can live without me, except when you want something; I can live without you too. I look after and love a certain number of people, but love is like tennis you know, on a major scale: it is played by two people, not by one saint and one pig. It is a relation between two equals. And I've never been able to go on loving people I don't respect – perhaps a handicap, perhaps a sign of a good, healthy instinct of self preservation.

I'm not bored, I'm dead tired, ill and worn out, but the jobs get done and the obligations are honored. But honey, you are neither a job nor obligation: you're a selfish, lazy, pointless young man, and you are responsible for yourself. I take no further blame. Over to you.

> Your
> Mum

To: Leonard Bernstein

> October 24 1969
> Naivasha
> Kenya

My dearest chauffeur; Thank you for that long drive on all the foul autobahns; that motel was no pleasure dome but provided a place for stupefied sleep. I haven't really felt awake except for the walking weeks in Switzerland and now here, gloriously, returning to my heaven home on earth. I can't get over it and I've learned the trick in life: expect the worst and then one's bound to be happily surprised (unless, of course, the worst comes true.) And I've also changed, in that now I consider it a miracle that I managed to build a house at all, this high up and this far away; and the fact that it stands is more remarkable than that it stands shakily. It seems I almost lost it on October 7 when a super forest fire swept over the unburned half of Longonot, a mountain rather like Popocatepetl, just behind me. Even the police came to fight it and finally they got a tractor and plow and dug a trench and so my house, with all its old and new defects, remains; and I have come to love it. In the end, I'll probably never leave, becoming the ancient eccentric of the African bush; but oh Lenny, the beauty of this land and sky. It does something to me, the minute I stop fretting over details such as the shower foolishly only running cold water and the moles eating my best plants and the porch pillars looking more and more detached. I've been largely in despair this beautiful summer. I felt lonely in the cities and sorry for all my friends, and there seemed too little joy to give or get anywhere. But now, I feel I want to live for years, having been tormented by the thought of all the dull years ahead, and the days can't be long enough; and at night, for a welcome change, I sleep.

Perhaps Africa would cure you. It is a true change of life. Perhaps the size and grandeur are healing: one gets a sense of proportion. Perhaps I am addicted to solitude and feel safe and easy in it, as if all were not being wasted while I ran in ever narrowing circles. I don't know about Africa except for me; for me it has Mexico beat, and Mexico was the best before this.

Two un-African thoughts: what if Nixon is the first homosexual President? I've always wondered about the curious Madame Tussaud effect he and Pat gave, and suddenly I read a news item about his knocking off work and playing squash, no, bowling with a 26 year old Negro White House employee, and then there's his Florida buddy to whom he seems incredibly attached. And the sense of mystery he creates, a non-mysterious man, because no one can seem to get near him or understand him. Ah, what a lovely idea for a story, and for a libel action too. And the other, but I've no space, is an addendum to our twenty year old annual talk entitled State of the Nation; remind me to tell you, it also concerns a man of colour. Bless you, and my love,

Martha

To: Sandy Gellhorn

October 26 1969
[Naivasha
Kenya]

Dearest old boy; I've decided to keep a sort of African journal for you and me. Instead of letters, I'll put down whenever I feel like it, some of the things I talk to you about in my head. And bung it off, again as the mood strikes me. A continuous conversation: news notes from the slopes of Longonot mountain.

The annoying thing is that the elation, the plain lovely silly dazzled joy I feel in being here and in living, has a tendency to leak away when I am faced by typewriter keys. So probably I can't convey to you (or in that novel which must start its interminable birth pangs soon) what it is really like. I keep saying how beautiful it is but I forget; so the actual sight of this immense sky – with great cumulus clouds now the size of a decent county drifting across it – and this immense land, great open plateau and the smooth high rolling mountains, amazes me: I think, My God it really is the most beautiful place on earth. It is beautiful, it is vast, it is unfailingly exciting (one way or the other) and it is all mine. The silence and the solitude are as remarkable as they are magical. A small greedy little bird, looks something like an English wren, has invaded my lawn, eating like pigs from the bird feeder and driving off all other comers: they peep a lot, by day the only sound.

. . . All summer, with rare good moments – both times in Switzerland notably – I have been thinking of death, and worrying very much about lasting too long and also fretting quite a lot at the basic fact of age: people fall apart, they are overtaken by bad luck, trouble seems to attach to them like moss. It didn't seem to be a bowl of cherries to be alive, at my age, in the civilized world. There was hardly a time when I wouldn't have settled for a sudden painless exit, in case this was all that remained. But here, ah no, I want to live many years; I can hardly wait to get up in the morning and see what's going to happen next. I have no age, neither old nor young; and I wonder if I have any sex. I was walking on the track leading up to the mountain at sunset yesterday, alone alone in a world where the view had changed, and the western sky was streaked with red, and suddenly thought: what do you feel like, you? The answer was: I feel like a man alone; with the shameless addition: a strong man alone. Luckily I have those small pearls in my ears to remind me of where I belong, in case I get dotty enough to forget.

. . . Try to imagine a very high plateau which grows only tall thick dry grass – lion grass it's called, I suppose because elsewhere lions hide in it, the perfect camouflage, the grass and the lions being the same color. It also grows a fierce little thorn tree, called whistling thorn, black with long stiletto silvery spikes, and covered with small round black balls, like walnuts in size, where ants make their homes. And a silvery grey scrub bush, less frequent, called leleshua. Nothing else grows: this is the true landscape of Africa, the bush, this is how it is meant to be. In this, alone, stands my house behind a fence made of dried sisal stalks, like a baby stockade in a Western movie, and inside this stockade I am trying to bring some color and some coolness and less dust – plants, grass, vines, even a few trees (which do not die and do not grow).

. . . So. Enough for tonight. I have been having a terrible stretch of insomnia, in Europe: dead tired but could only sleep with pills. Not quite finished here either, but I am reading Proust whom I've never dug at all, and who serves as a soporific. I have here all that is left of my books which have travelled over the years and the continents, given away, lost; and finally peeled down for shipment to Africa. A small three shelves of poetry, a biggish four shelves of fiction, a wide three shelves of non-fiction. If I read them all, I'd be a well educated woman. The tragedy is that I've read and read and read, I think not a day has passed since I learned how to read, except under most active war conditions, that I haven't read something. My annual intake is stupendous. And water in a sieve leaves as much mark; I remember nothing. Terrible waste. I will never be an educated woman.

But who knows, I may become a talented gardener.

Sleep well, my dearest boy. This will go on and on, I imagine.

. . . Later; I can't sleep. The wind sounds like heavy surf on the seashore and the windows rattle. The moon is not as bright tonight; too early. Last night, waking at 1 a.m. I got up to look at the world, and it seemed that

Africa lay under a coating of frost. At night, far away, I judge about fifty miles, I can see three lights and, insanely, resent them: I really do want this whole world to myself. Can you beat it? While I am considered mad, locally, for wishing to live in this totally isolated nearly inaccessible spot.

I think about you; not continuously but more than I think about anyone else.

I've got one piece of luck which you haven't; whereas you have many which I have not. I am a born activist (using the argot of the day.) Being one, I naturally found myself among others. The result of my youth (your age and later) in Paris was that half the young men I knew were in the Resistance and heroes thereof, half were collabos of the Germans and either shot or imprisoned or suicided when the Nazis lost. Activists all, started the same and branched, like good and evil. Unfortunately, for my comfort and ease and indeed popularity in life, I judge – though I am becoming more tolerant as I become older. I judge on behavior. Ernest wrote something once about 'grace under pressure'; as I remember it was his definition of courage. There are all kinds of courage: Omi, weary to death, trapped, not complaining, thinking of others, instantly ready to laugh if given half a chance – that's great courage. I suppose what I have always wanted to be was courageous, wanted that more than anything, as a value that included many other qualities, a blanket value of behavior. I've never got there, but it is a guide-line to conduct, I imagine; one can always try no matter how often one fails.

. . . I understand experimenting; my whole life has been an experiment. Equally, I understand taking risks, as you will agree, and the need for risks. It's a long long hangover from our ancestors who had to fight animals, stronger and faster than they. I have made as many mistakes as is possible in the time at hand; hopefully I do not make really wasteful, really damaging ones twice. And if I believe utterly in anything, it is in the human mind; I'd risk my neck far faster than my uncounted undecipherable brain cells. Therefore, it alarms – no, that's not the right word – fills me with questions as to why you have already progressed from pot to hash, since we know that hash is the stronger. Is that not right?

. . . Here's an account of two days, as far as I can remember them. I woke yesterday to no Josphat. Partly a nuisance and partly a pleasure, specially as he was due back in the afternoon. I sauntered around in my long hideous white flannel nightdress getting breakfast and feeling that I had achieved a stage of liberation in life: I would never never have to try to read Proust again. The night before was my final effort, a sporadic struggle starting my eighteenth year and finishing now.

A la Recherche du Temps Perdu is often described as the greatest novel of the century (all 4 or 5 volumes of it); but as far as I am concerned it is the most serious bore in literature. It bored me so much, the night before, that

I got cramps in my legs: and now I am through for good. Sometime I must have read the volume called *The Guermantes Way* because I vaguely remember what it was about, mainly parties in the *haut monde*, and people I detested. As I am sure I'd have loathed Proust in life. Very comforting to be quit of a duty to one's mind. Then I thought I'd wash my hair and at once found that the hot water was not working; the Sunday visit of the Hindu tinsmith having been successful for only one day. This annoyed me so I put on dirty clothes, being dirty, and went to the store room and got linseed oil and a paint brush and in a gale wind painted the cedar trunks which hold up the porch with a liberal dose of oil. The wind spattered oil over the porch (which is painted moss green inside) now the pillars look gleaming and lovely and the porch looks leprous. HAD I known about linseed oil, perhaps the pillars would not have split and shrunken (as my skin does) from the African sun.

I felt so competent about this that I decided to repair the hot water system and getting out instructions, reading them as I went, I switched over from the old gas cylinders and distributor head, to a new set I'd brought from Naivasha. To my astonishment this actually worked. By now I was drunk on my powers, and cleaned my typewriter keys with a toothbrush and alcohol, making a fine thin spray of ink over my desk and trousers the while but doing a great job on the keys. Then I settled on the front porch, filled with a desire to paint a beautiful picture of a vase of lupins.

Which I did. I am in my Impressionist (or slap-happy phase) now. It is much easier to sling paint around, suggesting lupins, than to be a Primitive, as I was before, trying like hell to make every single blossom look exactly like a lupin.

I raised my head from my finished painting and there was a young male giraffe eating a thorn bush just outside my fence. I cannot describe the feeling this gives; it is joy like a blow, a stopping of the breath with delight. It is magic and miracle. Not a sound in the world, neither from the giraffe nor me, and that lovely strange shape against the sky, and the slow chewing mouth and the eyelashes. It really is like the beginning of the world.

I went silently for my binoculars, wishing to see him better and as soon as I trained the glasses on him he turned his head – he'd not looked at me before – and slowly left. Lesson: do not be greedy. If I hadn't wanted to see more, I'd have seen longer.

. . . Personal rebellion has always seemed to me so natural and easy that it scarcely counts; it's as if one chose one's own clothes. The rebellions that matter are disinterested, beyond oneself; and they change everything: art, politics, science; religion, everything there is. The shooting stars make those. The personal rebellions have gone on forever; a casual friend of mine was a big shot at Oxford, being a roaring pansy, who walked the streets with a lobster on a leash, like a dog, and shocked one and all. So what? Of course it was funny; and he remained a roaring pansy, and nobody cared. At Harrow Cecil Beaton wore lipstick, you can imagine. People have been doing this sort of thing forever; it is amusing; it hurts no one. And people have been drinking too much, smoking opium, all the rest, since forever – and they simply ruin themselves and waste their lives, and who, finally, cares.

The rebels without a cause end being pathetic, that's all. I long for you to live. I want you to have the nerve to live. Once Tom (Dad) said to me angrily, enviously, bitterly, 'You only know headliners.' He was talking of my friends. But I knew them all young, we started together, and they were headliners because they took life head-on with gusto, fury, joy, whatever, and all their work and rebellion was for something beyond themselves.

I do not, repeat not, want you to be like me. I only want you to be the best of yourself, The very best. Using every inch of you and every drop of blood. Using it all intensely to be you.

October 31 6 p.m.

. . . Last night, I re-read *Men Without Women* by Ernest Hemingway, his 5th book, published in 1932. There's one story, called 'The Undefeated', which is so exciting that one's heart beats with pain while reading. It's about an old bullfighter who can't fight and won't stop, and how he fails. A wonder. All the rest good but none great, I think. I wanted to see again why Ernest had so captured his time, and influenced all writing throughout the world. (Now everyone has his discoveries under their belts and don't need them; but he made the discovery. Writing simply has not been the same since his flat accurate prose, but yet it's poetry too.) Funnily enough, Ernest makes several mistakes in simple grammar. You could not do this, nor I. It isn't only a question of education; it's a question of the language you have heard spoken around you since birth. I don't know any grammatical reasons for anything, but by ear, I know what sounds wrong. Poor Ernest, so much was left out in the early days. And though he conquered the world, he was really always a poor boy. At the height of his fame Omi astonished me by saying: 'I'm so sorry for him.'

He hated his mother, with reason. She was solid hell. A big false lying woman; everything about her was virtuous and untrue. Now I know enough to know that no woman should ever marry a man who hated his mother (just as the unlucky men who loved their mothers wrongly, or were perhaps – I'm not sure – too possessively loved by their mother, turn out to be fairies.) Deep in Ernest, due to his mother, going back to the indestructible first memories of childhood, was mistrust and fear of women. Which he suffered from always, and made women suffer; and which shows in his writing. But he loved his father and his father taught him to fish and shoot and live in the natural world. Then his father killed himself; and

Ernest's love turned to blinding contempt. He had nothing left to love. He called his father a coward and never forgave him. Isn't it strange. And then killed himself too; but his children are not the blaming kind, and besides he had hurt and damaged them so much before he died that they couldn't really care. Now, so late, Patrick is trying to resurrect both his parents, in his mind, because he needs them. He's too lonely with no roots, no one to love, no one to remember. So he is re-inventing them both . . .

And Ernest also made a simple mistake in French. How this fascinates me. When his accuracy is fierce, unique, and all his pride.

I'm going to have a reading problem. It really turns out that I've read the best of my library, or anyhow what I wanted to read; and all the remainder is a duty, carried across the years. But I suppose these books remain unread because, basically, they're unreadable, like Proust. So either I re-read or starve.

Wouldn't it be lovely if, by a miracle, when I got to Naivasha tomorrow, I found a postcard from you.

I love you. I believe in you. I hope for you. Try never to fail yourself. We could all be more than we are; but anyway we can't afford to be much less.

A huge goodnight kiss. I am now going to eat one of Josphat's dinners, which keep me thin and then try, grimly, to read Thackeray.

Your loving
Mum

To: George Paloczi-Horvath

November 3 1969
Naivasha
Kenya

Dear George: Ten easy ways to avoid work, by M. Gellhorn. Number one: write letters. . . .

I've just finished a novel, published by Penguin (number 1249) called *Pictures from an Institution* by Randall Jarrell. It made me think of you and I recommend it to you, it will give you pleasure. Jarrell is an American poet; or was; I seem to remember that he killed himself a few years ago. His book has the poet's defects; the prose is too witty, too erudite, too dense – one longs for air, for an easier stride. And it hasn't much shape, as to plot. Never mind. It is almost entirely a portrait of Mary McCarthy, very very thinly disguised under the name of Gertrude Johnson (or Mrs. Sidney Bacon), and Sidney Bacon is a thin disguise of Miss McCarthy's second husband. (She is on her third now.) The Institution is a girl's college, somewhere between

Sarah Lawrence and that costly progressive affair up in Vermont or New Hampshire, I forget the name.

Mr. Jarrell is eloquent and impressive on the subject of Miss Johnson-McCarthy's smile. I remember it on TV. Enough to freeze molten steel.

I came on this sentence by Mr. Jarrell: 'Yet a way of life is a way of escaping perception, as well as of perceiving.' Is it very good or am I being Germanic in liking it so much. It explains to me what I am doing now: escaping as best I can from perceiving a whole world of things, the perception of which I can no longer endure. (As we grow older, we grow more cowardly: that, at least, is certainly true.) And, in turn, perceiving a whole world of things I never truly put my mind to before.

I think I have now a good enough idea of my novel to go to work, in case Africa permits it. This a.m. all seems well, except for the fact that, to the west, a whole mountain range is burned black, and last night the line of fire, stretching for about 20 miles, was as terrible as it was beautiful.

I hope your Che [Guevara] book is going well; it is a fascinating subject.

Love

Martha

To: George Paloczi-Horvath

November 27 1969
Longonot
Naivasha

Nov 27 – the American Thanksgiving Day: precious little now for the Nation in the way of gratitude.

George dear;

. . . Ah Christ I am sick of this book,* of myself, of everything.

How can one decide when life is hell or which life is better? You have to write (writing is nothing; it is thinking which kills one) all the time, to keep eating, to keep carpets on the floor. No one would say your life is a bed of roses. Hardly safe as houses. (And who ever invented that idea? That houses were safe?) I, on the contrary, have enough money: I am careful not to have too much. I give it away; I refuse the better bargains in help whence help cometh. But still, unless I suddenly go mad and wish to travel first class in airplanes or buy Paris dresses, (and I am not tempted) I truly do not have to think about money. Having been so scamped always, despite my millionaire husbands, it is natural to me to behave like the rational and not rich intellectual classes. Yet, yet . . . Our problem is the same. The heroic days are over.

---

*Martha was working on a number of novellas, set in Africa.

That's the real problem. How to accept that newer younger voices will and must have their chance; that one's own voice (conceivably better) is not wanted because it has been heard too long. How? How? I read in the Observer about Hill 192 and now about Pinkville. George, these are two out of two thousand. This horrible true stuff is my meat; and I care about Vietnam more than about anything else in the world. And the kids who write up these appalling bits of history cannot write. But I have no place, no job, no outlet, no voice. . . . I remember in World War Two, there was Janet Flanner, in grey hair and correspondent's uniform, only in Paris, and she seemed absurd. It isn't only they who don't need one; it's one's own sense of seemliness.

Ah well. Thank you for the other letter. But do not fool yourself for a minute about me. Do not give me credit for anything. I act like a plaything of destiny, I move (something is very wrong there, I move too much) simply because there is neither absolute economic pressure nor emotional pressure to stay anywhere. I do not find a comfortable bed on the face of the globe. The Africans (now there are four) who live up here on this mountain with me drive me absolutely mad. They are making me hate the house and the life just the way the 24 passing servants did in Chester Square, before the Pamps came and brought order. This house is really something remarkable (my 19th, I believe). No one would have been so insane as to build it; its view and its isolation stun even old Africa hands. Inside I have made it (for my whole talent seems to be in making nests which I cannot endure) perhaps the prettiest house in the country.

And I am coming to detest it. The plain incessant fury of dealing with these Africans: lifelong cooks who go off leaving the gas taps on the stove open; gardeners who kill everything by watering it when the sun beats down; a semi-gardener, general dogsbody, who is found solemnly polishing the paint work of the car with chrome polish. It never ends. It is like living with chimpanzees who have been taught to paint but also eat the paint and throw it wildly around, since painting means nothing to them

And there is no one to laugh with — but is there anyone to laugh with anywhere? Is it not another function of one's age? That state of being I most loved in my life, helpless laughter among chums who were glad to be alive because they knew about death, that is all gone. Another feature of age: the weary ironic smile. I make people laugh — but what good is that? They don't make me laugh. Old Bernard Berenson, whom I questioned narrowly, thinking <u>he</u> must know, at his age, the answers, told me that in life there was only love and work — work was the building, love was the windows. I thought it tiringly simple, I'd always known this. But now twenty years have passed and I know he was right. I have no building and no windows.

Dear George, it's been a day to end days. All day long one scratch after the other. I decided I could not give thanks for anything but at least could pay bills, answer letters and send out all my Xmas checks. My Xmas checks are as political as I am a political animal: they go to an Italian orphanage, burned Vietnamese kids, an organization in the US against the war, a young man on the run from the FBI for his Vietnam protests, and so on. All done. I cannot even begin to make sense of my checkbooks in four countries. I only know that I have plodded through this day; planted some geraniums; shouted at my four Kikuyus (why don't they kill me? No one would know for weeks and they could be far away and no one would ever find them.) And I am filled with a sense of the end of things. [Graham] Greene wrote a book called *A Burned out Case*. I can't remember the book but have a ghastly feeling that this is what life does; it leaves one burned out.

But honestly George, you are all right. You have work, which in the end means work or starve. And you have love. You'll last. GOOD for you. I am always on your side.

Love,

Martha

To: Lucy Moorehead

December 1 1969

Naivasha

Kenya

Lucy dear chum; I finished the Nabokov.* It is the only book of his that I love (though it still hurts me: a lot of envy for his memory, a lot of envy for the blissfulness of his nature for he has been happy all along, even in exile, poor, so happy with his child – my nature is a black curse; and also the terrible nostalgia which I already feel for my mother). I could not bear *Lolita*, and failed to get on with any others; and hence rubbed him out for myself. But Lucy, it also horrifies me to see what a really good mind one needs to write, and I haven't one. His butterfly know-how, inventing chess problems, his languages; hell, he has enough brain for three people. I haven't enough for a gnome. Six hours yesterday, trying to get clear the difference between pride and vanity in a way which did not sound like baby talk, would be readable and suit the character. And it's a mess.

I also envy [Irwin] Shaw, with his vast memory and his talent for action and the way he keeps his characters running, not walking. My people, damn them, always seem to sit and think. Think badly, like me.

. . . They say that children bind up a marriage; me, I doubt it, but who am I to know. Though July is a long way off; Suki is only one month

---

*Probably *Speak Memory* (1969).

pregnant. Hardly counted even with us abortion girls. As for Martha,★ I know she's a world beater. Are the young not amazing; they go conventional almost as if superstitious. A christening indeed. They beat me. It may turn out we, our generation, were the really unconventional ones. Their ways are their own, new, but they all do follow the leader to a certain extent. Though I'm for them.

You're wrong about the US reaction to the massacres; and by the way, now the revelations have started, they will not stop. For the US atrocities are endless and innumerable (and I wait longingly for a long story about napalm on village children, another atrocity.) It is essential that all this horror come out, be admitted, and that shame sweep the U.S. Love,

Martha

To: Hortense Flexner

December 6 [1969]
Naivasha
Kenya

Teecher my little coconut: I implore you to listen to me and try to make sense. I did not send you the Florida check in order that you should frame it. I have more money than I know what to do with. It is no hardship; it is deducted from my check book without a pang. But all that would make me happy, and By God I am startlingly unhappy, is to think that for a week or two, you and Alice, whom you love, were having some fun. As a simple act of kindness, could you not do this for me? What is the use of your miserable money pride? I don't feel it. I take anything that's going from anybody, only regretting bitterly that my rich women friends aren't more my size so they can give their cast off clothes, thus saving me the vast trouble of getting any for myself . . . I was only tetchy about money with my husbands and then only because I didn't want them to get the notion that they had bought and paid for my freedom. But only with my husbands. I'm not menacing your freedom, darling. Why on earth can't you please for God's sake and my sake go off with Alice?

If I had anyone in the world that I wanted to make a trip with (I have only Laurence and he is not available), I would be beside myself with joy. There is no one and the awful fact is that I can't even think of anywhere to go. Here I am, doing what is the classic receipt for disaster: dreams come true: no pressures, no problems, no financial hardship, good health, a house in the place I want it. Everything is right. I am about to go mad with it . . .

★Suki was Lucy Moorehead's daughter-in-law, married to her eldest son, John. Martha was her first grandchild.

I do not work: my mind is like some dark grey sludge pit, no light glimmers, I keep asking myself a very basic question: why live?

The idea that my elderly classmates could envy me only proves that my elderly class mates are super boobs. Let them envy Miss [Katharine] Hepburn, hailed as an actress equal only to Bernhardt and making a splendid return to screen and stage. Diana Cooper and I went to see Kate's last film *A Lion in Winter*. It was somewhat complicated due to Diana having her chihuahua, who is a rather deformed little chihuahua, inside her coat against her breast, as always and against all movie theatre regulations, so all during films with her one feels and behaves like somebody smuggling extra cigarettes through customs. Miss Hepburn emoted a lot. Diana said, 'Oh no, please God, don't let her cry <u>again</u>.' Miss Hepburn cries more, on camera, than anybody I've ever seen. (Let all Bryn Mawr envy her forever.) I only wish to Christ I could make as many jokes, on a typewriter, as she makes tears. I'd feel very jolly then, as if this whole long stupid business of being alive (a quarter alive) was worthwhile.

Ah Teechie, for God's sake be a surrogate for me. Have some fun. I am perishing for the lack of it. If I had Alice, I'd be too lucky to be true; if Florida only tempted me, I'd dance in the streets. For pity's sake, (and I use the word pity advisedly), let your next communication be a post card from Florida.

Love always,

Gellhorn

To: Hortense Flexner

[?]
[?]

. . . You were not wrong to be happy with Wyncie,⋆ Teecher, and I do not think that can ever be called wasting time. It is using time, sanely and beautifully, as all people should; and if they did or could, do you think we would be so engrossed with the murderous occupations that use our days. People don't know how to be happy; in their frustration, they turn against others, and in their hypocrisy, they act as if they were helping others. You harmed no one ever, and you spread around you a lovely light, at which others could warm their spirit. Never think that was wasted living. I'd change with you like a shot; but I never had a Wyncie for me. Happy nations have no history, they say: lucky nations. Happy people are not goaded to spread their lives outward because the inward is bare and cold.

⋆Wyncie King had died while on holiday in Greece in 1961, and Alice was a close friend of theirs.

We are so made, darling Teechie, that we must always regret or be dissatisfied; but I'm getting old enough to accept what was and is and will be, knowing that my nature (or whatever the hell) is the way it is and I cannot do much about it. L.R. asked me, wonderingly, what I'd do when the Vietnam war ended – he meant, wouldn't I be lost, without a Cause. I said I'd dance in the streets and then I'd go back to Africa, when Mother and Sandy no longer need me, and take my joy from the animals and birds and fishies and the beauty of the natural world and be grateful.

I've so little energy left that I use it entirely each day, end up with a hollow well, start over again, and now I feel myself one with a large company of dissenters, not enough of us, ineffective but not silenced, and we are a bunch of boys with our fingers in the dike. I don't even give us 50/50 chances of keeping out the deluge.

A big kiss,

Gellhorn

To: Alvah Bessie

January 3 1970
temporarily at Pangani, Tanzania

Dear Alvah

. . . It's amazing that you think I have so much to say and can say it. I feel I can say nothing; my writing strikes me as dull and slow and boring. And as to having anything to say, even there I have no confidence. If I had a fine memory (one of the basic ingredients of talent), I might be able to write Memoirs, better than George Kennan for instance because, from my worm's eye view, I do believe I saw the world more truly. But I have absolutely no memory; this is not a joke. I honestly cannot recall whole hunks, months, years, of time: I remember only high spots and am never sure how accurately I remember and how much I have embroidered. And I never kept notes. I have the curious impression of my life as a sieve, once crowded or packed, but every day emptying again. And lately I have lost the sense that experience can be turned to account; I don't exactly know who is doing my semi-living for me. Who is this tall, fierce, irritable, impatient, sunburned driven woman?

Nothing in my life (or anyone's) that love and laughter wouldn't cure.

Love

Martha

To: Lucy Moorehead

January 4 1970
Tanzania, filthy place

Lucy darling: A literary note. Lillian Hellman is well named; hell on wheels. An odious woman. But the trick is to stay in the swim, keep knowing people, going about: then, as you grow old, you become sanctified. I think she didn't even write very good plays; but my God, she might be Racine the way she's treated in the U.S.

I am reading *The Mimic Men*.* There's a fellow I'd like to write like. (Follow my sentences if you can.) What a wonder, with everything got in, but not dragging. When I try to put anything in, anything extra, a reflection, it turns into cement and curds and whey. *Skin Deep*† was a marvel thriller; what excites me about thriller writers is, again, their knowledge, their expertise. Who wrote that was clearly a social anthropologist or anyhow knew the gen and techniques. I know absolutely nothing and also cannot write my way out of a paper bag.

But you know, I wouldn't care a damn if I could simply be happy; idle, lazy, easily pleased, enjoying myself. All earthly glory and ambition seem to me nothing compared to the two necessities: love and laughter. Love is in short supply, maybe gone; but what gets me is the way laughter too has gone down the drain. I can make people laugh sometimes (on the basis of laugh clown laugh) but damn few ever do it for me. I am starving for laughter.

Here at Patrick Hemingway's sewer dwelling where even the Indian Ocean isn't swimmable in; and 150 miles up the coast it is perfection. Poor Patrick, but he knows no better. I've again cleaned up and improved the accursed place and this is my absolute last visit. I'm going home early, in despair, having had almost no swimming and only medium sunburning and no writing; but probably good to be decompressed from 7000 feet to sea level.

But Lucy, what a bore it basically all is. I can't face the idea of going on looking after myself and preserving myself indefinitely. It's sillier than polishing furniture.

Love
Martha

---

*V. S. Naipaul's novel *The Mimic Men* (1967) had won the WH Smith Prize.
†By Peter Dickinson (1968), a detective story about the growth of an alien culture in the heart of London.

To: Winifred Hill★

January 5 1970
Naivasha
Kenya

Winnie darling:

. . . More and more, I realise that Cuernavaca was the golden time; and bitterly, I regret not having appreciated it more, not having enjoyed every second consciously, for the like really has not returned. It was a short oasis in a long life. I think the only house or place I have ever been homesick for was that small house, that place, during those years. I wish I had played more with Sandy; it is my loss, not his. I think of Mother there, coming home with a trail of little boys bearing flowers from the market; and how happy she was. And our swimming hours at your pool, and the addition of Lenny.

It seems to me that my whole life I have spent squirming around, wriggling, shifting, scratching, trying to find a way to be comfortable in my skin and on earth: and failing. But there, for those years, was as near as I've ever come to it. One's nature is somewhere fixed (genes and chromosomes, the position of the stars at one's birth, good and bad fairy godmothers?), and clearly my nature is wasteful and self destructive. I do not cling to blessings or good fortune: I move on, with equal speed, from what is right as well as from what is wrong.

My dearest Mum had her 91st birthday in St. Louis. I have failed her, and feel guilty; I pop in and out of St. Louis now, but literally fear for my reason if I stay – and what she really would like most is just to have me there, as daily company. I know that, and realise that I have selfishly abandoned her at this sad tail-end of her life: thus supplying myself with a further lifetime of remorse. That city does something to me which I cannot explain: I feel buried alive and now feel too often semi-dead to risk it. I am failing to write a novel, feel useless and pointless, while healthy, sunburned, bored.

LOVE,
Martha

★A friend from Cuernavaca in 1949.

To: Sandy Gellhorn

January 28 1970
Naivasha
[Kenya]

Dear Someone (you don't know and by now I don't know):
There has just been a hailstorm. In Africa at the top of the dry season. Lawn
covered with ice pellets; Africans looking white-eyed with awe. It has
rained for 23 days. I think it may be the beginning of the second Flood.
Teach us to muck about with the heavens, sprinkling the upper air with
satellites, fields of copper needles, eternally revolving astronaut's shit, teach
us to land on the moon. We are above ourselves, an egomaniac species; just
now Americans are well in the lead for the Conceit Trophy.

Well, what am I to say to you? I thought of saying nothing; after all,
silence might be golden. But there is the modern law: parents must always
understand, always put up with, always try to see the child's point of view
– no matter how idiot, slobby, stupid, senseless. I wonder if this modern
rule is all that hot stuff? Maybe us parents should rise up and say: you poor
half-assed boob, I've never heard such drivel in my life, stop insulting my
intelligence, and if yours is so inferior that this kind of muck pleases you,
then I can only pity you . . .

If you want to contemplate your navel <u>still</u> (I'd say you had been a
champion navel contemplator for far too long), go ahead. In the end, you
may anyhow know the shape of your navel, but not much else. It seems to
me a ghastly bore, when there's everything on earth to look at beside
oneself. But you're hooked on yourself; never fret, love, your ego will
never vanish. When you get right down to it, honestly, you cherish, worry
over, protect, consider, fear for and love no other human being on earth
except yourself.

As to your being hooked on that grotesque 45 year old flower child
Timothy Leary, that really finishes me. For God's sake if you want to go in
for Indian or Tibetan mysticism, why not go to the originals? Who, by the
way, never preached attaining Nirvana through drugs. No short cuts for
those boys: years and years of fasting, chastity, poverty and solitude: not
your cuppa? LSD is quicker? Oh heaven help us. I truly thought you had a
better mind than that. Nirvana is an almost unreachable state of Buddhist
beatitude; Buddhists don't go for drugs, honey. Leary is just a big hot-air
bunch of nothing words to excuse or exhort the use of LSD.

I assume from internal evidence in your quite shaming letter that you are
now busy with LSD. If so, what a copycat. Hash with Mavis (advancing
from pot) and LSD with Lee and Linda since that is their bag. Wait until
you meet a charming junkie; you'll be on the needle. Sandy, I can only
hope that someday you will get some character; you don't lack personality.

Enough character to stop yapping about stuff you don't understand and have never experienced – like 'society' which has done such awful things to you. Society never even noticed you, chum; the army got you, that's all. And the thing to do about society is learn about it, know how it works, live in it, and make it over or destroy it.

. . . The hailstorm has stopped, and also this hailstorm of a letter. Return to your silence, dear boy. You're quite right; we are not on the same wave length. (What makes you think we are on any similar material wave length; I haven't noticed you being any sort of partner or aide in any material affairs.) I despise your present wave length. It bores me; it depresses me. I hope to God you don't actually damage whatever brain you have, physiologically, by following your latest cheapest guru.

Love, but at a distance,
Mum

To: Robert Presnell

March 13, 1970
Naivasha
Kenya

My dearest P:

. . . Suddenly, as an alternative to suicide, I started writing in a hotel room in Dar. (I realise, at last, that hotels are where I write: why haven't I always lived in them; no kitchen of life.) Like an oil gusher and indeed someone else's skin and life; not the book I intended at all. Turned out a story, about 18,000 words in five days; never did such a thing. Have 12,000 words of the second story. Brain fog and nicotine poisoning. Am going to the coast, where swimming will keep me going, as a breather, in what has become an eight hour writing day. I think I can finish the first draft (about six weeks polishing needed later) of three long stories, to make a book, of the sort which repels publishers, called now tentatively *Package Tour*. Yes, easy as pie to write the totally made-up about people who have nothing whatever in common with me. And P, though I do feel pretty sick from cigs and etc., it is such relief to write at all. No idea if the stuff is good or banal, but oh my, just to write.

Next step is leave here on a charter flight on April 9 for London; the U.S. from April 16 book polishing and flat hunting and chums until end July; then two months in Vietnam – I have a book contract: instant book, two months for material, two months to write. (I think I only operate under impossible pressure, otherwise I slump into mush.) That's far enough to see ahead, indeed unusually far . . . So what, P? Life is bearable only under conditions of overwork? *Travail, opium unique* (Mauriac.) I am greedy: I still long for what I always wanted: love and laughter. Now that I am about to leave (until October probably), I am homesick for Africa. It is so beautiful, beautiful: but must be shared. Love, haste –

M

To: Sol Rabb★

April 2 1970
[?]

Dearest Sol; With this happy throng around, there will be no chance for a private chat. I want to say that I am overjoyed with your decision to resign. I am sure it is a <u>life-saving</u> decision. And I only hope you control the lovely sweetness of your nature enough to claim your rights: a solid gold handshake.

I spend a lot of time trying to figure out what life is about, and our purpose here below. And I think I have come to the conclusion that the <u>private</u> object of life is to be as much at peace with oneself as possible. If one cannot do all one wants in life, one can at least try not to do anything which is wrong for one's nature.

I wanted to tell Ruth a story but had no chance to. So you hand it on. In Paris, in the winter of 1944, I knew that I could never go back to Cuba and again be Ernest's wife. Divorce was unknown to my family; I was in despair, in a desperate tearful muddle. I went to see Diana [Cooper], then the Ambassadress, and found her taking a bath. I sat upon the toilet and poured out my misery, dripping tears. She sprang out of the bath, dripping water, and put her arms around me, saying, 'Don't cry, don't cry, you will look back on this as the happiest day of your life.' I know the value of resigning, you see.

Love always,
Martha

★Sol and Ruth Rabb had met Martha early on in Africa, and Sol had just resigned from a hotel organization. In her letters to them, she sometimes signed herself Alfie, after the name of a guest who came for a day and stayed three months.

To: Sandy Gellhorn

May 12 1970
[London]

Old boy; I stayed over to be in Washington* on Saturday with the people, more than 100,000 of them, all except me (I felt) young. I've just written a piece about it which I am sure no one will buy but I had to write it. It's not good, alas and alas, but I longed to say somewhere a declaration of love and faith. I never saw better people so I suppose they will kill more of them and make concentration camps for the others. They are strange, unseen before; it really is a new race or species or nation. I never felt so shy, so unable to touch or make contact: I only watched, listened, admired, all the boiling day, 90 degrees and more, no water; and how quiet they were and how generous and courteous. I wish I knew whether they felt anyone over forty was like some strange beast, a dinosaur, to whom they could never speak.

The President is a small cheap shit and there was a glorious moment when all 100,000 of us, in sight and hearing of the White House, loudly chanted 'FUCK NIXON.' Jolliest moment of the day.

Plain clothes cops, trying to look like demonstrators, taking photos madly. I wonder if the kids noticed. I enjoyed raising my clenched fist, the strike salute, the latest thing, and shouting Fuck Nixon whenever I saw one of them. My own age group has nothing to say to me or do with me; I find them pathetic and cowardly (except a very few chums). The young honestly aren't sure you can hear; they smile, they give you things, but they aren't able to talk to anyone who looks like me. So I left.

Love

Mum

To: Sydney ?†

June 17 1970
[London]

Dear Sydney; It is 5 a.m. which goes to show the high price of motherhood. I imagine I have been thinking of your suggested cure: amputate. Personally I mistrust major surgery, always have; even minor surgery. And it does not add to my enthusiasm that you have had to let your daughter sink. Not good enough. Why should they sink, for God's sake? Since neither you nor I sank (I mean without trace as it were; I rise and sink like a hippo in a lake,

---

*The March in Washington against the war in Vietnam was on May 9, 1970.
†Surname not known, but evidently a psychiatrist Martha consulted about Sandy.

myself) then why should our children sink? It really isn't good enough. In a very deep and angry way, this theory and type of action <u>bores</u> me.

I've no idea what Sandy has told you of his life, but factually, externally, he has probably been not so much given as obliged to take independence. A few years ago, when he was perhaps 18, he said to me, 'You've always treated me as if I were 35 and I'm not.' He went to boarding school at 10, and had a hellish time his first year; entirely on his own, no aid from Mum. He started having summer jobs when he was 14. (I got the job but did nothing about it, nor saw him on the job.) He learned to travel alone from the age of 11. Before that, to everyone's amazement, he was mooning around London on his own from the age of seven. He's had one summer holiday with me when 15. None since. I have blamed myself for absence, certainly not for presence; and above all blamed myself for not making a home-base for him since 1963. (Territory; I do believe that, like all animal species, we need it: a room of one's own.)

He has certainly made a muck of his independence but that can hardly be due to my presence, over-seeing, nagging, guiding. So I will not take that one; I will absolutely not take that responsibility or guilt. Got it, Doctor? And it is true that he returns to me always in need; but where else would he go? The trouble is that he <u>only</u> returns in need and that the need is so repetitive in style: the cop-out.

In a nutshell, the way you see it is that I have made a weakling of Sandy; and the counterpart is that Sandy has made a man of me. Well, I imagine he has a large amount of weakling in him and I have a large amount of man. But I would blame myself for lack of steady presence and lack of <u>demands</u>.

Now, to amputate is basically this: again, Sandy is relieved of responsibility. Amputated, his responsibility is only to himself: just make yourself into a fine free independent chap, and the hell with all others. I do not believe that is the way to go about it. I insist that I have responsibility to help him – though I more than agree that it should not be a material responsibility (I've told him that; if he wants to drug, he drugs alone, I really am through) – but help him with love, company, some steadiness in daily life. I equally insist that he has responsibility to me; again not material, but emotional. I need something from him as he needs something from me: neither of us has anyone else to be responsible to and for, and both need that.

I agree that it is bad that I am always the rescuer; it would be infinitely better if he rescued me for a change. But I do not believe in standing off and watching people sink for their own good if – as I do believe – he might choose not to sink from a sense of love and responsibility to me. (Do you really believe that our children are a new species and can have no feelings comparable to our feelings for our parents? I don't.)

Unless of course, despite everything he says (for he says he loves me and his greatest present wish is both to help me and earn my trust), he really loathes me. In which case, most certainly he should leave me; and furthermore he will, the minute this crisis is solved. But I am not going to boot him out.

I think Sandy needs two things: a girl and a job. He also needs an adult to love and be loved by. Until he finds a better parent, it better be me. I need a son – having really not had one to date, having only had a child who charmed me when he wanted something or landed on me when in trouble.

It is now 6 a.m. I write letters because I am a writer: I trust the written word as I don't trust the spoken word.

Martha

To: Lucy Moorehead

Sunday [1970]
St Louis

Lucy dear,

Here I am by my mother's death bed, waiting with her, day after day, for her escape. Her face never looked tormented in life, and now it looks as if exhaustion had become pain. She is thin as Belsen, bones and skin. I can't stop crying when I am with her – and the rest of the time I have a sensation of operating in somebody else's dream, not real. Nothing makes sense or is bearable. I think of you, 10 days beside Alan's bedside while he was in a coma. If you live long enough you will learn as much as you can endure. But I always think of the concentration camps in order to give myself a good long view on whatever strains I live through. Only this anguish is for her – when awake, though her eyes are closed & she is too weak to make words – I know she knows, and thinks with despair, will I never be allowed to depart.

I love her more than anything in the world & always have, my one unfailing love, and now I long for her to die, to be permitted not to stay where nothing is left except this overpowering weariness.

I will stay with her as long as she breathes. Maybe she knows my arms are around her & that I kiss her hands and maybe feels less lonely. I've seen so much death but it was all quick. Quick is lucky. There is no God and no justice. This superb human being should not have to struggle day after endless day to leave. Her only passionate act of free will was to refuse food – the fool nurses push a few spoonsful of milk down her throat, three times a day, but I know she is doing the only thing left for her to stop it all.

Oh Lucy – does one come back into life, after this, with any slight ability for laughter?

love
Martha

On September 24, 1970, Edna died. She was ninety-one. It had been a long, slow death and Martha blamed herself bitterly for not helping to hasten its end. She was dazed by grief and, talking to no one, crept into bed and spent a week sleeping, trying to adjust herself to a loss she had spent her entire life fearing. "Since she was the only person who ever possessed me," she told a friend, "life is unlivable without her." Sybille Bedford tried to comfort her: "You loved one another, and you did your best. In a sense both of you have this for ever." These were unhappy years. She had been right to fear her fifties and sixties for they brought her much sadness and uncertainty. She found writing increasingly hard and berated herself for lack of discipline and talent.

That year Martha had bought a flat in London, the top floor and attic of a tall, red brick Victorian house at number 72 Cadogan Square. It had large windows from which she could look out over London's skyline, and she furnished it in the simple, unpatterned colors and bamboo furniture that she most liked. She had also volunteered to work in Kew Gardens, picking up rubbish.

It was at about this time that, through their mutual friend Robert Presnell, she met Betsy Drake, actress and former wife of Cary Grant, who was moving to London from California to train as a therapist. This was the start of a long, close, affectionate friendship and it was to Betsy that Martha wrote some of her most intimate and confessional letters. More descriptive than analytical for the most part – Martha was fiercely hostile to self-analysis in any form, saying it was "not my bag" – she wrote to Betsy about love, loneliness, depression, writing, sex, and men. The first letters took the form of an autobiography. "Women," she told Betsy, "are much more reliable than men; but usually not as funny." The confidences had their drawbacks. Martha could be impatient, imperious, and bossy. Betsy told Martha one day that being with her was like "being friends with a rhinoceros who has no idea that he has stepped on your foot." Martha told her that once she reached eighty she would take more care and no longer tell her to fuck off.

Now that there was no longer any need for her to visit St. Louis, Martha divided her time between London – home to Sybille Bedford, Diana Cooper, and Betsy – Naivasha, and her travels. "Since I do not eat for my shape's sake," Martha wrote, "and have no sex life, I have sublimated the whole thing into love affairs with places." She loved exploring, but had no patience with ruins. "Nothing depresses me more than history," she once said, "always more of the ghastly same, only different clothes and weapons." From Duino, where, she reported, "Rilke wrote like a bird," she sent word that she herself was "writing like a cement mixer." In Phuket in Thailand, she adopted a small cat. In Costa Rica, she swam with sea turtles. Pausing in a hotel one day, she calculated that she had been to fifty-five countries, twenty-four of them more than once, and had established eleven permanent homes. However much she joked and complained, Martha needed to travel. It was, for her, freedom.

Martha visited Nadezhda Mandelstam in Moscow, having started what she called a "pen-pallery" with her after reading Hope Against Hope, Mrs. Mandelstam's account of the Soviet years of repression. Many of her letters to Martha survive, often

demanding, always opinionated, but none of Martha's to her. "If I had to live my
life from the beginning once more," she wrote to Martha one day, "I would have
become a nun. But when young I didn't think that clean life was possible. I would
have preferred to become a whore . . . The only thing I am glad for is that I have no
children. The young are not satisfactory. When I meet one of them I thank God that
they are not mine. The babies are nice. But when they become grown-ups they are
not what they ought to be – weaklings, nasty and so on." Martha loathed her week
in Moscow. She admired Mrs. Mandelstam, but she did not like her.

To: Lucy Moorehead

October 14 1971
72 Cadogan Square
London SW1

Lucy dear; The *élan vitale* has leaked away. Maybe leaked away in daily
kitchen of life errands; maybe leaked away by itself. The writing is a frost.
I have that one long story ready for you to cut to ribbons; but it has not
come off. And nothing else happens. The days go by, lost, wasted, and I
have no drive to write, no words come; cement has again settled on my
mind. I may just creep back to Kew. At least keep my leg muscles and some
happiness; nothing wrong with trees; nothing wrong with cleaning up a
corner of the world. Therapy.

And I grow more and more solitary. The truth is: there is no one to see.
Moura* dined here last night. She has got very deaf; she uses one simply as
a meal (she cannot bear to eat alone nor skip meals.) While I was getting
the food on to the table, she settled at the phone to make a few of her
check-in calls. ('You are back, dahleeng, we must meet soon.') After dinner
she had a good clean-up of her vast handbag. I had no sense that either of
us gave the faintest pleasure to the other. It is the same with everyone
though one doesn't feel as brutally used as with Moura. I don't know what
to do about this. It won't get better. I will certainly end sitting on a flagpole
like St. Simon Stylites; why not?

Should I write to Celia?† I hate to, of course; from my own experience,
I know words are futile. To me, they were worse, irrelevant, and a terrible
cross having to answer them. I bought masses of post cards, pretty flowers,
at the Vic and Albert, and scrawled thank yous. But I don't know;

---

*Moura Budberg (1892–1974), a famous beauty and an enigmatic figure, believed to have
been a spy. During the Russian Revolution she had an affair with Bruce Lockhart and later
became Maxim Gorky's secretary and mistress before living with H. G. Wells.
†Dame Celia Johnson (1908–1982), the actress, whose husband Peter Fleming, author of
Brazilian Adventure and *News from Tartary*, had just died.

sometimes people like to have jobs, like to hear. Tell me; and if I should, tell me where.

I can also see, in a way, that her armor now is a real protection. Again, only judging by myself: I found and still find that it is <u>worse</u> to talk. Of course, she has always been impenetrable, and darling, she got what she needed and came for, simply human company: voices, faces, activity. That was her comfort and you gave it.

I met Freya Stark★ yesterday. (Was it only yesterday? For me, it is never later than you think, I always think it is a lot later.) I got no impression of anything interesting or attractive. It was a terribly stiff boring lunch at Diana's [Cooper]. Everyone was boring. I thought Miss Stark a bit pissed off because I had been to Bodrum, where she went, just before her; took some of the shine off the travels, I guess. I could not understand what held you, about her. How does she get her letters; keep carbon copies or ask for them back? I'd have no idea where my roughly five million letters were scattered over the globe. I think what I don't like is the sense that she stands off and sees herself as someone.

. . . Solly† is coming to dinner and I shall listen, with undisguised envy, to his ceaseless activities. Just lately he was squiring the Emp. of Japan round the Zoo, in a tail coat. The Emp. actually smiled at ChiChi the giant panda. One does wonder whether Eliz Two would have been feted in Tokio, had we lost the war.

Love to all of you,

Martha

To: Daniel Ellsberg‡

[? 1971]

[?]

Dear Daniel Ellsberg,

I have just re-read the *Pentagon Papers* slowly, in the paperback *N.Y. Times* edition. It is a recommended exercise, bitter homework.

★Dame Freya Stark (1893–1993), traveler and writer, legendary for her hats, her conversation, and her sense of history. Lucy Moorehead was editing her letters.
†Solly Zuckerman (1904–1993), scientific adviser to the British government and leading figure in the Zoological Society, who carried out research into primates and was the author of a number of books, including his autobiography, *From Apes to Warlords*. Made a peer in 1971.
‡An open letter to Daniel Ellsberg – running to seventeen pages – the strategic analyst and State Department official who worked on the top secret McNamara study of U.S. decision making in Vietnam, and who in 1969 photocopied the 7,000-page report and gave it to the newspapers. Known as the Pentagon Papers, the revelations led to Ellsberg's prosecution in 1973, on twelve felony counts, but they were dismissed.

Unendurably bitter because the Vietnam war goes on, now an extended massacre from the air, while Mr. Nixon predicts that Vietnam will not be an issue in the 1972 election. Obviously Mr. Nixon realises that the *Pentagon Papers* did not rouse America as he must have feared when he tried to stop their publication. No other President ever tried to silence the press by injunction but then the times are full of broken precedents, such as war without benefit of Congress, a Presidential war. ('Nowhere are Presidential wars authorized.' Supreme Court). The same war we've still got. Mr. Nixon must have thought peace would be forced on him if the whole country knew how successive U.S. Administrations manufactured this war against small peasant nations half across the world. But not to worry, as it turns out. It is perfectly all right to go on killing these gooks at the increased average rate of 90,000 tons of bombs a month, as long as no American soldiers are killed. The President assumes that the American people are moral imbeciles. All is well. The *Pentagon Papers* weren't a 'grave and irreparable danger' to the war, after all.

This may be the first and last chance we ever have to learn how the Executive branch of our government really operates. We owe that to you and always will. It was an act of faith in your compatriots to risk your safety so that we might learn. You must have believed – it comes on the best authority – that 'the truth shall set ye free.' Well, not yet. But in time. And perhaps in time, these truths you brought to us will set us more free than any of us now can predict. Not only free of this abominable war but free of creeping distortions in our system of government.

The Founding Fathers cannot have intended a President and his small group of appointed advisors to perform like a monarch surrounded by his court. As if the people's representatives and the people themselves were a general nuisance, and the job is to keep the whole tiresome bunch quiet: manipulate them. How long has this been going on? It's not brand new evidently, as the *Pentagon Papers* show. For in 1954, at the time of the Geneva Conference on Indo China, our government made the fine public noises – 'The United States reiterates its traditional position that peoples are entitled to determine their own future' etc. – but at the same moment, the Eisenhower Administration was dispatching a Dirty Tricks Team to Vietnam, to begin sabotage and psychological warfare against Ho Chi Minh and his nation. Peoples are not to determine their own future, unless the U.S. Executive approves their future. We have seen where this kind of schizoid governing can lead us. The main lesson of the *Pentagon Papers* is that democracy needs to be re-invented in the United States . . .

. . . What a black historical irony if the Free World was lost due to the tyranny of the Leader of the Free World. No sane man (which seems to let out the men of the *Pentagon Papers*) would believe for a minute that you win the minds and hearts of the people by bombing them. Or by financing and arming rulers whom the people detest. The Russian government has wisely refrained from devastating its recalcitrant satellites, but no one assumes they have gained the love and loyalty of Hungarians, Poles, Czechs by sending in tanks.

Our country is founded on as decent principles as exist in human society, but of course principles become contemptible hypocrisy when they are only used for rhetoric, not as a faithful guide to action. If this unforgivable war has taught us to be eternally vigilant against the misuse of our power, then it will have served one valuable purpose: the education of Americans. But what a hideous price to pay for becoming an 'enlightened citizenry' – all the lives lost and all the lives spoiled, their children and ours.

Yours sincerely,
Martha Gellhorn

To: Robert Presnell

October 25 1971
[?]

Oh hell, P., I miss you too. But maybe it's best like this. The very last of the letter writers. We are, you know. Walpole and Sevigné, if they're the pair I mean.

I'll get George Garrett's *Death of a Fox* and recommend to you *Hope Against Hope* by Nadezhda Mandelstam; I think it is a miracle.

As for not showing Dracula getting a stake driven through his heart, any day here one can see Oliver Reed's testicles impaled in a film entitled *The Devils*. Goodness they are prissy in the U.S. about their horror. In fact, I haven't gone to see *The Devils* mainly because I really hate cruelty, am not purged by pity and terror but simply overwhelmed with sickness and despair, in life as in art.

No, I can't write about my Mum or St. Louis but have been, accidentally, doing a therapeutic act. I am always tidying up things, no doubt in preparation for death or simply because external disorder upsets me, I have enough inside. And thus got to work on my very few papers – I also throw away stuff so fast that I often throw or give away stuff I need. I found two short stories, probably saved (in an envelope marked short story notes) because I thought I could use the ideas later. They are better stories than I write now, so I tidied them up and sent them off; and thought angrily of the amount of stuff lost; also published stuff, no copies and no records. Anyway I then decided to look at about 15 years worth of diaries, never looked at since written. I've waded through 1949 (you'll appear in 1950.) Since it is absurd to weep, I can only laugh; but have learned more about

myself than any amount of costly babbling to psychiatrists; and suddenly seen a reason to keep a diary. These are to be burned in due course, but oh my, what a self-treatment. For P. I was <u>always</u> the way I am, only now with more lacks, mainly my mother, the one steady golden note in that morass of pages; and no more suitors. What I cannot get over is the number of men, whose names I no longer remember as belonging to anyone; and my constant refrain of being tired (now I'd be dead if I did so much) and of being solitary. In one year there were three major love affairs (I mean involving passion and the decision NOT to marry), four minor affairs and getting pregnant by an eighth (honest to God) and that year I spoke constantly to myself of knowing no one, being alone . . . Well, shit; the trouble with me has nothing to do with facts but only with my dark nature, born under Saturn by the light of a full moon (so Waldner, our great comical astrologer tells me). But I also worried, with reason, about money and told myself to spend less not earn more, the only road to freedom. I must say it beats me how I did manage, from typewriter to article to commercial story and with no margin. I no longer worry about money and spend as I always have, just on living, never on acquiring. Anyway, those diaries somehow taught me something about myself; maybe resignation. Nothing teaches me not to miss my Mum. I found an (unplaced) quotation; '*Un être me manque et tout est dépeuplé*' which basically explains the case.
LOVE,
M

To: Betsy Drake

January 15 1972
Longonot
[Naivasha]

Dear Betsy; I'm tired; it is *l'heure bleue*, no time to write a letter. I think I'll do a bits-and-pieces one, since even sustained letter writing is beyond me. Nothing else seems to be beyond me, including my latest operation: road building by hand. It is not good for the hands, nor the back. Carrying small boulders to fill erosion gullies in the damned seven mile track which passes for my road, and hoeing and shovelling dirt to cover same. But of course, always proud of a new skill. I even managed to mend the lawn mower; and aided by a magic book entitled *Casserole Treasury* and working like mad until 9:30 p.m. last night I made a very tasty lunch for the Israeli Ambassador and wife who came today and brought me a bottle of whiskey.

   . . . It bewilders me that you seem to feel it might be annoying or intrusive to write to me about my books. I know nothing about your two professions, acting and therapy, but surely they cannot be so different.

Would you be annoyed or feel your privacy violated if anyone wrote to you of your work? Especially when writing as you do, in a way that amazes me and gives me surely unjustified pride. I always write to writers. Not people I know, friends (though I am delighted if I can tell any of them that I approve.) But I always write to every writer, care his/her publisher, an immediate letter of praise and thanks when a book moves me. Because I know about being a writer and I know, as only those can who like me write in the dark, about the loneliness. You write by yourself and you are published. And you might as well have dropped the book into the middle of the Pacific, except for reviews which mean nothing. I always longed for a stranger to write to me, saying (in effect that's all I say), 'I heard you.'

There was no reason for you to be moved by either *His Own Man* or *The Lowest Trees Have Tops*. They were escape literature for me. Light as meringue. I wrote *His Own Man* about the middle of my last marriage, when literally dying of the thinness of life. I wrote it to amuse myself, while also trying to run one house in Spain and build another; while trying not to kill my then husband for his awful hypochondria and life-destroying; little did I know he was only having ulcer pains because of leading a double life and worried because, in Spain, he couldn't be double.

. . . The others, no. I have always written from compulsion (and maybe that is what is now lacking.) Not anything to do with my own life; compulsion about the lives of others. I wrote *The Wine of Astonishment*, which was titled and in my mind is always *Point of No Return* in order to get rid of Dachau. The whole book, for me, was that: to exorcise what I could not live with. (But Dachau, and all I afterwards saw: Belsen etc., changed my life or my personality. Like a water-shed. I have never been the same since. It's exactly like mixing paint. Black, real true solid black, was then introduced, and I have never again come back to some state of hope or innocence or gayety which I had before.) The article on Dachau was written immediately, the same week. The book was two years later. There is always a difference anyway between journalism and fiction. In journalism I spend my time trying to keep myself from screaming. By the way, the best of my articles is probably the one about the Eichmann Trial, not in that book.

In my opinion, which is very old-fashioned, the reporter should be there as little as possible: nothing about the reporter matters. What matters is the thing: the facts: what happened: how it was. And, again old-fashioned, I think it detracts from the effect – i.e. you want the reader to be there too – to underline or insist. I was always cutting and deleting from my articles, to eliminate as much as possible the sound of me screaming. And in a novel, since again I don't write about myself (and couldn't and am not interested) the problem was to make the external events true for the character.

Here I am again, some time later and a couple of drinks later, but still feeling chatty. Ah, the immense and repellent luxury of chatting about one's own work, something I've almost never done for the simple reason that no one wanted to hear. And now because there's nothing to say: no work. I think 'Till Death Us do Part'* is good. I wrote it again and again for some years; abortions. And finally it came right in three weeks. It was written in love and homesickness for the dead. I have no idea, never had, what it means: 'Let the dead bury the dead.' Try as I will, I cannot make sense of that famous sentence. Personally, I bury my own dead, or maybe make a private monument for a grave. Actually, thinking it over, I don't bury them at all; they stay with me. But if I can write something, then it's as if I could climb over a mountain, or get used to an empty valley. I have the feeling, ever more surely, that I will not be able to write anything until I can write (only for myself) my mother's death. Not her being dead, but how she died. Since I still have nightmares, I reckon I have to get it outside myself on paper – you know writing is really a form of vomiting what the mind cannot digest – and yet I cannot even face doing that. I can't face the pain yet. One day, either I will or I imagine I won't do anything else.

Mrs Hapgood† is what I did instead of therapy. I must believe that therapy is essential and valuable for some people, maybe for many. For me, it seems perfectly awful, like wallowing in self pity. When my second marriage busted, I was absolutely caved in. Not for good reasons, I now see: not the loss of a true and great love. But as if I had been kicked in the stomach. I had been lied to for at least five years, and lied to cruelly: in that I was given to understand that waning interest and a general sense of living in a well-furnished fridge was due to me. My husband pointed out that I was ageing; this was ten years ago; and anyway was not really much of a cuppa for men. I'd always had lots of men in my life but you know, one does not use one's noggin. I was easily brain-washed, more and more isolated, deadened; then found out that all this was cover for him. I nearly went crazy because I cannot handle lies, which is stupid. The world and people are full of them, and I ought to be able to handle anything – for after all, I have never been asked to handle anything like what others manage. (I was never in Dachau as an inmate: that's my real test.) So my darling old doctor got tired of prescribing sleeping pills and tranquillisers and sent me to a chum, a darling old psychiatrist: such a nice, kind, wise man. I talked to him five times; then said 'Darling Doctor, the sound of my own voice whining away makes me sick. The whole thing disgusts me. Fuck it. I am simply going to write it out and the hell with it.' So I sat down and wrote that story – while the Cuban Missile Crisis passed without my noticing

---

*Based on her friendship with Capa.
†In *The Fall and Rise of Mrs. Hapgood* Martha had written out her fury about the ending of her marriage to Tom Matthews.

same. I sat in a rented basement room and wrote and wrote and wrote. And cut that story in half: what you read is a compressed half. And when it was done, I went to call on the Other Woman (by the way, I never believed for an instant that any other woman or other man busted a marriage), whom I'd never seen and imagined, from my husband's finally joyful and also untruthful revelations, to be a young pathetic sort of touching refugee wisp. And found her to be a big stupid pretentious false-grand English lady, perhaps four years younger than I, and came home roaring with laughter and told him they really deserved each other; and I had my story and was free. So that's my therapy; it is the only one. I was brought up in a good tough school whose basic instruction is: Get on with it. Somehow.

I don't believe we are out of touch with ourselves, I think we are far too concerned with our own navels. I think we need, quite the opposite, to be committed to something beyond ourselves. Sublimation is maybe the absurdly fancy present-day word. What the hell does it matter all this learning about oneself? You learn by doing, not by sitting looking at your own innards. You are what you do; you learn by listening, <u>hearing</u>, feeling for others, putting yourself in the place and lives of others. It seems to me more important to get the hang of almost anyone else. I'll get the hang of me, for working purposes, as I move along; besides I change, with the times, with external events, such as passing time and greater experience. I think we are out of touch with others, with all others.

. . . One of the many reasons I was unhappy before, here, was that I could not get on any sort of real wave length with the Africans. They were <u>them</u>. I hated this but there it was. Now I still feel they are them, to the extent that I feel their foreignness (which is inevitable, and even a different language does this, let alone a difference in environment, wealth, culture, which is enormous) but I also feel them as people, in the sense that I know damn well their needs and wants are different and also their laughter and their pain; but I feel all of these, I recognize they are different from mine but <u>there</u>. So now something much better has happened, inside me; I will never know Africans, nor they me; but a vague dotty amiable bond has been established, I'm on the same planet with them now. And this is much more important to me than being in touch with myself. I can't help being in touch with myself, for God's sake, no matter how much I would like to meet someone in me who is not me.

. . . If you really want to go on reading Gellhorn, get *The Trouble I've Seen*. It's number two chronologically but actually number one. The first I wrote at 21, an ignorant and innocent baby; it was *The Group* long before Miss McCarthy, and a funny awful book. I knew nothing else and wrote what I knew. But as soon as I knew something more, I wrote what was right for me, not my group, not me: but others. There's a story in *The Trouble etc.* called 'Ruby' which I recently re-read, trying to con myself into feeling that if I'd once written I still could write. And I read it with wonder, and it didn't comfort me, it gave me the shakes. I couldn't write it now. But then I had found out my truth. That book is about the unemployed during the Great Depression. I found out that my interest and subject was people being pushed around, injustice, the suffering of the victims; and that I liked the victims, as people, forever more and always and could not bear the victors.

. . . But the two things I aimed for, I failed at. I wanted a great single man-woman love and to write a great book. So tough: I didn't have the quality needed. Most of the world does not have the quality needed; it's not like having your finger nails pulled out by someone who is entertained to do so. I cannot learn patience and feel that perhaps Sandy was sent, as Job was sent his boils, to try, test, and enlarge my minuscule capacity for patience. Intolerance is the word generally used but it is inaccurate. Impatience is the malady. Suddenly I wish to get away even from this remote place to something more remote and see more animals than I see here and stop being a pioneer housewife and be instead a pioneer Boy Scout. After this outing, I plan to be a part-time teacher in the village school. 200 little Africans, all from subsistence homes. It costs $6.08 a year to send a child to school so most families can't; and they go on having 8–10 children. You know, people spend a lot of time advising each other and themselves to 'forget it.' I cannot, not anywhere or about anything, and that, honey, is madness.

Well, you sure as hell needn't apologize to me about letter-writing; not after this example.

Did I say Happy New Year? Happy? Anyway, chin up, isn't it?

Martha

To: Betsy Drake

January 21 1972
Vipingo
Kenya

Betsy dear
. . . You think of looks always in relation to sex. I don't. I don't think I ever did. Now it strikes me as a huge joke that I bitterly resented the way men grabbed me, what the hell did they mean wanting my body when here I was with my immortal soul and much more important, the causes which were always the central concern of my life. I took my looks for granted, but they were an essential part of me – the body, face, brain are all oneself. I must have counted on them as a passport; everyone prefers good looks to ugliness, a beautiful building to a hideous one, a garden to a slum. It is

natural. And I am sure that, though I never used them for sexual attraction, my looks were a passport which somehow made tolerable the interruption of a furious woman, bullying powerful people to be concerned about unpowerful people. I think I had no self consciousness, on the basis of a built-in security about my looks; which is hard now to explain because I only began to think about and need and regret my looks, when they started to go. Does that explain to you? They don't mean love or sex to me; they mean, as I must have said before, confidence. Now I think: they will find an old woman absurd . . . I also feel the physical handicap of not being as strong, as sure as I was; I mean as to muscles and movements. Run indeed; I cannot run more than a few yards, I have no wind, decades of cigarettes, less muscle. I can thank God still walk forever and swim, ploddingly, forever, but speed is a thing of the past. But once I could and did set out alone in a cotton dress with a knapsack to climb alone among the snows of the Pyrenees. Only fairly lately has it been borne in upon me that there are actions I cannot do, that my body is definitely wearing out.

You wrote that a friend had died. I read this and took it in. No more. Then a cable came. A friend had died, like that, from perfect health to instant death, aged 64.★ A brave and rare man, a Hungarian, leaving a wife 20 years younger and an adored 17 year old son. I am sure I have written this to you. I mourn for them and me, not for him, except he would dearly have loved more life to watch his son longer. But a wonderful way to die. I wish it had been me, not him. I cannot think what I am to do with the time ahead; but he loved living. He told me once that after prison – he spent 5 years in solitary, 2 with four other men in prison in Budapest after the war – every minute of life was fascinating to him. It was. He was a happy man. So he's dead. My friends started dying when I was young, in Spain, and have died ever since steadily in all the wars and in accidents. But now I must nerve myself for their dying out of the blue because it is dying age. And the world gets emptier and I feel more and more a survivor.

. . . Meantime, count one's blessings. There is the sapphire sea, with white caps beyond the reef because the North East monsoon is blowing a treat. There is the moonstone sky by day and the brilliant moon-lit star-lit sky by night. The air is satin and soft and warm. There is no sound except the sea, the rattling of palms in the wind, and in the morning unseen African birds whose notes are the one certain proof to me that I am back here.

. . . I tell myself that I am of retirement age, and have done whatever I could and it's all done now, and for God's sake, grow old gracefully. Why is that so hard? I'm not even bored, not even restless. I am sad. Something else again. And I hate this goddamned sadness and never expect to lose it.

★Martha's great friend, George Paloczi-Horvath.

The truth is that everyone needs (and everyone loses) one person to love, a center point, or a rock to stand on. Without that, all is adrift, floating and the basic color is grey.

. . . I do not presume ever to speak to you of your mother's death. But I dare to disagree with you about suicide. I do not agree that it is murder and there is the hate and need for a victim. It might be, but I do not think one can generalize. The two suicides I know were not murdering themselves with hate, but simply leaving while there was time, from the empty ruins of life, because they knew – and I think rightly – that they had finished, and that what remained was going to be bleak and belittling. I speak of Ernest and a woman, aged I think 62, a painter of talent but not the largest talent, who had lost her husband, a worthless man she adored, and was now, some eight years later, losing what she believed (rightly I think) was her last lover, a man younger than she, also talented, very selfish, married. She knew she would not be any more of a painter, she knew she could not bear the loneliness of life without a man to love and be loved by; she did not want, as my mother so wisely said, simply to grow old. So she left. Ernest had every reason to leave. I cannot possibly blame them or think they were impelled by hate; they had made their accounts and reckoned that the whole operation was now finished, and they didn't want to stay around for a long rotting finale. I don't even pity them, now. I think they were very sane. Their evaluation of their futures was correct. Why stay until the evil present becomes a worse future and eats away all the value of the past?

Suicides terrify people. People are frightened to have it so clearly stated that life can fail, that it truly can be unlivable. It is not cheering news and those closest are usually infected with guilt, thinking they might have prevented, given more etc. But the basic reaction I think is fear. I used to find suicide perfectly unimaginable but that is always a question of age; where you are yourself, and how much you have worn out your own life. I think it takes some kind of desperate courage to commit suicide for after all, it is the totally unknown risk, and before that blank uncertainty, only one's own willful belief in nothingness is protection. I think, Betsey, that dying is a very hard business, however achieved. Even the dead I have seen in war, supposedly immediately dead, did not look as if the departure had been easy.

. . . So long. I must pull myself together and go down the beach to see some people who have a cottage to rent, smaller (therefore better) than here and certainly cheaper.

Love

M

To: Betsy Drake

February 3 1972
Naivasha
Kenya

Dear Betsy

I am going to take to drink. Lucy Moorehead wrote me that she found afternoons trying everywhere which astonished me. I had never thought of afternoons as separate but merely days: my life divides into day – the hours I am operational, and night, the hours I am sitting or lying and inert. But now afternoons have reached the screaming stage, due to the weather.

. . . Every bloody day for nearly two months, at 1 p.m. or 1:30 p.m. if lucky, the clouds move over. Very handsome, a remarkable sky. Water lilies carrying Alps is what they look like and each the size of Texas. A rare light, with the sun making fingers of God beyond belief, everything being outsize in Africa. Huge winds whip about, and miserable rain, about 20 inches, slants down. The sky remains every shade of grey, and there are vast stretches of brilliant cloud and pastel blue and always shifting lights on the mountains. Lovely for a painter maybe, and pure hell for me.

Returned from a solo safari of a dazzling nature, about 1000 miles of these fearsome red dust obstacle course roads. I went to see again, like going to the Prado to see the Goyas, a great herd of giraffe, far from the beaten track (not that there's anything much beaten) in the Serengeti. There they were, almost in the same place as three years ago, about 200 of them, a sight you cannot see on this earth, with nine other species from buffalo to banded mongoose cavorting around them. A great green plain dotted with trees and half circled by blue mountains. Not a soul anywhere, nor ever was or is: the beginning of the world. That was absolutely lovely and now I have that picture in my mind, so don't need to go again. The driving was something, the dust is a misery. But oh the land, the look of it, and the same beautiful busy wild animals everywhere. I got chased by a rhino, which is the nearest animal to humans, so filthy tempered it will charge out of sheer interior rage, though I had not even seen it nor in any way discommoded it. Slight increase of heart beat. However luckily the track was clear and I stepped hard on the gas and that was that. This was in another park, one that looks pure Douanier Rousseau, and also gives that strange tight sensation of joy: that such a thing exists, that one has eyes to see it.

. . . I do not believe in the perfectability of man any more. I believe that some men/women at some times (and a few most of their lives, a very few) achieve a state of such perfection it hardly seems possible. Bravery is the one I love most. A lady psychiatrist whom I liked a lot, but I am afraid I cannot trust them, they speak with too much God-omniscience, once told me I was so hipped on bravery because I was madly frightened all the time. I think that is balls myself, because I am not given to being frightened. I am afraid of jail, prison, anything which would close me in, always have been; and of the horrors of old age, another prison. This being said, I have never believed there was anything to do about fear except carry on and forget it. Applied to all things. Ah, I know about fear of course like all sane people exposed to immediate and evident danger. I know the exact physical symptoms and also their incredibly short duration: they cease the instant danger passes.

. . . Anyway, we cannot be perfect; we never were and never will be. Our species honest to God does have the mark of Cain; we are cursed with the blindness of stupidity and we are killers. The best of us can spend their lives fighting on any front against this, can learn to become kind, and generous, and brave. And thus perhaps keep us from perishing. But I fear that each age is the worst yet, each epoch is just as bad as the people then living can endure. However, I believe in saints, heroes, martyrs, and those who keep the record straight. <u>DO</u> read *Hope Against Hope* by Nadia Mandelstam. She's an example of what I mean: one human pretty damn near reaching perfection, under conditions of hell.

This is not a letter, it is a book. Go with God. I hope you are well and well occupied.

M

To: Sandy Gellhorn

February 13 [1972]
[Longonot?]

My dearest boy;

. . . I found this extra editorial about Omi; you said you wanted one. I send it to you as a sort of talisman. One needs, in life, heroes and models and they are hard to come by. Goodness, combined with brain, is a good deal rarer than rubies. I think your main luck is to have known Omi, for you have seen how lovely and lovable and admirable a woman can be, so it gives you faith in women.

I have been in such mental despair, no doubt due to being a physical disaster, that one day staying in bed feeling as if I had pus not blood in my veins, I took a solid look at myself as your mother. (You remember that on the wall facing my bed there is a variety of photos of you.) The big one of you as a very little boy, aged 4, leaning against me, smiling, shy but with sad eyes, is the one that breaks my heart. I decided I had been an absolute failure for you as a mother; not that I did not <u>provide</u>, and arrange, and guard your health; but I was joyless, uncosy, like that awful line in Milton or maybe Wordsworth (two poets I can do without) 'Stern daughter of the voice of God.' Of course, when one does wrong, the main person cheated and deprived is oneself. I wish to heaven I could start over. And that, my darling, is the very saddest most hopeless sentence that exists in any language.

Try to live so that you will have the minimum to regret. One doesn't regret material things for more than a minute, unless one is crazy. I have made so many material mistakes and walked away from them, riled, but quickly forgetful, that I never count them. But it's in human terms that regret eats one's innards.

Take care, please write to me, I am in need.

Love

Mum

To: Sandy Matthews

March 2, again 1972

[Longonot?]

Dearest Sandy; This is a birthday letter. But I shall bring your birthday present – African finery – because I no longer trust the mails, let alone customs.

I think (never sure) that between 30 and 45 is the great period of life, the full flowering. It seems to me the first 30 years are all too groping; as if experiments had to be made and re-made and one was maybe happily, maybe miserably, either skating on thin ice or slogging through swamp mud. But some workable certainties seem to happen in those exact middle years. Lucky people get a lot of certainties; I cannot exactly describe the sense of not being bought on approval by oneself, but accepting oneself forever, which does come in this time.

I wish you everything good in life, and I think – entirely due to yourself and no one else – you're on the right path. You're right about taking responsibility; how can one join the human condition as an observer only? It's too cold and too canny and too self-regarding to avoid all the trouble and pain, as well as the pitching-in satisfaction.

You've made me feel warmer in life, by caring about me. It is a comfort that you think well of me, a great comfort, and that you do not feel I failed you utterly, to the extent I have touched your life. I am more grateful to you than I can say, because I labor so heavily under the sense that I have failed Sandy G.; otherwise how could he so completely fail me? I would be much poorer were it not for you . . .

M

To: Robert Presnell

May 13 1972
72 Cadogan Square
London SW1

Dearest P; Now there is nothing to think about except Vietnam. And that isn't thinking, but mad fury and grief and shame to die. What can such bombing be like; and who lives there below? In the *Times* and *Paris Herald* Anthony Lewis is writing now splendidly and has just gone to Vietnam, after asking in vain for a visa for two years. (I fear they got him there to kill him.) I envy him alone of all people on earth: to have a voice and big powerful places to make it heard. I was talking to him on the phone and said, 'There is a new US policy, unique: it is, scorch their earth.' He liked the phrase and wrote an article of unanswerable condemnation.

Why does one write in the first place? Because one sees, feels and must speak; because one wants to know what one thinks; because it is the hardest work there is and thus, like Everest, it lures. I don't write any more. I am sure it is a question of compulsion – money necessity or something to say which is killing one inside. But also, it's a place to say it. Having none, one must be Emily Dickinson, which I am not. I do not think it a bad profession; I think it marvelous. How awful if it were like talking in one's sleep; that's being a shoe clerk; the boredom of repetition. It gets harder and harder because one knows more, the complexity in the brain is harder to put into words than the violence and clarity of youth; and because one has much better taste and fiercer self criticism. In the end, that does finish one; agony and doubt and the sense of never getting it right. But since there are no happy endings, that is no worse than any other. Everyone ends up with a handful of dust, I am sure of that, no matter where they start; and everyone feels failure in himself and his life, at the end. And believe me, there is nothing so terrible as old age. I have been seeing and knowing too much of it lately; it makes one pray to be hit by a timely bus or have the nerve to take oneself off, not from any special reason, but from good sense, not to stay around too long.

. . . Oh I wish you travelled or that I went your way. How many years since we've seen each other? Years and years; and maybe you'd get an awful shock for I am full of lines and sun damaged skin and there's lots of grey in my hair, and I cannot learn to be quiet about the human race and its fate now. One day I will be old but never serene, never wise, never gentle. So that, now I think of it, is even worse.

Love always,

M

To: Madame Binh*

May 20 1972
[?]

Dear Madame Binh; I hope you will remember me, please remember me. Long ago, just before the start of these hopeless Paris meetings, I came to see you there in Verrières-le-Buisson and wrote an interview about you for the London *Times*. I have thought of you often, during these bitter years, thinking also how sad and hard for you as a woman to be always away from your children. And I hope they are well and as safe as possible.

I am writing today only to tell you there are millions of us, in the U.S. as in Europe, who are in a state of fury and grief over this latest destruction of the lives and homes and land of the poor people of Vietnam. I cannot begin to tell you how this evil, unforgivable war darkens my life and I am sick with despair over the cruelty inflicted on your people.

For more than a year – 1970–1971 – I tried to get a visa to return to South Vietnam, again to write of the real life of ordinary people, but my articles of 1966 were too far ahead of general recognition of the suffering of your people, and were distasteful to the S. Vietnamese regime, so I was put off with bland remarks until finally, angry myself I made them angry and got my answer: writing the truth about real life bars a writer from returning. Now I am trying to get an assignment from a very good American paper to go to North Vietnam and if they will give me that assignment, I shall ask your help in getting a visa to North Vietnam. It is altogether possible that this paper would want to send someone younger, but I am anyway trying. For all of us, who have been against this war from the beginning and who have done whatever we could to stop it, it is heartbreaking to see how little effect we have on the decisions of a President.

Yours
Martha Gellhorn

To: Betsy Drake

September 3 1972
72 Cadogan Square
London SW1

Betsy dear,

. . . Four days after the N. Viets sadly and politely refused me, they got in

---

*Nguyen Thi Binh, member of the Central Committee for the National Front for the Liberation of the South, had attended the Paris peace talks in 1971. She later became Minister of Education and a deputy in Vietnam's National Assembly.

touch with MY paper (the St. Louis Post-Dispatch) out of the blue, and
gave a visa to a man reporter. This is how Women's Lib was born. I'd
rightly touted the paper and made an impassioned speech about their being
idiots to take applications in order; they needed every US reporter they
could get now, before the elections. Well, anyhow, I educated them. It is
a blow because the man they've chosen, Dudman, is a good man, but writes
only with his feet; an opportunity lost. However, I do not take my personal
blows as hard as I might since I am aware every minute of the really
horrendous blows falling on the innocent and helpless everywhere, the
Uganda Asians, the Jews in Russia and all poor Vietnamese.

Now, back to love and sex; what a fascinating topic. I don't know
whether I'm prim; I sure haven't lived it. I started living outside the sexual
conventions long before anyone did such dangerous stuff and I may say hell
broke loose and everyone thought unbridled sexual passion was the excuse.
Whereas I didn't like the sex at all; I only believed in honesty and besides
the man wanted it and what I wanted was to live at top speed, deep into
French politics, picketing with strikers, racing before the Garde Mobile and
bringing out a little French newspaper – maybe the first underground
paper. I never ever thought you got something for nothing in this life, and
fair's fair, and besides, all my life idiotically, I thought sex seemed to matter
so desperately to the man who wanted it that to withhold was like
withholding bread, an act of selfishness. But myself, I was not 'awakened',
if that's the word; often attracted, often horribly in love, but the bed part
didn't come off – I think partly due to the clumsiness of the men and partly
(largely?) due to a Victorian upbringing; sex and love were different. If I
practised sex, out of moral conviction, that was one thing; but to enjoy it
probably (in my subconscious) seemed a defeat. Anyway, I didn't; and
envied those who did, realising it made life so much easier.

Besides that, I believe, but never know, that what has always really
absorbed me in life is what is happening outside. I accompanied men and
was accompanied in action, in the extrovert part of life; I plunged into that;
that was something altogether to be shared. But not sex; that seemed to be
their delight and all I got was a pleasure of being wanted, I suppose, and the
sort of tenderness (not nearly enough) that a man gives when he is satisfied.
I daresay I was the worst bed partner in five continents. And the agile and
experienced men were always shits, which didn't endear sex to me as you
can imagine. So I just went on having abortions, because shits got me into
them, and being wanted; but I never in my life looked at a man and said,
that one is for me. So no, Betsy, there we are different; I cannot get myself
into any state about a man who is ugly or badly made, which is a pity and
a stupidity, but really, I am not even apt to think about sex until the actual
event is transpiring; we have different imaginations. And so, obviously, I do
not use men because there's nothing for me to use, I guess. . . .

Also, if sex isn't the number one excitement, one gets bored or intellectually outraged much quicker. I fear I start with my head and go to my heart and finally end up in the genital region. But my lover, my last and only, was a great change; the first man who didn't make any effort to own me because, morally, he couldn't, he had no right even to try. And somehow, to my intense amazement, sex is fine with him, perhaps because I feel absolutely safe. But of course, it is hardly existent; it's not sex, it's like a Xmas present or an Easter present, a delight which rarely happens. He is different because of his name and life and position in the world; he has less freedom than Prince Philip. He has no time, no leisure, a shocking amount of money; all kinds of handicaps. No, I would never have married him; no, I would never have lived with him – nor, ever again, with anyone. Freedom is the most expensive possession there is; it has to be paid for with loneliness, of course, and self reliance; but I value it most. I would love to have a few weeks holiday with him, but never will. He is there; I know he feels something special for me as I do for him; and in those hours (it is often only hours) we can get, we are merry together. I forgive him all his ignorance of how real life is down here on the ground, because he is honest and kind, and he can't help not having enough imagination not to understand what he has never come anywhere near experiencing.

But I don't know what you are afraid of. A man cannot do anything more than disappoint you; he can't destroy you. Not like prison, which can destroy anyone. I've been driven nearly round the bend by both my husbands, but both were odd creatures (and of course, so am I) but never really round the bend and all I had to do was escape. No one can prevent a woman from running for her life. I don't understand fear; I understand lack of opportunity. The men don't grow on trees; any man won't do.

Mrs. Mandelstam lived in the wilderness for nearly 30 years after the killing of her husband; alone in the provinces and you've no idea of the size of Russia – think that Yucatan was the capital and exile was somewhere in the Arctic Circle. She had no one and had to keep her connection with Osip secret; Stalin also wiped out witnesses. She had to earn her living as a provincial school teacher. She shows all this, old before her time and with shaky health. She learned to survive by cunning and camouflage. She still does. She is not a bit noble and I have a failing for nobility – I adore the heroic courage of Solzenitsyn; and she isn't even generous in her mind. I don't think I like her; I feel a protective duty to her and great pity for her and respect for her ability and her nerve, huge respect. So I have worked like a bitch ever since returning (here and in Paris and Geneva) and now have her literary and financial business on a sound professional footing and she will make some money, instead of being robbed by publishers or simply neglected – they get their money back and their kudos and don't care. It has been awful work and Mrs M., quite in character, did not even write to me spontaneously after I left Russia, not a word of mild thanks for that awful visit, laden like a Santa Claus mule, and hating it all; she wrote in answer to my letter upon my return (full of news of her affairs which I talk of as if they were mine.) And to thank me for six more books I sent. Ah well. And I don't think she liked me; I think she expected a hero worshipper, which I am not, not even with heroes.

And though I was only a listener (they can't learn anything about our world, it is simply too far away from their experience to be comprehensible or even interesting), she saw that I was a thinking listener. No, I don't think she liked me but I am sure she saw I was someone who can be counted on to keep her word, do what she is asked, a very true errand runner. No I speak not a word of Russian; English and French were the languages. I was there as much as I could be, about five hours every day, and towards the end I was simply out the rest of the time, naked on my hotel bed, done in from heat, awful food, exhaustion, and deep deep boredom. Because, you know, claustrophobia and fear can be very boring indeed.

She talks about paradise, a certain amount. I can't describe why the religion is so annoying; it's a late comer in her life; somehow I do not feel it to be utterly sincere. I can't explain it; it rings wrong. Oh, eat with her; well I brought bits of food, so does everyone; and you get it in scraps maybe at odd hours. Suddenly a plate of fried mushrooms at 5 p.m. and suddenly at 8 p.m. a plate of fried potatoes and fried mushrooms and that's dinner. We drank because I brought whiskey, there is no ice of course or soda. The Russians drank the whiskey like wine out of pottery coffee cups, in that heat; I drank it in a tooth glass with luke warm tap water. It was pretty good hell, I tell you. And now there are forest fires, spreading out from Moscow, covering an area the size of Great Britain . . . She must be nearly dead of the unending heat.

God what a volume, what a volume. And now back to the mines and the extra hours worth of business and duty letters and then happily to bed. I am dicting and working at Kew; I am disgusted by nine extra pounds like a large sausage around my middle, sign of failed discipline, failed hope, I get fat from despair which is really the limit. Despair would be much pleasanter if it made one thin and interesting like *La Dame aux Camélias*.

See you in the US somehow. And do have a lovely autumn in Cambridge. Shall I bring you woollen underwear from London?

> Always,
>
> Martha

Letter to the Editor

The Times   September 7 1972
                                                     72 Cadogan Square
                                                     London

Sir: I seek enlightenment. In the early stages of the abomination at Munich,* we saw on television the representative in London of the Palestinian Liberation Organization. Does the P.L.O. have open legal offices in any other city in the western world, besides London? And what is the open legal business of this organization in London? According to the P.L.O. representative, speaking on television, his organization represents all Palestinian patriotic groups, which necessarily includes Al Fatah, which in turn includes as its secret arm the Black September Group. The P.L.O. representative here, under repeated questioning, could not bring himself to condemn the cowardly murder of (at that time) two Israeli sportsmen at the Olympic Games but instead – by tricky and grotesque rhetoric – actually condoned this murder. What then is the place for such an organization in any civilized country?

I seek further enlightenment. I do not understand why it is impossible to prevent the free travel in the western world of these Arab gangsters who violate not only the laws we obey but the one law we most cherish. We read that eight million American tourists travel about Europe in the summer; but the number of Arab tourists must be minimal. Surely it is not beyond the massed power of the Intelligence and Security services of the western world to keep the closest check on possible Arab terrorists. I find it incomprehensible that Miss Khaled† can still move freely in Europe, as she was reported to be doing. Israelis must be forced to the bitter conclusion that Arab murderers are not all that important to us since, aside from firing a few oil tanks, their principle aim is to kill Israeli civilians.

                                                     Yours,
                                                     Martha Gellhorn

---

*On September 5, PLO terrorists took nine Israeli athletes hostage at the Munich Olympics and demanded the release of 234 Arab prisoners. The rescue plan failed and eleven Israelis, five terrorists, and one German policeman died.

†Leila Khaled had been released after an earlier plane hijacking, then undergone six months of plastic surgery to transform her appearance before attempting a second hijack. This time she was arrested after the plane landed in London but was exchanged by Edward Heath for fifty-six Western hostages.

To: Lucy Moorehead

5 November 1972
Naivasha
Kenya

Oh Lucy, I wish you'd come for both our sakes. Yes of course I'll be here in March, as if anyone knew where he/she would be, as far ahead as day after tomorrow . . . Health is all. Health is everything. I've been feeling lousy for three days and as a result my morale is gone, my mind numb, and despair rides around like the Four Horsemen. I think it is the altitude, I am dead tired for no reason, twitchy and nervous, and clearly at 7000 feet no oxygen at all is reaching my brain.

. . . I go to Nairobi tomorrow with a huge errand-shopping list. My one desire is to pamper myself in any way I can think of, but cannot think of any ways. The real truth is that the world is empty, and there's the snag: empty for me, less empty for you, but still fairly empty. Everyone is either dead or in trouble or busy or turned into an ageing bore. All the splendid comrades of one's youth, where are they? I never seem to meet anyone new; or else I fail to see them, if I do. The young are my whole hope, this generation of students, but I have nothing to do with them except admire and pray for them, at a distance. I don't like being an elder statesman to the young, which is the only possible role in case they ask one to have any. I want people my own age, but this last summer's venture into civilization convinced me that was pretty nearly a wash-out, a lost dream too. I remember Esmond Rothermere saying to me with delighted gratitude some years back, 'Thank God you look so young; everyone looks one hundred.' I thought he was daft; I now know what he was talking about. It's more than looks; it's the way people sound. Our age strikes me as all beasts of burden, myself included; and that doesn't lift my heart. So what? So what? The only answer is to feel violently well, and eat one's liver for nourishment.

I must get really into this book somehow, because otherwise I shall perish. If there's no world to live in, one must invent a world and live there. It may be that finally I shall become a worker, *faute de mieux*. I really always thought it better to live than do anything else; but my style of living is grotesque now. One cannot hurry to all the disaster areas of the world, though they still interest me most, when looking like an old lady. The kids are there, as once I was; one has to learn to retire gracefully. Well, I'm retired but not graceful; and bored with myself and my inadequate mind; and enraged that my body isn't acting like a strong cheerful motor, pumping vitality where needed.

. . . The thing is: I hate personal life and always have. I only like involvement in something large which contains lots of people, not on the buddy basis but the life and death basis. I can sublimate that, if coping with nature – that's large and impersonal too. But simply looking after my life bores me silly; all house necessities infuriate me; and I haven't a good enough mind to be what I should be: a student. So much to learn here, but I cannot find the energy for one hour a day at Swahili grammar. Shocking.

I thought always that I'd be dead of old age at forty; instead of which I am going to have <u>another</u> birthday in three days. Surely this longevity is exaggerated?

So you see, you're not alone in your slump, whatever it is. Be of good cheer, they are slumping in the Rift Valley too. I don't at all mind being a nerveless gutless whining pudding, to you; am without shame. People suffer from loneliness, I suffer from loneliness; and this strikes me as weird. Being lonely is as natural and inevitable as having lungs, liver, lights. There is a brief lovely odd period of youth, when one moves in a herd of like-minded energetic hopeful young animals – that's the only non-lonely period in life. What one can hope for, afterwards, is a very very few people in the world to whom one can talk. You're one of my very few.

Love,

Martha

To: Harry Redcay Warfel*

November 9 1972

Florence

Dear Dr. Warfel; I don't mean to be rude, I really don't. But I cannot understand what you are doing. It is like those weekly questionnaires one keeps getting from all over the country, enough to drive one mad, asking one what one likes in the theatre and why; whether one believes in marriage and what for, and etc etc. It is your book, why do I have to write it?

I feel you have not read anything of mine, and God knows there is no reason you should have (you are joined in this by most of the population of the US.) But then why bother with me? Are you doing a sort of literary Who's Who, or are you doing a book of criticism, evaluation. I cannot understand.

I have written what I thought essential about myself in Who's Who; it takes up exactly three lines. But it does say, perfectly simply, where I was at what times. As for the books, you cannot ask me to tell you about them. I wrote them; it is up to you to decide what they are about. I was only, in haste and despair, trying to correct such a hopeless misunderstanding of the

---

*Editor of *American Novelists Today* (1973).

last – a love story, you said – but if, after reading it, that is what you thought of it, that is your business and obviously the book failed, since it gave you no other reaction.

But dear Lord, if people in universities won't do things thoroughly (if in fact you also fall into the sinful ways of American publicizing, as opposed ever to thinking, feeling, discovering) we are lost.

I am terribly sorry and I wish you would just drop me out. Everyone is in Who's Who, if a reference is needed. Beyond that, we need understanding and criticism and a tremendously high standard of performance and appreciation of performance.

Please drop me. I'm a very very obscure writer, and no use to you.

Sincerely,

Martha Gellhorn

To: Sandy Matthews

November 15 1972
Naivasha
Kenya

Dear old son; I have no business writing to you. It is self indulgence. As Ernest used to say (rightly), you waste your juice on letters. Letters are out for a writer; all the juice has to be saved for where it counts. Like sperm. Do not throw same upon the ground etc. But I am scratchy and annoyed and instead of contemplating the ludicrous but unceasing horrors of trying to make Africans conform to our needs – all alien, all idiotic to them – I shall write to you.

Your letter came today, the long one about *Catch 22*. I've read *Catch 22* twice; I consider it a great book. It has 8 or 14 pages, maybe as much as 40 (I once knew exactly) which are a failure, when [Joseph] Heller did not control his immense original comic muse, but let it run wild: that's when he's off to the races about the whore who appears everywhere in a fury, wanting vengeance. Then he fell from the most beautiful and black humor into slapstick: but as for the rest . . . To me, it is a great war book: beneath all that comedy and laughter is the truest description of the Americans' war that anyone has written. I could hardly believe that book, I found it so accurate where accuracy really lies, in the emotion, the spirit, the sense that is deeper than the words. I met Heller at a party in New York and gave him hell for being there, hell to a total stranger; but you know my Moses complex. I said to him, for God's sake get out of here (Sardi's) and this world and stay away from it. You are a great writer, go home and write; and if you have to see anyone, see real people, not this job lot of NY celebrities, not in this fishy fake braggart place. He looked quite scared; later

I was much ashamed. But I could not figure how he knew what he knew, nor where their air base was; and he told me he'd been a tail gunner at 18 (I have ridden in the tail of nightfighters, from which they removed the machine guns because they were useless; it is the most horrible place to be on a mission, totally alone in the void); and the place was Corsica, which I instantly understood as soon as he said it.

Yossarian is not utilitarian; Yossarian is a poet and rebel, a man who knows with every drop of his blood and every milligram of bone that pleasure is better than pain, and life is a million thousand times better than death. And Yossarian also knew that all authority is shit and all orders are murderous. Yossarian is a hero.

The prose, by the way, is plainly glorious, and I see you know nothing at all about books. But you will learn. There are only two modern novels I wish to Christ I could have written; one is *Catch 22* and the other is *At Play in the Fields of the Lord.*★

Friendship is as remarkable as love and as rare. There are degrees. You know, from one to ten. I've had them all, and what saddens me now is that – and I attribute it to age, not mine as much as everyone else's (I am as free and loose and lost as anyone in their twenties, but my friends are not: they are rooted, responsible, burdened like mules with the lives they support) – my remaining friendships range from about five to ten. The ones are dead, every single friend of the one category is dead. Not from old age, but from war, accident, cancer. I suffer because the flame-like quality of the ones is gone. And one does not make that sort of friend, at my age, any more than one suddenly discovers the beautiful pure passionate great love.

But you, poor dope, have not even given yourself a chance. You have not stuck your nose out into the world, not to love, not to find friends. Your feet are not even damp from life.

. . . As for Xmas, it is a kiddies festival and all else is shaming. I send money, have for twenty years, to an Italian orphanage where the children have nothing and get nothing; at least, on this day, my money will buy them a bag of candy. I disapprove of Xmas for adults. If Christians, seriously so, they can go to church and thank God the Father for having given them the Son. That's enough. It is surely an obscene way to celebrate His birth to send baskets of fruit and food to people who are bursting with same anyway; it is worse to go in for competitive gift swapping. For the man who has everything, the mink-covered corkscrew . . .

I realise that all my books, and this one I am fiddling with when not gasping to survive my Africans, have no person in them that even mentions God, or finds religion any sort of concern or problem. I hadn't thought of that until now. Obviously, I can hardly create people with a type of

---

★By Peter Matthiessen (1927–), U.S. novelist, travel writer, naturalist, and explorer.

difficulty I do not feel or understand. I could bone up on nuclear physics enough to make a certain glib aura around a character labelled nuclear physicist but I can't bone up on religion. I can't, actually, ever seriously believe anyone believes in God; which goes to show that my mind is blinkered.

Now to bed. This hasn't been a best day, though it has rained, and any day with rain in it is pure gravy. The dust is laid, for the time being; the maddening wind has dropped; the earth doesn't feel as if painfully dying from thirst.

Love always
Martha

To: Frances Fitzgerald★

January 29 1973
Vipingo
Kenya

Dear Frankie; What Vietnamese did you see in Paris?[†] Not the Thieu lot? I must have told you I'm blackballed by them, and the N. Vietnamese gave my hoped-for visa to Dudman who cannot see, feel, understand or write. A general loss. But Mme. Binh is a friend. I beg you to keep me posted. If there's any way to get back I want to go too. The essential job remains: Americans must not be allowed to push this war under the rug. If there is any hope for a future in which the U.S. does not operate as the most dangerous and destructive power on earth then it will be because Americans have been made to see and feel and understand what was done in Vietnam, in their name. As after World War Two – although people did not have TV and then knew even less – it was essential to make true the Nazi horrors; there's a double reason I think. Perhaps the first is not to bury the victims without honour and mourning; and the other is to remind everyone that this did happen, what it means, and one hopes and prays thus warn them not to do it again. It will be a ferocious job with Americans who insanely insist on believing that they really cannot do evil. You do see the importance? I write with my feet, more and more.

Of course this isn't peace, not even a compromise. I thought when this

★Frances Fitzgerald was thirty-one when, in 1972, her first book *Fire in the Lake: The Vietnamese and the Americans* was published to huge praise. Even the *National Review*, which was critical, predicted that it would become the "gospel for the anti-war movement."
[†]On January 23, 1973, a peace agreement had been signed in Paris between the U.S. and the Democratic Republic of Vietnam. However, fighting continued between North and South until communist forces captured the Presidential Palace in Saigon on April 30, 1975.

filthy war ended a stone would lift from my heart and my mind would cease operating in a coal grey fog of depression. Well, it is better than having the bombers unleashed. But really it is a disgusting and deadly job of work. After 19 years, we officially depart, leaving behind a spoiled land and an uprooted (I'd think forever ruined) society, and in fact we are leaving Vietnam as we found it in 1954 only in far worse straits. Thieu not Diem, much better organized, beautifully (insanely) armed; and with the promise of 1 billion a year to keep himself there, since without the money all the arms wouldn't be effective. You know how well bribery works and of course all the guilty, the tarred, will naturally be forced to stick with him.

. . . I'm not in Mombasa but an hour away on a deserted beach. 24 hour a day solitude, no telephone, no papers, the mail becomes almost historic by the time it gets here (though your letter took only 8 days), and my radio, never healthy, is now totally busted. It's ideal for working for me, but the work has crumbled to ashes, all those pages, all those weeks. I am starting again from scratch but without that fine fire of confidence we like to see. I don't really know why I persist, having no sense that what I am trying to say is of immense value. Perhaps it's therapy or perhaps I am trying to see what I think. Fiction. I've no idea what will happen to it. In the last years I fill drawers with the unfinished, miscarriages; something is lacking. Probably it is because nothing, absolutely nothing one invents can even begin to touch what is.

Do you find writing easy? I used to; now it is hard forced labor. Sentences seem formed of concrete. I am physically exhausted, almost mindless, at the end of any working day. Reading it over, I cannot imagine why this was so incredibly hard to do. And it's not nearly good enough, just agony to produce a pea. The only thing I do like about it is the order of the days. The elimination of all non-essentials. After two months of this, I find myself dreading the thought of rejoining the human race. Even wearing clothes because this is life in a bikini. Maybe I'll hang on a bit; easier perhaps to face the unsatisfactory work than face daily life.

. . . I think Tolstoi was right about governments: a collection of men who do violence to the rest of us. Once I thought free people (i.e. people who could count on a vote, not rigged) were responsible for their governments. I no longer think so. I cannot believe that any people are as bad as their governments.

As to being pessimistic and not discouraged: even if you don't believe that the powers of good will overcome the powers of darkness, the point is that the powers of darkness have a huge free run in case one gives up. It is perhaps a futile holding action, and only ever partially successful; but an essential one. Silence is consent. Finally then everyone would be silenced. I cannot imagine anything more terrible. Governments everywhere in total control.

Please don't call me Miss Gellhorn. It makes me feel as old as I am.

I cherish the likes of you – in which category I include Tony [Lewis] and the women who run Another Mother for Peace and the Vietnam Veterans against the War and William Sloane Coffin and all – and without you, I would really despair.

Yours,

Martha Gellhorn

To: Betsy Drake

March 12 1973
72 Cadogan Square
London SW1

Betsy dear girl; I haven't written to you for weeks, owing to the various dramas which closed my African period. After all that stationary peace, suddenly: Sunday night (I cannot have told you this before) the verandah light went on, woke me, I rose and peered through the wooden slats of the windows, like large Venetian blinds, no glass; and there was a black in white underpants at 3:30 a.m. attempting to get in the door. I shouted at him, very Memsaab, and went to the back window slats and called for non-existent men, the houseboy and gardener paid to sleep on the premises but known never to do so. I then informed the marauder who was lingering on the verandah that he better beat it as the men were coming after him with pangas; so he took off. That was very serene. Tuesday night, sitting with the large door wide open and windows idem, reading at 10:30, I heard a noise on the verandah, walked out, and there about 12 feet away was a crouched naked black; and that did shake me. I rushed into the house, locking the door and beat it to call the male employees who by now had been told they must sleep in their house at the rear and had promised to do so. I was spooked and called and called: no answer. They were not there. So then I went around shutting the window slats which any child of 12 could have cut out with a panga at a stroke, and considered the new sensation of being alone, unarmed, beyond the sound of any human voice, and some lunatic was mooching around outside. Feeling a fool, I got a kitchen knife and went to bed. The man stayed about an hour and left.

Got home after a 15½ hour journey which is really too much, wedged 3 abreast in a plane with seats for kiddies; no question of straightening a leg, and found the flat freezing. Next, after 3 days here, I went into hospital for a curettage, as I had been bleeding all the time in Africa. I was sure I had uterine cancer and you will be surprised to hear I found this cheering; no old age, and with time limited it was bound to be more valuable and interesting. It took four days for the pathologist to make his report: no malignancy. I will live forever like my mother and grandmother and probably with a bad back.

The US Income Tax folk, who were auditing my 1970 return (first time in my life, alarming) have decided I am not a writer, since I make no money, and disallow all professional expenses, thus upping my tax 110%. I have to fight this on behalf of real hardworking long-writing writers but the expense and sweat is unnerving.

So you see I am full of beans. Actually today I have been putting in a rawl plug, screwing on a door handle and thus feel in my Pioneer woman phase which cheers me and am presently going to see *The Doll's House* with my one constant chum, the Lady Diana Cooper age 80 who really is my one buddy, so today life is not too dreary. But Betsy, what am I going to do with some 25 to 30 more years? I have decided, after again failing in Africa, that I really am through as a writer, not even bothering to try any more. What on earth is there to do? I am terrified of the bleak stretch of time, a cold tundra of time; I have a tendency to stay in bed and read, trying not to think.

Must get a manual labor job in an orphanage, working with small children, washing and feeding and dressing and undressing and playing with; it's all I can think of. I need a delightful merry funny pleasure-loving male playmate, someone to laugh with and make love with (as an antidote to freezing to death which I have been doing more and more and more), but won't find him. So what? So what? I used to think dying young was terrible and tragic; now I think dying old is the very worst.

Love

M

To: Betsy Drake

April 12 probably [1973]
72 Cadogan Square
London SW1

Betsy dearie; A brief chat. No energy for more.

. . . I think St. John of the Cross spoke first about 'the deep dark night of the soul' and Scott Fitzgerald said 'the deep dark night of the soul is at four in the morning.' Insidon, some type of brain pill, is keeping deep dark soul nights away, for me, or so I assume. One pill the size of a pin head every night.

My mother said that people were grown up at 80, not before, and if not then, not ever. You have a long way to go.

. . . Fear. Fear is the ruling human emotion, make no mistake. And from it, all evils flow; hate and prejudice and cruelty and just plain meanness.

Remember Roosevelt: we have nothing to fear but fear itself. It is the real enemy and also the mummy and daddy of stupidity, the other incurable human emotion. Think what the world would be, simply in terms of politics, if fear did not rule.

Oh yes, I fear prison. All my life, my guiding passion has been the desire for freedom. I've got it too; and had not considered that the price of freedom is loneliness. Also that people, on the whole, cannot endure freedom: it costs too much to get. And age is a prison, the final one.

I'm engaged in a strange occupation. Forcing myself to give dinner parties; six people at a time. The effort is incredible: telephoning them, shopping for food. The result does nothing much for me. But I am trying to oblige myself back into circulation, into contact with people I've lost track of, merely because they are people. My instinct is to become an urban hermit and I know I have to fight it. If one is working, then social life becomes a rest and recreation but in the present shape of my life it becomes a duty. I have short hair and wear long skirts like an 1890 anarchist; I am tossing around in life trying to find some way to be. As opposed to giving up.

Love,

M

To: Sandy Matthews

August 3 [1973]
72 Cadogan Square
London SW1

Dearest Sandy; I envy you the leaping flying impala and the early mornings and the sun and the sky and do you think I could get a job house sitting next winter; I am really superb with cats

I am finding two extremely worrying states of mind in myself; states of mind isn't right. I am finding two scary lacks. The first is that I have nothing to think about: I mean that when I am walking (as I have been with joy in rural England, miles and miles with my pedometer clicking at my side) I look at the world and rejoice in that, but my head is empty, I think of nothing since there is nothing I want to think about. And the second is a sense of unloving, as if my ability to love was withering to nil and of course that means being unloved, feeling unloved. Love has to go two ways; my idea has always been that the giving was more important than the getting. There is also no one to talk to; or rather, there are many people to talk to in bits about this or that, no one to talk to totally. I finish by not bothering to talk. This is the first letter that is more than ways and means or a few factual notes that I have written in months; I have no desire or temptation to try to talk. I listen as much as I can, but greyly; everything seems too small to bother with. The best to be hoped for is laughter; anyone who can make me laugh is like manna from heaven. Not much falling however. Well, this is a jolly letter.

Love always,

M

Early in September 1973, Martha was advised to have a hysterectomy. She had been bleeding for over six months and was feeling very low. She was surrounded, she told Alfred, by people "getting older, iller, sadder." "I must get used to the certainty that, even in health, my looks are now forever gone," she wrote to Betsy. "Find something else to rely on? Like my soul?" She now hated all photographs of herself, pointing out that Ingrid Bergman weighed at least fourteen pounds more than she did, yet looked thinner, and that though Lauren Bacall had far larger hips they did not show, while her own "ugly thickening through the center" gave her the look of a retired barmaid. Not even jokes and self-mockery shared with Diana Cooper, nor the affectionate exchanges and meetings with Laurence Rockefeller, could dispel her sense that she would never be attractive again. She was sleeping badly, sometimes taking first a Seconal and then a Valium, but still not falling asleep. She remained obsessed about the war in Vietnam, by the way the world was full of "evil little men" like Nixon and Brezhnev.

The hysterectomy did not go well. Martha had ten days of high fever and considerable pain before an abscess was discovered. She lay in bed remembering her mother and wishing again that she had had the courage to help her die. Finally, she sent a telegram to Betsy, who came over from California to look after her together with Shirlee, Sandy Matthews's wife. When Martha left the hospital, she wrote to Alfred: "Now I'm a frail, bowed, little old lady, aged 102."

To: Betsy Drake

January 2 1974
[72 Cadogan Square
London SW1?]

Betsy dear; I wrote to you at length yesterday but didn't get around to mailing the letter. Today your letter came, desperate letter. Do listen. All people are lonely everywhere. The bones of the skull separate all human beings, said my father to me when I was about aged eight. And the man speaking was perfectly married and perfectly loved by and in love with a perfect woman and his children were not yet old enough to disappoint him. . . . Loneliness is the basic universal human condition, and it is also the basic universal human fear. Not able to escape, all human beings spend their lives trying to escape from or alleviate their loneliness. This is the true reason for marriage, procreation and very possibly even sex. But there is no such thing as constant complete communication between humans. If very simple, people believe that bodies, presence, noise, voices work as an antidote to loneliness. Perhaps, for the simple and for the exact time of presence etc., this is a recipe. I don't find it so.

I think you have to accept loneliness as the ground you stand on. I made many foolish frantic efforts to escape it, in my time, though I never believed in my efforts, and they never worked. I had my mother and what she gave me was this: one person in the world was always ready to listen to me, no matter what. I believe that for these last eight years, probably the basic reason that I have so clung to the idea that Sandy would be my son and I his mother, was another futile effort to stave off loneliness, for him, too, I thought. For me, not to be responsible to or for any single human being is the definition of loneliness – each person must have a different definition. But I do accept that I have always been basically lonely; it is not only my nature but also my perception of life. I have never been lonelier than when I was married, both times; living with someone and utterly alone. And you, were you not lonely in marriage?

I have my own medicine against loneliness reaching the degree of despair: I read. I read as one swims to shore – when reading anything, I am not there, and therefore not alone; I am somewhere else, in the book, with those people. Probably the reason I read mainly novels; I join other lives. And also when writing because then too, I am not there, not me, not this special mass of blood and flesh with all its tedious problems; I am a conveyor, a tool, I am living in the lives I am making. Beyond these two medicines, I have nothing. But once you accept being lonely, dearest Betsy, it becomes much easier; one is not frightened of being alone.

As for doubting all your own ideas, that's surely healthy isn't it? It means they can change and grow, with each new piece of knowledge or insight or information. It means that, being doubted, they are not rigid nor ever will be. One <u>must</u> doubt and change and gasp and flounder; that too is the human condition. There are no answers; there's only learning more, and never enough. We keep our heads above water (and so does every one else) a day at a time. I do think the US Constitution, promising everyone the right to pursue happiness is idiotic. Happiness cannot be pursued; it is a grace, a gift, an accident, a miracle; and above all it is brief and spasmodic. The constitution should have said something serious like, the chance to struggle for sanity . . . Which is really what everyone is doing, and must do. Sanity also cannot be defined, being different for everyone.

. . . I hate to think of you flaying yourself, though I understand all that too; it is one of my many occupations. I hate more the sense of your being

afraid, though obviously I understand that too; only I know absolutely that
fear is useless, it is exhausting, and changes nothing for the better. I must
stop; I'm not a bit sure words are any use anyway to anyone. But you know
that you aren't unwanted and unneeded in the world.

Love,

Martha

To: Diana Cooper

January 29 1974

Kilifi

Kenya

Dearest Diana; I was going to give you a shock by writing you a <u>happy</u>
letter. Instead of which . . . This letter is between us two; this is not news
to share with anyone. But if I don't write it all to you, then I cannot write
at all.

To begin at the beginning. I arrived at Nairobi airport sodden with
Secconal and the dread night flight on Thursday morning Jan 10. From then
until the following Tuesday all was exhaustion, annoyance and effort. Then
on Tuesday I set off for the coast but stopped at Hunter's Lodge, some 2
1/2 hours from Nairobi. I swam my dutiful muscle building 20 minutes in
the kidney shaped pool and went to bed and slept with one pause, for 13
hours. Greatly refreshed, set off for the coast on Wednesday and on the way
suddenly, who knows how anything emerges from that compost heap in
the mind, a story came to me. This happening is by now a miracle to me,
hasn't happened easily like that since I watched my mother die. I stopped
at Voi just to write down names and birthdates so I could think back over
the lives of my characters because you have to know everything about them
before the iceberg tip of the story itself shows. Busy with this, I arrived here
at Kilifi at 6:30 p.m. on Wednesday Jan 16.

This house, which Peter found, is so appalling, so hopeless that it comes
under the heading of a black joke. I took one look and knew it might be a
disguised blessing, no chance to waste one minute on house-beautifying. I
never lived in such squalor. But on Thursday still full of hope, story
simmering inside me, I decided to make the main bedroom – done in
unmatching, stained, dirty bits of lavender – as clean as possible, unpack
everything in it, move in a desk, live and work in it, eat on the terrace and
avert my eyes from all the rest.

However, nothing destroys this satin air, the monsoon breeze, the color
of the sea, frangipani and bougainvillea, the sun and the night sky. I feel best
in this climate, better than in any other, and solitude in a bikini suits me
fine.

Friday, I began to write my story. I can't explain how much this means to me. I was writing with confidence, ease and excitement for the first time in over three years. Before, as duty, therapy, discipline, I had been trying, off and on, knowing I was on the sure road to failure. Writing like that again made me feel I could live, wanted to live, life had some point to it, all I needed. I felt I had emerged from limbo into some real place on earth.

. . . So, filled with hope and happiness, I set out Saturday morning to drive to Malindi, 42 miles away, to have lunch with the Mooreheads and Celia Johnson who were staying there in Jack Block's guest house. Consciously happy, you understand, and positively swollen with hope. At about 10:20 a.m. (I am not sure of this time), on a perfectly empty stretch of road, in bush country, no cars coming either way, no houses to be seen, no Africans walking or cycling along the road, a small African boy (about 6 to 10 years old, I'd guess) shot from the left across the road, like a tommy leaping from the bush, directly in front of my car, not more than three yards in front of me. I may have lost a second from pure horror shock, not more. I pulled the wheel as hard as I could to the right (we drive on the left here as in G.B.) trying to get away from him. I heard a soft thud behind me, as the car went off the tarmac onto the dirt verge and there teetered on the edge of a ditch. I pulled the car then hard left diagonally, far ahead of wherever the child could be and instantly saw myself plunging fast and straight down into the ditch (about 7 feet deep, I'd think.) I was knocked out as the car went over into the ditch and came to, covered in dust, even inside my clothes, and dead grass, stunned, in the passenger seat, and the car had apparently turned over twice onto its top then back on to its wheels and was now facing <u>back</u> the way I had come. There was absolute silence, nothing in the world, only me sitting dazed in the car in the ditch and a little body curled up in the road, more to the right of center than in the exact middle. And dead.

Slowly and for a long time, about three hours, everything else happened, people and police and the morgue and police station. But though I remember this very well, it passed in a sort of blur, due to numbness, shock, and the pain in my head. I showed up at Lucy's, late for lunch, filthy and of course quite crazy; in that I either could not stop talking or was a zombie. Not since Alan was struck down, had I seen Lucy so happy and carefree and filled with delight; they had 10 days on this coast and she was in a state of bliss. Then I arrived, like a spoiler – and she took over at once with great competence and selflessness and infinite kindness, but I'd say I'd pretty well ruined 24 hours for them and that too is a grief. She hasn't had much happiness to mention in these last 7 years.

I should of course have been as dead as the child, or anyway well broken up and cut. The windscreen did not break. The car is with the Malindi police and I saw it dully when we went to deliver a medical report on me. Old half blind doctor in Malindi said I didn't have concussion and no ribs broken, which I knew. A terrific blow on right temple, behind left ear and on left cheekbone must have knocked me out, and no doubt explain the constant stone headache that I still have all the time. And immense swollen purple and yellow bruises from both shoulders down elbows, on both sides of my back, on both hips, a great blow smack on the new loathsome scar and inner thighs above knees. My back is wrenched again but by now that's like ringing a doorbell, so frequent an occurrence. Nothing really. I don't know whether the police will prosecute or not (Lucy via Ruth Rabb, on telephone to Nairobi, got local lawyer, who says not.) I don't really care about that or anything.

After driving everywhere for over forty years, I had my first accident and it is this one, the one I can least bear. It is apparently not an unusual accident.

. . . There's only a little comfort. That doctor said the child could have felt nothing, being knocked out faster than I was and totally. Not even perhaps time to notice what was happening since he hadn't looked right or left at the road, and it was over in seconds – the whole thing can't have taken a minute from when I saw him until being in the ditch. And I did not run over him, that at least, the side of the car hit him, rear left side I am pretty sure. It isn't much comfort but something.

So here I am again, lying down – it seems to me I have done nothing else, lying down in London, lying down here – eating valium and aspirins on doctor's orders and back in limbo again. I believe that twice, in exactly four months, I should properly have died and that is perfectly all right with me, to be dead, I mean, but now it scares me because it looks to me as if I'm going to spread doom to others and that is not all right. So I'll just lie here or sit here and wait for time to pass. The days are long.

Dearest Diana, you see this is not the letter I ever meant to write. I won't write again for some time, having nothing to say, and feeling anyhow too lifeless. It seems two years not 20 days since I left. Please let nothing bad happen to you.

Love always,
Martha

A Life in Friendship, 1974–1998

The accident shook Martha profoundly. In the weeks that followed, she wrote about it again and again, in great detail, to Diana Cooper, to Betsy Drake, to Sandy Matthews, to Robert Presnell, repeating every stage of the little boy's death, as if only by writing it down could she make it possible to bear. Later, she told the story again, in a barely fictionalized novella, By the Sea, *but, as with* The Wine of Astonishment, *which she had hoped would exorcise her grief and horror over Dachau, even writing could not deal with the haunting she felt.*

Martha had been wondering for some time whether to give up her house at Naivasha. The altitude, the extreme solitariness, and the surprisingly difficult climate had removed many of the pleasures of the early days. The accident made it clear that the moment had come to leave Africa, for the time being at least. Characteristically, having decided to make the break, she was impatient for it to be done. After a number of rather acrimonious exchanges with the friends who had given her the land, she returned to England.

To: Betsy Drake

February 26 1974
Mombasa
Kenya

Dearest Betsy; I am two inches from the end of my rope, overcome with self pity and preparing to drown in a pool of tears. It is the malaria. I really can't stand it and though it is the least of my series of *malheurs* it is also the last, and I haven't any moral resistance.

. . . Lying here I have been thinking, having little else to do except read Trollope whom I am now renouncing because his style is hypnotic and I really cannot start copying lovely sonorous 19th century prose. So, my thoughts have finally almost jelled; I am going to pack Africa in. It has dawned on me that since 1967 I have had little except hardship here, and nothing consistently hard should be pursued because one is going against something, maybe Fate, maybe reality. I honestly know that the best writing is done with immense pleasure and _ease_; it dies when you have to grit your teeth and grind. Though there come grinding places naturally, but it must on the whole be possible, not climbing uphill on hands and knees. I think the same applies in life and with people. Pretty sure of that now, as I look back over the centuries.

The way I feel now I am ready to depart tomorrow. But one thing is sure; I _must_ finish this story. Another winter cannot be destroyed like last one, when a story became still born because I had to get an abortion for my maid. But you see what I mean; if it is not one thing it is another, each year I have been here; and I take this finally as a strong hint to get the hell out.

Feb 27: Dearest Betsy; I am sick and battered in spirit and I couldn't sleep last night for thinking of my mother. Bear those facts in mind and do not panic. If you heard someone talking in drunkenness or delirium you would make allowances for an abnormal state. Malaria is hell. But I want to talk.

Perhaps two years ago, Lady Reading died and there was a tremendous memorial service in Westminster Abbey; she was a friend inherited from Mrs. Roosevelt. I was uneasy as I always am during the practise of any religion, because I don't know what to do, when to rise, kneel, bow my head and I know none of the words in any faith. Opposite me in the swell part of the Abbey – such a welter of grandees, – between the screen and the altar I saw an old friend, Lady de Freitas, born Helen Bell, a classmate at Bryn Mawr. She is haggard and beautiful, married soon after college to a wildly energetic man named Geoffrey de Freitas; she has been an obedient wife in England all these years. She worked with Lady Reading. After the ceremony was over we filed out and met, leaning against a wall of the Abbey in sunshine as I remember. She said, 'One of the last, no one left, is there?' I said, 'Few.' She said, 'Were you thinking of your mother?' I said yes, and she said, 'I was thinking of mine.' Then she said suddenly, 'No one to write to.' We stood there, two tall women of a certain age and distinction with tears pouring down our faces. Then she pulled herself together, with her solid English training, and said, 'Goodbye, I am late for the hairdresser.'

The point is: not having someone to write to is torment. Now we have each other, and both of us see the value of that.

I have also thought out something else. The deterrent to killing myself will always be the same: animal fear. What I fear is definite; I do not know how suicide works, I do not know whether there are minutes of desperate suffocation, a hell of fear, before unconsciousness. I am afraid of that possibility which is odd since I have endured very great pain in my life and often, and am not on the whole a physical coward. The good reasons would be, for instance, not to hurt you, not to hurt (though I think it less probable) Sandy G; not to sadden my friends who would all feel, as I have felt, that they failed me in a moment of need. Not understanding, as I now understand (that's one guilt less) that this is an ignorant guilt; suicide is not a question of a <u>moment</u> when the balance of the mind is disturbed. It is cumulative; it is the total loss of hope, and no one can help that in another because no one was responsible for the long series of events which caused the piled-up hopelessness. I do not think suicide is irresponsible if no single person depends on you absolutely for continued existence. I would never have dreamed of suicide, for instance, when my mother was alive; she did depend on me for existence, I would never have done it for her sake. But otherwise, I do not think we owe our lives to anyone. For myself, I now wonder how much more I need to lose; because I really have no hope but I go on. And I imagine animal fear is stronger than any exhausted desire to get the hell out, to stop working, planning, battling away at all the trivia and tedium of life. I suppose I would have to feel myself physically incapacitated and know there was nothing left for me, except dependence and weariness. But I wonder; it interests me to find this plain fear of a few minutes which one has never experienced, which may not exist, this supposed suffocation, as the basic cause for my continued residence here below.

Your letters mean everything to me. It is not only that they carry messages of love but that they are a voice, speaking. This is a dialogue; I am not always talking to myself any more.

. . . Meanwhile, it becomes a sort of relief to think I am going to pack Kenya in. And it is the story of my life. The unremitting effort on the doomed enterprise; how many houses have I made, and left at a loss. And the marriages. I have invested more time, energy and money in failures than seems possible; to say nothing of the greatest failure of all, Sandy G. But if it is the story of my life, what the hell. I can't help it any more than your mother could help her cruelty.

Now I must try to work, but by God it is uphill slogging when you feel your insides sloshing around and your face hot and your skin cold. *Travail, opium unique*; and also the reason for getting up in the morning.

Love always,

M

To: Ruth Rabb

[?] February 1974
Naivasha
Kenya

. . . Went to doctor today; have amoebic dysentery on top of malaria; malaria presumably now cured having taken (on my own) the cure twice. But still very rocky. Doctor poked my tum, looked at my tongue; Leigh will be pleased to know I'd diagnosed amoebic dysentery on my own, privately, before the doctor did.

Have just been listening to the inconclusive 1 p.m. election news.* Anyway [Edward] Heath sure as hell isn't getting that national vote of confidence he was asking for. And I'm glad, though I heartily dislike Mr. Wilson. (Poor England, like everywhere else, there are midgets for leaders). But Heath disgraced Britain, to my mind, with that spare parts for Israel behavior and bottom licking the Arabs. I doubt if anyone voted Labor as protest on that score; but there it is, in my mind. If Labor gets in, Dick Crossman† will be in too and though he is an infuriating man and I would not willingly have a hot meal again with him, he is at least an understanding friend of Israel, unlike old [Alec] Douglas Hume.

Great God I haven't even told you that I got my passport back this a.m. I did. And the superintendent told me on his own the same story I'd heard that terrible day, Jan 19, in the Malindi police station. You remember there were ditches on both sides of road, reason I saw no one. The boy scrambled up on the left and I saw him for a split second only on the edge of the road, running. But his sisters were on the right side and had <u>called</u> to him to run across before the car came; I heard that in Malindi and thought it too horrible to be true. And there was no other car except mine on that road, either way, and not for minutes which seemed hours after the accident. There was no need to call to him. How awful it is. Are the parents to blame for not teaching their children anything about cars and roads? Or are children unteachable?

Oh God I am so fed up with living; it's too much work.

Love

M

---

*In January the militant tactics of the British coal miners forced Edward Heath to put industry on a three-day week. Heath called a general election in February, but failed to gain a majority and resigned, and the Labour leader Harold Wilson returned as head of a minority government.

†Richard Crossman had edited the *New Statesman* after the Labour government was defeated in 1970.

To: Sol and Ruth Rabb

April 28 1974
72 Cadogan Square
London SW1

Dearest Sol and Ruth;

I have started to believe, even, that there is justice here below –
somehow, somewhere, delayed, but justice: Watergate* and Nixon have
given me this new faith. Isn't that something to lift the heart. The deceivers
and crooks finally caught out; the scandal growing. Oh how it cheers me.
I don't think Nixon will be impeached; but even he, the superior to
Goebbels in the technique of lying, is not going to come out of this
unscathed.

. . . Meanwhile I have a new career here; I find I have a talent which is
to be a mass nanny. Over the Easter holidays, with 4 others (oldest 25, down
to 21) (young welfare workers from a settlement) I looked after 63 slum
kids, aged between 4 and 12 and believe me, I've never done harder
physical labor or enjoyed it more. Since we are all poor (I am just Martha,
seemingly a good-hearted poor old lady) we walked those kids everywhere.
To Trafalgar Square, St. James's Park, the playground by the Imperial War
Museum; the street crossings horrified me. One day we took them on an
ordinary bus to Greenwich Park. How we managed not to lose any of them
I'll never know. But I loved them all, and the young 'helpers' I admired and
respected and was so flattered to be accepted without question by them all.
And to have little kids, black and white, greet one with open arms, leap
upon one and shower kisses was about as comforting as anything that has
happened to me for years. Now that is over – to start again in the summer
– and meantime I work on Monday night at the Fulhalm Free Legal Advice
Center and am arranging to have a daily afternoon job in the Paddington
slums with 'commonwealth children', i.e. blacks and Asians – a small group,
maybe eight of them – in an effort to get them to talk. They are not
backward or autistic but no one ever talks to them so they simply do not
know how to use speech as communication. That's going to be very
exciting if I can do it. Having spent my life trying to communicate with
others, what a treat if I could teach others to communicate directly. And
then something about small children; they fill some very great need. . . . On
the last day in the last playground place for little ones I found myself being
nanny to perfectly strange two years olds, not in our lot, evidently couldn't

---

*The term used to describe the web of political scandals that took place in the U.S. between
1972 and 1974. In February 1974 a Senate committee launched an investigation and on
August 8 President Nixon resigned after recommendations by the committee that he be
impeached. It marked a brief – but large – moment of pleasure in Martha's hopes that
American politics might improve.

find their Mums, but who gravitated towards me, howling (usually a hurt finger) and stayed to be comforted and played with and I felt like the little old woman in the shoe and delighted with it.

Have also been giving and going to dinner parties; a huge effort to fight off my tendency to hermithood; and the spring has been so awful, freezing and wet that I've only been to Kew twice. So have missed the best moment of the year, those two or three weeks when the whole world starts hesitantly to come alive and grow.

Much much love and endless gratitude,

M

To: Betsy Drake

May 8 1974
c/o Moorehead
Porto Ercole
Italy

Dearest Betsy

. . . I had my hair cut. I closed my eyes and prayed (to whom?) thinking it can't be worse so it must be better or perhaps worse differently. I am like Samson about my hair. Considering that it matters to no one, not even to me, what I look like, this is absurd. Now I do know what it means to feel sexless; that's what being old must be about. It isn't the lack of <u>being</u> desired that counts; it's the lack of desire. Not seeing oneself and not being seen; I find myself invisible on the streets unless I happen to see a tall badly dressed figure in a shop window, mooning or striding along; someone, anyone, is that me? I was aware of being seen; often too much. When young it enraged me. Now it's ghostly, to myself, and to others non-existent.

As to writing. After 4 hours trying, whether it's failed or not, one is physically and mentally exhausted. I mean it. All I want to do is creep into bed, notably after failure. Also one cannot think coherently of anything else. It eats away in the brain, a ceaseless conversation with oneself. The smallest chore is horrendous to get through. People do not stimulate; they exhaust. But for more than a week I have not been trying to write. I stopped first because I felt I was close to some sort of new breakdown. Fascinatingly, Betsy, I was trying to write about a woman going mad, but was going mad myself. So I returned to Insidon and Valium and had a bearable vegetable week. Then slowed down and rested, I realised I have to start all over again. What I have to say, I must say: simply to get it out. The only therapy I know.

. . . You're wrong about Ernest's presence being a help. He wasn't present except in the flesh. He needed me to run his house and to copulate on (I use the adverb advisedly, not with but on) and to provide exercise in the way of a daily tennis game. There wasn't any fun or communication, none. When I thought I'd go mad from the loneliness and boredom, I slipped off to war: four times. To live at all, I had to write. I had to stay there for months at a time, and after I'd got over the usual agonies of house-running, I wrote. He enforced discipline because he was himself totally immersed in *For Whom The Bell Tolls*; so I had to make stories for myself.

My kind of loneliness now has no cure, you know; it is something I expect to live with until I die. Friends are heavenly kind, sometimes fun; it would be fatal not to have them. But I by no means need or want daily contact; perhaps it takes as much out of me as it gives, perhaps takes more. And when writing then I have nearly nothing to give. The problem wasn't people or the lack of: it was a flaw in my whole conception of the book, a ruinous flaw.

. . . Lillian Hellman, whom I have disliked for years, is quoted somewhere as saying, 'I get exhausted just walking around.' She claims to be 67. She is far more likely to be past 70. But the phrase is the first thing of hers that has charmed me. I get exhausted just peaceably staying alive. Having my hair cut, having a swim: my day's effort.

. . . Willy Brandt★ and Golda Meir† were the only two world leaders of real moral size; now both are gone. While Nixon stays. I read his transcripts daily and cannot believe my eyes. If the US Congress hasn't the nerve to rid the country of him, on its reading of the country's wishes, then I swear I think the U.S. is done for.

Love always,

M

To: Leonard Bernstein

July 9 1974
72 Cadogan Square
London SW1

Dearest Lennypot; Last night I saw and heard Mass‡ on the telly. It seems to me that it must be a lasting work of art. I don't know what the actual R.C. Mass is, or is about; and am ever more repelled by all religions and

---

★Willy Brandt (1913–1992), who had achieved international renown during the Berlin Wall crisis of 1961, had been forced to resign the chancellorship of Germany in April 1974 after the discovery that his close aide, Gunther Guillaume, had been an East German spy.
†Golda Meir (1898–1978), prime minister of Israel, resigned in 1974 after her efforts for peace in the Middle East were halted by the fourth Arab-Israeli war.
‡Mass commissioned for the opening of the Kennedy Center in Washington, D.C., on September 8, 1971.

surely do not believe in God, and as you well remember am in the underprivileged class re music. But the power of imagination in Mass, and the vitality, the plain strength of it must define it as permanent. I forgot beauty, taking that for granted. The words moved me more than anything, of course; and I had the records but could not listen to them (can't listen to music at all, willingly, alone, for years now); so I could follow the words in that booklet that comes with the records, whenever – in the choruses – I could not hear them all. I think the words are wonderful. Magical.

. . . No sense in saying to you that you can be proud because that's absolutely not the point. Nor say you might feel fulfilled because no one ever does. But glad; yes, you can feel a huge gladness.

. . . The introduction by you, the arriving plane, the row of waiting men – somewhere between a Mafia wedding and the French bestowing *Légions d'Honneur* – was a disaster. Suitable to Richard Burton. I think you are badly advised by P.R. men of no taste and no dignity, horribly advised. I don't blame you, I simply sorrow; you are coping with fame as best you can, and the 'image' is awful. But it really doesn't matter, in the long run, since the Work does surpass the Worker, and this dreadful image-making of you will vanish and be mercifully forgotten. I know you are a much better human being than this sort of crap which now surrounds you, as if you yourself needed advertising like a detergent or chocolate bar. You don't need it, and your work is cheapened by it; but all that is passing.

. . . There has never been a summer like this in living memory (as there never was such a soul destroying spring.) The sun shines every day, the whole place is a great green bouquet, and my life in no way matches or deserves this delight. I thought of coming to the US simply to stay glued to Watergate on the telly but paralysis of will intervened and now it's too late. Still Watergate is the most cheering event in years.

Love,

Marthy

To: Ruth Rabb

March 4 1975

[72 Cadogan Square

London SW1]

Dearest Ruth; I haven't time to breathe let alone write letters to loved ones. I am in such a frenzy of working as you can't believe. With a self imposed deadline. I mean to leave here about April 6 with a finished book, dump it on the publisher in NYC and go to the Caribbean to swim and sun for a few weeks. Have hardly been outside my pad all winter and am the color of goat cheese.

. . . Imagine my farm, in an area sort of between Elenmteita and Nakuru; say at 6000 feet. The time is 1950. I want these bits of gen:★

a) what sort of wild trees might grow there (not fever tree, there is no water, this is pure highlands stuff.) I am trying to imagine his garden, the area around his house. And also what would the watu be cutting for kuni?

b) His floors – an old simple house built in 1920; what wood.

c) His furniture made in 1920–23 by local Asian carpenter, what wood. All Kenya local wood obviously.

d) What shall I have growing on the walls of his house and pillars of verandah. (Note: would you call it verandah, remember the one at your/Pip's house at Naivasha and the one at the big house; terrace? porch? or verandah?) I've given him Virginia creeper, trumpet vine, clematis and bougainvillea. Can't give him wisteria; used that elsewhere.

e) does anyone grow fruit trees at that altitude, apples, cherries, plums? How long anyway from planting to getting fruit from them?

f) how would you say in Swahili worthless bum; I know *bure* is worthless but what is bum? Something the Africans would say of each other, not said to them, by a European.

No doubt I will think of more later. This book is a surprise to me. I was working on a novel; had 350 pages, a year's work, and a lot of research. While in Amsterdam at Xmas with Sandy, I suddenly saw it would never work; it was dead. So I returned and boiled the whole thing down to a 50 page story which I hope to God is good. I have an old finished story (these are novellas, between 13,000 and 23,000 words) and am working on the third, badly written and stuck once, in Nairobi at that hotel opposite the Israeli Embassy. Now rewritten from scratch and I hope it's coming off. So it will be a book of three very different novellas, set in Africa. Oh golly. What thrills me is that fact of writing. I have no idea if they are dreadful or not. Not up to me, as of now; up to me to finish.

Now I have to get ready to receive Lord Bangor[†] who says he remembers me from the war in Finland. (I can't remember anyone that far back; not even if I'd slept with him.) Point is: he was captured in the desert and had years as a P.O.W. and I need background gen on that for the hero of the present story. I pick brains everywhere. How could I be a writer if other people didn't actually know something. Myself, I know damn all.

I'll write decently when this orgy is over, but would be grateful for a prompt reply on the literary queries.

Love always,

Martha

★These kinds of questions, sent regularly to friends all over the world, give some idea of the detail and research that went into Martha's fiction.

†Edward Ward, 7th Viscount Bangor (1905–1993), Reuters' correspondent in China and the Far East and later an antiques dealer in the Portobello Road in London.

Early in 1976, when Martha was sixty-seven, her life finally began to pick up. She was once again writing, fast and with pleasure. She was working on the three novellas that would become The Weather in Africa, *and in a month she wore out two typewriter ribbons; though sometimes now, when she was traveling, she preferred to write by hand, saying that it changed her style for the better, made it plainer and even bleak, and that this was a good thing. "I am exhausted, fat, my legs are spaghetti, my back bent and I shuffle down the roads in this lovely hill country and sit by a clear stream," she wrote cheerfully from Nikki Dobrski's house in Switzerland, "listening to it, thinking of the next chapter."*

She had been asked to write a number of articles by various magazines and newspapers, and went off to do a piece on Spain after Franco's death for The New York Magazine. *And she had also started work on a book of horror journeys, laughing out loud as she wrote. "My memory is like an amputated arm," she told Betsy, "the part that is amputated, but flashes return." Only obsession, she wrote later, "makes writing really possible. You have to stop living, in order to write."*

The writing did not always flow. All writers have bad patches, but Martha suffered more than most. There were weeks on end when she wrote feverishly for twelve hours a day, only to find that what she had written was unusable. There were false starts, "cement sentences," times when she felt "blind and helpless with un-writing." "Writing a book is therapy," she told Betsy. "That's all it is. Nothing to do with the future, gains, rewards, nothing at all. Only here and now, a long absorbing act of vomiting." Friends answered her passionate cries of frustration: "Write fiction," advised Robert Presnell. "We are all professional — we are craftsmen — we need not only cross-examine ourselves."

For a while, it looked as if neither of her two books would find a publisher. Then Allen Lane and Penguin offered to take The Weather in Africa, *and what she had called* Travels with Myself and Another, *reissuing* The Honeyed Peace *at the same time.* Travels *became her most popular and bestselling book, and has been in print ever since.*

To: Betsy Drake

June 12 1975
Switzerland

Betsy dear; I have been slogging away, hours every day, since May 16 on the huge rambly ill-written second story of my book.* I am now at the end, which has to be entirely rewritten. And I just picked it up, a book size mss. and started re-reading from the beginning. AND IT WON'T DO. Christ,

---

In the Highlands.

what next. I want to weep. It is slow and wordy, dead, dead. All this work in vain. I really feel awful. Because I want more than anything to get this book done; it has to be done; and off to whatever publisher wants it; so I can get off to Vietnam. Yes, they'll let me in, if there's any logic anywhere in the world.

Aside from this ghastly blow today, of realising I've been doing a dismal job of writing, I am in the curious state of Lazarus, risen from the dead. I don't know how long Lazarus spent among the shades but it was almost exactly five years for me, I've dated it; it began on May 31, 1970 when Sandy showed up at midnight, crazy on LSD (I did not know) to two years ago this month, in France – on one of my many frantic efforts to escape from the tomb – walking along the Loire saying to myself, screaming to myself, I want to die, I MUST DIE – that's when I really knew about suicide and understood the madness of it.

What does baffle me is why this has ended; why I can see again, why I want to wake up, why time is no longer an unendurable burden. I have some ideas – the end of the war in Vietnam is a major cause for this lightening of color; I hated that war more than I can tell you, I felt it as a personal guilt and shame and horror. Now in one place on earth, people for whom I feel a private responsibility are not being killed and otherwise destroyed by Americans. That is something immense for me, growing more wonderful and releasing every day. Then too I think that finally writing out that accident – you realise it is 55 pages condensed from a total of well over 400 – also served, the way writing does, though I never before used it so personally: write it and put it outside where it no longer eats away at your liver. Not that I get over it; I only get some distance, some freedom to breathe. Those are the only two explicit causes I know. . . . Suddenly, here, I have come back to life. Every day I take my flabby legs and tar-coated lungs on a walk up the mountains. And there are the wildflowers, the Alpine wildflowers which I've never before seen, never having been here in spring – late spring this year. Great meadows of them, and every mountain trail lined with them. I find new ones each day; I cannot get over this bounty of the creation. Nothing has moved me in this way so much except for certain landscapes with wild animals in Africa. That was the great wild power of creation; this is the sweetness.

. . . About L., well, he is loving and tender and concerned. He is humble; he hasn't a drop of pomposity in him. He is muddled and searching. He wants and tries to be a good man. He laughs at himself; but is remarkably kind and tolerant of others. He is ashamed to be unhappy and that is a form of bravery; he has no opinion of himself at all. He is curiously innocent. What else? Enough to go on with? He telephones me here and talks forever (one person to whom I don't say, for God's sake stop wasting money). He is as thrilled, perhaps more thrilled, than I am by my sudden return to life.

I can, you see, talk to him about things like that. As I could talk of despair too. He understands more by instinct than through his brain, through words. I really don't know about his brain, only about his heart. I think (and I know he thinks) that we will not lose each other, this odd thing we have, as long as we live. Though I can't tell you exactly what we have.

Now I must pull up my socks, bury weariness and discouragement, and go back to this heavy immovable story. I shall rewrite the end and start all over from the beginning. It may be that a fierce slashing job is basically what is needed. So many words, loose ones; it's a mess.

I am glad for you, glad, glad, delighted you have two beaux and a cushion-eating dog and plenty of work and health and hope and the sense that you belong in your skin, in yourself, in the life you are making.

Love,

M

To: Alfred Gellhorn

November 11 1975
[72 Cadogan Square
London SW1]

Alfie darling; Your b-day letter came today. I don't remember your birthday or Walter's which makes me feel guilty but then I'd just as soon that no one including me remembered mine. It is a peculiar fact that I feel a solid year older on Nov 8 than I did on Nov 7. I know exactly how Lionel Trilling* (dead at 70) came to feel: the correct synonym for 'mature' is exhausted. Don't you fret, love; your passionate anger is a sign of health and sanity. I remember being shocked, when I was an ignorant (and I now realise totally heartless) girl by Dad saying he didn't want to hear or know any more – I can't remember what misery and outrage I was telling him about. I thought he was being selfish; he was simply exhausted. I cannot bear to read history, for example; it literally makes me sick. The horrible repetition of the same cruel stupidities. This last weekend (Dad and I have stylish birthday times; the Russian Revolution, the 1918 Armistice) I watched the Remembrance Services on the telly. Very old men, many blind, covered with medals, still parading before the Cenotaph; others, all very middle-aged (old really, the poor age faster) going back to Dunkirk every year and visiting the graves of their buddies; they remember in absolute detail, as if yesterday, every single thing that happened to them on

---

*Lionel Trilling (1905–1975), critic, author, and on the staff of Columbia University in New York for many years. His essays combined social, psychological, and political insights with literary criticism.

that day and every inch of the ground. The weekend TV was filled with this, which I watched in tears: thinking of all the waste and horror, the misery, the loss; to save us, to save our world. And look at it.

Well, outside my window miraculously the sky is blue. The autumn has been amazing, as was the summer; perhaps the end of the world is nearing. It gets dark at 4:30, winter coming in, but so far I don't mind. I seem slowly to have withdrawn into a singularly dotty way of life; I hardly see anyone – having got off the circuit, the only ones to see are my close friends, all women now, and I know in advance what each one is going to say, what I will say, and I find us all admirable bores. I prefer solitude and thrillers. Except for the Lady Diana who remains dotty and pleasure loving to the last (aged 82) and makes me laugh.

But work-wise (to use our elegant new idiom) things are looking up. Finally I corrected the mss. of my book to within a millimetre of possible perfection and sent it off airmail at great expense to a new U.S. publisher. . . . The New York Magazine (I don't admire it but it is, as they say, 'hot') telephoned and asked me to write a huge piece on Spain – quo vadis after Franco. This thrills me, the sort of journalism I love, three weeks to moon around getting ideas and impressions, plenty of room to write. I am waiting for the old swine to die; but obviously he is being kept breathing (no more) while the Right tightens its hold on the country. I intend to wait until he is buried and national mourning is over and Juan Carlos is crowned or whatever. There has to be something positive happening in order to see possible reactions. Meanwhile I build up contacts. Last evening 3 young Basques were here. They reminded me of the bravery, passion and total illogic of Spaniards though, as they insist, they are not Spaniards; a different race. The brother of one is in jail under death sentence being the leader of the ETA, *nom de guerre* Wilson. I have the names of their families in their villages, to visit . . . Tonight a Catalan comes. Diana meanwhile gives me letters to the ancient rich nobility. It will be interesting, no, madly exciting for me. But in my heart I have so little hope for our species; I think we are incurable. My only aim would be an amnesty for political prisoners; an end to torture by the state. That's nowadays a vast aim; it may be the only one to aim for.

Whilst waiting, I have also been involved (with a stone of pain in my stomach and nervous hysteria) in a fiasco of a telly program. Fellow named Knightley★ who has never been near a war has written a book about war correspondents (says none of them did much; naming at length only me for praise in Vietnam, can you beat it?). Said book is a Book of the Month Club

---

★When, in 1975, Philip Knightley published *The First Casualty*, about the reporter as hero and maker of myths, he speculated – as many others had – about whether Capa's celebrated photograph of the falling Republican soldier in the Spanish Civil War had been staged.

choice. In it, on rotten dubious conflicting and uncorroborated testimony he opines that Capa's great Spanish war picture of a militia man being hit is a fake. This roused me to such a passion of anger as I rarely feel; there are no laws of libel against the dead; and Capa was the bravest and best, and had the most compassionate vision of war, the real understanding. So I, who would rather be shot than go on TV, found myself there; in vain, it was all such a boring muddle that nothing came out of it. Except that, since we recorded it, I saw the program and I looked 108 years old. I don't see myself, cleverly, except when tooth brushing. This a.m. I decided I looked like Dotty Parker. The bags under her eyes were such that we always thought her related to the camel; a special arrangement for storing liquid. . . .

Having nothing else to do, while waiting for Franco to die, I decided to write a 'treatment' of one of my stories for a TV movie for Betty Bacall; she being interested and my agent being interested but they were all doing nothing – in NYC to get anything done you have to be there, nagging – while hoping to find an 'adaptor.' So I have done it, great fun; no idea if it works; and no idea how long it takes to play a written scene. This 'treatment' may work out at longer than the Russian *War and Peace*. Betty shows up here in two days and we solemnly discuss all this . . . Irwin Shaw has been here, brought by his publisher to promote his new book, and giving me lectures. 'Now listen kid, modesty is supposed to be a virtue – it is NOT – it is a serious mistake. You've got to stop running yourself down. Be imposing, be hard to get, talk of your work as if it was delivered from Mt. Sinai. I'm modest,' said Shaw laughing like mad, 'But I've got a lot of people to be immodest for me.' I am finding this advice hard to follow after a lifetime but mean to do my modest best.

. . . Darling, try not to kill yourself over your medical school. There have to be trail blazers in everything and they generally have a rotten life; then much later that blazed trail becomes the usual and accepted road. You have shown what can and should be done; please please don't kill yourself doing what time will do for you.

Love to you both,

M

I can't even write about Ford and Reagan – and Humphrey, indestructible as Mistinguett,* the Democrats likely choice. They ought to choose Presidents by lottery – couldn't do worse.

---

*The French cabaret singer Jeanne Marie Bourgeois, known as "La reine de Paris," who sang with Maurice Chevalier at Le Casino de Paris in the 1920s.

To: Gerry Brenner*

March 7 1976
Claviers
France

Dear Mr. Brenner;

Your idea about Ernest is very amusing and I am sure would have pleased him greatly. There used to be an extremely learned Russian who wrote lit. crit. about E. who showed me these profound articles with delight, saying who would ever have known I had all that stuff in me – but Aristotle's Poetics would really have thrilled him. He was not a scholarly man, you know, and his reading was far from ordered and I'd take a small bet he never read Aristotle's Poetics. Don't you think it more likely that art has a way of resembling other art? Or stemming without plan or study from the same sources of feeling? Again I find that finding a similarity between the *Bell* as you call it and *Paradise Lost* is enchanting but dotty. No reason to think E. had read Milton any more than Donne. Titles were searched for in that anthology, I think the *Oxford Book of Quotations*. When E. found that title he was overjoyed, saying, 'I can write em and Donne can title em.'

Myself, I think he made himself, really a self made artist. What did he read while writing? Anything. He was careful about reading stuff which might have an osmosis effect on his style – rather like the way I dare not read Henry James if writing because I find myself happily and insanely tied into sentences like pythons. But sometimes he found a fairly unknown writer and was like a man about to steal the neighbor's apples. He knew most about painting, I think. Anyway, I have no idea what that book was at Sun Valley, could have been, anything from an Almanac to some free book sent by a publisher. I seem to remember him reading in Cuba at that time *The History of the Peninsular Wars* a very long detailed accurate military study, many volumes, but would not swear to it. He didn't like talking about books. Just said they were great, good, lousy etc. He also didn't like me as a lit. crit. I hurt his feelings early on in the *Bell* by failing to be approving. I don't like the book at all actually. Same with articles. So, hurt and furious, he sought better audiences like his hunting and fishing chums. Very funny sweet scene in Cuba, E. reading aloud from the *Bell* to a bunch of grown-up well-off semi-illiterate pigeon shooting and fishing pals, they sitting on the floor spellbound.

So I can't help you. I guess he was secretive in lots of ways – but that was a character fault or fear, and I doubt whether he was hiding anything in writing except his own lack of formal education.

---

*Professor Emeritus of English at Montana University and a renowned Hemingway scholar.

Again, apologies for this delay. I don't usually answer any letters about E. but I also dislike bad manners about not acknowledging letters.

Yours sincerely

Martha Gellhorn

To: Betsy Drake

May 6 1976
72 Cadogan Square
London SW1

Honeychile; Sex news from all over. I have an admirer. It is funny and I could not admit anything so childish except to you. About two months ago, before I went to France, I gave dinner to the 2 old friends (Americans) from Spetsai and a dream funny man called Max Hayward, who translated Mme. Mandelstam and is an Oxford don and Russian expert. Then another man asked them if he could stop by after dinner, and did. There followed the funniest evening ever, I mean roll on the floor with laughter, as Max and John are both old Russian hands and spent the evening being Soviet Russians drunkenly. I knew that John was attracted, as one always does; since which he found a reason to write to me (twice) and yesterday came for a drink, which ended with breathless speed in close and passionate kissery and me protesting since he was en route to a dinner party. I imagine he will be back; and I imagine it will be a one night stand of some complexity as I am always shy in bed and never more than after 13 years of very little of one man. However, if I can steel myself to it, I shall do it, mad though it is, but rather as a test of nerve. He is of course an unusual man, and I am not surprised he is attracted as for most of my life I had also an insuperable lure for great womanizers which I have never thought about but know to be true. He's an ex-diplomat (last post ambassador in Spain), he speaks Arabic, Russian and all European languages, he is handsome, exceedingly witty and funny, probably a year or two younger than me, now a director of Rolls Royce, and I know he hasn't a principle in his mind, and has always viewed life as the finest comedy show imaginable which is scarcely my outlook. But as there would be nothing between us except sex, it doesn't much matter; and he does make me laugh like a drain. I would put as much faith in him as I could throw a herd of elephants from here to Marble Arch (if you understand the sentence) but why not just laugh and behave like a jolly pig and expect nothing more than to buck up one's non-existent sense of being a woman? Mum is the word. I'd never admit such folly to anyone but you. And he may have a good careful think and decide: better not even start, even once. But, to show how silly one is, I am delighted even to have roused this degree of animal passion, since I thought those days were long past.

. . . You know my theory about men: do not search, as it is useless, but wait and sooner or later, you will be found. Well, look, nothing startling: L. found me 13 years ago and J. found me yesterday; it isn't a world record but I think you'll be better off not hoping or looking and letting time and fate do their work or not, as the case may be. Though you have a problem I don't (and rather wish I did) which is an actual need for sex. Ah well, we must all bumble along as best we can.*

. . . I must hustle along. Your dog sounds lovely, so do your trees. Spring is here in a glory of blossom and with a searing cold wind to spoil the general effect. I want all the beauty of spring and balmy weather which never happens in England; but I have watched those baby leaves uncurl and the fruit trees and now the lilacs with the annual lifted heart.

Love, love

M

To: Moishe Pearlman†

July 12 1976
Comino
Malta

Moishie dearest; I have seen only one newspaper, on July 8, of which bits are enclosed; and so don't know the details of the Israeli rescue at Entebbe but only the fact.‡ It is a marvel and joy. Israel alone has any guts in this hijacking business and I, not naturally a killer, would have all hi-jackers shot at once, next to the plane they've hi-jacked. No matter who they are, of whatever political persuasion. And of course Amin is all bad, an insane savage, the ruin of his country; and I daresay Gaddafi is mad too. Dear God what a lot of powerful and dangerous loonies are loose.

I felt terribly sad, as I am sure you did, that awful circumstance forced Israel into some sort of deal or alliance with South Africa. It's all wrong and I blame it on Kissinger and a sense that he is constantly black-mailing Israel, for his own vanity, wishing to go down in history as the Author of the Middle East Peace. Just like that dandy peace he engineered in Vietnam

---

*The ex-diplomat, who Martha never named, did not return. Leonard Bernstein once told Martha that he had written the song "1,000 different ways to lose a man" with her in mind.
†Moishe Pearlman, historian and author of a series of books on the State of Israel and the Holy Land.
‡Very early on the morning of July 4, 1976, three Hercules transport planes bringing Israeli commandos from Tel Aviv arrived in Uganda to rescue 103 hostages, mostly Jews, held by pro-Palestinian hijackers. At Entebbe Airport all seven hijackers, twenty Ugandan soldiers, and three hostages died.

which meant more years of war. How do you feel about Jimmy Carter? I hope that, since he is a Bible thumper, he will be kindly inclined towards the Jews who invented the Bible.

I am wasting my time in an orgy of sloth here, most beautiful swimming I've ever seen outside certain Caribbean islands. I am supposed to be working on a book but have done damn all; wrote a short story in a day but otherwise I swim, sleep, read trash and eat. This would be pure heaven except the other guests are Krauts from Bearleen and I cannot stand them. Having avoided Krautland for decades I had forgotten how absolutely bloody awful they are, so noisy, so subhuman, and they act like owners of this place, outnumbering me 14 to 1. But I can avoid them and do, and my God the swimming is something. I feel about that the way you do about ski-ing.

> Dearest Moish, much love,
>
> Martha

To: Lucy Moorehead

> February 6 1977
> Anse Chastanet Hotel
> St Lucia

Lucy honey; 22 days ago I left London during which time I have:

1) Frozen with pain to my marrow. The cold never let up and was only comparable to Finland during that war.

2) Worked on my numbed feet for 5 ghastly days in Wash DC, then at typewriter for 4 ghastly days.

3) Gone to Waltham Mass., like going to Alaska, to read my letters to E.H. I browsed around in them for 2½ hours and felt depressed and disoriented. Kept thinking of that always incomprehensible sentence: Let the dead bury their dead. (Turns out it's from St. Matthew.) I think now that it means, leave the past alone. How can people bear to write autobiogs? My appalling memory is life saving, thank God I cannot remember the past. When it returns to me in any concrete form it only makes me feel regret and failure and sorrow. I wrote politely to Mary [Hemingway] asking if she would make these letters inaccessible until after my death. Why not? And I got a flash of anger, like old times, to find in a mishmash of unsorted papers, letters addressed to me by my friends, Mrs. Roosevelt, Bertrand, etc., which sure as hell don't belong in the Hemingway collection; he just cleaned out my desk, and the robbery annoyed me, so late, so late . . . I want it all buried. I cannot bear the past. I can bear each day now as it happens, and find it amusing or awful or whatever, but not a day ahead or a day behind.

4) Got myself to the Caribbean; at least lovely and hot. This is the most beautiful island I have ever seen and I think now I know them all. This

hotel is also enchanting, very small, very brilliantly and stylishly and originally done, and also good food and also by Carib standards cheap. The landscape is Douanier Rousseau jungle on hills and with twin peaks called the Pitons which are spectacular, and far below the blue blue sea. I love the weather, love the looks but today have felt too sick to do more than lie abed and read a rather bad thriller. And write to you and Diana. This must be the end of letters. I want to go to Vietnam but absolutely no one is interested in that. I had dinner with Kay Graham,* and sort of launched the idea and she responded with the enthusiasm of a cold cod. Funny woman. Known her since she was about 17 but never bothered with her before and both of us were baffled by the reunion.

The real with-it operator in Wash DC is Pam Churchill Harriman.† She is a US citizen with no trace of Brit accent and by next month she will be talking Southern. As she has no humor, she is cut out to win in Wash DC. I threw up at my first Georgetown dinner party (I never do) and did it gracefully, leaving the table with decorum and reaching the loo all right. Reason was attributed to the extreme cold and exhaustion. Real reason was battering noise of their talk, extreme boredom, and filthy corked white wine. Thereafter I carried Dramamine. How dull they all are. But I have great hopes of Mr. Carter though I know better than ever before the limits of power; an unmoveable bureaucracy, civil service, 3 million strong.

Love to you both,
Kisses,
Martha

To: Mary Hemingway

March 4 1977
72 Cadogan Square
London SW1

Dear Mary; Thank you for your letter which I found here.

. . . Something I always wanted to get straight with you, in case E. didn't tell you the truth. I couldn't understand why you two weren't immediately married upon return to Cuba and it later occurred to me that maybe he said I wasn't willing. That he had to wait a certain time (I don't know Cuban law) in order to divorce me for desertion. If he did, that is not true. He was free as air when he met you; I had told him I was through when I got to

---

*Katherine Graham (1917–2001), publisher of the *Washington Post* and famous for having supported the paper's coverage of the Pentagon Papers and Watergate in the early 1970s.
†Pamela Harriman (1920–1997), Washington hostess, celebrity, and diplomat. She had been married to Randolph Churchill before Averell Harriman and was legendary for her affairs with famous people.

England, that spring of 1944, having had 17 days on a dynamite ship to think it through to its final conclusion. He knew all along that I wanted my freedom and my name back, legally, but he never told me about you. Capa told me, one night in Paris after the Battle of the Bulge I think, when Capa found me weeping at 2 a.m. in my freezing room at the Lincoln. E. had convoked me to dinner with his band of nice kids from the 4th and wedged me on a banquette and talked like a cobra until the boys melted away with embarrassment and I could get out too. I was weeping because I didn't see how I'd ever get free, he had been threatening when I spoke of divorce. Capa told me to pick up the phone, call the Ritz and ask for your room; he sat on the floor counting his poker winnings and told me E. would answer the phone and what to say. I obeyed, shivering, and when E. began to vituperate Capa told me to hang up and said, 'It will be all right now.' I had never heard of you and I was (and am) deeply grateful.

I read your piece in the *Observer* and think you will be amused to know that E. also proposed to me, not at the third meeting but the third week in Madrid and not with witnesses, but while still married to Pauline. Innocently I imagined he knew what he was doing but the difference was that poor Pauline was not willing and had not been informed and God knows what she had to hear before she agreed to divorce, over two years later. But you know, no one (man or woman) breaks up a marriage from the outside; it is broken from the inside first. I knew that with Tom and never had the slightest feeling about, against Pam. On that basis, I have calmed my guilt about Pauline; if it hadn't been me, it would have been someone else.

. . . I won't read your book, I don't read any of the books about him, because I only get upset, even by snippets and hearing. How people are rewriting history (not you, I don't know) (but others); I read Miss Hellman's *An Unfinished Woman* and my goodness nothing was right and she sounded like La Passionaria and forgot to mention that she was in Madrid with Dotty Parker and Alan Campbell for a few perfectly calm days, no artillery, no nothing. It would be a whole career getting witnessed facts, only Herbert Matthews, if still alive (I don't even know that) and Sefton Delmer left to clear the record.

I dreamed about you last night, a long nice dream, you were very honest and clear and sensible.

Thank you about the letters, it is a great relief. I didn't want to be in that collection. I read, in the unsorted stuff, a carbon (he made carbons?) of an unsent letter to me, written I suppose after you'd been there a year or so, full of hate and lies, and it made me feel sick. I got up and left saying over and over to myself 'Let the dead bury their dead', as perhaps I told you. I wish you great success with your book.

Yours,

Martha

To: Robert Presnell

March 15 1977
72 Cadogan Square
London SW1

Dearest P;

. . . Today I am having drinks with a young lady who is a powerful editor at Penguin. (I don't know what this means.) She is a 'fan' (my agent's word) of mine; you probably didn't know that I have, with a limited youthful public, the position of the great dead. Long ago, meeting such a bunch (which included Edna O'Brien, young herself, you see how long ago) and being subjected to their breathless questions about the past, I told them at length about Rasputin whom I described as an absolutely beastly man, made one quite sick to eat with him, his table manners being worse than any known pig etc; and they believed me. It went to my head, I rambled on about Mayerling and dancing with Prince Rudolph; they believed that too. It's so funny about women's lib, to me, since I never thought there was any problem – I mean, there are enough problems for both sexes and all types of people to choke a horse, but I didn't see any problems for me. I knew what I wanted to do and went ahead doing it. Yes, I did earn less than men but as I earned enough for my needs and money was not the object, doing what I wanted was the object, I never thought about that one. My consciousness has always been raised far too high, about nearly everything, since infancy. Of course men can always get quiescent women to do the dirty work for them, the kitchen of life, and women can't find quiescent men to do the same – or if they can, who wants to be lumbered with a bore, and men endure boring women with an ease which always leaves me stunned. However, if the women don't want that job, they can shove, can't they? I keep thinking of the armies of men who are, for instance, life long shoe clerks; true, I'd rather be a shoe clerk than a hausfrau but there's not much in it. It seems to me that men and women are 'liberated' (no one is liberated) to the extent that they take the chances and accept the penalties. But, you see P., I am practically an original liberated woman – the very first (on record) in 'our class' to live openly in sin, and though I didn't enjoy the sin part, I got a colossal bad press everywhere. The first (in our time) woman war correspondent and I didn't notice it; I was just a war correspondent. I do believe in equal pay for equal work for everyone, male and female; but I find I am tired to death of this man/woman argument. Both sexes have been going on some time and will continue; outside circumstances change the conditions of life. Women can make children and usually want them; the one absolute responsibility (all else can be chucked) and if the reward is not worth the penalty, then they'll stop having children. Why does everyone scream so much? Or am I getting old?

The things that make me scream are always the same: I scream about Amin and I scream to read of an East German family, Dad, Mum, three kids, setting out in rubber dinghies on the Baltic in winter to escape from E. Germany; Dad and two girls drowning; Mum and son making it. I scream that societies exist which make such horrors possible. I scream about the Shah of Iran who says oh no, we're not really using that sort of torture now, we have new better methods. And etc.

Love, always
Martha

To: Diana Cooper

June 22 [1977]
Lindos
Rhodes

Dearest buddy; How I miss you. I am in a pretty pickle or better still a hideous pickle. I am a captive house guest, trapped by kindness. You know me, like Miss Garbo I want to be alone. (I also have in common with Miss Garbo the size of my feet and sun lust; there it ends.) John J's★ acquaintance, Mrs. Hope,† whom he described as 'really alarming to look at' is my hostess. The deal was that I'd spend ONE NIGHT, with heartfelt thanks, and the next day she would steer me towards a bed sitter that I could rent. But she is gregarious, she has actually had and enjoyed eleven house guests at a time (they must have been sleeping on top of each other like newts) and now she is alone, her husband being in Germany. She had no intention of helping me to solitude; she said the house is empty, use it. I could not think how to get away, short of saying I simply cannot stand human society, and since she doesn't know me she'd have taken that as a personal insult. So here I am, after a week, going mad.

This climate is the one I love best, where I blossom like a rose (last rose of summer, natch.) Boiling days, warm nights, cool smooth sea in which to swim marathons. But all over the world, the people who live in such climates are the world's biggest bores. It is some kind of natural law. During five years in Mexico, I had one friend,‡ a highly intelligent much older woman who was an insatiable and perceptive reader, and three acquaintances, and I saw even that large range with discretion. In thirteen years off and on in Africa I actually knew only twelve people, counting

---

★John Julius Norwich, writer and historian, was Diana Cooper's son.
†Polly Hope, an artist of collages, who lived for many years on Rhodes. To keep tourists from straying into her garden, she had a sign printed: "Danger: loose reptiles."
‡Winifred Hill, with whom Martha kept up a lifelong correspondence.

wives who didn't count. And saw them very seldom, at that. Here I already know five people and am feeling suffocated by them. I talk too much myself, if forced to spend time with them, mainly to stop them from boring me on the grounds that I am used to boring myself and can't stand the shock of strangers' boringness.

Sybille Bedford drives me mad when being either a *femme de lettres* or a wine authority but I don't think that's snobbery, I think that's her bag; she isn't showing off, she's just being tiresome on subjects she considers her specialty. Inexperienced as I am with the subject, I reckon Mrs. Hope comes under the category (as we spoke of it after that lecture) of snob; and it makes me blush to listen. It also makes me blush to see other locals being slightly crushed and respectful of such crapulous chat. Oh dear. And now my feet are swelling like elephantiasis (in need of a diuretic) and I sleep badly because the evenings so harass me and all I think of is how to break away from this very pretty over-adorned house and get off to a bare primitive bed sitter by myself.

. . . Mr. Bosanquet* of ITV† is next door (he's a nice drunk, you know, not a mean one) with three ladies; one coal black from Tobago whom I think is his, and a right bore too; and Mrs. Gall and a friend. I remembered how you'd liked your weekend with the Galls and told her so and she said, 'She's a sweet person.' Anyone who describes you like that has to be a half wit, you see what I mean about boredom. I think I may be going off my rocker so might as well get back to work. This is a real moan from the very center of the heart and intestines but do not share it because it will sure as hell get back.

Love always

Martha

To: Sandy Matthews

October 9 1977
Gozo
Malta

Dearest Sandy; You must be back at work now. How was it? I long to hear. Much of it must have been funny. Also, do you not think seriously that you ought to return to the US and make your life there? If you don't now, you never will; you will be a lifelong expatriate like me. I'm not sure it's a good thing. It is inevitably a permanent falling between stools. One is inevitably an outsider everywhere. Your roots must grow in air.

---

*Reginald Bosanquet and Sandy Gall were both newsreaders with ITN. Bosanquet was nicknamed Reginald Beaujolais.
†ITV is the British independent television channel.

. . . Things creep up. They don't happen, they drift into being. In this way, you suddenly find that you feel more alien in your own country than anywhere else. This irritates your compatriots more than somewhat, I can tell you. But you do not belong elsewhere; perhaps Eliot did, finally. I think Henry James never did. I've lived in England more than anywhere else in the world, longer in time; no English person ever mistakes me for English, not only in speech but in everything, in something deeper as if it were a smell recognized by members of the same herd. And as a foreigner, an alien, one cannot be effective in any communal way. One is an observer, must be; not a participant.

. . . Friends are roots too, not as strong as one might think. They die. I think, in my worst moments of desolation, that the ones I really loved are all dead. They also change with age; it is strange and unnerving to watch. At any one moment, I doubt if one has more than four friends. Many acquaintances, cared for in varying degrees. But if one wishes not to be bored, one must always be careful not to be boring; an unwritten law of friendship, I would guess. I find there is not anyone to talk to entirely; perhaps not even myself.

And there is that weird phenomenon, of which I've already written to you: nothing to think about. I believe people mostly think about facts: what they are going to do next, buy next, that sort of thing; ways and means. But if one is no longer interested in that, and totally without ability or interest in metaphysical speculation, this kind of calm void has a way of opening up . . . I walk for miles, for hours; I look at what is around me; I suggest to myself subjects for interior conversation; mostly I end by writing a letter in my head, to someone, describing what I am seeing.

. . . There must be solitary nights when you feel like talking to someone, so talk to me; as I do to you. You are one of my remaining roots, Sandy.

Love
Martha

To: Diana Cooper

February 16 1978
Hua Hin
Thailand

Dearest honeybun; Further adventures of Dick Dare in the Orient. I am now on a glorious beach, miles of wide empty white sand. The Gulf of Siam is out in front, sapphire with formal neat waves like Chinese paintings; smooth silver at sunrise, water clear as glass. Been here six days. No swimming. The cool clear water is infested with poisonous jelly fish, quite wrong, they should not be here at this season, but they are. A marine biologist would go mad with joy, the number, the varieties. I've seen one at least 33 inches in diameter. Their sting is said to be near fatal, leaving a lifelong gouged scar; no one puts toe in water. I am bored and frustrated. Will return to hateful Bangkok on the local bus (I really am a sporting traveller but it's all beginning to be a nuisance) and proceed back to the Andaman Sea and if it has jelly fish I give up.

As to degeneration, I want to brag a bit, you are only getting deaf and blind but you ought to see how I'm falling apart. A new item is sudden appearance on my arms of great blood bruises, look like birth marks, and are not the result of bumping into anything, they come by themselves. Back of my left hand is a solid dark purple bruise, different variety, also came by itself. My feet and ankles are swollen like elephantiasis almost all the time, they look like the black Queen of Togo, remember her? My back has been bum ever since I crashed in Greece last June and the London osteopath, who was exactly like the friendly neighborhood Gestapo for torture, didn't help. I just find it hot and dull in the glamorous Orient.

This place is good because there is no Thai pop music played on radio or tape recorder. I become hysterical when I hear it. This travel will be enough for a while. I want to find a nest on Gozo or near Almeria where I can grow vegetables and keep two cats and be dead sure I won't hear background music of any nationality.

Hang on, I may be home sooner than April 4.

Love love love,

Martha

To: The U.S. State Department*

August 8 1978
72 Cadogan Square
London SW1

Sir; I received a letter from you, dated June 13, enclosing a Xerox of a 'Confidential' document from the US Embassy in Mexico City to the State Department. The number stamped on the document is 680633. I am allowed to request amendment of this document. It is a matter of total indifference to me whether this nonsense is amended or not. But I am alarmed to think that such reporting – ignorant, unverified – may be the basis for any decisions or actions taken by the State Department. This is in fact the second report I've seen from the US Embassy in Mexico City; the

---

*When Martha discovered that under the Freedom of Information Act she could see her FBI files, she read that she was alleged to have had a long history of communist involvement.

first was of such vulgarity of tone, aside from being rubbish, that I was quite startled. However.

The reason the 'original Excelsior story' was missed by the rest of the press is because the rest of the press was more sensible and adhered to some of the tenets of journalism, such as checking a story. Of course this whole thing stems from McCarthyism, an ugly and shameful period of our history, but even so, your Embassy reporter only had to drive for an hour and a half to observe that Cuernavaca was what it always had been, a lazy pretty place, where people minded their own business and enjoyed life. The idea that anyone there, 'displaying red colors, singing of the Internationale, demonstrations against the United States and in favor of Russia and the like, had created an atmosphere of antagonism and division in Cuernavaca' etc etc. is too silly to bother with. If you want a very jokey highly imaginative view of Cuernavaca at that time, you might read my novel called *The Lowest Trees Have Tops* published in 1967. I knew slightly two and knew well four of the 'alleged Communists' among whom is my name. Ernest Ammann, and his wife were refugees from the Spanish war, Austrian Jews; Ernest was our beloved village doctor, for instance; two others – Charles McCabe and Ross Evans were probably as much Communists as you are; as for myself, I have traced my career via the Freedom of Information Act, which should rightly be called The Freedom of Partial Information Act. It began with the highly secret news that I was the very public honorary chairman of some group concerned with helping Spanish refugee children. Apparently the Attorney General had put that committee down as a Communist front. Well, too bad for the A.G.; its object was to help children and I am sure it did, homeless deprived children. From then on slowly, from that start, I became an alleged Communist and finally as I remember a Communist, according to the documents I have received. I've never belonged to any party; what I really am (you should note this) is a permanent and premature liberal – also a bad category during McCarthyism. I do whatever I believe, say what I think, write as I see the truth, and have been very lucky in life, being able always to do so.

However, I repeat my real concern which is: does the State Department receive this sort of idiot reporting generally, does it pay attention? That's a danger, isn't it?

Yours sincerely,
Martha Gellhorn

In the autumn of 1978, Martha decided that the moment had come to explore the English countryside. She found a cottage to rent in Dorset, in a village with a church and eleven houses, surrounded by small hills and rolling countryside, acquired two kittens, bought a secondhand red Renault and a gramophone and moved in. She agreed to appear on the Russell Harty *television show, and used the £100 fee on a greenhouse. When birds came to eat at her bird table, she began to think that this life might be the solution to her problems.*

The Dorset house came to an end sooner than she wished, with angry exchanges with its owners, and the summer of 1979 was particularly cold and windy, but Martha persevered. She spent several weeks driving backward and forward across Herefordshire, Wales, and Dorset, and finally settled on a 200-year-old cottage fifteen miles from Newport. It was small, "the size of a dolls house," stood on its own on a slope looking out across fields, and it cost £25,000. She spent £10,000 more on doing it up, putting in excellent heating, and on making a garden. She called it Catscradle, from the children's game with string in which everything ends in a "vast muddle, symbolic name and also factual." The weather in Wales, she complained "is subhuman and anti-human. It leads to neurosis, melancholia, probably schizophrenia," but she was soon gardening.

To: Moishe Pearlman

> January 28 1979
> Church Cottage
> Wareham
> Dorset

Dearest beloved Moishie, best of all Moishies in the world; The Bible industry in Israel is reaching epidemic proportions or does one say conditions. Yesterday I got a most beautifully printed and richly illustrated book entitled *Living with the Bible* by Moshe Dayan. Since he could not possibly have sent it, and certainly Weidenfeld wouldn't have given it to me, it must be a gift from you, and leads me to believe you wrote this <u>too</u>. Dear God, where will it end? You'll become one of those rare people who can quote from the Bible like knowing the London-Weymouth time table. The recognized basis of the culture of cultured English-speaking people is the Bible and Shakespeare, and I know neither, and truth to tell, in their original form, except for beautiful phrases, both rather turn me off. Too heroic for my taste. Or, better still, I am incurably uncultured and, as a friend recently said to me, 'Better stick to thrillers.'

. . . Do you know Betty Bacall? She's a chum of mine, in the way actors are chums; she's far better than any others I know, being funny and basically very kind. She's written her autobiography; she actually did write it, not ghosted. A feat. But there isn't much in it. However it is full of famous names and the death of Bogey is sadly interesting. She is said, on good authority, to have received $300,000 advance – even if you cut it in half, it's not peanuts. The result is such a tidal wave of publicity that you'd think she was at least Madame de Sévigné; the publishers must get their money back and they work at selling her. The form this takes nowadays, due to the hideous over-production of books, is to sell the author; it is known as 'exposure.' I've been feeling miffed about Betty's vast publicity and the certainty that her books will be on sale in bookstores, compared to mine, really (believe me) sunk without trace despite good reviews of the travel book and some of the African book. Reviews are only step one. Then last night I saw Betty on Michael Parkinson's talk show; he's the BBC top interviewer of celebrities, a Saturday night special, with an audience of millions. Betty was very good, funny, quick, lively; and it was, to me, like undressing in public. Felicia used to say Betty was a darling girl but couldn't talk about anything except herself – which is true – but the book has worked on her like a truth drug or psycho-analysis. (Ever known any psyched people; they have a tendency to tell all to everyone, unable to draw the line between that paid-up hour on the couch and the rest of life.) And I sat here, in my wee cottage, and thought: oh good, I don't have to fret any more. I would rather die than do any of the things needed to be a success. I'd felt the same watching Lenny's 60th birthday celebrations on telly – a vast paid musical performance, interlaced by stars paying tribute to a star. The price of success is too humiliating, that's all. It is a great relief to me to be absolutely sure in my mind that I prefer my obscurity and neglected work; and it is odd that the question only arose now, since nothing has changed in my condition over all these years.

I hated feeling <u>offended</u> by a lack of notice. Now I don't. I feel I'm sane and all right, and privacy is more valuable than this awful self exposure which is a modern necessity for success.

. . . I was sick of London, the hardship of surviving in a city is too much now. People have become snarly like overcrowded rats. I was also sick of airports and airlines. So I took this leap into the unknown and am hoping I can persuade the somewhat dotty owner to lease me this cottage for a year, giving me time to see whether it wears as well as up to now.

I am beginning to ponder a cheerful short story on the joys of a lonely old age. All you need is a) service and b) perfect health.

Now I must get on with the day's work. My one job is to replenish the grub and de-ice the water at my bird feeding station.

Love always,

Martha

P.S. I'm very very glad you liked the travel book. I started it to amuse myself and it was harder to do than anything before. Because of writing in the first person singular which I will never never do again.

To: Betsy Drake

March 24 [1979]
Church Cottage
Wareham
Dorset

Betsy honey; I am delighted that you are coming, mind made up, house rented, all signals Go as the saying is or was. If my present love affair with the country goes on, I'll hardly ever be there. Mainly due to the gardening; it's a derelict garden; anything I can do only makes it better. And gardening in a cold country is the trickiest thing you ever saw. I'll earn £100 for displaying myself (white slavery) on the Russell Harty show and mean to blow it on a green house. You need them here, I've got seed boxes all over the kitchen now which isn't good enough and besides I want so many more, I want to be filling seed boxes and then pricking out the small growths into seed pots and then into a cold frame and finally into the ground if it ever warms up.

Rumor has it (can rumor be believed) that my travel book is selling, by word of mouth is the expression. It sure has nothing to do with my sickening publisher. I only hope the bastards have the decency at least to answer the bookstores demand. I ordered it myself in the Wareham Bookshop anonymously to see how long it took; two weeks. Not what I'd call making much of an effort. Anyway, it is because he read it by chance that Mr. Harty has me on his show; he loved it. Mr. Harty is an absolute charmer, I hope I'll get him as a new friend for when I am in London but I daresay he's too busy and grand.

Tonight Roald's [Dahl] series, his stories, starts on TV. Star studded cast, no expense spared. He is described as 'the master of the short story', sometimes as 'the most masterful short story writer of our time.' You know that is balls. I sent Mr. Harty a copy of *The Honeyed Peace* and signed it Martha Dahl, mistress of the short story.

This leads me to *The Deer Hunter*.★ It is talked about as if it were at least Chekov, maybe Shakespeare. It illuminates or explains or resolves or some such high flown crap the Vietnam War. It is cheap, contemptible and above all absurd. Not one single thing in it, from the American bits to the Vietnamese bits, is true, bears any relation to reality.

I dread Boston and NYC (except for L. The darling man said, 'In general things are pretty good here, I mean apart from life and death.') But Jamaica and Grand Cayman have to be heaven. Now I am going to drink whiskey

---

★Directed by Michael Cimino and starring Robert de Niro and Meryl Streep, *The Deer Hunter* (1978) was a war drama looking at the way the Vietnam War had affected the lives of people in a small industrial town in the U.S.A.

and watch telly, including R. Dahl. It's called *Tales of the Unexpected*. The series is. He even has Gielgud amongst others. Yet I found him nicer than usual when I saw him on that ghastly book program TV thing and he walks with a limp, looks very old, no doubt has constant pain. He may mellow into a nice man; success may soften him.

Love,

M

To: Alvah Bessie

23 October 1979
Church Cottage
Wareham
Dorset

Alvah dear man; Do you hate Ernest? Why? I didn't name him in my travel book simply because I have avoided and mean forever to avoid membership in that group of grave robbers and corpse thieves who have been battening on the dead man all these years. They disgust me. I had to use him in the China chapter because we went there together; and this is a factual and all true book. I called him U.C., for Unwilling Companion; and wrote him as he then was on that trip. Personal feelings are long long dead. I do not forget the good he did in freeing the language; we are all his debtors.

. . . I don't understand Americans' reactions to President Carter. I think he is probably too good for Americans who really do want an imperial President with all the shit that implies. Carter has put human rights on the books, dear Alvah, and no one else has. He has also brought peace between Israel and Egypt and I seriously doubt if that can break down again. He behaves as an American President should, which is as a simple man, not a movie-star king-emperor. I'll vote for him.

Love

Martha

To: Bernard Perlin★

December 9 1979
[Church Cottage
Wareham
Dorset]

Dearest B; Would you, could you, paint a little picture of my cats? I don't know if cats fall within your scope. I think I'm going to lose them and it

---

★A painter friend, whom Martha admired greatly.

breaks my heart, I cannot find another furnished cottage though I've darkened my life and made all my time twitchy and tense with the effort since August. They'll then have to go to a cat orphanage and I may say I'll miss them more than people.

You can see their size by comparison with the iris leaves. I think their expressions very beautiful and regret only that I haven't got a clearer picture of the little black one's face which I find so delicious. If your answer is yes or no, I want these photos back in due course; very important.

I'd like them outdoors in a summer garden. Everything that grows here grows in your garden so you can just remember it in summer, as background, or is that bossily and wrongly instructive and am I getting in your way. I don't mean to and apologize if I am.

I talked again to L., about you who said he was going to ask Mary (his wife) to be in touch with you but he sounds somehow frantic and I doubt anything will happen. The fact is that now suddenly he has Nelson's family to look after – can it be easy? – and he is also, I know, heartbroken since Nelson (whom I always thought hell) was his darling brother and lifelong closest perhaps only friend.[*] I think he feels like a survivor. I know I do. After Felicia's death, Lucy Moorehead was killed in a car accident this summer. That's the end of my two nearest most needed women friends. I feel now so much older than everyone else and wise (a joke, isn't it?) and instead of being tolerant and gentle I'm filled with impatience and everyone bores me blind and I show it. Living alone in the country is all I like.

. . . The children are all unhappy and rudderless but Lenny is in one of his manic highs. Jamie,[†] who without knowing it is most like him, doesn't much care for him. She writes that Lenny finds everything wonderful and marvelous and talented and moving, her words, and she's steering clear of him. Oh those poor children. Lucy's children are also bereft and her daughter is nearly mad with grief and fear at being left alone without the support of her mother. 'I need her,' she writes.

I'm always sad at Xmas and this year specially sad, and feel useless for these young who turn to me for some sort of comfort. But I do not feel there is any comfort. I know you just live with loss, and never get over it, and nothing makes up for the loss; it's there, a permanent wound.

I hope you're still happy with Bud, and all goes calmly enough.

Love always,

M

---

[*]Nelson Rockefeller had died of a heart attack early in 1979.
[†]Jamie Bernstein, Leonard and Felicia Bernstein's daughter. Felicia had also died that year.

To: Leonard Bernstein

December 27 1979
72 Cadogan Square
London SW1

Dearest Lennypot of yore; Did you chaps manage Xmas all right? I've been suffering my usual Yuletide despair, perhaps worse than usual this year; I think it's like post-natal depression that seizes some women, only it's annual. At its blackest depth, I feel that everyone I really love is dead. Then I can't even remember love, what it is and does, and think: there it is, I have frozen up, I have become totally unloving. Well it's over now for another year and the hell with it.

I watched Itzak Perlman on TV, playing Bach in that bombed (repaired) Wren church in Smith Square where they have noon concerts. I didn't know he had no legs (polio? what?) and was so young. I hardly heard the music, I was so moved by his face, his expression. I would like to be the way Itzak Perlman looks. Do you know him? Amazing young chubby face, filled with joy, with hope and goodness.

Are you all right?

What happened to laughter? Do you know? I remember it as the central and loveliest fact of life. I remember when you came with Felie to Cuernavaca to the house of the woman who said, 'it's a short world.' I remember laughing constantly. Are other people doing it still or has it gone out of fashion? I'd give anything I have to meet someone who made me laugh.

A good New Year to you, old friend. Love,
Martha

Both The Weather in Africa *and* Travels with Myself and Another, *after slow starts, were selling well, and* Travels, *in particular, had come at a moment when the public was discovering a taste for the personal journey. Martha's life was getting better all the time. The period "spent like Lazarus among the shades," from the moment that Sandy deserted from the army in Germany, through the death of Edna, the car accident, and the war in Vietnam, seemed at last to be at an end. She was writing and she was less haunted by the thought of aging.*

And it was now that she was, as she wryly put it, "rediscovered," "by a little gang of funny young men." They were not of course all men — though Martha had always regarded friendship with men as funnier and in some ways more important — but they were writers and journalists, publishers and television reporters, who had read her books and articles and wanted to meet her. They brought her, as she said, "news of the Rialto," from places she could no longer so easily get to herself.

It started with Mary Blume, columnist and writer for the International Herald Tribune, and went on to include John Hatt, travel writer and founder of Eland Books. John introduced her to the biographer and novelist Victoria Glendinning, "my always friend," and "young Mr. Shakespeare," Nicholas, who had written two books of nonfiction. There was the author of White Mischief, James Fox; the writer and journalist Cynthia Kee; John Pilger, the Australian television documentary maker; Rosie Boycott, who was working with the magazine Spare Rib; and Jeremy Harding, after he made a television program about her for Omnibus. Martha felt affection and admiration for them all. They became "my chaps." She went to Partridges, up the road in Sloane Street, to get food to feed them – she was a truly terrible cook – and in the evenings and late into the night, over several glasses of Famous Grouse whiskey, they told her the story of their lives. Later, John Simpson and Jon Snow entered her life, bringing reports from warfronts. With a very few, she argued passionately about Israel, for Martha would hear no good spoken of the Palestinians, but most preferred to duck the subject. "I think friendship is like breathing," she said to Betsy. "One cannot live without it . . . I would only think it extraordinary, and a sign of oncoming insanity and death if there were no people one felt as friends."

When Bill Buford, editor of Granta, offered to act as Martha's agent, editor, and publisher, she was flattered and pleased. However, being published was never something Martha found easy and, in any case, she and Buford were temperamentally very different. So uncertain about her own talent as a writer, Martha was ferocious when it came to contracts, editorial changes, and the appearance of her books. A punctilious correspondent herself, hanging on to the manners of her youth, she was furious when her letters were not answered by return post. She and Buford had arguments so bitter that at one point she went to the Small Claims Court in Chepstow to sue him for royalties that he had failed to send.

Several of Martha's older close friends were now dead – George Paloczi-Horvath, Felicia Bernstein, Lucy Moorehead – and those whom she continued to see were disconcerted and hurt by her impatience and the speed and ease with which she sometimes dismissed them. Sybille Bedford was informed that she had become very boring; Leonard Bernstein was castigated for not being braver about being ill. But with Diana Cooper, Martha remained close and affectionate. One night, they took a thermos of consommé and vodka and some sandwiches and met at 12:30 to watch a special showing of the Russian film of War and Peace, which ended at seven the next morning.

The summer of 1983 was the best Martha had experienced in forty years in England. The sun shone for two months and she lived in her garden in Wales in a bathing suit, like a one-woman kibbutz, she told her friend from Cuernavaca, Winifred Hill, eating a surplus of vegetables from her garden, which bloomed "like a cross between Jack and the Beanstalk and The Day of the Triffids."

To: Mary Blume

February 2 [1980?]
72 Cadogan Square
London SW1

Dear Miss Blume; The thing about stories is: a person gives you an idea of a personnage and then the story grows. But they are not usually as recognizable as *The Honeyed Peace*; and I regret the recognizability.

I'm glad you like the war reporting.* Once everything grew out of everything else; novels grew from what I had seen as a reporter, stories too. Now I don't see anything much and am daily more sunk into despairing apathy as, like lemmings, we move towards World War Three. Mrs. Mandelstam in that superb book *Hope Against Hope* said: if there is nothing else to do one must scream. I long to scream. But where? But how? I am screaming all the time inside me and it will end by giving me severe stomach pains as it already gives me insomnia; useless screaming.

I do wish all of you who have a place to write would scream. In any way, in any words.

I wrote to that wicked Gloria† that I was going to be in NYC for 4 days and longed to see her. The result is total silence . . . But swimming and snorkeling are on. Do everything you long to do before 1984.

Yours,
Martha Gellhorn

To: Diana Cooper

June 28 [1980?]
Hotel Comino
Malta

Dearest Diana; Do you remember Miss Dietrich's most famous song? 'Men (something) round me/ Like mutts around a phlegm/ I cawn't helppit.' I was always fond of the mutts bit. What I want now is a handsome funny mutt with whom to swim, eat, drink and etcetera; as I ardently do not wish to work. Failing a mutt supply, however, I am absurdly happy as is. The travel brochure spoke of 'thyme scented air' which I took to be brochure guff. Not so. This limestone rock is entirely covered by clumps of purple

---

The Face of War, a collection of Martha's war pieces, originally published in 1959, but frequently reprinted.

†Gloria Emerson, foreign correspondent for the *New York Times*, whose book about Vietnam, *Winners and Losers*, won the National Book Award in 1978. In August 2004, feeling she had lost her battle against Parkinson's disease, Emerson killed herself. Like Martha, she had a huge aversion to self-publicity and a huge sympathy for the underdog.

thyme and that is how the air smells. Plus oleanders and various wildflowers unknown to me. I stumped across the island (thank God for my hefty Greek sandals) to the Blue Lagoon and set out with mask and snorkel on a voyage of discovery; marathon swimming here unlike Spetsai. I can hardly stay out of the water and must be getting giant muscles. Swimming just below the surface, the surface looks like a canopy of white and blue cloud, and the seabed is chalk white sand, so the water between is like azure veiling, with sun patterns in gold on the sand below. A few lonely fishies still float about and I greet them like old friends; I knew their relatives in the Indian Ocean.

The food is pretty awful but much more awful is the hungry way I eat it. There is local wine from the island of Gozo, a rosé that must have really high alcohol content as I tend to stagger back from dinner.

I wonder if the heat wave is still on. Please send me a bulletin on life on the Rialto.

Love always
Martha

To: George Plimpton★

August 2 1980
72 Cadogan Square
London SW1

Dear Mr Plimpton: Where on earth are you sending your letters? Mexico? Africa? Suddenly I realised that the second had followed the first into oblivion and time is running out, if I wish to state that Mr. Spender is an ass. He always was an ass but a nice timid type ass. In his advanced years he has become a pompous ass, which is deplorable. All true believers (in anything) should unite in war on pomposity . . .

Someone could make a riveting book entitled Hemingway Apocrypha Anthology, filled with fishy tales by famous names. If people feel that they gain lustre through inventing encounters with Hemingway, that is their problem and no business of mine. But I dislike being included in the nonsense.

So: 1) I never knew Mr Spender had a first wife.

2) I never had lunch in Paris with Mr Spender and his unknown first wife; therefore, logically, neither did Hemingway. I wonder whether Mr

---

★George Plimpton (1972–2003), editor and co-founder of The Paris Review, had invited Martha to comment on an article Stephen Spender had written for the magazine. In it, Spender had described a lunch at the Brasserie Lipp in Paris in the 1930s, apparently attended by both Hemingway and Martha, at which his wife, Inez, refusing to eat sweetbreads, had been called "yellow" by Hemingway, who then went on to say that he had cured Martha of being "yellow" in Spain by taking her to the morgue in Madrid every day before breakfast.

Spender ever had lunch with Hemingway anywhere; they did not seem faintly compatible during a brief meeting in Spain. This is not a criticism of either of them.

3) I did not know there was a morgue in Madrid but upon reflection, now, I see that there must have been one, as there is one in every big city. The only morgue I ever frequented was in Albany, NY. as a cub reporter on a Hearst newspaper in my distant youth. I assumed that someone buried the dead in Madrid where of course many died from the unnatural cause of war.

4) The very idea that anyone visited a morgue anywhere daily before breakfast proves that Mr Spender has a weird and wondrous imagination.

. . . It is risky to suggest that someone is a liar but it can do no harm to suggest that someone is a silly juggins.

Yours
Martha Gellhorn

To: George Plimpton

September 5 1980
1 Old Market Street
Usk
Gwent
Wales
for the moment

Dear Mr. P: Now your letters and the PR have arrived. When you told me on the telephone about daily dawn visits to the Madrid morgue, I just thought it was funny. But that whole paragraph makes me surprisingly cross. I am sick of the liars, a veritable horde, battening on that old corpse. I want to do better than the comments I banged out to you in a letter, better and at greater length. And there is, I see, no hurry; imagine telephoning from NYC about something that is going to become operational in two months. You're all mad, obviously.

I've sat on my hands, without too much effort, for what – almost 30 years isn't it, since Hemingway decided to depart. I avoid knowing about the apocrypha and read none of the Papa books. But suddenly, I realise I am the last person who not only knows the difference between truth and lies but should be believed, in the special area of Spain, owing to the provable fact that I really did know Hemingway. Unlike Spender for instance.

Now I am also involved (what a nasty busy life) with Miss McCarthy*

---

*On the *Dick Cavett Show* in the U.S.A., Mary McCarthy had stated that every word written by Lillian Hellman was "a lie, including the 'and' and the 'the.'"

whom I have never met and would certainly not wish to spend a desert island weekend with. But she has made a statement about Miss Hellman and is being sued for a million or so and wrote to me, asking if I would make some testimony as to Miss H. in Spain. I'd read those apocrypha (what a word to spell, easy to say) of Miss H. with a sneer, noting that Hemingway and Matthews and Sefton Delmer were all dead before she dared trot out that nonsense, leaving only me, a woman who had been outstandingly silent and also not likely to want to waste time on the subject. But obviously I must aid Miss McC in not being obliged to pay a million for a pretty accurate observation.

So now I am in the business of nailing the braggarts, the mythomanes, and the corpse vultures, and will be intensely pleased if this occupation ends with the PR and Miss McCarthy.

I have come to believe that the only work of non-fiction which can be trusted from beginning to end is the World Almanac. History is made by innumerable versions of Mr. Spender and Miss H. Their astounding words will remain on the record and in future be believed as fact; in the way we believe the past history we read. Me for fiction; that is believable, has to be in order to last.

So. As soon as I can force myself to it I'll write a tiny essay for you and you will get it long before two months.

Yrs.,
Martha Gellhorn

To: George Plimpton

January 27 1981
[72 Cadogan Square
London]

Dear Mr. Plimpton; Grim and horrible doubts are rising in my mind. WHY doesn't the Paris Review appear? Can it – heaven forbid – be due to some terrors relative to my magnum opus and Miss H? If you wait too long, the lady will be dead and there will be neither joy nor value in beating a dead horse. Please let me know what goes on, or rather why nothing goes on. When I think of the haste of getting it off, the cables and phone calls, I am sadly reminded of that ancient army rule: hurry up and wait.

I saw your co-founder, the lovely Prince,★ in Kenya on the coast and regaled him with the latest news from the battlefront which made him laugh. On the other hand, where is the battlefront?

★Prince Aga Khan.

I have added some comical ammunition, dealing with Miss H. and her heroic adventures in Russia at war. You'll also be interested to know that in the program notes for *Watch on the Rhine*,★ here, it states that Miss H lived through air raids (plural now) in Spain. My respect for Goebbels grows all the time; he was the smartest advertising man there ever was and he was bang-on about the power and success of lies.

Meanwhile, as a confirmed unbeliever, I am organizing a memorial service for Nadezhda Mandelstam in the Russian church here and trying to believe that the true and valuable in writing finally surfaces and remains, whereas the fishy and flashy does one day sink without trace.

I await word from you, almost breathlessly.

Yours,
Martha Gellhorn

To: George Plimpton

May 13 1981
The Cwm
Wales

Dear Mr. Plimpton; Well, good. If the only way to get an answer is to make you angry, then it's worth it to me. Though perhaps not for you.

As for losing Miss Hellman's friendship, I cannot possibly react to that in any useful way. (I think 'meaningful' is the in-word.) Self glorifying apocryphiars are what I dislike more than almost any other type of our species. My marriage to E.H. broke on that jagged rock. Miss Hellman has his worst characteristics without his talent or his charm, when he happened to be charming. Judging by her writing and by the way she treated Dotty Parker, I wouldn't say Miss H. had any great gift for friendship, apart from Hammett. The Julia† story is not about friendship (aside from being, I'd bet, entirely made-up, or something that partially happened to two other people). It is a story about Miss H. and her heroism.

I look forward eagerly to my copy of the Paris Review. Do you know Mary McCarthy? Maybe you would send her a copy of the mag when it comes out? I don't know her address. She is not a friend of mine; I simply agreed to testify because she happened to be saying in general what I know in particular, but I do not specially wish to be involved in a quarrel between the two Great American *Femmes de Lettres*. Only to do my duty versus

---

★A play by Lillian Hellman (1943), which was also made into a film.
†In *Pentimento* (1973) Lillian Hellman had written about a close friend she called Julia, very obviously referring to Muriel Gardiner, a socialist activist who later wrote her own book, *Code Name Mary*. Later Gardiner claimed that she had never met Hellman.

apocryphiars. Reporters are much nicer and better company than literary people, in my opinion.

Yours,

Martha G

To: Campbell Beckett

May 16 1981

Wales

Cam Dear

. . . You asked me if I believed in an after life. No. I don't bother myself with thinking about death at all, except to take the trouble to make a new will. Thinking about here and now is all I can manage. I think about old age from time to time, with dread, because of physical disabilities and because my grandmother and mother lived to a great age. The only thing that scares me is that: not being able to rush around and do what I want to. The afterlife either is or isn't and one will find out one way or the other in due time. Personally I hope very much that death is uninterrupted sleep and manure for the grass . . .

Dearest Cam, we've had our lives. If they were good enough, we are luckier than most. I think you think of me so much because I represent your youth and your one great wild departure from sobriety. Alice Longworth,★ sister-in-law (?) of Madame de Chambrun, recognized me in Washington, five–ten years ago because we were such a scandalous pair that even then, she recalled her sister's comments. It was fun, wasn't it. I remember it all. We were two of the most innocent people on earth and those worldlings thought we were the opposite. We were babes among the domes and turrets; do you remember that we <u>leapt</u> over streets at roof top level? I do. That's why you remember. You shouldn't have given up drink. You should anyway be thankful for your life. And you should NOT worry about money. There is plenty to see you and Elise through in comfort and that's all that counts.

. . . I'm spending money like water on the grounds that a) I don't care if any is left and b) after us, the sea of fire.

Love,

Martha

★Alice Roosevelt Longworth (1884–1980), the eldest of Theodore Roosevelt's children, of whom he once said: "I can either run the country or I can control Alice. I cannot possibly do both." Josée de Chambrun was the daughter of Pierre Laval of the Vichy government and herself of the far right.

To: Sandy Matthews

October 15 [1981?]
Catscradle
Wales

Dearest sonny; I loved your Amsterdam letter, filled with elation. That must be what works of art are meant to do: elate, make the lungs bigger and the eyes able to see farther and wider, and pump blood richly to the heart and brain. Hemingway (remember him) always said that painting related to writing, not music. Painting was what writers could learn from. True, when you think of it. True anyway of 'creative' (God what a word) writing, which is also trying to form a visual world.

. . . I got cat Valium from the Monmouth vet yesterday, in preparation for taking the cats to London, 2½ hours on the road, and 10 days in Cad Square. Thought that better than taking Valium myself. The cats, I realise, become over excited by any changes in their peaceful solitary life with me. Diana Cooper and Doggie, her microscopic Chihuahua, spent last weekend. Diana came on the bus from London; she is 89. The bus leaves Victoria at 10:05, due here at 1:05 p.m. Gales blew a tanker and a lorry across the carriage ways on the Severn Bridge, blocking same totally. She arrived at 4 p.m., without a coat or a complaint. Doggie, previously a charming funny dancing little dog, is suffering a serious inexplicable depression. She has gone lame like Diana and now has large black rimmed sad eyes. She paid no attention whatever to the cats. The cats, however, were terrified of this tiny unknown animal. They behaved abominably all weekend; ate furniture, peed on and then scratched up carpets (carpets are being slowly ruined), knocked over plants, leapt, scratched and generally drove me mad. The minute the company left, they sobered up. London may be a nightmare but I have to try it out because I'm pretty sure I'll have to spend much of January and February there unless something better happens with the weather. Like Doggie, I might get a depression.

A big kiss. I'll hope to see you in your English year.

Love
Martha

To: Nikki Dobrski

October 17 [1981?]
Catscradle
Wales

Nik honey; There's been an amazing series on the S.O.E.* on TV here. I don't know if there were others, I didn't catch on until Greece and then Italy. Next is Malaya. I thought of you and was fascinated and wondered how I'd go about finding out what happened to Major Charles Macintosh, of Florence S.O.E. spring 1944 (I think it was spring). He was their chap in charge and a delight and I would love to know if he survived the war or died in it; the series didn't say. Can one find out? I remember you always go to that S.O.E. club near Harrods and wonder if they'd have such records.

Major Macintosh was about 26 and tall and beautiful and funny and he and I went to bed in the empty Hotel Excelsior once (he and I and three young men from OSS who were Fogg School of Art from Harvard, saving works of art, were the only inhabitants). I had clambered across the ruins of the Ponte Vecchio into the city and our only and jolly coupling was accompanied by the sound of machine gun fire and mortars. I can hardly believe how funny war often was – nothing much is funny now.

I am tired. My life exhausts me. I've been here 10 days and never stopped. Outdoors and indoors; it's the Augean Stables. Shovel shovel, all day long. I feel like weeping. I need a secretary and a handyman and a nanny to tuck me in.

Must tell you great black joke. I went to Forest Mere, the grandest of the fat farms, determined to lose 7 pounds which are my overweight, cemented on. For three days ate: piece of fruit and cup of hot water with lemon for breakfast, cup of vegetable soup for lunch and dinner. Felt very weak, sick, tired, headachey and constipated natch. Then had salad for next day lunch. And what did I lose? Three quarters of one pound! Cost £250 . . . I guess that will teach me. I felt perfectly awful afterwards, came home and stuffed protein.

Plans: London for November; here for December; London for January; if I get a visa, Cuba and Nicaragua for February, then back here for spring planting.

Love,

M

---

*Special Operations Executive, set up to carry out sabotage and subversion behind enemy lines in WWII. The OSS, Office of Strategic Services, was a U.S. intelligence agency.

To: Moishe Pearlman

October 20 1981
Catscradle
Wales

My darling Moishie; I am so sad for you; you must be heartbroken to lose your loved and admired friend, Dayan.* He was too young and too necessary to die. And within a week of Sadat. Some evil fate at work; two men who wanted peace. Both deaths are terrible for Israel, to say nothing of every one else except those gleeful Arabs. I daresay the PLO rejoiced over Dayan's death too. Oh Moishie, Moishie. Life is too fragile.

Did you know that Dayan had a dicey heart? I think death is worse for the survivors and gets cumulatively worse as one grows older and becomes more and more a survivor oneself. I beg you not to die Moishie for any reason. Keep me company. I am going to live forever to my great dismay.

What is going to happen now? One of the reasons I have withdrawn to this tiny insane cottage in Wales – and worked to make it livable as if I were writing a great book – is because I could not stand the newspapers and worrying helplessly and steadily about the future of our species. Here in the silent countryside with nothing about except sheep, flies and my two cats, I worry about such things as the cess pit and why the tiny cats insist on peeing on or tearing down all the plants I stick in the ground. But what now? I can see that Mubarak would certainly follow in Sadat's footsteps until all Sinai was returned. And after? He can either revert to being a loyal Arab or be killed too.

Do you puzzle over the lemming quality in our species? SURELY even Arab fundamentalists must see that Iran is a disaster area? But no, they wish to go and do likewise. Surely anyone can see that Mrs. Thatcher's economics are ruining this country totally, perhaps beyond any future hope of recovery; yet Reagan wishes to go and do likewise. Could it be that old biz about whom the Gods wish to destroy etc.?

I wish I ever saw you. Would you want to be young now? I wouldn't; I'm quite pleased to be shelved and aged. But I do remember with tenderness our carefree youth, you and me and Lenny and Feli on a beach at where – Gaza? And you and me and Capa laughing. Lenny's an embarrassing bore now, like the intellectual's Liberace (wicked thing to say) and everyone except us is dead.

Love,
Martha

---

*Moshe Dayan, commander in chief of the Israeli army and later minister of defense had died on October 16. President Sadat of Egypt was shot by a gunman while watching a military parade on October 6. Mubarak became the next president of Egypt.

To: Robert Presnell

April 11 1982
Catscradle
Wales

Dearest P; I can't write letters, let alone anything else. Happy Easter. Think of your living in 85F. I doubt if it has ever been that warm here in the windblown north. Today is clear and of course cold. Spring has come. Outside my window white lambs leap and jump. There's faint green in the trees. The cherry trees are putting out pinkish buds; they are blooming elsewhere already but not up here on the hills. This morning I heard wood pigeons, surely one of the great sounds in the world.

. . . Lenny telephoned this afternoon. He is in London, about to do some huge thing and thence onwards to other big things. I envy him the work. The fame, I suddenly realised today, thrills him and I have the feeling he is always saying to himself: is this true? The fame, the surrounding bodies, would appall me; but I do envy the <u>demand</u> for his work. I'd probably work too, if anyone was out there saying, please, please, we can't wait for your next book, we hunger and thirst to publish you.

Have you read V.S. Naipul's *Among the Believers*? If not, hurry. I think he is a marvel, one of the finest observers now alive. He set out to see the Muslim world: a rational, humane, wise and just man. It is a delight to have one's own feelings expressed, from knowledge and close watching, so lucidly and so readably. I recommend his book on India and a much earlier one on the Caribbean. His novels vary; they don't affect me as much as his seeing eye books.

And now we have the Falkland Islands. I know what getting old means. It means that indignation turns into disgust and anger turns into despair. The repeated stupidity – and age is simply having been around for some time and seen again and again, repetition of stupidity – finally paralyzes me. I am sickened. I want to hide under all the beds, all the blankets; I cannot bear even to think about the idiocy which rules our species. Whom the Gods wish to destroy – it seems to me the stupidity has reached the degree of madness by now.

Last night, on our wonderful TV, without ads and really very good, I watched for a while *The Trials of Alger Hiss*.★ Did you see it? I had to switch off, I could not stand it. The TV reportage of the Un-American

---

★On August 3, 1948, Whittaker Chambers, an ex-Soviet agent and editor of *Time* magazine, identified Alger Hiss, a respected lawyer and senior figure of the New Deal, as having been a member of a communist cell set up to infiltrate the U.S. government. At the end of a series of hearings and trials, Hiss was found guilty of passing classified State Department documents and of lying.

Committee, the questions – all apparently hanging on what Hiss had done with an old 1929 car – caused me pain. The man is 77 now, and with hurt eyes, still trying to restore his good name. And though he doesn't understand why Whittaker Chambers and Richard Nixon were out to kill him, I do; he was the very embodiment of everything they were not and could not be, the educated upper class American, an American gentleman; they hated him. It had nothing to do with Communism; it was like a private vendetta. My reaction to seeing those hated old faces from the past – including Joe McCarthy – was a reaction of the old; I could not endure it. I could not look and listen, I despaired. Because McCarthyism has not died, but lives on and is now a permanent virus in American life. But when Hiss, talking now to some young questioner, said, 'During the New Deal, we didn't think about Communists, we didn't care, it didn't matter', he was speaking the truth. And when Truman, now revered, introduced the Loyalty Oath, he sold the pass for good: I have never forgotten or forgiven his two decisions: that, the Loyalty Oath, and dropping the H-Bomb on Japan instead of on to a Pacific atoll, with the Japanese naval command watching. It could have been done. Fact remains: the only country which has used the H-bomb is us; and furthermore, I believe that we – not the terrified Russians who know about war – will be the ones to use it again, if or when it is used.

What do I watch on TV? I watch a glorious range of documentaries, latest being a beauty on Tibet; Tibet before and after the Chinese. Incredible world, and touching, and destroyed. I watch the plays, done for British telly, and some movies. The news of course, but less and less the Think-Talk shows, though they are not contemptible, but they bore me. I still prefer either to think by myself or to read. It is a boon to me to have my tiny TV set in my bedroom and to creep to bed, with cats on my legs or stomach, wearing my flannel nightie and under the electric blanket, and watch. It has even happened that I laugh out loud, the best of all.

Dear P., there it is; no queue standing outside my door crying, Write, Write. But we are fine people, so that's a comfort. I said to the cats the other night, 'I'm tired of being an under-rated writer, I want to be an over-rated writer like everybody else.' But also, does it matter? Just now I'm more interested in weather.

Love always,

M

Letter to *The Times*

June 23 1982
72 Cadogan Square
London SW1

Sir: After the Six Day war, Jordan claimed that Israel had bombed hospitals and refugee camps on the West Bank and in Gaza, and 25,000 soldiers and civilians were dead. This figure was later reduced to 15,000. For three weeks at the end of that war, I retraced the course of the combat, looking for proof of these grave allegations. All hospitals and refugee camps were unharmed, untouched; no refugee anywhere was hurt or forced to flee from danger. There was fighting in only three inhabited areas on the West Bank and in the southern section of Gaza town; villages were not destroyed. I accepted Arab statements on the spot, wherever the Israeli army had passed, even though these statements denied visible evidence. The final civilian death toll was 127 Arabs and 23 Israelis. I wrote then that all deaths were to be mourned but none should be exploited for propaganda. Now the media are asserting that up to half a million people in Lebanon have been made homeless, or killed or wounded. The latest article I have seen in the Times states that 'almost 10,000 people' have been killed. Who has queried the sources of this information? Who has searched for proof of this appalling casualty count? It cannot be presumed that the half million or the 10,000 dead are all in Beirut where verification is impossible. Such numbers of people, dead or alive, cannot vanish. Detailed fact-finding is essential to serious journalism. I suggest that Israel again stands condemned on the basis of gross propaganda. I suggest also that a nation's frontier is unarguably sovereign territory and no nation will suffer indefinite attacks across its frontier. Why is it right for Britain but base and wrong for Israel to safeguard its sovereign territory?

Yours,
Martha Gellhorn

To: Valerie Forman*

October 30 1982
Catscradle
Wales

Dearest Valerie
 I hardly dare say it, Valerie, for fear of immediate bad luck, but I am as

---

*A new friend who had escaped Czechoslovakia after Hitler took over and settled in London. Mrs. Forman was already in her late eighties and Martha kept affectionately in touch with her.

happy now as I have ever been (only think of my dubious memory) in my life. It is different of course. But I think, at my age, one must define happiness as cheerfulness and contentment: and that is how I feel.

The Victorian ladies on your shawl note are too lovely. I presume Victorian, or that era? My doctor father would have looked with horror at the waists; the laced corsets, the terrible damage to the body. Funny. I was never allowed to wear a brassiere and did not own one until the age of forty and then, so baffled, I thought they had to be made to order. Nor of course was I allowed to wear a girdle. As a child, I had to wear (child and girl) appalling shoes called Ground Grippers, made to the real and proper shape of the human foot, therefore hideous, and laced above the ankle – as a result I have toes like fingers and bad luck to me, feet one half inch too long ever to be able to buy shoes. And I look at those graceful and feminine ladies on your card and realise that, among three brothers, I was only the obviously handicapped fourth boy who had to be tougher than anyone to be accepted as being good enough to associate with boys.

This present state of serenity cannot last; or else I am becoming gently senile . . . but while it does, how marvelous: to want nothing more, to repine over nothing in my own past. My sole remorse, regret, guilt, is that I was not far far better to my parents. But then, perhaps they understood that this never happens, it isn't a circular but a linear emotion: you hand on, you do not hand back. You are most fortunate in your daughter, Valerie, and never forget it. I was not one tenth as careful and helpful to my mother.

Love,

Martha

To: Betsy Drake

January 17 1983
72 Cadogan Square
London SW1

Dear Betsy; You are sensitive to your own feelings; you indulge yourself in feelings which are always and exhaustingly about your reactions to people and events. You haven't the faintest idea about other people's feelings – how you affect them. You invent complications, you analyse without reason or need very simple occurrences, and you analyse with very little true knowledge of people. It does not occur to you that this is an out-rageous burden on others; not friendship but emotional tyranny.

. . . Emotional tyranny, Betsy. The rule, your rule, is: tread softly, by God, or you will disturb my feelings. It's an enormous stupid tedious bore. You can have all the feelings you want, but the only practical way you can handle this is: cut out the people who distress your feelings and take the rest of the world at face value, the face the world presents, because everyone has enough real problems without getting bogged down in the problems you manufacture.

You have no idea why I won't travel with you again. Because, with all your feelings, you have never stopped to look at yourself: a woman who sulks when events don't work out as desired, who has innumerable absolute needs which are not life and death matters but your absolutes, who has to be kept happy or else by golly it's miseryville all round.

Friendship is fun and a loose mutual aid society. It isn't soul-picking (your soul, note) and you've made me as furious as I've ever been. I won't have this nonsense and this tyranny. I have never had it from anyone else and I'm not having it any more from you. Try growing up.

Love,

M

To: Marion Meade*

April 6 1983

[?]

Dear Miss Meade; Have a heart. I could talk to you about Dottie for hours, I knew her well, I knew her in Spain and afterwards she landed on my doorstep in Cuernavaca and knew Alan too, but I can't write a whole chapter for you, I haven't time to live let alone write letters. Not even those that grow moss in my TO ANSWER file.

Do not believe a word Hellman says on any subject. She is perhaps deranged and does not know truth from her self-serving fiction. She frightened Dottie in some way and Dottie, who had a talent for mistakes, named her as her lit executor which was the same as burying Dottie. Take therefore nothing from Hellman no matter what other sources you use.

Yours,

Martha Gellhorn

---

*Author of a biography of Dorothy Parker: *What Fresh Hell Is This?* (1987).

To: Gip Wells★

April 26 1983
Catscradle
Gwent

Dear Gip; Your handwriting reminds me of your papa's tiny neat script.

Now then: all women know that all men are silly and vain, but honestly this effort of Wells' takes the cookie. Consider: I was 26 or 27 when I met him; he was my father's age and not, you will agree, physically dazzling. I had a large constant supply of attractive young gents and have never been lured by men who were smaller than me. This must be due to having a tall father and tall brothers and also to being tall. I towered over Wells. He was fun unless he was bullying intellectually, and I was very fond of him but the rest is rubbish. He used me to annoy Moura [Budberg] and maybe came to believe his version. Moura, who became a lifelong friend, told me that Wells announced to her that 'I am not having her (me, that is) now.' Memorable phrase which caused me to rock with laughter. But that was the whole purpose for him, to enrage Moura or make her jealous or punish her, I don't know what.

He came self-invited to Connecticut and nearly drove me mad by talking for at least 10 hours a day when I was trying to write a book. Finally I sent secretly a telegram to Charlie Chaplin, who of course I didn't know, to tell him Wells was in Conn., and would probably like to come to Hollywood; and thus he was pried out of my borrowed country retreat.

Wells had some sort of vague crush on me and once suggested marriage. I bet he'd have been horrified if I hadn't gently and politely pointed out that it would look pretty funny, and wasn't a good idea. I may tell you I'd have swum the Pacific rather than get involved with him beyond friendship, and not too much of that. He did bully a lot, spent his time saying I must go to a polytechnic and study science, and I'd just started to enjoy life after Bryn Mawr.

I am a footnote in history, a passing reference in others' books and letters; and every time it's either factually wrong or pure apocrypha. I'm fairly sick of it and I do not wish to appear as a nut case, in this absurd version – and I wonder if you'll be doing Wells a favor by publishing this book – anyway, absolutely without me included. I won't stand for it. By the way, did Wells keep any of my letters? If so, you'd see they weren't love letters; loving

---

★In 1983, Gip, Wells's son, published his father's "Postscript" to his autobiography, written in the 1930s and never published. In it, H. G. Wells listed Martha as one of the "women I have kissed, solicited, embraced and lived with" – something Martha vehemently denied. Before publishing *On Loves and the Shadow-Lover*, Gip Wells showed Martha the manuscript. Martha wrote: "All the imaginary stuff connected with Hemingway is plenty to darken one's life. I don't need H.G. too."

letters maybe, but not more. How conceited he sounds. Imagine writing to Moura 'Either meet me in Southampton in token of entire submission . . .' I'm surprised she ever bothered to talk to him again. He also writes 'Moura took her presence very calmly . . .' Mine in London and not for three weeks either. Of course Moura did; she was not a fool, she knew perfectly well that Wells was playing games and there was nothing between us except friendship. It was funny because every night I was there I went out dancing almost all night with young gents of my acquaintance and every morning I was forced to get up at dawn because Wells insisted I have breakfast with him. Hardship.

Anyway there it is, Gip, and I wish I hadn't seen this because it makes me dislike Wells and I had fond memories and sad memories of him, at the end of his life during the war.

I imagine you are a nicer man than he was. I hope you're happy. Do you think he ever was?

Yours,

Martha

To: Betsy Drake

September 13 1983
Catscradle
Gwent

Betsy dear; As one who has been there before, please allow me to give you a warning about the sixties. It is a trying age. Neither fish nor fowl. My theory is that it is the second adolescence and lasts, like the first, according to the nature of the person. (Some people never get over their first adolescence.) The first adolescence is a transition to adulthood; the second to age. I wasted my sixties in destructive restlessness, trying to find a way to be comfortable in my life and my skin. Very stupid. I hope you'll avoid that.

I want to brag about my garden. I have many too many tomatoes, still have two huge cucumbers on the vine (12 on one plant), three dear little melons ripening and a fourth if it doesn't get too cold; parsley and dill; too much lettuce; just harvested (and froze) the last of the spinach; also carrots, courgettes still growing. The great wind that ended summer in one day blew down my spectacular corn crop which may or may not survive now staked up; but 4 ears per stalk is terrific, and I've been eating it and it's delicious. Strawberry bed will be even bigger next year and by then the asparagus will be ready. Isn't it colossal?

No I'm not going to send that awful Hemingway Wives* book, it's too

---

* *The Hemingway Women.* Those who loved him – the wives and others, by Bernice Kert.

fat for an envelope and I'm not up to buying paper, string and making a parcel. It's grisly anyway but I read about the other wives and I can't think why one of us, specially Mary, didn't shoot the bloody man. If you ever think you married the world's worst shit, you're wrong. I did. But, if Kert has her facts right and complete, E.H. must have slept with 4 women, his wives, and maybe a 5th during Pauline's reign. If any others, they must have been whores which he'd deny with his last breath. In fact, I think that's true and accounts for his being such a ghastly lover – wham bam thank you maam, or maybe just wham bam. No experience. Two virgin wives before me, and me not about to raise my voice in complaint because I imagined it was my fault, not ever getting anywhere. The great sex talker and writer must, in fact, have been terrified of women. Interesting. I hope never to hear about him again; this is the first and last book about him I'll ever read. I just want to be left out.

. . . Betsy, in case the world lasts you will one day reach my age. I want to tell you it's fine. This is not whistling in the dark. I have never been more contented and more aware of my enormous blessings. So do not waste your time squirming through the sixties; just live them as sanely as you can. They are not your last chance.

Love,
M

P.S. Sybille has been unwell ever since I've known her, 35 years I reckon. I feel sure she will outlive me. Please don't involve yourself or make a thing between us. Sybille does not need me; I served her wondrously well when she did need me and have no further obligation.

To: Valerie Forman

November 19 1983
[Catscradle
Gwent?]

Dearest Valerie; write to me any time, at any length, about anything you want to talk about, anything at all. It is important to have someone to write to.

I'm too busy to do 'real' writing. The kitchen of life in the country is constant and mostly amuses me. Now my garden and plants and vines are tucked in for the winter under a delicious thick coating of cow manure and straw. I like that sort of job. It looks a terrible mess and winter is nowhere near, except for the early dark. To my sorrow, I saw crocuses coming up, even what I think are daffodils; the earth hasn't got the message. But last year was normal until suddenly the place turned into Alaska.

. . . Yes, I watched the Marquez★ interview and was interested in how much he valued his work as a journalist. I feel the same way, and the lack of it does cut me off from life, real life of this moment. Bruce Chatwin, who wrote *On the Black Mountain*† came to call on me in London, for no reason; a young writer coming to see an old one. I was so surprised I didn't know how to treat him, was in a gloomy and sour mood, and regret it. I'm glad he's made such a success but am sure that telly cheapens writers and they should not do it. I refused to go on a TV program with him and Paddy Leigh Fermor, about travel books, because the interviewer named Frank Delaney† is a star-studded ass, phoney, pretentious, awful; and besides I don't think TV is a proper place for a writer. However, I am pre-TV Age, and was lucky to be a writer when writers were not supposed to sell their books by selling their personalities.

I don't feel like London. I am loving my life as a Welsh hermit.

Love,
Martha

To: James Fox

July 24 1984
Catscradle
Chepstow
Gwent

Dear James F; I could not put it down.‡ My plan was to nip in and out, to see how you wrote. Well, you write <u>felicitously</u>. I do not see how the style or tone could be bettered. But what dazzles me is your organization of the material. That mass of stuff, coherently ordered, and making a suspense. Bravo. It is spell-binding, despite the people involved.

I agree with Connolly's list headed: 'What a Set' and beginning, 'Shit E.' I mean people like that give money a bad name. As for titles, they make one wonder about the IQ level in the higher reaches.

The photos of Diana [Broughton] and Erroll, both young, show that they were meant for each other and really deserved each other; natural justice would have been served by their marriage. Their faces are to me very similar in looks of a peculiarly unattractive kind, suitable for advertisements of shampoo, sports cars etc. Very vulgar kind of looks. Two matched predators.

★Gabriel Garcia Marquez (1928–), author of *One Hundred Years of Solitude* (1967) and winner of the Nobel Prize.
†The title is *On the Black Hill*.
‡Frank Delaney (1942–), novelist, historian, and biographer.
§*White Mischief*, about the murder of Lord Erroll in Kenya, had been published in the U.K. in 1982.

Don't you think Diana stuck with Broughton after the trial because she had absolutely nowhere else to go? Who was going to pay the bills? Do you think the women who made a career of upwardly mobile marrying are a thing of the past; the career gold diggers? I wonder. You don't hear much of that kind of thing now but maybe there is a whole unknown set of girls moving upwardly between pop stars.

Also didn't you think it funny when Diana told you she never wore jewelry in the daytime considering what she had on? I wish I understood the passion for jewelry – do you think it is a very deep and spooky kind of self love: this glorious delectable me must be suitably adorned. Dunno. Cause for rumination.

I called Diana Cooper who needs cheering, to tell her of this book, so obviously her cuppa. She had read it; 'I adored it' she said, and the only cheerful note in our constant telephone chats was induced by the book and remembering 'little Idina', who was attractive not beautiful at all, 'but well known to be successful in flirtations. She was thought fast – well, indeed she was.' What a bunch of twits they all were.

. . . With your talent, you could write biography if you wanted to. Do you care about any angle of the human condition? Are you concerned or committed, as they say in the new dead language? Is there anything you believe for or against with passion? I am thinking about this matter of obsession, the need for, and whence obsession comes. I take it back, suggesting Harry and Caresse Crosby★ – really no, you ought to find something better – you could do them as an article for Vanity Fair or somebody who gives some space and some pay. But for a book, I feel you ought not to use that talent only on twits.

Yours,

Martha G.

To: James Fox

February 26 1986
Nyali
Mombasa
Kenya

My favorite James in all the world; What a treat to get your Valentine letter. And I'd written to you a day earlier which is ESP if ever there was. I've had

---

★Harry (1898–1929), poet, and Caresse (1891–1970), inventor of the modern brassiere, who together founded *Editions Narcisse*, which published James Joyce and Ezra Pound in the 1920s, were the models for Dick and Nicole Diver in Scott Fitzgerald's *Tender Is the Night*.

one letter from London since I left, from my 93 year old friend, telling me of the Ice Age but reporting my cats were all right. So it was too lovely that you had not forgot me.

I think those movie people are nuts and they better pray that Lady D. gets a second stroke because I doubt she will take kindly to a vulgar and lying scene, Broughton blowing out his brains at her feet.* The idiots. The truth is much more moving; the hotel room in frozen England. Why do they have such bad taste as well as a lack of understanding that the nearer you stay to truth, the greater the effect. I see your point about lying low, though I wish you were here with me on the boiling hot coast.

I want to tell you the story of my life because it's so stupid. For 6½ weeks I've been spoiling my pleasure in this perfect place and weather, obsessedly trying to write the new conclusion to *The Face of War*. It took me 4 months and a near nervous breakdown to write the 1986 introduction; some 240 pages to end up with 5 printed pages, which I have no great opinion of. So here I was doing the same thing; poisoned on nicotine, stomach shot, finally managing to get an abscessed gum and an earache and profound depression; and every version was worse than the last. Finally I tried writing by hand on the grounds that slow movement might match my slow brain. Finally on Feb 24, I woke up and said to myself: Fuck it. This is madness. I cannot write the stuff so I won't. And reminded myself that if you're a survivor, the thing to do is survive. Which I was definitely not doing. So now I mean to spend two weeks enjoying myself and working hard on leg muscles. I note an alarming general tendency to help me around, the hand on the elbow or stretched out, including strangers – clear sign that I move like the decrepit on my jello legs. This has to stop too. And when I feel old and ugly (another symptom of failure), I also know there's a nasty lurking suspicion of self pity.

So, if only you were here now – and I may say that's a unique invitation as I don't want anyone else, it would be an effort. But not you, who always make me laugh and whose low mumbling nearly inarticulate voice unfailingly gives me pleasure, as does your company. It's bliss, now that I've packed in the fucking work and the sickening knowledge of how shabbily and evilly the world is run. There's a fine silent competent man servant to do all the dirty work, and that alone is heaven. I am sick of household chores, normal life in Britain. And swimming under the stars in the pool. And now at last I'll get down to the 5 mile walk on the beach. The N.E. monsoon is dying, the start of the dead season between monsoons, but I'm not one to complain of heat. Life without underwear being my idea of the good life.

---

*In the film of *White Mischief*, starring Greta Scacchi and Charles Dance, events had been somewhat rearranged.

Oh yes, we will always be friends, always. We might prick our thumbs
and swear a blood oath. I love you dearly.

Martha

To: James Fox

May 18 1986
[Catscradle
Gwent]

Dearest James; I should not have been depressed on you. It is wrong for
olders to be depressed on youngers, it lowers morale, it spreads
despondency and alarm. Friday was a suicide day, feeling both hideous and
betrayed. Then yesterday I painted myself like *la folle de Chaillot* and dressed
in dirty clothes, the only kind I have here, and set out for Bristol Parkway
station and Oxford. After the Severn Bridge, I got an attack of near fatal
heartburn, due to narrowly missing a thunderous huge lorry, speeding up
on my right; I had not noticed it in the prevailing sheets of rain and was
swerving into its lane. I also feared I would never find the station since
Bristol affects my brain: I only have to go near it or in it to be helplessly
lost. But all obstacles were gallantly overcome and, rain damp, I got there
and bought my ticket and settled down to read and discovered I had left my
specs in Wales. This horrified me, as a sign of losing marbles, and I nearly
gave it all up but instead went on, found that British Rail had given me false
gloomy information and in fact it is only 1¼ hours from Bristol Parkway to
Oxford; I might as well go every day.

Rain in Oxford too. The undergraduates look pale grey and soiled. I was
thinking of the way we talk about the grubby glum appearance of people
and clothing in Communist countries but honest to God, there are few
sadder sights than British folk, forever under these grey skies.

The party was glorious.* I think it may be the second I've been to in 5
years and I had little hope. Instead everyone got slowly and gently drunk
on red wine and I had those frustratingly too short moments with a few
people and a bit too long with others and basked in a bubble bath of flattery
to which I am not accustomed – flattery due to drunkenness and my rarity
value; it would not happen if I was always on hand.

I realised how drunk I was when this a.m. I saw how I had parked my
car here. . . . Coming back last evening, still raining, I began to think of
Spain. Why not live there? 4 best months in London, the rest of the time
somewhere inland between Malaga and Almeria. I might have a swimming
pool, my one idea of luxe. Would the cats adjust? I like Spaniards and the

*Party given by *Granta*, the quarterly magazine edited by Bill Buford.

language and now they have a government that's okay, possible to live there.

I may come down to London this week, being bored here and just go to movies, an orgy of same.

Love,

Martha

To: Robert Presnell

May 23 1986
[Catscradle
Gwent]

My dearest P: I've just finished writing the tedium letters: 1) to a man who wants to know about Otto Katz of Spanish War days, a devoted communist, executed for treason after the Czech Trials. (Stalinist Communism was cannibal.) 2) A man who wants to know about Lillian Hellman. I think I get so many letters of this nature because I am practically the only living survivor. A very odd position. It is a pity that I never had any memory and am both bored and incompetent, I cannot help these dullish sounding seekers after historical truth.

May 25; time marches on . . . I have been watching on TV the reports of the final day of the Sport Aid week,★ Running against Time, all over the world. It has thrilled me. Bob Geldof is my hero and I specially enjoy admiring him so much because he's a new type of hero. First, a BBC reporter and camera man brought back news of the Ethiopian famine. Nobody paid much attention. How can we? After all, think what we see all the time. I've barely got over the skulls and bones of Cambodia, the rule of Pot Pol. But young Mr. Geldof, whose hair has never been washed, was horrified. . . . I love that young man. He speaks with a working class Irish accent and this is what he says: 'I don't think this kind of thing ought to be left to a pop musician, why aren't the politicians doing anything?' Mrs. Thatcher received him with her usual coo-ing condescending voice (I really am a snob, I cannot bear that counter jumper woman) and said of course it was all terrible but the government could do nothing and Bob Geldof said, simply, on camera to her, 'Why not?' As a result, he has had no honours here though they make a smarmy TV anchor man a knight. Today he spoke to some 200,000 people in Hyde Park, waiting to run and his last words were, 'You *can* effect the world you live in.' Oh P. Good for

★After the Live Aid concerts of July 1985 to raise money for the relief of Ethiopian famine, the pop singer Bob Geldof had launched Sport Aid, getting thirty million people in 132 countries running to raise money for the starving in Africa.

him and good for all the people who admire and follow him . . . the only trouble is: all the people who rule us are hopeless and pay no attention to us and we cannot find any good ones to vote for.

I am at some very low ebb and I'm not sure why. Not physical. Not professional because I'm too old to care, though it will be embarrassing if none of the stuff I've recently written – a piece about the Seychelles and 3 little short stories – finds a buyer. I don't know what it is. Joyless. My cottage is charming. I have no money problems. I have of course the usual inevitable boringness of managing my life, the Do-it-Yourself job which is tiresome, repetitive and time-spoiling. But who hasn't? So what is it?

The state of the world has reached such a point of idiocy and folly that I can't keep my mind on it. Here I believe Mrs. Thatcher will not return to us, but what she leaves behind is ruin; I think this country is dying, I think it will be on a par with Portugal.

Love,
M

P.S. I saw Lenny; he was here for a week called the Bernstein Festival. I wrote him a letter which will end our long relationship. I told him he was always an entertainment but not company, not companionship, because he never listened, there was no dialogue.

To: James Fox

July 3 1986
Lonjaron
[Spain]

Dearest James; I am quite drunk on two beers with dinner. Can you beat it? You are much on my mind. I fear I squashed you when I should have given you encouragement and praise which we all need. I was so busy with the mechanics of your piece that I forgot to tell you how strange and interesting it was. In fact, I know nothing of you. An interest in Mali singers is truly weird to me, makes you a phenomenon. What do I really know of you? Nothing. Yet you matter to me. I wish above all not to have depressed you for you seem to be desperately prone to depression. Yet that too may be error.

This was the year when everyone died. Diana [Cooper] of course though I was glad for her. For me, a hole in my life. My chosen and protected status is as outsider. I have never seen any place or group I wanted to join: not their taboos, rules, games, ambitions. I am an onlooker. Whereas Diana lived in a set and needed to be snuggled in a mass of people who spoke the same jargon. Our relation was odd but lasting. She kept saying, these last awful years in bed, 'You are the only person I like to see.' Within her permanent practise of flattery, there was some truth in it: I reminded her of a long past, I made her laugh. She is all but one the end of my old Brit world where I flitted in and out, welcomed as an outsider. Or accepted as an outsider. It's the people who really want to get in and belong, who nudge for a place, that annoy the insiders.

And a man who was my needed pen pal for 40 years died the next day in California.* And a few months before a woman, ten years younger than I, died of cancer in Washington; she also was both a pen pal and pal; a diplomat's widow (I was closer to him in some ways), she was either meringue inside or kept her own counsel, but for nearly 50 years, by mail and in company, we had reduced each other to helpless giggles; nobody was more whipped cream fun to be with.

What with the killing British spring and the deaths, I had reached a state where my spirit felt like dark grey flannel. Now I am alive again. Ponce de Léon† was a nut case: the fountain of youth is not a little spurt of water, but travel. I forget everything I know; otherwise I would have left much sooner, before I became suicidal. I have only to go to a different country, sky, language, scenery, to feel it is worth living; since I can go on looking.

I never heard of anyone ever going to Motril, a town on the coast east of Malaga. The map showed a place named Lonjaron, green for altitude, on the winding mountain road to Granada behind Motril. The Green Michelin, which John Hatt advised me to buy (I would not have thought of it) said Lonjaron (pop: nothing much) was a spa in a beautiful setting. Tourists do not go to spas. I got here the first day and it is heaven. For 6 days I did not leave this room except to eat and buy fruit. In my whole life I have never had enough cherries: 50 p. for a kilo. I reworked my Cuba piece which is now a year late. Very hard work.

Now I am free and simply rejoicing. I have a room that is aesthetically pleasing (unheard of), two huge windows and balconies and bath for $5.80 a day. The view is dazzling; counterpoint of mountains blue in the heat haze, with a ruined brown Arab castle on a peak in the foreground. A giant swimming pool in the hotel garden. The garden is neglected with waterfalls of geraniums and trees taller than the 5 story hotel. I recognize only palms and Mediterranean pines. The pool is surrounded by more trees and avalanches of purple bougainvillea. The water is from the hotel spring, feels like silk and no chlorine; it is not yet fully filled. That went on as I worked on Cuba. The Spanish disappear from 2 to 4 p.m. so I have the pool to

---

*Robert Presnell.
†Juan Ponce de Léon (1460?–1521) conquered Puerto Rico, discovered Florida, and started a settlement there.

myself when I want it, and plod up and down, gasping on a crawl, resting on a breast stroke. No muscles, less wind.

Off the main street little alleys, hardly wide enough for a car, cobbled, wind down to a retaining wall that keeps the town from slipping off the mountain side. The houses are white and adobe, I'd think, somehow rounded, no hard edges, and spill flowers and suddenly have grape arbors over spare space on second floors. Of course I at once want to live here but have the sense to see it is a no-no; would be icy in winter in these mountains and is really too far from anywhere.

. . . Right now the thought of either Wales or London makes me feel sick. The difference is waking each day to sun. The soft warm nights. Few clothes. What on earth am I doing in Britain? But on the other hand, what exactly am I doing anywhere? Travelling is the best answer. *Voyageur sur la terre*. No answers needed. Just look at the Creation.

Darling James, I hope you are happy.

Much love,

Martha

To: Ruth and Sol Rabb

December 15 1986
[Catscradle
Gwent?]

Honeybunnies:

. . . My news is spectacular. I thought 1986 was the worst year I could remember, so bleak, so sad that I was quite ready to think there had been enough years and I did not wish to go on ploughing through more of them. Then there was the US week, which I mainly dreaded. And it turned out to be a triumph, solid bliss. I went because my beau (we will soon be celebrating our illegal silver anniversary) insisted; and we played about like ancient kittens, because he finally had <u>time</u>. I'd given up on visits because it was nervously like a doctor's appointment, fixed hours, haste, tension. He makes me laugh, which to me is like pearls and rubies . . . Then, for years (maybe ten) I have felt myself to be a living dead, as a writer: nobody wants me, my stuff sells – the little there is – as if printing it was a favour. I talked to Bill Buford (who runs *Granta*) about this in London: saying that *The Face of War*, hideously published here – a shameful job – wasn't even wanted in the US. He said Nonsense and made one telephone call: a young top publisher called for drinks my first day in NY and the book was sold that night: plus the book I shall do at Nyali, a collection of my peacetime articles. Not only that (he's Atlantic Monthly Press, very classy) but Scribner's wanted me too and offered $10,000 more – and others came to see me. It turns out I am a smash hit with these young and the trouble has been the wrong agent, a charming man, who knows nothing of the publishing world; he's a theatrical agent, not that he ever sold any story to TV. Then returned, as I went, on Concorde (courtesy of my beau) after a week; exactly the right amount of time, and have been in a mood of cheerfulness ever since. Also wildly busy because I must get my stuff in order so I can work on it at Nyali.

. . . Merry Xmas if you can stand the event: I'm lucky to have it with cats and whiskey.

Love as always
Alfie

To: Bernard Perlin

January 2 1987
[Catscradle
Gwent?]

Dearest B; You are very much on my mind.* I think you are ruining yourself and your life, and no one can help you except yourself. And you seem incapable. You are locked into the tunnel vision that brings on nervous or mental collapse. Bud is the <u>only</u> wasted life; yours is the only inconsolable grief. You really cannot think beyond this: the world is narrowed to two people, one dead, one mourning. If you don't soon start to remember how many lives have been wasted, how many others have mourned and learned to live with a hole in their lives, then you'll be lost: your own life aimless, useless. You are being egocentric in the true meaning of the word: nothing is real outside your own disaster. I implore you to look outside yourself to a world full of suffering, and see what you can do for someone else. Think how you could use your talent to help others – I think of painting lessons – fun in children's hospitals, or even prisons – volunteer helping. Anything that makes you aware that you are not permitted to be so self-absorbed. This does not mean you will stop grieving; why should you? But does mean that you will remember you have obligations, outside yourself, as we all do; because we are the fortunate few who are able to give.

I think you were physically, as well as mentally and emotionally, worn out by the years of caring for Bud. Maybe above all you need a change of scene, something to look at that is new and without shared memories. I don't know what you need, but I do know that if you go on much longer like this, you'll become a psychiatric case, not yourself. Certainly you need courage, and perhaps you used up your supply in the months of nursing;

---

*Bernard Perlin's partner, Bud, had just died after a long illness.

but courage is a quality that renews itself after every stunning blow.

This isn't a kind letter but I don't think you need kindness; I think you need a sharp warning. And, as usual thumping in where angels would take care not to tread, I am giving it.

Bernard, leap four feet outside yourself and take a look.

Love always,

M

To: John Hatt

July 27 1987
[Catscradle
Gwent]

Dearest John; Forgive me. It isn't that I have mean ungrateful manners; it is that my mind is wobbling on the edge of crash or meltdown.* By the end of my working day I am fit only for TV or thrillers. Thank you for your invaluable lit crit. I've naturally re-written that Forties bit, and am now starting the Sixties. I hate every sentence I write with a deep sullen hatred. This is much increased by reading the articles themselves which I find to my amazement really good and written with natural free-flowing ease and life. Nor were they any great shakes to write; I mean no blood pouring from fingers. In fact, I don't remember any trouble as soon as I figured out what I wanted to say, the shape, how to manage the material. The writing was not a hurdle. Once, I was a natural writer. Now I am enslaved to the Thesaurus, the dictionary and terrible pauses when I gaze out the window and wonder how to say the very simplest statement. Also I find here and there the nasty weaseling face of clichés peeping in. After this book, I shall pack it in.

May come to London next week; 7 months of purdah may be too much.

Have you followed Irangate† in the snippets we get? America's mock heroes; the brave liars.

Love,

Martha

---

*Martha was working on a new series of introductions for *The View from the Ground*, her collection of peacetime articles.

†U.S. political scandal involving senior members of the Reagan administration in which it was revealed that the U.S. government had secretly sold weapons to Iran in 1985, trading them for hostages held in Lebanon by pro-Iranian militias, and used the profits to supply right-wing Contra guerrillas in Nicaragua with arms.

To: Victoria Glendinning

September 22 1987
Catscradle
Gwent

Dear Victoria; I read your 'Rebecca West'* in three goes in 3 days, and it is brilliant. I had never read anything of yours because I was not interested in those women. And I didn't know you had written about Rebecca, being as usual out of touch. What you do is to me the most impossible: seamlessly weaving the story but every word of it based on learned proven fact. Cleanly and elegantly written.

What an awful story it is too. I asked Rebecca why she had Anthony — the obvious thing, at aged 20, wasn't it, or thereabouts being to have Wells pay for a Swiss abortion. She said she was young and healthy and it seemed the reasonable and right thing. It was, of course, not. It seems to me that she had a constant instinct towards self destruction. Does one inherit these things? Your book has made me think about family, inheritance of genes, beginnings, which normally I never do: realising that I got everything in the world, the best of everything, on a plate; and took it for granted.

Neurotic is almost too mild a word for Rebecca, as one reads your book. Nearly mad, it seems to me. I knew so many of the people you write about and sometime I must tell you about me and Wells. The old fool asked me to marry him in 1935 when he was older than God and I was just 27. I've never told anyone; it seemed so ludicrous. I thought he was a bore too.

Doing arithmetic, I see that Rebecca had no sex life from the age of 43, apart from 2 walkouts. Well, better than that, but not of long duration. Did Henry stop because he had already started screwing around and the double job bothered him? Evidently she cannot have known about that. You use the word 'philandering,' do you mean only flirting, coy kisses etc. But of course, for Rebecca it must have been deeply unnerving to be unwanted or unused; since she cared so much about being or feeling attractive to men. And you know, the clothes mania is always a sign of someone insecure and usually (in an intelligent woman) someone who doesn't know about clothes. Like Freya Stark and hats. Perhaps the sexual unuse gave her the fierce driving energy to use for her mind. But her judgement seems weird to me; how <u>could</u> she have touched the witchhunting of the 50's even with an 80 foot pole? I'm glad I didn't know her then.

I love the way she wrote but I see her making that tedious usual trajectory of people, from left to right, that I find so disappointing (Sybille Bedford has done it.) And a passion for order, if that's what made Rebecca move rightwards, is a dangerous thing because the order of one's day is

---

*Victoria Glendinning's biography, *Rebecca West: A Life,* had just been published.

always suspect. I'm glad she did see that the New Deal in the U.S. was extraordinary: the only good period there in my lifetime.

We must have a long dinner and talk about all this. I live in the comfy notion that I don't know anyone but reading your book I see I've known the lot but I always lacked Rebecca's tendency to be dazzled. Did you like her gossiping? She must have found me sadly lacking; I'm no good at it and I find a great difference between malice and hate; the latter being respectable.

Many congratulations. This book has convinced me, if I needed it, that I cannot afford to die; I would so hate to be exposed in all my follies and failings and I know damn well it will happen when I am six feet under . . .

Your newfound friend

Martha

To: Victoria Glendinning

September 30 1987
Catscradle
Gwent

Dear Victoria; It is 8:10 p.m. and I have either done everything to close this dwelling for two months or I haven't, in all cases worn out. Time to chat. The best reason for letters; how I hate the telephone. And I've barely written a letter since January so now writing a letter is too lovely, like a Mars bar.

Further thoughts: *flâner* is the best French verb. It is a need for occupation, done sitting down or moving. I used to worry desperately about wasting time because I saw myself as basically lazy (which I am) and also saw my time wasting as proof of a second rate brain (which I also have.) Perhaps I also felt it was sinful because such a pleasure. I now think it is as necessary as solitude; that's how the compost heap grows in the mind. Anyway I intend to spend the rest of my life wasting time.

You astound me: your never having been alone. But of course the writing hours are alone, maybe that was enough. My mama remarked in passing, when I was about 40, that people should be careful of what they are when young because they only become more so when old. I said bitterly that she might have told me before; but I know she's right. From a non-gregarious child into a woman who has to be alone most of the time. My problem always used to be that I heard everything people said and most of it drove me up the wall. A friend known in London grandees' circles as being a superb conversationalist never listened at all and also rarely spoke; she listened with intent brown eyes, thinking all the while about such matters as wallpaper and clothes and her next dinner party and bills and such like. Surely to waste time properly one must do it alone?

The passion for order: I've always been exceedingly tidy and I know why. The disorder in my mind is such that if there is also physical disorder around me, I go off my nut. Considering the amount of time I've spent at wars, which are very disorderly, this also is weird. I cannot keep track of papers or valuable possessions perhaps because I hate both, but just now, as a celebration of finishing this work, I have cleaned this desk: 4 wastebaskets thrown out, and a sense of marvelous lightness and order. It is mixing up that with the *res publica* which makes reactionaries, I think. Now, as to Rebecca, the important point is: she was a wonderful writer. I feel (this is not kind to your chosen work) that writers are diminished by having their lives known: they should only be known by what they write. . . . And I have nothing important I want to say except as chat with chums if the mood suits. This last book I've been working on, 50 years of peacetime articles with comments on each decade, plus my war reporting, plus my fiction, is all I have to say of any importance. My statement, as it were; not that I feel the world will shift on its axis. . . .

Now that Gip Wells. He showed me what Wells had written and it seems Wells saved my letters. I know my love letters all right. I also told Gip that now his papa had destroyed himself in my memory by claiming me as a love affair. Why the hell would I sleep with a little old man when I could have any number of tall beautiful young men? My letters, sent to me by Gip, are good, amusing – I wrote letters instead of seeing people, like now; and specially when I was married because I was loneliest then. Gip had to admit that they were not love letters. I found it disgusting that Wells needed to add my scalp, and refused to play. Why should I, never having been anyone's 'lover-shadow' – the conceit of that idea makes me quite sick. Gip was getting money from some US university and Wells, to me, became a cheap nasty man by wanting to put all this in print. Before, I thought he was mostly a bore, but a serious man; and I could write to him about my endless preoccupations with the history of our time. Now I find that, since almost everyone is dead, I am hard up for anyone to whom to write when the news suffocates me with anger or grief or both.

Time for the 9 p.m. news. Don't worry, you're not going to be inundated with letters. It's just that everything is so tidy and done that I have the luxury of time, talking time. I am already homesick for my cats.

I'll be in London until Oct 7, then again from Oct 21 to Nov 19, this is my period (London) for rejoining the human race. You make a call, I'm in the directory, and come and smoke and drink any time. I'll really have time now.

Your verbose new friend,
Martha

To: Nicholas Shakespeare

November 17 1987
72 Cadogan Square
London SW1

Sweet Shakespeare; That was a lovely thing to do and a huge effort and I am deeply impressed by the way you whipped up and served a delicious and abundant meal. It would have taken me a week to organize and a nervous breakdown as well. I think men are improving enormously and am cross that I got the incompetent male chauvinist pig generation (not that we or they knew their name). Young females nowadays cannot compare and thus do not realise that they never had it so good.

It was a lovely party and I thank you.

Now I know why Vargas Llosa★ was not what I expected, took me all night and this a.m. to figure it out. I expected someone violent; signs of violence. Vague? That comes from his book, which I repeat is as vast and fierce and moving and good as Dostoevsky. I bet when you met Dostoevsky, you started running for the door; he must have given off a strong odour of madness if he wasn't cadging money. But V.L. is/seems a perfectly controlled well mannered civilized man and could easily be mistaken for almost anything except a writer. On the other hand, what are writers like? I know very few, maybe none.

I am now going out to buy garlic. I feel perfectly awful as I have now for a month and a half. The medical profession has done its best, in vain: garlic next.

Come and have a booze up and a fried egg when I get back from the snowbound U.S.

Yours,
Martha

To: Bill Buford

December 14 1987
[Catscradle
Gwent]

Dearest William: Just got a bound copy of *View From the Ground*. Apparently you are being sent five. <u>Don't</u> use them for sales. They are full of bad typos including actual word changes. I made a lot of important corrections on my new stuff. Also the book is not being printed in that

---

★Peruvian novelist, playwright, and essayist (1936–).

gimmicky way; copy starting in a narrow annoying single column – I'm talking about title pages of all articles.

. . . So funny, you and the young lady at *Village Voice* and the general tone is: the kids have discovered me, while previously I languished unknown in the literary shadows. But after all my books have always been reviewed and the size of reviews only changed as the size of all reviews changed – I doubt if I will have a larger public now than I've always had. I took myself out in hopelessness during 9 years of the Vietnam war, but there've been two books since and the good mags in the US seem few and far between. I'm beginning to feel condescended to by this why-hasn't-anyone-noticed-her-before stuff.

It's cold enough here to freeze your balls off; (female equivalent tits, do you think?) The widely advertised and incredibly costly electric central heating, the only kind I could have, keeps my residence at 60F, nice for Eskimos. I feel like a tired old fart, which I believe is a bisexual term.

Love,
Martha

To: Betsy Drake

Xmas Day 1987
[Catscradle
Wales]

Betsy honey;

. . . Your supposition about me/men/competing for/is rubbish – but I don't mind. I never competed, never set out to get any man, wouldn't know how; I was approached, to put it mildly, and agreed or not. I never looked at a man and said: that's for me. Also I had one lifelong rule, though being a specialist in married men. I never knew the wives, I was never a friend of the wives; the same applied to any woman who was a friend – her man was hers. Marian Shaw paid me the strange compliment of saying I was the only woman she wasn't jealous of – though Irwin, not Marian, was my friend; but I did know her, had accepted her hospitality etc. She didn't know that he had ever made a pass, which he did once, but I laughed him out of it, easily. Very clear on that rule of behavior. I met Mrs. R. once, same night I met L. in Africa; never spoke to her, never saw her again; she would never have been a friend in any case, not my bag. And so it goes. E.H. enjoyed blaming Pauline for 'taking' him from Hadley. Balls. He wanted to go; he was sick and tired of being so poor; he wanted a change – a man who had only slept with one woman, wanting a change of body and circumstances. To me, what was ugly was Pauline being an intimate friend of Hadley; that would not have been within my rules of engagement.

As soon as Pauline knew she was crazy about E.H. she should honorably have left the menage and declared herself first to Hadley. I disapprove of the behavior of both of them but E.H. putting all the blame on Pauline is typical E.H. Nasty.

One thing you always forget about me: I grew up with 3 brothers, I was treated like a second class male, by them, I got used to being one of the boys very early. Mainly I like the society of men because I'm interested in what they do; women's work – with exceptions – isn't my bag. I'm charmed by Victoria Glendinning for instance, a new female chum, because of her brain. Women are much more reliable than men; but usually not as funny. I've decided that what's wrong with me is (among a raft of other wrongnesses): I really want company for amusement value most of all. I outgrew loneliness long ago and never had it as a big problem, perhaps due to never having been accompanied by a man – my certain guard against loneliness, the real kind, was my mother. God knows E.H. and Tom, both, would teach any woman not to give in to loneliness; they were positively professors in how to be frozen cold lonely, and survive it.

Now, off to my dreary walk.

Love, you know, my kind, Cynara,

M

In 1988 Martha was eighty. Though absolutely determined to remain fit and active, forcing herself to exercise and dieting to keep her weight what it had been in her twenties, she was suffering from increasing ill health. A spot on her nose turned out to be cancerous and she received painful treatment for it. She had aches in her back and neck, controlled by walking and by swimming up and down every day in the pool she had built at Catscradle. She seldom complained. This code of courage, by which she had lived her entire life, kept her from being overwhelmed by a scene of violence that happened to her in Nyali, at the house belonging to her friends Ruth and Sol Rabb, in the spring of 1988.

She had also been much saddened by the deaths of Moishe Pearlman, Robert Presnell, and Diana Cooper. "I feel like a survivor on a raft," she wrote to Sandy Matthews. "I don't like it, like a lone antique monument, a small human Stonehenge."

Politics continued to obsess her, the way that they shaped the human condition "horribly, inexorably," and she felt pessimistic about the future, fearing, like Santayana, that the species, unable to learn from history, was doomed to keep making the same mistakes. "I feel madness in the air like a smell," she told Sandy Matthews. "Nothing strikes me as rational anywhere." Even at eighty, she continued to feel it her duty to "keep an eye on justice and injustice." Heroes – Gorbachev, Mandela – and villains – Kissinger, Reagan, Mrs. Thatcher – occupied her thoughts.

To: Bill Buford

> January 31 1988
> Nyali
> Kenya

Dearest William; You are behaving exactly like all the publishers in my life. They promise a girl the sun and the moon, feed her caviar and champagne, send American Beauty roses, until she signs on the dotted line. After which they are out to lunch. Anyway I don't even want to think about such matters now.

You forgot to enclose the letter that was going to terrify Doubleday. But here is a point: the letters to E.H. which appear in the fatal Bernice Kert book are copyrighted in my name. I do not know and cannot find out exactly how many words anyone may use of copyrighted material, without permission of the copyright owner. You might find out. I will of course not only not give permission but demand hefty compensation if my copyright is violated. That Kert conned me; she had to show me her mss. before publication but there were no letters quoted in what she showed me. She actually found the letters in the Kennedy Library and saw them before I did. Well, it's done now but will never be done again; all destroyed; no pickings for vultures.

I am so happy it is hardly decent. Last night, lying on the terrace in moonlight, drinking, I thought maybe I was going to die soon, this being a state of grace surely not meant for normal people or normal life. I'm also wonderfully well, which is probably why I'm so happy. I've got a workable back again and can walk and do, 5 miles a day on this beauty beach. And I do not lift my finger, everything is silently done for me including putting out the ice for my evening booze. Which booze, without effort, has cut itself in half; and cigarettes less than half; not by will but by not wanting.

I hope you are happy and I think you pretty well always are, operating at the speed of sound, over-extended to put it mildly, but enjoying the fierce exercise of it all. I wish you well.

> Love,
> Martha

To: Ruth and Sol Rabb

> March 7 1988
> Nyali
> Mombasa

Darlings: Listen carefully; this is important. My great happiness here, our heavenly holiday together, the loveliness of the place must not – in any way for a single minute – be smeared and spoiled by the Ugly Event on the stairs. Women have been raped all over the world since time began. Last year I remember reading about two old sisters, much older than I am, and two little girls, aged eight and nine, being raped <u>and</u> murdered. Simply because I was involved does not make this case special. In fact I got off lightly. I was afraid twice, but I have been frightened by high explosive far more often than that. Fear is only damaging if you let it change your attitudes and actions, which certainly I shall not.

Dr. Mohammed gave me a tetanus shot today (as well as yesterday antibiotics to take 4 times a day preventively). My array of scrapings and cuts, drenched in a new supply of iodine, will dry and heal in a few days. I'd bought a nasty little dark blue bikini at Deacons, for coolness. I hope it doesn't make Alex sick to his stomach; it makes me sick because of my stomach. But it turns out to be handy since it exposes the whole collection of superficial injuries, easy to see, and cover with iodine and expose to the air. Tomorrow I'll learn if there's any tasty bit like clap; and in 2–3 weeks (apparently can't be done sooner) a blood test in London. Dr. Mohammed, hotel doctor, is a nice man but cruelly ham-handed. Black comedy (always present), he has caused me more pain than anything else, by his examination last night and his swab taking today; so bad that I'm pessimistically swallowing pain killers to recover from Dr. Mohammed.

So that is that.

The notion (spoken by Ruth on the telephone) that you are 'somehow responsible' is certifiably insane and I order you to shred the nonsense and pop it up your jumpers. Is that clear?

I mean to try to finish the present chapter on Mrs. Farnham. I want to spend every minute of these few remaining days concentrated on the sun and heat, the moon and stars, the view, the ease and pleasure of life. You cannot imagine how I dread going back to London: the weather, wearing clothes and coping. Maybe coping is worst. The cottage industry of my life has grown too tiring for me; paper work alone drives me up the wall, not to mention manual labour. And I know I cannot survive 5 more years of that climate but my heart sinks at the prospect of house hunting in Spain.

I've only one thriller left; the rest are serious books and goddamit it's another that I've read before and so good that I remember it; but I'm reading it anyway. Mind resting. The moon is very beautiful and I mean to do some earnest drinking, then swim; then eat, not hungry, then read; and the days rush past, to my sorrow and real life looms ahead.

Love always
Martha

To: Bill Buford

April 21 1988
[72 Cadogan Square
London SW1]

Dearest William; I've decided to try to do this letter while drinking. Might be easier.

What horrifies and angers me is that you don't know what you did wrong. You claim you simply misunderstood words; while I claim the words were never said. But you didn't need words to understand or misunderstand me. You know how I feel about biography. You know that I wrote, with doubt and great difficulty, those autobiographical comments to follow each decade, explaining the preceding articles. You must, knowing this, knowing me, have realised I would NEVER in the world have let you print my personal comment on the Thirties. You had talked to me about the Hopkins piece for a probable issue of *Granta* about Home.★ Okay, I said. The Hopkins piece was about home and obviously had to be cut; though I would have insisted on cutting it myself, and better. But to take, out of context, and cut and use the autobiographical comment that seemed to be me, writing personal drool for *Granta* (not even noting in the back that this was an excerpt from a book) is intolerable, Bill. Intolerable. I feel myself and my book to be damaged. I feel you simply misused me for your purposes. And all the warm statements about taking my work seriously sound to me like a huckster.

Yes, you make things happen. What if you make bad things happen? What if you're in such a hurry and perhaps so dazzled (as you might well be) by your success that you cut corners, that you aren't absolutely straight? What if, for reasons of surprise, shock, whatever, you lose your grip on taste. (I do not forget your tasteless advert of my pirated book, nor do I forget the advert in the travel issue; Martha Gellhorn was stoned in Haiti – not exactly all that piece was about.)

The excuse of haste and last minute decisions for *Granta* won't wash; it just means you are badly organized and trying to be too many men. It is a quarterly. If you cannot manage on that time scale not to offend or infuriate your writers, then you are running a childish operation, or a naughty boy operation. I don't buy it. I don't excuse it either.

. . . What you have done, by making me feel cheapened and a fool, is lose my editorial trust in you – I care for you as a friend, but I care less for you as an editor. A lot less.

. . . I do see that you are sorry. I'd be happier if I thought you saw why

---

★*Granta* 33: *Home*, published on March 1, 1988, had included one of Martha's introductory essays for *The View from the Ground*.

you should be sorry and that you cannot, must never, fuck up writers: it is as wrong as fucking up miners or nurses or any people who work hard and honestly trying to do something seriously as well as they can.

Think of your soul, William.

Love,
M

To: Betsy Drake

April 25 1988
72 Cadogan Square
London SW1

Dearest Betsy; Thank you for Primo Levi's book.* I have read it with tears. We all failed that great and good man. We should have been writing to him every week to tell him that his voice is beautiful and needed and <u>heard</u>. I am sure he killed himself in despair; everything goes on being as cruel and blind as ever, no one learns, nothing changes. I cannot bear to think of his sense of failure and his loneliness. He writes like an angel and there cannot be any greater sanity and justice than in his thinking and his prose. I feel guilt towards him, together with unpayable gratitude.

A luminous spirit. That's what he had.

Love,
M

To Mary Blume

June 20 1988
Catscradle
[Gwent]

Dear Mary: What a welcome encouraging letter. I never expect anything from my books but they've always at least been reviewed. Since these were paperbacks, they were not; now reviews trickle in but the taboo holds . . . Now, as paperbacks, the books won't even get into libraries. I feel dispirited, sad. I did want them read in the US; I did think this long record had some value. But they've both pretty well fallen down a well. Nothing new, really; I feel I should be buried in Westminster Abbey as The Unknown Writer. But somehow, for once, I mind.

I cannot write backwards, Mary. I don't remember and I don't have notes. I also don't have the feeling really. Everything I write is hot off the

---

*If This is a Man, first published in 1958, is Levi's account of his time in Auschwitz.

griddle, the past truly is another country and I have forgotten it. Now I've agreed to write a preface to a collection of Mrs. R's [Roosevelt] columns, "My Day," but I am nervous since I don't remember whether she dictated to Tommy her secretary, or wrote them by hand herself; I'd guess dictated. I will simply try to remember her as she seemed to me; but I don't know anything about those times except what I saw and heard from the unemployed and that's best in *The Trouble I've Seen*. I saw everything spottily and with my usual dashing uninformed attention.

I could not, as well as would not, write an autobiography. Looking up what I earned at FERA in letters to my mother . . . I read with blank astonishment what my life was like. It doesn't sound real. It would sound, in a book, like crazy lying or bragging; it might even have the disgusting mythomaniac sound that Ernest invented for his life. It was hellish sweating nervy work to write those decade bits in the *View*, terrible fear of the cringe factor, horror of the use of the first person singular; but that's the total of autobiography I'm ever going to do . . .

Do you find it always harder to write or easier? I find it not only harder but much worse than I used to write. Lowering. On the other hand, I have a spiffing life so what the hell. Are you happy and healthy enough; one cannot hope for perfection,

As always,

Martha

To: James Fox

July 16 1988
72 Cadogan Square
London SW1

Dearest James; Have you been kidnapped and are the teen age abductors living in your house? Your answering machine says (in a boy's voice), 'If you want Damien' (or I think it was that) and gives you a number in the US. 'If you want Nick, I'll call back as soon as I can.' I said plaintively, 'And what about James? Where is he?' But no call replied . . .

Are you working in a cave in Outer Mongolia, determined to get your book underway?

Are you married and on your honeymoon on the Heinz island in the Caribbean?

Are you above all alive?

I've been here a week for daily dentistry. It has been a non-fun week. In Wales, it rains. I'm going back tomorrow and a week later, I agreed (madness clearly) to spend 3 days in Wales with Lord Snowdon, I think I'm an upmarket caption writer for his lordship who sure sounds a right shit on the telephone. Maybe better not on the telephone. $6000 to write 3000 words for Gully Wells,★ only way to do it is get drunk: fluff does not come easily to my typewriter.

I'm waiting for Bill Buford for dinner; it is strangely like waiting for Godot. He telephones en route to give progress reports. Mr. [Harold] Pinter, who plays tennis at your snazzy club, came to call. I could hardly believe how boring we both were.

Anyway I changed this typewriter ribbon today. I've had this machine upwards of 35 years. I still cannot dominate the ribbon. I was close to tears and with ink to my elbows but look at it, dreamy.

Love,
Martha

To: Bill Buford

November 6 1988
72 Cadogan Square
London SW1

Dearest William; Now I see you as a Russian Prince. Who but a Russian Prince would think of so magnificent a gesture? Prince Youssopov† to the reigning ballerina assoluta on the morning after her superb triumph . . . I am very touched by this splendour of roses, have boasted all over town and am, naturally, much concerned about your finances. I am covered in beautiful red roses and you are reduced to semi-starvation. It was <u>sweet</u>, William; and also funny; and it takes away the dread commemorative aspect of the occasion. I am glad to be leaving for the moment. I feared people might nail a plaque to me, the way things were going.

And also I am grateful to you for riding in like the cavalry to rescue the maiden from cattle rustling H. Evans.‡ But, seriously, I ask you: what has the magazine business come to when writers have to whine or bellow in order to be paid? And in vain anyway; in need of the cavalry.

Thank you William honey; this will be the 80 roses birthday.

Love,
M

★Then an editor with *Traveler* magazine.
†Prince Felix Youssopov, one of Rasputin's murderers.
‡Martha had written an article for Condé Nast's *Traveler* magazine, for which Harold Evans was then editor.

To: Victoria Glendinning

February 11 1989
Nyali
Mombasa
Kenya

Dear Victoria, my wonderful new friend; I wanted to write to you weeks ago but could not (explanation follows later at some dreary length). I wanted to talk to you about Rebecca's *Cousin Rosamund*.★ I read it with great emotion, twice gasping with sudden tears; and often laughter. This unfinished story is my idea of a novel deserving to be called art. Though I read the way an alcoholic drinks and always have, like an alcoholic I remember nothing so remain permanently at square one of ignorance. Thus I do not remember your fine biography of Rebecca. But I don't think she had a brother did she; perhaps longed for one? And I also don't remember that her relation to her mother was of deepest importance or have I got that wrong. But feel fairly sure she got on bad terms with her sister because of Wells. Is this all a muddle?

What I think marvelous about the book is the passion in it; I don't mean the sexual passion at the end which in fact didn't convince me. I mean the constant passion of grief, of loss, the almost physical pain of mourning the father, the mother, the brother. I can't think of any book (which means damn all because I can never think of any book) which tackled and triumphed with that emotion. For myself of course, I found the feeling about the mother – who was perfect, always right, made everything right for everyone, was adored by everyone – like something done for me, who have never been able to write a line about my mother, nor even read her letters since the loss does not cool, it is only accepted.

Now I think of Rebecca herself with tears. Because it seems to me she was longing for love, and mourning the lack of it, in mourning imagined people who gave it. One should not do this about writers and in a way it is wrong ever to know a writer (and my objection to biographies) because one mixes the writer with the writing and does this personal interpreting. But there is such a fever of loss, of longing that the book actually hurts.

I think of Rebecca also with awe. Did she know so much about music because she made me believe those girls were pianists and obsessed with perfection in their work. What a writer she was, not nearly recognized enough. Very few women can touch her, let alone men. She is also such a craftsman; the intricate brilliant prose is <u>caressing</u>; I felt soothed by it as I admired. Not infuriated the way I am by literariness.

. . . The climate has changed here; it's a world wide disaster. Instead of

---

★Posthumous third volume (1985) of Rebecca West's *Saga of the Century*.

the sure blazing summer it's always been, it's more like a tropical Wales. The monsoon blows from the north, reversing the season, this is the winter monsoon, May–October. There was rain in January, literally unheard of in living memory. I often wake to an overcast sky and who knows where the stars have vanished, but anyway swimming under the stars is out, it's far too chilly. Still I've forced myself into the big beautiful pool every day, except 5 when I was absolutely Eliz Barrett Browning, fainting on a chaise longue, and breast-stroked slowly up and down up and down. There must be some muscles somewhere as a result but don't feel muscular. I'm really pissed off with myself, letting my body turn into spaghetti from laziness and boredom with Welsh walks and weather. Serious resolve: exercise steadily from now on whether it bores me crazy or not.

Are you excited about your novel almost coming out? I look forward to reading it. As I remember, you think no one is grown-up and now I agree with you since I've totally failed and disappointed myself on that score. It may be that my mother was the only grown-up I've known in my life and perhaps my father was too but he died before I was old enough to know him. I expect he was or they wouldn't have been so completely in love; that has to be between equals.

Now my hands hurt and this is long enough anyway. When I get back I'll have a few days in London, can we have dinner? I miss seeing Terence★ who talks English in the best way of anyone I've ever known.

Love,
Martha

To: James Fox

March 20 1989
[Catscradle
Gwent]

Darling James;

    . . . You better read the book about loving too much again. It's really about possession, the need to possess and be possessed and, personally, I think that's a recipe for doom – though it is far from unusual. My mama sent me off to Bryn Mawr, aged 17, with a train note, quoting what she said was an old Chinese proverb: 'You only possess what you set free.'

Maybe who you have to set free first is yourself. That is a very tricky one. I do know about loneliness though I've long since outgrown it. It is a bad taskmaster, leading one into endless mistakes. I advise a funny loving dog,

---

★The writer, Terence de Vere White, Victoria Glendinning's husband.

so as not to live in an empty house; and give yourself time to behave rationally, not frantically.

Nobody can be possessed who is sane; there's always a separate part in everyone. And though we all know that the penis rules okay, there remains a smidgeon of brain; when the penis is fed enough, the brain moves in, full of discontents. I am giving you all this wisdom gratis and unasked and you are at liberty to chuck it into the nearest wastebasket.

Here I am, doing the same old thing: i.e. never going outdoors, feeling my leg muscles turn into spaghetti, maddened by the Welsh climate. I want to be outdoors. I want to be a tough old woman with strong legs and minimal lordosis trouble. I don't want to sit in my beloved cottage slowly turning into mush.

We have different problems at different ages, do we not.
                                   Undiluted love,
                                           Martha

To: Bill Buford

                                           April 28 1989
                                      72 Cadogan Square
                                           London SW1

Dearest William; I behaved badly and sat in the SLOW train feeling hideous and nasty, therefore. I told John Pilger I felt hideous and nasty because I'd been awful to you and how and why. He said, Yeah (the Australian yeah), you shouldn't have, it was wrong but he'll forgive you, you're his mate. He knows how you are. What, I said, what do you mean? Have I been awful to you? Now and again, he said, here and there. It's how you are. So now I see myself not as an old fart (normal perception) but as an old pain in the ass.

But having seen your office and your editorial conference and besides knowing you, I should not expect tidiness and order. The trouble is: I AM orderly, too late to change. I do not renege on the 20% but cannot stand the disorder. Therefore, this is what I suggest:

1) you 'generate' (great word) the business. The contracts are sent to you. You vet them, amend them if needed, and mail them PROMPTLY to me.

2) I send them to the publisher whoever he is myself directly. I inform the publisher that any future business, including the cheques, are to be sent promptly and directly to me. I then send you my cheque for 20%. This way I will know what money is due and when and will get it.

This way I will not be cross. If anything comes up that needs a furious phone call, I will ask you – but I see you hardly have time for phone calls or anything else. Your very real talent operates in disorder, your climate. Nothing wrong with that; only it is not mine.

Does this suit you.

But I do feel nasty about how I behaved to you at that moment. Your large innocent hurt very young brown eyes haunt me.

Love,

Martha

To: Leonard Bernstein

October 13 1989
[Catscradle
Gwent]

Dearest Lennypot; The first thing you have to do is get off those cancer anti-pain pills. I know all about them as I was given them in Perth Australia where I fetched up with a killer ear infection, poison boils in the canal of my ruined right ear. I would not go into hospital where I'd have been given morphine so instead I got those pills. For a time they were necessary as a notched knife was driving into my head, an ear pain is very special; but after a bit I found I could not walk, barely shuffle and could not think and only lie in a daze occasionally reading a page of a thriller. Same state as you are in. I do not like or approve of giving up, at least not while there is still something to do, so I got enormous injections of Vitamin B and electric physiotherapy, the kind where they run electricity through your legs and the almost dead muscles jump around like ball bearings. I got in operational shape within two weeks. Now listen, first of all, you are not in constant pain, so you should stop the pills at once. Then, if you do get a fierce attack of pain either you take a MUCH less strong pain killer or you get a shot of morphine. But you do NOT stay on those pills. I think they are more than body damaging; they may be brain damaging as well. So start now with Vitamin B shots and electro physiotherapy. You have to walk and you have to read. You cannot lie there, as a sorrowing vegetable. And you are not going to die now, and you cannot bump yourself off until I return and we discuss the pros and cons carefully. But first of all, you have to make an effort on your own behalf; and get back into some near human form.*

It seems to me more than possible that the medical profession did you in a lot more than you'd have been done in, without them. But that's past. You can easily live with the use of one lung. A friend of mine had a lung removed (for T.B.) when she was 22; she's in her mid seventies now and has spent her life, ski-ing, swimming, travelling with insane energy all over the world. Meantime, you did burn your candle at both ends, in the middle and wherever else a candle can be burned; and a bill was ultimately due. I

---

*Leonard Bernstein died a year later, on October 14, 1990.

want you to stop the self pity bit, it is undignified and prideless and a bad performance and make up your mind to bear some pain (come on, people do, you've seen worse than what you've got) and to get back into mobile rational shape. After which, if you think you cannot live without millions applauding, then okay – but we must discuss this when you are in shape, as you can be.

I know a lot about pain, Lennypot, and I know it is bad for people, eats away the spirit, but how about courage, what is it for if not to use when needed?

I expect to find you much changed when I get back; it is now a question of your will, and your pride. Not vanity, you've got far too much of that; this is different, this is pride. And keep all those kindly people away, you don't need sympathy, you need someone to say buck-up, since when are you the saddest creature on God's earth. You aren't. I don t think you've got cancer, for a start. I think you've had doctors. Love,

Marty

P.S. It is wonderful here.

To: James Fox

October 27 1989
Catscradle
Gwent

Dearest of all James's;

. . . I think I told you my birthday was Nov 7 – very interesting, that's my father's birthday; I'm the 8th. The 7th is the date of the Russian Revolution, the 11th is Armistice Day; we Scorpios belong in turbulent times. I feel like a crushed caterpillar myself, just now. Deeply glum. I'm about to subscribe to the *London Review of Books,* because they sent a demand and I remember you said it was good; but why don't they review my book? Why is that book simply sunk beneath the waves? Why are all my books like that? What's the matter? I think I've lacked the Literary manner. Last night I listened to the Booker Six talking about their books; I could not have done it, not for money, not for fame. Haven't the vocabulary. Does that make my books insignificant?

Did you read, or look at, my war novel that I gave you? I long for your opinion. I'd think maybe my fiction was unknown because too dark, but it isn't, not all of it. I wrote two really funny books, novels, and what about the short stories. It seems now that I'm going to be a smash hit in Germany of all places I detest. I feel lost, all the work ignored as if valueless.

This place is perfectly fine if you give up the idea of being outdoors and I don't much mind now. It is very warm (suffocating by local standards) and of course supremely comfortable having been designed for me and the cats. I love having time though there are always plenty of tedious chores connected with paper-work. The Augean stables are not full of shit but of paper. And I feel slowly better though lifeless, without energy. But so glum, so deeply glum.

For the first time this year I realise that I am very old, partly due to ill health, partly due to Jane Bown's photographs which showed such an old woman. One does not see oneself as others (and cameras) see one. Normally I don't see myself at all. Now I see myself as all looks gone and pointless.

Love love love

M

For all her fury at Bill Buford, Martha's writing was now back in print and in fashion. Her collection of war articles, The Face of War, *had gone into several editions and sold well in translation, as had her similar collection of peacetime articles,* The View from the Ground. Travels *continued to sell well. To a German editor and friend, Herwart Roseman, she wrote, somewhat irritably: "Late in life, to my rage, I've become a woman writer. Until they also speak of 'men writers,' this is an insult."*

Though her skin was now beginning to react badly to the sun, she kept on traveling – to Australia, to Fiji, to Copenhagen, Salzburg, Bimini, Virgin Gorda, Malta, and the Sinai Peninsula – telling John Hatt that she had to "keep moving, guaranteed cure for accidie." She talked of putting up a sign in her bathroom: "When things get bad, run." She was still writing articles, though her sight had almost gone in one eye and was poor in the other, making it nearly impossible either to read or to write. To strangers who wrote to her, she now sent back a short printed card:

> I appreciate your writing to me and I thank you. My eyesight has become so feeble, and my energy the same, that I can't any longer manage correspondence. Delighted to receive but unable to give. With apologies,
>
> *Martha Gellhorn*

Though she talked of being "the most elegant oldie on the trail" – which indeed she was – she found getting old extremely hard. Old age, she would say, is "the worst disease." "I have no problem except a solid and justified sense of futility, of lovelessness," she wrote one day, "and at my age the only way to love is to give it, diffused, wherever I am. I am making a real mess of growing old." This was not as others saw her. In public, with her younger friends, Martha was stylish, humorous, full of curiosity.

To: John Hatt

January 18 1990
San Pedro Town
Belize
Central America

Dearest John; You will be fascinated to know that fabled Ambergris is a dud. It is also an island sized clip joint; the main rippers off are foreigners but the natives (very charming people) are learning fast. More riveting news: I've been here 6 days and it has rained day and night like the monsoon, and blown a gale from the north. Natch I did not bring a sweater. I brought luggage like a curse, like a nightmare; I am trapped by my fucking luggage. But what I need, sweater, new typewriter ribbon, flashlight, I have not got. I hear that water pipes burst and froze in Houston, the citrus crop in Florida is lost and it snowed in Miami. But what I really think is that I have the evil eye for weather and wherever I go, the weather goes to hell. The wind seems at last to have blown the sky clear but I've lost confidence and think it will turn grey and rain again later.

As to the swimming, Paul Theroux is mad. You can only swim (I went in for a minute, bored by it, between cloudbursts) from a long pier to which you must trudge. The water is shallow and filled by turtle grass, nasty in itself and sharp, with a slimey bottom. To snorkel you take a boat ($7.50 per trip) with other tourists out to the reef about ¾ mile or a mile away. Not my idea.

. . . I've rented a large comfortable highly tasteless and very costly service flat for a month knowing I will be bored blind (I am) but also knowing this is the way to get writing done. I've only been settled for two days and have worked each day for four hours. I am writing too easily, too fast, so obviously it will be worthless stuff. I know my centerpiece but no idea how it will end and thus far I don't think my main character is believable. But I am steely fixed on this. I want to know a) if I can still write fiction and b) if I want to.

After this, I'll explore Belize which looks, in a lost tatty jungly way as if it might be interesting; and go to Tecal, the ruins, in Guatemala.

I'm reading, fascinated by your Marie of Roumania.* As a Royalty chum, you must have a sense of all this; to me it looks like lifelong prison. But I noticed at the end you did not list my *Weather in Africa*. If this means it is still out of print, take this letter as serious notice (author to publisher) that I will reclaim all rights if you haven't got it in print within three months. That was your promise: to keep books in print.

Please tell Nicholas [Shakespeare] that I have at last read *Utz* and I agree

---

*Eland Books had reprinted *Queen of Roumania* by Hannah Pakula in 1989.

with him about it. It is extraordinary. [Bruce] Chatwin was a real original and a polymath if that's what I mean: the range of knowledge is breath taking. I find the writing of *Utz* very beautiful, marble, carved and perfect. But I am right about Chatwin's coldness; he does not like his people, he feels no pity, he is an entymologist studying insects, freakish insects. Ask Nicholas if he has ever read the novels of Walker Percy and if not, he should. Walker P., an American, is another rare original, full of invention, mockery, anger hidden under laughter, but also full of love; and a magical writer. I've got *Love in the Ruins*, 1971, never read it before.

Now back to work. At least that makes me feel virtuous.

Much love,

Martha

To: Milton Wolff★

May 9 1990

Catscradle

Gwent

Dearest Milt; I have a better idea. Write your autobiography. You're a very interesting man and you've had a very interesting life. You don't have to write anything personal and private. You write of the ideas and events that influenced you, the actions you took, what you saw, what you learned and concluded. You can make a fascinating book and it would be published. It would give you the space to write what you wanted to say in the novel. Why not?

Otherwise, if the novel is your only dream, cut it down for a start. In the synopsis, in describing the two characters, explain the struggle between bravery and pragmatic cowardice. But you will have to have an agent. The reason I asked about writing is: it is very hard to do. I've been doing it since aged 14 and find it always harder. A novel needs very specially good writing and construction and the use of narrative suspense. Novels are just about the hardest thing there is to write. And I am sure that long novels are not good, and maybe even going out of style except for thrillers, where people like to get 3 books, no matter how padded and badly written, for the price of one.

You can put in an autobiography everything about you and E.H. and that angel Herbert Matthews. I blame myself for having lost touch with him. He was too attached in my mind to E.H. and I only wanted to flee from all that. You're a nut, Herbert was never in love with me, he loved

---

★Milton Wolff (1915–) arrived in Spain in 1937 and became commander of the Lincoln Battalion. It was there that Martha met him, but they did not renew their friendship until the 1980s. Wolff had become a peace activist and written three autobiographical novels.

me as he loved E.H.; we were probably his only buddies in life, that shy reserved man. I have so many guilts and regrets and remorses to live with; heavy luggage.

My Panama piece, cut down from 10,000 words will appear in the June issue of *Granta* which is distributed in the U.S. by Viking-Penguin; it's like a paperback book, ask your friendly bookseller to get cracking. Having written all my life on behalf of the abused, I am certain that not one word ever did the slightest good. But I am a writer and know nothing else to do. It is tiring and unrewarding. On the other hand, complete silence is worse, so even if it's only a mouse squeak it is better than nothing.

Please write your autobiography, you'll find it's the freedom you need.

Have fun in Berlin; I loathe Germans myself.

Love

Martha

To: William Walton★

September 28 1990

72 Cadogan Square

London SW1

Bill honey; I hear about you from Solly [Zuckerman]. I asked about your ankle operation. He said, 'He seemed perfectly steady to me.' From which I assume (hope) the operation went off well. Did it? Though he said you'd had a hideous time with an eye. Well, time's winged chariot seems to bring nothing more than bits and pieces of damage to the body.

. . . Now I want to ask you something. Did an academic creep named Carl Rollyson get in touch with you, maybe 2 years ago, to ask you to talk to him about me. He thanks a list of people, including me (the insolence) for acknowledging his request for info. I'm sure you turned him down.

But, did you ever say to someone called Denis Brian, author of the 1988 book *The True Gen; Hemingway by those who knew him intimately* the following: 'I knew Martha Gellhorn well. It takes two to tango, you know. Martha was a wild wicked bitch. Oh, the joint cruelties;' I cannot believe this, since you saw me and E.H. together only once, that night in Luxembourg City, and you did feel he was doing the dirty work. The point is; the vile Rollyson has written an unauthorized biography of me which has made me physically sick. It is vulgar and vicious and the whole point is to cash in on the bottomless Hemingway market. I'm trying to frighten the publisher into withdrawing it or demanding that he excise the worst; but

★In a note found among her papers after her death, Martha called Walton "a darling, a painter and now a potentate (alas)."

the whole thing is so mean, spiteful, ugly that I don't see how it could ever be more than awful. I never read the E.H. biographies and neither know nor care what they say about me, but this book is the first full biography purporting to be me; and books feed on books, the lies become fact with repetition and I find myself, at last, outraged. If I hadn't been married (4 years) to E.H., this creep would have left me alone. Hell hath no fury like E.H. scorned and I'll never escape from him and it really is bitterly unfair.

Global warming has done wonders for the British Isles so far. I'm loving Wales in steady sunshine. As to the almost-war in the Gulf, I find myself feeling as I did about the Korean war. *Ohne mich.* I think the blockade will do the job if given time but fear the gung-ho old men who are never there to pay for their hopeless policies. And the money is needed here (and surely there) desperately to rescue everything that matters and is falling apart.

I'm off to the Caribbean to swim.

Love,

Martha

To: Victoria Glendinning

January 3 1991
Catscradle
Gwent

Darling Victoria; The only answer to the Yuletide Season is mine; the beatific opt-out. The painlessness is incredible. I cannot even bear to do routine pre-Xmas shopping, due to the feeding frenzy in our one awful supermarket; the queues, the overladen trolleys. So I ran a bit short of food, no bad thing and made Xmas dinner of peanut butter sandwiches. But I adore the microwave, it was invented for me.* I do not of course try Creative cooking which I could not do on any machine but the joy of this instant food and no washing up is total. Since my usual dinner hour is around midnight, if I have the energy to eat at all, it is bliss to get the whole feeding thing done in max 4 mins.

Thank you for the Rebecca letter. I always secretly felt I had killed her. There was a terrible piece, an interview or some such with Anthony (who clearly inherited all Wells' shit blood) which someone sent to me. Rebecca had heard about it and wanted to see it. I said why bother with such tripe but she insisted and I did send it and as she died not long after, I was sure the shock and rage and horror of reading the vile stuff her son spewed out had done her in. What an unhappy life she had; so unjust, she deserved far

---

*Martha was an atrocious cook, not least because she had never been interested in food. Victoria Glendinning had the idea of introducing her to the microwave.

better. I hope being a Dame and praised and revered as a writer made up a bit. I don't know how old she was in the last years when I knew her, but the very old, of whom I have known many, are spooky – and it spooks me as I am heading that way, because of physical disabilities. She was so nearly blind and overweight and it was hard for her to move; nothing wrong with her brain but the body was a trap. I was crazy about being old and still am, only now the wear and tear factor enters in and alarms me. Mainly the spot of arthritis on my spine because it causes pain and makes me walk like a robot. If the Devil had shown up at my house, instead of calling on dreary Faust, and offered me a perfectly functioning body until death in exchange for my soul I'd have said it's a deal bud, with joy. I don't take to souls and all the propagandists for same; I believe in behavior and the mind that dictates it and fuzzy stuff like souls is balls.

Meantime I have found out how to dominate the stupefying boredom of plodding daily up and down my pool; an old tape recorder and classical music. I now swim to Chopin, Mozart, Brahms, the lot. Music lasts half an hour, just my reduced swimming time. Strange affair. I haven't listened to music for 21 years and didn't know why or think about it; I simply had no desire to hear any. Then I had a revelation, this does happen even to people who avoid introspection: my mother died slowly, a few terrible last weeks unable to speak; while gently classical music played on a super machine given to her by my 2nd husband, sounds from the sitting room. I told this to Lenny Bernstein and he said, 'You associate music with death.' No, but apparently with my mother's death. Now, complete turn-around, I associate it with a joke; my one woman swimming pool. Chopin is another revelation. As late as 1950, I remember being in uncontrollable tears at a concert in Mexico City, Rubinstein playing Chopin. I was in a box with a bunch of Eyetie grandees, *en visite* there and clearly they were embarrassed but that didn't matter to me. Chopin meant the death of the Republic in Spain, all that bravery and suffering for nothing, since we always opened the windows against blast and played Chopin on E's wind up gramophone during artillery bombardments of Madrid. Not defiance, I don't think, but a sort of reminder of there being such loveliness in the world. Now, swimming, I can listen to Chopin again, hugely noisy at top volume in that echo chamber glass house, with delight. I know nothing about music, having heard it all my life, but like all ignorant people I know what I like – and the liquid clarity and beauty of Chopin is my favorite.

My eyes aren't anything to dance in the streets about. Distance vision is better, hence safe to drive, but blurred, can't see road signs at all until on top of them, can't read them. Reading is the same with my magnifying specs from Boots and I am unable to cure myself of the deadly habit of reading until 3 and 4 a.m. Nightly, I promise reform and then cannot stop. Odd new quirks: I could see my TV before without specs; now only with distance specs (about 6 feet away) and blurred; if I have to read subtitles or want a clear picture I must get out of the covers and perch on the end of the bed, 2 ft away. When I come to re-read this and try to fix typos, I will find it nearly impossible, because direct down vision doesn't work, eyes don't focus; very trying if doing arithmetic on cheque stubs. Maybe it will get better, maybe it won't; nothing to do. I truly do not wail and weep over this.

Now a joke; on Xmas day I got into my swimsuit and went to turn on the pool lights (here in my tiny front hall.) Nothing doing. The entire electrical system of the pool was kaput. On Boxing Day I got an electrician from Chepstow, call-out charge £45, who found that the fuse box, the nerve center for it all, was filled with water – a wrong wiring set-up, conduits or some such. He put in a new piece and dried out the box with my hair dryer. I continue to keep the pool operational by using my hair dryer. Is this, do you think, further proof that Brits are not clued in on modern technology? Anyway I have kept it going and I do swim and someone will have to fix it some day. Now, at 5:45, dark night, I shall hurry out and do my daily half hour. Never say die.

I love you dearly. Let's have a spiffing private 1992 keeping a separate compartment in the brain for personal pleasure. Kiss Terence for me.

Always,
Martha

To: Milton Wolff

January 11 1991
Catscradle
Gwent

Dearest Milt; I am practising dictating letters. I have not got the hang of it yet, but intend to become like Henry James who dictated all his novels. This is my new system to get through mail so that I have time to write. I have started in a half hearted and picky way on an autobiography, doubting that I will ever finish. Rollyson has driven me to this, plus all the apocryphal stories I see here and there in other writing. Self defence, not the noblest motive.

I asked my publisher to send you a copy of the *Gellhorn Compendium*, 4 books in one 700 page volume. Which I am increasingly regarding as a mistake. Please ignore the photo slapped on the back of the dust jacket without either consultation or permission. I do not look like everyone's favourite granny in Ohio or like Helen Hayes★ at her most cloyingly sweet.

★Helen Hayes (1900–1993), U.S. actress who started work at the age of six.

The way to read the book, if you feel like reading it, is in bits, a few of the novellas at a time. Except for the first 4 they were never written consecutively but simply written, too long for any magazines, and kept in a drawer until they formed a book. To my surprise 4 of them being about marriage fitted the 4 marriage vows. To my greater surprise only the other day I realised that the next 3 were all about betrayal, although that does not appear in the title. The last 3 are considered to be about racism, which had nothing to do with my intention, I was simply writing about white people in Africa where I do not think they belong. This single volume should have had a health warning on the dust jacket: take in small doses.

You look too thin to me. Do you eat enough?

Love,

Martha

To: Milton Wolff

November 5 1991
Catscradle
Gwent

Milt honey; I wish you were here and we could get cosily sloshed together. My mail pisses me off. It is huge and insanely boring. People seem to think I have time on my hands whereas I am going mad from lack of time. They write from universities; they want interviews, information, God knows what. I have more than enough to do, too much, just managing my life, which also pisses me off because there's too much chore stuff, not enough luxury waste time. My dream, never fulfilled, is to do nothing except read thrillers, drink whiskey, loaf about.

I think Americans are exceptionally boring. They are sober-sided, don't mock enough (if at all) and of course this latest shaming display of boastful patriotic fervour is beyond words boring. What has happened to the nation? I remember Americans as great jokers in WW2. They were monsters in Vietnam, no question. But that vulgarity mixed with solemnity now seems par for the course. Present company excepted.

I have a little gaggle of chaps in London all half my age or less, who make me laugh. That's the only essential for company. I need people to laugh with, otherwise am fine alone. But I am beginning to wonder what I have done to deserve my mail. Just lived so long? I don't think survival is, in itself, cause for all this dreary stuff that pours in.

. . . I'm going to Spain on June 1, to join a charming Spaniard whom I met at the only Seminar I ever attended at Mich State U. He's an impenetrable cult writer but mainly a civil engineer; we are setting off with

picnic hamper from Harrod's to see his huge dam near Lerida, then up to
Navarra, and it will be fun unless Spain is as cold as here.

. . . So now I will have another drink and read a thriller. The evening sky
and now the night sky are beautiful. It is rare in Wales for either to be clear.
We are of course the most privileged people on earth.

Love,
Martha

To: James Fox

December 22 1991
Catscradle
Gwent

Dear Eternal Love; I've swum to Schubert since you told me how to open
the box. Now you'll have to tell me how to put back the cassette and close
the box. I can't get Mahler back in. I'm feeling very happy. In a force 7 gale,
I raked and swept dead leaves from the pool door and patio door, and took
the rubbish to the dust bins. At about 4 p.m. great black clouds streamed
from the west with pinkish sky, as from a distant fire, showing through. I
decided I was the most fortunate woman I knew and the winter in Wales
is going to be all right.

Thinking about you and your sex-romantic life, I conclude that you
haven't got the hang of it. You stop 'fancying' a woman and believe it's due
to your penis whereas I think it's due to your brain. You went off the Ph.D
because of how she talked about sex, talked in general, and her jealousy.
You went off her personality, not her body. Nothing is more anti-
aphrodisiac than boredom/irritation. Now you always speak of the teacher
as 'sweet.' Nothing wrong with sweet, except it can bore, cloy, leave one
feeling dull. Again, it's your brain that is dictating what you attribute to
your genitals.

My theory is that men are not interested in women, don't want to know
them as people, listen to them as separate human beings. Note by
percentage how much you talk about your things and how much you listen
to her (any woman), try to make said women operate as themselves, not
adjuncts. Women are afraid to talk, knowing full well the self absorption of
males and fearing to lose their attentions if they dare present their own lives
as separate and important. Women can be very interesting, talking to each
other. They conceal or suppress this with men, because long (maybe
millennial) experience has taught them that men are not concerned, don't
want to know; men want to be flattered, soothed, encouraged, helped and
listened to. Not the reverse.

Meantime, the woman – who is carefully concealing her own real self, hopes, fears, ideas – becomes a bore.

. . . I like men which is unusual; I mean like them as people. I find them touching and funny, on the whole. In my life, apart from men friends which always worked, men wanted me and became furious when they found out that I was and insisted upon being a person, separate from them, with my own ideas, needs, plans, actions. It is a great pity that the sexes cannot treat each other as equals, the same sex or no sex, when out of bed: they'd get on so much better. But at least you can make a start by trying to 'fancy' a woman as herself, as well as a body. On the other hand, I doubt very much whether you'll find the ideal woman for both bed and living. I know of 3 couples in my entire life who managed that. And of course you must search but you might search with more enlightenment.

This is enough Wisdom from Wales for now, maybe forever.

I love you dearly,

Martha

To: Victoria Glendinning

February 2 1992
Catscradle
Gwent

Dearest Victoria; I should have written to you days ago but I am paralyzed, body and mind, by the cold. To begin with, I told myself that this torpor was quite comfy and I was hibernating. But it's past that; endless freezing fog, a grey world visible for about three yards, iced-in claustrophobia.

. . . I've done 2 pieces, neither good, but very amazed I can write anything. One, about a childhood memory of something in the country, is 800 words for $2500. How I'd have longed for that some time ago. Now it's just pool upkeep. I swim to classical music on a big tape recorder, I must have told you, and it's fine for making one think about sentences. I try to think about my 'memoir' but find that almost impossible. Looking back is a misery. I don't remember what was fun and funny; I remember what I wish to forget, the wrong sad hurting things and I'm so pleased that normally, left to myself, I have a genius faculty for forgetting, good and bad alike, sign of a mediocre mind, but makes life easier. So now what. I have, for my whole life, 10 diaries, those cheap red books with a page a day, and those not filled. One page was too much trouble. But I read two from the seventies and felt suicidal. They are useless books; they don't tell me where I was or what I was doing since I knew that; they are only feelings and the feelings are coal black. I stopped because I couldn't bear to look back there and haven't had the nerve to go on with this. I really don't know what to do. Another unknown man is apparently getting ready to do another unauthorized job and various nice but untalented American women are writing books about my work.

I have become ugly. You may be surprised that at my age this both horrifies me and startles me. My idea of the bad part of old age was just that; getting ugly. I never thought at all about the inevitable decay of the body and what that could mean, I only thought about my face. Now it's plain hideous. The left operated eye, which is far from a miracle job, is so much smaller that I have a Picasso touch and all around my eyes is soggy and dreadful. I have to wear dark glasses to save my own feelings. The rest isn't much cop either. I am sure that vanity (physical) never dies in either men or women; all that happens is you feel unacceptable because there is nothing left to have vanity about.

Enough. I'm too cold even to think of trying to save myself. February is a disaster month, might as well disaster it out here. Darling Victoria, I hope T. is much better now and you have had some rest and respite. I think of you both, and with special love for you.

Martha

To: Victoria Glendinning

July 15 1992
Catscradle
Gwent

Victoria my honeybun: *Trollope* arrived. Now that's what I call a book. . . . You must feel proud when you see its size, to think you climbed that mountain.

. . . I've been going off my rocker trying to write a conclusion (the fifth and absolutely last) to *The Face of War*. Nobody will read it but I have been studying statistics about war for weeks now, and I am sick in my soul from my knowledge. The only good part about this awful job – it is not my kind of writing and a double agony – is a chance to praise and thank Mikhail Gorbachev whom I regard as a miracle. People who believe in God could thank Him for sending Comrade G. As an unbeliever I settle for miracles. But otherwise, it is a vile subject and I never want to touch it again. This Bosnian idiocy revolts me and I think everyone is guilty. I also don't like the way the Germans are throwing their weight around and think their unilateral recognition of Croatia helped start it all.

I'm coming down on the 21st but you are off the 23rd and I am off to Gatwick Park Hospital to have a tiny lump removed from under my nose, so we'll wait until we're both around later. I have a lot of eye surgeon meetings but intend mainly to go to movies and collect life necessities like loo paper before setting off for St. Petersburg. Maybe I've bitten off too much on that one and already I am looking ahead to travelling in Portugal. A great longing to travel, a great longing not to write a word about it. Even the pea-brained Florida piece took me three 8 hour days.

. . . Rebecca [West] said to me shortly before she died that she regretted not having written more books. I regret that I never had any discipline so I only wrote when I wanted to; and that leaves you with flabby muscles in the brain, not an outstanding brain for starters. But then again, does it matter?

I am specially glad Terence has no pain; I think that's the only unbearable. Otherwise one has to accept the wearing out and falling apart, or rather do one's best to keep it at bay (I suppose) but know it's there. Ernest either said to me or wrote, I can't remember which, 'There's nothing to dying. It's not being alive that matters.'

When I lived my old life in Africa I used to daydream about my beau but surely because I had little else to occupy me and I loved daydreaming. Now I've lost the art completely. Also I used to think it was wasteful but now see what a gift it was; I could travel with almost no books and no book-fear (which is now major, terror of being without) because I could tell myself stories endlessly, daydream stories. All gone. I'd go screaming dotty without books.

From where I sit, I can see the moon, it keeps coming out from cloud, at the moment it has a skein of cloud slanted across it, and I think: even with lousy weather I'd always rather live in the country. Though I must organize better so I have more time, less duties, chores, jobs, work – the stupid work with bills and a daily mail bag that harasses me. I get no letters, except yours, that are worth reading.

Love always,
Martha

To: Victoria Glendinning

November 9 1992
Catscradle
Gwent

Dearest Victoria;

. . . That book you chose, *The English Patient*.* It is beautiful, mesmerizing writing. When I got to the end and realised he learned all that, the desert, the Italian campaign, from books, I realised that's genius, that kind of imagination, to learn and transform and make entirely your own, just from

*By Michael Ondaatje.

reading. The Italian campaign was my war and I remember mines all right; it was like a land full of snakes. You'd hear them going off far behind and know some miserable peasant had blown himself up ploughing his field. . . . It was fought uphill, up mountains, through every walled or hill top village and town and mined mined mined. I must tell you mine stories with the Poles. But how beautiful the book is, hypnotic, and the two love stories; he is an astounding man that writer and I wish him well with all my heart. The desert part is brilliant. Do you know the desert? I know it only a little and only saw it once, in dawn light near Tibesti, as beyond belief beautiful. You did a fine job in selecting him.

I'll never do any show-offery again because there's no need to. It is only useful if selling a book and I won't have any more to sell. The U. of Nebraska wishes to adopt me and why not; they are very big on Indians and Willa Cather, I could lend light relief.

. . . I plan to be in London from Dec 1 if not earlier for almost a month and we will indeed drink. Having been away so long I have no friends and feel somewhat chilled. I cannot believe it is true but I was 84 yesterday and the only snag is that my body is too old for me though the man-made sight defect is unnecessary trouble. You're a good fine brave woman and I love you.

Martha

To: Bill Buford

March 14 1993
Catscradle
Gwent

Dear Bill; *Krauts*★ is a very good issue. We will be stoned in Germany. I read it all. When I came to my piece I was incoherent with rage. Days have passed and now I am coherent with rage. This is the second time you have done this: appropriated my published work as if you, not I, owned the copyright, and used this stolen goods as you saw fit. The first time was when you clobbered together stupidly two bits of unrelated writing, mine, copyrighted by me, and published it under my name as a piece in your *Home* issue. The piece made no sense and made me look a fool. I forgave you. Now I do not. You did not ask my permission to split up my piece and inset what you chose, because you knew I would refuse. Editorially, this combines insolence and dishonesty in equal parts. I think in fact that you have become a very shady character, glitzy-shady. I despise your

---

★*Granta* 42, December 1, 1992. Martha's piece was entitled "*Ohne Mich*: Why I Shall Never Return to Germany."

method of publishing a quarterly as if you were acting in Ben Hecht's play. I will not cut you dead in the street but I will never again have anything to do with you as an editor or a publisher. You will very likely survive.

Yours,

Martha

On November 8, 1993, when Martha was eighty-five, she gave a birthday party at the Groucho Club in Soho. Friends organized a cake, in the shape of James Fox's portable Olivetti, with a message printed out in marzipan. Martha had lost none of her sharpness with the years, saying of Bernard Levin that he was a critic "whose ego shows like a petticoat below a dress," and she seldom spoke of Nixon without calling him "our arsehole President." Politics, the corruption and venality of leaders, the catastrophes that befell the poor and the powerless, continued to enrage her.

She was at last on good terms with her adopted son Sandy, after many years' estrangement, and close to her stepson, the other Sandy, and his wife Shirlee. One day, Sandy Gellhorn, who was earning his living driving a minicab, took her to an exhibition on the Spanish Civil War at the Karl Marx library in Clerkenwell. "I think now," she wrote to Milton Wolff, whom she had first met in Madrid in 1937, "that the war in Spain was the only completely just war I have ever seen or known about in my lifetime."

Martha found the loss of most of her eyesight hard to bear, but she seldom complained, preferring to dismiss it humorously in her letters to friends. She was sick, she would say, of stopping strangers when traveling, to ask: "Is that a cloud or a mountain?" For the last ten years of her life, she was seldom not in pain.

In February 1996 – her eighty-eighth year – Martha, longing to swim, went off to Brazil, but the undertow pulled her down and she almost drowned. She wanted to write an article about street children and spent a month interviewing and taking notes, but when she returned to London, she couldn't see what she had written down, nor read back what she typed. "This is an historic document," she wrote on a piece of paper pinned to a copy of the article, "my last and my worst." She sold Catscradle, having burnt a number of letters, and sent the rest, together with all her papers, to Howard Gotlieb, curator of special collections at Boston University. With her younger friends, she remained unfailingly cheerful and funny. To Milton Wolff, she wrote: "I do nothing at all anymore for anyone and am simply taking up room on the surface of the earth."

To: Milton Wolff

December 5 1993
Catscradle
Gwent

Dearest Milt; Please tell me more about Cuba. How did you find it?
Hungry? I wish to God that in due course (he cannot do everything at
once) Clinton would change the evil bullying habits of US governments
and let people live their own way. Cuba. El Salvador where I'm told the
death squads are returning. Poor Nicaragua. Vietnam, above all Vietnam. It
is a great shame for us to bear, the Bully of the World.

I don't write letters much because though I can see the keys, because of
huge letters pasted over the regular ones, I cannot see what I write. This is
not exactly helpful to a writer or ex-writer.

Have you ever read *Naples '44* by Norman Lewis or *The Cattle Truck* by
Jorge Semprun. If not I will nerve myself to find a proper envelope and send
them. Superb books, both of them. You'll remember Naples well as I do
and Semprun was sent to Buchenwald as a Spanish Red. First class writers.

I spent all of November in celebrating my 85th Birthday. A delayed sense
of occasion, it seemed to me so impressive a number that I ought to give a
party and I did. 58 people all of whom said, wrote, that it was wonderful. I
have no idea. I was cold sober but seem to have passed the evening in a
daze, remembering nothing. Anyway I did it and spent the rest of the
month writing thank you cards for unforeseen presents. I'm off to Rome
for Xmas with my son, a nice chap who threw away his life by spending 20
vital years as a junkie and so, I fear, has forever lost his place in the queue.
Then in Jan Feb back to the Red Sea on the grounds that it cannot rain in
the Sinai desert but of course it can go mad like everywhere else and have
icy winds.

I follow all the doings of the disgusting government here and bits of
elsewhere, what's on our still good TV news. Cannot read newspapers,
small close print. Cannot read fairly worthless *Newsweek* because the paper
is shiny. Ah me. Aside from this, I know I am a fortunate or privileged
woman but my body does not suit my life. Does yours, much younger one?

Love,
Martha

To: Rosie Boycott

April 27 1994
Catscradle
[Gwent]

Darling Rosie Fixit,

I am ashamed to lean on you so much for aid and comfort. But about the cats' foster home: these are rich cats, they will be endowed for life, cost nobody for their food, and the caretakers will be rewarded. But my heart quails, Rosie, when I think of them alone, frightened, in a strange house. They have never met a dog. They have been my most constant companions for thirteen years and I feel about them as if I were abandoning old friends who count on me. But I cannot live here. Today was almost decent but it has been strong cold wind and rain, and my body hurts all over. Life in the country is also much more and harder work and I'm past it. There are no seasons any longer, only an ocean of paperwork. You know, it does get to the point where it seems too much trouble to be alive. If I weren't so interested in what happens in the world, though now only as a TV spectator, I'd see no point in it at all
love
Martha

To: Victoria Glendinning

August 13 1994
72 Cadogan Square
London SW1

Darling V;

. . . I'm off to Turkey at dawn tomorrow, really dawn, up at 5 a.m. It's a hardship journey, invented from my favourite book *The Rough Guide to Turkey.* I'll be at the airport at 6:30 a.m., at an unknown Turkish airport at around 12:30, then a 3½ hour busride to a village called, I think, Gumluslic. After a week, I start another bus journey to a luxury joint, which interests me because it's on a lagoon, said to be possible for swimming as early as April.

This is my Mexican Jumping Bean summer. Corsica (8 days were v. good, 6 were hell. It's wildly beautiful scenery but you must drive), then briefly Switzerland, now Turkey, back on August 28, off to Wales to see cats, then off to Sinai, Red Sea snorkelling. All this running around gives me the false impression that I am doing something, whereas I am doing nothing at all.

Warm today if greyish, pouring rain on Thursday. Got soaked to my underpants trying to get a cab. I hate this climate, it makes me nervous. If it is not boiling hot and sunny in Turkey I'll eat my huge suitcase. One effect of being functionally blind is that I take 2 paperbacks for 2 weeks and probably will not get through them.

This will not be proof read because that is a huge effort. I don't think I've said anything of value. I knew you would feel the loss of Terence's* love . . . Friends are invaluable but not the same of course because they have their own lives and problems. But you are fortunate because you have friends of your own generation, you have mates, people who know the same time of history that you do, have the same preoccupation, you can talk shorthand, you'll know the same things and jokes. Mates. I realise that is what I miss. I have no mates; they are all dead. Being a survivor is hard work. But you will survive, only you must not hurry yourself. Grieving, mourning takes time, it has to change slowly from turbulence to calm flowing. I think the missing someone loved is always there but it's simply another part of you, lived with. Sometimes I still wake in the night in tears, after 24 years, and it's from missing my mother.

Please just take your time, take it there where you feel safe and easy and I can tell you from long experience that you can go any amount of time without doing much more than brush your teeth and when you need to gussy up, it comes back quickly.

Much love, my darling V
Martha

To: Milton Wolff

October 14 1994
72 Cadogan Square
London SW1

Dear Milt: Your photograph looks very impressive, almost elder statesman. In return I send you an octogenerian bathing beauty. Mine looks as if I have an enormous right breast hanging almost to my knees and nothing on the left side. The camera lies. I've got two perfectly balanced reasonably sized droopy bosoms. It is awful what age does to the body. You seem to be having a good time as I get messages from you from different parts of the glamorous West. I've had a good summer swimming in three seas – the Med, the Aegean, the Red Sea. Now I'm just hanging about not sure what to do about my Welsh cottage which I've put up for sale, not that anyone wants it. I have to rehouse my cats and I'm very worried about that. Otherwise I plan to spend the winter in South Africa and as always I have

---

*Terence de Vere White, Victoria's husband, had recently died.

the kitchen of life to cope with. I wish I had your energy – or could see enough to work on a book. You're right, it's the best time-killer there is.

I have a letter from George Grunewald who's convinced that we met in WW2. Please thank him for sending me the New Yorker piece on the Roosevelts. It's too hard for me to read their type but as usual when you read about anyone or anything you know, you simply don't believe it. Do you read about the Spanish war? The little I've read seems to be about something we never saw.

I'm dull but I'm fond.

Love,
Martha

Dictated as you can tell

To: Ruth and Sol Rabb

December 7 1994
72 Cadogan Square
London SW1

Darlings: My darling brother Alfred came over for a weekend to check on my nose treatment,* and told me a lot of family news. I said thank God I live in London and never see any of them and never have to keep up with any family doings. This is known as the warm-hearted approach.

The radiology treatment turned into pure agony the week it was finished then went into acute pain and is now just bearably nasty. I think I've had all the experiences I want to have although it has also been interesting because it made me think a lot about napalm and, as you can imagine, about the napalm children of Vietnam. I also had a long interior discussion with myself as to whether pain of the mind or pain of the body is worse and decided firmly on pain of the body. But enough is enough. I pin all my hopes on sun and swimming and interesting people in South Africa.

Very much love,
Alfie

---

*A solar keratosis on her nose, kept under control by repeated courses of radiotherapy.

To: Howard Gotlieb

December 28 1994
72 Cadogan Square
London SW1

Darling Howard; What a grandee you are. The sumptuous smoked salmon, the delectable vodka all from Fortnum's which is so grand a store that I haven't set foot in it for years. I shall think of you with love while stuffing myself on the salmon and getting as drunk as possible on the vodka. And to top it all you send the handsomest Xmas card of anyone. Thank you thank you.

I fear for the U.S. (and the rest of the world since we have too much influence.) It looks to me sadly as if Clinton in despair is going to cave in to all his evil enemies. I do not blame him, I grieve. My idea of the future US is a Nazi state called Christian America. The people (the majority) who do not bother to vote will find there is no more voting.

I pick out each letter with difficulty for I am now as good as blind. I can't read anything unless there is a lot of white space between the lines. Few books and no papers or mags are printed like this. Not reading is torture, I have also just survived a season in hell; my body does nothing now except cause disaster. I've been through radiology for a rare cancer inside my nose and am lucky to have a nose though it looks a bit altered. Also I had pus-filled lungs from what started (I thought) as a bad cold last February.

The fact is: I am too old, the body just wears out and the mind seems pretty sluggish too.

Martha

To: Betsy Drake

May 20 1995
72 Cadogan Square
London

Saturday
Betsy honey; Let us make a covenant or pact never to talk to each other about ailments, medicines, doctors. Never. It is a fearful habit old women fall into. Mrs Forman called it 'Organ recitals' and told me how she dreaded her telephone calls. I think it makes everything worse and more depressing. I also have one last aim in life: not to be a bore and not to be bored. If I am both, I intend to do it privately. So please let's agree to talk about anything else but not our health problems . . . Alfred is coming over on May 29 for a week, to have his birthday here. Meanwhile I am now going to wash up a revolting sink full of dishes from giving the Rabbs a sandwich supper last

night and then go to the attic and look dully at my typewriter from which nothing flows. The unwritten articles weighs heavily on my mind but that's all they do. June will be here any minute and we'll go to the movies and if the weather decides to be summer, we'll go to Kew. My gym is the best idea I've had for years.

Much love,

M

To: James Fox

October 3 [1995?]
72 Cadogan Square
London

Dearest James; Thank you for comforting me with Bloody Marys, for wine tasting, for food choosing, for lunch, for your company, for being a sweet friend in need.

Love,
Martha

To: Milton Wolff

[November 1995]
72 Cadogan Square
London SW1

Dearest Milt: I'll try, kicking like a chicken, to answer you myself. Such a good letter. I think history as it happens is chance and accident. If Hitler had been accepted as a proper artist, he would not have branched out into destroying the world. There seems to be a law that more good leaders get assassinated than awful ones, no doubt because the awful ones expect to be killed and take precautions. My oldest Israeli friend in Jerusalem says the Rabin★ murder has had a deep traumatic effect: none of them (i.e. educated secular Jews) imagined there were as many religious fanatics as they now believe there are.

The Jews invented God, which is a terrible mistake and responsibility. It was okay when everyone had a lot of loony gods, no one seemed to insist on others adopting their gods. But this awful idea of one invisible all powerful God is what the Jews gave to the world and no good has come of it. I am sure that all religion is bad for people and I cannot understand why

---

★Yitzhak Rabin, born in 1922, Israeli soldier and statesman, prime minister between 1974 and 1977, and Nobel Prize winner, was assassinated on November 4, 1995, by a young Israeli extremist while attending a peace rally.

most people everywhere seem to need it. But it has caused more harm than any political ideology. Just now I am thinking about Ireland where Clinton has made an enormous hit. To think that white Irish people can tell on sight who is a Protestant and who is a Catholic among them and feel instant something – fear, distrust, alienation, whatever it is – baffles me. But given that, we should not be surprised that Arab Muslims and Jews cannot connect. I don't think they ever will but maybe in another 40 years they will reach the state of mutual tolerance of French and Germans. I've not yet met any French people who want to have a hot meal with Germans, there is the element of boredom basically. Now the difference between Palestinians and Jews seems to me comparable to the difference between white and black Americans.

I know I'm old because passionate anger has turned into weary disgust: nothing surprises me. Stupidity is king. The break-up of the Soviet Union is apt to be far more dangerous than the hideous family massacre in Bosnia. But I think the world will go on as it has, the real threat was nuclear war and I honestly believe that is out. Just a long unjust needless mess, as before, paid by the innocents.

Much love. Forgive rambling.

Martha

To: Milton Wolff

January 24 1996
72 Cadogan Square
London SW1

Dearest Milt; I am glad you liked that Bara story.* I think it's my favorite novella. I never knew anything about Capa's wife (she had been killed when I got to Madrid) or his life with her or his later love/sex life. I believe he never talked of his wife and his one real close friend, Shim, didn't either. I think I made a real character out of Capa's personality and an invented story. I've thought often of Capa and have two photos of him, one with Shim, which Ingrid Bergman gave me. A nice woman. She fell desperately in love with him when he went to Hollywood after the war and of course wanted to marry him and of course Capa never really wanted to marry anyone and fled. She told me she had never before met 'a free human being.' I loved him but not that way ever; he was my blood brother. I think he loved me too though we quarreled incessantly. One glorious scene in 1948 in Israel, coming back with another beloved now dead friend, Moishie Pearlman, from the Negev where we first met Captain Dayan. We ended

---

*"Till Death Do Us Part."

walking back to the hotel from wherever we'd been dropped, on different sides of the street, shouting at each other to shut up. I have now missed him for a bit more than forty years. But I think he would have hated to grow old though he need hardly have died so young. You know he stepped on a mine in Indo China when it was a French war and from hearing of it, I am sure he died due to boredom. He could not listen to the new war correspondents yammering about war tactics etc and said he'd just cross ahead, not on the road, and see them later.

. . . How are you? I'm able to type slowly but not read what I see, nor any books or papers; pure hell. I'm off to Brazil for the winter next week.

Much love,

Martha

To: Nicholas Shakespeare

[January ? 1996]
72 Cadogan Square
London SW1

WHERE ARE YOU? I AM DESPERATE. UNTIL NOW NOTHING FROM YOUR TELEPHONE, NOT EVEN A FAX WHINE. EVERY NUMBER YOU HAVE GIVEN ME FOR AMANDA IS WRONG. I HAVE BEEN WASTING TIME AND MONEY TO GET A DULL MALE VOICE SAYING HELLO HELLO HELLO AND THAT'S IT. I LEAVE ON FEB FOUR FOR ANGRA. I HAVE NO OTHER CONTACT IN ALL BRAZIL EXCEPT AMANDA. HAVE A HEART. GET THIS RIGHT FOR ME.

JUST BECAUSE YOU ARE FORTUNE'S FAVORED CHILD DOESN'T MEAN ALL GOES LIKE CLOCKWORK FOR EVERYONE ELSE, YOU OAF. PROBABLY YOU HAVE ALREADY DEPARTED. HELL. WHAT SHALL I DO?

DESPERATELY AND ALSO VERY IRRITABLY

Martha

To: Mary Blume

March 19 1996
72 Cadogan Square
London SW1

Dearest Mary; I was in Brazil when you were in London. Still recovering from it. A journey too far. I tried to call you but the operators, Brit and French, said I had the wrong number and you are ex-directory. I want to know about Gloria's [Steinem] operation but fear to call her directly. Has she a Fax. Have you? I've at last discovered how to make mine work incoming after some years. I'm here now with a word processor used as an electronic typewriter (with luck) that prints huge letters, few words to a page but I can read what I write which I cannot with this. So I have two pieces to write, then maybe spring will come. I feel very old, ugly, tired. So does Alfred (he feels bored, doesn't think about ugly). I told him that if we both got any more depressed our voices would be so weak and low we wouldn't hear each other.

Pam Harriman has asked me to visit her. I now realise I have seen her in every phase except this last for 53 years. So it has historical interest. I love Eurostar so when the weather gets human I'll drift over. Meantime no travel plans. Brazil cured me of wanderlust for some time.

Are you okay, survived the winter? Gets worse doesn't it?

Love,

Martha

To: Victoria Glendinning

June 8 1996
72 Cadogan Square
London SW1

Dearest Victoria; I have been listening to your life of E. [Elizabeth] Bowen on a tape from the Royal Blinds. It is read by a man with a torturing voice but I am getting skillful and can now separate words from voices. Your writing is fine, elegant but easy, like talk as one dreams it might be. I think the only real point in writing about writers is to make the reader want to read the original and you do that wonderfully with all you yourself read into and put into E.B.'s books. I do not think I would have liked her and do not regret never having met her but then that's not odd. I am dazed by her being able to write in the morning (on novels) and spend the rest of the day and night hostessing and guesting. Better at it than Edith Wharton by far. A few weeks ago I listened to *The Heat of the Day*, for I never know what is going to arrive in a cardboard box from Calibre or a plastic envelope from the Royal Blinds and I listen to whatever befalls. I did not believe that book. I did not think E.B. had the faintest notion of what a spy's life could be or his work (and who was the hero spying for, Nazis or Russians, it makes a difference.) I also did not believe the jump from the roof falling like a squashed tomato outside his lover's flat. You are right about E.B. being perfect on interiors, not as overpoweringly as Sybille is detailed about food in her books. *To the North* is a much better book, believable, except perhaps for the final finale . . . In a real accident there is no time for words or the thought words would need. There is the instant, only an instant, of appalling shock, an instant when you know it is happening and that's all.

When I could read, I read your *Vita* and I disliked her so much and found her such a bore that I could not like the book. Perhaps because of the subject, I felt the book lacked full life, like a vitamin deficiency. Not this one, because here you identify with your subject.

I am also listening to *Phineas Finn* and loving it. I love Trollope. I love the way he plods on with his story without fuss and you believe his people all the way. I cannot see their clothes exactly only by impression but I see them. And he had the real gift which is story telling so you must go on and on, what happens next. And then also listening, but saving both it and *P. Finn* to take away with me (they are on cassettes from Calibre) and Graham Greene's *Ways of Escape* which seems to be no. 2 of his autobiography. I do wish I had met him, he's the only one I regret. He and E.B. have in common, though Greene even more, the detailed knowledge of their own writing and a way of talking about their characters as if they were living people outside themselves. Badly put. It is the carefulness about their own work which impresses me, and I wonder if not having it is a bad sign. I have been thinking of this and tracing my own unknowledge and absent mindedness back to childhood with my brothers when the greatest sin was boasting, bragging. Telling on anyone was too inconceivable to be a sin but bragging was contemptible. The result is that I never knew what my older brother, barely dead, had done – the sheer range and importance, nationally and internationally of his work in law, until I read about it after his death. I'll never know about Alfred's pioneer work in medicine, in reforming and teaching, because I'll die first and though not long ago, the medical grandees gathered to praise him and to some sort of ceremony, I could not get from him copies of their speeches, I don't think he has them. Nobody bragged. What a pity.

You know I cannot see what I write so I hope this letter is understandable.

I have just finished a 42 page article, my last and very worst. It has driven me into exhaustion and despair. Typing and not seeing, trying to remember what I had already written and trying to get in a mass of information when also I could not read my own handwritten notes from Brazil. Then my reader read it back, again and again, maybe six times, four and five hours at a time, and I tried to correct verbally. There is not one sentence in it that is worth anything as writing. It is flat banal writing, a sad way to end one's writing life. I am not sure Ian Jack★ will take it because of the dullness of the writing which kills the subject. I am not going to try ever again, no need to suffer like that to produce work that shames me. Anyway I see that I

★Editor of *Granta*. The article eventually appeared in *The London Review of Books*.

won't be able to handle the typewriter if the sight in my usable eye fades any faster, or as fast as it is doing.

I'm off to Switzerland on Tuesday, today is Sunday, for a rest cure. Switzerland is the most reposeful country I know. Stupendously grand scenery and sweet toy architecture. I am going by train, a treat, and will find out if my field glasses work from a moving base. I now carry them everywhere in order to see the outside world. They weigh a ton and are very strong, and carry my tape recorder, a supply of batteries and cassettes.

From the age of 70 to 80, I was astonished by how delightful life had become, an unexpected golden plateau and was all set for a spiffing old age, irresponsible and self indulgent.

But exactly four years ago that plan was forever spoiled. Most people do not live as long as I have and certainly not without any grievous health problem and no money anxiety so I ought to count my blessings but instead I feel trapped and limited and disgusted and only hope that travel, even limited as it now is, will not fail me, will still revive me because it is change, because there is the chance of newness.

I felt like talking today and felt like talking about books. Now I am going to see what old clothes I can find for my journey and take the underground to St. James's Park for a sunlight walk and then back to you and E. Bowen.

I am glad you are happy as you were always meant to be. Do not marry though until I get back from Switzerland.

Much love as always,

Martha

On Saturday, February 16, 1998, at the age of eighty-nine, Martha took a special pill she had got hold of several years before for just this occasion, and died. She was still living on her own, and she had many devoted friends, but she did not care for the growing struggle that life had become. She could no longer see to read or write or travel, and she had cancer of the ovary and liver. She had failed to help her mother die quickly; but she had planned her own exit, at a moment and place of her own choosing, for many years.

In the few weeks before her death, she had several affectionate conversations with all her close friends and with Alfred. Mary Blume and Ward Just, whom she had known in Vietnam, came over from Paris for the day and took her out to lunch: they found her cheerful. Behind her, she left total order, the outside order she had once maintained was necessary to counterbalance the inner muddle and turmoil. Her affairs were up to date, her will clear and precise, her flat impeccably neat. On the chest of drawers in her bedroom, under photographs of her mother, the two Sandys, Capa and Bernard Perlin, Leonard and Felicia Bernstein, was a bowl of white tulips. "Death," she had once said to Betsy Drake, many years before, "is nothing. The only thing to fear is the manner of dying."

Acknowledgments

I most particularly would like to thank Sandy Matthews, Martha's stepson, and the Gellhorn literary estate for permission to edit and publish this selection of letters. Sandy and his wife, Shirlee, helped me at every stage of the process. My thanks also go to Alfred Gellhorn, Martha's brother, and to Sandy Gellhorn, her adopted son, for their help and for letting me use some of her many letters to them.

Most of Martha's vast correspondence is to be found at the Howard Gotlieb Archival Center at Boston University, and I would like to thank the late Dr. Gotlieb and his staff for their assistance over the course of many visits to Boston. This collection could never have been put together without their help. In particular, they hold Martha's letters to the following people: Edna Gellhorn, Campbell Bennett, John Gunther, Averell Harriman, Alexander Woollcott, Bill and Annie Davis, Gip Wells, H. G. Wells, Nelson Algren, Robert Sherrod, Adlai Stevenson, Evelyn Gendal, Iris Origo, Alvah Bessie, Levin Meyer, Virginia Deutsch, Winifred Hill, Daniel Ellsberg, and Valerie Forman.

I would also like to thank: Susan Wrynn, Hemingway Curator at the JFK Library in Boston, for Martha's letters to Ernest Hemingway and to William Walton; AnnaLee Pauls and Margaret Rich at the Special Collections Library at Princeton University, for those to Charles Scribner, Max Perkins, and William Walton; the staff of the Franklyn Roosevelt Library in Hyde Park, New York, for those to Eleanor Roosevelt; Eton College Library for those to Lady Diana Cooper; Jane Bernstein and the Library of Congress for those to Leonard Bernstein; Rob Grover, for the letters to his father, Allen Grover; Agi Paloczi-Horvath for those to herself and her husband, George; David Pearlman for those sent to Moishe, his brother; Sybille Bedford and the Harry Ransom Humanities Research Center at the University of Texas at Austin for those to Sybille Bedford; Fiorella Superbi at the Harvard University Center for Italian Renaissance Studies at I Tatti in Florence for those to Bernard Berenson; Marsha Presnell for those to her husband, Robert; Hugues de Jouvenel for those to his father, Bertrand; the Department of Rare Books and Special Collections at the University of Louisville in Kentucky for the letters to Hortense Flexner and Wyncie

King; the Manuscripts and Archives Division of the New York Public Library for the letters to Collier's Magazine and its editors.

John Hatt, James Fox, Bill Buford, Victoria Glendinning, Betsy Drake, Nikki Dobskri, Rosie Boycott, George Feifer, Bernard Perlin, Ruth and Sol Rabb, Nicholas Shakespeare, Raleigh Trevelyan, Milton Wolff, and Mary Blume were all kind enough to let me use some of Martha's letters to them, written over the years: I would like to thank them very much.

And, as always, my warm thanks go to Penny Hoare and Patrick Hargadon at Chatto & Windus, to Vanessa Mobley and Jennifer Barth at Henry Holt, and to my agent, Clare Alexander.

Index

About the Author

A distinguished biographer, CAROLINE MOOREHEAD has also served as a columnist on human rights for two British newspapers. More recently, she has worked directly with refugees by helping to establish a variety of services for African refugees in Cairo. She is the author of *Gellhorn: A Twentieth-Century Life* and *Human Cargo: A Journey Among Refugees,* which was a finalist for a National Critics Book Circle Award. She lives in London, where she is currently at work on a biography of Lucy Dillon, marquise de la Tour du Pin.